D0463349

EX LIBRIS

ESSENTIALS OF ECONOMETRICS

ESSENTIALS OF ECONOMETRICS

DAMODAR GUJARATI

Baruch College
City University of New York

McGRAW-HILL, INC.

New York   St. Louis   San Francisco   Auckland   Bogotá   Caracas
Lisbon   London   Madrid   Mexico   Milan   Montreal   New Delhi
Paris   San Juan   Singapore   Sydney   Tokyo   Toronto

Essentials of Econometrics

Copyright © 1992 by McGraw-Hill, Inc. All rights reserved. Printed in the United States of America. Except as permitted under the United States Copyright Act of 1976, no part of this publication may be reproduced or distributed in any form or by any means, or stored in a data base or retrieval system, without the prior written permission of the publisher.

1 2 3 4 5 6 7 8 9 0 DOC DOC 9 0 9 8 7 6 5 4 3 2 1

ISBN 0-07-025194-0

This book was set in Palatino by Arcata Graphics/Kingsport.
The editors were Scott D. Stratford and Peggy Rehberger;
the production supervisor was Leroy A. Young.
The cover was designed by Leon Bolognese.
R. R. Donnelley & Sons Company was printer and binder.

Library of Congress Cataloging-in Publication Data

Gujarati, Damodar N.
    Essentials of econometrics / Damodar Gujarati.
        p.   cm.
    Includes bibliographical references and index.
    ISBN 0-07-025194-0
    1. Econometrics.   2. Economics—Statistical methods.   I. Title.
HB 139.G85   1992
330'.01'5195—dc20   91-14189

ABOUT
THE
AUTHOR

Damodar Gujarati is a Professor of Economics and Finance, Baruch College of the City University of New York, where he has been since 1965. Dr. Gujarati received his M.B.A. and Ph.D. degrees from the University of Chicago. Dr. Gujarati has published extensively in recognized national and international journals, such as the *Review of Economics and Statistics*, the *Economic Journal*, the *Journal of Financial and Quantitative Analysis*, the *Journal of Business*, the *Journal of Industrial and Labor Relations*, and the *American Statistician*. Dr. Gujarati is an editorial referee to several journals and is a member of the Board of Editors of the *Journal of Quantitative Economics*, the official journal of the Indian Econometric Society. Dr. Gujarati is also the author of *Government and Business* (McGraw-Hill Book Company, 1984), *Pensions and New York City Fiscal Crisis* (American Enterprise Institute, 1978), and *Basic Econometrics*, 2d ed. (McGraw-Hill, 1988).

Dr. Gujarati was a Visiting Professor at the University of Sheffield, U.K. (1970–1971), a Visiting Fulbright Professor to India (1981–1982), a Visiting Professor in the School of Management of the National University of Singapore (1985–1986), a Visiting Professor, University of New South Wales, Australia, summer 1988, and a Visiting Professor of Economics, U.S. Military Academy, West Point, 1990–1991. As a regular participant in the USIA's lectureship program abroad, Dr. Gujarati has lectured extensively on micro- and macroeconomic topics in countries such as Australia, Bangladesh, Germany, India, Israel, Mauritius, the Republic of South Korea, and Sri Lanka.

TO MY WIFE PUSHPA,

who thinks that a subject with topics such as *autocorrelation, heteroscedasticity,* and *multicollinearity* must be exciting.

CONTENTS

PART II THE LINEAR REGRESSION MODEL

PART III   REGRESSION ANALYSIS IN PRACTICE

PREFACE

The importance of studying econometrics has increased dramatically in the last several years—as has the number of students taking beginning courses in it. I have written *Essentials of Econometrics* because I am convinced that there is a need for a brief, applied, and nonthreatening introduction to econometrics that is also authoritative. The most fundamental topics, presented accurately and motivated properly, can give a lasting foundation for economics majors and nonmajors alike.

As economists rely more and more heavily on econometric techniques, any student of the discipline must develop an appreciation for the power and versatility of econometric modelling. Those who go on to do professional work in economics have an additional goal—they must learn the fundamental techniques of econometrics, as accurately as possible, with respect to using them themselves in future courses.

Essentials of Econometrics has been written to address both these goals—appreciation of econometrics and learning the techniques needed for further work. It offers the most "user-friendly" introduction possible to beginning students, who need to understand the broad applications of the material throughout economics. At the same time, it provides a thorough and sound foundation for future courses in econometrics—with a focus on the most important and useful techniques of modelling. The audience for *Essentials of Econometrics* consists of undergraduate economics majors, undergraduate business administration majors, M.B.A. students, and others who wish to understand the fundamentals of econometrics. The book motivates students to *understand* technique through extensive examples, careful explanations, and a wide variety of problem material.

PLAN OF THE BOOK

After an introductory chapter, the book is organized into three parts. In Part I, which has three chapters, I discuss the fundamentals of probability and statistics. Although I assume that the students have taken an elementary course in statistics, it is my experience from several years of teaching that beginning students in econometrics need a good review of statistics. Because elementary courses in statistics are primarily descriptive, most students do not get a good grounding in inferential statistics, especially in the area of hypothesis testing. The three review chapters, although written in a relaxed and non-technical manner, will provide the reader with the background necessary to achieving an understanding of the fundamentals of econometrics. The statistical ideas introduced in these chapters are illustrated by several examples intended to give beginners a solid grasp of the fundamental concepts of probability and statistics without overwhelming them with theoretical fine points. To those students who already have some background in this material, these chapters will serve as a refresher course. Of course, the instructor can expand on some topics discussed in the three chapters.

Part II includes Chapters 5, 6, 7, 8, and 9. In these chapters I discuss the bread and butter tool of econometrics, namely, the *linear regression model.* In Chapter 5, I introduce the basic ideas of linear regression somewhat informally. And in Chapters 6 and 7, I discuss these ideas more formally, first with the two-variable regression model (Chapter 6) and then with the multivariable regression model (Chapter 7). These two chapters are the core of regression analysis. In Chapter 8, I discuss the functional form in which a linear regression model can be expressed. Contrary to intuition, the linear regression model requires *linearity in the parameters* of the model and not necessarily in the variables of the model. In Chapter 9, I show that the variables in a regression model need not always be quantitative (i.e., those measurable on some quantitative scale); *qualitative* variables such as sex, color, religion, nationality, etc., can be handled by the linear regression model.

In Part III, consisting of Chapters 10, 11, 12, 13, and 14, I discuss several practical aspects of the linear regression model. The linear regression model developed in Part II is known as the *classical linear regression model* (CLRM), which is the cornerstone of modern econometrics. Although it is a versatile model, the CLRM is based on several simplifying assumptions that may not always hold in practice. In this part, I consider several assumptions of the CLRM and discuss the consequences of relaxing one or more of the assumptions. The practitioner will find the discussion in this part particularly useful.

MATHEMATICAL REQUIREMENTS

In presenting the various topics, I have used very little matrix algebra or calculus. I firmly believe that econometrics can be taught to the beginner in an intuitive manner without a heavy dose of matrix algebra or calculus. Also, I have not given any proofs unless they are easily understood. I do not feel that the nonspecialist is particularly interested in the proofs. Of course, the instructor can supply the necessary proofs if the situation demands. My book, *Basic Econometrics,* 2d ed. (McGraw-Hill, 1988), gives proofs and more advanced discussion of the various topics included in this text.

COMPUTERS AND ECONOMETRICS

It cannot be overemphasized that what has made econometrics accessible to the beginner is the availability of several user-friendly computer packages. In Appendix A, I give a list of some popular statistical packages. Once the reader develops familiarity with one or more of these packages, he or she will discover that learning econometrics is really great fun.

All the data sets from problems in *Essentials of Econometrics* will be available, in ASCII-compatible diskettes, to instructors who adopt the book. McGraw-Hill will also make available a special, limited version of the popular SHAZAM econometrics package to adopters who wish to use a commercially successful program. Interested users of the book should contact their local McGraw-Hill representative for more details.

PROBLEM SOLVING APPROACH

I am a firm believer in learning by doing. Therefore, I have provided several questions and problems at the end of each chapter, a total of some 260 problems. Some of these problems arc based on small data sets that I have provided with the questions. The diversity of the problem material is reflective of the many uses of econometric modelling. I hope that students are better versed in those uses as a result of using the problems in this book.

For instructors, I have prepared an *Instructor's Manual* providing detailed solutions to all questions and problems in the text. Adopters may obtain the manual through their McGraw-Hill representative.

IN CLOSING

To sum up, in writing *Essentials of Econometrics* my primary objective has been to introduce the wonderful world of econometrics to the beginner in a relaxed but informative style. I hope the knowledge gained from this book will prove to be of lasting value in the reader's future academic or professional career.

ACKNOWLEDGMENTS

Although I am solely responsible for any errors that remain, I owe a great debt to several colleagues and reviewers for their very constructive suggestions. Without their help and encouragement, I would not have completed this book. In particular, I am indebted to: Dale Belman, University of Wisconsin at Milwaukee; Ashok Bhargava, University of Wisconsin at Whitewater; Sushila Gidwani-Buschi, Manhattan College; William H. Green, New York University; Ann Horowitz, University of Florida; Dennis Jansen, Texas A & M University; Salih Neftci, City University of New York; Neil Sheflin, Rutgers University; John Spitzer, State University of New York at Brockport; Vincent Su, Baruch College, City University of New York; Frank Tansey, Baruch College, City University of New York; Thomas Traynor, Wright State University; H. D. Vinod, Fordham University; and Albert Zucker, Baruch College, City University of New York.

I owe a special debt to my editor, Scott D. Stratford, for his encouragement and help through all phases of the book. I am also indebted to Peggy Rehberger, senior editing supervisor, for all her behind-the-scenes help.

I am grateful to Colonel James R. Golden, Head of the Department of Social Sciences, U.S. Military Academy, West Point, for inviting me as a Visiting Professor for the academic year 1990–1991. He provided me with all the comforts, especially a spacious office overlooking the Hudson River, to complete this book.

Finally, I am thankful to my daughter Diane for reading parts of this book and to my daughter Joan for her constant encouragement. One realizes the importance of family support only after the book is finished!

Damodar Gujarati

ESSENTIALS OF ECONOMETRICS

CHAPTER

1

THE NATURE
AND SCOPE
OF ECONOMETRICS

Research in economics, finance, management, marketing, and related disciplines is becoming increasingly quantitative. Beginning students in these fields are encouraged, if not required, to take a course or two in econometrics—a field of study that has become quite popular. The purpose of this chapter is to give the beginner an overview of what econometrics is all about.

1.1 WHAT IS ECONOMETRICS?

Simply stated, **econometrics** means economic measurement. Although quantitative measurement of economic concepts such as the gross national product (GNP), unemployment, inflation, imports, exports, etc. is very important, the scope of econometrics is much broader, as can be seen from the following definitions:

> **Econometrics** may be defined as the social science in which the tools of economic theory, mathematics, and statistical inference are applied to the analysis of economic phenomena[1]

> **Econometrics**, the result of a certain outlook on the role of economics, consists of the application of mathematical statistics to economic data to lend empirical support to the models constructed by mathematical economics and to obtain numerical results.[2]

---

[1] Arthur S. Goldberger, *Econometric Theory*, Wiley, New York, 1964, p. 1.

[2] P. A. Samuelson, T. C. Koopmans, and J. R. N. Stone, "Report of the Evaluative Committee for *Econometrica*," *Econometrica*, vol. 22, no. 2, April 1954, pp. 141–146.

1.2   WHY STUDY ECONOMETRICS?

As the preceding definitions suggest, econometrics makes use of economic theory, mathematical economics, economic statistics (i.e., economic data), and mathematical statistics. Yet, it is a subject that deserves to be studied in its own right for the following reasons.

Economic theory makes statements or hypotheses that are mostly qualitative in nature. For example, microeconomic theory states that, other things remaining the same (the famous *ceteris paribus* clause of economics), an increase in the price of a commodity is expected to decrease the quantity demanded of that commodity. Thus, economic theory postulates a negative or inverse relationship between the price and quantity demanded of a commodity—this is the widely known law of downward-sloping demand or simply *the law of demand*. But the theory itself does not provide any numerical measure of the strength of the relationship between the two; that is, it does not tell by how much the quantity demanded will go up or down as a result of a certain change in the price of the commodity. It is the job of the econometrician to provide such numerical estimates. Stated differently, econometrics gives empirical (i.e., based on observation or experiment) content to most economic theory. If we find in a study or experiment that when the price of a unit increases by a dollar and the quantity demanded goes down by, say, 100 units, we have not only confirmed the law of demand but in the process we have also provided a numerical estimate of the relationship between the two variables—price and quantity.

The main concern of mathematical economics is to express economic theory in mathematical form or equations (or models) without regard to measurability or empirical verification of the theory. Econometrics, as noted earlier, is primarily interested in the empirical verification of economic theory. As we will show shortly, the econometrician often uses mathematical models proposed by the mathematical economist but puts these models in forms that lend themselves to empirical testing. Economic statistics is mainly concerned with collecting, processing, and presenting economic data in the form of charts, diagrams, and tables. This is the job of the economic statistician. He or she collects data on the GNP, employment, unemployment, prices, etc. The data thus collected constitute the raw data for econometric work. But the economic statistician, not primarily concerned with using the collected data to test economic theories, does not go any further.

Although mathematical statistics provides many of the tools employed in the trade, the econometrician often needs special methods in view of the unique nature of most economic data, namely, the data are not usually generated as the result of a controlled experiment. The econometrician, like the meteorologist, generally depends on data that cannot be controlled directly. Thus, data on consumption, income, investment, savings, prices, etc., which are collected by public and private agencies, are nonexperimental in nature. The econometrician takes these data as given. This creates special problems not normally dealt with in mathematical statistics. Moreover, such data are likely to contain errors of measurement, of either omission or commission, and the econometrician may be called upon to develop special methods of analysis to deal with such errors of measurement.

For students majoring in economics and business there is a pragmatic reason for studying econometrics. After graduation, in their employment, they may be called upon to forecast sales, interest rates, and money supply, or to estimate demand and supply functions or price elasticities for products, etc. Quite often, economists appear as expert witnesses before federal and state regulatory agencies on behalf of their clients or the public at large. Thus, an economist appearing before a state regulatory commission that regulates prices of gas and electricity may be required to assess the impact of a proposed price increase on the demand for, say, electricity before the commission will approve the price increase. In situations like this the economist may need to develop a demand function for electricity for this purpose. Such a demand function may enable the economist to estimate the price elasticity of demand, that is, the percentage change in the quantity demanded for a percentage change in the price. A knowledge of econometrics is very helpful in estimating such demand functions.

It is fair to say that econometrics has become an integral part of training in economics and business.

1.3 THE METHODOLOGY OF ECONOMETRICS

How does one actually do an econometric study? Broadly speaking, econometric analysis proceeds along the following lines:

1. Statement of theory or hypothesis
2. Specification of the mathematical model
3. Specification of the statistical or econometric model
4. Collection of data
5. Estimation of the parameters of the chosen econometric model
6. Tests of the hypothesis derived from the model
7. Forecasting or prediction

To illustrate these steps, let us suppose that a producer hires a young econometrician to determine the effect of a proposed price increase on the demand for a product, say, coffee. Being trained in econometrics, he or she recalls the seven-step procedure and proceeds as follows:

Statement of Theory or Hypothesis: The Law of Demand

The first thing the econometrician does is find out what economic theory has to say about the effect of a price change on the quantity demanded, an effect enshrined in the famous **law of demand**, which states that:

> When the price of a commodity is raised (and other things are held constant), buyers tend to buy less of the commodity. Similarly, when the price is lowered, other things equal, quantity demanded increases.[3]

In short, there is an inverse relationship between the price of a commodity and its quantity demanded; that is, the demand curve is downward-sloping. But note carefully that this law holds true provided all other things, such as the tastes of the consumers, their income, prices of other goods, etc., are held constant; in other words, they do not change. As mentioned previously, this is the famous *ceteris paribus* caveat of economics.

Specification of the Mathematical Model of the Law of Demand

Although the law of downward-sloping demand (curve) postulates an inverse relationship between price and quantity, it does not indicate the precise form of the relationship between the two. That is, the law does not tell whether the relationship between quantity (Q) and price (P) is as that shown in Figure 1-1(a) or 1-1(b).[4]

The relationship between Q and P is *linear* (i.e., a straight line) in Figure 1-1(a), whereas it is *nonlinear* (i.e., not a straight line) in Figure 1-1(b).

If the relationship between Q and P is linear as shown in Figure 1-1(a), mathematically it can be expressed as

$$Q = B_1 + B_2P \qquad (1.1)$$

This expression is an example of a *linear* demand function. B_1 and B_2 are known as the *parameters* of the function.[5] B_1 is also known as the *intercept*; it gives the value of Q when P is zero.[6] And B_2 is also known as the *slope*—the

---

[3] Paul A. Samuelson and William D. Nordhaus, *Economics*, 13th ed., McGraw-Hill, New York, 1989, p. 57.

[4] Most economic textbooks show P on the vertical axis and Q on the horizontal axis. But that is primarily a convention. We put Q on the vertical axis because we are trying to explain how quantity demanded varies as price varies.

[5] Broadly speaking, a parameter is an unknown quantity that may vary over a certain set of values. In statistics a probability distribution function is often characterized by its *parameters*, such as its mean and variance. This topic is discussed in some detail in Chap. 2.

[6] In Chap. 5 we will give a more precise interpretation of the intercept in the context of regression analysis.

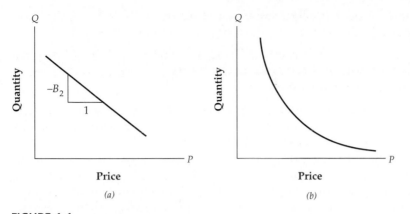

FIGURE 1-1
A linear (*a*) and nonlinear (*b*) demand curve.

slope measures the rate of change in Q for a unit (say, a dollar) change in P, as shown in Figure 1-1(*a*). If the law of demand holds, we would expect $B_2 < 0$ (i.e., negative) and $B_1 > 0$ (generally, who wouldn't demand a good if its price were zero?)

Equation (1.1) is an example of a mathematical model of the relationship between Q and P. In such a model the variable appearing on the left-hand side of the equality sign is called the **dependent variable** and the variable on the right-hand side is called the **independent**, or **explanatory, variable.** In the previous example Q is the dependent variable and P is the explanatory variable: We are trying to find out how quantity demanded changes as its price changes. Functionally, quantity demanded is dependent on price.[7]

A natural question that arises is: Why did we choose Eq. (1.1), the linear demand function, to represent the relationship between Q and P? What happens if the relationship between the two variables is as that shown in Figure 1-1(*b*)? Unfortunately, the law of demand (or economic theory in general) will not help as much here, for that law is simply a qualitative statement. The job of the econometrician is to choose a suitable mathematical function or mathematical model to represent economic relationships between variables. How econometricians actually develop such models will be the focus of our attention in this book. As a matter of fact, Chapters 8 and 13 are largely devoted

---

[7] An average consumer when he or she goes to the supermarket takes the price marked on the various goods as given and adjusts his or her consumption. We are explicitly assuming that there is no haggling over price.

to this topic. For the present, simply note that Eq. (1.1) is just one of the possible models to depict the relationship between Q and P.

Specification of the Statistical or Econometric Model of the Law of Demand

The purely mathematical model of the demand function, Eq. (1.1), although of prime interest to the mathematical economist, is of limited interest to the econometrician, for such a model assumes an *exact*, or *deterministic*, relationship between quantity and price; that is, for a given price there is a unique quantity demanded. In reality, one rarely finds such neat relationships between economic variables. Most often, the relationships are *inexact* or *statistical* in nature. To see this more concretely, consider the hypothetical data on Q and P given in Table 1-1. Let us plot these data in a diagram called the *scatter diagram* or *scattergram*, as shown in Figure 1-2.

Without question, the relationship between Q and P is inverse. It also seems that the relationship is *approximately* linear, that is, as shown in Eq. (1.1). But the relationship is not perfectly or exactly linear, for if we draw a straight line through the six points, not all of them will lie exactly on that straight line—recall that to draw a straight line we need only two points. Why don't all six data points lie exactly on the straight line specified by the mathematical model (1.1)? Keep in mind that our law of demand is a *ceteris paribus* law. That is, in deriving the demand curve, we assume that all other variables affecting the quantity demanded are held constant or fixed. However, when we have a concrete set of data as shown in Table 1-1, we have no way of knowing whether all these other influences are held constant. If they are not, then they are likely to exert some influence on Q even though the impact of P on Q is more dominant. As a result, the observed relationship between Q and P may be imprecise—we are not going to observe all data points lying exactly on the mathematical demand curve of Figure 1-1.

TABLE 1-1
Hypothetical data on quantity demanded (Q) and price (P)

P	Q
0	78
1	70
2	69
3	63
4	60
5	58

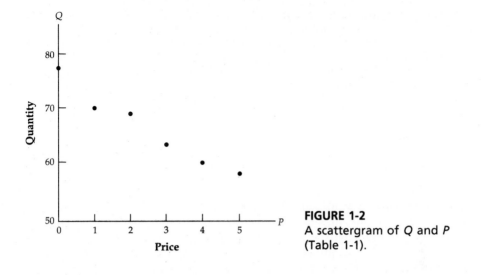

FIGURE 1-2
A scattergram of Q and P
(Table 1-1).

Let us allow for the influence of all other variables affecting Q in a catch-all variable u and write the demand function as

$$Q = B_1 + B_2P + u \tag{1.2}$$

where u is called the **random error term**, or simply the **error term**.[8] We let u represent all those forces (besides P) that affect Q but are not explicitly intro-duced in the model as well as purely random forces. As we will see in Part II of the text, the error term distinguishes econometrics from purely mathe-matical economics.

Equation (1.2) is an example of a *statistical* or *econometric model*. More precisely, it is an example of what is known as a **linear regression model**, which is a prime consideration of this book. In linear regression analysis, as we will see, our concern is to explain the behavior of one variable, say, Q (the dependent variable) in relation to the behavior of another variable(s), say, P (the independent or explanatory variable), allowing for the fact that the rela-tionship between the two is not exact because of the presence of other factors included in the error term, u.

Notice that the econometric model, Eq. (1.2), is derived from the math-ematical model, Eq. (1.1), which shows that mathematical economics and econ-ometrics are mutually complementary disciplines. This is clearly reflected in the definition of econometrics given at the outset.

---

[8] In statistical lingo, the random error term is known as the *stochastic error* term. We discuss this topic in Chap. 2.

Collection of Data

Before turning to the estimation of the chosen regression model (i.e., finding the numerical values of B_1 and B_2), we must first obtain the appropriate data. There are three types of data that are generally available for empirical analysis:

1. Time series
2. Cross-sectional
3. Pooled, that is, combination of time series and cross-sectional.

Times series data are collected over a period of time, such as the data on GNP, employment, unemployment, money supply, government deficits, etc. Such data may be collected at regular intervals—daily (e.g., stock prices), weekly (e.g., money supply), monthly (e.g., the unemployment rate), quarterly (e.g., GNP), or annually (e.g., government budget). These data may be **quantitative** in nature (e.g., prices, income, money supply) or **qualitative** (e.g., male or female, employed or unemployed, married or unmarried, white or black). As we will show, qualitative variables, also called *dummy* or *categorical* variables, can be every bit as important as quantitative variables.

Cross-sectional data are data on one or more variables collected at one point in time, such as the census of population conducted by the U.S. Census Bureau every 10 years (the most recent was on April 1, 1990), the surveys of consumer expenditures conducted by the University of Michigan, and the opinion polls such as those conducted by Gallup, Harris, and other polling organizations.

In **pooled data** we have elements of both time series and cross-sectional data. For example, if we were to collect data on the unemployment rate for 10 countries for a period of 20 years, the data will constitute an example of pooled data—data on the unemployment rate for each country for the 20-year period will form time series data, whereas data on the unemployment rate for the 10 countries for any single year will be cross-sectional data. In pooled data we will have 200 observations—20 annual observations for each of the 10 countries.

There is a special type of pooled data, the **panel**, or **longitudinal** data, also called **micropanel** data, in which the same cross-sectional unit, say, a family or firm, is surveyed over time. For example, the U.S. Department of Commerce conducts a census of housing at periodic intervals. At each periodic survey the same household (or the people living at the same address) is interviewed to find out if there has been any change in the housing and financial conditions of that household since the last survey. The panel data that results from repeatedly interviewing the same household at periodic intervals provide very useful information on the dynamics of household behavior.

Estimation of Parameters of the Chosen Econometric Model

Given data on Q and P, such as that in Table 1-1, how do we estimate the parameters of the model, namely, B_1 and B_2; that is, how do we find the numerical values, called the *estimates*, of these parameters? This will be the focus of our attention in Part II, where we develop the appropriate methods of computation. For now, take it on faith that the estimated demand function for our data in Table 1-1 is as follows:

$$\hat{Q} = 76.05 - 3.88P \qquad (1.3)$$

Note that we have put the symbol ^ on Q (read as Q hat) to remind us that Equation (1.3) is the estimated demand function (but more on this in Chapter 5). This estimated demand function is sketched in Figure 1-3.

As Eq. (1.3) shows, the estimated value of B_1 is ≈76 and that of B_2 is ≈ − 3.9, where the symbol ≈ means approximately. Thus, if P increases by one dollar, the quantity demanded is expected to decrease *on the average* by 3.9 units. We say "on the average" because the presence of the error term u, as noted earlier, is likely to make the relationship somewhat imprecise. This is clearly seen in Figure 1-3—the points not on the line are the actual Q and the (vertical) distance between them and the points on the line are the *estimated* u.[9] For example, corresponding to $P = 1$, the observed Q is 70 but the one shown by the estimated (regression) line is ≈72.2, an error of 2.2 units. (Do you see this? If not, see the section on prediction later). In short, the econometric model, Eq. (1.3), gives us the *average relationship* between Q and P— how on the average Q responds for a unit change in Q.[10] The value of 76.05 suggests that on the average about 76 units of the commodity will be demanded if its price were zero.[11]

Tests of the Hypothesis Derived from the Model

Having estimated the demand function, the econometrician may want to find out whether the estimated model makes economic sense, i.e., whether the results obtained conform with the underlying economic theory. For example, in the demand function the coefficient of the price variable is expected to be negative. (Why?) Is the observed value of the coefficient negative? In the lan-

---

[9] As we will show in Chap. 5, the estimated errors are called *residuals*.

[10] This point will be discussed more carefully in Part II.

[11] This is, however, a mechanical interpretation of the intercept. We will see in Chap. 5 how to interpret the intercept in a given context.

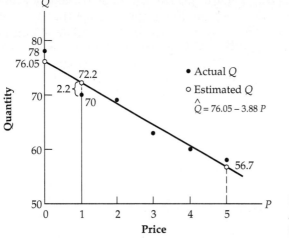

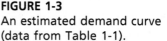

FIGURE 1-3
An estimated demand curve
(data from Table 1-1).

guage of statistics, is $B_2 < 0$? In other words, is the hypothesis $B_2 < 0$ sub-stantiated by the empirical results? Equation (1.3) shows that this is so. Similarly, is the hypothesis that $B_1 > 0$ substantiated by the observed results? (As noted before, who would not generally desire a commodity if its price were zero?) In the present case that is also true. Of course, some hypotheses will not be so readily verifiable. For example, if the hypothesis were $B_2 = -4.0$, can we say that the observed value of -3.88 is *practically* the same as the hypothesized value? To test such a hypothesis, we need to use the tools of probability theory, which are discussed in Chapters 2, 3, and 4.

As the preceding discussion shows, the econometrician is concerned not only with estimating the parameters of the chosen model but may also be interested in finding out to what extent the fitted model conforms with the underlying economic theory.

Forecasting or Prediction

Turning to our estimated demand function, Eq. (1.3), suppose the seller wants to know what the quantity demanded will be if he were to charge a price of $4.50, a price not shown in Table 1-1.[12] In other words, the seller wants to *forecast* the quantity demanded if the price were $4.50. If he plugs the value of $4.50 for P on the right-hand side of Eq. (1.3), he would obtain $\hat{Q} = 76.05 - 3.88 (4.50) = 58.59$ units. That is, the forecast value of Q is about 59 units

---

[12] Recall from elementary microeconomics that this represents a movement along the demand curve.

if the price is $4.50. Is this a legitimate procedure? In other words, can one use an estimated regression function such as Eq. (1.3) to predict the value of the dependent variable for a given value of the independent variable? This is the general problem of forecasting. As we will show later, under certain conditions one can use the estimated model for the purpose of prediction.

Let us summarize the steps involved in econometric analysis.

Step	Example
1. Statement of theory	The law of demand
2. Mathematical model of theory	$Q = B_1 + B_2P$ (e.g.)
3. Econometric model of theory	$Q = B_1 + B_2P + u$
4. Collection of data	Table 1-1
5. Parameter estimation	$\hat{Q} = 76.05 - 3.88P$
6. Testing of hypothesis	Is $B_2 < 0$? (i.e., is the slope negative?)
7. Forecasting	What is Q if $P = 4.50$

Although we examined econometric methodology using the demand-supply example, we should point out that a similar procedure can be employed to analyze quantitative relationships between any variables. To take an example from accounting, one may want to study the relationship between accounting rates on stocks and the market return. Accounting theory might suggest that the market rate is related to the accounting rate. This hypothesis can be tested by estimating a model similar to the linear regression model (1.3). As a matter of fact, such a model based on the cross-sectional data for 54 companies was estimated by Raymond Myers,[13] giving the following results:

$$\hat{Y} = 0.84801 + 0.61033X \tag{1.4}$$

where Y is the average market return (%) and X is the average yearly accounting rate (%), both averages computed over the period 1959 to 1974.

As these results indicate, if the accounting rate increases by, say, 1 percent, on the average the market rate increases by ≈ 0.6 of 1 percent.

As a noneconomic example, suppose a criminologist is interested in studying the relationship between the population density and the robbery rate. For this purpose, suppose he or she obtained a sample of 16 medium-sized cities and obtained the following regression results:[14]

---

[13] See Raymond H. Myers, *Classical and Modern Regression with Applications*, 2d ed., PWS-Kent Publishing, Boston, 1990, p. 16.

[14] The actual data are given in problem 1.6.

$$\hat{Y} = 182.97 + 0.2616X \qquad\qquad (1.5)$$

where Y = robbery rate (the number of robberies per 100,000 people) and X = population density of the city (the number of people per unit area).

These results seem to suggest that the higher the population density, the higher the crime rate, other things remaining the same. The criminologist has to determine the reasons for the positive association between the robbery rate and the population density.

As the preceding example shows, the methodology of regression analysis—the main tool of econometrics—goes beyond the field of economics.

1.4   THE ROAD AHEAD

Now that we have provided a glimpse at the nature and scope of econometrics, let us see what lies ahead. The book is divided into three parts.

Part I, consisting of Chapters 2, 3, and 4, reviews the basics of probability and statistics for the benefit of those readers whose knowledge of statistics has become rusty. It is assumed that the reader has some previous background in introductory statistics.

Part II introduces the reader to the bread-and-butter tool of econometrics, namely, the *classical linear regression model (CLRM)*. A thorough understanding of CLRM is a must in order to follow research in the general areas of economics and business.

Part III considers the practical aspects of regression analysis and discusses a variety of problems that the practitioner will have to tackle when one or more assumptions of the CLRM do not hold.

Throughout the book the needs of the beginner have been kept in mind. The discussion of most topics is straightforward, unencumbered with mathematical proofs, derivations, etc.[15] It is firmly believed that the apparently forbidding subject of econometrics can be taught to beginners in such a way that they can see the value of the subject without getting bogged down in mathematical and statistical niceties.

A final word. What has now made econometrics readily accessible to beginners is the availability of comparatively inexpensive computer software packages. Readers will be exposed to such packages throughout this text. Once students get used to one or two of the standard packages, they will soon realize that learning econometrics is really great fun, and in the bargain, they will get a better appreciation of the much maligned "dismal" science of economics.

---

[15] Some of the proofs and derivations are presented in my *Basic Econometrics*, 2d ed., McGraw-Hill, New York, 1988.

Key Terms and Concepts

The key terms and concepts introduced in this chapter are:

Econometrics
Law of demand
Linear regression model
  a) dependent variable
  b) independent, or explanatory, variables
  c) random error term (error term)

Data collection
  a) time series data—quantitative and qualitative
  b) cross-sectional data
  c) pooled and panel (longitudinal or micropanel) data

QUESTIONS

1.1. Suppose a local government decides to increase the tax rate on residential properties under its jurisdiction. What will be the effect of this on the prices of residential houses? Follow the seven-step procedure discussed in the text in answering this question.

1.2. How do you perceive the role of econometrics in decision making in business and economics?

1.3. Suppose you are an economic adviser to the Chairman of the Federal Reserve Board (the Fed) and he has asked you about the advisability of increasing the money supply to bolster the economy. What factors would you take into account in your advice? How would you use econometrics in your advice?

1.4. To reduce the dependence on foreign oil supplies, the government is thinking of increasing the federal taxes on gasoline. Suppose the Ford Motor Company has hired you to assess the impact of the tax increase on the demand for its cars. How would you go about advising the company?

1.5. What distinguishes econometrics from purely mathematical economics? And from economic theory?

PROBLEMS

1.6. The data underlying the robbery rate/population density regression given in Eq. (1.5) are listed in Table 1-2.

TABLE 1-2
Data on robbery rate (Y) and population density (X) in 16 U.S. cities

City	1	2	3	4	5	6	7	8
Y	209	180	195	192	215	197	208	189
X	59	49	75	54	78	56	60	82
City	**9**	**10**	**11**	**12**	**13**	**14**	**15**	**16**
Y	213	201	214	212	205	186	200	204
X	69	83	88	94	47	65	89	70

Source: John Neter, William Wasserman, and Michael H. Kutner, *Applied Linear Regression Models*, 2d ed., Irwin, Homewood, Ill., 1989, p. 59.

(*a*) Plot these data with the robbery rate on the vertical axis and population density on the horizontal axis.

(*b*) Does this plot indicate that the regression line shown in Eq. (1.5) approximately demonstrates the relationship between the two variables?

1.7. Table 1-3 gives data on per capita consumption expenditure (*Y*) and per capita disposable (i.e., after-tax) income (*X*) for the United States for 1979 to 1988; all data are in 1982 dollars.

TABLE 1-3

Per capita personal consumption expenditure (*Y*) and per capita disposable personal income (*X*), 1982 dollars

Year	Y	X
1979	8,904	9,829
1980	8,783	9,722
1981	8,794	9,769
1982	8,818	9,725
1983	9,139	9,930
1984	9,489	10,419
1985	9,840	10,625
1986	10,123	10,905
1987	10,303	10,970
1988	10,546	11,337

Source: Economic Report of the President, 1990, Table C-27, p. 325.

(*a*) A priori, or according to economic theory, what would you expect the relationship to be between *Y* and *X*?

(*b*) Plot the data given in Table 1-3 in a scattergram and see if the a priori expectations are borne out.

(*c*) "Eyeball" a regression line in the scattergram.

PART
I

BASICS OF
PROBABILITY
AND
STATISTICS

This part consists of three chapters that review the essentials of statistical theory that are needed to understand econometric theory and practice discussed in the remainder of the book.

Chapter 2 reviews the fundamental concepts of probability, probability distributions, and random variables.

Chapter 3 discusses four important probability distributions that are used extensively in econometrics: (1) the normal distribution, (2) the chi-square distribution, (3) the t distribution, and (4) the F distribution. In this chapter the main features of these distributions are outlined. With several examples, this chapter shows how these four probability distributions form the foundation of most statistical theory and practice.

Chapter 4 examines the two important branches of classical statistics, namely, estimation and hypothesis testing. A firm understanding of these two topics will considerably ease our study of econometrics in subsequent chapters.

These three chapters are written in a very informal yet informative style. The objective here is to brush up on the reader's knowledge of elementary statistics. Since students coming to econometrics may have different backgrounds in statistics, these three chapters provide a fairly self-contained introduction to this subject.

All the concepts introduced in these three chapters are well illustrated with several practical examples.

CHAPTER
2

A REVIEW OF BASIC STATISTICAL CONCEPTS

The purpose of this and the following two chapters is to review some fundamental statistical concepts that are needed to understand *Essentials of Econometrics*. These three chapters will serve as a refresher course for those students who have had a basic course in statistics and as a unified framework to follow discussions of material in the remaining parts of this book for those whose knowledge of statistics has become somewhat rusty. It is recommended that students who have had very little statistics supplement these three chapters with a good book on statistics. (Some references are given at the end of this chapter.) Note that the discussion in Chapters 2 through 4 is nonrigorous and is by no means a substitute for a basic course in statistics. It is simply an overview that is intended as a bridge to econometrics.

2.1 SOME NOTATION

In this chapter we come across several mathematical expressions that can often be expressed more conveniently in shorthand forms.

The Summation Notation

The Greek capital letter Σ (sigma) is used to indicate summation or addition. Thus,

$$\sum_{i=1}^{i=n} X_i = X_1 + X_2 + \cdots + X_n$$

where i is the index of summation and the expression on the left-hand side is the shorthand for "take the sum of the variable X from the first value ($i = 1$)

to the nth value $(i = n)''$; X_i stands for the ith value of the X variable. In practice, the full summation

$$\sum_{i=1}^{i=n} X_i \qquad (\text{or} \sum_{i=1}^{n} X_i)$$

is often abbreviated as

$$\sum X_i$$

where the upper and lower limits of the sum are known or can be easily determined or also expressed as

$$\sum_X X$$

which simply means take the sum of all the relevant values of X. We will use all these notations interchangeably.

Properties of the Summation Operator

Some important properties of Σ are as follows:

1. Where k is a constant

$$\sum_{i=1}^{n} k = nk$$

That is, a constant summed n times is n times that constant. Thus,

$$\sum_{i=1}^{4} 3 = 4 \times 3 = 12$$

In this example $n = 4$ and $k = 3$.

2. Where k is a constant

$$\sum k X_i = k \sum X_i$$

That is, a constant can be pulled out of the summation sign and put in front of it.

3.

$$\sum (X_i + Y_i) = \sum X_i + \sum Y_i$$

That is, the summation of the sum of two variables is the sum of their individual summations.

4.

$$\sum (a + b X_i) = na + b \sum X_i$$

where a and b are constants and where use is made of properties 1, 2, and 3.

We will make extensive use of the summation notation in what follows in this chapter and in the rest of the book.

We now discuss several important concepts from the probability theory.

2.2 EXPERIMENT, SAMPLE SPACE, SAMPLE POINT, AND EVENTS

Experiment

The first important concept is that of a **statistical** or **random experiment**. "A **random experiment** is a process leading to at least two possible outcomes with uncertainty as to which will occur." [1]

> **Example 2.1.** Tossing a coin, throwing a pair of dice, and drawing a card from a pack of cards are all experiments. It is implicitly assumed that in performing these experiments certain conditions are fulfilled, e.g., that the coin or the die is fair (i.e., it is not loaded). The *outcomes* of such experiments could be a head or a tail if a coin is tossed or any one of the numbers 1, 2, 3, 4, 5, and 6 if a die is thrown. Note that the outcomes are *unknown* before the experiment is performed. The objectives of such experiments may be to establish a law (e.g., how many heads one is likely to obtain in a toss of, say, 1000 coins) or to test the proposition that the coin is loaded (e.g., would one regard a coin loaded if one obtains 70 heads in 100 tosses of a coin?)

Sample Space or Population

The set of all possible outcomes of an experiment is called the **population** or **sample space**.

> **Example 2.2.** Consider the experiment of tossing two fair coins. Let H denote a head and T a tail. Then we have these outcomes: HH, HT, TH, TT, where HH means a head on the first toss and a head on the second toss, HT means a head on the first toss and a tail on the second toss, etc.

In this example the totality of the outcomes, or *sample space* or *population*, is 4—no other outcomes are logically possible (don't worry about the coin landing on its edge).

---

[1] Paul Newbold, *Statistics for Business and Economics*, Prentice-Hall, Englewood Cliffs, N.J., 1984, p. 83.

> **Example 2.3.** The New York Mets are scheduled to play a doubleheader. Let O_1 indicate the outcome that they win both games, O_2 that they win the first game but lose the second, O_3 that they lose the first game but win the second, and O_4 that they lose both games.

Here the sample space consists of four outcomes: (O_1, O_2, O_3, O_4).

Sample Point

Each member, or outcome, of the sample space (or population) is called a **sample point**. In Example 2.2 each outcome, *HH, HT, TH*, and *TT*, is a sample point. In Example 2.3 each outcome, O_1, O_2, O_3, and O_4, is a sample point.

Events

An **event** is a collection of the possible outcomes of an experiment; that is, it is a *subset* of the sample space.

> **Example 2.4.** Let event *A* be the occurrence of one head and one tail in the experiment of tossing two coins. From Example 2.2 we see that only outcomes *HT* and *TH* belong to event *A*. (*Note*: *HT* and *TH* are a subset of the sample space *HH, HT, TH*, and *TT*). Let *B* be the event that two heads occur in a toss of two coins. Then, obviously, only the outcome *HH* belongs to event *B*. (Again, note that *HH* is a subset of the sample space *HH, HT, TH*, and *TT*).

Events are said to be **mutually exclusive** if the occurrence of one event prevents the occurrence of another event at the same time. In Example 2.3, if O_1 occurs, i.e., the Mets win both the games, it rules out the occurrence of any of the other three outcomes. Two events are said to be **equally likely** if we are confident that one event is as likely to occur as the other event. In a single toss of a coin a head is as likely to appear as a tail. Events are said to be **collectively exhaustive** if they exhaust all possible outcomes of an experiment. In our two coin-tossing example, since *HH, HT, TH*, and *TT* are the only possible outcomes, they are (collectively) exhaustive events. Likewise, in the Mets example, O_1, O_2, O_3, and O_4 are the only possible outcomes, barring, of course, rain or natural calamities such as the earthquake during the 1989 World Series in San Francisco.

2.3 RANDOM VARIABLES

Although the outcome(s) of an experiment can be described verbally, such as a head or a tail, or the ace of spades, it would be much simpler if the results of all experiments could be described numerically, that is, in terms of numbers. As we will see later, for statistical purposes such representation is very useful.

Example 2.5.   Reconsider Example 2.2. Instead of describing the outcomes of the experiment by *HH*, *HT*, *TH*, and *TT*, consider the "variable" number of heads in a toss of two coins.[2] We have the following situation:

First Coin	Second Coin	Number of Heads
T	T	0
T	H	1
H	T	1
H	H	2

We call the variable "number of heads" a **stochastic** or **random variable** (r.v., for short). More generally, a variable whose (numerical) value is determined by the outcome of an experiment is called a **random variable**. In the preceding example the r.v., number of heads, takes three different values, 0, 1, or 2, depending on whether no heads, one head, or two heads were obtained in a toss of two coins. In the Mets example the r.v., the number of wins, likewise takes three different values, 0, 1, or 2.

By convention, random variables are denoted by capital letters, X, Y, Z, or X_1, X_2, X_3, etc.

An r.v. may be either discrete or continuous. A **discrete random variable** takes on only a finite (or countably infinite) number of values. Thus, the number of heads in a toss of two coins can take on only three values, 0, 1, or 2. Hence, it is a discrete r.v. Similarly, the number of wins in a doubleheader is also a discrete r.v. since it can take only three values, 0, 1, or 2 wins. A **continuous random variable**, on the other hand, is an r.v. that can take on any value in some interval of values. Thus, the height of an individual is a continuous variable—in the range of, say, 60 to 72 inches it can take any value, depending on the precision of measurement. Similarly, weight, rainfall, temperature, etc., can be regarded as continuous random variables.

2.4   PROBABILITY

Having defined experiment, sample space, sample points, events, and random variables, we now consider the important concept of probability. First, we

---

[2] Generally, a variable is any quantity that varies. More precisely, it is any quantity that may take any value of a specified set of values.

define the concept of probability of an event and then extend it to random variables.

Probability of an Event: The Classical or A Priori Definition

If an experiment can result in n *mutually exclusive* and *equally likely* outcomes, and if m of these outcomes are favorable to event A, then $P(A)$, the probability that A occurs, is the ratio m/n. That is,

$$P(A) = \frac{m}{n}$$

$$= \frac{\text{the number of outcomes favorable to } A}{\text{the total number of outcomes}}$$

(2.1)

Note the two features of this definition: The outcomes must be *mutually exclusive*—i.e., they cannot occur at the same time—and each outcome must have an *equal chance of occurring*—e.g., in a throw of a die any one of the six numbers has an equal chance of appearing.

Example 2.6.   In a throw of a die numbered 1 through 6, there are six possible outcomes: 1, 2, 3, 4, 5, and 6. These outcomes are mutually exclusive since in a single throw of the die two or more numbers cannot turn up simultaneously. These six outcomes are also equally likely. Hence, by the classical definition, the probability that any of these six numbers will show up is 1/6—there are six total outcomes and each outcome has an equal chance of occurring. Here $n = 6$ and $m = 1$.

Similarly, the probability of obtaining a head in a single toss of a coin is 1/2 since there are two possible outcomes, H and T, and each has an equal chance of coming up. Likewise, in a deck of 52 cards the probability of drawing any single card is 1/52. (Why?) The probability of drawing a spade, however, is 13/52. (Why?)

The preceding examples show why the classical definition is called an **a priori definition** since the probabilities are derived from purely *deductive* reasoning. One doesn't have to throw a coin to state that the probability of obtaining a head or a tail is 1/2, since logically these are the only possible outcomes.

But the classical definition has some deficiencies. What happens if the outcomes of an experiment are not finite or are not equally likely? What, for example, is the probability that the gross national product (GNP) next year will be such and such, or what is the probability that there will be a recession next year? The classical definition is not equipped to answer these questions.

TABLE 2-1
The distribution of marks received by 200 students in a microeconomics examination

Marks (1)	Midpoint of the interval (2)	Absolute frequency (3)	Relative frequency (4) = (3)/200
0–9	5	0	0
10–19	15	0	0
20–29	25	0	0
30–39	35	10	0.050
40–49	45	20	0.100
50–59	55	35	0.175
60–69	65	50	0.250
70–79	75	45	0.225
80–89	85	30	0.150
90–99	95	10	0.050
		Total 200	1.0

A more widely used definition that can handle such cases is the relative frequency definition of probability, which we now discuss.[3]

Relative Frequency or Empirical Definition of Probability

To introduce this concept of probability, consider the following example.

Example 2.7   Table 2-1 gives the distribution of marks received by 200 students in a microeconomics examination. Table 2-1 is an example of a **frequency distribution** showing how an r.v., marks in the present example, are distributed. The numbers in column 3 of the table are called **absolute frequencies**, i.e., the number of occurrences of a given event. The numbers in column 4 are called **relative frequencies**, that is, the absolute frequencies divided by the total number of occurrences (200 in the present case.) Thus, the absolute frequency of marks between 70 and 79 is 45 but the relative frequency is 0.225, which is 45 divided by 200.

---

[3] There is yet another definition of probability, called *subjective probability*, which is the foundation of *Bayesian statistics*. Under the subjective or "degrees of belief" definition of probability we can ask questions such as: What is the probability that Iraq will have a democratic government, what is the probability that President Bush will be reelected in 1992, or what is the probability that there will be a stock market crash in 1993.

Can we treat the relative frequencies as probabilities? Intuitively, it seems reasonable to consider the relative frequencies as probabilities provided the number of observations on which the relative frequencies are based is reasonably large. This is the essence of the *empirical*, or *relative frequency, definition of probability*.

More formally, if in *n* trials (or observations), *m* of them are favorable to event *A*, then *P(A)*, the probability of event *A*, is simply the ratio *m/n* (i.e., relative frequency) *provided n, the number of trials, is sufficiently large (technically, infinite)*.[4] Notice that, unlike the classical definition, we do not have to insist that the outcome be mutually exclusive and equally likely.

In short, if the number of trials is sufficiently large, we can treat the relative frequencies as fairly good measures of true probabilities. In Table 2-1 we can, therefore, treat the relative frequencies given in column 4 as probabilities.

Properties of probabilities. The probability of an event as defined earlier has the following important properties:

1. The probability of an event always lies between 0 and 1. Thus, the probability of event *A*, *P(A)*, satisfies this relationship:

$$0 \leq P(A) \leq 1 \qquad (2.2)$$

   $P(A) = 0$ means event *A* will not occur, whereas $P(A) = 1$ means event *A* will occur with certainty. Typically, the probability will lie somewhere between these numbers, as in the case of the probabilities shown in Table 2-1.

2. If *A, B, C, . . .* are *mutually exclusive events*, the probability that any one of them will occur is equal to the sum of the probabilities of their individual occurrences. Symbolically,

$$P(A + B + C + \cdots) = P(A) + P(B) + P(C) + \cdots \qquad (2.3)$$

   where the expression on the left-hand side of the equality means the probability of *A* or *B* or *C*, etc.

3. If *A, B, C, . . .* are *mutually exclusive and collectively exhaustive* set of events, the sum of the probabilities of their individual occurrences is 1. Symbolically,

$$P(A + B + C + \cdots) = P(A) + P(B) + P(C) + \cdots = 1 \qquad (2.4)$$

---

[4] What constitutes a large or small number depends on the context of the problem. Sometimes a number as small as 30 can be regarded as reasonably large. In presidential elections polls based on a sample of 800 people are fairly accurate in predicting the final outcomes although the actual number of voters runs into the millions.

Example 2.8. In Example 2.6 we saw that the probability of obtaining any of the six numbers on a die is 1/6 since there are six equally likely outcomes and each one of them has an equal chance of turning up. Since the numbers 1, 2, 3, 4, 5, and 6 form an exhaustive set of events, $P(1 + 2 + 3 + 4 + 5 + 6) = 1$, where 1, 2, 3, . . . means the probability of number 1 or number 2 or number 3, etc. And since 1, 2, . . . , 6 are mutually exclusive events in that two numbers cannot occur simultaneously in a throw of a single die, $P(1 + 2 + 3 + 4 + 5 + 6) = P(1) + P(2) + \cdots + P(6) = 1/6 + 1/6 + 1/6 + 1/6 + 1/6 + 1/6 = 1$.

In passing, note the following rules of probability that will come in handy later on.

If $A, B, C, . . .$ are any events, they are said to be *statistically independent events* if the probability of their occurring together is equal to the product of their individual probabilities. Symbolically,

$$P(ABC \cdots) = P(A)P(B)P(C) \cdots \tag{2.5}$$

where $P(ABC \cdots)$ means the probability of events $ABC \cdots$ occurring simultaneously or jointly. Hence, it is called a *joint probability*. In relation to the joint probability $P(ABC \cdots)$, $P(A)$, $P(B)$, etc. are called *unconditional, marginal, or individual probabilities*, for reasons that will become clear in Section 2.6.

Example 2.9. Suppose we throw two coins simultaneously. What is the probability of obtaining a head on the first coin and a head on the second coin? Let A denote the event of obtaining a head on the first coin and B on the second coin. We therefore want to find the probability $P(AB)$. Common sense would suggest that the probability of obtaining a head on the first coin is *independent* of the probability of obtaining a head on the second coin. Hence, $P(AB) = P(A)P(B) = (1/2)(1/2) = 1/4$ since the probability of obtaining a head (or a tail) is 1/2.

Let A and B be two events. Let us suppose we want to find out the probability that event A occurs knowing that event B has already occurred. This probability, called the *conditional probability of A, conditional on event B occurring*, and denoted by the symbol $P(A \mid B)$, is computed from the formula

$$P(A \mid B) = \frac{P(AB)}{P(B)} \tag{2.6}$$

That is, the conditional probability of A, given B, is the ratio of their joint probability to the marginal probability of B. In like manner,

$$P(B \mid A) = \frac{P(AB)}{P(A)} \tag{2.7}$$

Example 2.10.   In an introductory accounting class there are 500 students of which 300 are males and 200 are females. Of these, 100 males and 60 females plan to major in accounting. A student is selected at random from this class and it is found that this student plans to be an accounting major. What is the probability that the student is a male?

Let A denote the event that the student is a male and B that the student is an accounting major. Therefore, we want to find out $P(A\,|\,B)$. From the formula of conditional probability just given this probability can be obtained as

$$P(A\,|\,B) = \frac{P(AB)}{P(B)}$$

$$= \frac{\dfrac{100}{500}}{\dfrac{160}{500}}$$

$$= 0.625$$

From the data given previously it can be readily seen that $P(A) = 300/500 = 0.6$; that is, the unconditional probability of selecting a male student is 0.6, which is different from the preceding probability 0.625.

This example brings out an important point, namely, conditional and unconditional probabilities in general are different.[5]

Probability of Random Variables

Just as we assigned probabilities to sample outcomes or events of a sample space, we can assign probabilities to random variables, for as we saw, random variables are simply numerical representations of the outcomes of the sample space, as shown in Example 2.5. Since in this textbook we are largely concerned with random variables such as GNP, money supply, prices, wages, etc., we should know how to assign probabilities to random variables. Technically, we need to study the *probability distributions* of random variables, a topic we now discuss.

2.5   RANDOM VARIABLES AND PROBABILITY DISTRIBUTION FUNCTION (PDF)

By the probability distribution function or probability density function (PDF) of a random variable X we mean the values taken by that random variable and their

---

[5] But note that if the two events A and B are independent, $P(AB) = P(A) \cdot P(B)$, in which case $P(A\,|\,B) = P(AB)/P(B) = P(A)\,P(B)/P(B) = P(A)$. That is, if two events are independent, the conditional probability of A (given B) is the same as the unconditional probability of A.

associated probabilities. To understand this clearly, we first consider the PDF of a discrete r.v. and then consider the PDF of a continuous r.v.

PDF of a Discrete Random Variable

As noted before, a discrete r.v. takes only a finite (or countably infinite) number of values. To understand the meaning of the PDF of a discrete r.v., reconsider Example 2.5.

Example 2.11. Let the r.v. X represent the number of heads obtained in two tosses of a coin. Now consider the following table:

Number of heads X	PDF $f(X)$
0	1/4
1	1/2
2	1/4
	1.00

In this example the r.v. X (the number of heads) takes three different values—X = 0, 1, or 2. The probability that X takes a value of zero (i.e., no heads are obtained in a toss of two coins) is 1/4, for of the four possible outcomes of throwing two coins (i.e., the sample space), only 1 is favorable to the outcome *TT*. Likewise, of the four possible outcomes, only one is favorable to the outcome of two heads; hence, its probability is also 1/4. On the other hand, two outcomes, *HT* and *TH*, are favorable to the outcome of one head; hence, its probability is 2/4 = 1/2. Notice that in assigning these probabilities we have used the classical definition of probability.

The preceding table shows the likely values of X and their associated probabilities, which we denote by the function $f(X)$. This function is known as the **probability distribution** or **probability density function (PDF)**—*it shows how the probabilities are spread over or distributed over the various values of the random variable X.* Since the X variable in question is a discrete r.v., the PDF, $f(X)$, shown in the preceding table is known as the **PDF of a discrete random variable**. Incidentally, notice that the sum of the probabilities in the table is 1, for the three outcomes collectively exhaust all the possibilities. (Recall property 3 in Section 2.4.)

More formally, the function

$$f(X) = P(X = x_i) \qquad \text{for } i = 1, 2, 3, \ldots, n$$
$$= 0 \qquad\qquad\quad \text{for } X \neq x_i$$

(2.8)

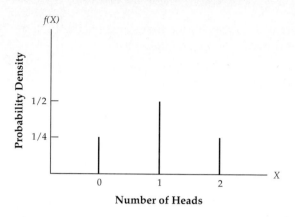

FIGURE 2-1
The probability density function (PDF) of the number of heads in two tosses of a coin (Example 2.11).

is called the PDF of the discrete r.v. X, where $P(X = x_i)$ means the probability that the discrete r.v. X takes the value of x_i. Thus, in the preceding example $P(X = 2)$ means the probability that the r.v., the number of heads in a throw of two coins, takes the value of 2.

Geometrically, the discrete PDF of this example is as shown in Figure 2-1.

PDF of a Continuous Random Variable

The PDF of a continuous r.v. is conceptually similar to the PDF of a discrete r.v. except that we now measure the probability of such an r.v. over a certain range or interval. Let X represent the continuous r.v. height, measured in inches, and suppose we want to find out the probability that the height of an individual lies in the interval, say, 60 to 68 inches. Further, suppose that the r.v. height has the PDF as shown in Figure 2-2.[6]

The probability that the height of an individual lies in the interval 60 to 68 inches is given by the shaded area lying between 60 and 68 marked on the curve in Figure 2-2. (How this probability is actually measured is shown in Chapter 3.) In passing, note that for a continuous r.v. the probability that such an r.v. takes a particular numerical value (e.g., 63 inches) is always zero; *the probability for a continuous r.v. is always measured over an interval*, say, between 62.5 and 63.5 inches.

---

[6] As we will see in Chap. 3, the PDF drawn in this figure is the PDF of the well-known normal probability distribution.

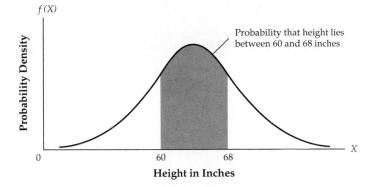

FIGURE 2-2
The PDF of a continuous random variable.

Cumulative Distribution Function (CDF)

Associated with the PDF of an r.v., X is its **cumulative distribution function (CDF)**, $F(X)$, which is defined as follows:

$$F(X) = P(X \leq x) \tag{2.9}$$

where $P(X \leq x)$ means the probability that the r.v. X takes a value of less than or equal to x, where x is given. (Of course, for a continuous r.v. the probability that such an r.v. takes the exact value of x is zero.) Thus, $P(X \leq 2)$ means the probability that the r.v. X takes a value less than or equal to 2.

Example 2.12.   What is the PDF and CDF of the r.v. number of heads obtained in four tosses of a fair coin? These functions are as follows:

Number of heads (X)	PDF Values of X	PDF f(X)	CDF Values of X	CDF F(X)
0	$0 \leq X < 1$	1/16	$X = 0$	1/16
1	$1 \leq X < 2$	4/16	$X \leq 1$	5/16
2	$2 \leq X < 3$	6/16	$X \leq 2$	11/16
3	$3 \leq X < 4$	4/16	$X \leq 3$	15/16
4	$4 \leq X$	1/16	$X \leq 4$	1

As this example and the definition of CDF suggest, a CDF is merely an "accumulation" or simply the sum of the PDF for the values of X less than or equal to a given x. That is,

$$F(X) = \sum^{x} f(X) \tag{2.10}$$

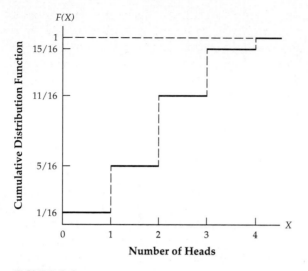

FIGURE 2-3
The cumulative distribution function (CDF) of a discrete random variable (Example 2.12).

where $\overset{x}{\Sigma} f(X)$ means the sum of the PDF for values of X less than or equal to the specified x, as shown in the preceding table. Thus, in this example the probability that X takes the value of less than 2 (heads) is 5/16, but the probability that it takes a value of less than 3 is 11/16. Of course, the probability that it takes a value of 4 or more than four heads is 1. (Why?)

Geometrically, the CDF of Example 2.12 looks like Figure 2-3. Since we

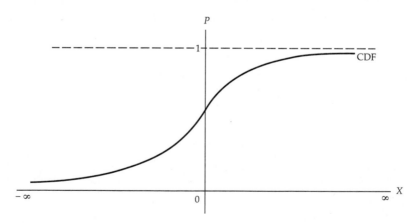

FIGURE 2-4
The CDF of a continuous random variable.

are dealing with a discrete r.v. in Example 2.12, its CDF is a discontinuous function, known as a **step function**. If we were dealing with the CDF of a continuous r.v., its CDF would be a continuous curve, as shown in Figure 2-4, which is the CDF corresponding to the PDF of the continuous r.v. shown in Figure 2-2.

2.6   MULTIVARIATE PROBABILITY DENSITY FUNCTIONS

So far we have been concerned with *single variable, or univariate,* probability distribution functions. Thus, the PDFs of Examples 2.11 and 2.12 are univariate PDFs, for we considered single random variables, such as the number of heads in a toss of two coins or the number of heads in a toss of four coins. However, we do not need to be so restrictive, for the outcomes of an experiment could be described by more than one r.v., in which case we must find their probability distributions. Such probability distributions are called **multivariate probability distributions**. The simplest of the multivariate PDFs is the *bivariate, or a two-variable PDF*. Let us illustrate with an example.

> **Example 2.13.**   Table 2-2 gives the rating (X) and yield to maturity $Y(\%)$ of 50 bonds, where the rating is measured at three levels: $X = 1$ (Bbb), $X = 2$ (Bb), and $X = 3$ (B). As per Standard & Poor's bond-rating scheme, Bbb, Bb, and B are all medium-quality bonds; Bb is of slightly higher quality than B; and Bbb is of slightly better quality than Bb. That is, the fewer the letters in the grading, the riskier is the bond.

In this example we have two random variables, X (bond rating) and Y (bond yield). The table shows that there are 13 bonds with a rating value of 1 (triple B), which yield a rate of return of 8.5 percent. Likewise, there are 14

TABLE 2-2
The frequency distribution of two random variables: Bond rating (X) and bond yield (Y)

Yield to maturity $Y(\%)$	1 (Bbb)	2 (Bb)	3 (B)	Total
8.5	13	5	0	18
11.5	2	14	2	18
17.5	0	1	13	14
Total	15	20	15	50

TABLE 2-3
Bivariate probability distribution

Y(%) \ X	1 (Bbb)	2 (Bb)	3 (B)	Total
8.5	0.26	0.10	0.00	0.36
11.5	0.04	0.28	0.04	0.36
17.5	0.00	0.02	0.26	0.28
Total	0.30	0.40	0.30	1.00

bonds with a rating of 2 (double B), which yield a rate of return of 11.5 percent, etc. In other words, Table 2-2 gives the absolute frequency distribution of two random variables, Y and X.

Let us divide each entry of the table by 50 to convert the absolute frequencies into relative frequencies, i.e., probabilities (for simplicity, assume that the population or sample space consists of 50 bonds only). The result is shown in Table 2-3.

Table 2-3 provides an example of what is known as a **bivariate** or **joint probability density function**, or **joint PDF**. Each entry in the body of the table is known as a **joint probability**—it gives the probability that the r.v. X takes a given value (e.g., 2) and Y takes a given value (e.g., 11.5 percent). The joint PDF may be denoted by $f(X, Y)$. Since in the previous example both X and Y take only discrete values, this is a discrete joint PDF.

More formally, let X and Y be two discrete random variables. Then the function

$$f(X, Y) = P(X = x \quad \text{and} \quad Y = y) \tag{2.11}$$
$$= 0 \qquad \text{when } X \neq x \quad \text{and} \quad Y \neq y$$

is known as the (*discrete*) *joint PDF*. This gives the joint probability that X takes the value of x and Y takes the value of y, where x and y are some specified values. Thus, in the preceding example the (joint) probability that X takes the value of 3 whereas Y assumes the value of 17.5 percent is 0.26. Other joint probabilities should be interpreted similarly.

The joint probability of two continuous random variables can be defined analogously, although their mathematical expressions are involved and best left for the references for interested readers.

Marginal Probability Density Function

We have studied the univariate PDFs, such as $f(X)$ or $f(Y)$, and the bivariate, or joint, PDF, $f(X, Y)$. Is there any relationship between the two? Yes, there is.

In relation to $f(X, Y)$, $f(X)$ and $f(Y)$ are called **univariate, unconditional,**

TABLE 2-4
**Marginal probability distributions
of X and Y**

Value of X (bond rating)	f(X)	Value of Y (bond yield, %)	f(Y)
1	0.30	8.5	0.36
2	0.40	11.5	0.36
3	0.30	17.5	0.28
Total	1.00	Total	1.00

individual, or **marginal PDFs**. More technically, the probability that X assumes a given value (e.g., 2) *regardless of the values taken by Y* is called the marginal probability of X and the distribution of these probabilities is called the marginal PDF of X. How do we compute these marginal PDFs? That is easy. In Table 2-3 we see from the column totals that the probability that X takes the value of 1 regardless of the values taken by Y is 0.30; the probability that it takes the value of 2 regardless of Y's value is 0.40; and the probability that it takes the value of 3, whatever Y's value, is 0.30. Therefore, the marginal PDF of X is as that shown in Table 2-4. Also Table 2-4 shows the marginal PDF of Y, which can be derived similarly. Note that the sum of each of the PDFs, $f(X)$ and $f(Y)$, is 1. (Why?)

The reader will easily note that to obtain the marginal probabilities of X, we sum the joint probabilities corresponding to the given value of X regardless of the values taken by Y. That is, we sum down the columns. Likewise, to obtain the marginal probabilities of Y, we sum the joint probabilities corresponding to the given value of Y regardless of the values taken by X. That is, we sum across the rows. Once such marginal probabilities are computed, finding the marginal PDFs is straightforward, as we just showed.

Conditional Probability Density Function

Continuing with our bond-yield/bond-rating example, let us now suppose we want to find the probability that the bond yield is 8.5 percent, given that it is rated 1, i.e., Bbb. In other words, what is the probability that $Y = 8.5$ percent, conditional upon the fact that $X = 1$? This is known as **conditional probability** (recall our earlier discussion of conditional probability of an event). This probability can be obtained from the **conditional probability density function** defined as

$$f(Y \mid X) = P(Y = y \mid X = x) \qquad (2.12)$$

where $f(Y \mid X)$ stands for the *conditional PDF* of Y; it gives the probability that Y takes on the value of y (e.g., 8.5 percent) conditional on the knowledge that X has assumed the value of x (e.g., 1) Similarly,

$$f(X|Y) = P(X = x | Y = y) \tag{2.13}$$

gives the conditional PDF of X.

Note that the preceding two conditional PDFs are for two discrete random variables, Y and X. Hence, they may be called *discrete conditional PDFs.* Conditional PDFs for continuous random variables can be defined analogously, although the mathematical formulas are slightly involved.

One simple method of computing the conditional PDFs is as follows:

$$f(X|Y) = \frac{f(X, Y)}{f(Y)} \tag{2.14}$$

$$= \frac{\text{the joint probability of } X \text{ and } Y}{\text{the marginal probability of } Y}$$

$$f(Y|X) = \frac{f(X, Y)}{f(X)} \tag{2.15}$$

$$= \frac{\text{the joint probability of } X \text{ and } Y}{\text{the marginal probability of } X}$$

In words, *the conditional PDF of one variable, given the value of the other variable, is simply the ratio of the joint probability of the two variables divided by the marginal or unconditional PDF of the other (i.e., the conditioning) variable.* [Compare this with the conditional probability of an event A, given that event B has happened, i.e., $P(A|B)$.]

Returning to our example, we want to find out $f(Y = 8.5 | X = 1)$, which is

$$f(Y = 8.5 | X = 1) = \frac{f(Y = 8.5 \text{ and } X = 1)}{f(X = 1)}$$

$$= \frac{0.26}{0.30} \quad \text{(from Table 2-3)}$$

$$\approx 0.8667$$

From Table 2-3 we observe that the unconditional probability that Y takes the value of 8.5 percent is 0.36, but knowing that the bond rating is 1 (i.e., Bbb, which is the highest in the given example), the probability that it takes a value of 8.5 percent increases to ≈ 0.87. Notice how knowledge about the other event, the conditioning event, changes our assessment of the probabilities.

In regression analysis, as shown in Chapter 5, we are interested in studying the behavior of one variable that is conditional on the values of another variable(s). Therefore, the knowledge of conditional PDFs is very important for the development of regression analysis.

TABLE 2-5
**Statistical independence
of two random variables**

		X			$f(Y)$
		1	2	3	
	1	1/9	1/9	1/9	3/9
Y	2	1/9	1/9	1/9	3/9
	3	1/9	1/9	1/9	3/9
	$f(X)$	3/9	3/9	3/9	1

Statistical Independence

Another concept that is vital for the study of regression analysis is the concept of **independent random variables**, which is related to the concept of independence of events discussed earlier. We explain this with an example.

Example 2.14.   A bag contains three balls numbered 1, 2, and 3, respectively. Two balls are drawn at random, with replacement, from the bag (i.e., every time a ball is drawn it is put back before another is drawn). Let the variable X denote the number on the first ball drawn and Y the number on the second ball. Table 2-5 gives the joint as well as the marginal PDFs of the two variables.

Now consider the probabilities $f(X = 1, Y = 1)$, $f(X = 1)$, and $f(Y = 1)$. As Table 2-5 shows, these probabilities are 1/9, 1/3, and 1/3, respectively. Now the first of these is a joint probability, whereas the last two are marginal probabilities. However, the joint probability in this case is equal to the product of the two marginal probabilities. When this happens, we say that the two variables are **statistically independent**. More formally, *two variables X and Y are statistically independent if and only if their joint PDF can be expressed as the product of their individual, or marginal, PDFs for all combinations of X and Y values.* Symbolically,

$$f(X, Y) = f(X)f(Y) \tag{2.16}$$

The reader can easily verify that for any other combination of X and Y values given in Table 2-5 the joint PDF is the product of the respective marginal PDFs; i.e., the two variables are statistically independent. *Bear in mind that Equation (2.16) must be true for all combinations of X and Y values.*

Example 2.15.   Are the bond rating and bond yield in Example 2.13 independent random variables? To determine this, let us apply the definition of independence given in Eq. (2.16). Let $X = 1$ (Bbb rating) and Y = yield of 8.5 percent. From Table 2-3 we see that $f(X = 1, Y = 8.5) = 0.26$; $f(X = 1) = 0.30$ and $f(Y = 8.5) = 0.36$. Obviously, in this case $0.26 \neq (0.30)(0.36)$. Hence, the bond rating and bond yield are not independent random variables, which is hardly surprising. (Why?)

2.7   CHARACTERISTICS OF PROBABILITY DISTRIBUTIONS

Although a PDF indicates the values taken by an r.v. and their associated probabilities, often we are not interested in the entire PDF. Thus, in the PDF of Example 2.11 we may not want the individual probabilities of obtaining no heads, one head, or two heads. Rather, we may wish to find out the *average number* of heads obtained in the toss of a coin several times. In other words, we may be interested in some summary characteristics, or more technically, the **moments** of the probability distribution. Two of the most commonly used summary measures or moments are the *expected value* (called the first moment of the distribution) and the *variance* (called the second moment of the distribution).

Expected Value: A Measure of Central Tendency

The **expected value** of a discrete r.v. X, denoted by the symbol $E(X)$ (read as E of X), is defined as follows:

$$E(X) = \sum_X Xf(X) \tag{2.17}$$

where $f(X)$ is the PDF of X and where $\sum_X$ means the sum over all values of X.[7]
   Verbally, the expected value of a random variable is a *weighted average* of its possible values, with the probabilities of these values [i.e., $f(X)$] serving as the *weights*. Equivalently, *it is the sum of products of the values taken by the r.v. and their corresponding probabilities.* The expected value of r.v. is also known as its *average* or *mean* value, although, more correctly, it is called the **population mean value** for reasons to be discussed shortly.

Example 2.16.   Suppose we roll a die numbered 1 through 6 several times. What is the expected value of the number shown? As given previously (see Example 2.6), we have the situation shown in Table 2-6.

---

[7] The expected value of a continuous r.v. can be defined similarly, with the summation symbol (Σ) being replaced by the integral symbol ($\int$) of calculus.

TABLE 2-6
The expected value of a random variable *X*, the number shown on a die

Number shown (1) X	Probability (2) $f(X)$	Number × Probability (3) $Xf(X)$
1	1/6	1/6
2	1/6	2/6
3	1/6	3/6
4	1/6	4/6
5	1/6	5/6
6	1/6	6/6
		$E(X) = 21/6 = 3.5$

Applying the definition of an expected value given in Eq. (2.17), we see that the expected value is 3.5.

Is it strange that we obtained this value, since the r.v. here is discrete and can take only one of the six values 1 through 6? The expected, or average, value of 3.5 in this example means that if we were to roll the die several times, then on the *average* we would obtain the number 3.5, which is between 3 and 4. If in a contest someone were to give you as many dollars as the number shown on the die, then in several rolls of the die you would anticipate receiving on the average $3.50 per roll of the die.

Geometrically, the expected value of the preceding example is shown in Figure 2-5.

Example 2.17.   In the bond-rating example, what is the expected value of the bond rating? This can be obtained easily from Table 2-4 by multiplying the various X values by their associated probabilities and summing the products obtained. This gives

$$1(0.30) + 2(0.40) + 3(0.30) = 2.0$$

That is, the expected value of the bond rating is 2.0, which is Bb.

Example 2.18.   In the previous example, what is the expected value of the bond yield? This value can also be obtained from Table 2-4 by multiplying the values of Y (yield) by their associated probabilities and summing the product. Thus,

$$8.5(0.36) + 11.5(0.36) + 17.5(0.28) = 12.10$$

which is the expected bond yield.

Properties of expected value. The following properties of expected value will prove very useful later on:

1. The expected value of a constant is that constant itself.
   Thus, if b is a constant,

$$E(b) = b \tag{2.18}$$

   For example, if $b = 2$, $E(2) = 2$.
2. The expectation of the sum of two random variables is equal to the sum of the expectations of those random variables. Thus, for the random variables X and Y[8]

$$E(X + Y) = E(X) + E(Y) \tag{2.19}$$

3. However,

$$E(X/Y) \neq \frac{E(X)}{E(Y)} \tag{2.20}$$

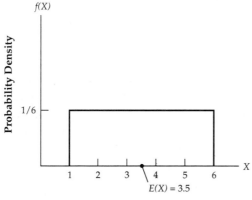

Discrete Random Variable

FIGURE 2-5
The expected value, $E(X)$, of a discrete random variable (Example 2.16).

---

[8] This property can be generalized to more than two random variables. Thus,

$$E(X + Y + Z + W) = E(X) + E(Y) + E(Z) + E(W)$$

That is, the expected value of the ratio of two random variables is not equal to the ratio of the expected values of those random variables.

4. Also, in general,

$$E(XY) \ne E(X)E(Y) \tag{2.21}$$

That is, in general, the expected value of the product of two random variables is not equal to the product of the expectations of those random variables. However, there is an exception to the rule. If X and Y are *independent random variables*, then it is true that

$$E(XY) = E(X)E(Y) \tag{2.22}$$

Recall that X and Y are said to be independent if and only if $f(X, Y) = f(X)f(Y)$, i.e., when the joint PDF is equal to the product of the individual PDFs of the two random variables.

5. If a is a constant, then

$$E(aX) = aE(X) \tag{2.23}$$

That is, the expectation of a constant times an r.v. is equal to the constant times the expectation of the r.v.

6. If a and b are constants, then

$$
\begin{aligned}
E(aX + b) &= aE(X) + E(b) \\
&= aE(X) + b
\end{aligned}
\tag{2.24}
$$

In deriving this result, (6), we use properties (1), (2), and (5). Thus, $E(4X + 7) = 4E(X) + 7$.

Variance: A Measure of Dispersion

The expected value of an r.v. simply gives its *center of gravity,* but it does not indicate how the individual values are spread, dispersed, or distributed around this mean value. The most popular numerical measure of this spread is called the **variance,** which is defined as follows.

Let X be an r.v. and $E(X)$ be its expected value, which for notational simplicity may be denoted by μ_x (where μ is the Greek letter mu). Then the variance of X is defined as

$$\text{var}(X) = \sigma_x^2 = E(X - \mu_x)^2 \tag{2.25}$$

where the Greek letter σ_x^2 (sigma squared) is the commonly used symbol for the variance. As Equation (2.25) shows, the variance of X (or any r.v.) is simply the expected value of the squared difference between an individual X value and its expected or mean value. The variance thus defined shows how the individual X values are spread or distributed around its expected, or mean, value. If all X values are precisely equal to $E(X)$, the variance will be zero, whereas if they are widely spread around the expected value, it will be rela-

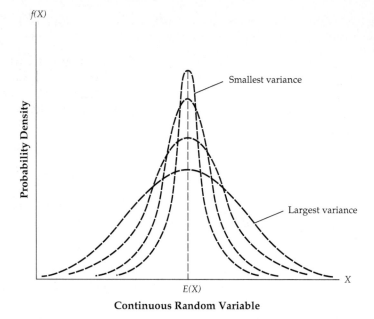

Continuous Random Variable

FIGURE 2-6
Hypothetical PDFs of continuous random variables all with the same expected value.

tively large, as shown in Figure 2-6. Notice that the variance cannot be a negative number. (Why?)

The positive square root of σ_x^2, σ_x, is known as the **standard deviation (s.d.)**.

Equation (2.25) is the definition of variance. To compute the variance, we use the following formula:

$$\text{var}(X) = \sum_X (X - \mu_x)^2 f(X) \tag{2.26}$$

if X is a discrete r.v. A similar formula can be obtained for a continuous r.v.

As Equation (2.26) shows, to compute the variance of a discrete r.v., we subtract the expected value of the variable from a given value of the variable, square the difference, and multiply the squared difference by the probability associated with that X value. We do this for each value assumed by the X variable and sum the products thus obtained. An example follows.

Example 2.19.   We continue with Example 2.16. There we showed that the expected value of the number in the repeated roll of a die is 3.5. To compute the variance for that problem, we set up Table 2-7.

TABLE 2-7
The variance of a random variable X, the number shown on a die

Number shown X	Probability $f(X)$	$(X - \mu_x)^2 \; f(X)$
1	1/6	$(1 - 3.5)^2 \; (1/6)$
2	1/6	$(2 - 3.5)^2 \; (1/6)$
3	1/6	$(3 - 3.5)^2 \; (1/6)$
4	1/6	$(4 - 3.5)^2 \; (1/6)$
5	1/6	$(5 - 3.5)^2 \; (1/6)$
6	1/6	$(6 - 3.5)^2 \; (1/6)$
		Sum = 2.9167

Thus, the variance of this example is 2.9167. Taking the positive square root of this value, we obtain the standard deviation (s.d.) as ≈ 1.7078.

Properties of variance. The variance as defined earlier has the following properties, which we will find useful in our later discussion of econometrics.

1. The variance of a constant is zero. By definition, a constant has no variability.

2. If X and Y are two *independent* random variables, then

$$\mathrm{var}(X + Y) = \mathrm{var}(X) + \mathrm{var}(Y)$$

and   (2.27)

$$\mathrm{var}(X - Y) = \mathrm{var}(X) + \mathrm{var}(Y)$$

That is, the variance of the sum or difference of two independent random variables is equal to the sum of their individual variances.

3. If b is a constant, then

$$\mathrm{var}(X + b) = \mathrm{var}(X) \qquad (2.28)$$

That is, adding a constant number to (the values of) a variable does not change the variance of that variable. Thus, $\mathrm{var}(X + 7) = \mathrm{var}(X)$.

4. If a is constant, then

$$\mathrm{var}(aX) = a^2 \, \mathrm{var}(X) \qquad (2.28a)$$

That is, the variance of a constant times a variable is equal to the square of that constant times the variance of that variable. Thus, $\mathrm{var}(5X) = 25 \, \mathrm{var}(X)$.

5. If a and b are constant, then

$$\text{var}(aX + b) = a^2\,\text{var}(X) \tag{2.28b}$$

which follows from properties (3) and (4). Thus,

$$\text{var}(5X + 9) = 25\,\text{var}(X)$$

6. If X and Y are *independent* random variables and a and b are constants, then

$$\text{var}(aX + bY) = a^2\,\text{var}(X) + b^2\,\text{var}(Y)$$

This property follows from the previous properties. Thus,

$$\text{var}(3X + 5Y) = 9\,\text{var}(X) + 25\,\text{var}(Y) \tag{2.29}$$

Covariance

The expected value and the variance are the two most frequently used summary measures of a univariate PDF—the former gives us the center of gravity and the latter tells us how the individual values are distributed around the center of gravity. But once we go beyond the univariate PDFs (e.g., the PDF of Example 2.13), we need to consider, in addition to the mean and variance of each variable, some additional characteristics, such as the **covariance** and **correlation,** which we now discuss.

Let X and Y be two random variables with means $E(X) = \mu_x$ and $E(Y) = \mu_y$. Then the covariance between the two variables is defined as

$$\text{cov}(X, Y) = E[(X - \mu_x)(Y - \mu_y)] \tag{2.30}$$
$$= E(XY) - \mu_x\mu_y$$

As Equation (2.30) shows, a covariance is a special kind of expected value and is a measure of how two variables vary or move together (i.e., co-vary), as shown in Example 2.20, which follows.

To compute the covariance as defined in Eq. (2.30), we use the following formula, assuming X and Y are discrete random variables:

$$\text{cov}(X, Y) = \sum_X \sum_Y (X - \mu_x)(Y - \mu_y)f(X, Y) \tag{2.31}$$
$$= \sum_X \sum_Y XY\,f(X, Y) - \mu_x\mu_y$$

Note the double summation sign in this expression because the covariance requires the summation of both variables over the range of their values. Using the integral notation of calculus, a similar formula can be devised to compute the covariance of two continuous random variables.

Example 2.20.   Let us compute the covariance between X (bond rating) and Y (bond yield) of Example 2.13. We use formula (2.31). First, using the data given in Table 2-3, we compute $\sum_X \sum_Y XY f(X, Y)$:

$$\sum_X \sum_Y XY f(X, Y) = (8.5)(1)(0.26) + (8.5)(2)(0.10) + (8.5)(3)(0.0)$$

$$+ (11.5)(1)(0.04) + (11.5)(2)(0.28) + (11.5)(3)(0.04)$$

$$+ (17.5)(1)(0.0) + (17.5)(2)(0.02) + (17.5)(3)(0.26)$$

$$= 26.54$$

As shown in Examples 2.17 and 2.18, $E(X) = \mu_x = 2.0$ and $E(Y) = \mu_y = 12.10$. Therefore, we have

$$cov (X, Y) = 26.54 - (2.0)(12.10) = 2.34$$

That is, the covariance between the bond rating and the bond yield is positive. This is understandable because of how we have coded bond rating: The bond rating 3 is given to the most risky bond (i.e., the B rating). Therefore, the higher the risk, the higher the expected yield.

In general, the covariance between two random variables can be *positive* or *negative*. If two random variables move in the same direction (e.g., if one increases, the other increases, too) as in Example 2.20, then the covariance will be positive, whereas if they move in the opposite direction (i.e., if one increases and the other decreases), the covariance will be negative.

Properties of covariance. The covariance as defined earlier has the following properties, which we will find quite useful in regression analysis in later chapters.

1. If X and Y are *independent* random variables, their covariance is zero. This is easy to verify. Recall that if two random variables are independent,

$$E(XY) = E(X)E(Y) = \mu_x\mu_y \qquad (2.32)$$

Substituting this expression into Eq. (2.30), we see at once that the covariance of two *independent* random variables is zero.

2.

$$cov (a + bX, c + dY) = bd \, cov(X, Y) \qquad (2.33)$$

where a, b, c, and d are constants.

3.

$$cov(X, X) = var(X) \qquad (2.34)$$

That is, the covariance of a variable with itself is simply its variance, which can be verified from the definitions of variance and covariance given previously. Obviously, then, $cov(Y, Y) = var(Y)$.

Correlation Coefficient

In the bond-rating example just considered we found that the covariance between the bond yield and the bond rating is +2.34, which suggests that the two variables are positively related. But the computed number of 2.34 does not give any idea of how "strongly" the two variables are positively related. If we are interested in finding out how strongly any two variables are related, we can do so in terms of what is known as the **coefficient of correlation,** which is defined as follows:

$$\rho = \frac{\text{cov}(X, Y)}{\sigma_x \sigma_y} \tag{2.35}$$

where ρ (rho) denotes the coefficient of correlation.

As is clear from Equation (2.35), the correlation between two random variables X and Y is simply the ratio of the covariance between the two variables divided by their respective standard deviations. The correlation coefficient thus defined is a measure of *linear* association between two variables, i.e., how strongly the two variables are linearly related.

Properties of correlation coefficient. The correlation coefficient just defined has the following properties:

1. Like the covariance, the correlation coefficient can be positive or negative. It is positive if the covariance is positive and negative if the covariance is negative. In short, it has the same sign as the covariance.
2. The correlation coefficient always lies between -1 and $+1$. Symbolically,

$$-1 \leq \rho \leq 1 \tag{2.36}$$

If the correlation coefficient is $+1$, it means that the two variables are perfectly positively correlated, whereas if the correlation coefficient is -1, it means they are perfectly negatively correlated. Typically, ρ lies between these limits.

Figure 2-7 gives some typical patterns of correlation coefficient.

Example 2.21.   Let us continue with the bond-rating example. In Example 2.20 we found that the covariance between the bond yield and the bond rating was 2.34. From the individual PDFs given in Table 2-4, the reader can readily check that the s.d. of X (bond rating) and Y (bond yield) are ≈ 0.77 and ≈ 3.60, respectively. Therefore, the correlation coefficient in the present instance is

$$\rho = \frac{2.34}{(0.77)(3.60)} \approx 0.844$$

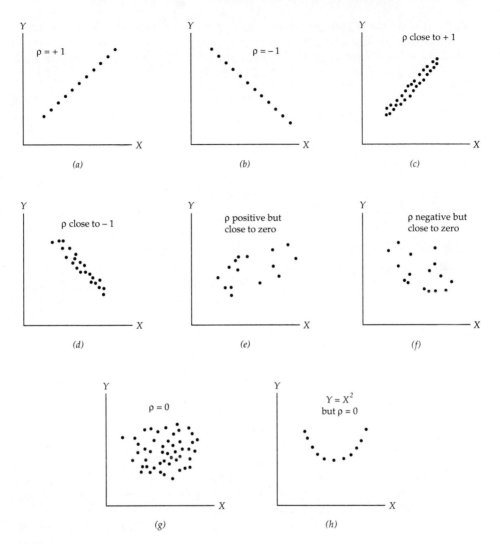

FIGURE 2-7
Some typical patterns of the correlation coefficient, ρ.

Notice that from the covariance of 2.34 alone we cannot tell whether the covariance between the two variables was "high" or "low." But from the correlation coefficient we can be a bit more assertive. Since ρ can be at most $+1$, the observed value of 0.844 suggests that the two variables are highly positively correlated, since 0.844 is close to 1.

The use of the correlation coefficient in the regression context is discussed in Chapter 5.

Variances of correlated variables. Earlier we discussed the formula for the variance of the sum or difference of two independent random variables. But what happens if the random variables are not independent; i.e., they are correlated? In this case we have the following formulas:

$$\text{var}(X + Y) = \text{var}(X) + \text{var}(Y) + 2\,\text{cov}(X, Y) \qquad (2.37)$$

$$\text{var}(X - Y) = \text{var}(X) + \text{var}(Y) - 2\,\text{cov}(X, Y) \qquad (2.38)$$

Of course, if the covariance between two random variables is zero, then $\text{var}(X + Y)$ and $\text{var}(X - Y)$ are both equal to $\text{var}(X) + \text{var}(Y)$, as we saw before.

It is left as an exercise for the student to find the variance of $(X + Y)$ of our bond-rating example.

Conditional Expectation

Another statistical concept that is especially important in regression analysis is the concept of **conditional expectation,** which is different from the expectation of an r.v. considered previously, which may be called the **unconditional expectation.** The difference between the two concepts of expectations can be explained as follows.

Return to our bond-rating example (Example 2.13). In this example X is the bond rating (measured 1, 2, or 3) and Y is the bond yield (8.5, 11.5, or 17.5 percent). What is the expected value of X? As we saw before from Table 2-4, $E(X) = 2.0$. Likewise, from Table 2-4 we can find $E(Y) = 12.10$ percent. Each of these expectations is called an *unconditional expectation.*

But now consider this question: What is the average value of the bond yield if you are told that the bond rating is 1? Put differently, what is the *conditional expectation* of Y given that $X = 1$? Technically, what is $E(Y \mid X = 1)$? This is known as the conditional expectation of Y. Similarly, we could ask: What is $E(X \mid Y = 8.5)$? That is, what is the conditional expectation of X knowing that the bond yield is 8.5 percent?

From the preceding discussion it should be clear that in computing the unconditional expectation of an r.v., we do not take into account information about any other r.v., whereas in computing the conditional expectation we do.

To compute such conditional expectations, we use the following definition of conditional expectation

$$E(X \mid Y = y) = \sum_X Xf(X \mid Y = y) \qquad (2.39)$$

which gives the conditional expectation of X, where X is a discrete r.v., $f(X \mid Y = y)$ is the conditional PDF of X given in Eq. (2.13), and $\sum_X$ means the sum over all values of X. In relation to Equation (2.39), $E(X)$ as considered earlier is called the *unconditional expectation.* Computationally, $E(X \mid Y = y)$ is similar to $E(X)$ except that instead of using the unconditional PDF of X, we use its conditional PDF, as seen clearly in comparing Eq. (2.39) with Eq. (2.17).

Similarly,

$$E(Y\,|\,X = x) = \sum_Y Yf(Y\,|\,X = x) \tag{2.40}$$

gives the conditional expectation of Y. Let us illustrate with an example.

Example 2.22. Let us compute $E(Y\,|\,X = 1)$ for the bond-rating example. That is, we want to find out the conditional expected bond yield for bonds whose bond rating is 1 (triple B).

Using formula (2.40), we have

$$E(Y\,|\,X = 1) = \sum_Y Y f(Y\,|\,X = 1)$$

$$= 8.5f(Y = 8.5\,|\,X = 1) + 11.5f(Y = 11.5\,|\,X = 1)$$

$$+ 17.5\,(f(Y = 17.5\,|\,X = 1)$$

$$= 8.5(0.87) + 11.5(0.13) + 17.5(0)$$

$$= 8.89^9$$

As the preceding computations show, the conditional expectation of Y, given that $X = 1$, is 8.89 percent, whereas, as shown previously, the unconditional expectation of Y was 12.10 percent. But this result should not be surprising—knowing that the bond rating is the highest (triple B), we expect the average yield to be lower. Just as we saw previously that the conditional PDFs and marginal PDFs are generally different, the conditional and unconditional expectations in general are different too.

2.8 FROM POPULATION TO THE SAMPLE

To compute the characteristics of probability distribution, such as the expected value, variance, covariance, correlation, conditional expected value, etc., we obviously need the PDF, that is, the whole sample space or population (i.e., the PDF). Thus, to find out the average income of all the people living in the city of New York at a given moment in time, obviously we need information on the whole population of New York City. Although conceptually there is some finite population of New York City at a given point in time, it is simply not practical to collect information about each member of the population (i.e., outcome, in the language of probability). What is done in practice is to draw

---

[9] *Note:* $f(Y = 8.5\,|\,X = 1) = f(Y = 8.5, X = 1)/f(X = 1) = 0.87$; i.e., the conditional density function is equal to the ratio of the joint density function divided by the marginal density function, as seen in Eq. (2.15).

a "representative" or a "random" sample from this population and to compute the average income of the people thus sampled.[10]

But would the average income obtained from the sample be equal to the true average income (i.e., expected value of income) in the population as a whole? Most likely not. Similarly, if we were to compute the variance of the income in the sampled population, would that equal the true variance that we would have obtained had we studied the whole population? Again, most likely not.

How then could we learn about population characteristics like expected value, variance, etc. if we only have one or two samples from a given population? And, as we will see throughout this book, in practice, invariably we have to depend on one or more samples from a given population.

The answer to this very important question will be the focus of our attention in Chapter 4. But meanwhile, we must find the sample counterparts, the **sample moments,** of the various population characteristics that we discussed in the preceding sections.

Sample Mean

Let X denote the number of cars sold per day by a car dealer. Assume that the r.v. X follows some PDF. Further, suppose we want to find out the average number [i.e., $E(X)$] of cars sold by the dealer in the first 10 days of each month. Assume that the car dealer has been in business for 10 years but has no time to look up the sales figures for the first 10 days of each month for the past 10 years. Suppose that he decides to pick at "random" one month from the past data and notes the sales figures for the first 10 days of that month, which are as follows: 9, 11, 11, 14, 13, 9, 8, 9, 14, 12. This is a *sample* of 10 values: Notice that he has data for 120 months and if he had decided to choose another month, he probably would have obtained 10 other values.

If the dealer adds up the 10 sales values and divides the sum by 10, the sample size, the number he would obtain is known as the **sample mean.**

The sample mean of a r.v. X is generally denoted by the symbol $\overline{X}$ (read as X bar) and is defined as

$$\overline{X} = \sum_{i=1}^{n} \frac{X_i}{n} \tag{2.41}$$

where $\sum_{i=1}^{n} X_i$, as usual, means the sum of the X values from 1 to n, where n is the sample size.

The sample mean thus defined is known as the **estimator** of $E(X)$, which we can now call the *population mean*. An *estimator is simply a rule or formula that tells us how to go about estimating a population quantity,* such as the population mean. In Chapter 3 we will show how $\overline{X}$ is related to $E(X)$.

---

[10] The precise meaning of a random sample will be explained later.

For the sample just given, the sample mean is

$$\overline{X} = \frac{9 + 11 + 11 + \cdots + 12}{10} = \frac{110}{10} = 11$$

which we call an **estimate** of the population mean. *An estimate is simply the numerical value taken by an estimator,* 11 in the preceding example. In our example the average number of cars sold in the first 10 days of the month is 11. But keep in mind that this number will not necessarily equal $E(X)$; to compute the latter, we will have to take into account the sales data for the first 10 days of each of the other 119 months. In short, we will have to consider the entire PDF of car sales. But as we show in Chapter 3, often the estimate, such as 11, obtained from a given sample is a fairly good "proxy" for the true $E(X)$.

Sample Variance

The ten sample values given previously are not all equal to the sample mean of 11. The variability of the ten values from this sample mean can be measured by the **sample variance,** denoted by S_x^2, which is an *estimator of* σ_x^2, *which we can now call the population variance.* The sample variance is defined as

$$S_x^2 = \sum_{i=1}^{n} \frac{(X_i - \overline{X})^2}{n - 1} \tag{2.42}$$

which is simply the sum of the squared difference of an individual X value from its mean value divided by the total number of observations less one.[11] The expression $(n - 1)$ is known as the *degrees of freedom,* whose precise meaning will be explained in Chapter 3.[12] S_x, the positive square root of S_x^2, is called the **sample standard deviation (s.d.).**

For the sample of $10X$ values given earlier the sample variance is

$$S_x^2 = \frac{(9 - 11)^2 + (11 - 11)^2 + \cdots + (12 - 11)^2}{9}$$

$$= \frac{44}{9} = 4.89$$

and the sample s.d. is $S_x = \sqrt{4.89} \approx 2.21$. Note that 4.89 is an *estimate* of the population variance and 2.21 is an *estimate* of the population s.d. Again, an estimate is a numerical value taken by an estimator in a given sample.

---

[11] If the sample size is large, the numerator of Eq. (2.42) can be divided by n rather than by $(n - 1)$.

[12] The reason for using the divisor $(n - 1)$ is Eq. (2.42) is that Eq. (2.42) provides an *unbiased* estimator of the true σ_x^2. That is, if we use formula (2.42) repeatedly, on the average the sample variance computed from Eq. (2.42) will be equal to the true population variance. On the concept of unbiasedness of an estimator, see Chap. 4.

Sample Covariance

Example 2.23. Suppose we have a bivariate population of two variables X (stock prices) and Y (consumer prices). Suppose further that from this bivariate population we obtain the random sample shown in the first two columns of Table 2-8. In this example stock prices are measured by the Dow-Jones average and consumer prices by the Consumer Price Index (CPI). The other entries in this table are discussed later.

Analogous to the population covariance defined in Eq. (2.30), the sample covariance between two random variables X and Y is defined as

$$\text{Sample cov}(X, Y) = \frac{\sum (X_i - \overline{X})(Y_i - \overline{Y})}{n - 1} \qquad (2.43)$$

TABLE 2-8
Sample covariance and sample correlation coefficient between Dow-Jones average (Y) and Consumer Price Index (X) over the period 1980–1989

Y (1)	X (2)	$(Y - \overline{Y})(X - \overline{X})$ (3)
891.4	82.4	$(891.4 - 1504.4)(82.4 - 104.64)$
932.42	90.9	$(932.42 - 1504.4)(90.9 - 104.64)$
884.36	96.5	— —
1190.34	99.6	— —
1178.48	103.9	— —
1328.23	107.6	— —
1792.76	109.6	— —
2275.99	113.6	— —
2060.82	118.3	$(2060.82 - 1504.4)(118.3 - 104.64)$
2508.91	124.0	$(2508.91 - 1504.4)(124.0 - 104.64)$
15044	1046.4	≈ 63234

$$\overline{Y} = \frac{15{,}044}{10} = 1504.4 \quad \text{Sample var}(Y) = 368{,}870$$

$$\overline{X} = \frac{1046.4}{10} = 104.64 \quad \text{Sample var}(X) = 161.18$$

Source: Data on Y and X are from the *Economic Report of the President*, 1990, Tables C-93 and C-58, respectively.

which is simply the sum of the cross products of the two random variables expressed as deviations from their (sample) mean values and divided by the degrees of freedom, $(n - 1)$. (If the sample size is large, we may use n as the divisor.) The sample covariance defined in Equation (2.43) is thus the estimator of the population covariance. Its numerical value in a given instance will provide an *estimate* of the population covariance, as in the following example.

In Table 2-8 we have given the necessary quantities to compute the sample covariance, which in the present case is

$$\text{Sample cov}(X, Y) = \frac{63234}{9} = 7026.20$$

Thus, in the present case the covariance between stock prices and consumer prices is positive. Some analysts believe that investment in stocks is a hedge against inflation; i.e., as inflation increases, stock prices increase, too. Apparently, for the period 1980 to 1989 that seems to be the case, although empirical evidence on this subject is not unequivocal.

Sample Correlation Coefficient

In Eq. (2.35) we defined the population correlation coefficient between two random variables. Its sample analogue, or *estimator*, which we denote by the symbol r, is as follows:

$$r = \frac{\sum_{i=1}^{n} (X_i - \overline{X})(Y_i - \overline{Y})/(n - 1)}{S_X S_Y} \tag{2.44}$$

$$= \frac{\text{sample cov}(X, Y)}{\text{s.d.}(X)\text{s.d.}(Y)}$$

The sample correlation thus defined has the same properties as the population correlation coefficient; they both lie between -1 and $+1$.

For the data given in Table 2-8 the reader can easily compute the sample standard deviations of Y and X, and therefore can compute the sample correlation coefficient r, an estimate of ρ, which turns out to be

$$r = \frac{7026.20}{(12.696)(607.40)}$$

$$= 0.9111$$

Thus, in our example stock prices and consumer prices are highly positively correlated because the computed value is very close to 1.

2.9   SUMMARY

In this chapter we introduced some fundamental concepts of probability, random variables, probability distributions, characteristics or moments of probability distributions, etc. The discussion of these concepts has been somewhat intuitive, for our objective here is not to teach statistics per se but simply to review some of its major concepts that are needed to follow the various topics discussed in the remainder of this book.

In this chapter we presented several important formulas. These formulas tell us how to compute the probabilities of random variables and how to estimate the characteristics of probability distributions (i.e., the moments), such as the expected or mean value, variance, covariance, correlation, conditional expectation; etc. In presenting these formulas, we made a careful distinction between the *population moments* and *sample moments* and gave the appropriate computing formulas. Thus, $E(X)$, the expected value of the r.v. X, is a population moment, i.e., the mean value of X if the entire population of the X values were known. On the other hand, $\overline{X}$ is a sample moment, i.e., the average value of X if it is based on sample values of X and not on the entire population. In statistics the dichotomy between the population and the sample is very important, for in most applications we have only one or two samples from some population of interest and often we want to draw inferences about the population moments on the basis of the sample moments. How this is done is explained in the following two chapters.

Key Terms and Concepts

The key terms and concepts introduced in this chapter are:

Statistical or random experiments

Population or sample space
    a) sample points
    b) events—mutually exclusive; equally likely; collectively exhaustive

Stochastic or random variables
    a) discrete random variables
    b) continuous random variables

Probability and properties of probability

A priori definition (classical definition) of probability

Frequency distribution; relative frequency; absolute frequency

Probability distribution functions or probability density functions (PDFs)

PDFs of discrete and continuous random variables

Cumulative distribution functions (CDFs)

Multivariate PDFs

    a) bivariate or joint PDF; joint probability
    b) marginal (or univariate, unconditional, or individual) PDF
    c) conditional PDF; conditional probability

Statistical independence; independent random variables

Characteristics (moments) of univariate PDFs
    a) expected value (population mean value)
    b) variance
    c) standard deviation (s.d.)

Characteristics of multivariate PDFs
    a) covariance
    b) correlation; coefficient of correlation
    c) conditional expectation
    d) unconditional expectation
    e) conditional variance[13]

---

[13] Conceptually, the conditional variance is similar to the unconditional variance except that we use the conditional mean and the conditional density function in computing it.

Population vs. sample
  a) sample moments
  b) sample mean
  c) estimator; estimate

d) sample variance
e) sample standard deviation
f) sample covariance
g) sample correlation

REFERENCES

As noted in the introduction to this chapter, the discussion presented here is, of necessity, brief and intuitive and not meant as a substitute for a basic course in statistics. Therefore, the reader is advised to keep on hand one or two of the many good books on statistics. The following short list of such references is only suggestive.

1. Newbold, Paul: *Statistics for Business and Economics* (latest ed.), Prentice-Hall, Englewood Cliffs, N.J. This is a comprehensive nonmathematical introduction to statistics with lots of worked-out examples.
2. Hoel, Paul G.: *Introduction to Mathematical Statistics* (latest ed.), Wiley, New York. This book provides a fairly simple introduction to various aspects of mathematical statistics.
3. Mood, Alexander M., Graybill, Franklin A., and Boes, Duane C.: *Introduction to the Theory of Statistics*, McGraw-Hill, New York, 1974. This is a standard but mathematically advanced book.
4. Mosteller, F., Rourke, R., and Thomas, G.: *Probability with Statistical Applications* (latest ed.), Addison-Wesley, Reading, Mass.

QUESTIONS

2.1. What is the meaning of
  (*a*) sample space
  (*b*) sample point
  (*c*) events
  (*d*) mutually exclusive events
  (*e*) PDF
  (*f*) joint PDF
  (*g*) marginal PDF
  (*h*) conditional PDF
  (*i*) statistical independence

2.2. *A* and *B* are two events. Can they be mutually exclusive and independent simultaneously?

2.3. What is meant by the moments of a PDF? What are the most frequently used moments?

2.4. Explain the meaning of
  (*a*) expected value
  (*b*) variance
  (*c*) standard deviation
  (*d*) covariance
  (*e*) correlation
  (*f*) conditional expectation

2.5. Explain the meaning of
  (*a*) sample mean
  (*b*) sample variance
  (*c*) sample standard deviation
  (*d*) sample covariance
  (*e*) sample correlation

2.6. Why is it important to make the distinction between population moments and sample moments?

2.7. Fill in the gaps in the manner of (*a*) below.

(*a*) The expected value or mean is a measure of central tendency.

(*b*) The variance is a measure of . . .

(*c*) The covariance is a measure of . . .

(*d*) The correlation is a measure of . . .

2.8. A random variable (r.v.) X has a mean value of $50 and its standard deviation (s.d.) is $5. Is it correct to say that its variance is $25 squared? Why or why not?

2.9. Explain whether the following statements are true or false. Give reasons.

(*a*) Although the expected value of an r.v. can be positive or negative, its variance is always positive.

(*b*) The coefficient of correlation will have the same sign as that of the covariance between the two variables.

(*c*) The conditional and unconditional expectations of an r.v. mean the same thing.

(*d*) If two variables are independent, their correlation coefficient will always be zero.

(*e*) If the correlation coefficient between two variables is zero, it means that the two variables are independent.

PROBLEMS

2.10. What do the following stand for?

(*a*) $\sum_{i=1}^{4} x^{i-1}$

(*e*) $\sum_{i=1}^{4} (i + 4)$

(*b*) $\sum_{i=2}^{6} ay_i$; a is a constant

(*f*) $\sum_{i=1}^{3} 3^i$

(*c*) $\sum_{i=1}^{2} (2x_i + 3y_i)$

(*g*) $\sum_{i=1}^{10} 2$

(*d*) $\sum_{i=1}^{3} \sum_{j=1}^{2} x_i y_j$

(*h*) $\sum_{x=1}^{3} (4x^2 - 3)$

2.11. Express the following in the Σ notation:

(*a*) $x_1 + x_2 + x_3 + x_4 + x_5$

(*b*) $x_1 + 2x_2 + 3x_3 + 4x_4 + 5x_5$

(*c*) $(x_1^2 + y_1^2) + (x_2^2 + y_2^2) + \cdots + (x_k^2 + y_k^2)$

2.12. It can be shown that the sum of the first n positive numbers is

$$\sum_{k=1}^{n} k = \frac{n(n + 1)}{2}$$

Use the preceding formula to evaluate

(*a*) $\sum_{k=1}^{500} k$

(*b*) $\sum_{k=10}^{100} k$

(*c*) $\sum_{k=10}^{100} 3k$

2.13. It can be proved that the sum of squares of the first n positive numbers is

$$\sum_{k=1}^{n} k^2 = \frac{n(n+1)(2n+1)}{6}$$

Using this formula, obtain

(a) $\displaystyle\sum_{k=1}^{10} k^2$ (b) $\displaystyle\sum_{k=10}^{20} k^2$ (c) $\displaystyle\sum_{k=1}^{10} 4k^2$

2.14. An r.v. X has the following PDF:

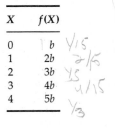

X	$f(X)$
0	b
1	$2b$
2	$3b$
3	$4b$
4	$5b$

(a) What is the value of b? Why?
(b) Find the prob$(X \le 2)$; prob$(X \le 3)$; prob$(2 \le X \le 3)$.
(c) Find the expected value of X, $E(X)$.
(d) Find the variance of X.

2.15. The *coefficient of variation* of an r.v. X, denoted by V, is defined as

$$V = \frac{E(X)}{\sigma_x}$$

$$= \frac{\text{the expected value of } X}{\text{the standard deviation of } X}$$

For problem 2.14, compute V. If X is measured in dollars, what is the unit of measurement of V? (*Note:* In practice, V is often multiplied by 100 to express it in percentage form.)

2.16. The following table gives the anticipated 1-year rates of return from a certain investment and their probabilities.

Rate of return $X(\%)$	$f(X)$
-20	0.10
-10	0.15
10	0.45
25	0.25
30	0.05
Total	1.00

(a) What is the expected rate of return on this investment?
(b) Find the variance and s.d. of the rate of return.

(c) Find the cumulative distribution function (CDF) and obtain the probability that the rate of return is 10 percent or less.

2.17. The following table gives the joint probability distribution, $f(X, Y)$, of two random variables X and Y.

Y \ X	1	2	3
1	0.03	0.06	0.06
2	0.02	0.04	0.04
3	0.09	0.18	0.18
4	0.06	0.12	0.12

(a) Find the marginal (i.e., unconditional) distributions of X and Y, namely, $f(X)$ and $f(Y)$.

(b) Find the conditional PDF, $f(X \mid Y)$ and $f(Y \mid X)$.

(c) Find the conditional expectations, $E(X \mid Y)$ and $E(Y \mid X)$.

(d) Find $E(X)$ and $E(Y)$.

(e) Are the conditional and unconditional expectations the same?

(f) Are X and Y statistically independent? How do you know?

2.18. The following table gives the joint PDF of random variables X and Y, where X = the first-year rate of return (%) expected from investment A and Y = the first-year rate of return (%) expected from investment B.

Y(%) \ X(%)	−10	0	20	30
20	0.27	0.08	0.16	0.00
50	0.00	0.04	0.10	0.35

(a) Calculate the expected rate of return from investment A.

(b) Calculate the expected rate of return from investment B.

(c) Are the expected rates of return of the two investments independent? *Hint:*

$$E(XY) = \sum_{X=1}^{4} \sum_{Y=1}^{2} X_i Y_i f(X_i, Y_i)$$

2.19. You are told that $E(X) = 8$ and $\text{var}(X) = 4$. What are the expected values and variances of the following expressions?

(a) $Y = 3X + 2$

(b) $Y = 0.6X - 4$

(c) $Y = X/4$

(d) $Y = aX + b$, where a and b are constants

2.20. Show that

(a) $\text{var}(X) = E[X - E(X)]^2 = E(X^2) - [E(X)]^2$
$$= E(X^2) - \mu_x^2$$

(b) $\text{cov}(X, Y) = E[(X - \mu_x)(Y - \mu_y)]$

$$= E(XY) - \mu_x\mu_y$$

where $\mu_x = E(X)$ and $\mu_y = E(Y)$.

How would you express these formulas verbally?

2.21. Using the definition of the population correlation coefficient given in Eq. (2.35), show that the formulas in Eqs. (2.37) and (2.38) can also be expressed as

$$\text{var}(X + Y) = \text{var}(X) + \text{var}(Y) + 2\rho\sigma_x\sigma_y \qquad (2.37a)$$

$$\text{var}(X - Y) = \text{var}(X) + \text{var}(Y) - 2\rho\sigma_x\sigma_y \qquad (2.38a)$$

2.22. Consider formula (2.37a) given in the previous problem. Let X stand for the rate of return on a security (say, IBM) and Y the rate of return on another security (say, General Foods). Let $\sigma_x^2 = 16$, $\sigma_y^2 = 9$, and $\rho = -0.8$. What is the variance $(X + Y)$ in this case? Is it greater than or smaller than $\text{var}(X) + \text{var}(Y)$? In this instance, is it better to invest equally in the two securities (i.e., diversify) than in either security exclusively? This problem, in a nutshell, is the essence of the modern portfolio theory of finance. (See, e.g., Richard Brealey and Steward Myers, *Principles of Corporate Finance*, McGraw-Hill, New York, 1981.)

2.23. Of 100 people, 50 are Democrats, 40 are Republicans, and 10 are Independents. The percentages of the people in these three categories who read the *Wall Street Journal* are known to be 30, 60, and 40 percent, respectively. If one of these people is observed reading the *Journal*, what is the probability that he or she is a Republican?

2.24. Table 2-9 gives data on the number of new business incorporations (Y) and the number of business failures (X) for the United States for 1979 to 1988.

TABLE 2-9
Number of new business incorporations (Y) and number of business failures (X), United States, 1979–1988

Year	Y	X
1979	524,565	7,564
1980	533,520	11,742
1981	581,242	16,794
1982	566,942	24,908
1983	600,400	31,334
1984	634,991	52,078
1985	662,047	57,253
1986	702,738	61,616
1987	685,572	61,622
1988	685,095	57,099

Source: Economic Report of the President,
1990, Table C-94, p. 402.

(*a*) What is the average value of new business incorporations? And the variance?

(*b*) What is the average value of business failures? And the variance?

(*c*) What is the covariance between Y and X? And the correlation coefficient?

(*d*) Are the two variables independent?

(*e*) If there is correlation between the two variables, does this mean that one variable "causes" the other variable. That is, do new incorporations cause business failures, or vice versa?

2.25. For the bond-rating Example 2.13, find out the var$(X + Y)$. How would you interpret this variance?

CHAPTER
3

SOME IMPORTANT PROBABILITY DISTRIBUTIONS

It was noted in the previous chapter that a random variable (r.v.) can be described by a few characteristics, or moments, of its probability density function (PDF), such as the expected value and variance. This, however, presumes that we know the PDF of that r.v.—a tall order, indeed, since there are all kinds of random variables. In practice, however, some random variables occur so frequently that statisticians have determined their PDFs and documented their properties. For our purpose, we will consider only those PDFs that are of direct interest to us. But keep in mind that there are several other PDFs that statisticians have studied that can be found in any standard textbook on statistics. In this chapter we discuss the following four probability distributions:

1. The normal distribution
2. The chi-square (χ^2) distribution
3. The t distribution
4. The F distribution

We examine the main features of each distribution and its properties, and the use of the four distributions for our purposes. The discussion will be as heuristic as possible. The reader is urged to master the material in this chapter because, as we will see, these probability distributions are at the core of much of econometric theory and practice.

3.1 THE NORMAL DISTRIBUTION

Perhaps the single most important probability distribution involving a continuous r.v. is the **normal distribution.** It's *bell-shaped* picture, as shown in Figure

2-2, should be familiar to anyone with a modicum of statistical knowledge. Experience has shown that the normal distribution is a reasonably good model for a continuous r.v. whose value depends on a number of factors, each factor exerting a comparatively small positive or negative influence. Thus, consider the r.v. body weight. It is likely to be normally distributed because factors such as heredity, bone structure, diet, exercise, metabolism, etc. are each expected to have some influence on weight, yet no single factor dominates the others. Likewise, variables such as height, grade-point average, etc. are also found to be normally distributed.

For notational convenience, we express a normally distributed r.v. X as

$$X \sim N(\mu, \sigma^2) \tag{3.1}[1]$$

where $\sim$ means distributed as, N stands for the normal distribution, and the quantities inside the parentheses are the *parameters* of the distribution, namely, its (population) mean or expected value μ and its variance σ^2. Note that X is a continuous r.v. and may take any value in the range $-\infty$ to $+\infty$

Properties of the Normal Distribution

1. The normal distribution curve, as Figure 2-2 shows, is symmetrical around its mean value μ.
2. The PDF of the distribution is the highest at its mean value (μ) but tails off at its extremities (i.e., in the tails of the distribution). That is, the probability of obtaining a value of a normally distributed r.v. far away from its mean value becomes progressively smaller. For example, the probability of someone exceeding the height of 7.5 feet is very small.
3. As a matter of fact, *approximately* 68 percent of the area under the normal curve lies between the values of ($\mu \pm \sigma$), ≈ 95 percent of the area lies between ($\mu \pm 2\sigma$), and ≈ 99.7 percent of the area lies between ($\mu \pm 3\sigma$), as shown in Figure 3.1. As noted in Chapter 2, and discussed further subsequently, these areas can be used as measures of probabilities.
4. A normal distribution is *fully described by its two parameters, μ and σ^2*. That is, once the values of these two parameters are known, one can find out the probability of X lying within a certain interval from the mathematical formula given in footnote 1. Fortunately, one does not have to undertake

---

[1] For the mathematically enterprising student, here is the mathematical equation of the PDF of a normally distributed r.v. X:

$$f(X) = \frac{1}{\sigma\sqrt{2\pi}} \exp\left\{-\frac{1}{2}\left(\frac{X-\mu}{\sigma}\right)^2\right\}$$

where $\exp\{\quad\}$ means e to the power of the expression inside $\{\quad\}$, $e = 2.71828$ (the base of natural logarithm), and $\pi = 3.14159$. μ and σ^2, known as the parameters of the distribution, are, respectively, the mean, or expected value, and the variance of the distribution.

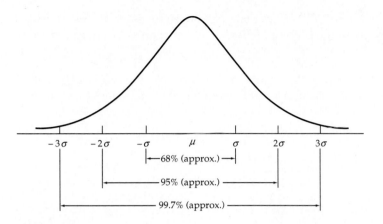

FIGURE 3-1
Areas under the normal curve.

the daunting task of computing the probabilities from this formula because these probabilities can be easily obtained from the specially prepared table (Table B-1) in Appendix B. We will explain how to use this table shortly.

5. A *linear combination (function) of two (or more) normally distributed random variables is itself normally distributed*—an especially important property of the normal distribution in econometrics. To illustrate, let

$$X \sim N(\mu_x, \sigma_x^2)$$

$$Y \sim N(\mu_y, \sigma_y^2)$$

and assume that X and Y are *independent*.[2]

Now consider the linear combination of these two variables: $W = aX + bY$, where a and b are constant (e.g., $W = 2X + 4Y$); then

$$W \sim N[\mu_w, \sigma_w^2] \tag{3.2}$$

where

$$\mu_w = (a\mu_x + b\mu_y) \tag{3.3}$$
$$\sigma_w^2 = (a^2\sigma_x^2 + b^2\sigma_y^2)$$

Note that in Eqs. (3.3) we have used some of the properties of the expectation operator E and the variances of independent random variables discussed in

---

[2] Recall that two variables are independently distributed if their joint PDF is the product of their marginal PDFs; i.e., $f(X, Y) = f(X)f(Y)$, for all values of X and Y.

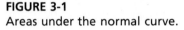

Chapter 2. (See Section 2.7.)[3] Incidentally, expression (3.2) can be extended straightforwardly to a linear combination of more than two normal random variables.

> **Example 3.1.** Let X denote the number of roses sold daily by a florist in uptown Manhattan and Y the number of roses sold daily by a florist in downtown Manhattan. Assume that both X and Y are *independently* normally distributed as $X \sim N(100, 64)$ and $Y \sim N(150, 81)$. What is the average value of the roses sold in two days by the two florists and the corresponding variance of sale? Here $W = 2X + 2Y$. Therefore, following expression (3.3), we have $E(W) = E(2X + 2Y) = 500$ and $\text{var}(W) = 4 \text{ var}(X) + 4 \text{ var}(Y) = 580$. Therefore, W is distributed normally with a mean value of 500 and a variance of 580: $[W \sim N(500, 580)]$.

The Standard Normal Distribution

Although a normal distribution is fully specified by its two parameters, (population) mean or expected value and variance, one normal distribution can differ from another in either its mean or variance, or both, as shown in Figure 3.2.

How do we compare the various normal distributions shown in Figure 3.2? Since these normal distributions differ in either their mean values or variances, or both, let us define a new variable, Z, as follows:

$$Z = \frac{X - \mu_x}{\sigma_x} \tag{3.4}$$

If the variable X has a mean μ_x and a variance σ_x^2, it can be shown that the Z variable defined previously has a mean value of zero and a variance of one (or unity). In statistics such a variable is known as a *unit* or *standardized* variable. If $X \sim N(\mu_x, \sigma_x^2)$, then the Z variable previously defined is known as a **unit** or **standard normal** variable, i.e., a normal variable with zero mean and unit variance. Symbolically,

$$Z \sim N(0, 1) \tag{3.5}[4]$$

Thus, any normally distributed r.v. with a given mean and variance can be converted to a standard normal variable, which greatly simplifies our task of computing probabilities, as shown later.

The PDF and CDF (cumulative distribution function) of the standard normal distribution are shown in Figure 3-3(a) and 3-3(b), respectively. (See

---

[3] It should be pointed out that if X and Y are normally distributed but are not independent, W is still normally distributed with the mean given in Eqs. (3.3), but with the following variance (cf. Eq. (2.37):

$$\sigma_w^2 = a^2\sigma_x^2 + b^2\sigma_y^2 + 2ab\text{cov}(X, Y)$$

[4] This can be easily proved by noting the property of the normal distribution that a linear function of a normally distributed variable is itself normally distributed.

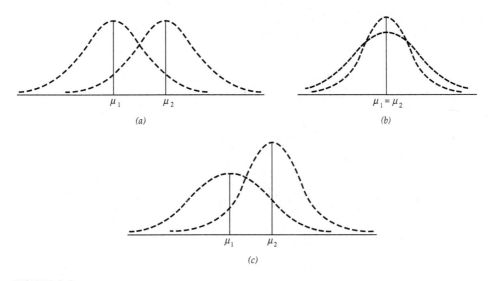

FIGURE 3-2
(a) Different means, same variance; (b) same mean, different variances; (c) different means, different variances.

Section 2.5 on the definitions of PDF and CDF.) The CDF, like any other CDF, gives the probability that the standard normal variable takes a value equal to or less than z (i.e., $P(Z \leq z)$, where z is a specific numerical value of Z.

To illustrate how we use the standard normal distribution to compute various probabilities, we consider several concrete examples.

Example 3.2. It is given that X, the daily sale of bread in a bakery, follows the normal distribution with a mean of 70 loaves and a variance of 9; i.e., $X \sim N(70, 9)$. What is the probability that on any given day the sale of bread is greater than 75 loaves?

Since X follows the normal distribution with the stated mean and variance, it follows that

$$Z = \frac{75 - 70}{3} = \approx 1.67$$

follows the standard normal distribution. Therefore, we want to find

$$P(Z > 1.67)^5$$

---

[5] *Note*: Whether we write $P(Z > 1.67)$ or $P(Z \geq 1.67)$ is immaterial because, as noted in Chap. 2, the probability that a continuous r.v. takes a particular value (e.g., 1.67) is always zero.

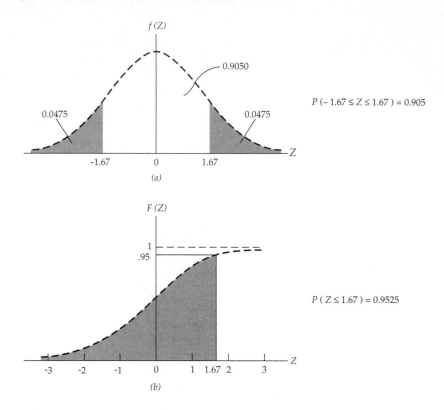

$P(-1.67 \leq Z \leq 1.67) = 0.905$

$P(Z \leq 1.67) = 0.9525$

FIGURE 3-3
(a) PDF and (b) CDF of the standard normal variable.

Now Table B.1 in Appendix B gives the CDF of the standard normal distribution between values of Z from 0 to 3.09. For example, this table shows us that the probability that Z lies between 0 and 1.3 is 0.4032 (or 40.32 percent) or the probability that it lies between 0 and 2.5 is 0.4938 (or 49.38 percent), etc. Since the normal distribution is symmetrical, the probability that Z lies between -1.3 and 0 is also 0.4032 or the probability that it lies between -2.5 and 0 is also 0.4938. Because of this symmetry, the standard normal distribution table is usually given for positive values of Z: The area lying to the right of $Z = 0$ and the area lying to the left of $Z = 0$ are both 0.50; together these areas (or probabilities) add up to 1, as they should.

In our example we want to find the probability that $Z > 1.67$. But that is easy, for we observe from the standard normal table that

$$P(0 \leq Z \leq 1.67) = 0.4525$$

therefore,

$$P(Z > 1.67) = 0.5000 - 0.4525$$
$$= 0.0475$$

That is, the probability of the daily sale of bread exceeding 75 loaves of bread is 0.0475 or ≈ 4.75 percent. [See Figure 3-3(a).]

Example 3.3. Continue with Example 3.2. But suppose we now want to find out the probability of a daily sale of bread of 75 or fewer loaves of bread.
The reader can easily verify that this probability is

$$0.5000 + 0.4525 = 0.9525$$

which is shown in Figure 3-3(b).

Example 3.4. Continue with Example 3.2 but now suppose we want to find out the probability that the daily sale of bread is between 65 and 75 loaves of bread.
To compute this probability, we first compute

$$Z_1 = \frac{65 - 70}{3} = \approx -1.67$$

and

$$Z_2 = \frac{75 - 70}{3} = \approx 1.67$$

Now from Table B.1 we see that

$$P(-1.67 \leq Z \leq 0) = 0.4525$$

and

$$P(0 \leq Z \leq 1.67) = 0.4525$$

because of symmetry.
Therefore,

$$P(-1.67 \leq Z \leq 1.67) = 0.4525 + 0.4525 = 0.9050$$

That is, the probability is ≈ 90.5 percent that the sales volume will lie between 65 and 75 loaves of bread per day, as shown in Figure 3-3(a).

Example 3.5. Continue with the preceding example but now assume that we want to find the probability that the sale of bread either exceeds 75 loaves or is less than 65 loaves per day.
If the reader has mastered the previous examples, he or she can see easily that this probability is 0.095, as shown in Figure 3-3(a).

As the preceding examples show, once we know that a particular r.v. follows the normal distribution with a given mean and variance, all we have to do is to convert that variable into the standard normal variable and compute the relevant probabilities from the standard normal table (Table B-1). It is indeed remarkable that just one standard normal distribution table suffices to deal with any normally distributed variable regardless of its specific mean and variance values.

As we have remarked earlier, the normal distribution is probably the single most important theoretical probability distribution because several (continuous) random variables are found to be normally distributed or at least approximately so. We now present some examples of this, which we will find very useful in our later development of econometrics.

3.2   THE SAMPLING, OR PROBABILITY, DISTRIBUTION OF THE SAMPLE MEAN $\overline{X}$

In the previous chapter we introduced the sample mean [see Eq. (2.41)] as an estimator of the population mean. But since the sample mean is based on a given sample, it will vary from sample to sample; that is, the sample mean can be treated as an r.v., which will have its own PDF. Can we find out the PDF of the sample mean? The answer is yes, provided the sample is drawn randomly. In Chapter 2 we described the notion of random sampling in an intuitive way by letting each member of the population have an equal chance of being included in the sample. In statistics, however, the term **random sampling** is used in a rather special sense. *We say that $X_1, X_2, . . . , X_n$ constitute a random sample of size n if all these Xs are drawn independently from the same probability distribution (i.e., each X_i has the same PDF).* The Xs thus drawn are known as *i.i.d. random variables,* i.e., *independently and identically distributed random variables.* In the future, therefore, the term *random sample* will denote a sample of i.i.d. random variables. For brevity, sometimes we will use the term *i.i.d. sample* to mean a random sample in the sense just described.

Thus, if each $X_i \sim N(\mu, \sigma^2)$ and if each X_i value is drawn independently, then we say that $X_1, X_2, . . . , X_n$ are i.i.d. random variables, the normal PDF being their common probability distribution. Note two things about this definition: First, each X included in the sample must have the *same* PDF and, second, each X included in the sample is drawn independently of the others.

Given the very important concept of a random sample, we now develop another very important concept in statistics, namely, the concept of the **sampling, or probability, distribution of an estimator,** such as, say, the sample mean, $\overline{X}$. A firm comprehension of this concept is absolutely essential in order to understand the topic of statistical inference in Chapter 4 and for our discussion of econometrics in succeeding chapters. Since many students find the concept of sampling distribution somewhat bewildering, let us explain it with an example.

TABLE 3-1

Possible samples of three observations from the population 51, 60, 70, 75, 80, and 90 and corresponding sample means

Sample	Sample mean $\overline{X}$	Sample	Sample mean $\overline{X}$
51, 60, 70	60.33	60, 75, 80	71.67
51, 60, 75	62.00	51, 75, 90	72.00
51, 60, 80	63.67	60, 70, 90	73.33
51, 70, 75	65.33	51, 80, 90	73.67
51, 60, 90	67.00	60, 75, 90	75.00
51, 70, 80	67.00	70, 75, 80	75.00
60, 70, 75	68.33	60, 80, 90	76.67
51, 75, 80	68.67	70, 75, 90	78.33
60, 70, 80	70.00	70, 80, 90	80.00
51, 70, 90	70.33	75, 80, 90	81.67

Example 3.6.   In an econometrics tutorial class an instructor gave a surprise quiz to his six students. The grade points scored by these six students were 51, 60, 70, 75, 80, and 90. Therefore, the average grade was 71 points, which is the true mean value (assume for simplicity that the six students constitute the entire population.) To introduce his students to the important concept of the sampling distribution of an estimator or statistic, the instructor asked his research assistant to draw a random sample of 3 students from the 6 students and to compute the (sample) mean grade point in each sample. In all, there are 20 samples.[6] The research assistant presented his results as shown in Table 3-1.

Column 1 of this table gives the various samples obtained and column 2 lists the (sample) mean values of the various samples. The research assistant also presented the various sample means in the form of a frequency distribution, as shown in Table 3-2.

Column 1 of Table 3-2 shows the values of the sample mean; column 2, the absolute frequencies; and column 3, the relative frequencies, which are simply the absolute frequencies divided by the total number of observations (i.e., samples), namely, 20. By the relative frequency definition of probability provided in Chapter 2, we see that Table 3-2 presents the probability distri-

---

[6] The number of combinations of n elements taken r at a time is given by the mathematical formula

$$\frac{n!}{(n-r)!\, r!}$$

where $n!$ (read as n factorial) is simply the product of $n(n-1)(n-2)\cdots 1$. In our example $n=6$ and $r=3$; therefore, the preceding formula gives $6!/(3!)(3!)$. Simplifying this gives the answer of 20 combinations. (*Note*: $6! = 6 \times 5 \times 4 \times 3 \times 2 \times 1 = 720$ and $3! = 3 \times 2 \times 1 = 6$.

TABLE 3-2
Probability or sampling distribution of the sample means from Table 3-1

Mean value $\overline{X}$ (1)	Absolute frequency (F) (2)	Relative frequency (f) (3)	$\overline{X} \cdot f$ (4) = (1) (3)	$(\overline{X} - 71)^2 f$ (5)
60.33	1	0.05	3.0165	$(60.33 - 71)^2 0.05$
62.00	1	0.05	3.1000	$(62.00 - 71)^2 0.05$
63.67	1	0.05		
65.33	1	0.05		
67.00	2	0.10		
68.33	1	0.05		
68.67	1	0.05		
70.00	1	0.05		
70.33	1	0.05		
71.67	1	0.05		
72.00	1	0.05		
73.33	1	0.05		
73.67	1	0.05		
75.00	2	0.10		
76.67	1	0.05		
78.33	1	0.05		
80.00	1	0.05	4.0000	$(80.00 - 71)^2 0.05$
81.67	1	0.05	4.0835	$(81.67 - 71)^2 0.05$
	Total 20	1.00	$E(\overline{X}) = 71$	var $(\overline{X}) = 32.673$

bution of the sample means. This probability distribution is called the *sampling distribution*—in this example the sampling distribution of the sample means. As Table 3-2 shows, the sampling distribution of an estimator is really like the probability distribution of any r.v. except that the r.v. in this case happens to be an estimator or a statistic. Stated differently, "A *sampling distribution* is a *probability distribution* where the random variable is a statistic."[7] The sampling distribution of the sample mean of Table 3-2 is depicted graphically in Figure 3-4.

Before proceeding further, let us raise an interesting question: What is $E(\overline{X})$, that is, the mean, or expected value, of the sample means shown in Table 3-2? Let us call $E(\overline{X})$ the *grand mean*. Since we have the probability distribution of $\overline{X}$, in order to compute $E(\overline{X})$, we only have to multiply the values of $\overline{X}$ given in column 1 of Table 3-2 by their probabilities given in column 3 and sum the products, as shown in the table. As the calculations indicate, this grand mean is 71. Can we equate the grand mean $E(\overline{X})$ with μ, the (popula-

---

[7] Richard S. Mills, *Statistics for Applied Economics and Business*, McGraw-Hill, New York, 1977, p. 151.

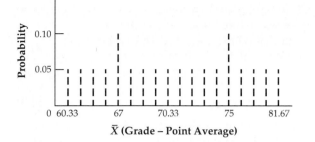

FIGURE 3-4
Probability distribution of $\overline{X}$ (Table 3-2).

tion) mean of $\overline{X}$? Intuition would suggest that we can. As a matter of fact, it can be proved that the mean of the sampling distribution of the sample mean (i.e., the grand mean) is equal to the population mean.[8] We already know that the population mean in our example was 71.

Let us continue with our example in Table 3-1. Just as we computed the (grand) mean of the sample means, we can also compute the variance of the sample means from formula (2.26) in Chapter 2. The necessary calculations are shown in Table 3-2. As the calculations show, this variance is 32.673. Can we equate this with the true variance of $\overline{X}$? Intuitively, it may not be obvious, but it can be proved that this is the case.[9] Incidentally, note that the positive square root of the variance, $\sqrt{32.673} = 5.716$, is known as the *standard error*.[10]

A practical question: Do we have to conduct the sampling experiment of Table 3-1 to find out the sampling distribution of an estimator, such as the sample mean? This would be an enormously time-consuming task, not to mention the costs involved in doing the necessary calculations (The research assistant has to be paid, however meagerly!). Fortunately, this is where statistical theory comes in handy. Without conducting the sampling experiment of Table 3-1, statistical theory shows the following:[11]

1. If $X_1, X_2, \ldots, X_n$ is a *random* sample of size n from some population (i.e., PDF), with mean μ and variance σ^2, the sample mean $\overline{X}$ is an r.v. with mean [i.e., $E(\overline{X})$] μ (the same as each X_i) and variance σ^2/n, which is $(1/n)$th

---

[8] For a rigorous proof, see any standard textbook on mathematical statistics. Some references are given at the end of Chapter 2.

[9] The proof of this can be found in any textbook on mathematical statistics. See some of the references at the end of Chapter 2.

[10] Just as we called the probability distribution of an estimator the sampling distribution, the s.d. of an estimator is known as the standard error. But conceptually, the terms *standard error* and *standard deviation* are the same.

[11] The proofs of the following statements can be found in any standard textbook on mathematical statistics. Some of the references are given at the end of Chapter 2.

the variance of X.[12] Therefore, as the sample size n increases, the PDF of $\overline{X}$ becomes more and more concentrated around its mean μ. The positive square root of the variance, $\sigma/\sqrt{n}$, as noted before, is known as the *standard error*. In our previous example the variance of 32.673 is in fact the value of σ^2/n.

2. If in item (1) it is assumed that the PDF of each X_i is $N(\mu, \sigma^2)$, i.e., each X_i follows the normal distribution with a mean μ and a variance σ^2, then

$$\overline{X} \sim N(\mu, \sigma^2/n) \tag{3.6}$$

In other words, the sampling (or probability) distribution of the sample mean $\overline{X}$, the estimator of μ, also follows the normal distribution with the same mean as that of X_i but with a variance equal to σ^2/n.

If in our Example 3.6 we were told at the outset that the r.v., grade-point average in the econometrics examination, was normally distributed with, say, mean = 71 and variance = 98.019, then we could have seen at once that the average grade obtained from any random sample of 3 students would have a (grand, or population) mean value of 71, a variance of 98.019/3 = 32.673, and a standard error of $\sqrt{32.673}$ = 5.716. We conducted the sampling experiment of Table 3-1 just to drive home the meaning of the sampling distribution of an estimator. In practice, one rarely has the luxury of conducting such sampling experiments.

3. If each X_i from a random sample of size n follows the normal distribution with a given mean and variance, the sample mean $\overline{X}$ also follows the normal distribution with the same mean but with the variance of σ^2/n, as we saw in item (2). But there is a remarkable theorem in statistics—the **central limit theorem (CLT)**—which states that if $X_1, X_2, \ldots, X_n$ is a random sample from *any* probability distribution with mean μ and variance σ^2, the sample mean $\overline{X}$ tends to be normally distributed with mean μ and variance σ^2/n as *the sample size n increases indefinitely.*

The difference between items (2) and (3) is that (2) holds true for any sample size, whereas (3) holds true as the sample size becomes large (tech-

---

[12] This is easy to prove. Note that

$$\overline{X} = \frac{1}{n}(X_1 + X_2 + \cdots + X_n)$$

Since the Xs are independent, following the properties of variance discussed in Chap. 2, we can write

$$\text{var}(\overline{X}) = \frac{1}{n^2}[\text{var}(X_1) + \text{var}(X_2) + \cdots + \text{var}(X_n)]$$

$$= \frac{1}{n^2}(n \times \sigma^2), \text{ since var. of each } (X_i) = \sigma^2$$

$$= \frac{1}{n}\sigma^2.$$

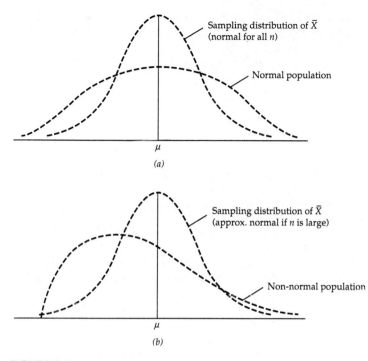

FIGURE 3-5
The central limit theorem: (*a*) Samples drawn from a normal population; (*b*) samples drawn from a non-normal population.

nically infinite.)[13] But what is remarkable about (3) is that this result holds true regardless of the original form of the PDF of the random variables; the main condition is that the sample size is sufficiently large.[14] The CLT can be visualized from Figure 3-5.

The upshot of the preceding discussion is that for a sufficiently large sample size the sample mean obtained from a random sample from any PDF will generally be approximately normally distributed, as in expression (3.6).[15]

---

[13] In practice, the normal approximation is good even for a sample size as small as 30 observations. As we show later in the chapter, the *t* distribution approaches the normal distribution as the number of observations exceed 30.

[14] There is even a more remarkable theorem in statistics, known as the Lindberg-Feller theorem, which states that if the Xs are distributed independently *each with its own PDF* (not all the PDFs necessarily different), then under certain conditions the sample mean still tends to be normally distributed as the sample size increases indefinitely.

[15] In our grade-point example, as can be seen from Figure 3-4, the sample means are not normally distributed. But this is because our sample size of three observations is small. One exception to the CLT is an r.v. that follows the Cauchy probability distribution.

In later chapters we will see how the CLT can make our (statistical) life simpler. In passing, note that from expression (3.6) it follows at once that

$$Z = \frac{\overline{X} - \mu}{\sigma/\sqrt{n}} \sim N(0, 1) \tag{3.7}$$

that is, a standard normal variable. Therefore, one can easily compute from the standard normal distribution the probabilities that a given sample mean is greater than or less than a given population mean. An example follows.

Example 3.7.   Let X denote the number of miles per gallon achieved by cars of a particular model. You are told that $X \sim N(20, 4)$. What is the probability that for a random sample of 25 cars, the average gallon per mile will be
(a) greater than 21 miles
(b) less than 18 miles
(c) between 19 and 21 miles?
Since X follows the normal distribution with mean = 20 and variance = 4, we know that $\overline{X}$ also follows the normal distribution with mean = 20 and variance = 4/25. As a result, we know that

$$Z = \frac{\overline{X} - 20}{\sqrt{4/25}} = \frac{\overline{X} - 20}{0.4} \sim N(0, 1)$$

That is, Z follows the standard normal distribution. Therefore, we want to find

(a)
$$P(\overline{X} > 21) = P\left(Z > \frac{21 - 20}{0.4}\right)$$
$$= P(Z > 2.5)$$
$$= 0.0062 \qquad \text{(From Table B-1)}$$

(b)
$$P(\overline{X} < 18) = P\left(Z < \frac{18 - 20}{0.4}\right)$$
$$= P(Z < -5)$$
$$= \text{almost zero}$$

(c)
$$P(19 \leq \overline{X} \leq 21) = P(-2.5 \leq Z \leq 2.5)$$
$$= 0.9876$$

3.3   THE CHI-SQUARE (χ^2) DISTRIBUTION

In statistics we often come across squared quantities such as X_i^2 or $\Sigma\, X_i^2$. For example, from Chapter 2, we know that the sample variance of an r.v. X is $S_x^2 = \Sigma(X_i - \overline{X})^2/(n - 1)$.

Do these quantities have their own sampling distributions, like the sampling distribution of the sample mean $\overline{X}$? It turns out that under certain conditions the sampling distributions of these quantities can be derived. Toward that end, we consider another well-known theoretical probability distribution, namely, the **chi-square distribution,** denoted by the Greek symbol, χ^2. In later chapters we will see the usefulness of this distribution.

Consider a normally distributed r.v. X with mean μ and variance σ^2; that is, $X \sim N(\mu, \sigma^2)$. Then we know that $Z = (X - \mu)/\sigma$ is a standard normal variable; that is, $Z \sim N(0, 1)$. Statistical theory shows that *the square of a standard normal variable is distributed as a chi-square (χ^2) distribution with one degree of freedom (d.f.)* Symbolically,

$$Z^2 = \chi^2_{(1)} \tag{3.8}$$

where the subscript (1) of χ^2 shows the *number of degrees of freedom (d.f.)*—1 in the present case. Just as the mean and variance are the parameters of the normal distribution, the d.f. is the parameter of the chi-square distribution. The term *degrees of freedom (d.f.)* in statistics has been used in different senses, but for our purpose here we define it as *the number of independent observations in a sum of squares.*[16] In Equation (3.8) there is only 1 d.f. since we are considering only the square of one standard normal variable.

Now let $Z_1, Z_2, \ldots, Z_k$ be *k-independent* unit normal variables (i.e., each Z is a normal r.v. with zero mean and unit variance). If we square each of these Zs, it can be shown that the sum of the squared Zs also follows a chi-square distribution with k d.f. That is,

$$\sum Z_i^2 = Z_1^2 + Z_2^2 + \cdots Z_k^2 \sim \chi^2_{(k)} \tag{3.9}$$

Note that the d.f. are now k since there are k-independent observations in the sum of squares shown in Equation (3.9).

Geometrically, the χ^2 distribution appears as in Figure 3-6.

Properties of the Chi-square Distribution

1. As Figure 3-6 shows, unlike the normal distribution, the chi-square distribution takes only positive values (after all, it is the distribution of a squared quantity) and ranges from 0 to infinity.
2. As Figure 3.6 also shows, unlike the normal distribution, the chi-square distribution is a *skewed distribution*, the degree of the skewness depending on the d.f. For comparatively few d.f. the distribution is highly skewed to

---

[16] In general, the number of d.f. means the number of independent observations available to compute a quantity, such as the sample mean or the sample variance. For example, the sample variance of an r.v. X is defined as $S^2 = \Sigma(X_i - X)^2/(n - 1)$. In this case we say that the number of d.f. is $(n - 1)$ because if we use the same sample to compute the sample mean $\overline{X}$ around which we measure the sample variance, so to speak, we lose one d.f.; i.e., we have only $(n - 1)$ independent observations. An example will clarify this further. Consider three X values: 1, 2, and 3. The sample mean is 2. Now since $\Sigma(X_i - \overline{X}) = 0$ always, of the three deviations $(1 - 2)$, $(2 - 2)$, and $(3 - 2)$, only two can be chosen arbitrarily; the third must be fixed in such a way that the condition $\Sigma(X_i - \overline{X}) = 0$ must be satisfied. Therefore, in this case, although there are three observations, the d.f. are only 2.

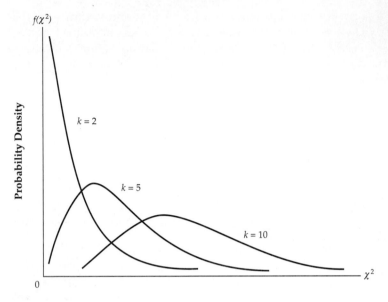

FIGURE 3-6
Density function of the χ^2 variable.

the right, but as the d.f. increase, the distribution becomes increasingly symmetrical and approaches the normal distribution. (Question 3.7 shows how one can approximate a chi-square variable by a normal variable as the sample size increases indefinitely.)

3. The expected, or mean, value of a chi-square r.v. is k and its variance is $2k$, where k is the d.f. This is a noteworthy property of the chi-square distribution in that its variance is twice its mean value.

4. If Z_1 and Z_2 are two *independent* chi-square variables with k_1 and k_2 d.f., then their sum $(Z_1 + Z_2)$ is also a chi-square variable with d.f. $= (k_1 + k_2)$.

Table B-4 in Appendix B tabulates the probabilities that a particular χ^2 value exceeds a given number, assuming the d.f. underlying the chi-square value are known or given. Although specific applications of the chi-square distribution in regression analysis will be considered in later chapters, for now let us see how to use the table.

Example 3.8. For 30 d.f., what is the probability that an observed chi-square value is greater than 13.78? Or greater than 18.49? Or greater than 50.89?

From Table B.4 in Appendix B we observe that these probabilitis are 0.995, 0.95, and 0.01, respectively. Thus, for 30 d.f. the probability of obtaining a chi-square value of ≈ 51 is very small, only ≈ 1 percent, but for the same d.f. the probability of obtaining a chi-square value of ≈ 14 is very high, ≈ 99.5 percent.

Example 3.9.   If S^2 is the sample variance obtained from a random sample of n observations from a normal population with the variance of σ^2, statistical theory shows that the quantity

$$(n-1)\left(\frac{S^2}{\sigma^2}\right) \sim \chi^2_{(n-1)} \tag{3.10}$$

That is, the ratio of the sample variance to population variance multiplied by the d.f. $(n-1)$ follows the chi-square distribution with $(n-1)$ d.f. Suppose a random sample of 20 observations from a normal population with $\sigma^2 = 8$ gave a sample variance of $S^2 = 16$. What is the probability of obtaining such a sample variance?

Putting the appropriate numbers in expression (3.10), we find that $19(16/8) = 38$ is a chi-square variable with 19 d.f. And from Table B-4 in Appendix B we find that for 19 d.f. if the true σ^2 were 8, the probability of finding a chi-square value of ≈ 38 is ≈ 0.005, a very small probability. There is doubt whether the particular random sample came from a population with a variance value of 8. But more on this in the next chapter.

3.4   THE t DISTRIBUTION

The probability distribution that we use most intensively in this book is the t distribution, also known as **Student's t distribution**.[17]

To introduce this distribution, recall that if $\overline{X} \sim N(\mu, \sigma^2/n)$, the variable

$$Z = \frac{\overline{X} - \mu}{\sigma/\sqrt{n}} \sim N(0, 1) \tag{3.11}$$

that is, the standard normal distribution. This is so provided both μ and σ^2 are known. But suppose we only know μ and estimate σ^2 by its (sample) estimator $S^2 = \dfrac{\Sigma(X_1 - \overline{X})^2}{(n-1)}$, given earlier in Eq. (2.42). Replacing σ by S, that is, replacing the population standard deviation (s.d.) by the sample s.d., in Equation (3.11), we obtain a new variable

$$t = \frac{\overline{X} - \mu}{S/\sqrt{n}} \tag{3.12}$$

Statistical theory shows that the t variable thus defined follows Student's t distribution with $(n-1)$ d.f. Like the chi-square distribution, the t distribution depends on the d.f. parameter, which in the present case is $(n-1)$. *Note:* Before we compute S^2 (and hence S) from Eq. (2.42), we must first compute $\overline{X}$. But since we use the same sample to compute $\overline{X}$, we have $(n-1)$, not n, independent observations to compute S^2; so to speak, we lose 1 d.f.

---

[17] *Student* was the pseudonym for W. S. Gosset, who used to work as a statistician for Guinness's Brewery in Dublin. He discovered this probability distribution in 1908.

In sum, if we draw random samples from a normal population with mean μ and variance σ^2 but replace σ^2 by its estimator S^2, the sample mean $\overline{X}$ follows the t distribution. A t-distributed r.v. is often designated as t_k, where k denotes the d.f. (To avoid confusion with the sample size n, we use the subscript k to denote the d.f. in general). Table B-2 in Appendix B tabulates the t distribution for various d.f. The use of this table will be demonstrated shortly.

Properties of the t Distribution

1. The t distribution, like the normal distribution, is symmetric, as shown in Figure 3.7.
2. The mean of the t distribution, like the standard normal distribution, is zero, but its variance is $k/(k - 2)$. Therefore, the variance of the t distribution is defined for d.f. greater than 2.

We have already seen for the standard normal distribution that the variance is always 1, which means that the variance of the t distribution is larger than the variance of the standard normal distribution, as shown in Figure 3.7. In other words, the t distribution is flatter than the normal distribution.

But as k increases, the variance of the t distribution approaches the variance of the standard normal distribution, namely, 1. Thus, if the d.f. are $k = 10$, the variance of the t distribution is $10/8 = 1.25$; if $k = 30$, the variance becomes $30/28 = 1.07$; and when $k = 100$, the variance becomes $100/98 = 1.02$, which is not much greater than 1. As a result, the t distribution, like the chi-square distribution, approaches the standard normal distribution as the d.f. increase. But notice that even for k as small as 30, there is no great difference in the variances of the t and the standard normal variable. Therefore, the

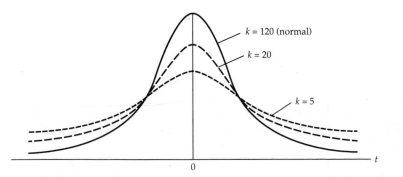

FIGURE 3-7
The t distribution for selected degrees of freedom (d.f.)

sample size does not have to be enormously large for the t distribution to approximate the normal distribution.

To illustrate the t table (Table B-2) given in Appendix B, we now consider a few examples.

Example 3.10. Let us revisit Example 3.2. In a period of 15 days the sale of bread averaged 74 loaves with a (sample) s.d. of 4 loaves. What is the probability of obtaining such a sale given that the true average sale is 70 loaves a day?

If we had known the true σ, we could have used the standard normal Z variable to answer this question. But since we know its estimator, S, we can use Equation (3.12) to compute the t value and use Table B-2 in Appendix B to answer this question as follows:

$$t = \frac{74 - 70}{4/\sqrt{15}}$$

$$= 3.873$$

Notice that in this example the d.f. are $14 = (15 - 1)$. (Why?)

As Table B-2 shows, for 14 d.f. the probability of obtaining a t value of 2.145 or greater is 0.025 (2.5 percent), of 2.624 or greater is 0.01 (1 percent), and of 3.787 or greater is 0.001 (0.1 percent). Therefore, the probability of obtaining a t value of as much as 3.873 or greater must be much smaller than 0.001.

Example 3.11. Let us keep the setup of Example 3.10 intact except to assume that the sale of bread averages 72 loaves of bread in the said 15-day period. Now what is the probability of obtaining such a sales figure?

Following exactly the same line of reasoning, the reader can verify that the computed t value is ≈ 1.936. Now from Table B-2 we observe that for 14 d.f. the probability of obtaining a t value of 1.761 or greater is ≈ 0.05 (or 5 percent) and that of 2.145 or greater is 0.025 (or 2.5 percent). Therefore, the probability of obtaining a t value of 1.936 or greater lies somewhere between 2.5 and 5 percent.

Example 3.12. Now assume that in a period of 15 days the average sale of bread was 68 loaves with an s.d. of 4 loaves a day. If the true mean sales are 70 loaves a day, what is the probability of obtaining such a sales figure?

Plugging in the relevant numbers in Equation (3.12), we find that the t value in this case is -1.936. But since the t distribution is symmetric, the probability of obtaining a t value of -1.936 or smaller is the same as that of obtaining a t value of $+1.936$ or greater, which, as we saw earlier, is somewhere between 2.5 and 5 percent.

Example 3.13.   Again, continue with the previous example. What is the probability that the average sale of bread in the said 15-day period was either greater than 72 loaves or less than 68 loaves?

From Examples 3.11 and 3.12 we know that the probability of the average sale exceeding 72 or being less than 68 is the same as the probability that a t value either exceeds 1.936 or is smaller than -1.936.[18] These probabilities, as we saw previously, are each between 0.025 and 0.05. Therefore, the total probability will be between 0.05 or 0.10 (or between 5 and 10 percent). In cases like this we would, therefore, compute the probability that $|t| > 1.936$, where $|t|$ means the absolute value of t, that is, the t value disregarding the sign.[19]

From the preceding examples it can be seen that once we compute the t **value** from Eq. (3.12), and once we know the d.f., computing the probabilities of obtaining a given t value involves simply consulting the t table. Further uses of the t table in the regression context will be considered at appropriate places later in the text.

Example 3.14.   For the years 1967 to 1990 the S.A.T. (Scholastic Aptitude Test) scores were as follows:

	Male	Female
Verbal (average)	440.42	434.50
	(142.08)	(303.39)
Math (average)	500.0	453.67
	(46.61)	(83.88)

Note: The figures in parentheses are the variances. The figures, computed by the author, were taken from the College Board statistics published in the *New York Times*, August 28, 1990, p. B-5. The actual data are given in Table 5-5, Chapter 5.

A random sample of 10 male S.A.T. scores on the verbal test gave the (sample) mean value of 440.60 and the variance of 137.60. What is the probability of obtaining such a score knowing that for the entire 1967 to 1990 period the (true) average score was 440.42?

---

[18] Be careful here: The number, say, -2.0 is smaller than -1.936 and the number -2.3 is smaller than -2.0.

[19] For example, the absolute value of 2 is 2 and the absolute value of -2 is also 2.

With the knowledge of the t distribution, we can now answer this question easily. Substituting the relevant values in Eq. (3.12), we obtain

$$t = \frac{440.60 - 440.42}{\sqrt{\dfrac{137.60}{10}}}$$

$$= 0.0485$$

This t value has the t distribution with 9 d.f. (Why?) From Table B-2 we observe that the probability of obtaining such a t value is greater than 0.25 or 25 percent.

3.5   THE F DISTRIBUTION

Another probability distribution that we will find extremely useful in econometrics is the F distribution. The motivation behind this distribution is as follows. Let $X_1, X_2, \ldots, X_m$ be a random sample of size m from a normal population with mean μ_x and variance σ_x^2, and let $Y_1, Y_2, \ldots, Y_n$ be a random sample of size n from a normal population with mean μ_y and variance σ_y^2. Assume that these two samples are independent. Suppose we want to find out if the variances of the two normal populations are the same, that is, whether $\sigma_x^2 = \sigma_y^2$. Since we cannot directly observe the two population variances, let us suppose we obtain their estimators as follows:

$$S_x^2 = \sum \frac{(X_i - \overline{X})^2}{m - 1} \tag{3.13}$$

$$S_y^2 = \sum \frac{(Y_i - \overline{Y})^2}{n - 1} \tag{3.14}$$

Now consider the following ratio:

$$F = \frac{S_x^2}{S_y^2}$$

$$= \frac{\sum (X_i - \overline{X})^2/(m - 1)}{\sum (Y_i - \overline{Y})^2/(n - 1)} \tag{3.15}[20]$$

---

[20] By convention, in computing the F value the variance with the larger numerical value is put in the numerator. That is why the F value is always 1 or greater than 1. Also, note that if a variable, say, W, follows the F distribution with m and n d.f. in the numerator and denominator, respectively, then the variable $(1/W)$ also follows the F distribution but with n and m d.f. in the numerator and denominator, respectively. More specifically,

$$F_{(1-\alpha),m,n} = \frac{1}{F_{\alpha,n,m}}$$

If the two population variances are in fact equal, the F ratio given in Equation (3.15) should be about 1, whereas if they are different, the F ratio should be different from 1; the greater the difference between the two variances is, the greater the F value will be.

Statistical theory shows that if $\sigma_x^2 = \sigma_y^2$ (i.e., the two population variances are equal), the F ratio given in Eq. (3.15) follows the **F distribution**[21] with $(m - 1)$ (numerator) d.f. and $(n - 1)$ (denominator) d.f.[22] And since the F distribution is often used to compare the variances of two populations, it is also known as the **variance ratio distribution.** The F ratio is often designated as $F_{k1,k2}$, where the double subscript indicates the parameters of the distribution, namely, the d.f. in the numerator and the denominator [in the preceding example $k_1 = (m - 1)$ and $k_2 = (n - 1)$].[23]

Properties of the F Distribution

1. Like the chi-square distribution, the F distribution is also skewed to the right and also ranges between 0 and infinity. (See Figure 3-8.)
2. Also, like the chi-square distribution, the F distribution approaches the normal distribution as k_1 and k_2, the d.f., become large (technically, infinite).
3. The square of a t-distributed r.v. with k d.f. has an F distribution with 1 and k d.f. in the numerator and denominator, respectively. That is,

$$t_k^2 = F_{1,k} \qquad (3.16)$$

We will see the usefulness of this property in Chapter 6.

The F distribution is tabulated in Table B-3 in Appendix B. Its specific uses in the context of regression analysis will be considered later, but in the meantime let us see how this table is used.

---

[21] To be precise,

$$\frac{S_x^2/\sigma_x^2}{S_y^2/\sigma_y^2}$$

follows the F distribution. But if $\sigma_x^2 = \sigma_y^2$, we have the F ratio given in Eq. (3.15).

[22] Note that the numerator sum of squares, $\Sigma(X_i - \bar{X})^2$, although based on m observations, has $(m - 1)$ d.f. because 1 d.f. is lost in computing the sample mean $\bar{X}$. Likewise, the denominator sum of squares, $\Sigma(Y_i - \bar{Y})^2$, although based on n observations again, has $(n - 1)$ d.f. because 1 d.f. is lost in computing the sample mean $\bar{Y}$. Recall our earlier discussion on d.f.

[23] The F distribution has two sets of d.f. because statistical theory shows that the F distribution is the distribution of the ratio of two *independent* chi-square random variables divided by their respective d.f.

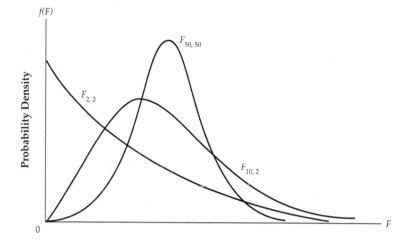

FIGURE 3-8
The F distribution for various d.f.

Example 3.15. Let us return to the S.A.T. example (Example 3.14). Assume that the verbal scores for males and females are each normally distributed. Further assume that average scores and their variances given in the preceding table represent sample values from a much larger population. Based on the two sample variances, can we assume that the two population variances are the same?

Since the verbal scores of the male and female populations are assumed to be normally distributed random variables, we can compute the F ratio given in Eq. (3.15) as

$$F = \frac{303.39}{142.08} = 2.1353$$

which has the F distribution with 23 d.f. in the numerator and 23 d.f. in the denominator. (*Note:* In computing the F value, we are putting the larger of the two variances in the numerator.) Although Table B-3 in Appendix B does not give the F value corresponding to d.f. of 23, if we use 24 d.f. for both the numerator and the denominator, the probability of obtaining an F value of ≈ 2.14 lies somewhere between 1 and 5 percent. If we regard this probability as "too" low (more about this in the next chapter), we could say that the two population variances do not seem to be equal; i.e., there is a difference in the variances of male and female scores on the verbal part of the S.A.T. test. Remember that if the two population variances are the same, the F value will be 1, but if they are different, the F value will be increasingly greater than 1.

Example 3.16.   An instructor gave the same econometrics examination to two classes, one consisting of 100 students and the other consisting of 150 students. He draws a random sample of 25 students from the first class and a random sample of 31 students from the other class and observes that the sample variances of the grade-point average in the two classes were 100 and 132, respectively. It is assumed that the r.v., grade-point average, in the two classes is normally distributed. Can we assume that the variances of grade-point average in the two classes is the same?

Since we are dealing with two independent random samples drawn from two normal populations, applying the F ratio given in Eq. (3.15), we find that

$$F = \frac{132}{100} = 1.32$$

follows the F distribution with 30 and 24 d.f., respectively. From the F values given in Table B-3 we observe that for 30 numerator d.f. and 24 denominator d.f. the probability of obtaining an F value of as much as 1.31 or greater is 25 percent. If we regard this probability as reasonably high, we can conclude that the (population) variances in the two econometrics classes are (statistically) the same.

3.6   SUMMARY

In Chapter 2 we discussed probability distributions in general terms. In this chapter, we considered four specific probability distributions—the normal, the chi-square, the t, and the F—and the special features of each distribution, in particular, the situations in which these distributions can be useful. As we will see in the remainder of this book, these four PDFs play a very pivotal role in econometric theory and practice. Therefore, a solid grasp of the fundamentals of these distributions is essential to follow the ensuing material. The reader may want to return to this chapter from time to time to consult specific points of these distributions when referred to in later chapters.

Key Terms and Concepts

The key terms and concepts introduced in this chapter are:

The normal distribution
    a) Unit, or standard normal variable
Random sampling; i.i.d. random variables
Sampling, or probability, distribution of an estimator (e.g., the sample mean)
Central limit theorem (CLT)

The chi-square (χ^2) distribution
The t distribution (Student's t distribution)
    a) t value

The F distribution
    a) variance ratio distribution
    b) numerator and denominator degrees of freedom (d.f.)

QUESTIONS

3.1. Explain the meaning of
(a) Degrees of freedom
(b) Sampling distribution of an estimator
(c) Standard error

3.2. Consider a random variable (r.v.) $X \sim N(8, 16)$. State whether the following statements are true or false:
(a) The probability of obtaining an X value of greater than 12 is ≈ 0.16.
(b) The probability of obtaining an X value between 12 and 14 is ≈ 0.09.
(c) The probability that an X is more than 2.5 standard deviations from the mean value is 0.0062.

3.3. Continue with question 3.2.
(a) What is the probability distribution of the sample mean $\overline{X}$ obtained from a random sample from this population?
(b) Does your answer to (a) depend on the sample size? Why or why not?
(c) Assuming a sample size of 25, what is the probability of obtaining $\overline{X}$ of 6?

3.4. What is the difference between the t distribution and normal distribution? When should you use the t distribution?

3.5. Consider an r.v. that follows the t distribution.
(a) For 20 degrees of freedom (d.f.), what is the probability that the t value will be greater than 1.325?
(b) And that the t value in 3.5(a) will be less than 1.325?
(c) What is the probability that a t value will be greater than or less than 1.325?
(d) Is there a difference between the statement in 3.5(c) and the statement, "What is the probability that the absolute value of t, $|t|$, will be greater than 1.325?"

3.6. True or false? For a sufficiently large d.f., the t, the chi-square, and the F distributions all approach the unit normal distribution.

3.7. Statistical theory shows that for sufficiently large d.f. the chi-square distribution can be approximated by a unit normal distribution as follows:
$$Z = \sqrt{2\chi^2} - \sqrt{2k - 1} \sim N(0, 1)$$
where k denotes the d.f. Suppose $k = 50$
(a) Use the chi-square table to find out the probability that a chi-square value will exceed 80.
(b) Determine this probability by using the given normal approximation.
(c) Assume that the d.f. are now 100. Compute the probability from the chi-square table as well as from the given normal approximation.
   What conclusions can you draw from using the normal approximation to the chi-square distribution?

3.8. What is the importance of the central limit theorem in statistics?

3.9. Give examples where the chi-square and F probability distributions can be used.

PROBLEMS

3.10. Profits (X) in an industry consisting of 100 firms are normally distributed with a mean value of $1.5 million and a standard deviation (s.d.) of $120,000. Calculate
(a) $P(X < \$1 \text{ million})$
(b) $P(800{,}000 \leq X \leq 1{,}300{,}000)$

3.11. In problem 3.10, if 10 percent of the firms are to exceed a certain profit, what is that profit?

3.12. The grade-point average in an econometrics examination was normally distributed with a mean of 75. In a sample of 10 percent of students it was found that the grade-point average was greater than 80. Can you tell what the s.d. of the grade-point average was?

3.13. The amount of toothpaste in a tube is normally distributed with a mean of 6.5 ounces and an s.d. of 0.8 ounces. The cost of producing each tube is 50 cents. If in a quality control examination a tube is found to weigh less than 6 ounces, it is to be refilled to the mean value at a cost of 20 cents per tube. On the other hand, if the tube weighs more than 7 ounces, the company loses a profit of 5 cents per tube.

If 1000 tubes were examined,
(a) How many tubes will be found to contain less than 6 ounces?
(b) In that case, what will be the total cost of the refill?
(c) How many tubes will be found to contain more than 7 ounces? In that case, what will be the amount of profits lost?

3.14. If $X \sim N(10, 3)$ and $Y \sim N(15, 8)$, and if X and Y are independent, what is the probability distribution of
(a) $X + Y$ (b) $X - Y$ (c) $3X$ (d) $4X + 5Y$

3.15. Continue with problem 3.14 but now assume that X and Y are positively correlated with a correlation coefficient of 0.6.

3.16. Let X and Y represent the rates of return (in percent) on two stocks. You are told that $X \sim N(15, 25)$ and $Y \sim N(8, 4)$, and that the correlation coefficient between the two rates of return is -0.4. Suppose you want to hold the two stocks in your portfolio in equal proportion. What is the probability distribution of the return on the portfolio? Is it better to hold this portfolio or to invest in only one of the two stocks? Why?

3.17. Return to Example 3.14. A random sample of 10 female S.A.T. scores on the math test gave a sample variance of 85.21. Knowing that the true variance is 83.88, what is the probability of obtaining such a sample value? Which probability distribution do you use to answer this question? What are the assumptions underlying that distribution?

3.18. The 10 economic forecasters of a random sample were asked to forecast the rate of growth of the real gross national product (GNP) for the coming year. Suppose the probability distribution of the r.v.—forecast—is normal.
(a) The probability is 0.10 that the sample variance of forecast is more than X percentage of the population variance. What is the value of X?
(b) If the probability is 0.95 so that the sample variance is between X and Y percent of the population variance, what will be the values of X and Y?

3.19. When a sample of 10 cereal boxes of a well-known brand was reweighed, it gave the following weights (in ounces):

16.13	16.02	15.90	15.83	16.00
15.79	16.01	16.04	15.96	16.20

(a) What is the sample mean? And the sample variance?
(b) If the true mean weight per box were 16 ounces, what is the probability of

obtaining such a (sample) mean? Which probability distribution do you use and why?

3.20. The same microeconomics examination was given to students in two different universities. The results were as follows:

$$\overline{X}_1 = 75, \qquad S_1^2 = 9.0, \qquad n_1 = 50$$
$$\overline{X}_2 = 70, \qquad S_2^2 = 7.2, \qquad n_2 = 40$$

where the $\overline{X}$s denote the grade averages in the two samples; the S^2s, the two sample variances; and the ns, the sample sizes. How would you test the hypothesis that the population variances of the test scores in the two universities are the same? Which probability distribution do you use? What are the assumptions underlying that distribution?

CHAPTER 4

STATISTICAL INFERENCE: ESTIMATION AND HYPOTHESIS TESTING

Equipped with the knowledge of probability; random variables; probability distributions; and characteristics of probability distributions, such as expected value, variance, covariance, correlation, conditional expectation, etc., we are now ready to undertake the important task of **statistical inference.** Broadly speaking, statistical inference draws conclusions about a population [i.e., probability density function (PDF)] from a random sample that has supposedly been drawn from that population.

4.1   THE MEANING OF STATISTICAL INFERENCE

As noted previously, the concepts of *population* and *sample* are extremely important in statistics. *Population,* as defined in Chapter 2, is the totality of all possible outcomes of a phenomenon of interest (e.g., the population of New York City). A *sample* is a subset of a population (e.g., the people living in Manhattan, which is one of the five boroughs of the city). Statistical inference, loosely speaking, is about the study of the relationship between a population and a sample drawn from that population. To understand what this means, let us consider a concrete example.

There are about 1758 common stocks listed on the New York Stock Exchange (NYSE) (as of September 4, 1990). Suppose we select a *random sample* of 50 stocks from this population on a particular day and compute the average *price to earnings ratio*—the famous *P/E ratio*—of these 50 stocks. (For example, if the price of a stock is $50 and its annual earnings are estimated at $5, the P/E ratio would be 10; that is, the stock is selling at a price 10 times its annual earnings.)[1] In statistical inference the question we raise is: Based on the average P/E ratio of the 50 stocks, can we tell what the average P/E ratio is in a population of 1758 stocks? In other words, if we let X = the P/E ratio of a stock and $\overline{X}$ = the average P/E ratio of the 50 stocks (= $\Sigma_{i=1}^{50} X_i/50$), can we tell what $E(X)$—the expected or average P/E ratio—is in the population as a whole? *This process of generalizing from the sample value ($\overline{X}$) to the population value $E(X)$ is the essence of statistical inference.* We now discuss this topic in some detail.

4.2 ESTIMATION AND HYPOTHESIS TESTING: TWIN BRANCHES OF STATISTICAL INFERENCE

From the preceding discussion it can be seen that statistical inference proceeds along the following lines. There is some population of interest, say, the 1758 stocks on the NYSE, and we are interested in studying some aspect of this population, say, the P/E ratio. Of course, we may not want to study each and every P/E ratio, but let us say, the average P/E ratio. Since collecting information on all 1758 P/E ratios needed to compute the average P/E ratio is expensive and time-consuming, one may obtain a *random sample* of only, say, 50 stocks, to get the P/E ratio of each of these sampled stocks and to compute the sample average P/E ratio, $\overline{X}$. $\overline{X}$ is an **estimator,** also known as a (sample) *statistics*, of the population average P/E ratio, $E(X)$, which is called the (population) **parameter.** [Recall from our discussion in Chapter 2 that a population (i.e., PDF) is characterized by its parameters.] For example, the mean and variance are parameters of the normal distribution. A particular numerical value of the estimator is called an *estimate* (e.g., an $\overline{X}$ of 10). Thus, *estimation is the first step in statistical inference.*

Having obtained an estimate of a parameter, we next need to find out how "good" that estimate is, for an estimate is not likely to equal the true parameter value: If we obtain two or more random samples of 50 stocks each and compute $\overline{X}$ for each of these samples, the two estimates will probably not be the same. This variation in estimates from sample to sample is known as

---

[1] What sample size one should use is a separate question. A specialized branch of statistics, known as *sampling theory*, discusses this question in depth. But it may be noted that if a sample is truly random, one does not have to draw a very large sample. As a matter of fact, most presidential election polls conducted in the United States are based on a sample size as small as 1000 or 1500 people, which is an extremely small portion of the U.S. population. Yet, several of these polls come within points of predicting the final result.

sampling variation or *sampling error.*[2] Are there any criteria by which we can judge the "goodness" of an estimator? In Section 4.4 we discuss some of the commonly used criteria to judge the goodness of an estimator.

Whereas estimation is one side of statistical inference, hypothesis testing is the other side. In *hypothesis testing* we may have a prior judgment or expectation about what value a particular parameter may assume. For example, a prior knowledge, or an expert opinion, tells us that the true average P/E ratio in the population of 1758 stocks is, say, 12. Suppose a particular random sample of 50 stocks gives this estimate as 11. Is this value of 11 "close" to the *hypothesized value* of 12? Obviously, the number 11 is different from the number 12. But the important question here is: Is 11 *statistically different* from 12? We know that because of sampling variation there is likely to be a difference between a (sample) estimate and its population value. It is possible that "statistically" the number 11 may not be very different from the number 12, in which case we may not reject the hypothesis that the true average of P/E ratio is 12. But how do we decide that? This is the topic of *hypothesis testing,* which we discuss in Section 4.5.

With these preliminaries, let us examine the twin topics of estimation and hypothesis testing in some detail.

4.3 ESTIMATION OF PARAMETERS

In the previous chapter we considered several theoretical probability distributions. Often we know or are willing to assume that a random variable X follows a particular distribution but do not know the value(s) of the parameter(s) of the distribution. For example, if X follows the normal distribution, we may want to know the values of its two parameters, namely, the mean $E(X) = \mu_x$ and the variance σ^2. To estimate these unknowns, the usual procedure is to assume that we have a *random sample* of size n from the known probability distribution and use the sample to estimate the unknown parameters. Thus, we can use the sample mean as an estimate of the population mean (or expected value) and the sample variance as an estimate of the population variance. This procedure is known as the *problem of estimation*. The problem of estimation can be broken down into two categories: **point estimation** and **interval estimation.**

To fix the ideas, assume that the random variable (r.v.), X (P/E ratio), is normally distributed with a certain mean and a certain variance, but for now we do not know the values of these parameters. Suppose, however, we have a random sample of 50 P/E ratios (50 Xs) from this normal population, as shown in Table 4-1.

---

[2] Notice that this sampling error is not deliberate but, rather, results from the fact that we have a random sample and that the elements included in the sample will vary from sample to sample. This is inevitable in any analysis based on a sample.

TABLE 4-1
Hypothetical sample
of 50 P/E ratios

P/E ratio	Frequency
6	2
7	2
8	5
9	6
10	5
11	7
12	5
13	4
14	3
15	4
16	6
18	1
Total	50

Mean = 11.5
Sample variance = 9.2755
Sample standard deviation = 3.0456
Median = mode = 11

How can we use this sample data to compute the population mean value $\mu_x = E(X)$ and the population variance σ^2? More specifically, suppose our immediate interest is in finding out μ_x.[3] How do we go about it? An obvious choice is the sample mean $\overline{X}$ of the 50 P/E ratios shown in Table 4-1, which is 11.5. We call this *single numerical value* the *point estimate* of μ_x and the formula $\overline{X} = \Sigma_{i=1}^{50} X_i/50$ we used to compute this point estimate is called the *point estimator, or statistic*. Notice that *a point estimator, or a statistic, is an r.v., as its value will vary from sample to sample.* (Recall our sampling experiment in Table 3-1.) Therefore, how reliable is a specific estimate such as 11.5 of the true μ_x? In other words, how can we rely on just one estimate of the true population mean? Would it not be better to state that although $\overline{X}$ is the single "best" guess of the true population mean, the interval, say, from 8 to 14, most likely includes the true μ_x? This is essentially the idea behind *interval estimation*. Now consider the actual mechanics of obtaining interval estimates.

The key idea underlying interval estimation is the notion of **sampling, or probability, distribution** of an estimator such as, e.g., the sample mean $\overline{X}$. In the previous chapter we saw that if an r.v. $X \sim N(\mu_x, \sigma^2)$, then

---

[3] This discussion can be easily extended to estimate σ^2.

$$\overline{X} \sim N\left(\mu_x, \frac{\sigma^2}{n}\right) \tag{4.1}$$

Or

$$Z = \frac{(\overline{X} - \mu_x)}{\sigma/\sqrt{n}} \sim N(0, 1) \tag{4.2}$$

That is, the sample distribution of the sample mean $\overline{X}$ also follows the normal distribution with the stated parameters.[4]

As pointed out in the previous chapter, σ^2 is not generally known, but if we use its (sample) estimator $S^2 = \Sigma(X_i - \overline{X})^2/(n - 1)$, then we know that

$$t = \frac{\overline{X} - \mu_x}{S/\sqrt{n}} \tag{4.3}$$

follows the t distribution with $(n - 1)$ degrees of freedom (d.f.).

To see how Equation (4.3) helps us to obtain an interval estimation of the μ_x of our P/E example, note that we have in all 50 observations and, therefore, 49 d.f. Now if we consult the t table (Table B-2) given in Appendix B, we notice that the t distribution is not given precisely for 49 d.f., but more extensive t tables given in other books will show that for 49 d.f.,

$$P(-2.0096 \le t \le 2.0096) = 0.95 \tag{4.4}$$

as shown in Figure 4-1. That is, for 49 d.f., the probability is 0.95 (or 95 percent) that the interval $(-2.0096, 2.0096)$ will include the t value computed from Eq. (4.3).[5] These t values, as we will see shortly, are known as **critical t values;** they show what percentage of the area under the t distribution curve (see

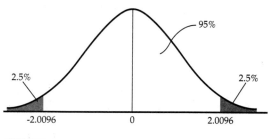

2.5%   95%   2.5%

-2.0096   0   2.0096

FIGURE 4-1
The t distribution for 49 d.f.

---

[4] Note that if X does not follow the normal distribution, $\overline{X}$ will follow the normal distribution à la the central limit theorem if n, the sample size, is sufficiently large.

[5] Needless to say, these values will depend on the d.f. as well as on the level of probability used. For example, for the same d.f. $(-2.68 \le t \le 2.68) = 0.99$.

Figure 4-1) lies between those values (note that the total area under the curve is 1). Now substituting the t value from Eq. (4.3) into Eq. (4.4), we obtain

$$P\left(-2.0096 \leq \frac{(\overline{X} - \mu_x)}{S/\sqrt{n}} \leq 2.0096\right) = 0.95 \qquad (4.5)$$

Simple algebraic manipulation will show that Equation (4.5) can be expressed *equivalently* as

$$P\left(\overline{X} - \frac{2.0096S}{\sqrt{n}} \leq \mu_x \leq \overline{X} + \frac{2.0096S}{\sqrt{n}}\right) = 0.95 \qquad (4.6)$$

Equation (4.6) provides an *interval estimator* of the true μ_x.

In statistics we call Eq. (4.6) a 95% **confidence interval** for the true but unknown population mean μ_x and 0.95 is called the **confidence coefficient.** In words, Eq. (4.6) says that the *probability is 0.95 that the random interval $(\overline{X} \pm 2.0096S/\sqrt{n})$ contains the true μ_x.* $(\overline{X} - 2.0096S/\sqrt{n})$ is called the **lower limit** of the interval and $(\overline{X} + 2.0096S/\sqrt{n})$ is the **upper limit** of the interval.

Before proceeding further, note this important point: The interval given in Eq. (4.6) is a **random interval** because it is based on $\overline{X}$ and $S/\sqrt{n}$, which will vary from sample to sample. The population mean μ_x, although unknown, is some fixed number and therefore is not random. Thus, *one should not say that the probability is 0.95 that μ_x lies in this interval. The correct statement, as noted earlier, is that the probability is 0.95 that the random interval, Eq. (4.6), contains the true μ_x. In short, the interval is random, and not the parameter μ_x.*

Returning to our P/E example of Table 4-1, we have $n = 50$, $\overline{X} = 11.5$, and $S = 3.0456$. Plugging these values into Eq. (4.6), we obtain

$$11.5 - 2.0096\left(\frac{3.0456}{\sqrt{50}}\right) \leq \mu_x \leq 11.50 + 2.0096\left(\frac{3.0096}{\sqrt{50}}\right)$$

or

$$10.63 \leq \mu_x \leq 12.36 \quad \text{(approx.)} \qquad (4.7)$$

as the 95% confidence interval for μ_x, as shown in Figure 4-2.

Equation (4.7) says, in effect, that if we construct intervals like Eq. (4-7), say, 100 times, then 95 out of 100 such intervals will include the true μ_x.[6] Incidentally, note that for our P/E example the lower limit of the interval is 10.63 and the upper limit is 12.36.

---

[6] Be careful again. We cannot say that the probability is 0.95 that the particular interval (4.7) includes the true μ_x; it may or may not. Therefore, statements like $P(10.63 \leq \mu_x \leq 12.36) = 0.95$ *are not permissible under the classical approach to hypothesis testing.* Intervals like (4.7) are to be interpreted in the repeated sampling sense in that if we construct such intervals a large number of times, then 95 percent of such intervals will include the true mean value; the particular interval (4.7) is just one realization of the interval estimator (4.6).

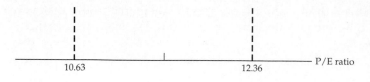

FIGURE 4-2
The 95% confidence interval for population average P/E ratio.

Thus, *interval estimation, in contrast to point estimation (such as 11.5), provides a range of values that will include the true value with a certain degree of confidence or probability (such as 0.95).*

More generally, suppose X is an r.v. with some PDF. Suppose further that we want to estimate a parameter of this distribution, say, its mean value μ_x. Toward that end, we obtain a random sample of n values, $X_1, X_2 \dots ,$ X_n, and compute two statistics (or estimators) L and U from this sample such that

$$P(L \leq \mu_x \leq U) = 1 - \alpha \qquad 0 < \alpha < 1 \qquad (4.8)$$

That is, the probability is $(1 - \alpha)$ that the *random interval* from L to U contains the true μ_x. L is called the lower limit of the interval and U is called the upper limit. This interval is known as a *confidence interval (CI)* of size $(1 - \alpha)$ for μ_x (or any parameter for that matter), and $(1 - \alpha)$ is known as the *confidence coefficient*. If $\alpha = 0.05$, $(1 - \alpha) = 0.95$, meaning that if we construct a confidence interval with a confidence coefficient of 0.95, then in repeated such constructions 95 out of 100 intervals can be expected to include the true μ_x. In practice, $(1 - \alpha)$ is often multiplied by 100 to express it in percent form, e.g., 95 percent. In statistics alpha (α) is known as the *level of significance*, or, alternatively, *the probability of committing a type I error*, which is defined and discussed in Section 4.5.

Now that we have seen how to establish confidence intervals, what do we do with them? As we will see in Section 4.5, confidence intervals make our task of testing a hypothesis—the twin of statistical inference—much easier.

4.4   PROPERTIES OF POINT ESTIMATORS

In the P/E example we used the sample mean $\overline{X}$ as a point estimator of μ_x, as well as to obtain an interval estimator of μ_x. But why did we use $\overline{X}$, for, as is well known, besides the sample mean, the (sample) median or the (sample) mode can also be used as point estimators of μ_x.[7] It can be shown for the

---

[7] The *median* is that value of a random variable that divides the total PDF into two halves such that half the values in the population exceed it and half are below it. To compute the median from a sample, arrange the observations in increasing order; the median is the middle value in

P/E sample given in Table 4-1 that the median and model values are both equal to 11.

In practice, the sample mean is the most frequently used measure of the population mean because it satisfies several properties that statisticians deem desirable. Some of these properties are:

1. Linearity
2. Unbiasedness
3. Efficiency
4. Best linear unbiased estimator (BLUE)
5. Consistency

We now discuss these properties somewhat heuristically.

Linearity

*An estimator is said to be a **linear estimator** if it is a linear function of the sample observations.* The sample mean is obviously a linear estimator because

$$\overline{X} = \sum_{i=1}^{n} \frac{X_i}{n} = \frac{1}{n}(X_1 + X_2 + \cdots + X_n)$$

is a linear function of the observations, the Xs (*Note*: The Xs appear with an index or power of 1 only).

In statistics a linear estimator is generally much easier to deal with than a nonlinear estimator.

Unbiasedness

If there are several estimators of a population parameter (i.e., several methods of estimating that parameter), and if one or more of these estimators *on the average* coincide with the true value of the parameter, we say that such estimators are **unbiased estimators** of that parameter. Put differently, if in repeated applications of a method the *mean* value of the estimators coincides with the true parameter value, that estimator is called an unbiased estimator. More formally, an estimator, say, $\overline{X}$, is an unbiased estimator of μ_x if

$$E(\overline{X}) = \mu_x \tag{4.9}$$

as shown in Figure 4-3. If this is not the case, however, then we call that estimator a *biased estimator*.

---

this order. For example, if we have observations 7, 3, 6, 11, 5, and rearrange them in increasing order, we obtain 3, 5, 6, 7, 11. The median, or the middlemost value, here is 6. The *mode* is the most popular or frequent value of the random variable. For example, if we have observations 3, 5, 7, 5, 8, 5, 9, the *modal value* is 5 since it occurs most frequently.

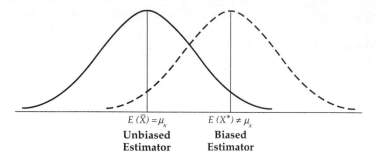

$$E\,(\overline{X}) = \mu_x \qquad\qquad E\,(X^*) \neq \mu_x$$

Unbiased   **Biased**
Estimator   **Estimator**

FIGURE 4-3
A biased (X^*) and unbiased ($\overline{X}$) estimator of population mean value, μ_x.

Example 4.1. Let $X_i \sim N(\mu_x, \sigma^2)$, then we know that $\overline{X}$ based on a random sample of size n from this population is distributed with mean $E(X) = \mu_x$ and var $(\overline{X}) = \sigma^2/n$. Thus, the sample mean $\overline{X}$ is an unbiased estimator of true μ_x: If we draw repeated samples of size n from this normal population and compute $\overline{X}$ for each sample, then on the average $\overline{X}$ will coincide with μ_x. But notice carefully that we cannot say that in a single sample, such as the one in Table 4-1, the computed mean of 11.5 will necessarily coincide with the true mean value. In the grade-point example of Table 3-1 we also cannot say that any single sample mean will be equal to the true mean.

Example 4.2. Again, let $X_i \sim N(\mu_x, \sigma^2)$, and suppose we draw a random sample of size n from this population. Let X_{med} represent the median value of this sample. It can be shown that $E(X_{med}) = \mu_x$; in words, the median from this population is also an unbiased estimator of the true mean. Notice also that unbiasedness is a *repeated sampling property*; that is, if we draw several samples of size n from this population and compute the median value for each sample, then the average of the median values obtained will tend to approach μ_x. We cannot guarantee that a single estimate of the median, such as 11 obtained from the sample of Table 4-1, is necessarily equal to the true mean value.

Efficiency

The property of unbiasedness, although desirable, is not by itself adequate. What happens if we have two or more estimators of a parameter and they are all unbiased? How do we choose among them?

Suppose we have a random sample of n values of an r.v. X such that each $X \sim N(\mu_x, \sigma^2)$. Let $\overline{X}$ and X_{med} be the mean and median values obtained from this sample. We already know that

$$\overline{X} \sim N(\mu_x, \sigma^2/n) \tag{4.10}$$

It can also be shown that *if the sample size is large,*

$$X_{\text{med}} \sim N(\mu_x, (\pi/2)(\sigma^2/n)) \tag{4.11}$$

where $\pi = 3.142$ (approx.). That is, in large samples, the median computed from a random sample of a normal population also follows a normal distribution with the same mean μ_x but with a variance that is larger than the variance of $\overline{X}$ by the factor $\pi/2$, which can be visualized from Figure 4-4. As a matter of fact, if we form the ratio

$$\frac{\text{var}(X_{\text{med}})}{\text{var}(\overline{X})} = \frac{\pi}{2}\frac{\sigma^2/n}{\sigma^2/n} = \frac{\pi}{2} = 1.571 \quad \text{(approx.)} \tag{4.12}$$

which shows that the variance of the sample median is ≈57 percent larger than the variance of the sample mean.

Now given Figure 4-4 and the preceding discussion, which estimator would you choose? Common sense suggests that we choose $\overline{X}$ over X_{med}, for although both estimators are unbiased estimators, $\overline{X}$ has a smaller variance than X_{med}. And therefore if we use $\overline{X}$ in repeated sampling, we will estimate μ_x more accurately than if we were to use the sample median. In short, $\overline{X}$ provides a more *precise* estimate of the population mean than the median X_{med}. In statistical language we say that $\overline{X}$ is an **efficient estimator.** Stated more formally, *if we consider only unbiased estimators of a parameter, the one with the smallest variance is called best, or efficient, estimator.*

Best Linear Unbiased Estimator (BLUE)

In econometrics the property that is frequently encountered is the **best linear unbiased estimator,** or **BLUE** for short. *If an estimator is linear, is unbiased, and*

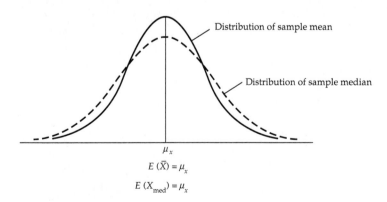

Distribution of sample mean

Distribution of sample median

μ_x

$E(\overline{X}) = \mu_x$

$E(X_{\text{med}}) = \mu_x$

FIGURE 4-4
An example of an efficient estimator (sample mean).

has a minimum variance in the class of all linear unbiased estimators of a parameter,
it is called a best linear unbiased estimator. Obviously, this property combines the
properties of linearity, unbiasedness, and minimum variance. In Chapter 6 we
will see the importance of this property.

Consistency

To explain the property of consistency, suppose $X \sim N(\mu_x, \sigma^2)$ and we draw
a random of size n from this population. Now consider two estimators of μ_x:

$$\overline{X} = \sum \frac{X_i}{n} \tag{4.13}$$

$$X^* = \sum \frac{X_i}{n+1} \tag{4.14}$$

The first estimator is the usual sample mean. Now, as already known

$$E(\overline{X}) = \mu_x$$

and it can be shown that

$$E(X^*) = \left(\frac{n}{n+1}\right)\mu_x \tag{4.15}[8]$$

Since $E(X^*)$ is not equal to μ_x, X^* is obviously a *biased estimator.*

But suppose we increase the sample size. What would you expect? The
estimators $\overline{X}$ and X^* differ only in that the former has n in the denominator
whereas the latter has $(n+1)$. But as the sample increases, we should not
find much difference between the two estimators. That is, as the sample size
increases, X^* will also approach the true μ_x. In statistics such an estimator is
known as a **consistent estimator.** Stated *more formally, an estimator (e.g., X^*) is*
said to be a consistent estimator if it approaches the true value of the parameter as
the sample size gets larger and larger. As we will see in later chapters, sometimes

---

[8] This is easy to show:

$$E(X^*) = \left(\frac{1}{n+1}\right)\{EX_1 + EX_2 + \cdots + EX_n\}$$

$$= \left(\frac{1}{n+1}\right)\{\mu_x + \mu_x + \cdots + \mu_x\}$$

$$= \left(\frac{1}{n+1}\right) \cdot n\mu_x$$

where use is made of the fact that each X_i has the same mean.

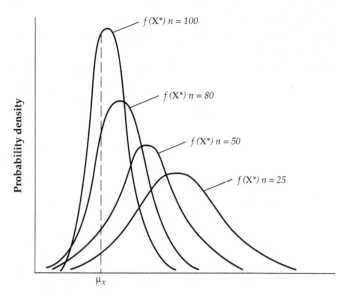

FIGURE 4-5
The property of consistency. The behavior of the estimator X^* of population mean μ_x as the sample size increases.

we may not be able to obtain an unbiased estimator but can obtain a consistent estimator.[9] The property of consistency is depicted in Figure 4-5.

4.5   STATISTICAL INFERENCE: HYPOTHESIS TESTING

Having studied in some detail the estimation branch of statistical inference, we now consider its twin, hypothesis testing. Although the general nature of hypothesis testing was discussed earlier, we study it here in some detail.

Let us return to the P/E example given in Table 4-1. In Section 4.3, based on a random sample of 50 P/E ratios, we established a 95% confidence interval for μ_x, the true but unknown average P/E ratio in the population of 1758 stocks listed on the NYSE. Now let us reverse our strategy. Instead of establishing a confidence interval, suppose we *hypothesize* that the true μ_x takes a

---

[9] Note the critical difference between an unbiased and a consistent estimator. If we fix the sample size and draw several random samples of an r.v. from some probability distribution to estimate a parameter of this distribution, then unbiasedness requires that *on the average* we should be able to obtain the true parameter value. In establishing consistency, on the other hand, we see the behavior of an estimator as the sample size increases. If a sample size is reasonably large and the estimator based on that sample size approaches the true parameter value, then that estimator is a consistent estimator.

particular numerical value, e.g., $\mu_x = 13$. Our task now is to "test" this hypothesis.[10] How do we test this hypothesis?—that is, support or refute the hypothesis?

In the language of hypothesis testing a hypothesis such as $\mu_x = 13$ is called the **null hypothesis** and is generally denoted by the symbol H_0. Thus, H_0: $\mu_x = 13$. The null hypothesis is usually tested against an **alternative hypothesis,** denoted by the symbol H_1. The alternative hypothesis can take one of these forms:

H_1: $\mu_x > 13$, which is called a **one-sided** alternative hypothesis, or

H_1: $\mu_x < 13$, also a **one-sided** alternative hypothesis, or

H_1: $\mu_x \neq 13$, which is called a **two-sided** alternative hypothesis. That is, the true mean value is either greater than or less than 13.[11]

To test the null hypothesis (against the alternative hypothesis), we use the sample data (e.g., the sample average P/E ratio of 11.5 obtained from the sample in Table 4-1) and statistical theory to develop decision rules that will tell us whether the sample evidence supports the null hypothesis. If the sample evidence supports the null hypothesis, we do not reject H_0, but if it does not, we reject H_0. In the latter case we can accept the alternative hypothesis, H_1.

How do we develop these decision rules? There are two complementary approaches: (1) the confidence interval approach and (2) the test of significance approach. We illustrate each with the aid of our P/E example and assume that

$$H_0: \mu_x = 13$$

$$H_1: \mu_x \neq 13 \qquad \text{(a two-sided hypothesis)}$$

The Confidence Interval Approach
to Hypothesis Testing

To test the null hypothesis, suppose we have the sample data given in Table 4-1. From these data we computed the sample mean of 11.5. We know from our discussion in Section 4.3 that the sample mean is distributed normally with mean μ_x and variance σ^2/n. But since the true variance is unknown, we replace it with the sample variance, in which case we know that the sample

---

[10] A *hypothesis* is "something considered to be true for the purpose of investigation or argument" (Webster), or a "supposition made as a basis for reasoning, or as a starting point for further investigation from known facts" (*Oxford English Dictionary*).

[11] There are various ways of stating the null and alternative hypotheses. For example, we could have H_0: $\mu_x \geq 13$ and H_1: $\mu_x < 13$.

mean follows the t distribution, as shown in Eq. (4.3). Based on the t distribution, we obtained the following 95% confidence interval for μ_x:

$$10.63 \leq \mu_x \leq 12.36 \quad \text{(approx.)} \tag{4.7}$$

We know that confidence intervals provide a range of values within which the true μ_x will lie with a certain degree of confidence, such as 95 percent. Therefore, if a particular null hypothesized value such as $\mu_x = 13$ does not lie within this interval, could we not reject this null hypothesis? Yes, we can, with 95% confidence.

From the preceding discussion it should be clear that the topics of confidence interval and hypothesis testing are intimately related. In the language of hypothesis testing, the (95%) confidence interval shown in inequality (4.7) (see Figure 4-2) is called the **acceptance region** and the area outside the acceptance region is called the **critical region, or the region of rejection,** of the null hypothesis. The lower and upper limits of the acceptance region are called **critical values.** In this language, if the value of the parameter under H_0 lies inside the acceptance region, we do not reject the null hypothesis. But if it falls outside the acceptance region (i.e., it lies within the rejection region), we reject the null hypothesis. In our example we reject the null hypothesis that $\mu_x = 13$ since this value lies within the critical region; it is greater than the upper critical value of 12.36 and the probability of that happening is very small—less than 2.5 percent. In short, the null hypothesis is rejected if the value of the parameter under the null hypothesis either exceeds the upper critical value or is less than the lower critical value of the acceptance region. It should be clear now why the boundaries of the acceptance region are called critical values, for they are the dividing line between accepting or rejecting a null hypothesis.

Type I and Type II Errors: A Digression

In our P/E example we rejected H_0: $\mu_x = 13$ because our sample evidence of $\overline{X} = 11.5$ does not seem to be compatible with this hypothesis. Does this mean that the sample shown in Table 4-1 could not have come from a normal population whose mean value was 13? It is possible that in fact the sample did; remember that the confidence interval given in inequality (4.7) is 95 and not 100 percent. If that is the case, we would be making an error in rejecting H_0: $\mu_x = 13$. In this case we are said to commit a **type I error,** that is, *the error of rejecting a hypothesis when it is true.* By the same token, suppose H_0: $\mu_x = 12$, in which case, as inequality (4.7) shows, we would not reject this null hypothesis. But quite possibly the sample in Table 4-1 did not come from a normal distribution with a mean value of 12. Thus, we are said to commit a **type II error,** that is, *the error of accepting a false hypothesis.*

Ideally, we would like to minimize both these errors. But, unfortunately, for any given sample size, it is not possible to minimize both errors simultaneously. The classical approach to this problem, embodied in the work of statisticians Neyman and Pearson, is to assume that a type I error is likely to be more serious in practice than a type II error. Therefore, one should try to keep the probability of committing a type I error at a fairly low level, such as 0.01 or 0.05, and then try to minimize a type II error as much as possible.[12]

In the literature the probability of committing a type I error is designated as α and is called the **level of significance,** and the probability of committing a type II error is designated as β. Symbolically,

$$\text{Type I error} = \alpha = \text{prob. (rejecting } H_0 \mid H_0 \text{ is true)}$$

$$\text{Type II error} = \beta = \text{prob. (accepting } H_0 \mid H_0 \text{ is false)}$$

The probability of not committing a type II error is $(1 - \beta)$; that is, rejecting H_0 when it is false, which is called the **power of the test.**

The standard, or classical, approach to hypothesis testing is to fix α at levels such as 0.01 or 0.05 and then try to maximize the power of the test; that is, to minimize β. How this is actually accomplished is involved, and so we leave the subject for the references. Suffice it to note, in practice, the classical approach simply specifies the value of α without worrying too much about β.

The reader will recognize that the **confidence coefficient** $(1 - \alpha)$ discussed earlier is simply one minus the probability of committing a type I error. Thus, a 95% confidence coefficient means that we are prepared to accept at the most a 5 percent probability of committing a type I error—we do not want to reject the true hypothesis by more than 5 out of 100 times. *In short, a 5% level of significance or a 95% level or degree of confidence means the same thing.*

Let us consider another example to illustrate further the confidence interval approach to hypothesis testing.

Example 4.3   The number of peanuts contained in a jar follows the normal distribution but we do not know its mean and standard deviation, both measured in ounces. Twenty jars were selected randomly and it was found that the sample mean was 6.5 ounces and the sample standard deviation was 2 ounces. Test the hypothesis that the true mean value was 7.5 ounces against the hypothesis that it is different from 7.5. Use $\alpha = 1\%$.

Answer: Letting X denote the number of peanuts in a jar, we are given that $X \sim N(\mu_x, \sigma^2)$, both parameters being unknown. Since the true variance is unknown, it follows that

---

[12] To Bayesian statisticians this procedure sounds rather arbitrary because it does not consider carefully the relative seriousness of the two types of errors. For further discussion of this and related points, see Robert L. Winkler, *Introduction to Bayesian Inference and Decision*, Holt, Rinehart and Winston, New York, 1972, Chap. 7.

$$t = \frac{\overline{X} - \mu_x}{S/\sqrt{20}} \sim t_{19} \tag{4.16}$$

That is, the t distribution with 19 d.f.

From the t distribution table given in Table B-2 in Appendix B, we observe that for 19 d.f.,

$$P(-2.861 \le t \le 2.861) = 0.99 \tag{4.17}$$

Then from expression (4.6) we obtain

$$P\left(\frac{\overline{X} - 2.861S}{\sqrt{20}} \le \mu_x \le \frac{\overline{X} + 2.861S}{\sqrt{20}}\right) = 0.99 \tag{4.18}$$

Substituting $\overline{X} = 6.5$, $S = 2$, and $n = 20$ into Equation (4.18), we obtain

$$5.22 \le \mu_x \le 7.78 \quad \text{(approx.)} \tag{4.19}$$

as the 99% confidence interval for μ_x. [See Figure 4-6(a)]. Since the interval, expression (4.19), includes the hypothesized value of 7.5, we do not reject the null hypothesis that the true $\mu_x = 7.5$.

Example 4.4.   Suppose in Example 4.3 we decide to fix α at the 5% level; that is, we decide to accept a higher risk of committing a type I error. What now?

Answer: From the t table we find that for 19 d.f. and $\alpha = 5\%$, the critical t values are now -2.093 and $+2.093$ because

$$P(-2.093 \le t \le 2.093) = 0.95 \tag{4.20}$$

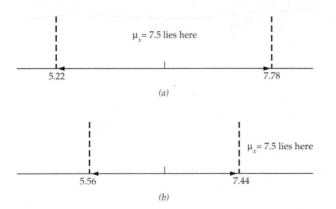

FIGURE 4-6
(a) 99% confidence interval for μ_x; (b) 95% confidence interval for μ_x of Examples 4.3 and 4.4.

Next, following the procedure of Example 4.3, the reader should be able to verify that

$$5.56 \le \mu_x \le 7.44 \quad \text{(approx.)} \tag{4.21}$$

And since this interval, as shown in Figure 4-7(b), does not include 7.5, we can reject the hypothesis that the true $\mu_x = 7.5$.

   The difference between expressions (4.19) and (4.21) is that the latter confidence interval is narrower than the former, but this should not be surprising because in establishing inequality (4.21) we are willing to take a higher risk of committing a type I error, that is, rejecting the null hypothesis even though it might be true.

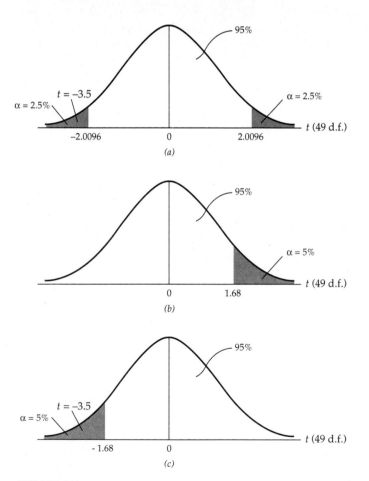

FIGURE 4-7
The *t* test of significance: (*a*) Two-tailed; (*b*) right-tailed; (*c*) left-tailed.

As Examples 4.3 and 4.4 illustrate, the decision to accept or reject a null hypothesis depends critically on both the d.f. and the probability of committing a type I error.

The Test of Significance Approach to Hypothesis Testing

The test of significance is an alternative, but complementary, and perhaps a shorter approach to hypothesis testing. To see the essential points involved, return to the P/E example and Eq. (4.3). We know that

$$t = \frac{\overline{X} - \mu_x}{S/\sqrt{n}} \tag{4.3}$$

follows the t distribution with $(n - 1)$ d.f. In any concrete application we will know the values of $\overline{X}$, S, and n. The only unknown value is μ_x. But if we specify a value for μ_x, as we do under H_0, then the right-hand side of Eq. (4.3) is known, and therefore we will have a unique t value. And since we know that the t of Eq. (4.3) follows the t distribution with $(n - 1)$, we simply look up the t table to find out the probability of obtaining such a t value. Observe that if the difference between $\overline{X}$ and μ_x is small (in absolute terms), then, as Eq. (4.3) shows, the $|t|$ value will also be small, where $|t|$ means the absolute t value. In the event that $\overline{X} = \mu_x$, t will be zero, in which case we can accept the null hypothesis. Therefore, as the $|t|$ value deviates from zero, increasingly we will tend to reject the null hypothesis: As the t table shows, for any given d.f., the probability of obtaining an increasingly higher $|t|$ value becomes progressively smaller. Thus, as $|t|$ gets larger, we will be more and more inclined to reject the null hypothesis. But how large must $|t|$ be before we can reject the null hypothesis? The answer depends on α, the probability of committing a type I error, as well as on the d.f., as we will demonstrate shortly.

This is the general idea behind the test of significance approach to hypothesis testing. The key idea here is the **test statistic**—the t **statistic**—and its probability distribution under the hypothesized value of μ_x. Appropriately, in the present instance the test is known as the t **test** since we use the t distribution. (For details of the t distribution, see Section 3.4).

In our P/E example $\overline{X} = 11.5$, $S = 3.0456$, and $n = 50$. Let H_0: $\mu_x = 13$ and H_1: $\mu_x \neq 13$, as before. Therefore,

$$t = \frac{(11.5 - 13)}{3.0456/\sqrt{50}} = -3.4826$$

Is the computed t value such that we can reject the null hypothesis? We cannot answer this question without first specifying what chance we are willing to take if we reject the null hypothesis when it is true. In other words, to answer this question, we must specify α, the probability of committing a type I error.

Suppose we fix α at 5 percent. And since the alternative hypothesis is two-sided, we want to divide the risk of a type I error equally between the two tails of the t distribution—the two critical regions—so that if the computed t value lies in either of the rejection regions, we can reject the null hypothesis.

Now for 49 d.f., as we saw earlier, the 5% *critical t values* are -2.0096 and $+2.0096$, as shown in Figure 4-1: The probability of obtaining a t value equal to or smaller than -2.0096 is 2.5 percent and that of obtaining a t value equal to or greater than $+2.0096$ is also 2.5 percent, giving the total probability of committing a type I error of 5 percent.

As this Figure 4-1 also shows, the computed t value for our example is about -3.5, which obviously lies in the left tail critical region of the t distribution. We therefore reject the null hypothesis that the true average P/E ratio is 13: If that hypothesis were true, we would not have obtained a t value as large as 3.5 (in absolute terms); the probability of our obtaining such a t value is much smaller than 5 percent—our prechosen probability of committing a type I error. Actually, the probability is much smaller than 2.5 percent. (Why?)

In the language of the test of significance we frequently come across the following two terms:

1. A test (statistic) is *statistically significant*.
2. A test (statistic) is *statistically insignificant*.

When we say that a test is statistically significant, we generally mean that we can reject the null hypothesis. That is, the observed difference between the sample value and the hypothesized value cannot be due to mere chance; in this case the test statistic lies in the rejection region. We regard the test statistic as statistically significant if the probability of our obtaining it is equal to or less than α, the probability of a type I error. By the same token, when we say that a test is statistically insignificant, we do not reject the null hypothesis. In this case the observed difference between the sample value and the hypothesized value can very well be due to sampling variation.

One or two-tailed test? In all the examples considered so far the alternative hypothesis was two-sided, or two-tailed. Thus, if the average P/E ratio were equal to 13 under H_0, it was either greater than or less than 13 under H_1. In this case if the test statistic fell in either tail of the distribution (i.e., the rejection region), we rejected the null hypothesis, as is clear from Figure 4-7(a).

However, there are occasions when the null and alternative hypotheses are one-sided, or one-tailed. For example, if for the P/E example we had H_0: $\mu_x = 13$ and H_1: $\mu_x < 13$, the alternative hypothesis is one-sided. How do we test this hypothesis?

The testing procedure is exactly the same as that used in previous cases except that instead of finding out two critical values we determine only a single critical value of the test statistic, as shown in Figure 4-7. As this figure illustrates, the probability of committing a type I error is now concentrated only in one tail of the probability distribution, t in the present case. For 49 d.f. and $\alpha = 5\%$, the extended t table will show that the one-tailed critical t value is 1.6766 (right tail) or -1.6766 (left tail), as shown in Figure 4-7. For our P/E example, as noted before, the computed t value is -3.4826 or ≈ -3.50. Since the t value lies in the critical region of Figure 4-7(c), this t value is statistically significant. That is, we reject the null hypothesis that the true average P/E ratio is equal to (or greater than) 13; the chances of that happening are much smaller than our prechosen probability of committing a type I error of 5 percent.

Table 4-2 summarizes the (t) test of significance approach to testing the two-tailed and one-tailed null hypothesis.

In practice, whether one uses the confidence interval approach or the test of significance approach to hypothesis testing is a matter of personal choice and convenience. In the confidence interval approach we specify a plausible range of values (i.e., confidence interval) for the true parameter and find out if the hypothesized value of that parameter lies inside or outside that interval. If it lies inside, we do not reject that null hypothesis, but if it lies outside, we can reject the hypothesis. In the test of significance approach, instead of specifying a range of plausible values for the unknown parameter, we pick a specific value of the parameter suggested by the null hypothesis, compute a test statistic, such as the t statistic, and find its sampling distribution and the probability of obtaining a specific value of such a test statistic. If this probability is very low, say, less than $\alpha = 5$ or 1%, we reject the particular null hypothesis. If this probability is greater than the prechosen α, we do not reject the null hypothesis.

TABLE 4-2
A summary of the t test

Null hypothesis H_0	Alternative hypothesis H_1	Critical region Reject H_0 if
$\mu_x = \mu_0$	$\mu_x > \mu_0$	$t = \dfrac{\overline{X} - \mu_0}{S/\sqrt{n}} > t_{\alpha,\text{d.f.}}$
$\mu_x = \mu_0$	$\mu_x < \mu_0$	$t = \dfrac{\overline{X} - \mu_0}{S/\sqrt{n}} < -t_{\alpha,\text{d.f.}}$
$\mu_x = \mu_0$	$\mu_x \neq \mu_0$	$|t| = \dfrac{\overline{X} - \mu_0}{S/\sqrt{n}} > t_{\alpha/2,\text{d.f.}}$

Note: μ_0 denotes the particular value of μ_x assumed under the null hypothesis.
    The first subscript on the t statistic shown in the last column is the level of significance and the second subscript is the d.f. These are critical t values.

A Word on Choosing the Level of Significance, α, and the p Value

The Achilles heel of the classical approach to hypothesis testing is its arbitrariness in selecting α. Although 1, 5, and 10 percent are the commonly used values of α, there is nothing sacrosanct about these values. As noted earlier, unless we examine the consequences of committing both type I and type II errors, we cannot come to grips with the appropriate choice of α. In practice, it is preferable to find the *p* **value** (i.e., the probability value), also known as the *exact significance level*, of the test statistic. This may be defined *as the lowest significance level at which a null hypothesis can be rejected.*

To illustrate, in an application involving 20 d.f. a t value of 3.552 was obtained. The t table given in Appendix B shows that the p value for this t is 0.001 (one-tailed) or 0.002 (two-tailed). That is, this t value is statistically significant at the 0.001 (one-tailed) or 0.002 level (two-tailed).

For our P/E example we found that if $t \approx -3.5$ under the null hypothesis that the true average P/E ratio is 13. Now for 49 d.f., the extended t table will show that

$$P(t < -3.5) = 0.0005$$

This is the p value of the t statistic. We say that this t value is statistically significant at the 0.0005 or 0.05% level. Put differently, if we were to fix $\alpha = 0.0005$, at that level we can reject the null hypothesis that the true $\mu_x = 13$. Of course, this is an extremely small probability, much smaller than the conventional α values. As a matter of fact, in this example the probability of committing a type I error is only 0.0005 (one-tailed). Therefore, we can reject the null hypothesis much more emphatically than if we were to choose, say, $\alpha = 0.05$.

One virtue of quoting the p value is that it avoids the arbitrariness involved in fixing α at artificial levels, such as 1, 5, or 10 percent. If, e.g., in an application the p value of a test statistic (such as t) is, say, 0.135, and if one is willing to accept an $\alpha = 13.5\%$, this p value is statistically significant (i.e., one rejects the null hypothesis at this level of significance). Nothing is wrong if one wants to take a chance of being wrong 13.5 percent of the time if one rejects the true null hypothesis.

Nowadays several statistical packages routinely compute the p values of various test statistics, and it is recommended that the researcher report these p values.

The χ^2 and F Tests of Significance

Besides the t test of significance discussed previously, in subsequent chapters we will need tests of significance based on the χ^2 distribution and the F probability distribution considered in Chapter 3. Since the philosophy of testing is the same, we will simply present here the actual mechanism with a couple of illustrative examples; further examples will be presented in subsequent chapters.

The χ^2 test of significance. In Chapter 3 we showed that if S^2 is the sample variance obtained from a random sample of n observations from a normal population with variance σ^2, then the quantity

$$(n - 1) \left(\frac{S^2}{\sigma^2} \right) \sim \chi^2_{(n-1)} \tag{3.10}$$

That is, the ratio of the sample variance to population variance multipled by the d.f. $(n - 1)$ follows the χ^2 distribution with $(n - 1)$ d.f. If the d.f. and S^2 are known but σ^2 is not known, we can establish a $(1 - \alpha)$ % confidence interval for the true but unknown σ^2 using the χ^2 distribution. The mechanism is similar to that for establishing confidence intervals on the basis of the t test.

But if we are given a specific value of σ^2 under H_0, we can directly compute the χ^2 value from expression (3.10) and test its significance against the critical χ^2 values given in the χ^2 table. An example follows.

Example 4.5. Suppose a random sample of 31 observations from a normal population gives a (sample) variance of $S^2 = 12$. Test the hypothesis that the true variance is 9 against the hypothesis that it is different from 9. Use $\alpha = 5\%$.

Here $H_0: \sigma^2 = 9$ and $H_1: \sigma^2 \neq 9$.

Answer: Putting the appropriate numbers in expression (3.10), we obtain: $\chi^2 = 30(12/9) = 40$, which has 30 d.f. From the χ^2 table given in Appendix B, we observe that the probability of obtaining a χ^2 value of ≈ 40 (for 30 d.f.) is 0.10 or 10 percent. Since this probability is greater than our level of significance of 5 percent, we do not reject the null hypothesis that the true variance is 9.

Table 4-3 summarizes the χ^2 **test** for the various types of null and alternative hypotheses.

The F test of significance. In Chapter 3 we showed that if we have two randomly selected samples from two normal populations, X and Y, with m and n observations, respectively, then the variable

$$F = \frac{S_x^2}{S_y^2}$$
$$= \frac{\Sigma(X_i - \overline{X})^2/(m - 1)}{\Sigma(Y_i - \overline{Y})^2/(n - 1)} \tag{3.15}$$

follows the F distribution with $(m - 1)$ and $(n - 1)$ d.f., *provided the variances of the two normal populations are equal.* In other words, the H_0 is $\sigma_x^2 = \sigma_y^2$. To test this hypothesis, we use the F **test** given in Eq. (3.15). An example follows.

TABLE 4-3
A summary of the χ^2 test

Null hypothesis H_0	Alternative hypothesis H_1	Critical region Reject H_0 if
$\sigma_x^2 = \sigma_0^2$	$\sigma_x^2 > \sigma_0^2$	$\dfrac{(n-1)\,S^2}{\sigma_0^2} > \chi^2_{\alpha,(n-1)}$
$\sigma_x^2 = \sigma_0^2$	$\sigma_x^2 < \sigma_0^2$	$\dfrac{(n-1)\,S^2}{\sigma_0^2} < \chi^2_{(1-\alpha),(n-1)}$
$\sigma_x^2 = \sigma_0^2$	$\sigma_x^2 \neq \sigma_0^2$	$\dfrac{(n-1)\,S^2}{\sigma_0^2} > \chi^2_{\alpha/2,(n-1)}$
		or $< \chi^2_{(1-\alpha/2),(n-1)}$

Note: σ_0^2 is the value of σ_x^2 under the null hypothesis. The first subscript on χ^2 in the last column is the level of significance and the second subscript is the d.f. These are critical χ^2 values.

Example 4.6.   Refer to the S.A.T. math scores for male and female students given in Example 3.14. The variances of these scores were (46.61) for male and (83.88) for female. The number of observations were 24 or 23 d.f. each. Assuming that these variances represent a sample from a much larger population of S.A.T. scores, test the hypothesis that the male and female population variances on the math part of the S.A.T. scores are the same. Use $\alpha = 1\%$.

Answer: Here the F value is $83.88/46.62 = 1.80$ (approx.). This F value has the F distribution with 23 d.f. each. Now from the F table we see that for 24 d.f. (23 d.f. is not given in the table), the *critical* F value at the 1% level of significance is 2.74. Since the observed F value of 1.80 is less than 2.74, it is not statistically significant. That is, at $\alpha = 1\%$ we do not reject the hypothesis that the two population variances are the same.

Table 4-4 summarizes the F test.

To conclude this chapter, we summarize the steps involved in testing a statistical hypothesis:

Step 1: State the null hypothesis H_0 and the alternative hypothesis H_1 (e.g., H_0: $\mu_x = 13$ and H_1: $\mu_x \neq 13$ for our P/E example).

Step 2: Select the test statistic (e.g., $\overline{X}$)

Step 3: Determine the probability distribution of the test statistic (e.g., $\overline{X} \sim N(\mu_x, \sigma^2/n)$).

Step 4: Choose the level of significance α, that is, the probability of committing a type I error. (But keep in mind our discussion about the p value.)

TABLE 4-4
A summary of the F statistic

Null hypothesis H_0	Alternative hypothesis H_1	Critical region Reject H_0 if
$\sigma_1^2 = \sigma_2^2$	$\sigma_1^2 > \sigma_2^2$	$\dfrac{S_1^2}{S_2^2} > F_{\alpha, ndf, ddf}$
$\sigma_1^2 = \sigma_2^2$	$\sigma_1^2 \neq \sigma_2^2$	$\dfrac{S_1^2}{S_2^2} > F_{\alpha/2, ndf, ddf}$
		or $< F_{(1-\alpha/2), ndf, ddf}$

Notes:
1. σ_1^2 and σ_2^2 are the two population variances.
2. S_1^2 and S_2^2 are the two sample variances.
3. ndf and ddf denote, respectively, the numerator and denominator d.f.
4. In computing the F ratio, put the larger S^2 value in the numerator.
5. The critical F values are given in the last column. The first subscript of F is the level of significance and the second subscript is the numerator and denominator d.f.
6. Note that $F_{(1-\alpha/2),ndf,ddf} = \dfrac{1}{F_{\alpha/2,ddf,ndf}}$

Step 5:   Choose the confidence interval or the test of significance approach.

The confidence interval approach. Using the probability distribution of the test statistic, establish a $100(1-\alpha)\%$ confidence interval. If the **null-hypothesized value** lies in this interval (i.e., the acceptance region), do not reject the null hypothesis. But if it falls outside this region (i.e., the rejection region), you can reject the null hypothesis.

The test of significance approach. Alternatively, you can follow this approach by obtaining the relevant test statistic (e.g., the t statistic) under the null hypothesis and find out the probability of obtaining a specific value of the test statistic from the appropriate probability distribution (e.g., the t, F, or the χ^2 distribution). If this probability is less than the prechosen value of α, you can reject the null hypothesis. But if it is greater than α, do not reject it. If you do not want to preselect α, just present the p value of the statistic.

Whether you choose the confidence interval or the test of significance approach, *always keep in mind that in rejecting or not rejecting a null hypothesis you are taking a chance of being wrong $\alpha\%$ of the time.*

Further uses of the various tests of significance discussed in this chapter will be illustrated throughout the rest of this book.

4.6   SUMMARY

Estimation of population parameters on the basis of sample information and testing hypothesis about them in light of the sample information are the two main branches of (classical) statistical inference. In this chapter we examined the essential features of these aspects.

Key Terms and Concepts

The key terms and concepts introduced in this chapter are:

Statistical inference
Parameter estimation
 a) point estimation
 b) interval estimation
Sampling (probability) distribution
Critical t (test) values
Confidence interval
 a) confidence coefficient
 b) random interval (upper limit, lower limit)
Properties of estimators
 a) linearity
 b) unbiasedness
 c) efficiency (efficient estimator)
 d) best linear unbiased estimator (BLUE)
 e) consistency (consistent estimator)
Hypothesis testing
 a) null hypothesis
 b) alternative hypothesis

 c) one-sided; one-tailed
 d) two-sided; two-tailed
Confidence interval (approach to hypothesis testing)
 a) acceptance region
 b) critical region; region of rejection
 c) critical values
Level of significance
Type I error (α)
 a) confidence coefficient ($1 - \alpha$)
Type II error (β)
 a) power of the test ($1 - \beta$)
Tests of significance (approach to hypothesis testing)
 a) Test statistic; t statistic; t test
 b) χ^2 test
 c) F test
The p value
"Accepting" or rejecting a null hypothesis

QUESTIONS

4.1. What is the distinction between each of the following pairs of terms:
  (*a*) Point estimator and interval estimator
  (*b*) Null and alternative hypotheses
  (*c*) Type I and type II errors
  (*d*) Confidence coefficient and level of significance
  (*e*) Type II error and power

4.2. What is the meaning of
  (*a*) Statistical inference
  (*b*) Sampling distribution
  (*c*) Acceptance region
  (*d*) Test statistic
  (*e*) Critical value of a test
  (*f*) The level of significance
  (*g*) The p value

4.3. Explain carefully the meaning of
  (*a*) An unbiased estimator
  (*b*) A minimum variance estimator
  (*c*) A best, or efficient, estimator
  (*d*) A linear estimator
  (*e*) A best linear unbiased estimator (BLUE)

4.4. State whether the following statements are true, false, or uncertain. Justify your answers.

(a) An estimator of a parameter is a random variable, but the parameter is non-random, or fixed.

(b) An unbiased estimator of a parameter, say, μ_x, means that it will always be equal to μ_x.

(c) An estimator can be a minimum variance estimator without being unbiased.

(d) An efficient estimator means an estimator with minimum variance.

(e) An estimator can be BLUE only if its sampling distribution is normal.

(f) An acceptance region and a confidence interval for any given problem means the same thing.

(g) A type I error occurs when we reject the null hypothesis even though it is false.

(h) A type II error occurs when we reject the null hypothesis even though it may be true.

(i) As the degrees of freedom (d.f.) increase indefinitely, the t distribution approaches the normal distribution.

(j) The central limit theorem states that the sample mean is always distributed normally.

(k) The terms *level of significance* and *p value* mean the same thing.

4.5. Explain carefully the difference between the confidence interval and test of significance approaches to hypothesis testing.

4.6. Suppose in an example with 40 d.f. that a t value of 1.35 was obtained. "Since its p value is somewhere between a 5 and 10% level of significance (one-tailed), it is not statistically very significant." Do you agree? Why or why not?

PROBLEMS

4.7. Find the critical Z values in the following cases:
(a) $\alpha = 0.05$ (two-tailed test)   (c) $\alpha = 0.01$ (two-tailed test)
(b) $\alpha = 0.05$ (one-tailed test)   (d) $\alpha = 0.01$ (one-tailed test)

4.8. Find the critical t values in the following cases:
(a) $n = 4, \alpha = 0.05$ (two-tailed test)
(b) $n = 4, \alpha = 0.05$ (one-tailed test)
(c) $n = 14, \alpha = 0.01$ (two-tailed test)
(d) $n = 14, \alpha = 0.01$ (one-tailed test)
(e) $n = 60, \alpha = 0.05$ (two-tailed test)
(f) $n = 200, \alpha = 0.05$ (two-tailed test)

4.9. Assume that the per capita income of residents in a country is normally distributed with mean $\mu = \$1000$ and variance $\sigma^2 = 10{,}000$ (\$ squared).

(a) What is the probability that the per capita income lies between \$800 and \$1200?

(b) What is the probability that it exceeds \$1200?

(c) What is the probability that it is less than \$800.

(d) Is it true that the probability of per capita income exceeding \$5000 is practically zero?

4.10. Continue with problem 4.9. Suppose based on a random sample of 1000 members that the sample mean income, $\overline{X}$, was found to be \$900.

(a) Given that μ = $1000, what is the probability of obtaining such a sample mean value?

(b) Based on the sample mean, establish a 95% confidence interval for μ and find out if μ = $1000 lies in this confidence interval. If it does not, what conclusions would you draw?

(c) Using the test of significance approach, decide whether you want to accept or reject the hypothesis that μ = $1000. Which test do you use and why?

4.11. The number of peanuts contained in a jar follows the normal distribution with mean μ and variance σ^2. Quality control inspection over several periods shows that 5 percent of the jars contain less than 6.5 ounces of peanuts and 10 percent contain more than 6.8 ounces.

(a) find μ and σ^2.

(b) What percentage of bottles contain more than 7 ounces?

4.12. The following random sample was obtained from a normal population with mean μ and variance = 2.

$$8, 9, 6, 13, 11, 8, 12, 5, 4, 14$$

(a) Test: μ = 5 against $\mu \neq 5$

(b) Test: μ = 5 against $\mu > 5$

Note: use α = 5%.

(c) What is the p value in part (a)?

4.13. Based on a random sample of 10 values from a normal population with mean μ and standard deviation σ, it was calculated that $\overline{X}$ = 8 and the sample standard deviation = 4. Estimate a 95% confidence interval for the population mean. Which probability distribution do you use? Why?

4.14. You are told that $X \sim N$ (μ = 8, σ^2 = 36). Based on a sample of 25 observations, it was found that $\overline{X}$ = 7.5.

(a) What is the sampling distribution of $\overline{X}$?

(b) What is the probability of obtaining an $\overline{X}$ = 7.5 or less?

(c) From your answer in part (b), could such a sample value have come from the preceding population?

4.15. Compute the p values in the following cases:

(a) $t \geq 1.72$, d.f. = 24

(b) $Z \geq 2.9$

(c) $F \geq 2.59$, d.f. = 3 and 20, respectively

(d) $\chi^2 \geq 19$, d.f. = 30

Note: If you cannot get an exact answer from the various probability distribution tables, obtain the best possible approximation.

4.16. In an application involving 30 d.f. a t statistic of 0.68 was obtained. "Since this t value is not statistically significant even at the 10% level of significance, one can safely accept the relevant hypothesis." Do you agree with this statement? What is the p value of obtaining such a statistic?

4.17. Let $X \sim N$ (μ, σ^2). A random sample of three observations was obtained from this population. Consider the following estimators of μ:

$$\hat{\mu}_1 = \frac{X_1 + X_2 + X_3}{3} \quad \text{and} \quad \hat{\mu}_2 = \frac{X_1}{6} + \frac{X_2}{3} + \frac{X_3}{2}$$

(a) Is $\hat{\mu}_1$ an unbiased estimator of μ? What about $\hat{\mu}_2$?

(b) If both estimators are unbiased, which one would you choose? (Hint: Compare the variances of the two estimators).

4.18. Refer to problem 3.10 in Chapter 3. Suppose a random sample of 10 firms gave a mean profit of $900,000 and a (sample) standard deviation of $100,000.

(a) Establish a 95% confidence interval for the true mean profit in the industry.

(b) Which probability distribution do you use? Why?

4.19. Refer to Example 3.9 in Chapter 3.

(a) Establish a 95% confidence interval for the true σ^2.

(b) Test the hypothesis that the true variance is 8.2.

4.20. Sixteen cars were first driven with a standard fuel and then with Petrocoal, a gasoline with a methanol additive. The results of the nitrous oxide emissions (NO_x) test are as follows:

Type of fuel	Average NO_x	Standard deviation of NO_x
Standard	1.075	0.5796
Petrocoal	1.159	0.6134

Source: Michael O. Finkelstein and Bruce Levin, *Statistics for Lawyers*, Springer-Verlag, New York, 1990, p. 230.

(a) How would you test the hypothesis that the two population standard deviations are the same?

(b) Which test do you use? What are the assumptions underlying that test?

PART

II

THE LINEAR REGRESSION MODEL

T
he objective of Part II, consisting of five chapters, is to introduce the reader to the "bread-and-butter" tool of econometrics, namely, the linear regression model.

Chapter 5 discusses the basic ideas of linear regression in terms of the simplest possible linear regression model, in particular, the two-variable model. We make an important distinction between the population regression model and the sample regression model and estimate the former from the latter. This estimation is done by the method of least squares, one of the popular methods of estimation.

Chapter 6 considers hypothesis testing. As in any hypothesis testing in statistics, we try to find out whether the estimated values of the parameters of the regression model are compatible with the hypothesized values of the parameters. We do this hypothesis testing in the context of the classical linear regression model (CLRM). We discuss why the CLRM is used and point out that the CLRM is a useful starting point. In Part III we will reexamine the assumptions of the CLRM to see what happens to the CLRM if one or more of its assumptions are not fulfilled.

Chapter 7 extends the idea of the two-variable linear regression model developed in the previous two chapters to multiple regression models, that is, models having more than one explanatory variable. Although in many ways the multiple regression model is an extension of the two-variable model, there are differences when it comes to interpretation of the coefficients of the model and in the hypothesis-testing procedure.

The linear regression model, whether two-variable or multivariable, only requires that the parameters of the model be linear; the variables entering the model need not themselves be linear. **Chapter 8** considers a variety of models that are linear in the parameters (or can be made so) but are not necessarily linear in the variables. With several illustrative examples, we point out how and where such models can be used.

Often the explanatory variables entering into a regression model are qualitative in nature, such as sex, color, and religion. **Chapter 9** shows how such variables can be "measured" and how they enrich the linear regression model by taking into account the influence of variables that otherwise cannot be quantified.

Throughout this part an effort has been made to "wed" practice to theory. It is true that the availability of user-friendly regression packages can enable one to estimate a regression model without knowing much theory. But remember the adage that "a little knowledge is a dangerous thing." Therefore, even though theory may be "boring," it is absolutely essential in understanding and interpreting regression results. Besides, by omitting all mathematical derivations, we have made the theory "less boring."

CHAPTER 5

BASIC IDEAS OF LINEAR REGRESSION: THE TWO-VARIABLE MODEL

In Chapter 1 we noted that in developing an econometric model of an economic phenomenon (e.g., the law of demand) econometricians make heavy use of a statistical technique known as **regression analysis.** The purpose of this and the next chapter is to introduce the basics of regression analysis in terms of the simplest possible linear regression model, namely, the two-variable model. Subsequent chapters will consider various modifications and extensions of the two-variable model.

5.1 THE MEANING OF REGRESSION

Regression analysis is concerned with the study of the relationship between one variable called the **explained,** or **dependent, variable** and one or more other variables called **independent,** or **explanatory,** variables.

Thus, we may be interested in studying the relationship between the quantity demanded of a commodity in terms of the price of that commodity, income of the consumer, and prices of other commodities competing with this commodity. Or, we may be interested in finding out how sales of a product (e.g., automobiles) are related to advertising expenditure incurred on that product. Or, we may be interested in finding out how defense expenditure varies in relation to the gross national product (GNP). In all these examples there may be some underlying theory that specifies why we would expect one variable to be dependent or related to one or more other variables. In the first example cited, e.g., the *law of demand* provides the rationale for the dependence of the quantity demanded of a product on its own price and several other variables previously mentioned.

For notational uniformity, from now on we will let Y represent the dependent variable and X the independent, or explanatory, variable. If there is more than one explanatory variable, we will show the various Xs by the appropriate subscripts (e.g., X_1, X_2, X_3, etc.)

It is very important to bear in mind that although regression analysis deals with relationship between a dependent variable and one or more independent variables, *it does not necessarily imply causation*; that is, it does not necessarily mean that the independent variables are the *cause* and the dependent variable is the *effect*. If causality between the two exists, it must be justified on the basis of some (economic) theory. As noted earlier, the law of demand suggests that if all other variables are held constant, the quantity demanded of a commodity is (inversely) dependent on its own price. Here microeconomic theory suggests that the price may be the causal force and the quantity demanded the effect. *Always keep in mind that regression does not necessarily imply causation. Causality must be justified, or inferred, from the theory that underlies the phenomenon that is tested empirically.*

The objective of regression analysis may be either

1. To estimate the *mean*, or *average*, value of the dependent variable, given the values of the independent variables.

2. To test hypotheses about the nature of the dependence—hypotheses suggested by the underlying economic theory. For example, in the demand function mentioned previously, one may want to test the hypothesis that the price elasticity of demand is, say, -1.0; that is, the demand curve has unitary price elasticity. If the price of the commodity goes up by 1 percent, the quantity demanded on the average goes down by 1 percent, assuming all other factors affecting demand are held constant.

3. To predict, or forecast, the mean value of the dependent variable, given the values of the independent variable(s). Thus, in the S.A.T. example discussed in the previous chapter one may wish to predict the average score on the verbal part of the S.A.T. of a group of students knowing their scores on the math part of the test.

4. One or more of the preceding objectives combined.

5.2   THE POPULATION REGRESSION FUNCTION (PRF): A HYPOTHETICAL EXAMPLE

To illustrate what all of this means, we consider a more extended example of the *law of demand* discussed in Chapter 1. Recall that the law of demand postulates an inverse relationship between the quantity demanded of a commodity and its price, provided all other variables affecting demand are held constant, the famous *ceteris paribus* clause of economics. These other variables are the income of the consumer, his or her tastes, prices of other commodities competing or complementary to the commodity in question, etc.

Consider the demand for the textbook mythical commodity, the *widget*. Assume that we have a tiny town with a total population of 55 consumers. The quantities of the widget demanded by these consumers for prices ranging between $1 per unit to $10 per unit are given in Table 5-1.

Table 5-1 is to be interpreted as follows: At price $1 per unit there are seven consumers who purchase the widget in quantities ranging from 45 to 51 units. The average quantity demanded by these seven consumers is, however, 48 units—this figure is obtained by taking the arithmetic average of the seven demand figures. Similarly, at price $7 per unit, there are five consumers who purchase the widget in amounts ranging from 32 to 40 units. The average quantity demanded at this price, however, is 36 units. Other figures are to be interpreted similarly.

Let us plot the data of Table 5-1 in a *scattergram* (see Figure 5-1) with quantity (Y) on the vertical axis and price (X) on the horizontal axis.

As this scattergram shows, corresponding to any given X there are several values of Y. For example, for X = $1 there are seven Y values and for X = $4 there are six Y values, etc. In other words, each X has associated with it a Y *population*—the totality of Y corresponding to that X (recall the definition of population from Chapter 2).

What does the scattergram reveal? The impression that one gets is that Y *generally* decreases as X increases, and vice versa. This tendency is all the more pronounced if we concentrate on the circled points, which give the **expected**, or **population mean**, or **population average value** of Y corresponding to the various Xs. As we can see, the *average* value of Y decreases linearly

TABLE 5-1
The demand schedule for widgets

Price (X) (1)	Quantity demanded (Y) (2)	Number of consumers (3)	Average Y demanded (4)
1	45, 46, 47, 48, 49, 50, 51	7	48
2	44, 45, 46, 47, 48	5	46
3	40, 42, 44, 46, 48	5	44
4	35, 38, 42, 44, 46, 47	6	42
5	36, 39, 40, 42, 43	5	40
6	32, 35, 37, 38, 39, 42, 43	7	38
7	32, 34, 36, 38, 40	5	36
8	31, 32, 33, 34, 35, 36, 37	7	34
9	28, 30, 32, 34, 36	5	32
10	29, 30, 31	3	30
	Total	55	

(i.e., in a straight line) with X. If we draw a line through these mean values, the line we obtain is called the **population regression line (PRL).** *The PRL gives the average, or mean, value of the dependent variable (Y in the present case) corresponding to each value of the independent variable (X here).* In our example it tells us that if X is $2, the average quantity demanded is 46 units, although we know from Table 5-1 that at this price the quantity demanded varies from 44 to 48 units. In short, the PRL is a line that tells us how the *average* value of Y (or any dependent variable) is related to each value of X (or any independent variable).

Since the PRL sketched in Figure 5-1 is linear, we can express it mathematically in the following functional form:

$$E(Y\,|\,X_i) = B_1 + B_2X_i \qquad\qquad (5.1)$$

which is the mathematical equation of a straight line. In Equation (5.1), $E(Y\,|\,X_i)$ means the mean, or expected, value of Y corresponding to, or *conditional* upon, a given value of X. As we know from Chapter 2, this is nothing but the **conditional expectation** or **conditional expected value** of Y. The subscript i refers to the ith subpopulation. Thus, in Table 5-1 $E(Y\,|\,X_i = 2)$ is 46, which is the mean, or expected, value of Y in the second subpopulation (i.e., corresponding to X = 2).

The last column in Table 5-1 gives the conditional expectation, or conditional mean, values of Y. It is very important to note that $E(Y\,|\,X_i)$ is a function of X_i (linear in the present example). This means that the dependence of Y on X, technically called the *regression of Y on X*, can be defined simply as the mean of the distribution of Y values (as in Table 5-1), which has the given X. In other words, *the population regression line (PRL) is a line that passes through*

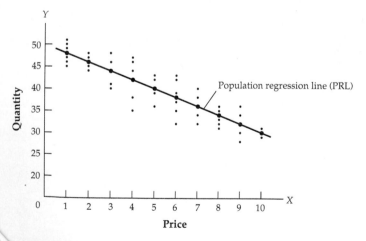

FIGURE 5-1
Scattergram of price and quantity.

the conditional means of Y. The mathematical form in which the PRL is expressed, such as Eq. (5.1), is called the **population regression function (PRF),** which in the present instance is linear. (The more technical meaning of linearity is discussed in Section 5.6).

In Eq. (5.1) B_1 and B_2 are called the **parameters,** also known as the **regression coefficients.** B_1 is also known as the **intercept** (coefficient) and B_2 as the **slope** (coefficient). The *slope coefficient measures the rate of change in the (conditional) mean value of Y per unit change in X.* If, e.g., the slope coefficient were -2, it would suggest that if the price increases, say, by a dollar, the (conditional) mean value of Y decreases by two units; that is, on the average the quantity demanded will go down by two units. B_1 is the (conditional) mean value of Y if X is zero; it gives the average value of the quantity demanded if the price were zero. But we will have more to say about this interpretation of the intercept in later chapters.

How do we go about finding out the estimates, or numerical values, of the intercept and slope coefficients? We explore this question in Section 5.8.

Before moving on, a word about terminology. Since in regression analysis, as noted in Chapter 1, we are concerned with examining the behavior of the dependent variable *conditional upon the given values of the independent variable(s), our approach to regression analysis can be termed* **conditional regression analysis.** As a result, there is no need to use the adjective "conditional" all the time. Therefore, in the future expressions like $E(Y \mid X_i)$ will be simply written as $E(Y)$, with the explicit understanding that the latter in fact stands for the former. Of course, where there is cause for confusion, we will use the more extended notation.

5.3   STOCHASTIC SPECIFICATION OF THE POPULATION REGRESSION FUNCTION (PRF)

As we just discussed, the PRF gives the average value of the dependent variable corresponding to each value of the independent variable. Let us take another look at Table 5-1. We know, e.g., that corresponding to X = $1, the average Y is 48. But if we pick one consumer at *random* from the seven consumers corresponding to this price, we know that the quantity demanded by that consumer will not necessarily be equal to the mean value of 48 units. To be concrete, take the last consumer in the group. His or her demand for widgets is 51 units, which is above the mean value. By the same token, if you take the first consumer in that group, her consumption is 45 units, which is below the average value. How do you explain the demands of the individual consumer in relation to the price? The best we can do is to say that any individual's demand is equal to the average for that group plus or minus some quantity. Let us express this mathematically as

$$Y_i = B_1 + B_2 X_i + u_i \tag{5.2}$$

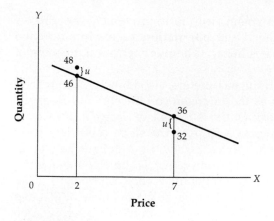

FIGURE 5-2

where u is known as the **stochastic, or random error, term,** or simply the error term.[1] We have already encountered this term in Chapter 1. The error term is a *random variable* (r.v.), for its value cannot be controlled or known a priori. As we know from Chapter 2, an r.v. is usually characterized by its probability distribution (e.g., the normal or the t distribution).

How do we interpret Expression (5.2)? We can say that the demand of an individual consumer, say, the ith individual, corresponding to a specific price can be expressed as the sum of two components: (1) $(B_1 + B_2X_i)$, which is simply the mean, or average, quantity demanded by the ith subpopulation, that is, the point on the PRL corresponding to the specific price. This component may be called the *systematic*, or *deterministic*, component, and (2) u_i, which may be called the *nonsystematic*, or random component (i.e., determined by factors other than price).

To see this clearly, consider Figure 5-2, which is based on the data of Table 5-1.

As this figure shows, at $X = \$2$, one consumer demands 48 units of the widget, whereas the average quantity demanded at this price is 46 units. Thus, this consumer's demand exceeds the systematic component (i.e., the mean for the group) by 2 units. So to speak, his u component is 2 units. On the other hand, at $X = \$7$ a randomly chosen consumer demands 32 units, whereas the average for this group is 36. This consumer's demand is less than the systematic component by 4 units; her u component is -4.

---

[1] The word *stochastic* comes from the Greek word *stokhos* meaning a "bull's eye." The outcome of throwing darts onto a dart board is a stochastic process, that is, a process fraught with misses. statistics, the word implies the presence of a random variable—a variable whose outcome is mined by a chance experiment.

Equation (5.2) is called the **stochastic PRF,** whereas Eq. (5.1) is called the **deterministic,** or **nonstochastic, PRF.** The latter represents the means of the various Y values corresponding to the specified prices, whereas the former tells us how individual demands vary around their mean values due to the presence of the stochastic error term, u.

What is the nature of this "beast," the u term?

5.4   THE NATURE OF THE STOCHASTIC ERROR TERM

1. The error term may represent the influence of those variables that are not explicitly included in the model. In our widget example, e.g., it may very well represent influences, such as the consumer's income, prices of other products competing with widgets, etc.
2. Even if we included all the relevant variables determining the demand for widgets, some "intrinsic" randomness in quantity demanded is bound to occur that cannot be explained no matter how hard we try. Human behavior, after all, is not totally predictable, if not totally irrational. Thus, u may reflect this inherent randomness in human behavior.
3. u may also represent errors of measurement. For example, the data on Y, quantity demanded, may be rounded to the nearest digit, or the nearest 100 units, etc.
4. The *principle of Occam's razor*—that descriptions be kept as simple as possible until proved inadequate—would suggest that we keep our regression model as simple as possible.[2] Therefore, even if we know what other variables might affect Y, their combined influence on Y may be so small and nonsystematic that one can incorporate it in the random term, u.

It is for one or more of these reasons that the demand of an individual consumer will deviate from his or her group average (i.e., the systematic component). And as we will soon discover, this error term plays an extremely crucial role in regression analysis.

5.5   THE SAMPLE REGRESSION FUNCTION (SRF)

How do we estimate the PRF of Eq. (5.1), that is, obtain the values of B_1 and B_2? If we have the data of Table 5-1, the whole population, this would be a relatively straightforward task. All we have to do is to find the conditional

---

[2] Remember that a model is a simplification of reality. If we truly want to build reality into a model it may be too unwieldy and complex to be of any practical use. In model-building, therefore, some abstraction from reality is inevitable.

TABLE 5-2
A random sample from the population of Table 5-1

Y	X
49	1
45	2
44	3
39	4
38	5
37	6
34	7
33	8
30	9
29	10

TABLE 5-3
Another random sample from Table 5-1

Y	X
51	1
47	2
46	3
42	4
40	5
37	6
36	7
35	8
32	9
30	10

means of Y corresponding to each X and then join these means. Unfortunately, in practice, we rarely have the entire population at our disposal. Often we only have a *sample* from this population. (Recall from Chapters 1 and 2 our discussion regarding the population and the sample). Our task here is to estimate the PRF on the basis of the sample information. How do we accomplish this?

Pretend that you have never seen Table 5-1. Rather, you had the data given in Table 5-2, which presumably represent a randomly selected sample of Y values corresponding to the X values shown in Table 5-1. Unlike Table 5-1, we now have only one Y value corresponding to each X. The important question that we now face is: From the sample data of Table 5-2, can we estimate the average quantity demanded in the population as a whole corresponding to each X? In other words, can we estimate the PRF from the sample data? As the reader can well surmise, we may not be able to estimate the PRF "accurately" because of *sampling fluctuations*, or *sampling error*, a topic we discussed in Chapter 4. To see this clearly, suppose another random sample is drawn from the population of Table 5-1, which is shown in Table 5-3. If we plot the data of Tables 5-2 and 5-3, we obtain the scattergram shown in Figure 5-3.

Through the scatterpoints we have drawn visually two straight lines that "fit" the scatterpoints reasonably well. Let us call these lines the **sample regression lines (SRLs).** Which of the two SRLs represents the "true" PRL? If we avoid the temptation of looking at Figure 5-1, which represents the PRL, there is no way we can be sure that either of the SLRs shown in Figure 5-3 represents the true PRL. For if we had yet another sample, we would obtain a third SRL, etc. Supposedly, each SRL represents the PRL, but because of sampling variation, each is at best an approximation of the true PRL. In general, we would get K different SRLs for K different samples and all these SRLs are not likely to be the same.

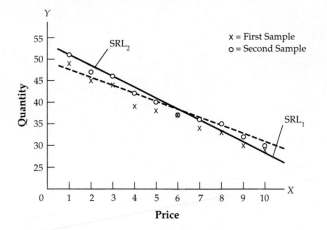

FIGURE 5-3
Sample regression lines based on two independent samples.

Now analogous to the PRF that underlies the PRL, we can develop the concept of the **sample regression function (SRF)** to represent the SRL. The sample counterpart of Eq. (5.1) may be written as

$$\hat{Y}_i = b_1 + b_2 X_i \qquad (5.3)$$

where ^ is read as "hat" or "cap," and where

$\hat{Y}_i$ = the estimator of $E(Y \mid X_i)$, the estimator of
       the population conditional mean

b_1 = the estimator of B_1

b_2 = the estimator of B_2

As noted in the preceding chapter, an *estimator,* or a *sample statistic,* is a rule or a formula that indicates how to estimate the population parameter at hand. A particular numerical value obtained by the estimator in an application, as we know, is an *estimate.* (Recall from Chapter 4 the discussion on point and interval estimators.)

If we look at the scattergram of Figure 5-3, we observe that not all the sample data lie exactly on the respective sample regression lines. Therefore, just as we developed the stochastic PRF, Eq. (5.2), we need to develop the stochastic version of Eq. (5.3), which we write as

$$Y_i = b_1 + b_2 X_i + e_i \qquad (5.4)$$

where e_i = the estimator of u_i.

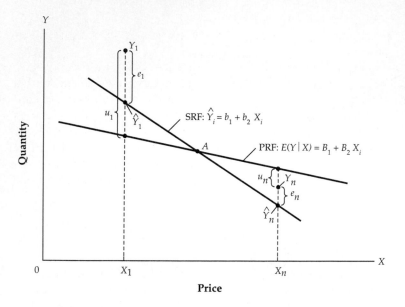

FIGURE 5-4
The population and sample regression lines.

We call e_i the **residual term,** or simply the **residual.** Conceptually, it is analogous to u_i and can be regarded as the estimator of the latter. It is introduced in the SRF for the same reasons as u_i was introduced in the PRF.

To summarize, our primary objective in regression analysis is to estimate the (stochastic) PRF

$$Y_i = B_1 + B_2X_i + u_i \qquad (5.2)$$

on the basis of the SRF

$$Y_i = b_1 + b_2X_i + e_i \qquad (5.4)$$

because more often than not our analysis is based on a single sample from some population. But because of sampling variation, our estimate of the PRF based on the SRF is only approximate. This approximation is shown in Figure 5-4.

For a given X_i, shown in this figure, we have one (sample) observation, Y_i. In terms of the SRF, the observed Y_i can be expressed as

$$Y_i = \hat{Y}_i + e_i \qquad (5.5)$$

and in terms of the PRF it can be expressed as

$$Y_i = E(Y \mid X_i) + u_i \qquad (5.6)$$

Obviously, in Figure 5-4, $\hat{Y}_i$ overestimates the true mean value $E(Y \mid X_i)$ for the shown therein. By the same token, for any Y to the right of point A in

Figure 5-4, the SRF will *underestimate* the true PRF. But the reader can readily see that such over- and underestimation is inevitable due to sampling fluctuations.

The important question now is: Granted that the SRF is only an approximation of the PRF, can we find a method or a procedure that will make this approximation as "close" as possible? In other words, how should we construct the SRF so that b_1 is as close as possible to B_1 and b_2 is as close as possible to B_2 because generally we do not have the entire population at our disposal. As we will show in Section 5.8, we can indeed find a "best-fitting" SRF that will mirror the PRF as "faithfully" as possible. Indeed, it is fascinating to consider that this can be done even though we never actually determine the PRF itself.

5.6 THE SPECIAL MEANING OF THE TERM "LINEAR" REGRESSION

Since in this text we are concerned primarily with "linear" models like Eq. (5.1), it is essential to know what the term *linear* really means, for it can be interpreted in two different ways.

Linearity in the Variables

The first and perhaps the more "natural" meaning of linearity is that the conditional mean value of the dependent variable is a linear function of the independent variable(s) as in Eq. (5.1) or Eq. (5.2) or in the sample counterparts, Eqs. (5.3) and (5.4).[3] In this interpretation, the following functions are not linear:

$$E(Y) = B_1 + B_2 X_i^2 \tag{5.7}$$

$$E(Y) = B_1 + B_2 \frac{1}{X_i} \tag{5.8}$$

because in Equation (5.7) X appears with a power of 2 and in Equation (5.8) it appears in the inverse form. For regression models linear in the explanatory variable(s), the rate of change in the dependent variable remains constant for a unit change in the explanatory variable; that is, the slope remains constant. But for a regression model nonlinear in the explanatory variables the slope does not remain constant.[4] This can be seen more clearly from Figure 5-5.

---

[3] A function $Y = f(X)$ is said to be linear in X if (1) X appears with a power of 1 only; that is, terms such as X^2 and $\sqrt{X}$ are excluded; (2) X is not multiplied or divided by another variable (e.g., $X \cdot Z$ and X/Z, where Z is another variable.)

[4] Consider $Y = a + bX$. For this function, $dY/dX = b$, which is a constant. But now consider $Y = a + bX^2$. For this function $dY/dX = 2bX$, which is not constant as its value will depend on X. Here dY/dX (derivative of Y with respect to X) measures the rate of change of Y for a unit change in X. Geometrically, the derivative measures the slope of the function.

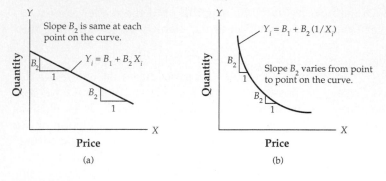

FIGURE 5-5
(*a*) Linear demand curve; (*b*) nonlinear demand curve.

As Figure 5-5 shows, for the regression (5.1), the slope—the rate of change in $E(Y)$—the mean of Y, remains the same, namely, B_2 no matter at what value of X one measures the change. But for regression, say, Eq. (5.8), the rate of change in the mean value of Y varies from point to point on the regression line, actually a curve here.[5]

Linearity in the Parameters

The second interpretation of linearity is that the conditional mean of the dependent variable is a linear function of the parameters, the Bs; it may or may not be linear in the variables. Analogous to a linear-in-variable function, a function is said to be linear in the parameter, say, B_2 if B_2 appears with a power of 1 only. On this definition, models (5.7) and (5.8) are both linear models because B_1 and B_2 enter the models linearly. It does not matter that the variable X enters nonlinearly in both models. However, a model of the type

$$E(Y) = B_1 + B_2^2 X_i \qquad (5.9)$$

is nonlinear in the parameter model since B_2 enters with a power of 2.

In this book we are primarily concerned with models that are linear in the parameters. Therefore, from now on the term **linear regression** will mean a regression that is linear in the parameters, the Bs (i.e., the parameters are raised to the power of 1 only); it may or may not be linear in explanatory variables.[6]

---

[5] Those who know calculus will recognize that in the linear model the slope, that is, the derivative of Y with respect to X, is constant, equal to B_2, but in the nonlinear model (5.8) it is equal to $-B_2(1/X_i^2)$, which obviously will depend on the value of X at which the slope is measured, and is therefore not constant.

[6] This is not to suggest that nonlinear (in-the-parameter) models like Eq. (5.9) cannot be estimated or that they are not used in practice. As a matter of fact, in advanced courses in econometrics models are studied in depth.

5.7 TWO-VARIABLE VERSUS MULTIPLE LINEAR REGRESSION

So far in this chapter we have considered only the **two-variable,** or simple, **regression** models in which the dependent variable is a function of just one explanatory variable. This was done just to introduce the fundamental ideas of regression analysis. But the concept of regression can be easily extended to the case where the dependent variable is a function of more than one explanatory variable. For instance, if the demand for widgets is a function of their price (X_2), income of the consumer (X_3), and the price of a competing product (X_4), we can write the extended demand function as

$$E(Y) = B_1 + B_2X_{2i} + B_3X_{3i} + B_4X_{4i} \qquad (5.10)$$

Equation (5.10) is an example of a **multiple linear regression**, a regression in which more than one independent, or explanatory, variable is used to explain the behavior of the dependent variable. Model (5.10) states that the (conditional) mean value of the quantity of widgets demanded is a linear function of the price of the widget, income of the consumer, and the price of a product competing with the widget. The demand function of an individual consumer (i.e., the stochastic PRF) can be expressed as

$$\begin{aligned} Y_i &= B_1 + B_2X_{2i} + B_3X_{3i} + B_4X_{4i} + u_i \\ &= E(Y) + u_i \end{aligned} \qquad (5.11)$$

which shows that the individual demand will differ from the group mean by the factor u, which is the stochastic error term. As noted earlier, even in a multiple regression we introduce the error term because we cannot take into account all the umpteen forces that might affect the demand for widgets.

Notice that both Eqs. (5.10) and (5.11) are linear in the parameters and are therefore *linear regression models*. The explanatory variables themselves do not need to enter the model linearly, although in the present example they do.

5.8 ESTIMATION OF PARAMETERS: THE METHOD OF ORDINARY LEAST SQUARES (OLS)

As noted in Section 5.5, we have to estimate the population regression function (PRF) on the basis of the sample regression function (SRF) since, in practice, we only have a sample (or two) from a given population. How then do we estimate the PRF? And how do we find out whether the estimated PRF (i.e., the SRF) is a "good" estimate of the true PRF. We will answer the first question in this chapter and take up the second question—of the "goodness" of the estimated PRF—in the following chapter.

To introduce the fundamental ideas of estimation of the PRF, we consider the simplest possible linear regression model, namely, the two-variable linear regression in which we study the relationship of the dependent variable Y to a single explanatory variable X. In Chapter 7 we extend the analysis to the multiple regression, where we will study the relationship of the dependent variable Y to more than one explanatory variable.

The Method of Ordinary Least Squares (OLS)

Although there are several methods of obtaining the SRF as an estimator of the true PRF, in regression analysis the method that is used most frequently is that of *least squares (LS)*, more popularly known as the method of **ordinary least squares (OLS)**.[7] We will use the terms LS and OLS methods interchangeably. To explain this method, we first explain the **least squares principle**.

The least squares principle. Recall our two-variable PRF, Eq. (5.2):

$$Y_i = B_1 + B_2 X_i + u_i \qquad (5.2)$$

Since the PRF is not directly observable (why?), we estimate it from the SRF

$$Y_i = b_1 + b_2 X_i + e_i \qquad (5.4)$$

which we can write as

$$e_i = \text{actual } Y_i - \text{predicted } Y_i$$

$$= Y_i - \hat{Y}_i$$

$$= Y_i - b_1 - b_2 X_i \text{ [using Eq. (5.3)]} \qquad (5.12)$$

which shows that the residuals are simply the differences between the actual and estimated Y values, the latter obtained from the SRF, Eq. (5.3). This can be seen more vividly from Figure 5-4.

Now the best way to estimate the PRF is to choose b_1 and b_2, the estimator of B_1 and B_2, in such a way that the residual e_i is as small as possible. There are several methods of doing this, but in regression analysis the one that is used most frequently is the method of **ordinary least squares (OLS)**, which states that b_1 and b_2 should be chosen in such a way that the residual sum of squares (RSS) Σe_i^2 is as small as possible.

Algebraically, the least squares principle states

$$\text{Minimize: } \Sigma e_i^2 = \Sigma (Y_i - \hat{Y}_i)^2$$

$$= \Sigma (Y_i - b_1 - b_2 X_i)^2 \qquad (5.13)$$

---

[7] Despite the name, there is nothing ordinary about this method. As a matter of fact, as we will show, this method has some extraordinary properties. It is called OLS because there is another method, called the generalized least squares (GLS), of which OLS is a special case.

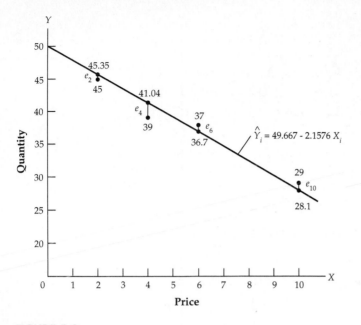

FIGURE 5-6

Deviations (e_i) of actual Y from the estimated Y. Ordinary least squares (OLS) minimizes the sum of the deviations squared.

In words, the least squares principle states that the SRF should be fixed in such a way that the sum of the squared distance between the actual Y and the Y obtained from that SRF is the smallest one.[8] (See Figure 5-6.)

Before finding out how this minimization can be achieved, let us consider a concrete example to see what is going on.

A Numerical Example: The Demand for Widgets

Let us revisit our demand schedule for widgets given in Table 5-2, which for convenience is reproduced along with other calculations in Table 5-4. Recall that the demand schedule given in Table 5-4 is a random sample from the (population) demand schedule given in Table 5-1. The data given in Table 5-4 are plotted in Figure 5-6. This figure shows the actual SRF fitted to these data by the method of least squares (the actual mechanics of doing that is

---

[8] Note that the smaller the e_i is, the smaller the sum of their squares will be. The reason for considering the squares of e_i and not of e_i themselves is that this procedure avoids the problem of the sign of the residuals. Note that e_i can be positive as well as negative.

TABLE 5-4
Least squares computations of the widget example

Y_i	X_i	X_iY_i	X_i^2	x_i	y_i	y_i^2	x_i^2	x_iy_i	$\hat{Y}_i$	e_i	e_i^2	e_iX_i
49	1	49	1	-4.5	11.2	125.44	20.25	-50.4	47.509	1.4909	2.2228	1.4909
45	2	90	4	-3.5	7.2	51.84	12.25	-25.2	45.352	-0.3515	0.1236	-0.7030
44	3											
39	4											
38	5											
37	6											
34	7											
33	8											
30	9	270	81	3.5	-7.8	60.84	12.25	-27.3	30.248	-0.2484	0.0617	-2.2356
29	10	290	100	4.5	-8.8	77.44	20.25	-39.6	28.091	0.9091	0.8265	8.2650
Sum: 378	55	1901.0	385	0	0	393.60	82.50	-178.0	378.00*	0*	9.5515	0*

Slope: $b_2 = \dfrac{\sum x_iy_i}{\sum x_i^2} = \dfrac{-178}{82.5} = -2.1576$

Intercept: $b_1 = \bar{Y} - b_2\bar{X} = 37.8 - (-2.1576)(5.5) = 49.667$

Notes: * means approximately due to rounding.

$\bar{Y} = \dfrac{378}{10} = 37.8$

$\bar{X} = \dfrac{55}{10} = 5.5$

$x_i = (X_i - \bar{X}) \qquad y_i = (Y_i - \bar{Y})$

$\hat{Y}_i$ is computed from Eq. (5.3)

The blank entries in the table are to be filled in by the reader in the manner suggested.

explained below). The vertical distances between the actual Y and the estimated Y_i from the SRF are simply the e_i. In OLS these vertical distances are squared and then added up to obtain the RSS $\Sigma\, e_i^2$, as shown in Eq. (5.13). It is this RSS that OLS tries to minimize.

As you can see from Eq. (5.13), the RSS, $\Sigma\, e_i^2$, is a function of b_1 and b_2. For a given set of data, such as that of Table 5-4, choosing different values for b_1 and b_2 will give different es and hence different values of RSS: To see this, just rotate the SRF shown in Figure 5-6 any way you like. For each rotation, you will get a different intercept (i.e., b_1) and a different slope (i.e., b_2). (Try to sketch several regression lines through the scattergram of Figure 5-6).

Does this mean that for a given data set we cannot fix a definite SRF? That is, for a given data set, is it not possible to find unique values of b_1 and b_2 so that we are guaranteed the least possible RSS? Herein lies the beauty of the method of OLS, for it gives us unique values of b_1 and b_2 for a given data set. For the data given in Table 5-4, these unique values of b_1 and b_2 are, respectively, 49.6670 and -2.1576, which are shown in Figure 5-6. (Recall that the numerical value taken by an estimator in a concrete application is called an estimate.)

How did we actually determine these values? This is now simply a matter of arithmetic and involves the technique of differential calculus. Without going into detail, it can be shown that the values of b_1 and b_2 that actually minimize the RSS given in Eq. (5.13) are obtained by solving the following two simultaneous equations:[9]

$$\Sigma\, Y_i = nb_1 + b_2\, \Sigma\, X_i \tag{5.14}$$

$$\Sigma\, Y_iX_i = b_1\, \Sigma\, X_i + b_2\, \Sigma\, X_i^2 \tag{5.15}$$

where n is the sample size. These simultaneous equations are known as the (least squares) **normal equations**.

In Equations (5.14) and (5.15) the unknowns are the bs and the knowns are the quantities involving sums, the sums of squares, and the sums of cross products of the variables Y and X, which can be obtained from the sample at hand. Now solving these equations simultaneously (using any high school algebra trick you know), we obtain the following solutions for b_1 and b_2:

$$b_1 = \overline{Y} - b_2\overline{X} \tag{5.16}$$

which is the estimator of the population intercept, B_1:

---

[9] The necessary proofs can be found in Damodar N. Gujarati, *Basic Econometrics*, 2d ed., McGraw-Hill, 1988, pp. 81–82. Those who know calculus can obtain the following results by (partially) differentiating Eq. (5.13) with respect to b_1 and b_2, setting the resulting equations to zero (the first-order conditions for minimization or maximization), and simplifying the resulting expressions. This will give Eqs. (5.14) and (5.15) shown in the text.

$$b_2 = \frac{\sum x_i y_i}{\sum x_i^2}$$

$$= \frac{\sum (X_i - \overline{X})(Y_i - \overline{Y})}{\sum (X_i - \overline{X})^2} \tag{5.17}$$

$$= \frac{\sum X_i Y_i - n\overline{X}\overline{Y}}{\sum X_i^2 - n\overline{X}^2}$$

which is the estimator of the population slope coefficient, B_2. Note that $x_i = (X_i - \overline{X})$ and $y_i = (Y_i - \overline{Y})$; that is, the small letters denote deviations from the sample mean values, a convention we will adopt in this book.

Notice that Equation (5.17) provides various alternatives to compute the slope coefficient, the choice depending on the ease of computation, which is not a problem in this age of high-speed computers.

The estimators given in Eqs. (5.16) and (5.17) are known as **OLS estimators**, for they are obtained by the method of OLS.

Returning to our widget example, Table 5-4 gives all the necessary calculations to compute the OLS estimators b_1 and b_2 as derived in Eqs. (5.16) and (5.17). From the computations given there, we can see that the estimated demand function for our widget example (i.e., the SRF) is

$$\hat{Y}_i = 49.667 - 2.1576X_i \tag{5.18}$$

It is this SRF that is depicted in Figure 5-6.

Interpretation of the Estimated Demand Function for Widgets

The estimated demand function is interpreted as follows: Other things remaining the same, if the price of widgets goes up by, say, a dollar, the *mean* or *average* quantity of widgets demanded decreases by about 2.16 units (i.e., the slope of the demand curve is -2.16). Similarly, if the price of the widget were zero, the *average* quantity of widgets demanded is about 49.7 units (i.e., the intercept of the demand curve is 49.7 units). Of course, this is the purely mechanical interpretation of the *intercept* term. In reality, the price of a good is never zero, unless it is a "free" good, like the air we breathe (but note that pollution-free air is not a free good!). As we will see throughout this book, often the intercept has no particular economic meaning.

Before proceeding further, we should note a few interesting features of the OLS estimators given in Eqs. (5.16) and (5.17):

1. The SRF obtained by the method of OLS always passes through the sample mean values of X and Y, which should be evident from Eq. (5.16), for it can be written as

$$\overline{Y} = b_1 + b_2\overline{X} \tag{5.19}$$

2. $\bar{e} = \Sigma\ e_i/n$, that is, the mean value of the residuals is always equal to zero, which provides a check on the arithmetical accuracy of the calculations (see Table 5-4). (For proof, see problem 5.11.)
3. The sum of the product of the residuals e and the explanatory variable X is zero; that is, these two variables are uncorrelated (on the definition of correlation, see Chapter 2). Symbolically,

$$\Sigma\ e_iX_i = 0 \qquad (5.20)$$

This provides yet another check on the least squares calculations.

5.9 SOME ILLUSTRATIVE EXAMPLES

Now that we have discussed the OLS method and learned how to estimate a PRF, let us provide some concrete applications.

Example 5.1. Based on a random sample of 212 families, the following OLS regression was obtained:[10]

$$\hat{Y}_i = -1.924 + 0.19X_i \qquad (5.21)$$

where Y is federal income taxes paid by the family and X is the family income, both measured in thousands of dollars.

In this example $b_1 = -1.924$ and $b_2 = 0.19$. This regression says that, holding other things constant, for every $1000 increase in family income, taxes paid on the average go up by $190. We could also have said that per unit increase in the family income, say, a dollar, the average taxes paid increase by about 0.19 dollars, or 19 cents. In this example, however, income is measured in thousands of dollars (e.g., if $X = 2$, it means $2000 dollars, etc.).

As remarked earlier, the intercept has no visible economic meaning in most cases, as in the present example. Literally interpreted, the value -1.924 means that if the family income were zero, the amount of taxes paid would be $(-)$ $1924. This does not make much economic sense, unless we interpret this figure as "negative" income tax; in other words, the government in this case is actually paying the family $1924!

Example 5.2. Table 5-5 gives data on the S.A.T. scores on both the verbal and math parts of the test for both males and females for the period 1967 to 1990. Suppose we want to predict the male verbal score (Y) on the basis of the male math score (X). Using the data of Table 5-5 and applying the OLS method, we obtained the following results:

---

[10] See Richard G. Lipsey, Peter O. Steiner, and Douglas D. Purvis, *Economics*, 8th ed., Harper & Row, New York, 1987. The notation has been changed to conform with our notation. Note that for brevity we will sometimes use the expression *OLS regression* to mean a regression obtained by the method of ordinary least squares.

$$\hat{Y}_t = -380.48 + 1.6418X_t \tag{5.22}$$

Since the data are time series, we have put the time subscript t on the variables. In all, we have data for 24 years ($t = 24$).

What does this regression show? Here the slope is 1.6418, meaning that if the math score goes up by a unit, on the average the verbal score goes up by about 1.64 units. It seems that the two variables are positively related. The intercept of about -380 has no particular physical meaning, for there is no such thing as a negative verbal score even if the math score is zero—unless, of course, the College Board, which administers the S.A.T. examination, decides to impose a penalty of 380 points on the verbal score if the math score is zero!

Example 5.3.   What is the relationship between the female verbal (Y) and female math (X) S.A.T. scores?

TABLE 5-5

S.A.T. Scores

Mean Scholastic Aptitude Test scores for college-bound seniors; 1967–1990, 1967–1971 data are estimates

Year	Verbal			Math		
	Males	Females	Total	Males	Females	Total
1967	463	468	466	514	467	492
1968	464	466	466	512	470	492
1969	459	466	463	513	470	493
1970	459	461	460	509	465	488
1971	454	457	455	507	466	488
1972	454	452	453	505	461	484
1973	446	443	445	502	460	481
1974	447	442	444	501	459	480
1975	437	431	434	495	449	472
1976	433	430	431	497	446	472
1977	431	427	429	497	445	470
1978	433	425	429	494	444	468
1979	431	423	427	493	443	467
1980	428	420	424	491	443	466
1981	430	418	424	492	443	466
1982	431	421	426	493	443	467
1983	430	420	425	493	445	468
1984	433	420	426	495	449	471
1985	437	425	431	499	452	475
1986	437	426	431	501	451	475
1987	435	425	430	500	453	476
1988	435	422	428	498	455	476
1989	434	421	427	500	454	476
1990	429	419	424	499	455	476

Source: The College Board. The *New York Times*, Aug. 28, 1990, p. B-5.

Using the data of Table 5-5 and the OLS, we obtain the following results:

$$\hat{Y}_t = -336.06 + 1.6985X_t \tag{5.23}$$

Here $b_1 = -336.06$ and $b_2 = 1.6985$. The interpretation is that, holding other things the same, if the female math score increases by a unit, the female verbal score increases on the average by about 1.70 units, which is a slightly higher value than that obtained for male students. Again, the intercept of -336 has no particular practical significance.

Example 5.4. Okun's law Based on the U.S. data for 1947 to 1960, the late Arthur Okun of the Brookings Institution and a former chairman of the President's Council of Economic Advisers obtained the following regressions, known as Okun's law:

$$\hat{Y}_t = -0.4(X_t - 2.5) \tag{5.24}$$

where

Y_t = the change in the unemployment rate, percentage points

X_t = the percent growth rate in real output, as measured by real GNP

2.5 = the long-term, or trend, rate of growth of output historically observed in the United States

In this regression the intercept is zero and the slope coefficient is -0.4. Okun's law says that for every percentage point of growth in real GNP above 2.5 percent, the unemployment rate declines by 0.4 percentage points.

Okun's law has been used to predict the required growth in real GNP to reduce the unemployment rate by a given percentage point. Thus, a growth rate of 5 percent in real GNP will reduce the unemployment rate by 1 percentage point, or a growth rate of 7.5 percent is required to reduce the unemployment rate by 2 percentage points. (Verify these calculations.)

This example shows how sometimes a regression result can be used for policy purposes.

A Word about Computations

The regression results presented in Equations (5.22) and (5.23) can be obtained by applying the OLS formulas (5.16) and (5.17) to the data given in Table 5-5. Of course, this would be tedious and very time-consuming if done manually. Today such calculations are made with the aid of ready-made statistical packages that can estimate regressions such as Eqs. (5.22) and (5.23) quickly. As noted in Chapter 1, in this book we will use such statistical packages routinely. A description of some of the available statistical packages is given in Appendix A. Where convenient, we will reproduce the output of these packages so that the reader can see what these packages actually do.

5.10   SUMMARY

In this chapter we introduced some fundamental ideas of regression analysis. Starting with the key concept of population regression function (PRF), we developed the concept of linear PRF. This book is primarily concerned with linear PRFs, that is, regressions that are *linear in the parameters* regardless of whether or not they are linear in the variables. We then introduced the idea of stochastic PRF and discussed in detail the nature and role of the stochastic error term u. PRF is, of course, a theoretical or idealized construct because in practice all we have is only a sample(s) from some population. This necessitated the discussion of the sample regression function (SRF).

We then considered the question of how one actually goes about obtaining the SRF. Here we discussed the popular method of ordinary least squares (OLS) and presented the appropriate formulas to estimate the parameters of the PRF. We illustrated the OLS method with a fully worked out numerical example as well as with several practical examples.

Our next task is to find out how good the SRF obtained by OLS is as an estimator of the true PRF. This important task is undertaken in the following chapter.

Key Terms and Concepts

The key terms and concepts introduced in this chapter are:

Regression analysis
  a) explained, or dependent, variable
  b) independent, or explanatory, variable
Population regression function (PRF)
Population regression line (PRL)
  a) population average value
  b) conditional expected, or mean, value
Regression coefficients; parameters
  a) intercept
  b) slope
Conditional regression analysis
Stochastic, or random error, term u
  a) stochastic PRF

  b) deterministic, or nonstochastic, PRF
Sample regression function (SRF)
Sample regression line (SRL)
Residual term e
Linearity in variables
Linearity in parameters
  a) linear regression
Two-variable vs. multiple regression
Estimation of parameters
  a) the method of ordinary least squares (OLS)
  b) the least squares principle
  c) normal equations
  d) OLS estimators

QUESTIONS

5.1 Explain carefully the meaning of each of the following terms:
  (*a*) Population regression function (PRF)
  (*b*) Sample regression function (SRF)
  (*c*) Stochastic PRF
  (*d*) Linear regression model
  (*e*) Stochastic error term (u_i)
  (*f*) Residual term (e_i)
  (*g*) Conditional expectation
  (*h*) Unconditional expectation
  (*i*) Regression coefficients or parameters
  (*j*) Estimators of regression coefficients

5.2 What is the difference between a stochastic population regression function (PRF) and a stochastic sample regression function (SRF)?

5.3 "Since we do not observe the PRF, why bother studying it?" Comment.

5.4 State with reasons whether the following statements are true, false, or uncertain. Be precise.
  (*a*) The stochastic error term u_i and the residual term e_i mean the same thing.
  (*b*) The PRF gives the value of the dependent variable corresponding to each value of the independent variable.
  (*c*) A linear regression model means a model linear in the variables.
  (*d*) In the linear regression model the explanatory variable is the cause and the dependent variable is the effect.
  (*e*) The conditional and unconditional mean of a random variable are the same things.
  (*f*) In Eq. (5.2) the regression coefficients, the Bs, are random variables, whereas the bs in Eq. (5.4) are the parameters.
  (*g*) In Eq. (5.1) the slope coefficient B_2 measures the slope of Y per unit change in X.
  (*h*) In practice, the two-variable regression model is useless because the behavior of a dependent variable can never be explained by a single explanatory variable.

5.5 The following table gives pairs of dependent and independent variables. State in each case whether you would expect the relationship between the two variables to be positive, negative, or uncertain. In other words, tell whether the slope coefficient will be positive, negative, or neither. Give a brief justification in each case.

Dependent variable	Independent variable
(*a*) GNP	Rate of interest
(*b*) Personal savings	Rate of interest
(*c*) Yield of crop	Rainfall
(*d*) U.S. defense expenditure	Soviet Union's defense expenditure
(*e*) Number of home runs hit by a star baseball player	His annual salary
(*f*) A president's popularity	Length of stay in office
(*g*) A student's first-year grade-point average	His or her S.A.T. score
(*h*) A student's grade in econometrics	His or her grade in statistics
(*i*) Imports of Japanese cars	U.S. per capita income

PROBLEMS

5.6 State whether the following models are linear regression models:

(a) $Y_i = B_1 + B_2(1/X_i)$ *lin on Parameter*

(b) $Y_i = B_1 + B_2 \ln X_i + u_i$ *lin on Parameter not var*

(c) $\ln Y_i = B_1 + B_2 X_i + u_i$ *lin on Parmento*

(d) $\ln Y_i = B_1 + B_2 \ln X_i + u_i$ *lin on Par not var*

(e) $Y_i = B_1 + B_2 B_3 X_i + u_i$ *not lin on Paramete*

(f) $Y_i = B_1 + B_2^3 X_i + u_i$ *lin on Var not Par*

Note: ln stands for the natural log, that is, log to the base e. (More on this in Chapter 8).

5.7 The following table gives data on weekly family consumption expenditure (Y) (in dollars) and weekly family income (X) (in dollars).

Weekly income (X)	Weekly consumption expenditure (Y)
80	55, 60, 65, 70, 75
100	65, 70, 74, 80, 85, 88
120	79, 84, 90, 94, 98
140	80, 93, 95, 103, 108, 113, 115
160	102, 107, 110, 116, 118, 125
180	110, 115, 120, 130, 135, 140
200	120, 136, 140, 144, 145
220	135, 137, 140, 152, 157, 160, 162
240	137, 145, 155, 165, 175, 189
260	150, 152, 175, 178, 180, 185, 191

(a) For each income level, compute the mean consumption expenditure, $E(Y \mid X_i)$, that is, the conditional expected value.

(b) Plot these data in a scattergram with income on the horizontal axis and consumption expenditure on the vertical axis.

(c) Plot the conditional means derived in part (a) in the same scattergram.

(d) What can you say about the relationship between Y and X and between mean Y and X.

(e) Write down the PRF and the SRF for this example.

(f) Is the PRF linear or nonlinear?

5.8 From the data given in the preceding problem, a random sample of Y was drawn against each X. The result was as follows:

Y	70	65	90	95	110	115	120	140	155	150
X	80	100	120	140	160	180	200	220	240	260

(a) Draw the scattergram with Y on the vertical axis and X on the horizontal axis.

(b) What can you say about the relationship between Y and X?

(c) What is the SRF for this example? Show all your calculations in the manner of Table 5-4.

(d) On the same diagram, show the SRF and the PRF obtained in problem 5.7.

(e) Are the PRF and SRF identical? Why or why not?

5.9 Suppose someone has presented the following regression results for your consideration:

$$\hat{Y}_t = 2.6911 - 0.4795X_t$$

where

Y = the coffee consumption in the United States (cups per person per day)

X = the retail price of coffee ($ per pound)

t = the time period

(a) Is this a time series regression or a cross-sectional regression?
(b) Sketch the regression line.
(c) What is the interpretation of the intercept in this example? Does it make economic sense?
(d) How would you interpret the slope coefficient?
(e) Is it possible to tell what the true PRF is in this example?
(f) The *price elasticity* of demand is defined as the percentage change in the quantity demanded for a percentage change in the price. Mathematically, it is expressed as

$$\text{Elasticity} = \text{slope}\left(\frac{X}{Y}\right)$$

That is, elasticity is equal to the product of the slope and the ratio of X to Y, where X = the price and Y = the quantity. From the regression results presented earlier, can you tell what the price elasticity of demand is for coffee? If not, what additional information would you need to compute the price elasticity?

5.10 The following table gives data on the Consumer Price Index (CPI) for all items (1982–1984 = 100) and Standard & Poor (S&P) company's index of 500 common stocks prices (Base of index: 1941–1943 = 10).

Year	CPI	Index
1978	65.2	96.02
1979	72.6	103.01
1980	82.4	118.78
1981	90.9	128.05
1982	96.5	119.71
1983	99.6	160.41
1984	103.9	160.46
1985	107.9	186.84
1986	109.6	236.34
1987	113.6	286.83
1988	118.3	265.79
1989	124.0	322.84

Source: Economic Report of the President, 1990, Table 6-58, p. 359 for CPI and Table C-93, p. 401 for the S&P index.

(a) Plot the data on a scattergram with the S&P index on the vertical axis and CPI on the horizontal axis.

(b) What can you say about the relationship between the two indexes?

(c) Consider the following regression model:

$$(S\&P)_t = B_1 + B_2 CPI_t + u_t$$

Use the method of least squares to estimate this equation from the preceding data and interpret your results.

(d) Do the results obtained in part (c) make economic sense?

(e) Do you know why the S&P index dropped in 1988?

5.11 Prove that $\Sigma e_i = 0$, and hence show that $\bar{e} = 0$.

5.12 Prove that $\Sigma e_i x_i = 0$.

5.13 prove that $\Sigma e_i \hat{Y}_i = 0$; that is, the sum of the product of residuals e_i and the estimated Y_i is always zero.

5.14 The following table gives data on the nominal interest rate (Y) and the inflation rate (X) for the year 1988 for nine industrial countries:

Country	Y (%)	X (%)
Australia	11.9	7.7
Canada	9.4	4.0
France	7.5	3.1
Germany	4.0	1.6
Italy	11.3	4.8
Mexico	66.3	51.0
Switzerland	2.2	2.0
United Kingdom	10.3	6.8
United States	7.6	4.4

Source: Rudiger Dornbusch and Stanley Fischer, *Macroeconomics*, 5th ed., McGraw-Hill, New York, 1990, p. 652. The original data are from the various issues of the *International Financial Statistics*, published by the International Monetary Fund (IMF).

(a) Plot these data with the interest rate on the vertical axis and the inflation rate on the horizontal axis. What does the scattergram reveal?

(b) Do an OLS regression of Y on X. Present all your calculations.

(c) If the real interest rate is to remain constant, what must be the relationship between the nominal interest rate and the inflation rate? That is, what must be the value of the slope coefficient in the regression of Y on X? And the value of the intercept? Do your results suggest that this is the case? For a theoretical discussion of the relationship among the nominal interest rate, the inflation rate, and the real interest rate, see any textbook on macroeconomics, such as the Dornbusch and Fischer text just mentioned, and look up the topic of the Fisher equation, named after the famous American economist, Irving Fisher.

CHAPTER 6

THE TWO-VARIABLE MODEL: HYPOTHESIS TESTING

In the previous chapter we showed how the method of least squares works. By applying that method to our widget sample data given in Table 5-2, we obtained the following demand function:

$$\hat{Y}_i = 49.667 - 2.1576X_i \qquad (5.18)$$

This is the estimation stage of statistical inference. We now turn our attention to its other stage, namely, hypothesis testing. The important question that we raise is: How "good" is the estimated regression line (i.e., the demand curve) given in Eq. (5.18)? That is, how do we tell that it really is a good estimator of the true PRF? How can we be sure just on the basis of a single sample given in Table 5-2 that the estimated regression function (i.e., the SRF) is in fact a good approximation of the true PRF?

We cannot answer this question definitely unless we are a little more specific about our PRF, Eq. (5.2). As Eq. (5.2) shows, Y_i depends on both X_i and u_i. Now we have assumed that the X_i values are known or given—recall from Chapter 5 that our analysis is conditional regression analysis, conditional upon the given Xs. In short, we treat the X values as *nonstochastic*. The error term u is of course random, or stochastic. (Why?) Since a stochastic term (u) is added to a nonstochastic term (X) to generate Y, Y becomes stochastic, too. (Do you see this?) All this means that unless we are willing to assume how the stochastic u terms are generated, we will not be able to tell how good an SRF is as an estimate of the true PRF. In deriving the ordinary least squares (OLS) estimators so far, we did not say how the u_i are generated, for the derivation of OLS estimators did not depend on any assumption about the error terms. But in testing statistical hypotheses based on the SRF, we cannot make further progress, as we show shortly, unless we make some specific assumptions about how u_i are generated. This is precisely what the so-called **classical linear regression model (CLRM)** does, which we now discuss. Again, to explain the fundamental ideas, we consider the two-variable regression model introduced in Chapter 5. In Chapter 7 we extend the ideas developed here to the multiple regression model.

6.1 THE CLASSICAL LINEAR REGRESSION MODEL (CLRM)

The CLRM makes the following assumptions:

A6.1. The explanatory variable(s) X is nonstochastic; that is, its values are fixed numbers.

This is not a new assumption for us because in Chapter 5 we stated that our regression analysis is *conditional regression* analysis, conditional upon the given X values.

A6.2. The expected, or mean, value of the disturbance term u is zero. That is,

$$E(u_i) = 0 \tag{6.1}$$

Since u_i is a random term, this assumption means only that *on the average* the error term u has no effect on Y one way or the other. So to speak, positive and negative values of u cancel each other out. Geometrically, what this means is shown in Figure 6-1.

A6.3. The variance of each u_i is constant, or **homoscedastic** (*homo* means equal and *scedastic* means variance). That is

$$\text{var}(u_i) = \sigma^2 \tag{6.2}$$

Geometrically, this assumption is as shown in Figure 6-2(*a*). This assumption simply means that the conditional distribution of each Y population corresponding to the given value of X has the same variance; that is, the individual Y values are spread around their mean values with the same

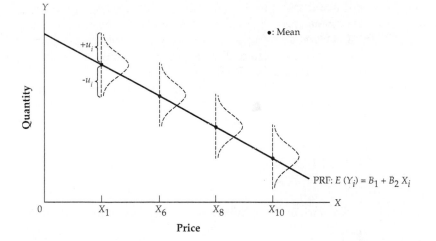

FIGURE 6-1
Conditional distribution of disturbances u_i.

variance.[1] If this is not the case, then we have **heteroscedasticity**, or **unequal variance**, which is depicted in Figure 6-2(*b*). As this figure shows, the variance of each Y population is different, which is in contrast to Figure 6-2(*a*), where each Y population has the same variance. The CLRM assumes that the variance of u is as shown in Figure 6-2(*a*).

A6.4.   There is no correlation between two error terms. This is the assumption of **no autocorrelation.**

Algebraically, this assumption can be written as

$$\operatorname{cov}(u_i, u_j) = 0 \qquad i \neq j \tag{6.3}$$

Here *cov* stands for covariance (see Chapter 2) and i and j are any two error terms. (*Note*: If $i = j$, Eq. (6.3) will give the variance of u, which by Eq. (6.2) is a constant.)

Geometrically, Eq. (6.3) can be shown in Figure 6-3. Assumption A6.4 means that there is no systematic relationship between two error terms. If one

---

[1] Since the X values are assumed to be given, or nonstochastic, the only source of variation in Y is from u. Therefore, given X_i, the variance of Y_i is the same as that of u_i. In short, the (conditional) variance of u_i = (conditional) variance of Y_i = σ^2. Note, however, that the unconditional variance of Y is $E[Y_i - E(Y)]^2$, as shown in Chap. 2. The sample counterpart of the unconditional variance of Y is $\Sigma(Y_i - \overline{Y})^2/(n - 1)$.

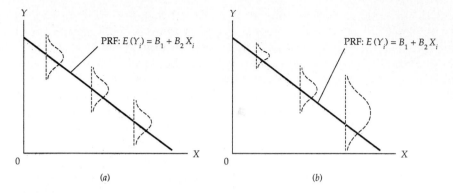

FIGURE 6-2
(a) Homoscedasticity (equal variance); (b) heteroscedasticity (unequal variance).

u is above the mean value, it does not mean that another error term u will also be above the mean value (for positive correlation), or that if one error term is below the mean value, it does not mean another error term has to be above the mean value, or vice versa (negative correlation). In short, the assumption of no autocorrelation means that the error terms u_i are random.

The reader might wonder about all these assumptions. Why are they needed? How realistic are they? What happens if they are not true? How do we know that a particular regression model in fact satisfies all these assumptions? Although these questions are certainly pertinent, at this stage of the development of our subject matter, we cannot provide totally satisfactory answers to all of them. However, as we progress through the book, we will

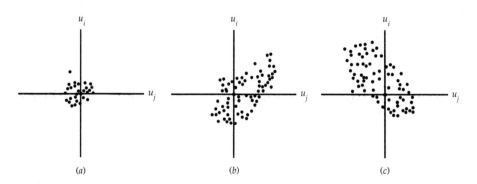

FIGURE 6-3
Patterns of autocorrelation: (a) No autocorrelation; (b) positive autocorrelation; (c) negative autocorrelation.

see the utility of these assumptions. As a matter of fact, the whole of Part III is devoted to finding out what happens if one or more of the assumptions of CLRM are not fulfilled. But keep in mind that in any scientific inquiry we make certain assumptions because they facilitate the development of the subject matter in gradual steps, not because they are necessarily realistic. An analogy might help here. Students of economics are generally introduced to the model of perfect competition before they are introduced to the models of imperfect competition. This is done because the implications derived from this model enable us to appreciate better the models of imperfect competition, not because the model of perfect competition is necessarily realistic. Besides, there are markets that may be reasonably perfectly competitive, such as the stock market or the foreign exchange market.

6.2 VARIANCES AND STANDARD ERRORS OF ORDINARY LEAST SQUARES (OLS) ESTIMATORS

One immediate consequence of the assumptions just introduced is that they enable us to estimate the variances and standard errors of the OLS estimators given in Eqs. (5.16) and (5.17). In Chapter 4 we discussed the basics of estimation theory, including the notions of (point) estimators, their sampling distributions, and the concepts of the variance and standard error of the estimators. Recalling that knowledge, we know that the OLS estimators given in Eqs. (5.16) and (5.17) are *random variables*, for their values will change from sample to sample. Naturally, we would like to know something about the sampling variability of these estimators, that is, how they vary from sample to sample. These sampling variabilities, as we know now, are measured by the variances of these estimators, or by their *standard errors* (se), which are the square roots of the variances. The **variances** and **standard errors of the OLS estimators** given in Eqs. (5.16) and (5.17) are as follows:[2]

$$\text{var}(b_1) = \frac{\sum X_i^2}{n \sum x_i^2} \cdot \sigma^2 \tag{6.4}$$

(*Note*: This formula involves both small x and capital X.)

$$\text{se}(b_1) = \sqrt{\text{var}(b_1)} \tag{6.5}$$

$$\text{var}(b_2) = \frac{\sigma^2}{\sum x_i^2} \tag{6.6}$$

$$\text{se}(b_2) = \sqrt{\text{var}(b_2)} \tag{6.7}$$

---

[2] The proofs can be found in Damodar N. Gujarati, *Basic Econometrics*, 2d ed., McGraw-Hill, New York, 1988, pp. 83–84.

where var = the variance and se = the standard error, and where σ^2 is the variance of the disturbance term u_i, which by the assumption of homoscedasticity is assumed to be the same for each u.

Once σ^2 is known, then all the terms on the right-hand sides of the preceding equations can be easily computed, which will give us the numerical values of the variances and standard errors of the OLS estimators. The homoscedastic σ^2 is estimated from the following formula:

$$\hat{\sigma}^2 = \frac{\sum e_i^2}{n - 2} \tag{6.8}$$

where $\hat{\sigma}^2$ is an estimator of σ^2 (recall we use ^ to indicate an estimator) and $\sum e_i^2$ is the RSS (residual sum of squares), that is, $\Sigma(Y_i - \hat{Y}_i)^2$, the sum of the squared difference between the actual Y and the estimated Y. (See the next to the last column of Table 5-4.)

The expression $(n - 2)$ is known as the *degrees of freedom* (d.f.), which, as noted in Chapter 3, is simply the number of independent observations.[3]

Once e_i is computed, as shown in Table 5-4, Σe_i^2 can be easily computed. Incidentally, in passing, note that

$$\hat{\sigma} = \sqrt{\hat{\sigma}^2} \tag{6.9}$$

That is, the positive square of $\hat{\sigma}^2$ is known as the **standard error of the estimate** or the **standard error of the regression,** which is simply the standard deviation of the Y values about the estimated regression line.[4] This standard error of estimate is often used as a summary measure of the *goodness of fit* of the estimated regression line, a topic discussed in Section 6.6.

Variances and Standard Errors of the Widget Example

Using the preceding formulas, let us compute the variances and standard errors of our widget example. These calculations are presented in Table 6-1. The necessary raw data were already given in Table 5-4.

---

[3] Notice that we can compute e_i only when $\hat{Y}_i$ is computed. But to compute the latter, we must first obtain b_1 and b_2. In estimating these two unknowns, we lose, so to speak, 2 d.f. Therefore, although we have n observations, the d.f., are only $(n - 2)$.

[4] Note the difference between the standard error of estimate $\hat{\sigma}$ and the standard deviation of Y. The latter is measured, as usual, from its mean value, as

$$S_y = \sqrt{\sum \frac{(Y_i - \bar{Y})^2}{n - 1}}$$

whereas the former is measured from the estimated mean value (i.e., $\hat{Y}_i$) from the sample regression. See also footnote 1.

TABLE 6-1
Computations for the widget example

Estimator	Formula	Answer	Equation number
$\hat{\sigma}^2$	$\sum \dfrac{e_i^2}{n-2} = \dfrac{9.5515}{8}$	1.1939	(6.10)
$\hat{\sigma}$	$\sqrt{\hat{\sigma}^2} = \sqrt{1.1939}$	1.0926	(6.11)
var (b_1)	$\dfrac{\sum X^2 \cdot \sigma^2}{n \sum x_i^2} = \dfrac{(385)(1.1939)}{10\,(82.5)}$	0.5572	(6.12)
se (b_1)	$\sqrt{\text{var}(b_1)} = \sqrt{0.5572}$	0.7464	(6.13)
var (b_2)	$\dfrac{\sigma^2}{\sum x_i^2} = \dfrac{1.1939}{82.5}$	0.0145	(6.14)
se (b_2)	$\sqrt{\text{var}(b_2)} = \sqrt{0.0145}$	0.1203	(6.15)

Note: The raw data underlying the calculations are given in Table 5.4.
In computing the variances of the estimators, σ^2 has been replaced by its unbiased estimator, $\hat{\sigma}^2$.

Summary of Demand Function for Widgets

Let us express the estimated demand function for widgets in the following form:

$$\hat{Y}_i = 49.6670 - 2.1576 X_i$$
$$\text{se} = (0.7464) \quad (0.1203) \tag{6.16}$$

where the figures in the parentheses are the estimated standard errors. Regression results are sometimes presented in this format (but more on this in Section 6.7). Such a presentation indicates immediately the estimated parameters and their standard errors. For example, it tells us that the estimated slope coefficient of the demand function (i.e., the coefficient of the price variable) is -2.1576 and its standard deviation, or standard error, is 0.1203—this is a measure of variability of b_2 from sample to sample. What use can we make of this finding? Can we say, e.g., that our computed b_2 lies within a certain number of standard deviation units from the true B_2? If we can do that, we can state with some confidence (i.e., probability) how good the computed SRF, Eq. (6.16), is as an estimate of the true PRF. This is, of course, the topic of hypothesis testing.

But before discussing hypothesis testing, we need a bit more theory. In particular, since b_1 and b_2 are random variables, we must find out their **sampling**, or **probability distributions**: Recall from Chapters 3 and 4 that a random variable (r.v.) has a probability distribution associated with it. Once we determine the sampling distributions of our two estimators, as we will show in Section 6.5, the task of hypothesis testing becomes straightforward. But even before that we answer an important question: Why do we use the OLS method?

6.3   WHY ORDINARY LEAST SQUARES (OLS)? THE PROPERTIES OF OLS ESTIMATORS

Although intuitively quite appealing and easy to use, the OLS method is used popularly because it has some very strong theoretical properties, which are stated in the following theorem, known as the **Gauss-Markov theorem**:

> **Gauss-Markov theorem.**   Given the assumptions of the classical linear regression model, the OLS estimators, in the class of unbiased linear estimators, have minimum variance; that is, they are **BLUE** (best linear unbiased estimators).

We have already discussed in Chapter 4 the BLUE property. In short, the OLS estimators b_1 and b_2 are:

1. Linear; that is, they are linear functions of the random variable Y, which is clear from formulas (5.16) and (5.17).[5]
2. They are unbiased; that is,[6]

$$E(b_1) = B_1$$

$$E(b_2) = B_2$$

(see Figure 4-3), and

$$E(\hat{\sigma}^2) = \sigma^2$$

Therefore, in repeated applications on the average b_1 and b_2 will coincide with their true values B_1 and B_2, and $\hat{\sigma}^2$ will concide with true σ^2.
3. They have minimum variance; that is,[7]

   $\text{var}(b_1)$ is less than the variance of any other unbiased linear estimator of B_1.

   $\text{var}(b_2)$ is less than the variance of any other unbiased linear estimator of B_2.

---

[5] Consider, e.g., $b_2 = \Sigma\, x_i y_i / \Sigma\, x_i^2$. Let $w_i = x_i / \Sigma\, x_i^2$. Therefore, we can write $b_2 = \Sigma\, w_i y_i$, which shows that b_2 is a linear function of y since y appears with a power of 1 only. Notice that we are treating x_i as nonstochastic, or fixed, numbers.

[6] For proofs, see Damodar N. Gujarati, *Basic Econometrics*, 2d ed., McGraw-Hill, New York, 1988, pp. 82–83.

[7] For proof, see footnote 6.

The implication of this finding is that we will be able to estimate the true B_1 and B_2 more accurately if we use the OLS method rather than any other method that also gives unbiased linear estimators of the true parameters.

The upshot of this discussion is that the OLS estimators possess many desirable statistical properties that we have discussed in Chapter 4. It is for this reason that the OLS method has been used popularly in regression analysis, as well as its intuitive appeal and ease of use.

6.4   THE SAMPLING, OR PROBABILITY, DISTRIBUTIONS OF OLS ESTIMATORS

Now that we have seen how to compute the OLS estimators and their standard errors and have also studied the statistical properties of these estimators, we need to find out the sampling distributions of these estimators. Without that knowledge we cannot tell how "close" these estimators are to their population values. The general notion of sampling distribution of an estimator has already been discussed in Chapter 3 (see Section 3.2).

To derive the sampling distributions of the OLS estimators b_1 and b_2, we need to add one more assumption to the list of assumptions of the CLRM. This assumption is:

A6.5.   In the PRF $Y_i = B_1 + B_2X_i + u_i$ the error term u_i follows the *normal distribution* with mean zero and variance σ^2. That is

$$u_i \sim N(0, \sigma^2) \tag{6.17}$$

What is the rationale for this assumption? There is a celebrated theorem in statistics, known as the **central limit theorem (CLT),** which we have already discussed in Chapter 3 (see Section 3.2), which states that:

Central limit theorem.   If there is a large number of independent and identically distributed random variables, then, with a few exceptions, the distribution of their sum tends to be a normal distribution as the number of such variables increases indefinitely.

Recall from Chapter 5 our discussion about the nature of the error term, u_i. As shown in Section 5.4, the error term represents the influence of all those umpteen forces that affect Y but are not specifically included in the regression model because there are so many of them and the individual effect of any one such force (i.e., variable) on Y may be too minor. If all these umpteen forces are random, and if we let u represent the sum of all these forces, then by invoking the CLT we can assume that the error term u follows the normal distribution. We have already assumed that the mean value of u is zero and that its variance, following the homoscedasticity assumption, is the constant σ^2. Hence, we have Equation (6.17).

But how does the assumption that u follows the normal distribution help us to find out the probability distributions of b_1 and b_2? Here we make use of another property of the normal distribution discussed in Chapter 3, namely, *any linear function of a normally distributed variable is itself normally distributed.* Does this mean that if we prove that b_1 and b_2 are linear functions of the normally distributed variable u, they themselves are normally distributed? You guessed it right! It can indeed be proved that these two OLS estimators are in fact linear functions of the normally distributed u_i.[8]

Now we know from Chapter 3 that a normally distributed r.v. has two parameters, the mean and the variance. What are the parameters of the normally distributed b_1 and b_2? They are as follows:

$$b_1 \sim N(B_1, \sigma_{b_1}^2) \qquad (6.18)$$

where

$$\sigma_{b_1}^2 = \operatorname{var}(b_1) = \frac{\sum X_i^2 \cdot \sigma^2}{n \sum x_i^2} \qquad (6.4)$$

$$b_2 \sim N(B_2, \sigma_{b_2}^2) \qquad (6.19)$$

where

$$\sigma_{b_2}^2 = \operatorname{var}(b_2) = \frac{\sigma^2}{\sum x_i^2} \qquad (6.6)$$

In short, b_1 and b_2 each follow the normal distribution with their means equal to true B_1 and B_2 and their variances given by formulas (6.4) and (6.6) developed previously.

Geometrically, the distributions of these estimators are as shown in Figure 6-4.

---

[8] In footnote 5 we showed that

$$b_2 = \sum w_i y_i$$

That is, b_2 is a linear function of y. But Y is itself a linear function of u, which is obvious from Eq. (5.2) (*Note:* the Bs and X are constants or nonstochastic). If u is assumed to be normally distributed, then Y, a linear function of u, is also normally distributed. But since b_2 is a linear function of y, ultimately b_2 is a linear function of u, and is therefore also normally distributed. The same is true of b_1. *Note:* $y_i = Y_i - \bar{Y}$.

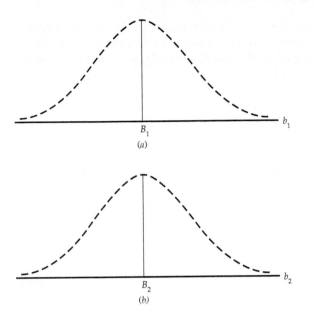

FIGURE 6-4
(Normal) sampling distributions of b_1 and b_2.

6.5   HYPOTHESIS TESTING

Let us return to our widget example. The estimated demand function is given in Eq. (6.16). Suppose someone suggests that the price has no effect on the quantity demanded. That is, our *null hypothesis* is that

$$H_0: B_2 = 0$$

In applied regression analysis such a "zero" null hypothesis, the so-called straw man hypothesis, is deliberately chosen to find out whether Y is related to X at all. If there is no relationship between Y and X to begin with, then testing a hypothesis that $B_2 = -2$ or any other value is meaningless. Of course, if the zero hypothesis is sustainable, there is no point at all in including X in the model. Therefore, if X really belongs in the model, one would fully expect to reject the zero null hypothesis H_0 in favor of the *alternative hypothesis H_1*, which says, e.g., that B_2 is different from zero.

Our numerical results show that $b_2 = -2.1576$. One would therefore expect that the zero null hypothesis is not tenable in this case. But we cannot look at the numerical results alone, for we know that because of sampling fluctuations, the numerical values will change from sample to sample. Obviously, we need some formal testing procedure to reject or not reject the null hypothesis. How do we proceed?

This should not be a problem now, for in equation (6.19) we have shown that b_2 follows the *normal distribution* with mean $= B_2$ and $var(b_2) = \sigma^2/\Sigma\, x_i^2$. Then following our discussion about hypothesis testing in Chapter 4, Section 4.5, we can use either:

1. The confidence interval approach or
2. The test of significance approach to test any hypothesis about B_2 as well as B_1.

Since b_2 follows the normal distribution, with the mean and the variance stated in expression (6.19), we know that

$$Z = \frac{b_2 - B_2}{se(b_2)}$$

$$= \frac{b_2 - B_2}{\sigma/\sqrt{\Sigma\, x_i^2}} \sim N(0, 1) \tag{6.20}$$

is the *standard normal distribution*. From Chapter 3 we know the properties of the standard normal distribution, particularly, the property that ≈ 95 percent of the area of the normal distribution lies within two standard deviation units of the mean value, etc. Therefore, if our null hypothesis is $B_2 = 0$ and the computed $b_2 = -2.1576$, we can find out the probability of obtaining such a value from the Z, or standard normal, distribution (Appendix B, Table B-1). If this probability is very small, we can reject the null hypothesis, but if it is large, say, greater than 10 percent, we may not reject the null hypothesis. All this is familiar material from Chapters 3 and 4.

Alas, there is a hitch! To use Equation (6.20) we must know the true σ^2. This is not known, but we can estimate it by using $\hat{\sigma}^2$ given in Eq. (6.8). However, if we replace σ in Eq. (6.20) by its estimator $\hat{\sigma}$, then, as shown in Chapter 3, Eq. (3.12), the right-hand side of Eq. (6.20) follows the *t distribution* with $(n - 2)$ d.f., not the standard normal distribution; that is,

$$\frac{b_2 - B_2}{\hat{\sigma}/\sqrt{\Sigma\, x_i^2}} \sim t_{n-2} \tag{6.21}$$

Or, more generally,

$$\frac{b_2 - B_2}{se(b_2)} \sim t_{n-2} \tag{6.22}$$

Note that we lose 2 d.f. in computing $\hat{\sigma}^2$ for reasons stated earlier.

Therefore, to test the null hypothesis in the present case, we have to use the t distribution in lieu of the (standard) normal distribution. But the procedure of hypothesis testing remains the same, as explained in Chapter 4.

Testing H_0: $B_2 = 0$ versus H_1: $B_2 \neq 0$: The Confidence Interval Approach

For our widget example we have 10 observations, hence the d.f. are $(10 - 2) = 8$. Let us assume that the level of significance α, the probability of committing a type I error, is fixed at 5 percent. Since the alternative hypothesis is two-sided, from the t table given in Appendix B, Table B-2, we find that for 8 d.f.,

$$P(-2.306 \leq t \leq 2.306) = 0.95 \tag{6.23}$$

That is, the probability that a t value (for 8 d.f.) lies between the limits $(-2.306, 2.306)$ is 0.95 or 95 percent; these, as we know, are the critical t values. Now by substituting for t from expression (6.21) into the preceding equation, we obtain

$$P\left(-2.306 \leq \frac{b_2 - B_2}{\hat{\sigma} / \sqrt{\sum x_i^2}} \leq 2.306\right) = 0.95 \tag{6.24}$$

Rearranging inequality (6.24), we obtain

$$P\left(b_2 - \frac{2.306\hat{\sigma}}{\sqrt{\sum x_i^2}} \leq B_2 \leq b_2 + \frac{2.306\hat{\sigma}}{\sqrt{\sum x_i^2}}\right) = 0.95 \tag{6.25}$$

Or, more generally,

$$P[(b_2 - 2.306 \ se(b_2) \leq B_2 \leq b_2 + 2.306 \ se(b_2)] = 0.95 \tag{6.26}$$

which provides *a 95% confidence interval for B_2:* In repeated applications 95 out of 100 such intervals will include the true B_2. As noted previously, in the language of hypothesis testing such a confidence interval is known as the *region of acceptance* (of H_0) and the area outside the confidence interval is known as the *rejection region* (of H_0).

Geometrically, the 95% confidence interval is shown in Figure 6-5(a).

Now following our discussion in Chapter 4, if the null-hypothesized value of B_2 lies in such an interval (i.e., in the acceptance region), we do not reject the hypothesis. But if it lies outside the confidence interval (i.e., it lies in the rejection region), we reject the null hypothesis, bearing in mind that in making either of these decisions we are taking a chance of being wrong a certain percent (say, 5 percent) of the time.

All that remains to be done for our widget example is to obtain the numerical value of this interval. But that is now easy, for we have already obtained $se(b_2) = 0.1203$, as shown in Eq. (6.15). Substituting this value in Equation (6.26), we now obtain the 95% confidence interval as [see Figure 6-5(b)]

$$-2.1576 - 2.306(0.1203) \leq B_2 \leq -2.1576 + 2.306(0.1203)$$

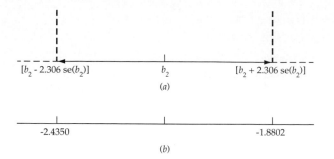

FIGURE 6-5
(*a*) 95% confidence interval for B_2 (8 d.f.); (*b*) 95% confidence interval for the slope coefficient of the widget demand function.

That is,

$$-2.4350 \le B_2 \le -1.8802 \qquad (6.27)$$

Since the null-hypothesized value of 0 does not lie in this interval, we can reject the null hypothesis that price has no effect on the quantity of widgets demanded. In other words, price does determine the quantity demanded.

A cautionary note: As noted in Chapter 4, although the statement given in Eq. (6.26) is true, we *cannot say* that the probability is 95 percent that the particular interval (6.27) includes the true B_2, for unlike Eq. (6.26), expression (6.27) is not a random interval; it is fixed. Therefore, the probability is either 1 or 0 that B_2 lies in interval (6.27). We can only say that if we construct 100 intervals like interval (6.27), 95 out of 100 such intervals will include the true B_2; we cannot guarantee that this particular interval will necessarily include B_2.

Following a similar procedure exactly, the reader should verify that the 95% confidence interval for the intercept term B_1 is

$$47.946 \le B_1 \le 51.388 \qquad (6.28)$$

If, e.g., H_0: $B_1 = 0$ vs. H_1: $B_1 \ne 0$, obviously this null hypothesis will be rejected too, for 0 does not lie in the preceding 95% confidence interval. On the other hand, if the null hypothesis were that the true intercept term is 50, we cannot reject this null hypothesis because this value lies in the 95% confidence interval.

The Test of Significance Approach to Hypothesis Testing

The key idea underlying this approach to hypothesis testing is that of a *test statistic* (see Chapter 4) and the *sampling distribution* of the test statistic under the null hypothesis, H_0. The decision to accept or reject H_0 is made on the basis of the value of the test statistic obtained from the sample data.

To illustrate this approach, recall that

$$t = \frac{b_2 - B_2}{se(b_2)} \quad (6.22)$$

follows the t distribution with $(n - 2)$ d.f. Now if we let

$$H_0: B_2 = B_2^*$$

where B_2^* is a *specific numerical value* of B_2 (e.g., $B_2^* = 0$), then

$$t = \frac{b_2 - B_2^*}{se(b_2)} \quad (6.29)$$

can be readily computed from the sample data. Since all the quantities in Equation (6.29) are now known, we can use the t value computed from Eq. (6.29) as the test statistic, which follows the t distribution with $(n - 2)$ d.f. Appropriately, the testing procedure is called the **t test**.[9]

Now to use the t test in any concrete application, we need to know three things:

1. The d.f., which are always $(n - 2)$ for the two-variable model
2. The level of significance, α, which is a matter of personal choice, although 1, 5, or 10% levels have been usually used in empirical analysis[10]
3. Whether we use a one-tailed or two-tailed test (see Table 4-2 and Figure 4-7).

The Demand for Widgets Continued

1. *A two-tailed test.* Assume that $H_0: B_2 = 0$ and $H_1: B_2 \neq 0$. Using (6.29), we find that

$$t = \frac{-2.1576 - 0}{0.1203} \quad (6.30)$$
$$= -17.94 \quad \text{(approx.)}$$

---

[9] The difference between the confidence interval and the test of significance approaches lies in the fact that in the former we do not know what the true B_2 is and therefore try to guess it by establishing a $(1 - \alpha)$ confidence interval. In the test of significance approach, on the other hand, we hypothesize what the true B_2 $(= B_2^*)$ is and try to find out if the sample value b_2 is "sufficiently" close to (the hypothesized) B_2^*.

[10] But keep in mind our discussion about the level of significance and the *p value* (i.e., the exact level of significance) in Chapter 4. It is generally a good practice to give the *p* value of the test statistic.

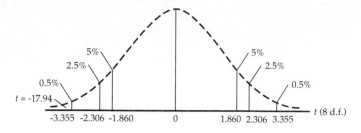

FIGURE 6-6
The t distribution for 8 d.f.

Now from the t table given in Appendix B, we find that for 8 d.f. we have the following critical t values (two-tailed) (see Fig. 6.6):

Level of significance	0.01	0.05	0.10
Critical t	3.355	2.306	1.860

Now in Table 4-2 we stated that in the case of the two-tailed t test if the computed $|t|$, the absolute value of t, exceeds the critical t value at the chosen level of significance, we can reject the null hypothesis. Therefore, in the present case we can reject the null hypothesis that the true B_2 (i.e., the price coefficient) is zero because the computed $|t|$ of 17.94 far exceeds the critical t value even at the 1% level of significance. We reached the same conclusion on the basis of the confidence interval (6.27), which should not be surprising because the confidence interval and the test of significance approaches to hypothesis testing are merely two sides of the same coin.

Incidentally, in the present example the p $value$ (i.e., probability value) of the t statistics of 17.94 obtained in Equation (6.30) is much smaller than even the 0.002 level. As the t table shows, the probability of obtaining a t value of as much as 4.501 or greater (for 8 d.f.) is 0.002 (two-tailed); and since the value of 17.94 is far greater than 4.501, the probability of obtaining such a high value must indeed be much smaller than 0.002. (Using a computer, we can obtain the p value of obtaining a t value of 17.94 as $\approx$ 0.00000005).

2. *A one-tailed test.* Since the price coefficient in a demand function is expected to be negative, a realistic set of hypotheses would be H_0: $B_2 = 0$ and H_1: $B_2 < 0$; here the alternative hypothesis is one-sided.

The t-testing procedure remains exactly the same as before, except, as noted in Table 4-2, the probability of committing a type I error is not divided equally between the two tails of the t distribution but is concentrated in only one tail, either left or right. In the present case it will be the left tail. (Why?)

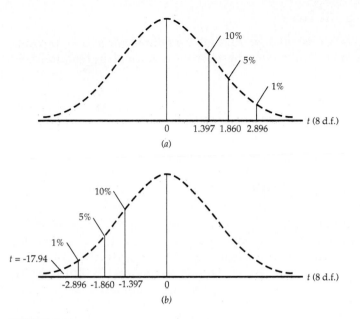

FIGURE 6-7
One-tailed t test: (a) Right-tailed; (b) left-tailed.

Now for 8 d.f. we observe from the t table that the critical t value (left-tailed) is

Level of significance	0.01	0.05	0.10
Critical t	-2.896	-1.860	-1.397

For the widget example, under the null hypothesis that $B_2 = 0$, we have already seen that

$$t = -17.935 \qquad (6.30)$$

Since this t value is much smaller than the 1% critical t value of -2.896, following the rules laid down in Table 4-2 we can reject the null hypothesis that the true price coefficient is zero (see Figure 6.7).[11] In other words, we can accept the alternative hypothesis that the price coefficient is negative, which is what economic theory would suggest [see Figure 6.7(b)]. Needless to say, we can apply the t test to test hypotheses about the true intercept term in similar fashion.

---

[11] Some authors would say that the computed t value is *highly statistically significant*. This simply means that the probability of obtaining such a t value is extremely small.

The χ^2 Test of Significance

Recall that in Example 3.9 we pointed out that the sample variance S^2 obtained from a random sample of n observations from a normal population with variance σ^2 is distributed as

$$\frac{(n-1)S^2}{\sigma^2} \sim \chi^2_{(n-1)} \tag{3.10}$$

In the regression context $\hat{\sigma}^2$ is an estimator of σ^2. Therefore, assuming a random sample from a normal population, it can be shown that

$$\frac{(n-2)\hat{\sigma}^2}{\sigma^2} \sim \chi^2_{(n-2)} \tag{6.31}$$

follows the χ^2 distribution with $(n-2)$ d.f. Therefore, if the value of σ^2 is a specified number under the null hypothesis, one can use the χ^2 test to test hypotheses about the true σ^2. Let us illustrate with our widget example.

For our example, $\hat{\sigma}^2 = 1.1939$, as shown in Eq. (6.10). Suppose we hypothesize that true $\sigma^2 = 1.5$. Can we accept this hypothesis? Using (6.31), we find that

$$\frac{8(1.1939)}{1.5} = 6.3675 \tag{6.32}$$

Now, from the χ^2 table given in Appendix B-4, we find that for 8 d.f. the probability of obtaining a χ^2 value of ≈ 6.37 or greater is somewhere between 0.75 and 0.50, which is much higher than the conventional 0.01 or 0.05. (Using a computer, we can obtain the p value of obtaining a χ^2 value of ≈ 6.37 as ≈ 0.61.) Hence, if we fix α, the level of significance, at the conventional 0.05 or even 0.10 level, we cannot reject the hypothesis that the true σ^2 is 1.5. In other words, the sample value of 1.1939 and the true value of 1.5 are not *statistically* different.

As the preceding discussion indicates, once we know that a given estimator follows a particular probability, or sampling, distribution, testing statistical hypotheses about the true values of such estimators is relatively straightforward.

6.6   HOW GOOD IS THE FITTED REGRESSION LINE: THE COEFFICIENT OF DETERMINATION, r^2

Our finding in the preceding section that on the basis of the t test both the estimated intercept and slope coefficients are *individually* statistically significant (i.e., significantly different from zero) suggests that the SRF, Eq. (6.16), shown in Figure 5-6 seems to "fit" the data "reasonably" well. Of course, not each actual Y value lies on the estimated PRF. That is, not all $e_i = (Y_i - \hat{Y}_i)$ are zero; as Table 5-4 shows, some e are positive and some are negative. Can we develop an overall measure of "goodness of fit" that will tell us how well

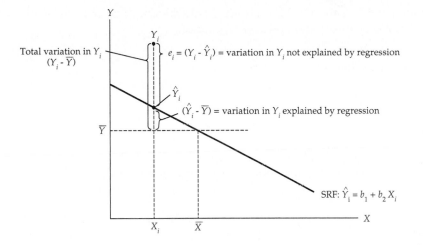

FIGURE 6-8
Breakdown of total variation in Y_i.

the estimated regression line, Eq. (6.16), fits the actual Y values? Indeed, such a measure has been developed and is known as the **coefficient of determination,** denoted by the symbol r^2 (read as r squared). To see how r^2 is computed, we proceed as follows.

Recall that

$$Y_i = \hat{Y}_i + e_i \tag{5.5}$$

Let us express this equation in a slightly different but equivalent form as (see Figure 6-8)

$$(Y_i - \overline{Y}) \quad = \quad (\hat{Y}_i - \overline{Y}) \quad + \quad (Y_i - \hat{Y}_i) \text{ (i.e., } e_i) \tag{6.33}$$

| Variation in Y_i from its mean value | Variation in Y_i explained by X ($=\hat{Y}_i$) around its mean value (*Note:* $\overline{Y} = \overline{\hat{Y}}$) | Unexplained or residual variation |

Now letting small letters indicate deviations from mean values, we can write the preceding equation as

$$y_i = \hat{y}_i + e_i \tag{6.34}$$

(*Note:* $y_i = (Y_i - \overline{Y})$, etc. Also, note that $\overline{e} = 0$, as a result of which $\overline{Y} = \overline{\hat{Y}}$; that is, the mean values of the actual Y and the estimated Y are the same.)
Or

$$y_i = b_2 x_i + e_i \tag{6.35}[12]$$

---

[12] Note that the SRF: $Y_i = b_1 + b_2 X_i + e_i$, in deviation form (i.e., each variable expressed as a deviation from its sample mean value) becomes $y_i = b_2 x_i + e_i$ and $\hat{y}_i = b_2 x_i$. In this deviation form the intercept term b_1 does not appear explicitly in the model.

Now squaring Equation (6.34) on both sides and summing over the sample, we obtain, after simple algebraic manipulation,

$$\sum y_i^2 = \sum \hat{y}_i^2 + \sum e_i^2 \qquad (6.36)$$

Or, equivalently,

$$\sum y_i^2 = b_2^2 \sum x_i^2 + \sum e_i^2 \qquad (6.37)^{13}$$

This is an important relationship, as we will see.

The various sums of squares appearing in Equation (6.36) can be defined as follows:

$\sum y_i^2 =$ the total variation[14] of the actual Y values about their sample mean $\overline{Y}$, which may be called the **total sum of squares (TSS).**

$\sum \hat{y}_i^2 =$ the total variation of the estimated Y values about their mean value ($\overline{\hat{Y}} = \overline{Y}$), which may be called appropriately the *sum of squares due to regression* [i.e., due to the explanatory variable(s)], or simply the **explained sum of squares (ESS).**

$\sum e_i^2 =$ *as before, the* **residual sum of squares (RSS)** or residual or unexplained variation of the Y values about the regression line.

Put simply, then, Eq. (6.36) is

$$\text{TSS} = \text{ESS} + \text{RSS} \qquad (6.38)$$

and shows that the total variation in the observed Y values about their mean value can be partitioned into two parts, one attributable to the regression line and the other to random forces because not all actual Y observations lie on the fitted line. All this can be seen clearly from Figure 6-8.

Now if the chosen SRF fits the data quite well, ESS should be much larger than RSS: If all the actual Y lie on the fitted SRF, ESS will be equal to TSS and RSS will be zero. On the other hand, if the SRF fits the data poorly, RSS will be much larger than ESS; in the extreme, if X explains no variation at all in

---

[13] Squaring Eq. (6.34) on both sides and summing over the sample size, we obtain

$$\sum y_i^2 = \sum \hat{y}_i^2 + \sum e_i^2 + 2 \sum \hat{y}_i e_i$$
$$= b^2 \sum x_i^2 + \sum e_i^2$$

since $\Sigma \hat{y}_i e_i = b_2 \Sigma x_i e_i = 0$, as shown in Eq. (5.20). Note that:

$$x_i = X_i - \overline{X}$$

[14] The terms *variation* and *variance* are different. Variation means the sum of squares of deviations of a variable from its mean value. Variance is this sum divided by the appropriate d.f. In short, variance = variation/d.f.

Y, ESS will be zero and RSS will equal TSS. These are, however, polar cases. Typically, neither ESS nor RSS will be zero. If ESS is relatively larger than RSS, the SRF will explain a substantial proportion of the variation in Y; if RSS is relatively larger than ESS, the SRF will explain only some part of the variation of Y. All these qualitative statements, although intuitively easy to understand, can be readily quantified. If we divide Equation (6.38) by TSS on both sides, we obtain

$$1 = \frac{\text{ESS}}{\text{TSS}} + \frac{\text{RSS}}{\text{TSS}} \tag{6.39}$$

Now let us define

$$r^2 = \frac{\text{ESS}}{\text{TSS}} \tag{6.40}$$

The quantity r^2 thus defined is known as the (sample) *coefficient of determination* and is the commonly used measure of the goodness of fit of a regression line. Verbally,

r^2 measures the proportion or percentage of the total variation in Y explained by the regression model.

Two properties of r^2 may be noted:

1. It is a non-negative quantity. (Why?)
2. Its limits are $0 \le r^2 \le 1$ since a part (ESS) cannot be greater than the whole (TSS). An r^2 of 1 means a "perfect fit," for the entire variation in Y is explained by the regression. An r^2 of zero means no relationship between Y and X whatsoever.

Formulas to Compute r^2

Using Equation (6.40), Equation (6.39) can be written as

$$1 = r^2 + \frac{\text{RSS}}{\text{TSS}}$$

$$= r^2 + \frac{\sum e_i^2}{\sum y_i^2} \tag{6.41}$$

Therefore,

$$r^2 = 1 - \frac{\sum e_i^2}{\sum y_i^2} \tag{6.42}$$

There are several equivalent formulas to compute r^2, which are given in problem 6.5.

r^2 for the Widget Example

From the data given in Table 5-4, and using formula (6.42), we obtain the following r^2 value for our widget example:

$$r^2 = 1 - \frac{9.5515}{393.60}$$

$$= 0.9757$$

(6.43)

Since r^2 can at most be 1, the computed r^2 is very high. In our demand function X, the price variable, explains about 98 percent of the variation in the quantity demanded. In this case we can say that the sample regression (6.16) gives an excellent fit.

The Coefficient of Correlation, r

In Chapter 2, Section 2.8, we introduced the **coefficient of correlation, r,** as a measure of the strength of the linear relationship between two variables Y and X and showed that r can be computed from formula (2.44), which can also be written as

$$r = \frac{\sum (X_i - \overline{X})(Y_i - \overline{Y})}{\sqrt{\sum (X_i - \overline{X})^2 \sum (Y_i - \overline{Y})^2}}$$

(6.44)

$$= \frac{\sum x_i y_i}{\sqrt{\sum x_i^2 \sum y_i^2}}$$

(6.45)

But this coefficient of correlation can also be computed from the coefficient of determination, r^2, as follows:

$$r = \pm \sqrt{r^2}$$

(6.46)

Since most regression computer packages routinely compute r^2, r can be easily computed. The only question is about the sign of r. However, that can be easily determined from the nature of the problem. In our widget example, since quantity and price are expected to be negatively related, the r value in this case will be negative. In general, though, r has the same sign as the slope coefficient, which should be clear from formulas (5.17) and (6.45). Thus, for our demand example,

$$r = - \sqrt{0.9757} = - 0.9878$$

(6.47)

Using the data given in Table 5-4 and formula (6.45), the reader can easily confirm the r value given in Equation (6.47), except for the rounding errors. We have already discussed the properties of r in Section 2.8 and also have shown some likely patterns of r in Figure 2-7.

In the regression context r^2, the coefficient of determination, is a more meaningful measure than r. r^2 tells us the proportion of the variation in the dependent variable explained by the explanatory variable(s), and therefore provides an overall measure of the extent to which the variation in one variable determines the variation in the other, but r does not have such a value. Besides, as we will see, the interpretation of r (= R) in a multiple regression is of dubious value.

6.7   REPORTING THE RESULTS OF REGRESSION ANALYSIS

There are various ways of reporting the results of regression analysis, but in this text we will use the following format, employing the widget example as an illustration:

$$\hat{Y}_i = \quad 49.6670 \quad - \quad 2.1576X_i \qquad r^2 = 0.9757$$
$$\text{se} = \quad (0.7464) \qquad (0.1203) \qquad \text{df} = 8 \qquad\qquad (6.48)$$
$$t = \quad (66.538) \qquad (-17.935)$$

In Equation (6.48) the figures in the first set of parentheses are the estimated standard errors (se) of the regression coefficients and those in the second set of parentheses are the estimated t values computed from expression (6.22) *under the null hypothesis that the true population value of each regression coefficient individually is zero*; e.g., 66.538 = 49.6670/0.7464. In short, the t values given are simply the ratios of the estimated coefficients to their standard errors.[15]

One advantage of reporting regression results in the preceding format is that we can see at once whether each estimated coefficient is individually statistically significant, that is, significantly different from zero. As a rule of thumb, if d.f. are greater than 20, a t value of ≈ 2 is statistically significant at the 5% level (two-tailed test) and a t value of ≈ 1.7 is statistically significant at the 5% level (one-tailed test.) Needless to say, these critical t values will change if we choose α at 1 or 10 percent or any other level. *As a matter of convention, from now on, if we do not specify a specific null hypothesis, then we will assume that it is the zero null hypothesis (i.e., the population parameter assumes zero value). And, if we reject it (i.e., when the test statistic is significant), it means that the true population value is different from zero.*

Any other null hypothesis can be easily tested by making use of the t

---

[15] As pointed out in Chap. 4, if the computer program you are using gives the p value of each t ratio, by all means quote that p value.

test discussed earlier. Thus, if the null hypothesis is that the true intercept term is 49 and if H_1: $B_1 \neq 49$, the t value will be

$$t = \frac{49.6670 - 49}{0.7464}$$

$$= 0.8931$$

The reader can easily verify that at, say, $\alpha = 5\%$, this t value is not statistically significant on the basis of a two-tailed t test (the critical $t_{0.025,8} = 2.306$). The zero null hypothesis, as mentioned before, is essentially a kind of straw man. It is usually adopted for strategic reasons—to "dramatize" the statistical significance (i.e., importance) of an estimated coefficient.

6.8 A WORD ON COMPUTATION: COMPUTER REGRESSION PACKAGES

In this and the previous chapters we provided several computational formulas. These are the formulas that one would use to compute the various regressions employing the old-fashioned hand calculator. But the computer has made our life so much easier. Not only are there several excellent computer regression packages commercially available today, but even computer hardware, thanks to the personal computer, is now within the reach of most readers. Therefore, in this age of computers, one would hardly use the hand calculator to do complex calculations. Initially, though, readers should use the hand calculator to do some simple regression problems just to familiarize themselves with the various formulas given in this chapter. Besides, these are the formulas, with some short-cuts, that are built into most regression packages. A list of some of the most popular regression packages, such as *ET*, *SHAZAM*, *TSP*, *SAS*, *SPSS*, and *MINITAB*, is given in Appendix A. Most illustrative examples in this book use one or more of these packages.

6.9 AN ILLUSTRATIVE EXAMPLE: THE U.S. EXPENDITURE ON FOREIGN IMPORTS

We conclude our discussion of the two-variable model by presenting an example based on concrete economic data. These data pertain to the U.S. expenditure on imported, or foreign, goods (durable and nondurable) and the U.S. personal disposable (i.e., after-tax) income (PDI), all in billions of 1982 dollars, and are given in Table 6-2 for the years 1968 to 1987. By expressing data in constant dollars (i.e., the dollar value of a particular year such as 1982), we avoid the problem of inflation.

The celebrated Keynesian consumption function theory states that personal consumption expenditure (PCE) is positively related to PDI. Since expenditure on foreign goods is part of the aggregate consumption expendi-

TABLE 6-2
U.S. expenditure on imported goods (Y) and personal disposable income (X), 1968–1987*

Year	Y	X	Year	Y	X
1968	135.7	1551.3	1978	274.1	2167.4
1969	144.6	1599.8	1979	277.9	2212.6
1970	150.9	1668.1	1980	253.6	2214.3
1971	166.2	1728.4	1981	258.7	2248.6
1972	190.7	1797.4	1982	249.5	2261.5
1973	218.2	1916.3	1983	282.2	2331.9
1974	211.8	1896.9	1984	351.1	2469.8
1975	187.9	1931.7	1985	367.9	2542.8
1976	229.9	2001.0	1986	412.3	2640.9
1977	259.4	2066.6	1987	439.0	2686.3

Source: Economic Report of the President, 1989. Data on Y from Table B-21, p. 331, and data on X from Table B-27, p. 333.
* In billions of 1982 dollars.

ture, one would also expect a positive relationship between expenditure on imports and PDI. To see if a model like

$$Y_t = B_1 + B_2X_t + u_t \tag{6.49}$$

(where Y = the consumption expenditure on imports and X = the PDI, and where the subscript t denotes that the data are time series data) fits the data given in Table 6-2, and to see if the relationship between the two variables is linear, one can plot the data on Y and X in a scattergram as shown in Figure 6-9.

This scattergram shows that the relationship between the two variables is approximately linear, and therefore the linear model (6.49) might be appropriate. In a later chapter we will reexamine this model to determine if it violates any of the assumptions of the CLRM. But for now, march on!

Before presenting the OLS results based on the data in Table 6-2, let us find out what economic theory has to say about the expected values of B_1 and B_2. Mathematically, B_2 is the slope of the (regression) line, but, economically speaking, it represents the **marginal propensity to spend (MPS)** on imported goods; that is, it represents the change in the mean expenditure on imported goods following, say, a dollar's increase in PDI. If, e.g., the MPS were 0.25 and the PDI increases by a dollar, the mean or average consumption expenditure on imported goods will go up by 25 cents. Economic theory tells us that the MPS is expected to be positive but less than one; that is, $0 < B_2 < 1$. This is because as our income increases, we do not spend the entire increase in income on consumption; some of it is saved.

What about the intercept, B_1? As we know, the intercept represents the average value of Y when X takes the value of zero. In the present instance

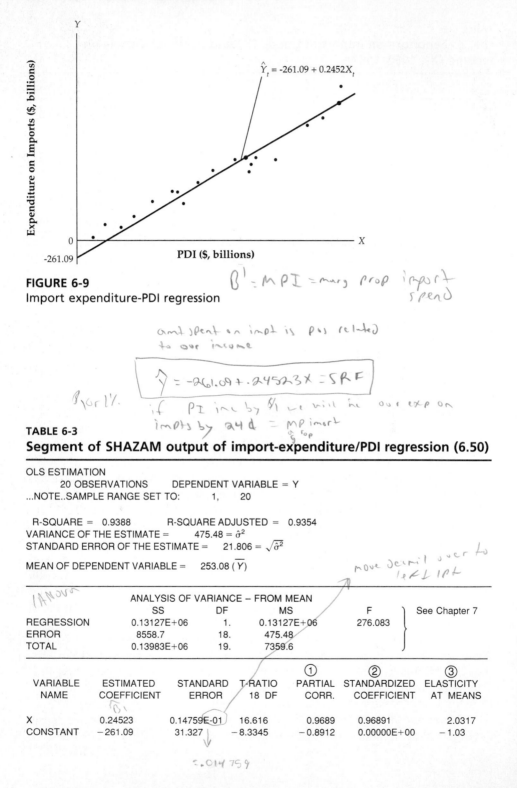

FIGURE 6-9
Import expenditure-PDI regression

(handwritten notes)

$\beta' = MPI =$ marg prop import spend

amt spent on impt is pos related to our income

$\hat{Y} = -261.09 + .24523X = SRF$

β or 1%.   if PI inc by $1 we will inc our exp on impts by 24¢ = MP import

TABLE 6-3
Segment of SHAZAM output of import-expenditure/PDI regression (6.50)

OLS ESTIMATION
      20 OBSERVATIONS   DEPENDENT VARIABLE = Y
...NOTE..SAMPLE RANGE SET TO: 1,   20

  R-SQUARE = 0.9388   R-SQUARE ADJUSTED = 0.9354
VARIANCE OF THE ESTIMATE = 475.48 = $\hat{\sigma}^2$
STANDARD ERROR OF THE ESTIMATE = 21.806 = $\sqrt{\hat{\sigma}^2}$

MEAN OF DEPENDENT VARIABLE = 253.08 $(\bar{Y})$

(handwritten) move decimal over to left 1 pt

(handwritten) IANOVA

ANALYSIS OF VARIANCE – FROM MEAN				
	SS	DF	MS	F
REGRESSION	0.13127E+06	1.	0.13127E+06	276.083
ERROR	8558.7	18.	475.48	
TOTAL	0.13983E+06	19.	7359.6	

See Chapter 7

VARIABLE NAME	ESTIMATED COEFFICIENT	STANDARD ERROR	T-RATIO 18 DF	① PARTIAL CORR.	② STANDARDIZED COEFFICIENT	③ ELASTICITY AT MEANS
X	0.24523	0.14759E-01	16.616	0.9689	0.96891	2.0317
CONSTANT	-261.09	31.327	-8.3345	-0.8912	0.00000E+00	-1.03

(handwritten) =.014759

[handwritten: ŷ predicted y   OLY Y x/list]

[handwritten: zero line]

OBS. NO.	OBSERVED VALUE (Y_i)	PREDICTED VALUE ($\hat{Y}_i$)	CALCULATED RESIDUAL (= e_i)	⑦
1	135.70	119.34	16.364	I *
2	144.60	131.23	13.370	I *
3	150.90	147.98	2.9212	I*
4	166.20	162.77	3.4338	I*
5	190.70	179.69	11.013	I *
6	218.20	208.85	9.3548	I *
7	211.80	204.09	7.7123	I *
8	187.90	212.62	−24.722	* I
9	229.90	229.62	0.28372	*
10	259.40	245.70	13.697	I *
11	274.10	270.42	3.6772	I*
12	277.90	281.51	−3.6072	*I
13	253.60	281.92	−28.324	* I
14	258.70	290.34	−31.636	* I
15	249.50	293.50	−43.999	* I
16	282.20	310.76	−28.563	* I
17	351.10	344.58	6.5193	I*
18	367.90	362.48	5.4174	I*
19	412.30	386.54	25.760	I *
20	439.00	397.67	41.327	I *

④DURBIN-WATSON = 0.5951   ④VON NEUMAN RATIO = 0.6264   ④RHO = −0.73339
RESIDUAL SUM = −0.17764E−12   RESIDUAL VARIANCE = 475.48 ($\hat{\sigma}^2$)
SUM OF ABSOLUTE ERRORS= 321.70 = $|e_i|$
⑤R-SQUARE BETWEEN OBSERVED AND PREDICTED = 0.9388 (= R^2)
⑥RUNS TEST: 5 RUNS,   14 POSITIVE,   6 NEGATIVE, NORMAL STATISTIC = −2.4326

Source: SHAZAM output based on Table 6-2.
Notes: ① See Chap. 10.

② Obtained by regressing $[(Y_i - \overline{Y})/s_y]$ on $[(X_i - \overline{X})/s_x]$. These are called standardized variables. In such a regression the intercept value is zero.

③ Elasticity = slope $(\overline{X}/\overline{Y})$ where $\overline{X}$ and $\overline{Y}$ are means of X and Y.
④ Discussed in Chap. 12.
⑤ See problem 6.5.
⑥ See Chap. 12.
⑦ Residual graph (see Chaps. 11 and 12).

[handwritten: e should not have any systematic pattern in its behavior. There should be no pattern]

this would mean the average consumption expenditure on imported goods if the PDI is zero. Common sense suggests that in this case the expenditure should also be zero. (Why?) Unfortunately, the estimated intercept usually turns out to be different from zero, and therefore frequently it has no concrete economic meaning. Most often it is just a mathematical entity, although in some cases it can be given specific economic meaning. We will have more to say about the intercept when we discuss specific examples.

Although the raw data needed to estimate the regression are given in problem 6.16, the calculations presented here are based on the *SHAZAM* computer package, of which the actual *SHAZAM* printout follows (see Table 6-3).

Following the format of Eq. (6.48), the regression results are

$$\hat{Y}_t = -261.09 + 0.24523X_t \qquad r^2 = 0.9388$$

$$\text{se} = \quad (31.327) \qquad (0.0148) \qquad \text{d.f.} = 18 \qquad\qquad (6.50)$$

$$t = (-8.334) \qquad (16.6160)$$

The estimated regression line is also shown in Figure 6-9.

Interpretation of Regression Results

As regression (6.50) and Figure 6-9 show, as expected, there is a positive relationship between the expenditure on imports and the PDI. The slope coefficient of 0.2452 means that the *marginal propensity to spend* on imported goods is ≈24 cents, meaning that if the PDI increases by a dollar, on the average the consumption expenditure on imports goes up by ≈24 cents. Also, as expected, the MPS, although positive, is less than 1.

The intercept value of ≈ −261 means that the average expenditure on imports would be minus (−) $261 billions if the PDI were zero. As remarked several times, the intercept term may not have any economic significance, as in this case.

The r^2 value of 0.9388 means that ≈94 percent of the variation in expenditure on imported goods is explained by our model, that is, by the single explanatory variable PDI. Considering that r^2 at most can be 1, the observed r^2 is quite high, indicating that the model we have chosen fits the actual data quite well.

Statistical Significance of Results

Are the estimated regression coefficients statistically significant; that is, are they statistically significantly different from zero? The answer to this question can be obtained quickly from the estimated regression, Eq. (6.50). First, consider the slope coefficient. Under the null hypothesis that the true slope coefficient is zero, we see that the computed t value is 16.616. (See the discussion in Section 6.7.) Do we reject this null hypothesis? As discussed earlier, if the computed t value exceeds the *critical t* value for a given α and d.f., we can reject the null hypothesis. For our example, the d.f. are 18 (why?), and if we choose $\alpha = 5\%$ and assume the alternative hypothesis H_1—that the true B_2 is greater than zero (why this hypothesis?)—then the *right-tailed* critical t value is

$$t_{0.05,18} = 1.734$$

Since the computed t value of 16.62 far exceeds the critical t value, following our t-testing procedure, we can reject the null hypothesis that PDI has no impact on the expenditure on imported goods. (The exact p value of obtaining a t value of 16.62 or greater is $1.125/10^{12}$, an extremely small number.) The same conclusion is reached if we use the *confidence interval approach*. To establish this interval, we use Eq. (6.26) to obtain

$$P[b_2 - t_{a/2,\text{df}} \, \text{se}(b_2) \leq B_2 \leq b_2 + t_{a/2,\text{df}} \, \text{se}(b_2)] = (1 - \alpha) \qquad (6.51)$$

If we use $\alpha = 5\%$, then $t_{a/2,18} = 2.101$ and Eq. (6.51) becomes

$$[0.24523 - 2.101(0.014759) \leq B_2 \leq 0.24523 + 2.101(0.014759)]$$

That is,

$$0.2142 \leq B_2 \leq 0.2762 \qquad (6.52)$$

which is the 95% confidence interval for B_2. Obviously, the null-hypothesized value of $B_2 = 0$ does not lie in the 95% confidence interval, or the region of acceptance; it lies in the region of rejection. Hence, we reject this particular null hypothesis.

In short, the confidence interval and the t test of significance approaches yield the identical conclusion in the present example, which is not surprising. (Why?)

It is left to the reader to show that the estimated intercept is also statistically significant on the basis of the confidence interval and the t test, although in the present instance the intercept does not have an economic meaning.

6.10 A WORD ABOUT FORECASTING

Based on the historical data for the period 1968 to 1987, we obtained the import demand function (actually, consumption expenditure on imported goods), shown in Eq. (6.50). Can we use it for *forecasting*, that is, for predicting what the average, or mean, consumption expenditure on imported goods will be if the PDI were a given number? This may be called the *mean forecast*. The answer is yes.

To fix the ideas, assume that the variable X (PDI) takes the value X_0, where X_0 is a *specified* numerical value of X, e.g., $X_0 = \$2800$, say, for the year 1988. Now suppose we want to estimate $E(Y \mid X_0)$ for 1988, that is, the true mean consumption expenditure for 1988 corresponding to the given level of PDI.

Now let

$$\hat{Y}_0 = \text{the estimator of } E(Y \mid X_0) \qquad (6.53)$$

How do we obtain this estimate? Under the assumptions of the CLRM, it can be shown that Eq. (6.53) can be obtained by simply putting the given value of X in Eq. (6.50) as follows:

$$\hat{Y}_{1988} = -261.09 + 0.24523(2800)$$
$$= 425.556 \qquad (6.54)$$

That is, the forecasted mean expenditure on imported goods for 1988 is about 426 billions of (1982) dollars.

Although econometric theory shows that under CLRM $\hat{Y}_{1988}$ or, more generally, $\hat{Y}_0$, is an unbiased estimator of the true mean value (i.e., a point on the population regression line), it is not likely to be equal to the latter in any given sample. (Why?) The difference between them is called the **forecasting** or **prediction error.** To assess this error, we need to find out the sampling distribution of $\hat{Y}_0$.[16] Given the assumptions of the CLRM, it can be shown that $\hat{Y}_0$ is *normally distributed* with the following mean and variance:

$$\text{Mean} = E(Y \mid X_0) = B_1 + B_2 X_0 \tag{6.55}$$

$$\text{var} = \sigma^2 \left[\frac{1}{n} + \frac{(X_0 - \overline{X})^2}{\sum x_i^2} \right] \tag{6.56}$$

where

$\overline{X}$ = the sample mean of X values in the historical regression (6.50)

$\sum x_i^2$ = their sum of squared deviations from $\overline{X}$

σ^2 = the variance of u_i

n = sample size

The positive square root of Equation (6.56) gives the standard error of $\hat{Y}_0$, $se(\hat{Y}_0)$.

Since in practice σ^2 is not known, if we replace it by its unbiased estimator $\hat{\sigma}^2$, $\hat{Y}_0$ follows the t distribution with $(n - 2)$ d.f. (Why?) Therefore, we can use the t distribution to establish a 100 $(1 - \alpha)\%$ confidence interval for the true (i.e., population) mean value of Y corresponding to X_0 in the usual manner as follows:

$$P[b_1 + b_2 X_0 - t_{a/2} \, se(\hat{Y}_0)] \leq B_1 + B_2 X_0 \leq b_1 + b_2 X_0 + t_{a/2} \, se(\hat{Y}_0) \tag{6.57}$$
$$= (1 - \alpha)$$

Let us continue with our import expenditure/PDI example. First, we compute the variance of $\hat{Y}_{1988}$ from Eq. (6.56):

$$\text{var } \hat{Y}_{1988} = 475.48 \left[\frac{1}{20} + \frac{(2800 - 2096.7)^2}{2182851} \right] \tag{6.58}$$
$$= 131.5243$$

Therefore,

$$se(\hat{Y}_0) = \sqrt{131.5243} = 11.46840 \tag{6.59}$$

Note: In the present example $\overline{X} = 2096.7$, $\sum x_i^2 = 2{,}182{,}851$ and $\hat{\sigma}^2 = 475.48$.

---

[16] Note that $\hat{Y}_0$ is an estimator and therefore will have a sampling distribution.

The preceding result suggests that given the estimated PDI of $2800 billions, the mean predicted import consumption expenditure, as shown in Eq. (6.54), is $425.47 billions and the standard error of this predicted value is ≈$12.4 billions.

Now if we want to establish, say, a 95% confidence interval for the population mean consumption expenditure for 1988, we obtain it from expression (6.57) as

$$425.556 - 2.101(11.4684) \le E(Y \mid X_0 = 2800) \le 425.556 + 2.101(11.4684)$$

That is,

$$401.4609 \le E(Y \mid X_0 = 2800) \le 449.651 \tag{6.60}$$

Note: For 18 d.f., the 5 percent two-tailed t value is 2.101.

Given the PDI of $2800 billions for 1988, Equation (6.60) states that although the single best, or point, estimate of the mean consumption expenditure on imports for 1988 is $425.56 billions, it is expected to lie in the interval $401.46 to $449.65 billions with 95% confidence. Therefore, with 95% confidence, the forecast error will be between $24.10 (401.46 − 425.56) and $24.10 (449.46 − 425.55) billions.

If we obtain a 95% confidence interval like Eq. (6.60) for each X value shown in Table 6-2, we obtain what is known as the *confidence interval* or

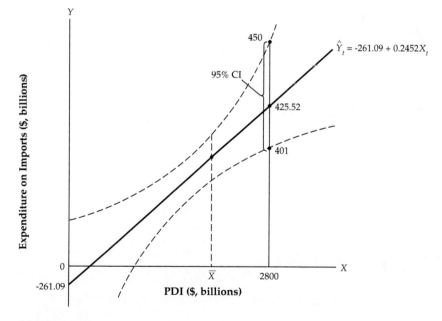

FIGURE 6-10
95% confidence interval for mean import expenditure.

confidence band for the true mean consumption expenditure for each X, that is, for the entire population regression line. This can be seen clearly from Figure 6-10.

Notice some interesting aspects of Figure 6-10. The width of the confidence band is smallest when $X_0 = \overline{X}$, which should be apparent from the variance formula given in Eq. (6.56). However, the width widens sharply (i.e., the prediction error increases) as X_0 moves away from $\overline{X}$. This suggests that the predictive ability of the historical regression, such as regression (6.50), falls markedly as X_0 (the X value for which the forecast is made) departs progressively from $\overline{X}$. The message here is clear: *One should exercise great caution in "extrapolating" the historical regression line to predict the mean value of Y associated with any X that is far removed from the sample mean of X. In more practical terms, one should not use the import expenditure regression (6.50) to predict the average import expenditure in the year, say, 2001.*

6.11   SUMMARY

In the previous chapter we showed how to estimate the parameters of the two-variable linear regression model. In this chapter we showed how the estimated model can be used for the purpose of drawing inferences about the true population regression model. Although the two-variable model is the simplest possible linear regression model, the ideas introduced in these two chapters are the foundation of the more involved multiple regression models that we discuss in ensuing chapters. As we will see, in many ways the multiple regression model is a straightforward extension of the two-variable model.

Key Terms and Concepts

The key terms and concepts introduced in this chapter are:

Classical linear regression model
   (CLRM)
Homoscedasticity or equal variance
Heteroscedasticity or unequal variance
Autocorrelation and no autocorrelation
Variances of OLS estimators
Standard errors of OLS estimators
   a) standard error of estimate, or
      standard error of the regression
BLUE property; Gauss-Markov theorem
Sampling, or probability, distributions
   of OLS estimators

Central limit theorem (CLT)
The t test of significance
   a) two-tailed t test
   b) one-tailed t test
χ^2 test of significance
The coefficient of determination, r^2
Total sum of squares (TSS)
Explained sum of squares (ESS)
Residual sum of squares (RSS)
The coefficient of correlation, r
Marginal propensity to spend (MPS)
Forecasting, or prediction, error

QUESTIONS

6.1. Explain the meaning of

(a) Least squares

(b) OLS estimators

(c) The variance of an estimator

(d) Standard error of an estimator

(e) Homoscedasticity

(f) Heteroscedasticity

(g) Autocorrelation

(h) Total sum of squares (TSS)

(i) Explained sum of squares (ESS)

(j) Residual sum of squares (RSS)

(k) r^2

(l) Standard error of estimate

(m) BLUE

(n) A test of significance

(o) The t test

(p) One-tailed test

(q) Two-tailed test

(r) Statistically significant

6.2. State with brief reasons whether the following statements are true, false, or uncertain.

(a) OLS is an estimating procedure that minimizes the sum of the errors squared, Σu_i^2.

(b) The assumptions made by the classical linear regression model (CLRM) are not necessary to compute OLS estimators.

(c) The theoretical justification for OLS is provided by the Gauss-Markov theorem.

(d) In the two-variable PRF b_2 is likely to be a more accurate estimate of B_2 if the disturbances u_i follow the normal distribution.

(e) The OLS estimators b_1 and b_2 each follow the normal distribution only if u_i follows the normal distribution.

(f) r^2 is the ratio of TSS/ESS.

(g) For a given α and d.f., if the computed $|t|$ exceeds the critical t value, we should accept the null hypothesis.

(h) The coefficient of correlation, r, has the same sign as the slope coefficient b_2.

6.3. Fill in the appropriate gaps in the following statements:

(a) If $B_2 = 0$, $b_2/\text{se}(b_2) = \ldots$

(b) If $B_2 = 0$, $t = b_2/\ldots$

(c) r^2 lies between . . . and . . .

(d) r lies between . . . and . . .

(e) TSS = RSS + $\cdots$

(f) d.f. (of TSS) = d.f. (of . . .) + d.f. (of RSS)

(g) $\hat{\sigma}$ is called . . .

(h) $\Sigma y_i^2 = \Sigma(Y_i - \cdots)^2$

(i) $\Sigma \hat{y}_i^2 = b^2 (\ldots)$

6.4. Consider the following regression:

$$\hat{Y}_i = -66.1058 + 0.0650\, X_i$$

$$\text{se} = \quad (10.7509) \quad (\quad) \qquad r^2 = 0.9460$$

$$t = \quad (\quad) \quad (18.73) \qquad n = 20$$

Fill in the missing numbers. Can you accept the hypothesis that true B_2 is zero at $\alpha = 5\%$? Tell whether you are using a one-tailed or two-tailed test and why.

6.5. Show that all the following formulas to compute r^2 are equivalent:

$$r^2 = 1 - \frac{\sum e_i^2}{\sum y_i^2}$$

$$= \frac{\sum \hat{y}_i^2}{\sum y_i^2}$$

$$= \frac{b_2^2 \sum x_i^2}{\sum y_i^2}$$

$$= \frac{\left(\sum y_i \hat{y}_i\right)^2}{\left(\sum y_i^2\right)\left(\sum \hat{y}_i^2\right)}$$

6.6. Show that $\sum e_i = n\overline{Y} - nb_1 - nb_2\overline{X} = 0$

PROBLEMS

6.7. Based on the data for the years 1962 to 1977 for the United States, Dale Bails and Larry Peppers[17] obtained the following demand function for automobiles:

$$\hat{Y}_t = 5807 + 3.24X_t$$

$$se = \qquad (1.634) \qquad r^2 = 0.22$$

where Y = retail sales of passenger cars (thousands) and X = the real disposable income (billions of 1972 dollars).

Note: se for b_1 is not given.

(a) Establish a 95% confidence interval for B_2.

(b) Test the hypothesis that $B_2 = 0$ lies in this interval. If not, would you accept this null hypothesis?

(c) Compute the t value under H_0: $B_2 = 0$. Is it statistically significant at the 5% level? Which t test do you use, one tailed or two-tailed, and why?

6.8. The *characteristic line* of modern investment analysis involves running the following regression:

$$r_t = B_1 + B_2 r_{mt} + u_t$$

where

r = the rate of return on a stock or security

r_m = the rate of return on the market portfolio represented by a broad market index such as S&P 500

t = time

---

[17] See Dale G. Bails and Larry C. Peppers, *Business Fluctuations: Forecasting Techniques and Applications*, Prentice-Hall, Englewood Cliffs, N.J., 1982, p. 147.

In investment analysis B_2 is known as the *beta coefficient* of the security and is used as a measure of market risk, that is, how developments in the market affect the fortunes of a given company.

Based on 240 monthly rates of return for the period 1956–1976, Fogler and Ganapathy obtained the following results for IBM stock; the market index used by the authors is the market portfolio index developed at the University of Chicago:[18]

$$\hat{r}_t = 0.7264 + 1.0598 r_{mt}$$

$$se = (0.3001) \quad (0.0728) \qquad r^2 = 0.4710$$

(a) Interpret the estimated intercept and slope.
(b) How would you interpret r^2?
(c) A security whose beta coefficient is greater than 1 is called a volatile or aggressive security. Set up the appropriate null and alternative hypotheses and test them using the t test.

Note: Use $\alpha = 5\%$.

6.9. You are given the following data based on 10 pairs of observations on Y and X.

$$\sum Y_i = 1110; \quad \sum X_i = 1680; \quad \sum X_i Y_i = 204{,}200$$
$$\sum X_i^2 = 315{,}400; \quad \sum Y_i^2 = 133{,}300$$

Assuming all the assumptions of CLRM are fulfilled, obtain
(a) b_1 and b_2
(b) standard errors of these estimators
(c) r^2
(d) Establish 95% confidence intervals for B_1 and B_2
(e) On the basis of the confidence intervals established in (d), can you accept the hypothesis that $B_2 = 0$?

6.10. Based on the data for the United States for the period 1970 to 1983, the following regression results were obtained:

$$\widehat{GNP}_t = -787.4723 + 8.0863 \, M_{1t}$$

$$se = (\quad) \quad (0.2197) \qquad r^2 = 0.9912$$
$$t = (-10.10001) \quad (\quad)$$

where GNP is the gross national product ($, in billions) and M_1 is the money supply ($, billions).
Note: M_1 includes currency, demand deposits, travelers checks, and other checkable deposits.
(a) Fill in the blank parentheses.
(b) The monetarists maintain that money supply has a significant positive impact on GNP. How would you test this hypothesis?
(c) What is the meaning of the negative intercept?
(d) Suppose M_1 for 1984 is $552 billion. What is the mean forecast value of GNP for that year?

---

[18] H. Russell Fogler and Sundaram Ganapathy, *Financial Econometrics*. Prentice-Hall, Englewood-Cliffs, N.J., 1982, p. 13.

6.11. *Political business cycle*: Do economic events affect presidential elections? To test this so-called political business cycle theory, Gary Smith[19] obtained the following regression results based on the U.S. presidential elections for the four yearly periods from 1928 to 1980 (i.e., the data are for years 1928, 1932, etc.):

$$\hat{Y}_t = 53.10 - 1.70X_t$$

$$t = (34.10) \quad (2.67) \qquad r^2 = 0.37$$

where Y is the % vote received by the incumbent and X is the unemployment rate change—unemployment rate in an election year minus the unemployment rate in the preceding year.

(a) A priori, what is the expected sign of X?

(b) Do the results support the political business cycle theory? Support your contention with appropriate calculations.

(c) Do the results of the 1984 and 1988 presidential elections support the preceding theory?

(d) How would you compute the standard errors of b_1 and b_2?

6.12. To study the relationship between capacity utilization in manufacturing and inflation in the United States, Thomas A. Gittings[20] obtained the following regression results based on the annual data from 1971 to 1988:

$$\hat{Y}_t = -70.85 + 0.8880X_t$$

$$t = (-5.89) \quad (5.90) \qquad r^2 = 0.685$$

where Y = changes in inflation as measured by the wholesale price index and X = the capacity utilization rate.

(a) A priori, would you expect a positive relationship between Y and X? Why?

(b) How would you interpret the slope coefficient?

(c) Is the estimated slope coefficient statistically significant?

(d) Is it statistically different from unity?

(e) The natural rate of capacity utilization is defined as the rate at which Y is zero. What is this rate for the period under study?

6.13. Table 6-4 gives data on X [net profits after tax in U.S. manufacturing industries ($, in millions)] and Y [cash dividend paid quarterly in manufacturing industries ($, in millions)] for years 1974 to 1986.

(a) What relationship, if any, do you expect between cash dividend and after-tax profits?

(b) Plot the scattergram between Y and X.

(c) Does the scattergram support your expectations in part (a)?

(d) If so, do an OLS regression of Y on X and obtain the usual statistics.

(e) Establish a 99% confidence interval for the true slope and test the hypothesis that the true slope coefficient is zero; that is, there is no relationship between the dividend and the after-tax profit.

---

[19] Gary Smith, *Statistical Reasoning*, Allyn & Bacon, Boston, Mass., 1985, p. 488. Change in notation was made to conform with our format. The original data were obtained by Ray C. Fair, "The Effect of Economic Events on Votes for President," *The Review of Economics and Statistics*, May 1978, pp. 159–173.

[20] See Thomas A. Gittings, "Capacity Utilization and Inflation," *Economic Perspectives*, Federal Reserve Bank of Chicago, May/June 1989, p. 4.

TABLE 6-4

Cash dividend (Y) and after-tax profits (X), in U.S. manufacturing industries, 1974–1986

Year	Y	X	Year	Y	X
	($, in millions)				($, in millions)	
1974	19,467	58,747	1981	40,317	101,302
1975	19,968	49,135	1982	41,259	71,028
1976	22,763	64,519	1983	41,624	85,834
1977	26,585	70,366	1984	45,102	107,648
1978	28,932	81,148	1985	45,517	87,648
1979	32,491	98,698	1986	46,044	83,121
1980	36,495	92,579			

Source: Business Statistics, 1986, U.S. Department of Commerce, Bureau of Economic Analysis, December 1987, p. 72.

6.14. *Earnings-productivity relationship.* Table 6-5 gives data on indexes (1977 = 100) of real compensation per hour (Y) and output per hour of all persons (X) for the U.S. business sector for the period 1973 to 1987.
   (a) Economic theory postulates a positive relationship between earnings and productivity. Plot a scattergram of Y against X and see if the postulated relationship holds.
   (b) If it does, do an OLS regression of Y on X.
   (c) How do you decide whether earnings is a function of productivity or productivity is a function of earnings?

6.15. *Regression through the origin: Regression model without the intercept.* There are occasions when the two-variable PRF assumes the following form:

$$Y_i = B_2 X_i + u_i$$

TABLE 6-5

Indexes of real compensation per hour (Y) and output per hour (X) (1977 = 100), U.S. business sector, 1973–1987

Year	Y	X	Year	Y	X
1973	96.8	95.9	1981	95.8	100.7
1974	95.4	93.9	1982	97.3	100.3
1975	96.0	95.7	1983	98.2	103.0
1976	98.8	98.3	1984	97.9	105.5
1977	100.0	100.0	1985	98.8	107.7
1978	100.9	100.8	1986	101.2	110.1
1979	99.4	99.6	1987	101.5	111.0
1980	96.7	99.3			

Source: Economic Report of the President, 1989, Table B-46, p. 360

TABLE 6-6
Rate of return on a security (Y) and the market rate of return (X)

Y	X
67.5	19.5
19.2	8.5
−35.2	−29.3
−42.0	−26.5
63.7	61.9
19.3	45.5
3.6	9.5
20.0	14.0
40.3	35.3

In this model the intercept term is absent or zero. The model is therefore known as *regression through the origin* or *zero-intercept model*. For this model it can be shown that

$$b_2 = \frac{\sum X_i Y_i}{\sum X_i^2}$$

$$\text{var}(b_2) = \frac{\sigma^2}{\sum X_i^2}$$

$$\hat{\sigma}^2 = \frac{\sum e_i^2}{n - 1}$$

Warning: For the regression through the origin, the usual r^2 formula to compute the coefficient of determination is not applicable.[21]

(a) Compare this model with the usual two-variable model and point out the difference between the two.

(b) Why are the d.f. for this model $(n - 1)$ and not $(n - 2)$?

(c) Consider the data in Table 6-6, where Y is the rate of return on a security and X is the rate of return on a market index, both in percentages, for a period of 10 years.

   (1) Fit a regression through the origin model to these data.
   (2) Fit a regression model with the intercept present.
   (3) Based on your results, which model would you prefer? And why?

---

[21] On this topic, see Dennis J. Aigner, *Basic Econometrics*, Prentice-Hall, Englewood Cliffs, N.J., 1971, pp. 85–90.

6.16. The raw data underlying the expenditure on imports and PDI regression given in Eq. (6.50) are as follows: Using these data, verify the regression results given in Eq. (6.50), keeping in mind that because of roundoffs there will be some differences in the two answers.

$$\bar{Y} = 253.08; \quad \bar{X} = 2096.7; \quad \sum(Y_i - \bar{Y})^2 = 139{,}830$$

$$\sum(X_i - \bar{X})^2 = 2{,}182{,}900; \quad \sum(Y_i - \bar{Y})(X_i - \bar{X}) = 535{,}300; \quad n = 20$$

6.17. Refer to the S.A.T. data given in Table 5-5. Suppose you want to predict the male math scores on the basis of the female math scores by running the following regression:

$$Y_t = B_1 + B_2X_t + u_t$$

where Y and X denote the male and female math scores, respectively.
(a) Estimate the preceding regression, obtaining the usual summary statistics.
(b) Test the hypothesis that there is no relationship between Y and X whatsoever.
(c) Suppose the female math score in 1991 is expected to be 460. What is the predicted (average) male math score?
(d) Establish a 95% confidence interval for the predicted value in part (c).

6.18. Repeat the exercise in problem 6.17 but let Y and X denote the male and the female verbal scores respectively. Assume a female verbal score for 1991 of 425.

6.19. Consider the following regression results:[22]

$$\hat{Y}_t = -0.17 + 5.26X_t$$

$$t = (-1.73)\ (2.71) \qquad \bar{R}^2 = 0.10, \text{Durbin-Watson} = 2.01$$

where

$Y =$ the real return on the stock price index from January of the current year to January of the following year

$X =$ the total dividends in the preceding year divided by the stock price index for July of the preceding year

$t =$ times

The time period covered by the study was 1926 to 1982.
Note: $\bar{R}^2$ stands for the adjusted coefficient of determination. The Durbin-Watson value is a measure of autocorrelation. Both measures are explained in subsequent chapters.
(a) How would you interpret the preceding regression?
(b) If the previous results are acceptable to you, does that mean the best investment strategy is to invest in the stock market when the dividend/price ratio is high?
(c) If you want to know the answer to part (b), read Shiller's analysis.[23]

---

[22] See Robert J. Shiller, *Market Volatility*, MIT Press, Cambridge, Mass., 1989, p. 32–36.
[23] *Ibid.*

CHAPTER
7

MULTIPLE REGRESSION: ESTIMATION AND HYPOTHESIS TESTING

In the two-variable linear regression model that we have considered so far there was a single independent, or explanatory, variable. In this chapter we extend that model by considering the possibility that more than one explanatory variable may influence the dependent variable. A regression model with more than one explanatory variable is known as a **multiple regression model,** multiple because *multiple influences* (i.e., variables) affect the dependent variable.

For example, consider the recent S&L (savings and loan) crisis resulting from the bankruptcies of some S&L institutions in several states. Suppose we want to develop a regression model to explain bankruptcy, the dependent variable. Now a phenomenon such as bankruptcy is too complex to be explained by a single explanatory variable; several variables may be entailed in the explanation, such as the ratio of primary capital to total assets, ratio of loans that are more than 90 days past due to total assets, ratio of nonaccruing loans to total assets, ratio of renegotiated loans to total assets, ratio of net income to total assets, etc.[1] To include all these variables in a regression model to allow for the multiplicity of influences affecting bankruptcies, we have to consider a multiple regression model.

Needless to say, one could cite hundreds of examples of multiple regression models. In fact, most regression models are multiple regression models

---

[1] As a matter of fact, these were some variables that were considered by the Board of Governors of the Federal Reserve system in their internal studies of bankrupt banks.

because very few economic phenomena can be explained by only a single explanatory variable, as in the case of the two-variable model.

In this chapter we discuss the multiple regression model with a view to seeking answers to the following questions:

1. How do we estimate the multiple regression model? Is the estimating procedure any different from that for the two-variable model?
2. Is the hypothesis-testing procedure any different from the two-variable model?
3. Are there any unique features of multiple regression that we did not encounter in the two-variable case?
4. Since a multiple regression can have any number of explanatory variables, how do we decide how many variables to include in any given situation?

To answer these and other related questions, we first consider the simplest of the multiple regression models, namely, the three-variable model in which the behavior of the dependent variable Y is examined in relation to two explanatory variables, X_2 and X_3. Once the three-variable model is clearly understood, the extension to the four, five, or more variables case is quite straightforward, although the arithmetic gets a bit tedious. (But in this age of high-speed computers, that should not be a worrisome problem.) It is interesting that the three-variable model itself is in many ways a clear-cut extension of the two-variable model, as the following discussion reveals.

7.1 THE THREE-VARIABLE LINEAR REGRESSION MODEL

Generalizing the two-variable population regression function (PRF), we can write the three-variable population regression function (PRF) in its nonstochastic form as

$$E(Y_t) = B_1 + B_2 X_{2t} + B_3 X_{3t} \qquad (7.1)^2$$

and in the stochastic form as

$$Y_t = B_1 + B_2 X_{2t} + B_3 X_{3t} + u_t \qquad (7.2)$$

$$= E(Y_t) + u_t \qquad (7.3)$$

where

---

[2] Equation (7.1) can also be written as

$$E(Y_t) = B_1 X_{1t} + B_2 X_{2t} + B_3 X_{3t}$$

with the understanding that $X_{1t} = 1$ for each observation. The presentation in Eq. (7.1) is for notational convenience in that the subscripts on the parameters or their estimators match the subscripts on the variables to which they are attached.

$$Y = \text{the dependent variable}$$

$$X_2 \text{ and } X_3 = \text{the explanatory variables}$$

$$u = \text{the stochastic disturbance term}$$

$$t = \text{the } i\text{th observation}$$

In case the data are cross-sectional, the subscript i will denote the ith observation. Note that we introduce u in the three-variable, or, more generally, in the multivariable model for the same reason that it was introduced in the two-variable case.

B_1 is the intercept term. As before, it represents the average value of Y when X_2 and X_3 are set equal to zero. The coefficients B_2 and B_3 are called *partial regression coefficients*, whose meaning will be explained shortly.

Following the discussion in Chapter 5, Equation (7.1) gives the *conditional mean* value of Y conditional upon the given or fixed values of the variables X_2 and X_3. Therefore, as in the two-variable case, multiple regression analysis is *conditional regression* analysis, conditional upon the given or fixed values of the explanatory variables, and we obtain *the average, or mean, value of Y for the fixed values of the X variables*: Recall that the PRF gives the (conditional) means of the Y populations corresponding to the given levels of the explanatory variables, X_2 and X_3.[3]

The stochastic version, Eq. (7.2), states that any individual Y value can be expressed as the sum of two components:

1. A systematic, or *deterministic*, component, $(B_1 + B_2 X_{2t} + B_3 X_{3t})$, which is simply its mean value $E(Y_t)$ (i.e., the point on the population regression line, PRL),[4] and
2. u_t, which is the *nonsystematic*, or *random*, component, determined by factors other than X_2 and X_3.

All this is familiar territory from the two-variable case; the only point to note is that we now have two explanatory variables instead of one explanatory variable.

Notice that Eq. (7.1), or its stochastic counterpart Eq. (7.2), is a *linear regression model*—a model that is *linear in the parameters*, the Bs. As noted in Chapter 5, our concern in this book is with regression models that are linear in the parameters; such models may or may not be linear in the variables (but more on this in Chapter 8).

---

[3] Unlike the two-variable case, we cannot show this diagrammatically because to represent the three variables Y, X_2, and X_3, we have to use a three-dimensional diagram, which is difficult to visualize on two-dimensional paper. But by stretching the imagination, we can visualize a diagram similar to Figure 5-1.

[4] Geometrically, the PRL in this case represents what is known as a plane.

The Meaning of Partial Regression Coefficient

As mentioned earlier, the regression coefficients B_2 and B_3 are known as **partial regression** or **partial slope coefficients.** The meaning of the partial regression coefficient is as follows: B_2 measures the *change* in the mean value of Y, $E(Y)$, per unit change in X_2, holding the value of X_3 constant. Likewise, B_3 measures the change in the mean value of Y per unit change in X_3, holding the value of X_2 constant. This is the unique feature of a multiple regression; in the two-variable case, since there was only a single explanatory variable, we did not have to worry about the presence of other explanatory variables in the model. In the multiple regression we want to find out what part of the change in the average value of Y can be "directly" attributable to X_2 and what part to X_3. Since this point is so crucial to understanding the logic of multiple regression, let us explain it by a simple example. Suppose we have the following PRF:

$$E(Y_t) = 15 - 1.2\,X_{2t} + 0.8X_{3t} \tag{7.4}$$

Let X_3 be held constant at the value 10. Putting this value in Equation (7.4), we obtain

$$\begin{aligned} E(Y_t) &= 15 - 1.2X_{2t} + 0.8(10) \\ &= (15 + 8) - 1.2X_{2t} \\ &= 23 - 1.2X_{2t} \end{aligned} \tag{7.5}$$

Here the slope coefficient $B_2 = -1.2$ indicates that the mean value of Y decreases by 1.2 per unit increase in X_2 when X_3 is held constant—in this example it is held constant at 10 although any other value will do.[5] This slope coefficient is called the *partial regression coefficient.*[6] Likewise, if we hold X_2 constant, say, at the value 5, we obtain

$$\begin{aligned} E(Y_t) &= 15 - 1.2(5) + 0.8X_{3t} \\ &= 9 + 0.8X_{3t} \end{aligned} \tag{7.6}$$

Here the slope coefficient $B_3 = 0.8$ means that the mean value of Y increases by 0.8 per unit increase in X_3 when X_2 is held constant—here it is held constant at 5, but any other value will do just as well. This slope coefficient too is a partial regression coefficient.

In short, then, a partial regression coefficient reflects the (partial) effect of one explanatory variable on the mean value of the dependent variable when the values of other explanatory variables included in the model are held constant. This unique feature of multiple regression enables us not only to include more than one explanatory variable in the model but also to "isolate" or "disentangle" the

---

[5] As the algebra of Eq. (7.5) shows, it does not matter at what value X_3 is held constant, for that constant value multiplied by its coefficient will be a constant number, which will simply be added to the intercept.

[6] The mathematically minded reader will notice at once that B_2 is the partial derivative of $E(Y)$ with respect to X_2 and that B_3 is the partial derivative of $E(Y)$ with respect to X_3.

effect of each X variable on Y from the other X variables included in the model.

We will consider a concrete example in Section 7.4.

7.2 ASSUMPTIONS OF MULTIPLE LINEAR REGRESSION MODEL

As in the two-variable case, our first order of business is to estimate the regression coefficients of the multiple regression model. Toward that end, we continue to operate within the framework of the classical linear regression model (CLRM) first introduced in Chapter 6 and to use the method of ordinary least squares (OLS) to estimate the coefficients.

Specifically, for model (7.2), we assume (cf. Section 6.1):

A7.1. X_2 and X_3 are nonstochastic; that is, their values are fixed in repeated sampling.

A7.2. The error term u has a zero mean value; that is,

$$E(u_i) = 0 \tag{7.7}$$

A7.3. Homoscedasticity, that is, the variance of u, is constant:

$$\text{var}(u_i) = \sigma^2 \tag{7.8}$$

A7.4. No autocorrelation exists between the error terms u_i and u_j:

$$\text{cov}(u_i, u_j) \quad i \neq j \tag{7.9}$$

A7.5. No exact collinearity exists between X_2 and X_3; that is, there is no exact linear relationship between the two explanatory variables. This is a new assumption and is explained later.

A7.6. For hypothesis testing, the error term u follows the normal distribution with mean zero and (homoscedastic) variance σ^2. That is,

$$u_i \sim N(0, \sigma^2) \tag{7.10}$$

Except for assumption 7.5, the rationale for the other assumptions is the same as that discussed for the two-variable linear regression. As noted in the previous chapter, we make these assumptions to facilitate the development of the subject. In Part III we will revisit these assumptions and see what happens if one or more of them are not fulfilled in actual applications.

Assumption 7.5 that there is no exact linear relationship between the explanatory variables X_2 and X_3, technically known as the assumption of *no collinearity*, or no **multicollinearity**, if more than one exact linear relationship is involved, is new and needs some explanation.

Informally, no perfect collinearity means that a variable, say, X_2, cannot be expressed as an exact linear function of another variable, say, X_3. Thus, if we can express

$$X_{2i} = 3 + 2X_{3i}$$

or

$$X_{2i} = 4X_{3i}$$

then the two variables are **collinear,** for there is an **exact linear relationship** between X_2 and X_3. Assumption 7.5 states that this should not be the case. The logic here is quite simple. If, e.g., $X_2 = 4X_3$, then substituting this in Eq. (7.1), we see that

$$
\begin{aligned}
E(Y_i) &= B_1 + B_2(4X_{3i}) + B_3 X_3 i \\
&= B_1 + (4B_2 + B_3)X_{3i} \\
&= B_1 + AX_{3i}
\end{aligned}
\tag{7.11}
$$

where

$$A = 4B_2 + B_3 \tag{7.12}$$

Equation (7.11) is a two-variable model, not a three-variable model. Now even if we can estimate Eq. (7.11) and obtain an estimate of A, there is no way that we can get individual estimates of B_2 or B_3 from the estimated A. Note that since Eq. (7.12) is one equation with two unknowns we need two equations to obtain unique estimates of B_2 and B_3.

The upshot of this discussion is that in cases of perfect collinearity we cannot estimate the individual partial regression coefficients B_2 and B_3; in other words, we cannot assess the individual effect of X_2 and X_3 on Y. But this is hardly surprising, for we really do not have two independent variables in the model.

Although, in practice, the case of perfect collinearity is rare, the cases of **high** or **near perfect collinearity** abound. In a later chapter (see Chapter 10) we will examine this case more fully. For now we merely require that two or more explanatory variables do not have exact linear relationships among them.

7.3   ESTIMATION OF PARAMETERS OF MULTIPLE REGRESSION

To estimate the parameters of Eq. (7.2), we use the OLS method whose main features have already been discussed in Chapters 5 and 6.

Ordinary Least Squares (OLS) Estimators

To find the OLS estimators, let us first write the sample regression function (SRF) corresponding to the PRF Eq. (7.2), as follows:

$$Y_t = b_1 + b_2 X_{2t} + b_3 X_{3t} + e_t \qquad (7.13)$$

where, following the convention introduced in Chapter 5, e is the *residual term*, or simply the *residual*—the sample counterpart of u—and where the bs are the *estimators* of the population coefficients, the Bs. More specifically,

$$b_1 = \text{the estimator of } B_1$$

$$b_2 = \text{the estimator of } B_2$$

$$b_3 = \text{the estimator of } B_3$$

The sample counterpart of Eq. (7.1) is

$$\hat{Y}_t = b_1 + b_2 X_{2t} + b_3 X_{3t} \qquad (7.14)$$

which is the *estimated* population regression line (PRL) (actually a plane).

As explained in Chapter 5, the OLS principle chooses the values of the unknown parameters in such a way that the residual sum of squares (RSS) $\Sigma\, e_t^2$ is as small as possible. To do this, we first write Eq. (7.13) as

$$e_t = Y_t - b_1 - b_2 X_t - b_3 X_{3t} \qquad (7.15)$$

Squaring this equation on both sides and summing over the sample observations, we obtain

$$\text{RSS: } \sum e_t^2 = \sum (Y_t - b_1 - b_2 X_{2t} - b_3 X_{3t})^2 \qquad (7.16)$$

And in OLS we minimize this RSS (which is simply the sum of the squared difference between actual Y_t and estimated Y_t).

The minimization of Eq. (7.16) involves the calculus technique of differentiation. Without going into detail, this process of differentiation gives us the following equations, known as (least squares) *normal equations*, to help estimate the unknowns[7] [compare them with the corresponding equations given for the two-variable case in Eqs. (5.14) and (5.15)]:

---

[7] The mathematical details can be found in Damodar N. Gujarati, *Basic Econometrics*, 2d ed., McGraw-Hill, New York, 1988, pp. 205–206.

$$\overline{Y} = b_1 + b_2 X_2 + b_3 X_3 \tag{7.17}$$

$$\sum Y_t X_{2t} = b_1 \sum X_{2t} + b_2 \sum X_{2t}^2 + b_3 \sum X_{2t} X_{3t} \tag{7.18}$$

$$\sum Y_t X_{3t} = b_1 \sum X_{3t} + b_2 \sum X_{2t} X_{3t} + b_3 \sum X_{3t}^2 \tag{7.19}$$

where the summation is over the sample range 1 to n. Here we have three equations with three unknowns—the knowns are the variables Y and the Xs and the unknowns are the bs. Ordinarily, we should be able to solve three equations with three unknowns. By simple algebraic manipulations of the preceding equations, we obtain the three OLS estimators as follows:

$$b_1 = \overline{Y} - b_2 \overline{X}_2 - b_3 \overline{X}_3 \tag{7.20}$$

$$b_2 = \frac{\left(\sum y_t x_{2t}\right)\left(\sum x_{3t}^2\right) - \left(\sum y_t x_{3t}\right)\left(\sum x_{2t} x_{3t}\right)}{\left(\sum x_{2t}^2\right)\left(\sum x_{3t}^2\right) - \left(\sum x_{2t} x_{3t}\right)^2} \tag{7.21}$$

$$b_3 = \frac{\left(\sum y_t x_{3t}\right)\left(\sum x_{2t}^2\right) - \left(\sum y_t x_{2t}\right)\left(\sum x_{2t} x_{3t}\right)}{\left(\sum x_{2t}^2\right)\left(\sum x_{3t}^2\right) - \left(\sum x_{2t} x_{3t}\right)^2} \tag{7.22}$$

where, as usual, lowercase letters denote deviations from sample mean values (e.g., $y_t = Y_t - \overline{Y}$).

The reader will notice the similarity between these equations and the corresponding ones for the two-variable case given in Eqs. (5.16) and (5.17). Also, notice the following features of the preceding equations: (1) Equations (7.21) and (7.22) are symmetrical in that one can be obtained from the other by interchanging the roles of X_2 and X_1, and (2) the denominators of these two equations are identical.

Variance and Standard Errors of OLS Estimators

Having obtained the OLS estimators of the intercept and partial regression coefficients, we can derive the variances and standard errors of these estimators in the manner of the two-variable model. These variances or standard errors give us some idea about the variability of the estimators from sample to sample. As in the two-variable case, we need the standard errors for two main purposes: (1) to establish confidence intervals for the true parameter values and (2) to test statistical hypotheses. The relevant formulas, stated without proof, are as follows:

$$\text{var}(b_1) = \left[\frac{1}{n} + \frac{\overline{X}_2^2 \sum x_{3t}^2 + \overline{X}_3^2 \sum x_{2t}^2 - 2\overline{X}_2 \overline{X}_3 \sum x_{2t} x_{3t}}{\sum x_{2t}^2 \sum x_{3t}^2 - \left(\sum x_{2t} x_{3t} \right)^2} \right] \cdot \sigma^2 \qquad (7.23)$$

$$\text{se}(b_1) = \sqrt{\text{var}(b_1)} \qquad (7.24)$$

$$\text{var}(b_2) = \frac{\sum x_{3t}^2}{\left(\sum x_{2t}^2 \right) \left(\sum x_{3t}^2 \right) - \left(\sum x_{2t} x_{3t} \right)^2} \cdot \sigma^2 \qquad (7.25)$$

$$\text{se}(b_2) = \sqrt{\text{var}(b_2)} \qquad (7.26)$$

$$\text{var}(b_3) = \frac{\sum x_{2t}^2}{\left(\sum x_{2t}^2 \right) \left(\sum x_{3t}^2 \right) - \left(\sum x_{2t} x_{3t} \right)^2} \cdot \sigma^2 \qquad (7.27)$$

$$\text{se}(b_3) = \sqrt{\text{var}(b_3)} \qquad (7.28)$$

In all these formulas σ^2 is the (homoscedastic) variance of the population error term u_t. The OLS estimator of this unknown variance is

$$\hat{\sigma}^2 = \frac{\sum e_t^2}{n - 3} \qquad (7.29)$$

This formula is a straightforward extension of its two-variable companion given in Eq. (6.8) except that now the degrees of freedom (d.f.) are $(n - 3)$. This is because in estimating RSS, $\sum e_t^2$, we must first obtain b_1, b_2, and b_3, which consume, so to speak, 3 d.f. This argument is quite general: In the four-variable case the d.f. will be $(n - 4)$; in the five-variable case, $(n - 5)$; etc.

Also, note that the (positive) square root of $\hat{\sigma}^2$

$$\hat{\sigma} = \sqrt{\hat{\sigma}^2} \qquad (7.30)$$

is the *standard error of the estimate*, or the *standard error of the regression*, which, as noted in Chapter 6, is the standard deviation of Y values around the estimated regression line.

A word about computing $\sum e_t^2$. Since $\sum e_t^2 = (Y_t - \hat{Y}_t)^2$, to compute this expression, one has first to computer $\hat{Y}_t$, which the computer does very easily. But there is a shortcut to computing the RSS, which is

$$\sum e_t^2 = \sum y_t^2 - b_2 \sum y_t x_{2t} - b_3 \sum y_t x_{3t} \qquad (7.31)$$

which can be readily computed once the partial slopes are estimated.

Properties of OLS Estimators of Multiple Regression

In the two-variable case we saw that under assumed conditions the OLS estimators are *BLUE,* that is, they are best linear unbiased estimators. This property continues to hold for the multiple regression. Thus, each regression coefficient estimated by OLS is linear and unbiased—on the average it coincides with the true value. Among all such linear unbiased estimators, the OLS estimators have the least possible variance so that the true parameter can be estimated more accurately than by competing linear unbiased estimators.

As the preceding development shows, in many ways the three-variable model is an extension of its two-variable counterpart, although the estimating formulas are a bit involved. These formulas get much more involved and cumbersome once we go beyond the three-variable model. In that case, willy-nilly, one has to use matrix algebra, which expresses various estimating formulas more compactly. Of course, in this text matrix algebra is not used. Besides, today one rarely computes the estimates by hand; let the computer do all the work.

7.4 THE DEMAND FOR ROSES: AN ILLUSTRATIVE EXAMPLE

Let us take time out to illustrate all the preceding theory with an example. Consider the sample data given in Table 7-1. This table gives data on the quantity of roses demanded (Y), the price of roses (X_2), and the price of carnations (X_3). Suppose we want to estimate the quantity of roses demanded as a function of the price of roses and the price of carnations.[8] With Y and Xs thus defined, we want to estimate Eq. (7.2).

Now to use the various OLS formulas presented earlier, we will need the various sums of squares, cross products, etc. of the three variables. The necessary quantities, derived from the raw data of Table 7-1, are given in Table 7-2.

In Table 7-3 we give the computer output for our example.

---

[8] Economic theory suggests that the demand for a product is generally a function of the price of the product, the income of the consumer, and the prices of products competing or complementary with the given product. Unfortunately, we do not have data on the income of the consumer in this example. Therefore, the demand function considered here is not completely adequate. But for illustrative purposes, it will do.

TABLE 7-1
The demand for roses

Year and Quarter	Y	X_2	X_3
1971-III	11,484	2.26	3.49
-IV	9,348	2.54	2.85
1972-I	8,429	3.07	4.06
-II	10,079	2.91	3.64
-III	9,240	2.73	3.21
-IV	8,862	2.77	3.66
1973-I	6,216	3.59	3.76
-II	8,253	3.23	3.49
-III	8,038	2.60	3.13
-IV	7,476	2.89	3.20
1974-I	5,911	3.77	3.65
-II	7,950	3.64	3.60
-III	6,134	2.82	2.94
-IV	5,868	2.96	3.12
1975-I	3,160	4.24	3.58
-II	5,872	3.69	3.53

Source: The data were collected by my student Joe
Walsh from a wholesaler in the Detroit metropolitan
area.

Notes: Y = the quantity of roses sold (dozen); X_2 =
the average wholesale price of roses ($ per dozen);
X_3 = average wholesale price of carnations ($ per
dozen).

TABLE 7-2
Numerical calculations based on Table 7-1

$\sum Y_t = 122{,}320;$ $\sum X_{2t} = 49.71$ $\sum X_{3t} = 54.91$

$\sum y_t^2 = 62{,}596{,}000;$ $\sum y_t x_{2t} = -12{,}923;$ $\sum y_t x_{3t} = -225.87$

$\sum x_{2t}^2 = 4.3385;$ $\sum x_{3t}^2 = 1.5836$

$\sum x_{2t} x_{3t} = 1.2385$

$n = 16$

Based on the computer output presented in Table 7–3, we see that the
estimated demand function for roses is as follows:

$$\hat{Y}_t = 9734.2 - 3782.2X_{2t} + 2815.3X_{3t} \tag{7.32}$$
$$\text{se} = (2888.1) \ (572.45) \qquad (947.51) \qquad R^2 = 0.7706$$

TABLE 7-3
Computer output of the rose demand function (7.32)

OLS ESTIMATION
     16 OBSERVATIONS   DEPENDENT VARIABLE = Y
...NOTE..SAMPLE RANGE SET TO: 1,   16

  R-SQUARE = 0.7706   R-SQUARE ADJUSTED = 0.7354
VARIANCE OF THE ESTIMATE = 0.11044E+07 − $\hat{\sigma}^2$
STANDARD ERROR OF THE ESTIMATE = 1050.9
MEAN OF DEPENDENT VARIABLE = 7645.0

ANALYSIS OF VARIANCE – FROM MEAN

	SS	DF	MS	F	(See Section 7.8)
REGRESSION	0.48240E+08	2.	0.24120E+08	21.841 = F	
ERROR	0.14357E+08	13.	0.11044E+07	Not crit	
TOTAL	0.62596E+08	15.	0.41731E+07	F-value △	

VARIABLE NAME	ESTIMATED COEFFICIENT	STANDARD ERROR	T-RATIO 13 DF	PARTIAL CORR.	STANDARDIZED COEFFICIENT	ELASTICITY AT MEANS
X2	−3782.2	572.45	−6.6070	−0.8778	−0.99573	−1.5371
X3	2815.3	947.51	2.9712	0.6360	0.44779	1.2638
CONSTANT	9734.2	2888.1	3.3705	0.6829	0.00000E+00	1.2733

OBS. NO.	OBSERVED VALUE	PREDICTED VALUE	CALCULATED RESIDUAL	
1	11484.	11012.	472.32	I *
2	9348.0	8150.9	1197.1	I *
3	8429.0	9552.8	−1123.8	* I
4	10079.	8975.5	1103.5	I *
5	9240.0	8445.8	794.22	I *
6	8862.0	9561.4	−699.36	* I
7	6216.0	6741.5	−525.48	* I
8	8253.0	7343.0	910.05	I *
9	8038.0	8712.2	−674.25	* I
10	7476.0	7812.5	−336.48	* I
11	5911.0	5751.0	159.99	I*
12	7950.0	6101.9	1848.1	I *
13	6134.0	7345.3	−1211.3	* I
14	5868.0	7322.5	−1454.5	* I
15	3160.0	3776.3	−616.31	* I
16	5872.0	5715.8	156.25	I*

DURBIN-WATSON = 2.2100   VON NEUMAN RATIO = 2.3573   RHO = −0.11381
RESIDUAL SUM = −0.12449E−10   RESIDUAL VARIANCE = 0.11044E+07
SUM OF ABSOLUTE ERRORS=   13283.
R-SQUARE BETWEEN OBSERVED AND PREDICTED = 0.7706
RUNS TEST: 9 RUNS,   8 POSITIVE,   8 NEGATIVE, NORMAL STATISTIC =   0.0000

Source: SHAZAM output of Eq. (7.2) fitted to the data of Table 7-1. For details, see Table 6-3.

where, following the convention introduced in Chapter 6, the figures in the parentheses are the estimated standard errors. The R^2 value, the multiple regression analog of the two-variable r^2, is explained in Section 7.5.

From the various formulas given previously and the raw data presented in Table 7-2, the reader should verify that the estimates of the regression parameters and their standard errors given in regression (7.32) are correct, except for the roundoff errors.

Intrepretation of the Rose Demand Function

The partial slope coefficient of -3782.2 means that if all other variables are held constant (here the price of carnations), the average quantity of roses demanded will decrease by ≈ 3782 dozens if the price of roses per dozen goes up by a dollar. As expected, the relationship between the quantity of roses demanded and its own price is inverse.

Likewise, the partial slope coefficient of 2815.3, holding other variables constant (here the price of rose), means that if the price of carnations goes up by a dollar per dozen, the average quantity of roses demanded will increase by ≈ 2815 dozens. Economic theory suggests that if the price of one product goes up and the quantity demanded of another product goes up, then the two products are said to be *substitute or competing* products. In our example it seems that roses and carnations are competing products. (Sorry, rose lovers!)

If the prices of roses and carnations are fixed at zero, regression (7.32) shows that the average quantity of roses demanded will be $\approx 9,734$ dozens. As usual, this mechanical interpretation of the intercept has to be taken with a grain of salt. One would hardly expect the prices of the two flowers to be zero. Certainly, in our sample of Table 7-1 they were not zero.

What can we say about the estimated rose demand function? So far we have only obtained OLS estimators of the demand function and their standard errors. Insofar as economic theory is concerned, our results are in accord. As expected, the coefficient of the rose price variable is negative (the downward-sloping law of demand). And the positive coefficient of the carnation price variable suggests that from the consumer's viewpoint the two products (flowers) seem to be substitute products. Are the estimated coefficients statistically significant? What is the overall goodness of fit of the estimated regression (7.32)? The answers follow.

7.5   GOODNESS OF FIT OF ESTIMATED MULTIPLE REGRESSION: MULTIPLE COEFFICIENT OF DETERMINATION, R^2

In the two-variable case we say that r^2 as defined in Eq. (6.40) measures the goodness of fit of the fitted sample regression line (SRL); that is, it gives the *proportion* or *percentage of the total variation in the dependent variable Y explained by the single explanatory variable X.* This concept of r^2 can be extended to regression models containing any number of explanatory variables. Thus, in the three-variable case we would like to know the proportion of the total variation in $Y(= \Sigma\ y_t^2)$ explained by X_2 and X_3 jointly. The quantity that gives this information is known as the **multiple coefficient of determination** and is denoted by the symbol R^2; conceptually, it is akin to r^2.

As in the two-variable case, we have the identity (cf. Eq. 6.38):

$$TSS = ESS + RSS \tag{7.33}$$

where

TSS = the total sum of squares of the dependent variable $Y(= \Sigma\ y_t^2)$

ESS = the explained sum of squares (i.e., explained by all the X variables)

RSS = the residual sum of squares

Also, as in the two-variable case, R^2 is defined as

$$R^2 = \frac{ESS}{TSS} \tag{7.34}$$

That is, it is the ratio of the explained sum of squares to the total sum of squares; the only change is that the ESS is now due to more than one explanatory variable.

Now it can be shown that

$$ESS = b_2 \sum y_t x_{2t} + b_3 \sum y_t x_{3t} \tag{7.35}$$

and, as shown before,

$$RSS = \sum y_t^2 - b_2 \sum y_t x_{2t} - b_{3t} \sum y_t x_{3t} \tag{7.31}$$

Therefore, R^2 can be computed as

$$R^2 = \frac{b_2 \sum y_t x_{2t} + b_3 \sum y_t x_{3t}}{\sum y_t^2} \tag{7.36}[9]$$

All these quantities can be obtained from the data given in Table 7-2. Of course, the computer will do this calculation in a jiffy. For our rose demand function, as regression (7.32) shows, the computed R^2 is 0.7706. The interpretation is that ≈ 77 percent of the variation in the quantity of roses demanded can be explained by the two explanatory variables—the prices of roses and carnations. Like r^2, R^2 also lies between 0 and 1. (Why?) The closer R^2 is to 1,

---

[9] R^2 can also be computed as

$$1 - \frac{RSS}{TSS} = 1 - \frac{\sum e_t^2}{\sum y_t^2}$$

the better is the fit of the estimated regression line. In our example the value of 0.77 seems "reasonably" high.

In passing, note that R, the positive square root of R^2, is known as the **coefficient of multiple correlation**, the two-variable analogue of r. Just as r measures the degree of linear association between Y and X, R can be interpreted as the degree of linear association between Y and all the X variables jointly. Although r can be positive or negative, R is always taken to be positive. In practice, however, R is of little importance. In our example, $R = \sqrt{0.7706} = 0.8778$.

7.6 HYPOTHESIS TESTING IN A MULTIPLE REGRESSION: GENERAL COMMENTS

Although R^2 gives us an overall measure of goodness of fit of the estimated regression line, by itself R^2 does not tell us whether the estimated partial regression coefficients are statistically significant, that is, statistically different from zero. Some of them may be and some may not. How do we find out?

To be specific, let us suppose we want to entertain the hypothesis that the price of roses has no effect on the quantity of roses demanded. In other words, we want to test the null hypothesis: $H_0: B_2 = 0$. How do we go about it? From our discussion of hypothesis testing for the two-variable model given in Chapter 6, in order to answer this question we need to find out the sampling distribution of b_2, the estimator of B_2. What is the sampling distribution of b_2? And the sampling distribution of b_1 and b_3?

In the two-variable case we saw that the OLS estimators b_1 and b_2 are normally distributed if we are willing to assume that the error term u follows the normal distribution. Now in assumption A7.6 we have stated that even for multiple regression we will continue to assume that u is normally distributed with zero mean and constant variance σ^2. Given this and the other assumptions listed in Section 7.2, it can be proved that b_1, b_2, and b_3 *each* follows the normal distribution with means equal to B_1, B_2, and B_3, respectively, and the variances given by Eqs. (7.23), (7.25), and (7.27), respectively.

However, as in the two-variable case, if we replace the true but unobservable σ^2 by its unbiased estimator $\hat{\sigma}^2$ given in Eq. (7.29), the OLS estimators follow the t distribution with $(n - 3)$ d.f., not the normal distribution. That is,

$$t = \frac{b_1 - B_1}{se(b_1)} \sim t_{(n-3)} \tag{7.37}$$

$$t = \frac{b_2 - B_2}{se(b_2)} \sim t_{(n-3)} \tag{7.38}$$

$$t = \frac{b_3 - B_3}{se(b_3)} \sim t_{(n-3)} \tag{7.39}$$

Notice that the d.f. are now $(n - 3)$ because in computing the RSS, $\Sigma\, e_i^2$, and hence $\hat{\sigma}^2$, we first need to estimate the intercept and the two partial slope coefficients; so to speak, we lose 3 d.f.

The knowledge that by replacing σ^2 with $\hat{\sigma}^2$ the OLS estimators follow the t distribution can now be used fruitfully to establish confidence intervals as well as to test statistical hypothesis about the true partial regression coefficients. The actual mechanics in many ways resemble the two-variable case, which we now illustrate with our demand for roses example.

7.7 TESTING HYPOTHESES ABOUT INDIVIDUAL PARTIAL REGRESSION COEFFICIENTS

Suppose in our demand for roses regression given in Eq. (7.32) we hypothesize that

$$H_0: B_2 = 0 \quad \text{and} \quad H_1: B_2 \neq 0$$

That is, the null hypothesis states that holding X_3—the price of carnations—constant, X_2—the price of roses—has no effect on the quantity of roses demanded. The alternative hypothesis states that this is not the case: The price of roses does have a definite effect on the quantity of roses demanded, positive or negative (economic theory would suggest a negative effect). Thus, the alternative hypothesis is two-sided.

Under the preceding null hypothesis we know that

$$t = \frac{b_2 - B_2}{\text{se}(b_2)} \tag{7.38}$$

$$= \frac{b_2}{\text{se}(b_2)} \quad (\textit{Note: } B_2 = 0)$$

follows the t distribution with $(n - 3) = 13$ d.f., since $n = 16$. From the estimated regression given in Eq. (7.32), we obtain

$$t = \frac{-3782.2}{572.45}$$

$$= -6.6070 \tag{7.40}$$

which has a t distribution with 13 d.f.

On the basis of the computed t value, do we reject the null hypothesis that the price of roses has no effect on the quantity of roses demanded? To answer this question, we can use either the *test of significance approach* or the *confidence interval approach,* as we did for the two-variable regression.

The Test of Significance Approach

Recall that in the test of significance approach to hypothesis testing we develop a test statistic, find out its sampling distribution, choose a level of significance α, and determine the critical value(s) of the test statistic at the chosen level of significance. Then we compare the value of the test statistic obtained from the sample at hand with the critical value(s) and reject the null hypothesis if the computed value of the test statistic exceeds the critical value(s).[10] The approach that we followed for the two-variable case also carries over to the multiple regression.

Returning to our illustrative example, we know that the test statistic in question is the t statistic, which follows the t distribution with $(n - 3)$ d.f. Therefore, we use the t *test of significance*. The actual mechanics are now straightforward. Suppose we choose $\alpha = 0.05$ or 5%. Since the alternative hypothesis is two-sided, we have to find the critical t value at $\alpha/2 = 2.5\%$ (why?) for $(n - 3)$ d.f., which in the present example is 13. Then from the t table we observe that for 13 d.f.,

$$P(-2.160 \le t \le 2.160) = 0.95 \tag{7.41}$$

That is, the probability that a t value lies between the limits -2.160 and $+2.160$ (i.e., the critical t values) is 95 percent.

From Equation (7.40) we observe that the computed t value under the null hypothesis that true $B_2 = 0$ is -6.6070, or 6.6070 in absolute terms, which obviously exceeds the critical t value of 2.160 in absolute terms. We therefore reject the null hypothesis. The price of a rose *has* definite influence on its quantity demanded.

The Confidence Interval Approach to Hypothesis Testing

The basics of the confidence interval approach to hypothesis testing have already been discussed in the previous chapter. Here we merely illustrate it with our numerical example. We showed previously that

$$P(-2.160 \le t \le 2.160) = 0.95 \tag{7.41}$$

We also know that

$$t = \frac{b_2 - B_2}{\text{se}(b_2)} \tag{7.38}$$

If we substitute this t value into Equation (7.41), we obtain

$$P\left(-2.160 \le \frac{b_2 - B_2}{\text{se}(b_2)} \le 2.160 \right) = 0.95$$

---

[10] If the test statistic has a negative value, we consider its absolute value and say that if the absolute value of the test statistic exceeds the critical value, we will reject the null hypothesis.

which after rearranging becomes

$$P[b_2 - 2.160 \, se(b_2) \leq B_2 \leq b_2 + 2.160 \, se(b_2)] = 0.95 \qquad (7.42)$$

which is a 95% confidence interval for B_2. (cf. Eq. 6.26). Recall that under the confidence interval approach, if the null-hypothesized value lies in the confidence interval, which we call the *acceptance region*, we do not reject the null hypothesis. On the other hand, if the hypothesized value lies outside the confidence interval, that is, in the *region of rejection*, we can reject the null hypothesis. But always bear in mind that in making either decision we are taking a chance of being wrong $\alpha\%$ (say, 5%) of the time.

For our illustrative example, Equation (7.42) becomes

$$-3782.2 - 2.160(572.45) \leq B_2 \leq -3782.2 + 2.160(572.45)$$

that is,

$$-5018.692 \leq B_2 \leq -2545.708 \qquad (7.43)$$

which is a 95% confidence interval for true B_2. Since the null-hypothesized value of zero does not lie in this interval, we can reject the null hypothesis: If we construct confidence intervals like expression (7.43), then 95 out of 100 such intervals will include the true B_2, but, as noted in Chapter 6, *we cannot say that the probability is 95% that the particular interval (7.43) does or does not include the true B_2.*

Needless to say, we can use the two approaches to test statistical hypotheses about the other coefficients of our demand for roses function. As a matter of fact, we can present our estimated demand function for roses given in Eq. (7.32) in the manner of Eq. (6.48).

$$\hat{Y}_t = 9734.2 - 3782.2 X_{2t} + 2815.3 X_{3t}$$

$$se = (2888.1) \quad (572.45) \quad (947.51) \qquad R^2 = 0.7706$$

$$t = (3.3705) \quad (-6.6070) \quad (2.9712)$$

$$\text{Adjusted } R^2 = 0.7354 \qquad (7.44)$$

Note: The adjusted R^2 is discussed in Section 7.10.

where the t values presented are computed under the null hypothesis that each relevant true population regression coefficient is zero. Such a presentation enables us to see at a glance which of the coefficients are *statistically significant*, that is, significantly different from zero. From the reported t values we can observe that each estimated regression coefficient is *individually statistically significant*, for the critical t value for 13 d.f. at the 5% level of significance is 2.160 (two-tailed) or 1.771 (one-tailed) and each computed $|t|$ value shown in Eq. (7.44) exceeds either of these critical t values.

To summarize: The procedure for testing a hypothesis about an individual partial regression coefficient is exactly identical to the testing procedure of the two-variable case. We can use either the t test or the confidence interval based on the t distribution to test any individual null hypothesis.

7.8   TESTING THE JOINT HYPOTHESIS THAT $B_2 = B_3 = 0$ OR $R^2 = 0$

In regression (7.44) we saw that *individually* the partial slope coefficients b_2 and b_3 are statistically significant; that is, *individually* each partial slope coefficient is significantly different from zero. But now consider the following null hypothesis:

$$H_0: B_2 = B_3 = 0 \tag{7.45}$$

This null hypothesis is a **joint hypothesis** that B_2 and B_3 are *jointly* or *simultaneously* (and not individually or singly) equal to zero. This hypothesis states that the two explanatory variables *together* have no influence on Y; so to speak, demand for roses is independent of the prices of roses and carnations. Put differently, the variables X_2 and X_3 have no influence on Y whatsoever. This is the same as saying that

$$H_0: R^2 = 0 \tag{7.46}$$

That is, the two explanatory variables explain zero percent of the variation in the dependent variable (recall the definition of R^2). Therefore, the two sets of hypotheses (7.45) and (7.46) are equivalent; one implies the other. A test of either hypothesis is called a test of the **overall significance** of the *estimated* population regression line, that is, whether Y is linearly related to both X_2 and X_3.

How do we test, say, the hypothesis given in hypothesis (7.45)? The temptation here is to state that since individually b_2 and b_3 were statistically different from zero in regression (7.44), then jointly or collectively they also must be statistically different from zero [i.e., we reject H_0 given in Equation (7.45)]. In other words, since the price of roses as well as the price of carnations *each* has a significant effect on the quantity of roses demanded, *together* they also must have a significant effect on the quantity of roses demanded. But one should be careful here for, as we show more fully in Chapter 10 on multicollinearity, in practice, in a multiple regression one or more variables *individually* have no effect on the dependent variable but *collectively* they have a significant impact on Y. This means that the t-testing procedure discussed previously, *although valid for testing the statistical significance of an individual regression coefficient, is no longer valid for testing the joint hypothesis.*

How then do we test a hypothesis like hypothesis (7.45)? This can be done by using a technique known as **analysis of variance (ANOVA)**. To see how this technique is employed, recall the following identity:

$$TSS = ESS + RSS \tag{7.33}$$

That is,

$$\sum y_t^2 = b_2 \sum y_t x_{2t} + b_3 \sum y_t x_{3t} + \sum e_t^2 \tag{7.47}$$

Equation (7.47) decomposes the TSS into the components, one explained by the (chosen) regression model (ESS) and the other not explained by the model (RSS). *A study of these components of TSS is known as the analysis of variance (ANOVA) from the regression viewpoint.*

As noted in Chapter 4 every sum of squares has associated with it degrees of freedom (d.f.)—that is, the number of independent observations on the basis of which the sum of squares is computed. Now each of the preceding sum of squares has these d.f.:

Sum of squares	d.f.	
TSS	$n-1$	(always, why?)
RSS	$n-3$	(three-variable model)
ESS	2	(three-variable model)*

* An easy way to find the d.f. for ESS is to subtract the d.f. for RSS from the d.f. for TSS.

Let us arrange all these sums of squares and their associated d.f. in a tabular form, known as the ANOVA table, as shown in Table 7-4.

TABLE 7-4
ANOVA table for the three-variable regression

Source of variation	Sum of squares (SS)	d.f.	$MSS = \dfrac{SS}{d.f.}$
Due to regression (ESS)	$b_2 \sum y_t x_{2t} + b_3 \sum y_t x_{3t}$	2	$\dfrac{b_2 \sum y_t x_{2t} + b_3 \sum y_t x_{3t}}{2}$
Due to residual (RSS)	$\sum e_t^2$	$n-3$	$\dfrac{\sum e_t^2}{n-3}$
Total (TSS)	$\sum y_t^2$	$n-1$	

Note: MSS = mean, or average, sum of squares.

Now given the assumptions of the CLRM (and assumption A7.6) and the null hypothesis: H_0: $B_2 = B_3 = 0$, it can be shown that the variable

$$F = \frac{\text{ESS}/\text{d.f.}}{\text{RSS}/\text{d.f.}} \tag{7.48}$$

$$= \frac{\text{variance explained by } X_2 \text{ and } X_3}{\text{unexplained variance}}$$

$$= \frac{\left(b_2 \sum y_t x_{2t} + b_3 \sum y_t x_{3t}\right)\Big/2}{\sum e_t^2/(n-3)} \tag{7.49}$$

follows the F distribution with 2 and $(n - 3)$ d.f. in the numerator and denominator, respectively. (see Chapter 3 for a general discussion of the F distribution and Chapter 4 for some applications). *In general, if the regression model has k explanatory variables including the intercept term, the F ratio has $(k - 1)$ d.f. in the numerator and $(n - k)$ d.f. in the denominator.*[11]

How can we use the F ratio of Equation (7.49) to test the joint hypothesis that both X_2 and X_3 have no impact on Y? The answer is evident in Eq. (7.49). If the numerator of Eq. (7.49) is larger than its denominator—if the variance of Y explained by the regression (i.e., by X_2 and X_3) is larger than the variance not explained by the regression—the F value will be greater than 1. Therefore, as the variance explained by the X variables becomes increasingly larger relative to the unexplained variance, the F ratio will be increasingly larger, too. Thus, an increasingly large F value will be evidence against the null hypothesis that the two (or more) explanatory variables have no effect on Y.

Of course, this intuitive reasoning can be formalized in the usual framework of hypothesis testing. As shown in Chapter 3, Section 3.5, we compute F as given in Eq. (7.49) and compare it with the critical F value for 2 and $(n - 3)$ d.f. at the chosen level of α, the probability of committing a type I error. As usual, if the computed F value exceeds the critical F value, we reject the null hypothesis that the impact of all explanatory variables is simultaneously equal to zero. If it does not exceed the critical F value, we do not reject the null hypothesis that the explanatory variables have no impact whatsoever on the dependent variable.

To illustrate the actual mechanics, let us return to our rose demand function. The computer output given in Table 7-3 shows the ANOVA table and the computed F value, which is 21.841. Under the null hypothesis $B_2 = B_3 = 0$ this F value follows the F distribution with 2 and 13 d.f. in the numerator and denominator, respectively.

---

[11] A simple way to remember this is: The numerator d.f. of the F ratio is equal to the number of *partial slope coefficients* in the model and the denominator d.f. is equal to n minus the total number of parameters estimated (i.e., partial slopes plus the intercept).

If we choose $\alpha = 1\%$, then from the F table we see that for the given d.f., the *critical F* value is 6.70. Since the computed F of ≈ 22 far exceeds the critical F value, our conclusion is to reject the null hypothesis: Collectively, both X_2 and X_3, the prices of roses and carnations, respectively, do affect the quantity of roses demanded. It so happens in this example that X_2 and X_3 *each individually* also has influence on the quantity of roses demanded, as shown very clearly in (7.44). But this does not always need to be the case. We will come across cases (see the example in Section 7.12) where not all explanatory variables individually have much impact on the dependent variable (i.e., some t values may be statistically insignificant) yet all explanatory variables *collectively* impact the dependent variables (i.e., the F test will reject the null hypothesis that all partial slope coefficients are simultaneously equal to zero). But more on this in the chapter on multicollinearity (see Chapter 10).

An Important Relationship between F and R^2

There is an important relationship between the coefficient of determination R^2 and the F ratio used in ANOVA. This relationship is as follows (see problem 7.16):

$$F = \frac{R^2/(k-1)}{(1 - R^2)/(n-k)} \qquad (7.50)$$

where n = the number of observations and k = the number of explanatory variables including the intercept.

Equation (7.50) shows how F and R^2 are related. These two statistics vary directly. When $R^2 = 0$ (i.e., no relationship between Y and the X variables), F is zero ipso facto. The larger R^2 is, the greater the F value will be. In the limit when $R^2 = 1$, the F value is infinite.

Thus the **F test** discussed earlier, which is a measure of the overall significance of the estimated regression line, is also a test of significance of R^2— that is, whether R^2 is different from zero. In other words, testing the null hypothesis (7.45) is equivalent to testing the null hypothesis that (the population) R^2 is zero.

One advantage of the F test expressed in terms of R^2 is the ease of computation: All we need to know is the R^2 value, which is routinely computed by most regression programs. Therefore, the overall F test of significance given in Eq. (7.48) can be recast in terms of R^2 as shown in Eq. (7.50) and the ANOVA Table 7-4 can be equivalently expressed as Table 7-5.

For our demand for roses function, $R^2 = 0.7760$. Therefore, the F ratio of Equation (7.50) becomes

$$F = \frac{0.7706/2}{(1 - 0.7706)/13} = 21.83 \qquad (7.51)$$

which is about the same F as shown in Table 7-3, except for rounding errors.

TABLE 7-5
ANOVA table in terms of R^2

Source of variation	Sum of squares (SS)	d.f.	MSS = SS/d.f.
Due to regression (ESS)	$R^2 \left(\sum y_t^2 \right)$	2	$\dfrac{R^2 \left(\sum y_t^2 \right)}{2}$
Due to residuals (RSS)	$(1 - R^2) \left(\sum y_t^2 \right)$	$n - 3$	$\dfrac{(1 - R^2) \left(\sum y_t^2 \right)}{n - 3}$
Total (TSS)	$\sum y_t^2$	$n - 1$	

Note: In computing the F value, we do not need to multiply R^2 and $(1 - R^2)$ by $\sum y_t^2$ since it drops out, as can be seen from Eq. (7.50).

Note: In the k-variable model the d.f. will be $(k - 1)$ and $(n - k)$, respectively.

7.9   TWO-VARIABLE REGRESSION IN CONTEXT OF MULTIPLE REGRESSION

Let us return to our roses data in Table 7-1. Suppose someone believes that the price of carnations has no effect on the demand for roses, and therefore estimates the following two-variable regression, regressing the quantity of roses demanded (Y) on its own price (X_2):

$$\hat{Y}_t = 16899 - 2978.5X_{2t}$$

$$\text{se} = (1984.6) \quad (629.98) \qquad r^2 = 0.6149 \hspace{3cm} (7.52)$$

$$t = (8.5152) \quad (-4.7280)$$

What now? If you compare this regression with the three-variable regression (7.44), you will notice the following. Although the quantity of roses demanded is still significantly negatively related to its price, the two rose price coefficients are not the same: In absolute terms (i.e., disregarding the sign), the coefficient of the rose price in Eq. (7.52) is smaller than that in Eq. (7.44), 2978 vs. 3782, suggesting that a unit increase in the price of roses has greater impact on its quantity demanded in Eq. (7.44) than in Eq. (7.52). How can we explain this difference? Remember, in Eq. (7.44) in deriving the impact of the price of roses on its quantity demanded we held the price of carnations constant, whereas in Eq. (7.52) we simply neglected the price of carnations. Put differently, in Eq. (7.44) the rose price effect is *net* of the effect of the carnation price, whereas in Eq. (7.52) the effect of the price of carnations has not been netted out. Thus, the price coefficient in Eq. (7.52) reflects the *gross effect*—the *direct effect* of the price of roses as well as the *indirect effect* of the price of carnations.

The preceding discussion should help to clarify the meaning of a partial regression coefficient.

7.10   COMPARING TWO R^2 VALUES: THE ADJUSTED R^2

By examining the R^2 values of our two-variable [Eq. (7.52)] and three-variable [Eq. (7.44)] regressions for roses, you will notice that the R^2 value of the former (0.6149) is smaller than that of the latter (0.7706). Is this always the case? Yes! An important property of R^2 is that the larger the number of explanatory variables is, the higher the R^2 will be. It would then seem that if one wants to explain a substantial amount of the variation in a dependent variable, one merely has to go on adding more explanatory variables!

However, do not take this "advice" too seriously. This is because the definition of $R^2 = ESS/TSS$ does not take into account the d.f. Note that in a k-variable model including the intercept term the d.f. for ESS is $(k - 1)$. Thus, if you have a model with 5 explanatory variables including the intercept, the d.f. associated with ESS will be 4, whereas if you had a model with 10 explanatory variables including the intercept, the d.f. for the ESS will be 9. But the conventional R^2 formula does not take into account the differing d.f. in the various models. Note that the d.f. for TSS is always $(n - 1)$. (Why?) Therefore, comparing the R^2 values of two models with the *same* dependent variable but with differing numbers of explanatory variables is essentially like comparing apples and oranges.

Thus, what we need is a measure of goodness of fit that is adjusted for (i.e., takes into account explicitly) the number of explanatory variables in the model. Such a measure has been devised and is known as the **adjusted R^2**, denoted by the symbol $\overline{R}^2$. This (adjusted) $\overline{R}^2$ can be derived from the conventional R^2 as follows:

$$\overline{R}^2 = 1 - (1 - R^2)\frac{n - 1}{n - k} \tag{7.53}$$

Note that the R^2 we have considered previously is also known as the *unadjusted* R^2 for obvious reasons.

The features of the adjusted R^2 are:

1. If $k > 1$, $\overline{R}^2 \leq R^2$; that is, as the number of explanatory variables increases, the adjusted R^2 becomes increasingly less than the unadjusted R^2. There seems to be a "penalty" involved in adding more explanatory variables to a regression model.
2. Although the unadjusted R^2 is always positive, the adjusted R^2 can on occasion turn out to be negative. For example, in a regression model involving $k = 3$ and $n = 30$, if an R^2 is found to be 0.06, $\overline{R}^2$ can be negative (-0.0096).

At present, most computer regression packages compute both the adjusted and unadjusted R^2 values. This is a good practice, for the adjusted

R^2 will enable us to compare two regression models that have the *same* dependent variable but a different number of explanatory variables.[12]

In passing, note that for our rose demand function, the adjusted R^2 value is 0.7354, which is smaller than the unadjusted R^2 value of 0.7706, which can be seen from Eq. (7.44). For the two-variable rose demand function given in Eq. (7.52), the reader can verify from Eq. (7.53) that the adjusted R^2 value is 0.5874.

7.11   WHEN TO ADD AN ADDITIONAL EXPLANATORY VARIABLE TO THE MODEL

In practice, in order to explain a particular phenomenon, a researcher is often faced with the problem of deciding among several competing explanatory variables. The common practice is to add variables as long as the adjusted R^2 increases (even though its numerical value may be less than the unadjusted R^2.) But when does $\overline{R}^2$ increase? It can be shown that $\overline{R}^2$ *will increase if the* $|t|$ *(absolute t) value of the coefficient of the added variable is larger than 1, where the t value is computed under the hypothesis that the population value of the said coefficient is zero.*

For our demand for roses example we just saw that the adjusted R^2 values were 0.5874 (two-variable model) and 0.7354 (three-variable model). The adjusted R^2 value has increased, but this should not be surprising because the $|t|$ value of the X_3 variable [see Eq. (7.44)] exceeds 1. Therefore, X_3 should be added to the model. Incidentally, the t value of X_3 not only is greater than 1 in this example, but it is also statistically significant.[13]

7.12   ILLUSTRATIVE EXAMPLES

In this section we consider several examples involving multiple regressions. Our objective here is to show the reader how the multiple regression model is used in a variety of applications.

Example 7.1. Does tax policy affect corporate capital structure?   To find out the extent to which tax policy has been responsible for the recent trend in U.S. manufacturing toward increasing use of debt capital in lieu of equity capital—that is, toward an increasing debt/equity ratio (called leverage in the financial literature)—Pozdena[14] has estimated the following regression model:

---

[12] As we will show in Chap. 8, if two regression models have different dependent variables, we cannot compare their R^2 values directly, adjusted or unadjusted.

[13] But whether or not a particular t value is significant, the adjusted R^2 will increase so long as $|t|$ of the coefficient of the added variable is greater than 1.

[14] Randall Johnston Pozdena, "Tax Policy and Corporate Capital Structure," *Economic Review*, Federal Reserve Bank of San Francisco, Fall 1987, pp. 37–51.

$$Y_t = B_1 + B_2X_{2t} + B_3X_{3t} + B_4X_{4t} + B_5X_{5t} + B_6X_{6t} + u_t \qquad (7.54)$$

where

Y = the leverage (= debt/equity) in percent

X_2 = the corporate tax rate

X_3 = the personal tax rate

X_4 = the capital gains tax rate

X_5 = nondebt-related tax shields

X_6 = the inflation rate

Economic theory suggests that coefficients B_2, B_4, and B_6 will be positive and coefficients B_3 and B_5 will be negative.[15] Based on the data for U.S. manufacturing corporations for the years 1935 to 1982, Pozdena obtained the OLS results that are presented in tabular form (Table 7-6) rather than in the usual format [Eq. (7.44)]. (Results are sometimes presented in this form for ease of reading.)

Discussion of Regression Results

The first fact to note about the preceding regression results is that all the coefficients have the signs that are expected by economic theory. For instance, the corporate tax rate has a positive effect on leverage—holding other things the same, as the corporate tax rate goes up by one percentage point, on the average the leverage ratio (i.e., the debt/equity ratio) goes up by 2.4 percentage points. Likewise, if the inflation rate goes up by one percentage point, on the average leverage goes up by 1.4 percentage points, other things remaining the same (*Question*: Why would you expect a positive relation between leverage and inflation?). Other partial regression coefficients should be interpreted similarly.

Since t values are presented underneath each partial regression coefficient under the null hypothesis that each population partial regression coefficient is *individually* equal to zero, we can easily test whether such a null hypothesis stands up against the (two-sided) alternative hypothesis that each true population coefficient is different from zero. Hence, we use the two-tailed t test. The d.f. in this example are 42, which are obtained by subtracting from

---

[15] See Pozdena's article (footnote 14) for the theoretical discussion of expected signs of the various coefficients. It should be pointed out that in the United States the interest paid on debt capital is tax deductible, whereas the income paid as dividends is not. This is one reason that corporations may prefer debt to equity capital.

TABLE 7-6
Leverage in manufacturing corporations, 1935–1982

Explanatory variable	Coefficient (t value in parentheses)
Corporate tax rate	2.4
	(10.5)
Personal tax rate	−1.2
	(−4.8)
Capital gains tax rate	0.3
	(1.3)
Nondebt shield	−2.4
	(4.8)
Inflation rate	1.4
	(3.0)

$$n = 48 \text{ (number of observations)}$$
$$R^2 = 0.87$$
$$\bar{R}^2 = 0.85$$

Source: Randall Johnston Pozdena, "Tax Policy and Corporate Capital Structure," *Economic Review*, Federal Reserve Bank of San Francisco, Fall 1987, Table 1, p. 45 (adapted).

Notes:

1. The author does not present the estimated intercept.

2. The adjusted R^2 is calculated using Eq. (7.53).

3. The standard errors of the various coefficients can be obtained by dividing the coefficient value by its t value (e.g., 2.4/10.5 = 0.2286 is the se of the corporate tax rate coefficient.)

$n \ (= 48)$ the number of parameters estimated, which are 6 in the present instance (*Note*: The intercept value is not presented in Table 7-6, although it was estimated.) If we choose $\alpha = 0.05$ or 5%, the two-tailed *critical t value* is about 2.021 for 40 d.f. (*Note*: This is good enough for present purposes since the t table does not give the precise t value for 42 d.f.) If α is fixed at 0.01 or a 1% level, the critical t value for 40 d.f. is 2.704 (two-tailed). Looking at the t values presented in Table 7-6, we see that each partial regression coefficient, except that of the capital gains tax variable, is statistically significantly different from zero at the 1% level of significance. The coefficient of the capital gains tax variable is not significant at either the 1 or 5% level. Therefore, except for this variable, we can reject the *individual* null hypothesis that each partial regression coefficient is zero. In other words, all but one of the explanatory variables *individually* has an impact on the debt/equity ratio. In passing, note that *if an estimated coefficient is statistically significant at the 1% level, it is also significant at the 5% level but the converse is not true.*

What about the overall significance of the estimated regression line? That is, can we accept the null hypothesis that all partial slopes are *simultaneously* equal to zero or, equivalently, is $R^2 = 0$? This hypothesis can be easily tested by using Eq. (7.50), which in the present case gives

$$F = \frac{R^2/(k-1)}{(1-R^2)/(n-k)}$$

$$= \frac{0.87/5}{0.13/42} \qquad (7.55)$$

$$= 56.22$$

This F value has an F distribution with 5 and 42 d.f. If α is set at 0.05, the F table (Appendix B) shows that for 5 and 40 d.f. (the table has no exact value of 42 d.f. in the denominator), the *critical F value* is 2.45. The corresponding value at $\alpha = 0.01$ is 3.51. The computed F of ≈ 56 far exceeds either of these critical F values. Therefore, we reject the null hypothesis that all partial slopes are simultaneously equal to zero or, alternatively, $R^2 = 0$. *Collectively*, all five explanatory variables influence the dependent variable. *Individually*, however, as we have seen, only four variables have an impact on the dependent variable, the debt/equity ratio. Example 7-1 again underscores the point made earlier that the (individual) t test and the (joint) F test are quite different.[16]

Example 7.2. The demand for imports in Jamaica. To explain the demand for imports in Jamaica, J. Gafar[17] obtained the following regression based on annual data for 19 years:

$$\hat{Y}_t = -58.9 + 0.20X_{2t} - 0.10X_{3t}$$

se =	(0.0092)	(0.084)	$R^2 = 0.96$	(7.56)
t =	(21.74)	(-1.1904)	$\bar{R}^2 = 0.955$	

where

$$Y = \text{the quantity of imports}$$

$$X_2 = \text{the personal consumption expenditure}$$

$$X_3 = \text{the import price/domestic price}$$

---

[16] In the two-variable linear regression model, however, there is a connection between the two, which is

$$t_k^2 = F_{1,k}$$

That is, the square of a t value with k d.f. is equal to an F value with 1 d.f. in the numerator and k d.f. in the denominator [see Eq. (3.16)].

[17] J. Gafar, "Devaluation and the Balance of Payments Adjustment in a Developing Economy: An Analysis Relating to Jamaica," *Applied Economics*, vol. 13, 1981, pp. 151–165. Notations were adapted. Adjusted R^2 computed.

Economic theory would suggest a positive relationship between Y and X_2 and a negative relationship between Y and X_3, which turns out to be the case. Individually the coefficient of X_2 is statistically significant but that of X_3 is not at, say, the 5% level. But since the absolute t value of X_3 is grater than 1, $\bar{R}^2$ for this example will drop if X_3 were dropped from the model (why?). Together, X_2 and X_3 explain about 96 percent of the variation in the quantity of imports into Jamaica.

Example 7.3. The demand for alcoholic beverages in the United Kingdom.   To explain the demand for alcoholic beverages in the United Kingdom, T. McGuinness[18] estimated the following regression based on annual data for 20 years:

$$\hat{Y}_t = -0.014 - 0.354X_{2t} + 0.0018X_{3t} + 0.657X_{4t} + 0.0059X_{5t}$$

$$se = \quad (0.012) \quad (0.2688) \quad\quad (0.0005) \quad\quad (0.266) \quad\quad (0.0034)$$

$$t = (-1.16) \quad (1.32) \quad\quad\quad (3.39) \quad\quad\quad (2.47) \quad\quad\quad (1.73)$$

$$R^2 = 0.689 \quad (7.57)$$

where

$Y =$ the annual change in pure alcohol consumption per adult

$X_2 =$ the annual change in the real price index of alcoholic drinks

$X_3 =$ the annual change in the real disposable income per person

$X_4 = \dfrac{\text{the annual change in the number of licensed premises}}{\text{the adult population}}$

$X_5 =$ the annual change in real advertising expenditure on alcoholic drinks per adult

Theory would suggest that all but the variable X_2 will be positively related to Y. This is borne out by the results, although each coefficient is not statistically significant. For 15 d.f. (why?), the 5% critical t value is 1.753 (one-tailed) and 2.131 (two-tailed). Consider the coefficient of X_5, the change in advertising expenditure. Since the advertising expenditure and the demand for alcoholic beverage are

---

[18] T. McGuinness, "An Econometric Analysis of Total Demand for Alcoholic Beverages in the United Kingdom," *Journal of Industrial Economics*, vol. 29, 1980, pp. 85–109. Notations were adapted.

expected to be positive (otherwise, it is bad news for the advertising industry), one can entertain the hypothesis that H_0: $B_5 = 0$ vs. H_1: $B_5 > 0$, and therefore can use the one-tailed t test. The computed t value of 1.73 is very close to being significant at the 5% level.

It is left as an exercise for the reader to compute the F value for this example to test the hypothesis that all partial slope coefficients are simultaneously equal to zero.

7.13 SUMMARY

In this chapter we considered the simplest of the multiple regression models, namely, the three-variable linear regression model—one dependent variable and two explanatory variables. Although in many ways a straightforward extension of the two-variable linear regression model, the three-variable model introduced several new concepts, such as partial regression coefficients, an adjusted and unadjusted multiple coefficient of determination, and multicollinearity.

Insofar as estimation of the parameters of the multiple regression coefficients was concerned, we still worked within the framework of the method of ordinary least squares (OLS). The OLS estimators of multiple regression, like the two-variable model, possess several desirable statistical properties summed up in the Gauss-Markov property of best linear unbiasedness (BLUE).

With the assumption that the disturbance term follows the normal distribution with zero mean and constant variance σ^2, we saw that, as in the two-variable case, each estimated coefficient in the multiple regression follows the normal distribution with a mean equal to the true population value and the variances given by the formulas developed in the text. Unfortunately, in practice, σ^2 is not known and has to be estimated. The OLS estimator of this unknown variance is $\hat{\sigma}^2$. But if we replace σ^2 by $\hat{\sigma}^2$, then, as in the two-variable case, each estimated coefficient of the multiple regression follows the t distribution, not the normal distribution.

The knowledge that each multiple regression coefficient follows the t distribution with d.f. equal to $(n - k)$, where k is the number of parameters estimated (including the intercept), means we can use the t distribution to test statistical hypotheses about each multiple regression coefficient individually. This can be done on the basis of either the t test of significance or the confidence interval based on the t distribution. In this respect, the multiple regression model does not differ much from the two-variable model, except that proper allowance must be made for the d.f., which now depend on the number of parameters estimated.

However, when testing the hypothesis that all partial slope coefficients are simultaneously equal to zero, the individual t testing referred to earlier is of no help. Here we should use the analysis of variance (ANOVA) technique and the attendant F test. Incidentally, testing the fact that all partial slope coefficients are simultaneously equal to zero is the same as testing the fact that the multiple coefficient of determination R^2 is equal to zero. Therefore, the F test can also be used to test this latter but equivalent hypothesis.

All the concepts introduced in this chapter have been illustrated by a numerical example and by concrete economic applications.

Key Terms and Concepts

The key terms and concepts introduced in this chapter are:

Multiple regression model
Partial regression coefficients; partial
    slope coefficients
Collinearity; exact linear relationship
    a) high or near perfect collinearity
Multicollinearity
Multiple coefficient of determination,
    R^2

Coefficient of multiple correlation, R
Individual hypothesis testing
Joint hypothesis testing or test of
    overall significance of estimated
    multiple regression
    a) analysis of variance (ANOVA)
    b) F test
Adjusted R^2 ($\bar{R}^2$)

QUESTIONS

7.1. Explain carefully the meaning of
    (a) Partial regression coefficient
    (b) Coefficient of multiple determination, R^2
    (c) Perfect collinearity
    (d) Perfect multicollinearity
    (e) Individual hypothesis testing
    (f) Joint hypothesis testing
    (g) Adjusted R^2

7.2. Explain step by step the procedures involved in
    (a) Testing the statistical significance of a single multiple regression coefficient
    (b) Testing the statistical significance of all partial slope coefficients.

7.3. State with brief reasons whether the following statements are true (T), false (F), or uncertain (U).
    (a) The adjusted and unadjusted R^2s are identical only when the unadjusted R^2 is equal to 1.
    (b) The way to determine whether a group of explanatory variables exerts significant influence on the dependent variable is to see if any of the explanatory variables has a significant t statistic; if not, they are statistically insignificant as a group.
    (c) When $R^2 = 1$, $F = 0$, and when $R^2 = 0$, $F = $ infinite.
    (d) When the d.f. exceed 120, the 5% critical t value (two-tailed) and the 5% critical Z (standard normal) value are identical, namely, 1.96.

*(e) In the model $Y_i = B_1 + B_2X_{2i} + B_3X_{3i} + u_i$, if X_2 and X_3 are negatively correlated in the sample and $B_3 > 0$, omitting X_3 from the model will bias b_{12} downward [i.e., $E(b_{12}) < B_2$] where b_{12} is the slope coefficient in the regression of Y on X_2 alone.

(f) When we say that an estimated regression coefficient is statistically significant, we mean that it is statistically different from 1.

(g) To compute a critical t value, we need to know only the d.f.

(h) By the overall significance of a multiple regression we mean the statistical significance of any single variable included in the model.

(i) Insofar as estimation and hypothesis testing are concerned, there is no difference between simple regression and multiple regression.

(j) The d.f. of the total sum of squares (TSS) are always $(n - 1)$ regardless of the number of explanatory variables included in the model.

7.4. What is the value of $\hat{\sigma}^2$ in each of the following cases?

(a) $\Sigma e_i^2 = 880$, $n = 25$, $k = 4$ (including intercept)

(b) $\Sigma e_i^2 = 1220$, $n = 14$, $k = 3$ (excluding intercept)

7.5. Find the critical t value(s) in the following situations:

Degrees of freedom (d.f.)	Level of significance (%)	H_1
12	5	Two-sided
20	1	Right-tailed
30	5	Left-tailed
200	5	Two-tailed

7.6. Find the critical F values for the following combinations:

Numerator d.f.	Denominator d.f.	Level of significance (%)
5	5	5
4	19	1
20	200	5

PROBLEMS

7.7. You are given the following data:

Y	X_2	X_3
1	1	2
3	2	1
8	3	-3

* Optional.

Based on these data, estimate the following regressions:
(a) $Y_i = A_1 + A_2 X_{2i} + u_i$
(b) $Y_i = C_1 + C_3 X_{3i} + u_i$
(c) $Y_i = B_1 + B_2 X_{2i} + B_3X_{3i} + u_i$
Note: Do not worry about estimating the standard errors.
(1) Is $A_2 = B_2$? Why or why not?
(2) Is $C_3 = B_3$? why or why not?
What general conclusion can you draw from this exercise?

7.8. You are given the following data based on 15 observations:

$$\bar{Y} = 367.693; \quad \bar{X}_2 = 402.760; \quad \bar{X}_3 = 8.0; \quad \sum y_i^2 = 66,042.269$$
$$\sum x_{2i}^2 = 84,855.096; \quad \sum x_{3i}^2 = 280.0; \quad \sum y_ix_{2i} = 74,778.346$$
$$\sum y_ix_{3i} = 4,250.9; \quad \sum x_{2i}x_{3i} = 4,796.0$$

where lowercase letters, as usual, denote deviations from sample mean values.
(a) Estimate the three multiple regression coefficients.
(b) Estimate their standard errors.
(c) Obtain R^2 and $\bar{R}^2$
(d) Estimate 95% confidence intervals for B_2 and B_3.
(e) Test the statistical significance of each estimated regression coefficient using $\alpha = 5\%$ (two-tailed).
(f) Test at $\alpha = 5\%$ that all partial slope coefficients are equal to zero. Show the ANOVA table.

7.9. A three-variable regression gave the following results:

Source of variation	Sum of squares (SS)	d.f.	Mean sum of squares (MSS)
Due to regression (ESS)	65,965	—	—
Due to residual (RSS)	—	—	—
Total (TSS)	66,042	14	

(a) What is the sample size?
(b) What is the value of the RSS?
(c) What are the d.f. of the ESS and RSS?
(d) What is R^2? And $\bar{R}^2$?
(e) Test the hypothesis that X_2 and X_3 have zero influence on Y. Which test do you use and why?
(f) From the preceding information, can you tell what is the individual contribution of X_2 and X_3 toward Y?

7.10. Recast the ANOVA table given in problem 7.9 in terms of R^2.

7.11. To explain what determines the price of air conditioners, B. T. Ratchford,[19] obtained the following regression results based on a sample of 19 air conditioners:

---

[19] B.T. Ratchford, "The Value of Information for Selected Appliances," *Journal of Marketing Research*, vol. 17, 1980, pp. 14–25. Notations were adapted.

$$\hat{Y}_i = -68.236 + 0.023\,X_{2i} + 19.729X_{3i} + 7.653X_{4i} \quad R^2 = 0.84$$
$$se = \qquad\qquad (0.005) \qquad (8.992) \qquad (3.082)$$

where

$$Y = \text{the price, in dollars}$$
$$X_2 = \text{the BTU rating of air conditioner}$$
$$X_3 = \text{the energy efficiency ratio}$$
$$X_4 = \text{the number of settings}$$
$$se = \text{standard errors}$$

(a) Interpret the regression results.

(b) Do the results make economic sense?

(c) At $\alpha = 5\%$, test the hypothesis that the BTU rating has no effect on the price of an air conditioner vs. that it has a positive effect.

(d) Would you accept the null hypothesis that the three explanatory variables explain a substantial variation in the prices of air conditioners? Show clearly all your calculations.

7.12. Based on the U.S. data for 1965-IQ to 1983-IVQ ($n = 76$), James Doti and Esmael Adibi[20] obtained the following regression to explain personal consumption expenditure (PCE) in the United States.

$$\hat{Y}_t = -10.96 + \qquad 0.93X_{2i} - 2.09X_{3i}$$
$$t = (-3.33) \qquad (249.06) \quad (-3.09) \qquad R^2 = 0.9996$$
$$F = 83{,}753.7$$

where

$$Y = \text{the PCE (\$, in billions)}$$
$$X_2 = \text{the disposable (i.e., after-tax) income (\$, in billions)}$$
$$X_3 = \text{the prime rate (\%) charged by banks}$$

(a) What is the marginal propensity to consume (MPC)—the amount of additional consumption expenditure from an additional dollar's personal disposable income?

(b) Is the MPC statistically different from 1? Show the appropriate testing procedure.

(c) What is the rationale for the inclusion of the prime rate variable in the model? A priori, would you expect a negative sign for this variable?

(d) Is b_3 significantly different from zero?

(e) Test the hypothesis that $R^2 = 0$.

(f) Compute the standard error of each coefficient.

7.13. In the illustrative Example 7.2 given in the text, test the hypothesis that X_2 and X_3 together have no influence on Y. Which test do you use? What are the assumptions underlying that test?

7.14. You are given the data in Table 7-7 for the United States for years 1973 to 1987. To explain the civilian labor-force participation rate (i.e., the civilian labor force

---

[20] See James Doti and Esmael Adibi, *Econometric Analysis: An Applications Approach*, Prentice-Hall, Englewood Cliffs, N.J., 1988, p. 188. Notations were adapted.

$Y = B_0 + B_2 x_2 + B_3 x_3 + B_4 x_4$
$\quad \hookrightarrow$ constant

TABLE 7-7

Data on civilian labor-force participation, unemployment rate, and earnings, United States, 1973–1987

Year	Y	X_2	X_3	X_4
1973	60.8	4.9	101.1	74.1
1974	61.3	5.6	98.3	80.0
1975	61.2	8.5	97.6	86.7
1976	61.6	7.7	99.0	92.9
1977	62.3	7.1	100.0	100.0
1978	63.2	6.1	100.5	108.2
1979	63.7	5.8	97.4	116.8
1980	63.8	7.1	93.5	127.3
1981	63.9	7.6	92.6	138.9
1982	64.0	9.7	93.4	148.5
1983	64.0	9.6	94.8	155.4
1984	64.4	7.5	94.6	160.3
1985	64.8	7.2	94.1	165.2
1986	65.3	7.0	95.0	169.4
1987	65.6	6.2	94.0	173.5

Source: Economic Report of the President, 1989. Data on Y from Table B-37, p. 350; X_2 from Table B-39, p. 352; X_3 and X_4 from Table B-44, p. 358.

Y = the civilian labor-force participation rate (%), seasonally adjusted

X_2 = all civilian workers' unemployment rate (%), seasonally adjusted

X_3 = the index of average hourly earnings in 1977 dollars, total private nonagricultural sector (1977 = 100)

X_4 = the index of average hourly earnings in current dollars, total private nonagricultural sector (1977 = 100)

as a percent of civilian noninstitutional population), consider the following two models:

$$Y_t = B_1 + B_2X_{2t} + B_3X_{3t} + u_t \qquad \text{Model I}$$
$$Y_t = A_1 + A_2X_{2t} + A_4X_{4t} + u_t \qquad \text{Model II}$$

(a) A priori, which of these models will you choose? Why?

(b) For Model I, what are the expected signs of the coefficients? Why?

(c) For Model II, what are the expected signs of the coefficients? Why?

(d) Estimate the parameters of both models and obtain the usual regression output.

(e) Based on the results in part (d), which model do you prefer and why?

(f) Do the regression results suggest that there is *money illusion* in the U.S. economy? Money illusion occurs when people make economic decisions (e.g., to enter the labor force) on the basis of nominal rather than real income or real earnings.

(g) The *discouraged worker hypothesis* in labor economics states that people are discouraged from participating in the labor force if the unemployment rate is high. Do the regression results support this hypothesis?

(h) Another hypothesis from labor economics is the *added worker hypothesis* that, in contrast to the discouraged worker hypothesis, states that when the unemployment rate is high, secondary or part-time workers enter the market to supplement family income. Do the regression results support this hypothesis if they do not support the discouraged worker hypothesis?

7.15. Use formula (7.53) to answer the following question:

Value of R^2	n	k	$\bar{R}^2$
0.83	50	6	—
0.55	18	9	—
0.33	16	12	—
0.12	1,200	32	—

What conclusion do you draw about the relationship between R^2 and $\bar{R}^2$?

7.16. Establish the relation in Eq. (7.50)

7.17. For the illustrative Example 7.3, compute the F value. If that F value is significant, what does that mean?

7.18. For Example 7.2, set up the ANOVA table and test that $R^2 = 0$. Use $\alpha = 1\%$.

CHAPTER

8

FUNCTIONAL FORMS OF REGRESSION MODELS

Until now we have considered models that were linear in parameters as well as in variables. But recall that in this textbook our concern is with models that are linear in parameters; variables Y and Xs do not necessarily have to be linear. As a matter of fact, as we show in this chapter, there are many economic phenomena for which the linear-in-parameters/linear-in-variables (LIP/LIV, for short) regression models may not be adequate or appropriate.

For example, suppose for the LIP/LIV widget demand function given in Eq. (6.48) we want to estimate the *price elasticity of demand*, that is, the percentage change in the quantity of widgets demanded for a percentage change in the price of widgets. We cannot estimate this elasticity from Eq. (6.48), for the slope coefficient of that model simply gives the absolute change in the (average) quantity demanded for a unit change in the price of widgets, but this is not elasticity. Such elasticity, however, can be readily computed from the so-called *log-linear* models discussed in Section 8.1. As we will show, this model, although linear in parameters, is not linear in variables.

For another example, suppose we want to find out the *rate of growth*[1] over time of an economic variable, such as gross national product (GNP) or

---

[1] If Y_t and Y_{t-1} are values of a variable (say, GNP) at time t and $(t - 1)$, say, 1990 and 1989, then the rate of growth of Y between the two time periods is measured as

$$\frac{Y_t - Y_{t-1}}{Y_{t-1}} \cdot 100$$

which is simply the relative, or proportional, change in Y multiplied by 100. It is shown in Section 8.4 how the semilog regression model can be used to measure the growth rate over a longer period of time.

money supply or unemployment rate, or what have you. As we show in Section 8.4, this growth rate can be measured by the so-called *semilog* model, which while linear in parameters, is nonlinear in variables.

The point to note is that even within the confines of the linear-in-parameter regression models, a regression model can assume a variety of *functional forms*. In particular, in this chapter we discuss the following types of regression models:

1. Log-linear or constant elasticity models. (Section 8.1)
2. Semilog models (Sections 8.4 and 8.5)
3. Reciprocal models (Section 8.6)
4. Polynomial regression models (Section 8.7)

An important feature of all these models is that they are all linear in parameters (or can be made so by simple algebraic manipulations), but they are not necessarily linear in variables. In Chapter 5 we have already discussed the technical meaning of linearity in both variables and parameters. Briefly, for a regression model linear in explanatory variable(s) the rate of change (i.e., the slope) of the dependent variable remains constant for a unit change in the explanatory variable, whereas for regression models nonlinear in explanatory variable(s) the slope does not remain constant.

To introduce the basic concepts, and to illustrate them graphically, initially we will consider two-variable models and then extend the discussion to multiple regression models.

8.1 HOW TO MEASURE ELASTICITY: THE LOG-LINEAR MODEL

Let us revisit our widget demand function discussed in Chapters 5 and 6. But now consider the following functional form of the demand function. (To ease the algebra, we will introduce the error term u_i later.)

$$Y_i = AX_i^{B_2} \tag{8.1}$$

where Y is the quantity of widgets demanded and X its price.

This model is nonlinear in the variable X.[2] But let us express Equation (8.1) in an alternative, but equivalent, form, as follows:

$$\ln Y_i = \ln A + B_2 \ln X_i \tag{8.2}$$

---

[2] Using calculus, it can be shown that

$$\frac{dY}{dX} = AB_2 \, X^{(B_2-1)}$$

which shows that the rate of change of Y with respect to X is not independent of X; that is, it is not constant. By definition, then, model (8.1) is not linear in variable X.

where ln = the natural log, that is, logarithm to the base e.[3] Now if we let

$$B_1 = \ln A \qquad (8.3)$$

we can write Equation (8.2) as

$$\ln Y_i = B_1 + B_2 \ln X_i \qquad (8.4)$$

And for estimating purposes, we can write this model as

$$\ln Y_i = B_1 + B_2 \ln X_i + u_i \qquad (8.5)$$

This is a linear regression model, for the parameters B_1 and B_2 enter the model linearly.[4] It is of interest that this model is also linear in the logarithms of the variables Y and X [*Note*: The original model (8.1) was nonlinear in X]. Because of this linearity, models like Equation (8.5) are called **double-log** (because both variables are in the log form) or **log-linear** (because of linearity in the logs of the variables) models.

Notice how an "apparently" nonlinear model (8.1) can be converted into a linear (in the parameter) model by suitable transformation, here the *logarithmic transformation*. Now letting $Y_i^* = \ln Y_i$ and $X_i^* = \ln Y_i$, we can write model (8.5) as

$$Y_i^* = B_1 + B_2 X_i^* + u_i \qquad (8.6)$$

which resembles the models we have considered in the previous chapters; it is linear in both the parameters and the transformed variables Y^* and X^*.

If the assumptions of the classical linear regression model (CLRM) are satisfied for the transformed model, regression (8.6) can be easily estimated with the usual ordinary least squares (OLS) routine and the estimators thus obtained will have the usual best linear unbiasedness (BLUE) property.[5]

One attractive feature of the double-log, or log-linear, model that has made it popular in empirical work is that *the slope coefficient B_2 measures the elasticity of Y with respect to X, that is, the percentage change in Y for a given (small) percentage change in X.*

---

[3] The appendix to this chapter discusses logarithms and their properties for the benefit of those who need it.

[4] Note that since $B_1 = \ln A$, A can be expressed as

$$A = \text{antilog } (B_1)$$

which is, mathematically speaking, a nonlinear transformation. In practice, however, the intercept A often does not have much economic meaning.

[5] Any regression package now routinely computes the logs of (positive) numbers. So, there is no additional computational burden involved.

Symbolically, if we let ΔY stand for a small change in Y and ΔX for a small change in X, we define the elasticity coefficient, E, as

$$E = \frac{\%\ \text{change in } Y}{\%\ \text{change in } X}$$

$$= \frac{\Delta Y/Y \cdot 100}{\Delta X/X \cdot 100}$$

$$= \frac{\Delta Y}{\Delta X} \cdot \frac{X}{Y}$$

$$= \text{slope} \left(\frac{X}{Y}\right)$$

(8.7)[6]

Thus, if Y represents the quantity of a commodity demanded and X represents its unit price, B_2 measures the *price elasticity of demand*.

All this can be shown graphically. Figure 8-1(a) represents the function (8.1) and Figure 8-1(b) shows its logarithmic transformation. The slope of the straight line shown in Figure 8-1(b) gives the estimate of price elasticity, $(-B_2)$. An important feature of the log-linear model should be apparent from Figure 8-1(b). Since the regression line is a straight line (in the logs of Y and X), its slope $(-B_2)$ is constant throughout. And since this slope coefficient is equal to the elasticity coefficient, for this model, the elasticity is also constant throughout—it does not matter at what value of X this elasticity is computed.[7]

Because of this special feature, the double-log or log-linear model is also known as the **constant elasticity model.** Therefore, we will use all these terms interchangeably.

---

[6] In calculus notation

$$E = \frac{dY}{dX} \cdot \frac{X}{Y}$$

where dY/dX means the derivative of Y with respect to X, that is, the rate of change of Y with respect to X. $\Delta Y/\Delta X$ is an approximation of dY/dX.
Note: For the transformed model (8.6),

$$B_2 = \frac{\Delta Y^*}{\Delta X^*} = \frac{\Delta \ln Y}{\Delta \ln X} = \frac{\Delta Y/Y}{\Delta X/X} = \frac{\Delta Y}{\Delta X} \cdot \frac{X}{Y}$$

which is the elasticity of Y with respect to X as per Eq. (8.7). As noted in the appendix to this chapter, a change in the log of a number is a relative or proportional change. For example,

$$\Delta \ln Y = \frac{\Delta Y}{Y}$$

[7] Note carefully, however, in general, elasticity and slope coefficients are different concepts. As Eq. (8.7) makes clear, elasticity is equal to the slope times the ratio of X/Y. It is only for the double-log, or log-linear, model that the two are identical.

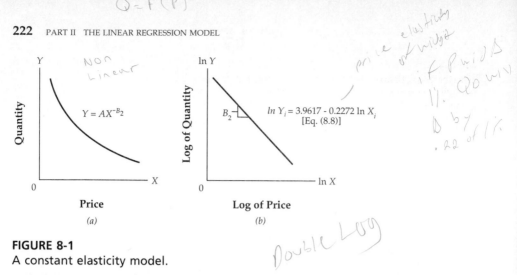

FIGURE 8-1

A constant elasticity model.

Example 8.1. The demand for widgets revisited. In Eq. (6.48) we presented the linear (in variables) demand function for widgets. But recall that the scattergram showed that the relationship between the quantity and the price of widgets was approximately linear because not all points were really on a straight line. Equation (6.48) was, of course, developed for pedagogy. Let us see if the log-linear model fits the data given in Table 5-4, which for convenience is reproduced in Table 8-1.

The OLS regression based on these data gave the following results:

$$\widehat{\ln Y_i} = 3.9617 - 0.2272 \ln X_i$$

$$se = (0.0416) \quad (0.0250) \tag{8.8}$$

$$t = (95.261) \quad (-9.0821) \qquad r^2 = 0.9116$$

As these results show, the (constant) price elasticity is ≈ -0.23, suggesting that if the price of widgets increases by 1 percent, the quantity of widgets demanded *on the average* decreases by ≈ 0.23 percent. By definition, a product whose price elasticity is less than 1 in absolute value has inelastic demand. Therefore, in our example the demand for widgets is price inelastic since the absolute value of the elasticity coefficient is ≈ 0.23.

The interpretation of the intercept of ≈ 3.96 means that the average value of $\ln Y$ is 3.96 if the value of $\ln X$ is zero. Again, this mechanical interpretation of the intercept may not have concrete economic meaning.[8]

The interpretation of $r^2 = 0.9116$ is that ≈ 91 percent of the variation in the log of Y is explained by the log of X.

The regression line (8.8) is sketched in Figure 8-1(b).

---

[8] Since $\ln Y = 3.9617$ when $\ln X$ is zero, if we take the antilog of this number, we obtain 52.5466. Thus, the average quantity of widgets demanded is ≈ 53 units if the price of widgets is zero. For the linear model (6.48) this number was 49.667 or ≈ 50 units.

TABLE 8-1
The demand for widgets

Quantity Y	Price X	ln Y	ln X
49	1	3.8918	0.0000
45	2	3.8067	0.6931
44	3	3.7842	1.0986
39	4	3.6636	1.3863
38	5	3.6376	1.6094
37	6	3.6109	1.7918
34	7	3.5264	1.9459
33	8	3.4965	2.0794
30	9	3.4012	2.1972
29	10	3.3673	2.3026

Hypothesis Testing in Log-Linear Models

There is absolutely no difference between the linear and log-linear models insofar as hypothesis testing is concerned. Under the assumption that the error term follows the normal distribution with mean zero and constant variance σ^2, it follows that each estimated regression coefficient is normally distributed. Or, if we replace σ^2 by its unbiased estimator $\hat{\sigma}^2$ each estimator follows the t distribution with degrees of freedom (d.f.) equal to $(n - k)$, where k is the number of parameters estimated including the intercept. k is 2 in the two-variable case, 3 in the three-variable case, etc.

From the regression (8.8), the reader can readily check that each estimated coefficient is statistically significantly different from zero, for the t values of -9.08 (for b_2) and 95.26 (for b_1) exceed the critical t value of 2.306 for 8 d.f. at the 5% level of significance (two-tailed).

8.2   COMPARING LINEAR AND LOG-LINEAR REGRESSION MODELS

We take this opportunity to consider an important practical question. We have fitted a linear (in variables) demand function, Eq. (6.48), to our widget data as well as a log-linear demand function, Eq. (8.8). Which model should we choose? Although economic theory suggests that the price and quantity demanded are negatively related, as noted in Chapter 1, the theory is often not *robust* enough to tell us the particular **functional form** of the relationship between the two. That is, theory is not strong enough to suggest whether we should fit the linear model or the log-linear model or some other model. The functional form of the regression model then becomes essentially an *empirical question*. Are there any guidelines or rules of thumb that one can follow in choosing among competing models?

One guiding principle is to plot the data. If the scattergram shows that the relationship between two variables looks reasonably linear (i.e., a straight line), the linear specification might be appropriate. But if the scattergram shows a nonlinear relationship, plot the log of Y against the log of X. If this plot shows an approximately linear relationship, a log-linear model may be appropriate. Unfortunately, this guiding principle works only in the simple case of two-variable regression models and is not very helpful once we consider multiple regressions; it is not easy to draw scattergrams in multiple dimensions. We need other guidelines.

Why not choose the model on the basis of r^2, that is, choose the model that gives the highest r^2. Although intuitively appealing, this criterion has its own problems. First, as noted in Chapter 7, *to compare the r^2 values of two models, the dependent variable must be in the same form.*[9] For model (6.48), the dependent variable is Y, whereas for the model (8.8), it is ln Y, and these two dependent variables are obviously not the same. Therefore, $r^2 = 0.9757$ of the linear model (6.48) and $r^2 = 0.9116$ of the log-linear models are not directly comparable.

The reason that we cannot compare these two r^2 values is not difficult to grasp. By definition, r^2 measures the proportion of the variation in the dependent variable explained by the explanatory variable(s). In the linear model (6.48) r^2 thus measures the proportion of the variation in Y explained by X, whereas in the log-linear model (8.8) it measures the proportion of the variation in the log of Y explained by the log of X. Now the *variation in Y and the variation in the log of Y* are conceptually different. *The variation in the log of a number measures the relative or proportional change* (or percent change if multiplied by 100) and the variation in a number measures the *absolute change.*[10] Thus, for the linear model (6.48) $\approx$ 98 percent of the variation in Y is explained by X, whereas for the log-linear model, $\approx$ 91 percent of the variation in the log of Y is explained by the log of X. If one wants to compare the two r^2s, one can use the method discussed in problem 8.16.

Even if the dependent variable in the two models is the same so that two r^2 values can be directly compared, one is well-advised against choosing a model on the basis of a **high r^2 value criterion.** This is because, as pointed out in Chapter 7, an $r^2 (= R^2)$ can always be increased by adding more explanatory variables to the model. Rather than emphasizing the r^2 value of a model, the researcher should consider factors such as the relevance of the explanatory variables included in the model (i.e., the underlying theory), the expected signs of the coefficients of the explanatory variables, their statistical significance, and certain derived measures like the elasticity coefficient. These should be the guiding principles in choosing between two competing models. If based

---

[9] It does not matter what form the independent or explanatory variables take; they may or may not be linear.

[10] If a number goes from 45 to 50, the absolute change is 5, but the relative change is $(50 - 45)/45 = 0.1111$ or $\approx$ 11.11 percent.

on these criteria one model is preferable to the other, and if the chosen model also happens to have a higher r^2 value, then well and good. But *avoid the temptation of choosing a model only on the basis of the* r^2 *value alone.*

Comparing the results of the log-linear demand function (8.8) vs. the linear demand function (6.48), we observe that in both models the slope coefficient is negative, as per economic theory. Also, both slope coefficients are statistically significant. However, we cannot compare the two slope coefficients directly, for in the LIV model it measures the absolute rate of change in the quantity demand for a unit change in price, whereas in the log-linear model it measures price elasticity—the percentage change in quantity demanded for a percentage change in price.

If for the LIV model we can measure price elasticity, then it is possible to compare the two slope coefficients. To do this, we can use Eq. (8.7), which shows that elasticity is equal to the slope times the ratio of X to Y—that is, of price to quantity. Although for the linear model the slope coefficient remains the same (why?), which is -2.1576 in our example, the elasticity changes from point to point on the linear demand curve because the ratio X/Y changes from point to point. From Table 8-1 we see that there are 10 different price and quantity combinations. Therefore, in principle we can compute 10 different price elasticity coefficients. In practice, however, the elasticity coefficient for the linear model is often computed at the sample mean values of X and Y to obtain a measure of *average price elasticity*. That is,

$$\text{Average price elasticity} = \frac{\Delta Y}{\Delta X} \cdot \frac{\overline{X}}{\overline{Y}} \tag{8.9}$$

where $\overline{X}$ and $\overline{Y}$ are sample mean values. For the data given in Table 8-1, $\overline{X} = 5.5$ and $\overline{Y} = 37.8$. Thus, the average price elasticity for the widget sample is

$$\text{Average price elasticity} = -2.1576 \cdot \frac{5.5}{37.8}$$

$$= -0.314$$

It is interesting to note that for the log-linear demand function the price elasticity coefficient was -0.2272, which remains the same no matter at what price the elasticity is measured [see Figure 8-1(b)]. This is why such a model is called a constant elasticity model. For the LIV, on the other hand, the elasticity coefficient changes from point to point on the demand curve.[11]

The fact that for the linear model the elasticity coefficient changes from point to point and that for the log-linear model it remains the same at all points on the demand curve means that one has to exercise some judgment in choosing between the two specifications, for, in practice, both these assump-

---

[11] Notice this interesting fact: For the LIV model, the slope coefficient is constant but the elasticity coefficient is variable. However, for the log-linear model, the elasticity coefficient is constant but the slope coefficient is variable, which can be seen at once from the formula given in footnote 2.

tions may be extreme. It is possible that over a small segment of the demand curve the price elasticity remains constant but that over some other segment(s) it is variable.

8.3 MULTIPLE LOG-LINEAR REGRESSION MODELS

The two-variable log-linear model can be easily generalized to models containing more than one explanatory variable. For example, a three-variable log-linear model can be expressed as

$$\ln Y_i = B_1 + B_2 \ln X_{2i} + B_3 \ln X_{3i} + u_i \tag{8.10}$$

In this model the partial slope coefficients B_2 and B_3 are also called the partial elasticity coefficients.[12] Thus, B_2 measures the elasticity of Y with respect to X_2 holding the influence of X_3 constant; that is, it measures the percentage change in Y for a percentage change in X_2, holding the influence of X_3 constant. Since the influence of X_3 is held constant, it is called a partial elasticity. Similarly, B_3 measures the (partial) elasticity of Y with respect to X_3, holding the influence of X_2 constant. In short, *in a multiple log-linear model, each partial slope coefficient measures the partial elasticity of the dependent variable with respect to the explanatory variable in question, holding all other variables constant.*

> **Example 8.2 The Cobb-Douglas production function.** As an example of model (8.10), let Y = output, X_2 = labor input, and X_3 = capital input. In that case model (8.10) becomes a *production function*—a function that relates output to labor and capital inputs. As a matter of fact, regression (8.10) represents the famous **Cobb-Douglas production function.** As an illustration, based on the data for Taiwan for the period 1958 to 1972, the following regression results were obtained:[13]
>
> $$\widehat{\ln Y_t} = -3.3385 + 1.4988 \ln X_{2t} + 0.4899 \ln X_{3t}$$
>
> $$t = (-1.3629) \quad (2.7765) \quad (4.8005) \tag{8.11}$$
>
> $$R^2 = 0.8890$$

---

[12] The calculus-minded reader will recognize that the partial derivative of $\ln Y$ with respect to $\ln X_2$ is

$$B_2 = \frac{\partial \ln Y}{\partial \ln X} = \frac{\partial Y/Y}{\partial X/X} = \frac{\partial Y}{\partial X} \cdot \frac{X}{Y}$$

which by definition is elasticity of Y with respect to X_2. Likewsie, B_3 is the elasticity of Y with respect to X_3.

[13] For details, see Damodar N. Gujarati, *Basic Econometrics*, 2d ed., McGraw-Hill, New York, 1988, pp. 189–192.

where

Y = the real gross product (in \$, millions of NT)

X_2 = millions of man-days

X_3 = the real capital input (in \$, millions of NT)

where NT \$ is the new Taiwanese dollar.

The interpretation of this regression is as follows. The partial slope coefficient of 1.4988 measures the partial elasticity of the output with respect to the labor input. Specifically, this number states that, holding the capital input constant, if the labor input increases by 1 percent on the average, the output goes up by $\approx$ 1.50 percent. Likewise, holding the labor input constant, if the capital input increases by 1 percent on the average, output goes up by $\approx$ 0.5 percent. If we add the two elasticity coefficients, we obtain an economically important parameter called the **returns to scale** parameter, which gives the response of output to a proportional change in inputs. If the sum of the two elasticity coefficients is 1, we have the case of **constant returns to scale** (e.g., doubling the inputs doubles the output); if it is greater than 1, we have **increasing returns to scale** (i.e., doubling the inputs more than doubles the output); if it is less than 1, we have **decreasing returns to scale** (i.e., doubling the inputs less than doubles the output).

For the regression given in Equation (8.11), the sum of the two elasticity coefficients is 1.9887, suggesting that for the Taiwanese economy for the aforementioned period, there were increasing returns to scale—doubling the inputs more than doubles the output; that is, the productivity growth in the economy was quite fast.

Example 8.3. The demand for roses revisited. In Chapter 7 we estimated the LIV demand function for roses given in Eq. (7.44). For the same example, the log-linear demand function was estimated as follows:

$$\widehat{\ln Y_t} = 9.2278 - 1.7607 \ln X_{2t} + 1.3398 \ln X_{3t}$$

$$
\begin{array}{llll}
\text{se} = & (0.56839) & (0.29821) & (0.52737) \\
t = & (16.235) & (-5.9044) & (2.5407)
\end{array}
\qquad (8.12)
$$

$$R^2 = 0.7292$$
$$\overline{R}^2 = 0.6875$$

As this regression shows, the *own-price* elasticity of demand for roses is -1.7693. It means, holding all other things constant, if the price of roses increases by 1 percent, the average quantity of roses demanded will decrease by $\approx$ 1.76 percent. The reader can easily check that this price elasticity is not only statistically significant (i.e., different from zero), but it is actually statistically greater than 1 in absolute value, at, say, the 5% level. In economics a commodity whose price elasticity coefficient is greater than 1 (in absolute value) is said to have elastic demand. In our example it seems that the demand for roses is (price) elastic.

The partial elasticity of 1.3499 means, holding other things the same, if the price of carnations goes up by 1 percent, the average quantity of roses demanded increases by ≈ 1.35 percent. In economics this is called the *cross-price elasticity* of demand, which is the percentage change in the quantity demanded of a product for a percentage change in the price of another product. If the cross-price elasticity is positive, it means the two products are *competing* or *substitute* products. If, on the other hand, this elasticity is negative, the two products are complementary (e.g., if the price of gasoline goes up, the demand for automobiles goes down). In our example roses and carnations seem to be competing products. The reader should check that the measured cross-price elasticity is statistically significantly different from zero but not significantly different from 1. A product whose elasticity coefficient is unity or 1 is said to have *unitary elasticity*.

8.4   HOW TO MEASURE THE GROWTH RATE: THE SEMILOG MODEL

As noted in the introduction to this chapter, economists, businesspeople, and the government are often interested in finding out the rate of growth of certain economic variables. For example, the projection of the government budget deficit (surplus) is based on the projected rate of growth of the GNP, the single most important economic indicator of economic activity. Likewise, the Fed keeps a strong eye on the rate of growth of consumer credit outstanding (auto loans, installment loans, etc.) to monitor its monetary policy.

In this section we show how regression analysis can be used to measure such growth rates.

Example 8.4. The growth of consumer credit outstanding in the United States, 1973 to 1987. Table 8-2 gives the data on consumer credit outstanding in the United States over the period 1973 to 1987.

We want to measure the rate of growth of consumer credit outstanding (Y) over this period. Now consider the following well-known compound interest formula from your introductory courses in money, banking, and finance:

$$Y_t = Y_0(1 + r)^t \qquad (8.13)[14]$$

---

[14] Suppose you deposit $Y_0 = \$100$ in a passbook account in a bank, paying, say, 6 percent, interest per year. Here $r = 0.06$, or 6 percent. At the end of the first year this amount will grow to $Y_1 = 100(1 + 0.6) = 106$; at the end of the second year it will be $Y_2 = 106(1 + 0.06) = 100 (1 + 0.06)^2 = 112.36$ because in the second year you get interest not only on the initial $100 but also on the interest earned in the first year. In the third year this amount grows to $100(1 + 0.06)^3 = 119.1016$, etc.

where

$$Y_0 = \text{the beginning, or initial, value of } Y$$

$$Y_t = Y\text{'s value at time } t$$

$$r = \text{the compound (i.e., over time) rate of growth of } Y$$

Let us manipulate Equation (8.13) as follows. Take the (natural) log of (8.13) on both sides to obtain

$$\ln Y_t = \ln Y_0 + t \ln(1 + r) \tag{8.14}$$

Now let

$$B_1 = \ln Y_0 \tag{8.15}$$

$$B_2 = \ln(1 + r) \tag{8.16}$$

Therefore, we can express model (8.14) as

$$\ln Y_t = B_1 + B_2 t \tag{8.17}$$

Now if we add the error term u_t to model (8.17); we will obtain[15]

$$\ln Y_t = B_1 + B_2 t + u_t \tag{8.18}$$

This model is like any other linear regression model in that parameters B_1 and B_2 are linear. The only difference is that the dependent variable is the logarithm of Y and the independent, or explanatory, variable is "time," which will take values of 1, 2, 3, etc.

Models like regression (8.18) are called **semilog models** because only one variable (in this case the dependent variable) appears in the logarithmic form. How do we interpret semilog models like regression (8.18)? Before we do that, note that model (8.18) can be estimated by the usual OLS method, assuming of course that the usual assumptions of OLS are satisfied. For the data of Table 8-2, we obtain the following regression results:

$$\widehat{\ln Y_t} = 12.007 + 0.0946t$$

$$se = (0.0319) \quad (0.0035) \tag{8.19}$$

$$t = (376.12) \quad (26.954) \quad r^2 = 0.9824$$

The estimated regression line is sketched in Figure 8-2(a).

The interpretation of regression (8.19) is as follows. The slope coefficient of 0.0946 means on the average the *log of* Y (consumer credit outstanding) has been increasing at the rate of 0.0946 per year. In plain English, Y has been increasing at the rate of 9.46 percent per year, for *in a semilog model like regression (8.19) the slope coefficient measures the proportional or relative change in Y for a given absolute*

---

[15] The reason we add the error term is that the compound interest rate formula will not exactly fit the data of Table 8-2.

change in the explanatory variable, time in the present case.[16] If this relative change is multiplied by 100, we obtain the percentage change or the growth rate (see footnote 1). In our example the relative change is 0.0946, and hence the growth rate is 9.46 percent.

Because of this, semilog models like (8.19) are known as *growth models* and such models are routinely used to measure the growth rate of many variables, whether or not economic.

The interpretation of the intercept term 12.007 is as follows. From (8.15) it is evident that

$$b_1 = \text{the estimate of } \ln Y_0 = 12.007$$

TABLE 8-2
Consumer credit outstanding (Y), United States, 1973–1987*

Year	Y	Year	Y
1973	190,601	1981	366,597
1974	199,365	1982	381,115
1975	204,963	1983	430,382
1976	228,162	1984	511,768
1977	263,808	1985	592,409
1978	308,272	1986	646,055
1979	347,507	1987	685,545
1980	349,386		

Source: Economic Report of the President, 1989, Table B-75, p. 396.
* In millions of dollars, seasonally adjusted.

SHAZAM

---

[16] Using differential calculus, it can be shown that

$$B_2 = \frac{d \ln Y}{dt}$$

$$= \left(\frac{1}{Y}\right)\left(\frac{dY}{dt}\right)$$

$$= \frac{\frac{dY}{Y}}{dt}$$

$$= \frac{\text{relative change in } Y}{\text{absolute change in } t}$$

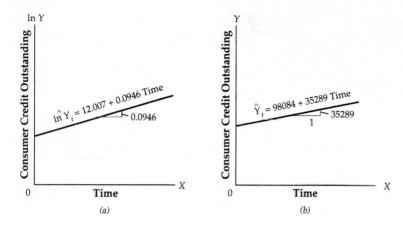

FIGURE 8-2
Growth of consumer credit outstanding: (a) Semilog model; (b) linear trend model.

Therefore, if we take the antilog of 12.007 we obtain

$$\text{antilog}(12.007) \approx 163{,}911.7 \qquad (8.20)$$

which is the value of Y when $t = 0$, that is, at the beginning of the period. As Table 8-2 shows, at the end of 1973, which is the beginning period of our analysis, the value of Y was 190,000 ($, in millions). Perhaps we can interpret the value of 163,912 ($, in millions) as the value of consumer credit outstanding at the beginning of 1973. But remember the warning given previously, namely, often the intercept term has no particular physical meaning.

Instantaneous versus Compound Rate of Growth

Notice from Eq. (8.16) that

$$b_2 = \text{the estimate of } B_2 = \ln(1 + r)$$

Therefore,

$$\text{antilog}(b_2) = (1 + r)$$

which means that

$$r = \text{antilog}(b_2) - 1 \qquad (8.21)$$

And since r is the compound rate of growth, once we have obtained b_2 we can easily estimate the compound rate of growth of Y from Equation (8.21). For our example, we obtain

$$r = \text{antilog}(0.0946) - 1 \qquad (8.22)$$
$$= 1.0922 - 1 = 0.0992$$

That is, over the sample period *the compound rate of growth in consumer credit outstanding had been at the rate of 9.92 percent per year.*

Earlier we said that the growth rate in Y was 9.46 percent but now we say it is 9.92 percent. What is the difference? The growth rate of 9.46 percent [or, more generally, the slope coefficient in regressions like Eq. (8.19), multiplied by 100] gives the **instantaneous** (at a point in time) **growth rate**, whereas the growth rate of 9.92 percent [or, more generally, that obtained from Equation (8.22)] is the **compound** (over a period of time) **growth rate**.

In practice, though, one generally quotes the instantaneous growth rate, although the compound growth rate can be easily computed, as just shown.

The Linear Trend Model

Sometimes, as a quick and ready method of computation, researchers estimate the following model:

$$Y_t = B_1 + B_2 t + u_t \qquad (8.23)$$

That is, regress Y on time itself, where time is measured chronologically. Such a model is called, appropriately, the **linear trend model** and the time variable t is known as the **trend variable**.[17] If the slope coefficient in the preceding model is positive, there is an *upward trend* in Y, whereas if it is negative, there is a *downward trend* in Y.

For the data of Table 8-2, the results of fitting Equation (8.23) were as follows:

$$\hat{Y}_t = \ 98084 \ + \ 35289t$$
$$se = (23095) \quad (2540.1) \qquad (8.24)$$
$$t = (4.2470) \quad (13.893) \qquad r^2 = 0.9369$$

As these results show, over the sample period the consumer credit outstanding had been increasing at the absolute (note, not relative) rate of $35,289 (millions) per year. Thus, over that period there was an upward trend in consumer credit outstanding [See Figure 8-2(b)].

In practice, both the linear trend and growth models have been used extensively. For comparative purposes, however, the growth model is more useful. People are often interested in finding out the relative performance and not the absolute performance of economic measures, such as GNP, money supply, etc.

Incidentally, note that we cannot compare r^2 values of the two models because the dependent variables in the two models are not the same (but see

---

[17] By trend we mean a sustained upward or downward movement in the behavior of a variable.

problem 8.16). Statistically speaking, both models give fairly good results, judged by the usual t test of significance.

Recall that for the log-linear, or double-log, model the slope coefficient gives the elasticity of Y with respect to the relevant explanatory variable. For the growth model and the linear trend models, we can also measure such elasticities. As a matter of fact, once the functional form of the regression model is known, one can compute elasticities from the basic definition of elasticity given in Eq. (8.7). Table 8-6 at the end of this chapter summarizes the elasticity coefficients for the various models we have considered in this chapter.

8.5 THE LIN-LOG MODEL: WHEN THE EXPLANATORY VARIABLE IS LOGARITHMIC

In the previous section we considered the growth model in which the dependent variable was in log form but the explanatory variable was in linear form. For descriptive purposes, one can call such a model a **log-lin**, or **growth**, **model**. In this section we consider a model where the dependent variable is in linear form but the explanatory variable is in log form. Appropriately, we call this model the **lin-log model**.

We introduce this model with a concrete example.

Example 8.5. The relationship between GNP and money supply in the United States, 1973 to 1987.   Suppose the Fed is interested in finding out the response of GNP to a percentage change in the money supply, which the Fed can control. Toward that end, suppose we have data on the GNP and the money supply (as measured by M_2) given in Table 8-3.

Now consider the following model:

$$Y_t = B_1 + B_2 \ln X_{2t} + u_t \qquad (8.25)$$

where Y = the GNP and X_2 = the money supply.

In contrast to the log-lin model (8.18) where the dependent variable is in log form, the independent variable here is in log form. Before interpreting this model, we present the results based on this model:

$$\hat{Y}_t = -16329.0 + 2584.8 \ln X_t$$
$$t = (-23.494) \qquad (27.549) \qquad r^2 = 0.9832 \qquad (8.26)$$

Interpreted in the usual fashion, the slope coefficient of ≈ 2585 means that if the log of money supply increases by a unit, the absolute change in the GNP is $\approx \$2585$ billions. What does it mean in everyday language?

Recall that a change in the log of a number is a relative change. Therefore, the slope coefficient in model (8.25) measures[18]

$$B_2 = \frac{\text{absolute change in } Y}{\text{relative change in } X}$$

$$= \frac{\Delta Y}{\Delta X / X}$$

(8.27)

TABLE 8-3
GNP and money supply, United States, 1973–1987

Year	GNP ($, in billions)	M_2
1973	1359.3	861.0
1974	1472.8	908.5
1975	1598.4	1023.2
1976	1782.8	1163.7
1977	1990.5	1286.7
1978	2249.7	1389.0
1979	2508.2	1500.2
1980	2723.0	1633.1
1981	3052.6	1795.5
1982	3166.0	1954.0
1983	3405.7	2185.2
1984	3772.2	2363.6
1985	4014.9	2562.6
1986	4240.3	2807.7
1987	4526.7	2901.0

Source: *Economic Report of the President*, 1989, GNP data from Table B-1, p. 308, and M_2 data from Table B-67, p. 385.

Notes: The GNP figures are quarterly at seasonally adjusted annual rates.

M_2 = currency + demand deposits + travelers checks
    + other checkable deposits + overnight RPs and Eurodollars
    + MMMF balances + MMDAs + savings and small deposits

These are average daily figures, seasonally adjusted.

---

[18] If $Y = B_1 + B_2 \ln X$, using calculus, it can be shown that

$$\frac{dY}{dX} = B_2 \left(\frac{1}{X} \right)$$

Therefore,

$$B_2 = X \cdot \frac{dY}{dX} = \frac{dY}{dX/X} = \text{Eq. (8.27)}$$

where, as before, ΔY and ΔX represent (small) changes in Y and X. Equation (8.27) can be written, equivalently, as

$$\Delta Y = B_2 \left(\frac{\Delta X}{X} \right) \tag{8.28}$$

This equation states that the absolute change in $Y(= \Delta Y)$ is equal to B_2 times the relative change in X. If the latter is multiplied by 100, then Equation (8.28) gives the absolute change in Y for a percentage change in X. Thus, if $\Delta X/X$ changes by 0.01 unit (or 1 percent), the absolute change in Y is 0.01 (B_2). Thus, if in an application we find that $B_2 = 674$, the absolute change in Y is (0.01)(674), or 6.74. Therefore, when regressions like (8.25) are estimated by OLS, multiply the value of the estimated slope coefficient B_2 by 0.01, or what amounts to the same thing, divide it by 100.

Returning to the GNP/money regression given in model (8.26), we then see that if the money supply increases by 1 percent, on the average the GNP increases by $\approx$\$25.84 billions (*Note*: Divide the estimated slope coefficient by 100.)

Lin-log models like Eq. (8.25) are thus used in situations where the interest lies in studying the absolute change in the dependent variable for a percentage change in the independent variable. Needless to say, models like regression (8.25) can have more than one X variable in the log form. Each partial slope coefficient will then measure the absolute change in the dependent variable for a percentage change in the given X variable, holding all other X variables constant.

8.6 RECIPROCAL MODELS

Models of the following type are known as **reciprocal models**:

$$Y_i = B_1 + B_2 \left(\frac{1}{X_i} \right) + u_i \tag{8.29}$$

This model is nonlinear in X because it enters the model *inversely* or *reciprocally*, but it is a linear regression model because the parameters are linear.[19]

The salient feature of this model is that as X increases indefinitely, the term $(1/X_i)$ approaches zero (why?) and Y approaches the limiting or **asymptotic value** of B_1. Therefore, models like regression (8.29) have built into them an *asymptote* or *limit value* that the dependent variable will take when the value of the X variable increases indefinitely.

Some likely shapes of the curve corresponding to Eq. (8.29) are shown in Figure 8-3.

---

[19] If we let $X_i^* = (1/X_i)$, then Eq. (8.29) is linear in the parameters as well as in the variables Y_i and X_i^*.

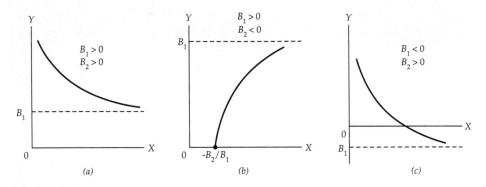

FIGURE 8-3
The reciprocal model: $Y_i = B_1 + B_2(1/X_i)$

In Figure 8-3(a) if we let Y stand for the average fixed cost (AFC) of production, that is, the total fixed cost divided by the output, and X for the output, then as economic theory shows, AFC declines continuously as the output increases (because the fixed cost is spread over a large number of units) and eventually becomes asymptotic with the output axis at level B_1.

An important application of Figure 8-3(b) is the **Engel expenditure curve** (named after the German statistician Ernst Engel, 1821–1896), which relates a consumer's expenditure on a commodity to his or her total expenditure or income. If Y denotes expenditure on a commodity and X the total income, then certain commodities have these features: (1) There is some critical or *threshold level* of income below which the commodity is not purchased (e.g., an automobile). In Figure 8-3(b) this threshold level of income is at the level $-(B_2/B_1)$. (2) There is a satiety level of consumption beyond which the consumer will not go no matter how high the income (even millionaires do not generally own more than two or three cars at a time). This level is nothing but the asymptote B_1 shown in Figure 8-3(b). For such commodities, the reciprocal model of this figure is the most appropriate.

One important application of Figure 8-3(c) is the celebrated **Phillips curve** of macroeconomics. Based on the British data on the percent rate of change of money wages (Y) and the unemployment rate (X) in percent, Phillips obtained a curve similar to Figure 8-3(c).[20] As this figure shows, there is asymmetry in the response of wage changes to the level of unemployment: Wages rise faster for a unit change in unemployment if the unemployment rate is below U^N, which is called the *natural rate of unemployment* by economists, than they fall for an equivalent change when the unemployment rate is above the natural level, B_1 indicating the asymptotic floor for wage change. (See Figure 8-4 later.) This particular feature of the Phillips curve may be due to institutional factors, such as union bargaining power, minimum wages, unemployment insurance, etc.

---

[20] A. W. Phillips, "The Relation between Unemployment and the Rate of Change of Money Wages in the United Kingdom, 1861–1957," *Economica*, November 1958, pp. 283–299.

Example 8.6. The Phillips curve for the United States, 1958 to 1969. Because of its historical importance, and to illustrate the reciprocal model, we have obtained data, shown in Table 8-4, on percent change in the index of hourly earnings (Y) and the civilian unemployment rate, percent, (X) for the United States for years 1958 to 1969.

Model (8.29) was fitted to the data in Table 8-4, and the results were as follows:

$$\hat{Y}_t = -0.2594 + 20.5880 \left(\frac{1}{X_t}\right)$$

$$t = (-0.2572) \qquad (4.3996) \qquad r^2 = 0.6594$$

(8.30)

This regression line is shown in Figure 8-4(a).

As Figure 8-4 shows, the wage floor is -0.26 percent, which is not statistically different from zero. (Why?) Therefore, no matter how high the unemployment rate is, the rate of growth of wages will be at most zero.

For comparison we present the results of the following linear regression based on the same data [see Figure 8-4(b)]:

$$\hat{Y}_t = 8.0147 - 0.7883X_t$$

$$t = (6.4625) \quad (-3.2605) \qquad r^2 = 0.5153$$

(8.31)

Observe these features of the two models. In the linear model (8.31) the slope coefficient is negative, for the higher the unemployment rate is, the lower the rate of growth of earnings will be, *ceteris paribus*. In the reciprocal model, however, the slope coefficient is positive, which should be the case because the X variable enters inversely (so to speak, two negatives make one positive). In other words, a positive slope in the reciprocal model is analogous to the negative slope in the linear model. The linear model suggests that as the unemployment rate increases by one percentage point, on the average the percent point change in the earnings is a constant amount of ≈ -0.79 no matter at what X we measure it. On the other hand, in the reciprocal model the percentage point rate of change in the earnings is not constant, but rather depends on at what level of X (i.e., the unemployment rate) the change is measured (see Table 8-6).[21] The latter assumption seems economically more plausible. Since the dependent variable in the two models is the same, we can compare the two r^2 values. The r^2 for the reciprocal model is higher than that for the linear model, suggesting that the former model fits the data better than the latter model.

As this example shows, once we go beyond the LIV/LIP models to those models that are still linear in the parameters but not necessarily so in the variables, one has to exercise considerable care in choosing a suitable model in a given situation. In this choice the theory underlying the phenomenon of

---

[21] As shown in Table 8-6, for the reciprocal model the slope is $-B_2(1/X_t^2)$, which obviously is not constant.

TABLE 8-4
Year-to-year percentage change in the index of hourly earnings (Y) and the unemployment rate (%) (X), United States, 1958–1969

Year	Y	X
1958	4.2	6.8
1959	3.5	5.5
1960	3.4	5.5
1961	3.0	6.7
1962	3.4	5.5
1963	2.8	5.7
1964	2.8	5.2
1965	3.6	4.5
1966	4.3	3.8
1967	5.0	3.8
1968	6.1	3.6
1969	6.7	3.5

Source: *Economic Report of the President*, 1989, data on Y from Table B-39, p. 352, and data on X from Table B-44, p. 358.

interest is often a big help in choosing the appropriate model. There is no denying that model-building involves a good dose of theory, some introspection, and considerable hands-on experience. But the latter comes with practice.

8.7   POLYNOMIAL REGRESSION MODELS

In this section we consider regression models that have found extensive use in applied econometrics relating to production and cost functions. In particular, consider Figure 8-5, which depicts the total cost of production (TC) as a function of output as well as the associated marginal cost (MC) and the average cost (AC) curves.

Letting Y stand for TC and X for the output, mathematically, the total cost function can be expressed as

$$Y_i = B_1 + B_2 X_i + B_3 X_i^2 + B_4 X_i^3 \tag{8.32}$$

which is called a **cubic function**, or, more generally, a **third-degree polynomial** in the variable X—the highest power of X represents the degree of the polynomial (three in the present instance).

Notice that in these types of polynomial functions there is only one explanatory variable on the right-hand side, but it appears with various powers, thus making them multiple regression models.[22] (*Note*: We add the error term u_i to make model (8.32) a regression model.)

---

[22] Of course, one can introduce other X variables and their powers, if needed.

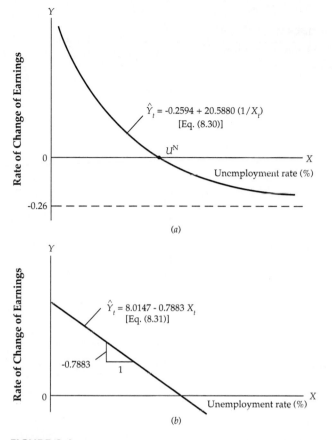

FIGURE 8-4
The Phillips curve for the United States, 1958–1969; (a) Reciprocal model;
(b) linear model.

Although model (8.32) is nonlinear in the variable X, it is linear in the
parameters, the Bs, and is therefore a linear regression model. Thus, models
like regression (8.32) can be estimated by the usual OLS routine. The only
"worry" about the model is the likely presence of the problem of *collinearity*
because the various powered terms of X are functionally related. But this
concern is more apparent than real, for the terms X^2 and X^3 are *nonlinear
functions of* X and do not violate the assumption of no perfect collinearity, that
is, no perfect *linear* relationship between variables. In short, polynomial regression models can be estimated in the usual manner and do not present any
special estimation problems.

TABLE 8-5
Hypothetical cost-output data

Y($)	193	226	240	244	257	260	274	297	350	420	Total cost
X	1	2	3	4	5	6	7	8	9	10	Output

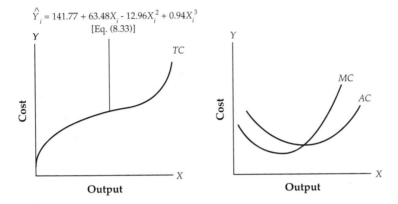

$$\hat{Y}_i = 141.77 + 63.48X_i - 12.96X_i^2 + 0.94X_i^3$$
[Eq. (8.33)]

FIGURE 8-5
Cost-output relationship.

Example 8.7. Hypothetical total cost function. To illustrate the polynomial model, consider the hypothetical cost-output data given in Table 8-5.

The OLS regression results based on these data are as follows (see Figure 8-5):

$$\hat{Y}_i = 141.7667 + 63.4776X_i - 12.9615X_i^2 + 0.9396X_i^3$$

$$\text{se} = (6.3753) \qquad (4.7786) \qquad (0.9857) \qquad (0.0591)$$

$$R^2 = 0.9983 \quad (8.33)$$

If cost curves are to have the U-shaped average and marginal cost curves shown in price theory texts, then the theory suggests that the coefficients in model (8.32) should have these a priori values:[23]

---

[23] For the economics of this, see Alpha C. Chiang, *Fundamental Methods of Mathematical Economics*, 3d ed., McGraw-Hill, New York, 1984, pp. 205–252. The rationale for these restrictions is that to make economic sense the total cost curve must be upward-sloping (the larger the output is, the higher the total cost will be), as well as the marginal cost of production must be positive.

1. B_1, B_2, and B_4, each is greater than zero
2. $B_3 < 0$
3. $B_3^2 < 3B_2B_4$

The regression results given in regression (8.33) clearly are in conformity with these expectations.

8.8   SUMMARY OF FUNCTIONAL FORMS

In this chapter we discussed several regression models that, although linear in the parameters, were not necessarily linear in variables. For each model, we noted its special features and also the circumstances when it might be appropriate. In Table 8-6 we summarize the various functional forms that were discussed in terms of a few salient features, such as the slope coefficients and the elasticity coefficients. Although for double-log models the slope and elasticity coefficients are the same, this is not the case for other models. But even for these models, we can compute elasticities from the basic definition given in Eq. (8.7).

As Table 8-6 shows, for the linear-in-variable (LIV) models, the slope coefficient is constant but the elasticity coefficient is variable, whereas for the log-log, or log-linear, model, the elasticity coefficient is constant but the slope coefficient is variable. For other models shown in Table 8-6, both the slope and elasticity coefficients are variable.

TABLE 8-6
Summary of functional forms

Model	Form	Slope $= \dfrac{dY}{dX}$	Elasticity $= \dfrac{dY}{dX} \cdot \dfrac{X}{Y}$
Linear	$Y = B_1 + B_2 X$	B_2	$B_2 \left(\dfrac{X}{Y}\right)^*$
Log-linear	$\ln Y = B_1 + B_2 \ln X$	$B_2 \left(\dfrac{Y}{X}\right)$	B_2
Log-lin	$\ln Y = B_1 + B_2 X$	$B_2\,(Y)$	$B_2\,(X)^*$
Lin-log	$Y = B_1 + B_2 \ln X$	$B_2 \left(\dfrac{1}{X}\right)$	$B_2 \left(\dfrac{1}{Y}\right)^*$
Reciprocal	$Y = B_1 + B_2 \left(\dfrac{1}{X}\right)$	$-B_2 \left(\dfrac{1}{X^2}\right)$	$-B_2 \left(\dfrac{1}{XY}\right)^*$

Note: * indicates that the elasticity coefficient is variable, depending on the value taken by X or Y or both. When no X and Y are specified, in practice, these elasticities are often measured at the mean values $\overline{X}$ and $\overline{Y}$.

8.9   SUMMARY

In this chapter we considered models that are linear in parameters or can be rendered as such with suitable transformation but are not necessarily linear in variables. There are a variety of such models, each having special applications. We considered five major types of nonlinear-in-variables but linear-in-parameter models, namely:

1. The log-linear model, in which both the dependent variable and the explanatory variable are in logarithmic form
2. The log-lin or growth model, in which the dependent variable is logarithmic but the independent variable is linear
3. The lin-log model, where the dependent variable is linear but the independent variable is logarithmic
4. The reciprocal model, in which the dependent variable is linear but the independent variable is not[24]
5. The polynominal model, where the independent variable enters with various powers

Of course, there is nothing that prevents the researcher from combining the features of one or more of these models. Thus, one can have a multiple regression model in which the dependent variable is in log form and some of the X variables are also in log form, but some are in linear form.

We studied the properties of these various models in terms of their relevance in applied research, their slope coefficients, and their elasticity coefficients. We also showed with several examples the situations in which the various models could be used. Needless to say, we will come across several more examples in the remainder of the text.

It cannot be overemphasized that in choosing among the competing models the overriding objective should be the economic relevance of the various models and not merely the summary statistics, such as R^2. Model-building requires a proper balance of theory, availability of the appropriate data, a good understanding of the statistical properties of the various models, and the elusive quality that is called practical judgment. Since the theory underlying a topic of interest is never perfect, there is no such thing as a perfect model. What we hope for is a reasonably good model that will balance all preceding criteria.

---

[24] The dependent variable can also be reciprocal and the independent variable linear, as problem 8.15 shows.

Key Terms and Concepts

The key terms and concepts introduced in this chapter are:

Linear vs. log-linear regression model
    a) functional form
    b) high r^2 value criterion
Log-linear, double-log, or constant
    elasticity model
Cobb-Douglas production function
    a) returns to scale parameter
    b) constant returns to scale
    c) increasing and decreasing
       returns to scale
Semilog models
Log-lin, or growth, model
    a) instantaneous growth rate
    b) compound growth rate

Lin-log model
Linear trend model
    a) trend variable
Reciprocal models
    a) asymptotic value
    b) Engel expenditure curve
    c) the Phillips curve
Polynomial regression models
    a) cubic function or third-degree
       polynomial

QUESTIONS

8.1. Explain briefly what is meant by
    (*a*) Log-log model   (*d*) Elasticity coefficient
    (*b*) Log-lin model   (*e*) Elasticity at mean value
    (*c*) Lin-log model

8.2. What is meant by a slope coefficient and an elasticity coefficient? What is the relationship between the two?

8.3. Fill in the blanks in the following table:

Model	When appropriate
$\ln Y_i = B_1 + B_2 \lin X_i$	—
$\ln Y_i = B_1 + B_2 X_i$	—
$Y_i = B_1 + B_2 \lin X_i$	—
$Y_i = B_1 + B_2 \left(\dfrac{1}{X_i}\right)$	—

8.4. Complete the following sentences:
    (*a*) In the double-log model the slope coefficient measures . . .
    (*b*) In the lin-log model the slope coefficient measures . . .
    (*c*) In the log-lin model the slope coefficient measures . . .
    (*d*) Elasticity of Y with respect to X is defined as . . .
    (*e*) Price elasticity is defined as . . .
    (*f*) Demand is said to be elastic if the absolute value of the price elasticity is . . . , but demand is said to be inelastic if it is . . .

8.5. State with reason whether the following statements are true (T) or false (F):
    (*a*) For the double-log model, the slope and elasticity coefficients are the same.
    (*b*) For the linear-in-variable (LIV) model, the slope coefficient is constant but the

elasticity coefficient is variable, whereas for the log-log model, the elasticity coefficient is constant but the slope is variable.

(c) The R^2 of a log-log model can be compared with that of a log-lin model but not with that of a lin-log model.

(d) The R^2 of a lin-log model can be compared with that of a linear (in variables) model but not with that of a double-log or log-lin model.

(e) Model A: $\widehat{\ln Y} = -0.6 + 0.4X;$ $r^2 = 0.85$

      Model B: $\hat{Y} = 1.3 + 2.2X;$ $r^2 = 0.73$

      Model A is a better model because its r^2 is higher.

8.6. The *Engel expenditure curve* relates a consumer's expenditure on a commodity to his total income. Letting Y = the consumption expenditure on a commodity and X = the consumer income, consider the following models:

(a) $Y_i = B_1 + B_2 X_i + u_i$

(b) $Y_i = B_1 + B_2(1/X_i) + u_i$

(c) $\ln Y_i = B_1 + B_2 \ln X_i + u_i$

(d) $\ln Y_i = B_1 + B_2(1/X_i) + u_i$

(e) $Y_i = B_1 + B_2 \ln X_i + u_i$

Which of these models would you choose for the Engel curve and why? (*Hint:* Interpret the various slope coefficients, find out the expressions for elasticity of expenditure with respect to income, etc.)

8.7. The growth model (8.18) was fitted to several U.S. economic time series and the following results were obtained:

Time series and period	B_1	B_2	r^2
Real GNP (1954–1987)	7.2492	0.0302	0.9839
(1982 dollars)	$t = $ (529.29)	(44.318)	
Labor force participation rate	4.1056	0.053	0.9464
(1973–1987)	$t = $ (1290.8)	(15.149)	
S&P 500 index	3.6960	0.0456	0.8633
(1954–1987)	$t = $ (57.408)	(14.219)	
S&P 500 index	3.7115	0.0114	0.8524
(1954–1987 quarterly data)	$t = $ (114.615)	(27.819)	

(a) In each case find out the instantaneous rate of growth.

(b) What is the compound rate of growth in each case?

(c) For the S&P data, why is there a difference in the two slope coefficients? How would you reconcile the difference?

PROBLEMS

8.8. Refer to the cubic total cost (TC) function given in Eq. (8.33)

(a) The marginal cost (MC) is the change in the TC for a unit change in output; that is, it is the rate of change of the TC with respect to output. (Technically, it is the derivative of the TC with respect to X, the output.) Derive this function from regression (8.33).

(b) The average variable cost (AVC) is the total variable cost (TVC) divided by the total output. Derive the AVC function from regression (8.33).

(c) The average cost (AC) of production is the TC of production divided by total output. For the function given in regression (8.33), derive the AC function.

(d) Plot the various cost curves previously derived and confirm that they resemble the stylized textbook cost curves.

8.9. Are the following models linear in the parameters? If not, is there any way to make them linear-in-parameter (LIP) models?

(a)
$$Y_i = \frac{1}{B_1 + B_2 X_i}$$

(b)
$$Y_i = \frac{X_i}{B_1 + B_2 X_i^2}$$

8.10. Based on 11 annual observations, the following regressions were obtained:

$$\text{Model A: } \hat{Y}_i = 2.6911 - 0.4795 X_t$$
$$\text{se} = (0.1216) \ (0.1140) \quad r^2 = 0.6628$$

$$\text{Model B: } \ln \hat{Y}_t = 0.7774 - 0.2530 \ln X_t$$
$$\text{se} = (0.0152) \ (0.0494) \quad r^2 = 0.7448$$

where Y = the cups of coffee consumed per person per day and X = the price of coffee, dollars per pound.

(a) Interpret the slope coefficients in the two models.

(b) You are told that $\overline{Y} = 2.43$ and $\overline{X} = 1.11$. At these mean values, estimate the price elasticity for model A.

(c) What is the price elasticity for model B?

(d) From the estimated elasticities, can you say that the demand for coffee is price inelastic?

(e) How would you interpret the intercept in model B? (*Hint:* Take the antilog.)

(f) "Since the r^2 of model B is larger than that of model A, model B is preferable to model A." Comment.

8.11. Refer to the Cobb-Douglas production function given in regression (8.11).

(a) Interpret the coefficient of the labor input X_2. Is it statistically different from 1?

(b) Interpret the coefficient of the capital input X_3. Is it statistically different from zero? And from 1?

(c) What is the interpretation of the intercept value of -3.3385?

(d) Test the hypothesis that $B_2 = B_3 = 0$.

8.12. In their study of the demand for international reserves [i.e., foreign reserve currency such as the dollar or International Monetary Fund (IMF) drawing rights], Moshen Bhahmani-Oskooee and Margaret Malixi[25] obtained the following regression results for a sample of 28 LDCs (less developed countries):

$$\widehat{\ln(R/P)} = 0.1223 + 0.4079 \ \ln(Y/P) + 0.5040 \ \ln \sigma_{BP} - 0.0918 \ \ln \sigma_{EX}$$
$$t = (2.5128) \ \ (17.6377) \qquad (15.2437) \qquad (-2.7449)$$

[25] See Moshen Bhahami-Oskooee and Margaret Malixi, "Exchange Rate Flexibility and the LDCs Demand for International Reserves," *Journal of Quantitative Economics*, vol. 4, no. 2, July 1988, pp. 317–328.

$$R^2 = 0.8268$$
$$F = 1151$$
$$n = 1120$$

where

R = the level of nominal reserves in U.S. dollars
P = U.S. implicit price deflator for GNP
Y = the nominal GNP in U.S. dollars
σ_{BP} = the variability measure of balance of payments
σ_{EX} = the variability measure of exchange rates

(*Notes*: The figures in parentheses are t ratios. This regression was based on quarterly data from 1976 to 1985 (40 quarters) for each of the 28 countries, giving a total sample size of 1120.)

(*a*) A priori, what are the expected signs of the various coefficients? Are the results in accord with these expectations?

(*b*) What is the interpretation of the various partial slope coefficients?

(*c*) Test the statistical significance of each estimated partial regression coefficient (i.e., the null hypothesis is that *individually* each true or population regression coefficient is equal to zero).

(*d*) How would you test the hypothesis that all partial slope coefficients are simultaneously zero?

8.13. Based on the U.K. data on annual percentage change in wages (Y) and the percent annual unemployment rate (X) for the years 1950 to 1966, the following regression results were obtained:

$$\hat{Y}_t = -1.4282 + 8.7243 \left(\frac{1}{X_t}\right)$$

$$\text{se} = (2.0675) \qquad (2.8478) \qquad r^2 = 0.3849$$
$$F(1,15) = 9.39$$

(*a*) What is the interpretation of 8.7243?

(*b*) Test the hypothesis that the estimated slope coefficient is not different from zero. Which test do you use?

(*c*) How would you use the F test to test the preceding hypothesis?

(*d*) Given that $\overline{Y} = 4.8$ percent and $\overline{X} = 1.5$ percent, what is the rate of change of Y at these mean values?

(*e*) What is the elasticity of Y with respect to X at the mean values?

(*f*) How would you test the hypothesis that the true $r^2 = 0$?

8.14 Table 8-7 gives data on the Consumer Price Index, Y (1980 = 100), and the money supply, X (billions of Deutsche marks), for Germany for the years 1971 to 1987.

(*a*) Regress
  (1) Y on X
  (2) $\ln Y$ on $\ln X$
  (3) $\ln Y$ on X
  (4) Y on $\ln X$

(*b*) Interpret each estimated regression.

(*c*) For each model, find out the rate of change of Y with respect to X.

(*d*) For each model, find out the elasticity of Y with respect to X. For some of these models, the elasticity is to be computed at the mean values of Y and X.

TABLE 8-7
Consumer Price Index (Y) (1980 = 100) and the money
supply (X),* Germany, 1971–1987

Year	Y	X
1971	64.1	110.02
1972	67.7	125.02
1973	72.4	132.27
1974	77.5	137.17
1975	82.0	159.51
1976	85.6	176.16
1977	88.7	190.80
1978	91.1	216.20
1979	94.9	232.41
1980	100.0	237.97
1981	106.3	240.77
1982	111.9	249.25
1983	115.6	275.08
1984	118.4	283.89
1985	121.0	296.05
1986	120.7	325.73
1987	121.1	354.93

Source: International Economic Conditions, Annual Ed., June 1988, The Federal Reserve Bank
of St. Louis, p. 24.
* In billions of Deutsche marks.

(e) Based on all these regression results, which model would you choose and
why?

8.15. Based on the following data, estimate the model:

$$\left(\frac{1}{Y_i}\right) = B_1 + B_2 X_i + u_i$$

Y	86	79	76	69	65	62	52	51	51	48
X	3	7	12	17	25	35	45	55	70	120

(a) What is the interpretation of B_2?
(b) What is the rate of change of Y with respect to X?

(c) What is the elasticity of Y with respect to X?

(d) For the same data, run the regression

$$Y_i = B_1 + B_2 \left(\frac{1}{X_i}\right) + u_i$$

(e) Can you compare the r^2s of the two model? Why or why not?

(f) How do you decide which is a better model?

8.16 *Comparing two r^2s when dependent variables are different.*[26] Suppose you want to compare the r^2 values of the growth model (8.19) with the linear trend model (8.24) of the consumer credit outstanding regressions given in the text. Proceed as follows:

(a) Obtain $\widehat{\ln Y_t}$, that is, the estimated log value of each observation from model (8.19).

(b) Obtain the antilog values of the values obtained in step (a).

(c) Compute r^2 between the values obtained in step (b) and the actual Y values using the definition of r^2 given in Problem 6.5.

(d) This r^2 value is comparable with the r^2 value obtained from linear model (8.24).

Use the preceding steps to compare the r^2 values of models (8.19) and (8.24).

8.17. Based on the GNP/money supply data given in Table 8-3, the following regression results were obtained (Y = GNP, X = M2):

Model		Intercept	Slope	r^2
Log-linear		0.5531	0.9882	0.9926
	$t =$	(3.1652)	(41.889)	
Log-lin		6.8616	0.00057	0.9493
(Growth model)	$t =$	(100.05)	(15.597)	
Lin-log		−16329.0	2584.8	0.9832
	$t =$	(−23.494)	(27.549)	
Linear		101.20	1.5323	0.9915
(LIV model)	$t =$	(1.369)	(38.867)	

(a) For each model, interpret the slope coefficient.

(b) For each model, estimate the elasticity of the GNP with respect to money supply and interpret it.

(c) Are all r^2 values directly comparable? If not, which ones are?

(d) Which model will you choose? What are the criteria that you consider in your choice?

(e) According to the monetarists, there is a one-to-one relationship between the rate of changes in the money supply and the GNP. Do the preceding regressions support this view? How would you test this formally?

---

[26] For additional details and numerical computations, see Damodar N. Gujarati, *Basic Econometrics*, 2d ed., McGraw-Hill, New York, 1988, pp. 183–186.

Appendix to Chapter 8: Logarithms

Consider the numbers 5 and 25. We know that

$$25 = 5^2 \tag{A.1}$$

We say that the *exponent* 2 is the *logarithm* of 25 to the *base* 5. More formally, the logarithm of a number (e.g., 25) to a given base (e.g., 5) is the power (2) to which the base (5) must be raised to obtain the given number (25).

More generally, if

$$Y = b^X \quad (b > 0) \tag{A.2}$$

then

$$\log_b Y = X \tag{A.3}$$

In mathematics the function (A.2) is called an *exponential function* and (A.3) is called the *logarithmic function*. As is clear from Eqs. (A.2) and (A.3), one function is the inverse of the other function.

Although any (positive) base can be used, in practice, the two commonly used bases are 10 and the mathematical number $e = 2.71828. \ldots$

Logarithms to base 10 are called *common logarithms*. Thus,

$$\log_{10} 100 = 2 \qquad \log_{10} 30 \approx 1.48$$

That is, in the first case $100 = 10^2$ and in the latter case $30 \approx 10^{1.48}$.

Logarithms to the base e are called *natural logarithms*. Thus,

$$\log_e 100 \approx 4.6051 \quad \text{and} \quad \log_e 30 \approx 3.4012$$

All these calculations can be done routinely on a hand calculator.

By convention, the logarithm to base 10 is denoted by the letters log and to the base e by ln. Thus, in the preceding example, we can write log 100 or log 30 or ln 100 or ln 30.

There is a fixed relationship between the common log and natural log, which is

$$\ln X = 2.3026 \log X \tag{A.4}$$

That is, the natural log of the number X is equal to 2.3026 times the log of X to the base 10. Thus,

$$\ln 30 = 2.3026 \log 30 = 2.3026(1.48) = 3.4012 \quad \text{(approx.)}$$

as before. Therefore, it does not matter whether one uses common or natural logs. But in mathematics the base that is usually preferred is e, that is, the natural logarithm. Hence, in this book all logs are natural logs, unless stated explicitly. Of course, we can convert the log of a number from one basis to the other using Eq. (A.4).

It should be kept in mind that logarithms of negative numbers are not defined. Thus, the log of (-5) or the ln (-5) is not defined.

Some properties of logarithms are as follows: If A and B are any positive numbers, then it can be shown that:

1. $\ln (A \cdot B) = \ln A + \ln B$ $\hfill$ (A.5)

   That is, the log of the product of two (positive) numbers A and B is equal to the sum of their logs.

2. $\ln (A/B) = \ln A - \ln B$ $\hfill$ (A.6)

   That is, the log of the ratio of A to B is the difference in the logs of A and B.

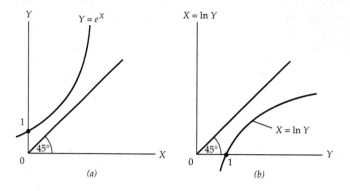

FIGURE 8A-1
Exponential and logarithmic functions: (a) Exponential function; (b) logarithmic function.

3. $\ln (A \pm B) \neq \ln A \pm \ln B$ (A.7)

That is, the log of the sum or difference of A and B is not equal to the sum or difference of their logs.

4. $\ln (A^k) = k \ln A$ (A.8)

That is, the log of A raised to power k is k times the log of A.

5. $\ln e = 1$ (A.9)

That is, the log of e to itself as a base is 1 (as is the log of 10 to the base 10).

6. $\ln 1 = 0$ (A.10)

That is, the natural log of the number 1 is zero (so is the common log of numer 1).

7. If $Y = \ln X$,

$$\frac{dY}{dX} = \frac{1}{X}$$ (A.11)

That is, the rate of change (i.e., the derivative) of Y with respect to X is 1 over X.

The exponential and (natural) logarithmic functions are depicted in Figure 8A-1.

Although the number whose log is taken is always positive, the logarithm of that number can be positive as well as negative. It can be easily verified that if

$$0 < Y < 1 \quad \text{then } \ln Y < 0$$
$$Y = 1 \quad \text{then } \ln Y = 0$$
$$Y > 1 \quad \text{then } \ln Y > 0$$

Also note that although the logarithmic curve shown in Figure 8A-1(b) is positively sloping, implying that the larger the number is, the larger its logarithmic value will be, the curve is increasing at a decreasing rate (mathematically, the second derivative of the function is negative). Thus, $\ln(10) = 2.3026$ (approx.) and $\ln (20) = 2.9957$ (approx.). That is, if a number is doubled, its logarithm does not double.

This is why the logarithm transformation is called a nonlinear transformation. This can also be seen from Equation (A.11), which notes that if $Y = \ln X$, $dY/dX = 1/X$. This means that the slope of the logarithmic function depends on the value of X; that is, it is not constant (recall the definition of linearity in the variable).

REGRESSION ON DUMMY EXPLANATORY VARIABLES

In all the linear regression models considered so far the explanatory variables, the Xs, have been numerical or quantitative. But this may not always be the case; there are occasions when the explanatory variable(s) can be **qualitative** in nature. These qualitative variables, often known as **dummy variables,** have some alternative names used in the literature, such as *indicator variables, binary variables, categorical variables*, and *dichotomous variables*. In this chapter we show with several illustrations how the dummy variables enrich the linear regression model.

9.1 THE NATURE OF DUMMY VARIABLES

Frequently in regression analysis the dependent variable is influenced not only by variables that can be quantified on some well-defined scale (e.g., income, output, costs, prices, weight, temperature) but also by variables that are basically qualitative in nature (e.g., sex, race, color, religion, nationality, strikes, political party affiliation, marital status). For example, some researchers have reported that, *ceteris paribus*, female college teachers are found to earn less than their male counterparts, and, similarly, that the average score of female students on the math part of the S.A.T. examination is less than their male counterparts. (See Table 5-5.) Whatever the reason for this difference, qualitative variables such as sex should be included among the explanatory variables when problems of this type are encountered. Of course, there are other examples that could also be cited.

Such qualitative variables usually indicate the presence or absence of a "quality" or an attribute, such as male or female, black or white, Catholic or non-Catholic, citizens or noncitizens. One method of "quantifying" these attributes is by constructing *artificial variables* that take on values of 1 or 0, 0 indicating the absence of an attribute and 1 indicating the presence (or possession) of that attribute. For example, 1 may indicate that a person is a female and 0 may designate a male; or 1 may indicate that a person is a college graduate and 0 that he or she is not; or 1 may indicate membership in the Democratic party and 0, membership in the Republican party; etc. "Variables" that assume values such as 0 and 1 are called **dummy variables.** We denote the dummy explanatory variables by the symbol D rather than by the usual symbol X to emphasize that we are dealing with a qualitative variable.

Dummy variables can be used in regression analysis just as readily as quantitative variables. As a matter of fact, a regression model may contain only dummy explanatory variables. Regression models that contain only dummy explanatory variables are called **analysis-of-variance (ANOVA) models.** As an example of the ANOVA model, consider the following example:

$$Y_i = B_1 + B_2 D_i + u_i \tag{9.1}$$

where

$$Y = \text{the annual starting salary}$$

$$D = 1 \text{ if college graduate}$$

$$= 0 \text{ otherwise (i.e., noncollege graduate)}$$

Note that model (9.1) is like the two-variable regression models encountered previously except that instead of a quantitative explanatory variable X, we have a qualitative or dummy variable D; as noted earlier, from now on we will use D to denote a dummy variable.

Assuming that the disturbances u_i in model (9.1) satisfy the usual assumptions of the classical linear regression model (CLRM), we obtain from model (9.1) the following:[1]

Mean starting salary of noncollege graduates:

$$E(Y_i \mid D_i = 0) = B_1 + B_2(0) \tag{9.2}$$
$$= B_1$$

Mean starting salary of college graduates:

$$E(Y_i \mid D_i = 1) = B_1 + B_2(1) \tag{9.3}$$
$$= B_1 + B_2$$

---

[1] Since dummy variables generally take on values of 1 or 0, they are nonstochastic; that is, their values are fixed. And since we have assumed all along that our X variables are nonstochastic, the fact that one or more of these X variables are dummies does not create any special problems insofar as estimation of model (9.1) is concerned. In short, dummy explanatory variables do not pose any new estimation problems and we can use the customary OLS method to estimate the parameters of models that contain dummy variables.

From these regressions we see that the intercept term B_1 gives the average or mean starting salary of noncollege graduates and that the "slope" coefficient B_2 tells us by how much the mean salary of college graduates differs from the mean salary of their noncollege counterparts; $(B_1 + B_2)$ gives the mean salary of college graduates.

A test of the null hypothesis that college education does not pay (i.e., $B_2 = 0$) can be easily made by running regression (9.1) in the usual ordinary least squares (OLS) manner and finding out whether or not on the basis of the t test the computed b_2 is statistically significant.

Example 9.1. Starting salaries of college and noncollege graduates. Table 9-1 gives hypothetical data on starting salaries of 10 people by the level of education. The OLS results corresponding to model (9.1) are as follows:

$$\hat{Y}_i = 18.00 + 3.28D_i$$

$$se = (\ 0.31) \quad (0.44) \tag{9.4}$$

$$t = (57.74) \quad (7.444) \qquad r^2 = 0.8737$$

As we can see, the estimated mean salary of noncollege graduates is $18,000 ($= b_1$) and that of college graduates is $21,280 ($b_1 + b_2$). From the data given in Table 9-1, we can easily calculate that the average salaries of noncollege and college graduates are, respectively, $18,000 and $21,280, which are precisely the same as those estimated from regression (9.4).

From the reported t statistic in regression (9.4), it is easy to verify that b_2 is statistically significant (i.e., significantly different from zero), suggesting a difference in the starting salaries of noncollege and college graduates; actually the college graduates on the average earn more than those without the college degree. Higher education does pay!

TABLE 9-1
Hypothetical data on starting salaries

Starting salary, Y (Dependent) ($, in thousands)	Education (1 = college, 0 = noncollege)
21.2	1
17.5	0
17.0	0
20.5	1
21.0	1
18.5	0
21.7	1
18.0	0
19.0	0
22.0	1

Not being measured quantitatively its qualitative.

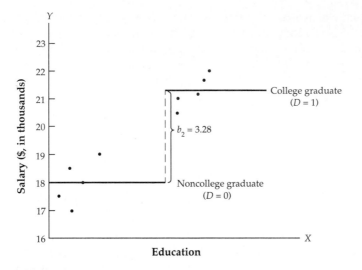

FIGURE 9-1
Starting salary by level of education.

Incidentally, it is interesting to see regression (9.4) graphically, as illustrated in Figure 9-1. As this figure shows, the regression function is a *step function*—the average salary of a noncollege graduate is $18,000 and that of a college graduate jumps by $3,280 (= b_2) to $21,280; the salaries of the individual people in the two groups hover around their respective average salaries.

Example 9.2 The effect of right-to-work laws on union membership. In order to study the effect of *right-to-work laws,* which make mandatory union membership contracts for collective bargaining purposes illegal, Brennan et al.[2] considered union membership (percent of workers belonging to unions) as a function of the right-to-work laws for the year 1980. The study covered the 50 states of the union, with 19 states having right-to-work laws and 31 states allowing union shops (i.e., unions are allowed to bargain for mandatory union memberhip contracts). The results were as follows:

$$\hat{Y}_i = 26.68 - 10.51D_i$$

$$\text{se}= \quad (1.00) \qquad (1.58) \qquad r^2 = 0.4790$$

(9.5)

where

---

[2] See Michael J. Brennan and Thomas M. Carroll, *Preface to Quantitative Economics and Econometrics,* 4th ed., South-Western Publishing, Cincinnati, Ohio, 1987. Notations were altered to suit our notation.

> $Y =$ the percent of workers belonging to unions in 1980
>
> $D = 1$ for states that have right-to-work laws
>
> $= 0$ for states that do not have such laws
>
> From these results we see that the average union membership in union-shop states is 26.68 percent and that in nonunion, or right-to-work, states it is 16.17 percent ($26.68 - 10.51$). This difference is significant, for the coefficient of the dummy variable is statistically different from zero (check this). These results suggest that in those states that permit union shops the union membership is on the average higher than in those states in which union shops are banned, which is not very surprising.

ANOVA models like regressions (9.4) and (9.5), although common in fields such as sociology, psychology, education, and market research, are not that common in economics. In most economic research a regression model contains some explanatory variables that are quantitative and some that are qualitative. Regression models containing a combination of quantitative and qualitative variables are called **analysis-of-covariance (ANCOVA) models,** and in the remainder of this chapter we will largely deal with such models.

9.2 REGRESSION WITH ONE QUANTITATIVE VARIABLE AND ONE QUALITATIVE VARIABLE WITH TWO CATEGORIES

As an example of the ANCOVA model, consider the following example:

$$Y_i = B_1 + B_2 D_i + B_3 X_i + u_i \tag{9.6}$$

where

$Y_i =$ the annual salary of a college teacher

$X_i =$ years of teaching experience

$D_i = 1$ if male

$= 0$ otherwise (i.e., female)

Model (9.6) contains one numerical or quantitative variable X (years of teaching experience) and one qualitative variable (sex), which has two categories (or classes, levels, or classifications), namely, male and female.

The meaning of model (9.6) is as following. Assuming, as usual, $E(u_i) = 0$, we see that:

Mean salary of a female college teacher:

$$E(Y \mid X, D_i = 0) = B_1 + B_3 X_i \tag{9.7}$$

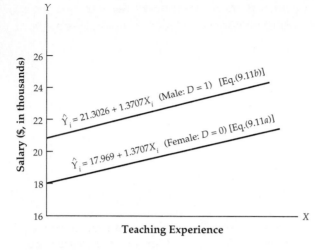

FIGURE 9-2
Hypothetical scattergram.

Mean salary of a male college teacher:

$$E(Y_i \mid X_i, D_i = 1) = (B_1 + B_2) + B_3 X_i \tag{9.8}$$

Geometrically, we have the situation shown in Figure 9-2 (for illustration, we assume that $B_1 > 0$).

In words, model (9.6) states that the male and female college teachers' mean salary functions in relation to the years of teaching experience have the same slope (B_3) but different intercepts. Put differently, it is assumed that the level of the male teacher's mean salary is different from that of the female teacher's mean salary (by B_2), but that the rate of change in the mean annual salary by years of experience (i.e., the slope) is the same for both sexes. If the hypothesis of common slope is valid,[3] a test of the null hypothesis that the two regressions (9.7) and (9.8) have the same intercept (i.e., there is no sex discrimination) can be made easily by running regression (9.6) and noting the statistical significance of b_2 on the basis of the usual t test. If the t test shows that b_2 is statistically significant, we can reject the null hypothesis that male and female teachers' levels of mean annual salary are the same.

Before proceeding to illustrate this model, note the following features of the dummy variable regression model presented earlier:

1. To distinguish the two categories, male and female, we have introduced only one dummy variable, D_i. For if $D_i = 1$ denotes a male, then when $D_i = 0$, we know it is a female since there are only two possible categories

---

[3] The validity of this assumption can be tested by the procedure discussed in Section 9.6.

here. Hence, one dummy variable suffices to distinguish the two categories. Assuming that the regression model contains an intercept term, if we were to write the model (9.6) as

$$Y_i = B_1 + B_2X_i + B_3D_{1i} + B_4D_{2i} + u_i \qquad (9.9)$$

where Y and X are as defined before, and where

$$D_{1i} = 1 \text{ if a male teacher}$$

$$= 0 \text{ otherwise}$$

$$D_{2i} = 1 \text{ if a female teacher}$$

$$= 0 \text{ otherwise}$$

model (9.9) as it stands cannot be estimated because of perfect collinearity (i.e., perfect linear relationship) between D_2 and D_3. To see this clearly, suppose we have a sample of three male teachers and two female teachers. The data matrix will look something like the following:

		D_1	D_2	X
Male	Y_1	1	1	0	X_1
Male	Y_2	1	1	0	X_2
Female	$Y_3 =$	1	0	1	X_3
Male	Y_4	1	1	0	X_4
Female	Y_5	1	0	1	X_5

The first column on the right-hand side of this data matrix represents the common intercept term, B_1. Now it is easy to verify that $D_1 = (1 - D_2)$ or $D_2 = (1 - D_1)$; that is, D_1 and D_2 are perfectly collinear. And, as we noted in Chapter 7, in cases of perfect collinearity or multicollinearity it is not possible to obtain unique estimates of the various parameters.

There are various ways to resolve the problem of perfect collinearity. But the simplest one is to assign the dummies the way we did in model (9.6), namely, to use only one dummy variable if there are two categories of a qualitative variable, such as sex. In this case the preceding data matrix will not have the column labeled D_2, thus avoiding the problem of perfect collinearity. *The general rule is: If a qualitative variable has m categories, introduce only (m − 1) dummy variables.* In our example sex has two categories, and hence we introduced only a single dummy variable in model (9.6). If this rule is not followed, we will fall into what is known as the **dummy variable trap,** that is, the situation of **perfect multicollinearity.**

2. The assignment of 1 and 0 values to two categories, such as male and female, is arbitrary in that in our example we could have assigned $D = 1$ for female and $D = 0$ for male; of course, the coefficients would change in logical fashion.

3. The category that is assigned the value of 0 is often referred to as the **base, bench mark, control, comparison,** or **omitted category.** It is the bench mark in that comparisons are made with that category. Thus, in model (9.6) the female teacher is the base category. Note that the (common) intercept term B_1 is the intercept term for the base category in that if we run the regression with $D = 0$, that is, on female teachers only, the intercept will be B_1. Also, note that the category that is treated as the base category is a matter of choice sometimes dictated by the objective of study.

4. The coefficient B_2 attached to the dummy variable D can be called the *differential intercept coefficient* because it tells by how much the value of the intercept term of the category that receives the value of 1 differs from the intercept coefficient of the base category. Thus, as model (9.8) shows, B_2 tells by how much the intercept of the male college teacher's salary regression differs from that of the female college teacher's salary regression.

Example 9.3.   An illustrative example: teacher's salary in relation to years of experience and sex.   To illustrate the ANCOVA model (9.6) we have obtained a hypothetical set of data as shown in Table 9-2.

The OLS results based on these data are as follows:

$$\hat{Y}_i = 17.969 + 1.3707X_i + 3.3336D_i$$

$$se = (0.1919) \quad (0.0356) \quad\quad (0.1554) \quad\quad\quad\quad\quad\quad\quad\quad (9.10)$$

$$t = (93.6120) \quad (38.454) \quad\quad (21.455) \quad\quad R^2 = 0.9933$$

The interpretation of this regression is as follows. Holding the sex variable constant, the average salary increases by $\approx\$1371$ per year of service. Holding the length of service constant, the male teacher's average salary is $\approx\$3334$ higher than the female teacher's salary. Since the coefficient of the dummy variable is statistically significant (why?), we can say that there is a difference in the average salaries of the two groups of teachers, although they both experience the same rate of increase of $1371 per year of service.[4]

As shown in models (9.7) and (9.8), we can derive the salary functions of the two categories of teachers from regression (9.10) as follows:

Mean salary of female college teachers:

$$\hat{Y} = 17.969 + 1.3707X_i \quad\quad\quad\quad\quad\quad\quad (9.11a)$$

Mean salary of male college teachers:

$$\hat{Y}_i = (17.969 + 3.3336) + 1.3707X_i$$

$$= 21.3026 + 1.3707X_i \quad\quad\quad\quad\quad\quad (9.11b)$$

---

[4] It is possible that the rate of salary increase per year of service may also be different for the two categories. In Section 9.6 we will show how to find out whether that is in fact the case.

These regressions are shown in Figure 9-2.

Notice that the two regression lines are *parallel* because we are (implicitly) assuming that the rate of progression of average salary per year of service is the same for both groups of teachers. The difference is in their average level of starting salary, which is $17,969 for female teachers and $21,303 for male teachers; these values are simply the intercepts of the two preceding regressions. (Recall that the intercept measures the average value of the dependent variable when the explanatory variable takes the value of zero.)[5]

TABLE 9-2
Hypothetical data on salaries of college teachers in relation to years of teaching experience and sex

Starting salary, Y ($, in thousands)	Years of teaching experience, X_2	Sex (1 = male) (0 = female)
23.0	1	1
19.5	1	0
24.0	2	1
21.0	2	0
25.0	3	1
22.0	3	0
26.5	4	1
23.1	4	0
25.0	5	0
28.0	5	1
29.5	6	1
26.0	6	0
27.5	7	0
31.5	7	1
29.0	8	0

Example 9.4   The impact of product differentiation on rate of return on equity.   To find out whether firms selling differentiated products (i.e., brand names) experience higher rates of return on their equity capital, J. A. Dalton and

---

[5] Although generally the intercept term may not have much economic meaning, in some cases it does; in the present case the intercept represents the starting average salary (i.e., salary without any teaching experience.)

S. L. Levin[6] obtained the following regression results based on a sample of 48 firms:

$$\hat{Y}_i = 1.399 + 1.490D_i + 0.246X_{2i} - 9.507X_{3i} - 0.016X_{4i}$$

$$se = \qquad (1.380) \quad (0.056) \quad (4.244) \qquad (0.017) \quad R^2 = 0.26 \quad (9.12)$$

where

Y = the rate of return on equity

D = 1 for firms with high or moderate product differentiation

X_2 = the market share

X_3 = the measure of firm size

X_4 = the industry growth rate

As this regression shows, holding the values of X variables constant, firms that practice high or moderate product differentiation experience a higher rate of return on equity by ≈ 1.49 percentage points than those who do not practice such product differentiation. But since the coefficient of the dummy variable is not statistically significant (do you see this?), statistically speaking, we cannot say that there is any difference in the average level of the rate of return between the two groups of firms, holding the values of X variables constant.

9.3   REGRESSION ON A QUANTITATIVE VARIABLE AND A QUALITATIVE VARIABLE WITH MORE THAN TWO CLASSES OR CATEGORIES

Suppose that based on cross-sectional data we want to regress the annual expenditure on vacation travel by an individual on the income and education of the individual. Since the variable *education* is qualitative in nature, suppose we consider three mutually exclusive levels of education: less than high school, high school, and college. Now, unlike the previous case, we have more than two categories of the qualitative variable education. Therefore, *following the rule that the number of dummies should be one less than the number of categories of the variable*, we introduce two dummies to represent the three levels of education.

Assuming that the three educational groups have a common slope but

---

[6] See J. A. Dalton and S. L. Levin, "Market Power: Concentration and Market Share," *Industrial Organization Review*, vol. 5, 1977, pp. 27–36. Notations were altered to conform with our notation.

different intercepts in the regression of annual expenditure on vacation travel on annual income, we can use the following model:[7]

$$Y_i = B_1 + B_2 D_{2i} + B_3 D_{3i} + B_4 X_i + u_i \qquad (9.13)$$

where

Y_i = the annual expenditure on vacation travel

X_i = the annual income

D_2 = 1 if high school education

= 0 otherwise

D_3 = 1 if college education

= 0 otherwise

Notice that in the preceding assignment of dummy variables we are treating "less than high school education" as the bench mark category.[8] Therefore, the intercept B_1 represents the intercept for this category. The *differential intercepts* B_2 and B_3 tell by how much the intercepts of the other two categories differ from the intercept of the base category, which can be readily verified as follows. Assuming $E(u_i) = 0$, which is the standard assumption, we obtain from regression (9.13):

Mean travel expenditure of less than high school education:

$$E(Y_i \mid D_2 = 0, D_3 = 0, X_i) = B_1 + B_4 X_i \qquad (9.14)$$

Mean travel expenditure of high school graduates:

$$E(Y_i \mid D_2 = 1, D_3 = 0, X_i) = (B_1 + B_2) + B_4 X_i \qquad (9.15)$$

Mean travel expenditure of college graduates:

$$E(Y_i \mid D_2 = 0, D_3 = 1, X_i) = (B_1 + B_3) + B_4 X_i \qquad (9.16)$$

These three regression lines are depicted in Figure 9-3. (The actual lines are based on Example 9.5.)

---

[7] For expositional purposes, we are assuming that the rate of change of annual expenditure on vacation travel with respect to annual income (i.e., the slope) remains the same; that is, regardless of the level of education, as income increases by a dollar the mean expenditure on travel increases by the same amount. Of course, this may not be the case, which means the slope can change too. But this situation can be handled by the method discussed in Section 9.6.

[8] Of course, any other category of education could serve as the bench mark. The choice is purely personal, although the objectives of a particular study may suggest which category to treat as the bench mark.

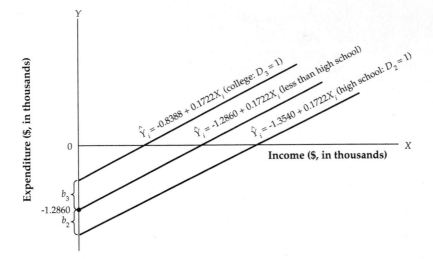

FIGURE 9-3
Travel expenditure in relation to income and by level of education.

After estimating the regression (9.13), one can easily find out whether the *differential* intercepts B_2 and B_3 are individually statistically significant (i.e., different from zero) on the basis of the usual t test.

A question: Instead of running regression (9.13), why not run the three regressions (9.14), (9.15), and (9.16), separately? There is no question that we can do that. But if we do, how can we find out whether there is any difference in the three regressions? Although we will discuss this question shortly (see Section 9.6), one advantage of regression (9.13) is that from the single regression alone we can derive the three regressions (9.14) to (9.16), as previously shown.

Example 9.5. A hypothetical example of travel expenditure in relation to income and education. To illustrate the model (9.13), consider the hypothetical data given in Table 9-3. Based on these data the regression results were as follows:

$$\hat{Y}_i = -1.2860 + 0.1722X_i - 0.0680D_{2i} + 0.4472D_{3i}$$
$$\text{se} = (0.2694) \quad (0.0147) \quad (0.1708) \quad (0.3956) \tag{9.17}$$
$$t = (-4.7738) \quad (11.7280) \quad (-0.3982) \quad (1.1304) \quad R^2 = 0.9965$$

These regression lines are shown in Figure 9-3.

As this regression shows, *ceteris paribus*, as income increases, say, by a dollar, the average expenditure on travel goes up by ≈ 17 cents. For our purpose,

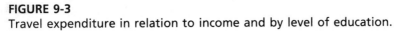

$n = 15$

TABLE 9-3
Expenditure on travel (Y), income (X), and education

Y ($, in thousands)	X	High school education $D_2 = 1$	College education $D_3 = 1$
6.0	40	0	1
3.9	31	1	0
1.8	18	0	0
1.9	19	0	0
7.2	47	0	1
3.3	27	1	0
3.1	26	1	0
1.7	17	0	0
6.4	43	0	1
7.9	49	0	1
1.5	15	0	0
3.1	25	1	0
3.6	29	1	0
2.0	20	0	0
6.2	41	0	1

Note: When $D_2 = D_3 = 0$, that observation represents a non-high school graduate. (Why?)

the more interesting result is the effect of education on travel. Since both dummy variables are individually statistically insignificant at the 5% level (check this), it seems education per se has no statistically discernible effect on average travel expenditure, holding income constant. In other words, the intercepts of the three groups do not differ statistically from one another. Therefore, in Figure 9-3, although the individual intercepts are numerically different, statistically they are the same.

9.4 REGRESSION ON ONE QUANTITATIVE VARIABLE AND TWO QUALITATIVE VARIABLES

The technique of dummy variables can be easily extended to handle more than one qualitative variable. Let us return to the college teacher's salary regression (9.6), but now assume that in addition to years of teaching experience and sex, the color of the teacher is also an important determinant of salary. For simplicity, assume that color has two categories, white and non-white. We can now write model (9.6) as

$$Y_i = B_1 + B_2 D_{2i} + B_3 D_{3i} + B_4 X_i + u_i \tag{9.18}$$

where

$$Y_i = \text{the annual salary}$$
$$X_i = \text{years of teaching experience}$$
$$D_{2i} = 1 \text{ if male teacher}$$
$$= 0 \text{ otherwise (i.e., female)}$$
$$D_{3i} = 1 \text{ if white}$$
$$= 0 \text{ otherwise (i.e., nonwhite)}$$

Notice that each of the two qualitative variables, sex and color, has two categories, and hence each category needs one dummy variable (to avoid the dummy variable trap). Note that the bench mark or omitted category now is "nonwhite female teacher."

Assuming $E(u_i) = 0$, we can obtain the following mean salary regressions from model (9.18):

Mean salary for nonwhite female teacher:

$$E(Y_i \mid D_2 = 0, D_3 = 0, X_i) = B_1 + B_4 X_i \tag{9.19}$$

Mean salary for nonwhite male teacher:

$$E(Y_i \mid D_2 = 1, D_3 = 0, X_i) = (B_1 + B_2) + B_4 X_i \tag{9.20}$$

Mean salary for white female teacher:

$$E(Y_i \mid D_2 = 0, D_3 = 1, X_i) = (B_1 + B_3) + B_4 X_i \tag{9.21}$$

Mean salary for white male teacher:

$$E(Y_i \mid D_2 = 1, D_3 = 1, X_i) = (B_1 + B_2 + B_3) + B_4 X_i \tag{9.22}$$

Once again, we are assuming that the preceding regressions differ only in the intercept coefficient and not in the slope coefficient, B_4.

An OLS estimation of model (9.18) will enable us to test a variety of hypotheses. For instance, if the *differential* intercept b_3, the estimator of B_3, is statistically significant, it means that color does affect a teacher's salary. Similarly, if the *differential* intercept b_2 is statistically significant, it suggests that sex also affects a teacher's salary. Finally, if both differential intercepts are statistically significant, it indicates that sex as well as the color of the teacher is an important determinant of teachers' salaries. Thus, we can determine which of these possibilities exist without having to run individual regressions for each combination of sex and color, for these individual regressions can be easily derived from model (9.18), as previously shown.

9.5   A GENERALIZATION

As the reader can well imagine, we can extend our model to include more than one quantitative variable and more than two qualitative variables. However, care must be exercised that the *number of dummies for each qualitative variable is one less than the number of categories of that variable.* An example follows.

Example 9.6. Campaign contributions by political parties.[9] In a study of party contributions to congressional elections in 1982, Wilhite and Theilmann obtained the following regression results, which are given in tabular form (Table 9.4) using the authors' symbols. The *dependent variable* in this regression is PARTY$ (campaign contributions made by political parties to local congressional candidates). In this regression $GAP, VGAP, and PU are (three) quantitative variables and OPEN, DEMOCRAT, and COMM are three qualitative variables, each with two categories.

What do these results suggest? The larger the $GAP is (i.e., the opponent has substantial funding), the less is the support by the national party to the local candidate. The larger the VGAP is, that is, the larger the margin by which the opponent won the previous election is, the lesser will be the amount of money the national party is going to spend on this candidate (this expectation is not borne out by the results for 1982). An open race is likely to attract more funding from the national party to secure that seat for the party, which expectation is supported by the regression results. The greater the party loyalty (PU) is, the greater the party support will be, which is also supported by the results. Since the Democratic party has a smaller campaign money chest than the Republican party, the Democratic dummy is expected to have a negative sign, which it does (the intercept term for the Democratic party's campaign contribution regression will be smaller than that of its rival). The COMM dummy is expected to have a positive sign, for if you are up for election and happen to be a member of the national committees that distribute the campaign funds, you are more likely to steer money for your own election proportionately in greater amounts.

9.6 COMPARING TWO REGRESSIONS[10]

In the models considered so far in this chapter we have assumed that qualitative variables affect the intercept but not the slope coefficient of the various subgroup regressions. But, what if the slopes are also different? Thus, in the teacher's salary regression in relation to years of teaching experience and sex given in model (9.9) we implicitly assumed that the rate of change of salary in relation to years of experience is the same for the two categories of teachers (i.e., the two regression lines are parallel); the two regressions differ only in

---

[9] This example is taken from Al Wilhite and John Theilmann, "Campaign Contributions by Political Parties: Ideology versus Winning," *Atlantic Economic Journal,* vol. XVII, June 1989, pp. 11–20.

[10] Another test that is used to compare two or more regressions, known as the **Chow test,** is discussed in Damodar N. Gujarati, *Basic Econometrics,* 2nd ed., McGraw-Hill, New York, 1988, pp. 443–444. But the results based on that test and the dummy variable test discussed later are qualitatively the same.

TABLE 9-4
Aggregate contributions by political parties, 1982

Explanatory variable	Coefficient
$GAP	−8.189*
	(1.863)
VGAP	0.0321
	(0.0223)
OPEN	3.582*
	(0.7293)
PU	18.189*
	(0.849)
DEMOCRAT	−9.986*
	(0.557)
COMM	1.734*
R^2	0.70
F	188.4

Source: Al Wilhite and John Theilmann, "Campaign Contributions by Political Parties: Ideology versus Winning." *Atlantic Economic Journal*, vol. XVII, June 1989, pp. 11–20. p. 15, Table 2 (adapted).

Notes: Standard errors are in parentheses.
* means significant at the 0.01 level.

$GAP = a measure of the candidate's finances

VGAP = the size of the vote differential in the previous election

OPEN = 1 for open seat races
0 otherwise

PU = party unity index as calculated by *Congressional Quarterly*

DEMOCRAT = 1 for members of the Democratic party
0 otherwise

COMM = 1 for representatives who are members of the Democratic Congressional Campaign Committee or the National Republican Congressional Committee
= 0 otherwise (i.e., those who are not members of such committees.

their intercept values. However, the assumption that the two slopes are the same may not be appropriate in every situation. Therefore, we need to develop a general methodology to find out whether two (or more) regressions are different; the difference may be in the intercepts or the slopes or both. To see how this can be done, let us consider the savings-income data for the United States given in the first two columns of Table 9-5.

In 1982 the United States suffered one of its worst recessions. To see if the savings-income relationship, the *savings function*, has changed since the

TABLE 9-5
Personal savings (Y) and personal income (X), United States, 1970–1987

Year	Y	X	D	DX
		($, billions)		
(1)	(2)	(3)	(4)	(5) = (3) (4)
1970	57.7	831.8	0	0
1971	66.3	894.0	0	0
1972	61.4	981.6	0	0
1973	89.0	1101.7	0	0
1974	96.7	1210.1	0	0
1975	104.6	1313.4	0	0
1976	95.8	1451.4	0	0
1977	90.7	1607.5	0	0
1978	110.2	1812.4	0	0
1979	118.1	2034.0	0	0
1980	136.9	2258.5	0	0
1981	159.4	2520.9	0	0
1982	153.9	2670.8	1	2670.8
1983	130.6	2836.6	1	2836.6
1984	164.1	3108.7	1	3108.7
1985	125.4	3325.3	1	3325.3
1986	121.7	3531.1	1	3531.1
1987	104.2	3780.0	1	3780.0

Source: Economic Report of the President, 1989, data on Y and X are from Table B-26, p. 338. These are quarterly data at seasonally adjusted annual rates.

1982 recession, we have divided the data into two periods, 1970 to 1981 (call it the prerecession period) and 1982 to 1987 (call it the postrecession period). Economic theory suggests that there is a positive relationship between personal savings and personal income; *ceteris paribus*, the higher the income is, the higher the savings will be. To find out if the savings function has changed between the two periods, we can run the following two regressions:

Prerecession period, 1970 to 1981:

$$Y_t = A_1 + A_2 X_t + u_{1t} \tag{9.23}$$

Postrecession period, 1982 to 1987:

$$Y_t = B_1 + B_2 X_t + u_{2t} \tag{9.24}$$

where

$$Y = \text{savings}$$

$$X = \text{income}$$

$$u = \text{the error terms in the two equations}$$

Now regressions (9.23) and (9.24) present the following four possibilities. (See Figure 9-4.)

1. $A_1 = B_1$ and $A_2 = B_2$; that is, the two regressions are identical. This is the case of *coincident regressions*. In this case there is no need to run two separate regressions. [See Figure 9-4(a).]
2. $A_1 \neq B_1$ but $A_2 = B_2$; that is, the two regressions differ only in their locations—their intercepts. This is the case of *parallel regressions*, the case we have considered until now. [See Figure 9-4(b).]

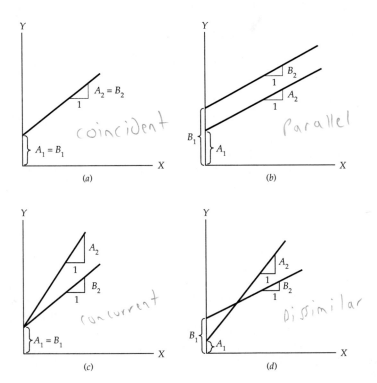

FIGURE 9-4
Possible differences in two regressions: (*a*) Coincident regressions; (*b*) parallel regressions; (*c*) concurrent regressions; (*d*) dissimilar regressions.

3. $A_1 = B_1$ but $A_2 \neq B_2$; that is, the two regressions have the same intercepts but different slopes. This is the case of *concurrent regressions*. [See Figure 9-4(c).]

4. $A_1 \neq B_1$ and $A_2 \neq B_2$; that is, the two regressions are completely different. This is the case of *dissimilar regressions*. [See Figure 9-4(d).]

In our savings-income example, how do we find out whether the relationship between savings and income is one of the preceding possibilities? The technique of dummy variables can be adapted to check this. To do this, consider the following regression:

$$Y_t = C_1 + C_2 D_t + C_3 X_t + C_4 (D_t \cdot X_t) + u_t \qquad (9.25)$$

where

$$Y = \text{savings income}$$

$$D_t = 1 \text{ for observations beginning in 1982}$$

$$= 0 \text{ otherwise (i.e., for observations through}$$

$$1981, \text{ as shown in Table 9-5)}$$

To see the implication of regression (9.25), and assuming $E(u_t) = 0$, we obtain

$$E(Y_t \mid D_t = 0, X_t) = C_1 + C_3 X_t \qquad (9.26)$$

$$E(Y_t \mid D_t = 1, X_t) = (C_1 + C_2) + (C_3 + C_4) X_t \qquad (9.27)$$

which are, respectively, the (mean) savings functions for the prerecession and the postrecession periods. In other words, regression (9.26) is the same as (9.23) and (9.27) is the same as (9.24) with

$$A_1 = C_1 \qquad \text{and} \quad A_2 = C_3$$

$$B_1 = (C_1 + C_2) \quad \text{and} \quad B_2 = (C_3 + C_4)$$

Thus, from the single regression (9.25) we can obtain the two subperiod regressions easily, again showing the flexability of the dummy technique.

In regression (9.25) C_2 is the **differential intercept,** as before, and C_4 is the **differential slope coefficient,** indicating by how much the slope coefficient of the postrecession period's savings function differs from the slope coefficient of the prerecession period's savings function.[11] Note how the introduction of the dummy variable D in the **interactive,** or **multiplicative, form** (D multi-

---

[11] In general, the differential slope coefficient tells by how much the slope coefficient of the category that receives the value of 1 differs from the base category.

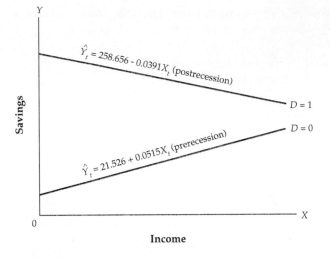

FIGURE 9-5
U.S. savings-income relationship, 1970 to 1987.

plied by X) enables us to differentiate between the slope coefficients of the two periods, just as the introduction of the dummy variable in the **additive form** enabled us to distinguish between the intercepts of the two periods. (See columns 4 and 5 of Table 9-5.)

Example 9.7. Savings-income relation, United States, 1970 to 1987. Returning to the savings-income data given in Table 9-5, the regression results based on model (9.25) are as follows:[12]

$$\hat{Y}_t = 21.526 \ + 237.13D_t \ + 0.0515X_t \ - 0.0906(D_t X_t)$$
$$se = (10.610) \quad (43.437) \quad (0.0067) \quad (0.0146) \quad R^2 = 0.8777 \quad (9.28)$$
$$t = (2.0289) \quad (5.4592) \quad (7.7343) \quad (-6.1888) \quad F = 33.476$$

Regression (9.28) should be interpreted as any other multiple regression. As the reader can easily verify, the *differential intercept* and the *differential* slope coefficients are both individually statistically significant, strongly suggesting that the savings functions post- and pre-1982 recessions are different, as shown in Figure 9-5 [see also Figure 9-4(*d*)]. The intercept of the postrecession period is higher

---

[12] In running this regression we assumed that

$$\text{var}(u_{1t}) = \text{var}(u_{2t}) = \text{var}(u_t)$$

but the slope coefficient is smaller than the prerecession savings function. Using regressions (9.26) and (9.27), we can now derive the savings function of the two periods as follows:

Mean savings function, 1970 to 1981:

$$\hat{Y}_t = 21.526 + 0.0515X_t \qquad (9.29)$$

Mean savings function, 1982 to 1987:

$$\hat{Y}_t = (21.526 + 237.130) + (0.0515 - 0.0906)X_t$$
$$= 258.656 - 0.0391X_t \qquad (9.30)$$

As these results suggest, the 1982 recession was obviously severe and its effect seems to have lingered on for some time. What is surprising is that the coefficient of the income variable is negative, which is contrary to economic theory. But keep in mind that the sample size for the second period is rather small. As more data become available, hopefully, the savings-income relationship will resume its historical, and economically logical, positive relationship.

Example 9.8. What happened to the United States Phillips curve? To illustrate further the use of differential intercept and differential slope coefficients in testing for differences in two regressions,[13] recall the Phillips curve presented in regression (8.30). That regression covered the period 1958 to 1969. Since then economists have observed that the inverse trade-off between the rate of change in earnings and the unemployment rate no longer exists. Some economists have gone so far as to declare that the Phillips curve no longer exists. To see if that is in fact the case, we extended the sample data given in Table 8-4 to the year 1977 and estimated the following regression:

$$Y_t = B_1 + B_2 D_t + B_3 \left(\frac{1}{X_t}\right) + B_4 D_t \left(\frac{1}{X_t}\right) + u_t \qquad (9.31)$$

where

Y = the year-to-year percentage change in the index of hourly earnings

X = the percent unemployment rate

D_t = 1 for observations through 1969

= 0 otherwise (i.e., for observations from 1970 through 1977)

---

[13] The technique can be easily generalized to compare more than two regressions. For example, if we want to compare three regressions, we will have to introduce two dummies, one less than the number of categories to be compared.

The regression results were as follows:

$$\hat{Y}_t = 10.078 - 10.337D_t - 17.549\left(\frac{1}{X_t}\right) + 38.137D_t\left(\frac{1}{X_t}\right)$$

$$\text{se} = (1.4024) \quad (1.6859) \quad (8.3373) \quad (9.3999) \tag{9.32}$$

$$t = (7.1860) \quad (-6.1314) \quad (-2.1049) \quad (4.0572) \quad R^2 = 0.8787$$

As these results show, the differential intercept and slope coefficients are both individually statistically significantly different from zero, suggesting there has been a statistically visible change in the Phillips curve since 1969. To see this more clearly, let us derive from regression (9.32) the Phillips curve for the two periods individually as follows:

Phillips curve for 1958 to 1969:

$$\hat{Y}_t = (10.078 - 10.337) + (-17.549 + 38.137)\left(\frac{1}{X_t}\right)$$

$$\tag{9.33} = (8.30)$$

$$= -0.259 + 20.588\left(\frac{1}{X_t}\right)$$

Phillips curve for 1970 to 1977

$$\hat{Y}_t = 10.078 - 17.549\left(\frac{1}{X_t}\right) \tag{9.34}$$

What is significant to note is that for the 1970 to 1977 period the Phillips curve is positively sloping! (*Note*: The variable X enters inversely, and therefore a priori its coefficient should be positive, as for the 1958 to 1969 period.) This suggests that the higher the unemployment rate is, the greater the increase in hourly earnings will be, which does not make economic sense. It does seem that the Phillips curve has broken down.[14]

9.7 THE USE OF DUMMY VARIABLES IN SEASONAL ANALYSIS

Many economic time series based on monthly or quarterly data exhibit **seasonal patterns** (regular oscillatory movements). Examples are sales of department stores at Christmas time, demand for money (cash balances) by households at holiday times, demand for ice cream and soft drinks during the summer, and demand for travel during holiday seasons. Often it is desirable

---

[14] There is now considerable empirical evidence that the Phillips curve has broken down not only in the United States but in most industrialized countries.

to remove the seasonal factor, or *component,* from a time series so that one may concentrate on the other components of times series, such as the *trend,*[15] which is increase or decrease fairly steadily over an extended time period. The process of removing the seasonal component from a time series is known as **deseasonalization,** or **seasonal adjustment,** and the time series thus obtained is called **deseasonalized,** or *seasonally adjusted, time series.* The U.S. government publishes important economic time series on a seasonally adjusted basis.

There are several methods of deseasonalizing a time series, but we will consider one of these methods, namely, the *method of dummy variables,*[16] which we now illustrate.

Example 9.9. Expenditure-income relationship, Australia, 1977-I–1980-IV. To illustrate how the dummy variable method can be used to deseasonalize economic time series, Table 9-6 gives data on Y [value of retail sales of clothing, hardware, electrical appliances, and furniture, call it personal consumption expenditure (PCE)] and X [personal disposable income (PDI)] for the Australian economy for the quarterly period 1977-I to 1980-IV; the data are in Australian hundred millions of dollars. To see if each of the quarterly data exhibit any seasonal pattern (i.e., if each quarter exhibits its own unique pattern of expenditure in relation to PDI), consider the following model:

$$Y_t = B_1 + B_2 D_{2t} + B_3 D_{3t} + B_4 D_{4t} + B_5 X_t + u_t \qquad (9.35)$$

where Y and X are as defined earlier and where the *seasonal dummies,* the Ds, are defined as:

$D_{2t} = 1$ if the observation lies in the
IInd quarter

$= 0$ otherwise

$D_{3t} = 1$ if the observation lies in the
IIIrd quarter

$= 0$ otherwise

$D_{4t} = 1$ if the observation lies in the
IVth quarter

$= 0$ otherwise

---

[15] A time series may contain four components: a *seasonal,* a *cyclical,* a *trend* (or long-term component), and one that is strictly random.

[16] Some other methods are the ratio-to-moving average method, link-relative method, and percentage-of-annual-average method. For a nontechnical discussion, see Paul Newbold, *Statistics for Business and Economics,* Prentice-Hall, Englewood Cliffs, N.J., 1984, Chap. 17.

Note that we assume that the variable "season" has four classes, the four quarters of a year, thereby requiring the use of three dummies; in the present example we let quarter I represent the base, or bench mark, quarter, although any other quarter would do just as well. Thus, if there is a seasonal pattern present in the various quarters, the estimated *differential intercepts*, B_2, B_3, and B_4 if statistically significant, will reflect it. Each of these *differential intercepts* tells us by how much the level of Y (i.e., the mean value of Y) differs from that of the base quarter I. To see this clearly, and assuming $E(u_t) = 0$, as usual, we obtain:

Mean consumption expenditure in quarter I:

$$E(Y_t \mid D_2 = 0, D_3 = 0, D_4 = 0, X_t) = B_1 + B_5 X_t \qquad (9.36)$$

Mean consumption expenditure in quarter II:

$$E(Y_t \mid D_2 = 1, D_3 = 0, D_4 = 0, X_t) = (B_1 + B_2) + B_5 X_t \qquad (9.37)$$

Mean consumption expenditure in quarter III:

$$E(Y_t \mid D_2 = 0, D_3 = 1, D_4 = 0, X_t) = (B_1 + B_3) + B_5 X_t \qquad (9.38)$$

Mean consumption expenditure in quarter IV:

$$E(Y_t \mid D_2 = 0, D_3 = 0, D_4 = 1, X_t) = (B_1 + B_4) + B_5 X_t \qquad (9.39)$$

Table 9-6 shows how the dummy variables are set up.

The regression results based on regression (9.35) are as follows:

$$\hat{Y}_t = 3.2706 + 4.2128 D_{2t} + 1.1866 D_{3t} + 3.5306 D_{4t} + 0.0946 X_t$$

$$\text{se} = (0.9345) \quad (0.3729) \qquad (0.3901) \qquad (0.4706) \qquad (0.0055)$$

$$t = (3.4998) \quad (11.296) \qquad (3.0417) \qquad (7.5023) \qquad (17.278)$$

$$R^2 = 0.9870 \qquad (9.40)$$

As this regression shows, all differential intercepts are individually statistically significant, suggesting that the average level of Y differs among the quarters. It seems that there are four distinct "seasons," if we allow seasons to be measured by the various quarters. For example, the average value of Y in the fourth quarter is higher than that in the first, the base quarter, by ≈3.5 (hundred millions). It is not surprising that the coefficient of PDI is statistically significant and that it has the correct sign; a priori, one would expect a positive relationship between PCE and PDI.

A cautionary note is in order here. In regression (9.40) we have implicitly assumed that the seasonal effect, if any, only affects the intercept term and not the slope coefficient. But how do we find out if that is in fact the case? This is easily accomplished by the technique of the *differential slope and differential intercept method* discussed in the previous section.

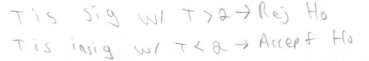

Let us apply that method to the present example. We now write the model (9.35) in the extended form as follows:

$$Y_t = B_1 + B_2 D_{2t} + B_3 D_{3t} + B_4 D_{4t} + B_5 X_t + B_6(D_{2t}X_t) +$$
$$B_7(D_{3t}X_t) + B_8(D_{4t}X_t) + u_t \tag{9.41}$$

Notice carefully how the multiplicative dummies have been created, following the discussion in the previous section. The *differential slope* coefficients B_6, B_7, and B_8 tell by how much the slope coefficient of the second, third, and fourth quarters differs from that of the base (i.e., first) quarter, which is B_5. Applying model (9.41) to the Australian data given in Table 9-6, we obtain the following results shown in tabular form (Table 9-7) for ease of reading and interpretation.

By comparing the results given in regression (9.40) and those in regression (9.42) (in Table 9-7), we see some dramatic changes. The coefficient of the income variable, PDI, is positive and statistically significant in both regressions and its numerical value is about the same. But the differential intercept coefficients, which were individually statistically significant in Eq. (9.40), are individually statistically insignificant in Eq. (9.42). Not only that, in Eq. (9.42) none of the differential slope coefficients are individually statistically significant.

TABLE 9-6
Personal consumption expenditure,
PCE (Y) and PDI (X)*,
Australia, 1977-I–1980-IV

Year and Quarter	Y	X	D_2	D_3	D_4
1977-I	16.63	136.5	0	0	0
-II	19.91	132.1	1	0	0
-III	19.41	157.5	0	1	0
-IV	24.01	177.7	0	0	1
1978-I	17.55	152.4	0	0	0
-II	21.97	150.7	1	0	0
-III	20.90	173.0	0	1	0
-IV	25.61	199.8	0	0	1
1979-I	19.46	179.1	0	0	0
-II	22.72	167.4	1	0	0
-III	22.14	191.6	0	1	0
-IV	27.42	227.0	0	0	1
1980-I	21.42	187.3	0	0	0
-II	25.41	185.0	1	0	0
-III	25.49	219.2	0	1	0
-IV	32.07	261.5	0	0	1

Source: Data provided by Dr. Eric Sowey of the University of New South Wales.
* Australian dollars in hundred million.

TABLE 9-7
**Regression results based
on Eq. (9.41),
the Australian economy**

Explanatory variable	Coefficient	
b_1 (constant)	4.4526	
	$t = (1.8193)^*$	
D_{2t}	2.4082	
	(0.69332)	
D_{3t}	-0.42336	
	(-0.12213)	
D_{4t}	2.2891	
	$(0.70819)^*$	
X_t	0.0874	(9.42)
	$(5.8931)^*$	
$D_{2t}X_t$	0.0111	
	(0.52084)	
$D_{3t}X_t$	0.0095	
	(0.4.8067)	
$D_{4t}X_t$	0.0075	
	$(0.42337)^*$	
	$R^2 = 0.9875$	

Notes: Only the t ratios are presented in parentheses.
* denotes statistically significant at the 5% level (one-tailed).

An important question: Which results do we trust—regression (9.40) or regression (9.42)? Remember that regression (9.40) was based explicitly on the assumption that the intercept and not the slope coefficient varies among quarters. In other words, the regression assumed that the four regression lines, one for each quarter, are parallel regression lines, as in Figure 9-4(b). On the other hand, model (9.42) assumes that all regression lines are dissimilar, as in Figure 9-4(d), which is a much more general assumption. If regression (9.42) is in fact true but we use regression (9.40), then we commit what is known as **model specification error** or **model specification bias,** that is, fitting the wrong model. The consequences of such bias, as our regression results suggest, can be serious. (But more on this in Chapter 13.) The best practical strategy is to run the more general model (9.42). If, e.g., all *differential slope dummies* are individually statistically insignificant, then one can fit model (9.40) to find out if the *differential intercepts* are statistically significant. Of course, if the differential intercepts are individually insignificant, then in relation to the bench mark category there is no difference in the regression of that category and the other categories; that is, we have the situation of *coincident regressions*, as in Figure 9-4(a).

Following this strategy, the overall conclusion for the present study is that the rate of change (i.e., slope) of mean PCE in relation to the PDI is the

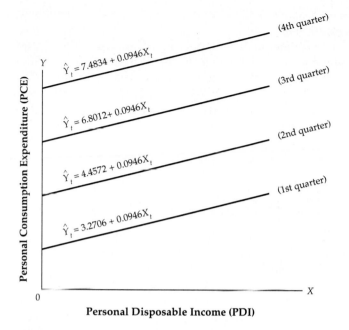

FIGURE 9-6
PCE-PDI relationship, Australia, 1977-I to 1980-IV.

same for all four quarters but the average level (i.e., intercept) is different for each quarter, as shown in Figure 9-6.

9.8 WHAT HAPPENS IF THE DEPENDENT VARIABLE IS DICHOTOMOUS OR DUMMY

Now that we have allowed for the possibility that one or more of the explanatory variables can be qualitative or dummy variables, a question that arises naturally is: Can the dependent variable Y be a dummy variable, too? In principle there is no reason that Y cannot be qualitative. For example, suppose we want to study the labor-force participation of adult males as a function of the unemployment rate, average wage rate, family income, education, etc. Now a person either is or is not in the labor force. Hence, the dependent variable, labor-force participation, can take only two values, 1 if the person is in the labor force and 0 if he or she is not.

As another example, consider home ownership as a function of annual earnings, level of education, family wealth, number of children in the family, mortgage interest rate, etc. Now a person either owns or does not own a home. Therefore, the dependent variable, home ownership, is dichotomous and takes only two values, 1 (owns a house) or 0 (does not own a house). Obviously, such examples can be multiplied.

Can we use the conventional OLS methodology to estimate the regression model where the dependent variable is a dummy variable? As a matter of sheer routine, this can be done. But, unfortunately, the estimators thus obtained do not have the usual optimal properties; that is, the OLS estimators are not necessarily best linear unbiased (BLUE). Therefore, such models should not be routinely estimated with the usual ordinary least squares (OLS) procedure. Some special techniques have been designed to estimate such models. One such technique is discussed in Chapter 14 as a special topic.

9.9 SUMMARY

In this chapter we showed how qualitative, or dummy, variables taking values of 1 and 0 can be introduced into regression models alongside quantitative variables. As the various examples in the chapter showed, the dummy variables are essentially a data-classifying device in that they divide a sample into various subgroups based on qualities, or attributes (sex, marital status, race, religion, etc.), and *implicitly* run individual regressions for each such subgroup. Now if there are differences in the response of the dependent variable to the variation in the quantitative variables in the various subgroups, they will be reflected in the differences in the intercepts or slope coefficients, or both, of the various subgroups.

Although a versatile tool, the dummy-variable technique has to be handled carefully. First, if the regression model contains a constant term (as most models usually do), the number of dummy variables *must be one less than the number of classifications of each qualitative variable.* Second, the coefficient attached to the dummy variables *must always be interpreted in relation to the control, or bench mark, group—the group that gets the value of zero.* Finally, if a model has several qualitative variables with several classes, introduction of dummy variables can consume a large number of degrees of freedom (d.f.). Therefore, one should weigh the number of dummy variables to be introduced into the model against the total number of observations in the sample.

In this chapter we also discussed the possibility of committing a *specification error,* that is, of fitting the wrong model to the data. If intercepts as well as slopes are expected to differ among groups, we should build a model that incorporates both the *differential* intercept and slope dummies. In this case a model that introduces only the differential intercepts is likely to lead to a specification error. Of course, it is not always easy a priori to find out which is the true model. Thus, some amount of experimentation, willy-nilly, is required in a concrete study, especially in situations where theory does not provide much guidance. The topic of specification error is discussed further in Chapter 13.

Key Terms and Concepts

The key terms and concepts introduced in this chapter are:

Qualitative vs. quantitative variables
Dummy variables
Analysis-of-variance (ANOVA) models
Analysis-of-covariance (ANCOVA) models
  a) base, bench mark, control, comparison, or omitted category (category assigned value of 0)
The dummy variable trap; perfect multicollinearity
Differential intercept dummies
  a) additive form
  b) coincident regressions

Differential slope dummies
  a) interactive, or multiplicative, form
Seasonal dummies
  a) seasonal patterns
  b) deseasonalization, or seasonal adjustment
Model specification bias or error
Dummy dependent variables

QUESTIONS

9.1. Explain briefly the meaning of
  (*a*) Categorical variables
  (*b*) Qualitative variables
  (*c*) Analysis-of-variance (ANOVA) models
  (*d*) Analysis-of-covariance (ANCOVA) models
  (*e*) The dummy variable trap
  (*f*) Differential intercept dummies
  (*g*) Differential slope dummies

9.2. Are the following variables quantitative or qualitative?
  (*a*) U.S. balance of payments
  (*b*) Political party affiliation
  (*c*) U.S. exports to the Republic of China
  (*d*) Membership in the United Nations
  (*e*) CPI (Consumer Price Index)
  (*f*) Education
  (*g*) People living in the EC (European Community)
  (*h*) Membership in GATT (General Agreement on Tariffs and Trade)
  (*i*) Members of the U.S. Congress
  (*j*) Social security recipients

9.3. If you have monthly data over a number of years, how many dummy variables will you introduce to test the following hypotheses?
  (*a*) All 12 months of the year exhibit seasonal patterns.
  (*b*) Only February, April, June, August, October, and December exhibit seasonal patterns.

9.4. What problems do you foresee in estimating the following models:
  (*a*) $Y_t = B_0 + B_1 D_{1t} + B_2 D_{2t} + B_3 D_{3t} + B_4 D_{4t} + u_t$
  where

$D_{it} = 1$ for observation in the ith quarter, $i = 1, 2, 3, 4$
$\quad = 0$ otherwise

(b) $\text{GNP}_t = B_1 + B_2M_t + B_3M_{t-1} + B_4 (M_t - M_{t-1}) + u_t$

where

$\text{GNP}_t =$ gross national product (GNP) at time t

$M_t =$ the money supply at time t

$M_{t-1} =$ the money supply at time $(t - 1)$

9.5. State with reasons whether the following statements are true or false.
  (a) In the model $Y_i = B_1 + B_2D_i + u_i$, letting D_i take the values of $(0, 2)$ instead of $(0, 1)$ will *halve* the value of B_2 and will also *halve* the t value.
  (b) When dummy variables are used, ordinary least squares (OLS) estimators are unbiased only in large samples.

9.6. Consider the following model:

$$Y_i = B_0 + B_1X_i + B_2D_{2i} + B_3D_{3i} + u_i$$

where

$Y =$ annual earnings of MBA graduates

$X =$ years of service

$D_2 = 1$ if Harvard MBA

$\quad = 0$ otherwise

$D_3 =$ Wharton MBA

$\quad = 0$ otherwise

  (a) What are the expected signs of the various coefficients?
  (b) How would you interpret B_2 and B_3?
  (c) If $B_2 > B_3$, what conclusion would you draw?

9.7. Continue with question 9.6 but now consider the following model:

$$Y_i = B_0 + B_1X_i + B_2D_{2i} + B_3D_{3i} + B_4(D_{2i}X_i)$$
$$+ B_5(D_{3i}X_i) + u_i$$

  (a) What is the difference between this model and the one given in question 9.6?
  (b) What is the interpretation of B_4 and B_5?
  (c) If B_4 and B_5 are individually statistically significant, would you choose this model over the previous one? If not, what kind of bias or error are you committing?
  *(d) How would you test the hypothesis that $B_4 = B_5 = 0$?

PROBLEMS

9.8. Based on quarterly observations for the United States for the period 1961-I through 1977-II, H. C. Huang, J. J. Siegfried, and F. Zardoshty[17] estimated the following demand function for coffee. (The figures in parentheses are t values.)

---

* Optional. (See Chapter 14 on restricted OLS.)

[17] See H. C. Huang, J. J. Siegfried, and F. Zardoshty "The Demand for Coffee in the United States, 1963–1977," *Quarterly Review of Economics and Business*, Summer 1980, pp. 36–50.

$$\widehat{\ln Q_t} = 1.2789 - \underset{(-2.14)}{0.1647} \ \ln P_t + \underset{(1.23)}{0.5115} \ \ln I_t + \underset{(0.55)}{0.1483} \ \ln P_t'$$
$$t =$$

$$\underset{t = (-3.36)}{-0.0089T} \ \underset{(-3.74)}{-0.0961D_{1t}} \ \underset{(-6.03)}{-0.1570D_{2t}} - \underset{(-0.37)}{0.0097D_{3t}} \quad R^2 = 0.80$$

where

Q = pounds of coffee consumed per capita

P = the relative price of coffee per pound at 1967 prices

I = per capita PDI, in thousands of 1967 dollars

P' = the relative price of tea per quarter pound at 1967 prices

T = the time trend with $T = 1$ for 1961-I, to $T = 66$ for 1977-II

D_1 = 1 for the first quarter

D_2 = 1 for the second quarter

D_3 = 1 for the third quarter

$\ln$ = the natural log

(a) How would you interpret the coefficients of P, I, and P'?

(b) Is the demand for coffee price elastic?

(c) Are coffee and tea substitute or complementary products?

(d) How would you interpret the coefficient of T?

(e) What is the trend rate of growth or decline in coffee consumption in the United States? If there is a decline in coffee consumption, what accounts for it?

(f) What is the income elasticity of demand for coffee?

(g) How would you test the hypothesis that the income elasticity of demand for coffee is not significantly different from 1?

(h) What do the dummy variables represent in this case?

(i) How do you interpret the dummies in this model?

(j) Which of the dummies are statistically significant?

(k) Is there a pronounced seasonal pattern in coffee consumption in the United States? If so, what accounts for it?

(l) Which is the bench mark quarter in this example? Would the results change if we choose another quarter as the base quarter?

(m) The preceding model only introduces the *differential intercept* dummies. What implicit assumption is made here?

(n) Suppose someone contends that this model is *misspecified* because it assumes that the slopes of the various variables remain constant between quarters. How would you rewrite the model to take into account *differential slope* dummies?

(o) If you had the data, how would you go about reformulating the demand function for coffee?

9.9. In a study of the determinants of direct air fares to Cleveland, Paul W. Bauer and Thomas J. Zlatoper obtained the following regression results (in tabular form) to explain one-day air fare for first class, coach, and discount air fares. (The dependent variable is one-way air fare in dollars).

Explanatory variable	First class	Coach	Discount
Carriers	−19.50	−23.00	−17.50
	*t = (−0.878)	(−1.99)	(−3.67)
Carriers^2	2.79	4.00	2.19
	(0.632)	(1.83)	(2.42)
Miles	0.233	0.277	0.0791
	(5.13)	(12.00)	(8.24)
Miles^2	−0.0000097	−0.000052	−0.000014
	(−0.495)	(−4.98)	(−3.23)
Pop	−0.00598	−0.00114	−0.000868
	(−1.67)	(−4.98)	(−1.05)
INC	−0.00195	−0.00178	−0.00411
	(−0.686)	(−1.06)	(−6.05)
Corp	3.62	1.22	−1.06
	(3.45)	(2.51)	(−5.22)
Pass	−0.000818	−0.000275	0.853
	(−0.771)	(−0.527)	(3.93)
Stop	12.50	7.64	−3.85
	(1.36)	(2.13)	(−2.60)
Slot	7.13	−0.746	17.70
	(0.299)	(−0.067)	(3.82)
Hub	11.30	4.18	−3.50
	(0.90)	(0.81)	(−1.62)
Meal	11.20	0.945	1.80
	(1.07)	(0.177)	(0.813)
EA	−18.30	5.80	−10.60
	(−1.60)	(0.775)	(−3.49)
CO	−66.40	−56.50	−4.17
	(−5.72)	(−7.61)	(−1.35)
Constant term	212.00	126.00	113.00
	(5.21)	(5.75)	(12.40)
R^2	0.863	0.871	0.799
Number of observations	163	323	323

Source: Paul W. Bauer and Thomas J. Zlatoper, *Economic Review*, Federal Reserve Bank of Cleveland, vol. 25, no. 1, 1989, Tables 2, 3, and 4, pp. 6–7.
* Figures in parentheses represent *t* values.

The explanatory variables are defined as follows:

Carriers = the number of carriers
    Pass = the total number of passengers flown on route (all carriers)
    Miles = the mileage from the origin city to Cleveland
    Pop = the population of the origin city
    Inc = per capita income of the origin city
    Corp = the proxy for potential business traffic from the origin city
    Slot = the dummy variable equaling 1 if the origin city has a slot-restricted airport
        = 0, otherwise

Stop = the number of on-flight stops
Meal = the dummy variable equaling 1 if meal is served
     = 0 otherwise
 Hub = the dummy variable equaling 1 if the origin city has a hub airline
     = 0 otherwise
  EA = the dummy variable equaling 1 if the carrier is Eastern Airlines
     = 0 otherwise
  CO = the dummy variable equaling 1 if the carrier is Continental Airlines
     = 0 otherwise

(a) What is the rationale for introducing both carriers and squared carriers as explanatory variables in the model? What does the positive sign for carriers and negative sign for carrier squared suggest?
(b) As in part (a), what is the rationale for the introduction of miles and squared miles as explanatory variables? Do the observed signs of these variables make economic sense?
(c) The population variable is observed to have a negative sign. What is the implication here?
(d) Why is the coefficient of the per capita income variable negative in all the regressions?
(e) Why does the stop variable have a positive sign for first-class and coach fares but a negative sign for discount fares? Which makes economic sense?
(f) The dummy for Continental Airlines consistently has a negative sign. What does this suggest?
(g) Assess the statistical significance of each estimated coefficient. *Note*: Since the number of observations is sufficiently large, use the normal approximation to the t distribution at the 5% level of significance. Justify your use of one-tailed or two-tailed tests.
(h) Why is the slot dummy significant only for discount fares?
(i) Since the number of observations for coach and discount fare regressions is the same, 323 each, would you pull all 646 observations and run a regression similar to the ones shown in the preceding table? If you do that, how would you distinguish between coach and discount fare observations (*Hint*: dummy variables).
(j) Comment on the overall quality of the regression results given in the preceding table.

9.10. In a regression of weight on height involving 51 students, 36 males and 15 females, the following regression results were obtained:[18]

1. $\widehat{Weight_i} = -232.06551 + 5.5662 height_i$
   $t = \quad (-5.2066) \quad\quad (8.6246)$

2. $\widehat{Weight_i} = -122.9621 + 23.8238 dumsex + 3.7402 height_i$
   $t = \quad (-2.5884) \quad\quad (4.0149) \quad\quad\quad (5.1613)$

3. $\widehat{Weight_i} = -107.9508 + 3.5105 height_i + 2.0073 dumsex_i + 0.3263 dumht.$
   $t = \quad (-1.2266) \quad\quad (2.6087) \quad\quad\quad (0.0187) \quad\quad\quad (0.2035)$

---

[18] Data were collected by and various regressions were run by my colleague Albert Zucker.

where weight is in pounds, height is in inches, and where

$$Dumsex = 1 \text{ for male}$$
$$= 0 \text{ otherwise}$$
$$Dumht. = \text{the interactive or differential slope dummy}$$

(*a*) Which regression would you choose, 1 or 2? Why?

(*b*) If 2 is in fact preferable but you choose 1, what kind of error are you committing?

(*c*) What does the dumsex coefficient in 2 suggest?

(*d*) In model 2 the differential intercept dummy is statistically significant whereas in model 3 it is statistically insignificant? What accounts for this change?

(*e*) Between models 2 and 3, which would you choose? Why?

(*f*) In models 2 and 3 the coefficient of the height variable is about the same but the coefficient of the dummy variable for sex changes dramatically. Any idea what is going on?

    To answer questions (*d*), (*e*), and (*f*) you are given the following *correlation matrix*.

	Height	Dumsex	Dumht.
Height	1	0.6276	0.6752
Dumsex	0.6276	1	0.9971
Dumht.	0.6752	0.9971	1

The interpretation of this table, e.g., is that the coefficient of correlation between height and dumsex is 0.6276 and that between dumsex and dumht. is 0.9971.

9.11. The following table gives *nonseasonally* adjusted quarterly data on the retail sale of apparel and accessories for the period 1983 to 1986.

Sale of apparel and accessory stores

Year	Quarter			
	I	II	III	IV
		($, in millions)		
1983	4190	4927	6843	6912
1984	4521	5522	5350	7204
1985	4902	5912	5972	7987
1986	5458	6359	6501	8607

Source: Business Statistics, 1986, U.S. Department of Commerce, A Supplement of the Survey of Current Business, p. 37 (quarterly averages computed from monthly data).

Consider the following model:

$$Sales_t = B_1 + B_2 D_{2t} + B_3 D_{3t} + B_4 D_{4t} + u_t$$

where

$D_2 = 1$ in the second quarter; $= 0$ otherwise

$D_3 = 1$ in the third quarter; $= 0$ otherwise

$D_4 = 1$ in the fourth quarter; $= 0$ otherwise

(a) Estimate the preceding regression.

(b) What is the interpretation of the various coefficients?

*(c) How would you use the estimated regression to deseasonalize the data?

9.12. Use the data of problem 9.11 but estimate the following model:

$$\text{Sales}_t = B_1 D_{1t} + B_2 D_{2t} + B_3 D_{3t} + B_4 D_{4t} + u_t$$

In this model there is a dummy assigned to each quarter.

(a) How does this model differ from the one given in problem 9.11?

(b) To estimate this model, will you have to use a regression program that suppresses the intercept term? In other words, will you have to run a regression through the origin?

(c) Compare the results of this model with the previous one and determine which model you prefer and why.

9.13. Refer to Example 9.3 in the text. How would you set up the regression model that allows for the possibility that both the intercept and slope coefficients of the starting salary in relation to years of experience differ for male and female teachers?

9.14. Refer to regression (9.12). How would you interpret the nondummy variables in this model?

9.15. How would you modify the regression (9.13) so as to allow for the possibility that the slope coefficients are also different?

9.16. Consider the following model:

$$Y_i = B_1 + B_2 D_{2i} + B_3 D_{3i} + B_4 (D_{2i} D_{3i}) + B_5 X_i + u_i$$

where

$Y = $ the annual salary of a college teacher

$X = $ years of teaching experience

$D_2 = 1$ if male

$\quad = 0$ otherwise

$D_3 = 1$ if white

$\quad = 0$ otherwise

(a) The term $(D_{2i} D_{3i})$ represents the *interaction effect*. What does this expression mean?

(b) What is the meaning of B_4?

(c) Find $E(Y_i | D_2 = 1, D_3 = 1, X_i)$ and interpret it.

9.17. Suppose in the regression (9.1) we let

$D_i = 1$ for a college graduate

$\quad = -1$ for a noncollege graduate

---

* Optional.

Using the data given in Table 9-1, estimate regression (9.1) with this dummy set-up and compare your results with those given in regression (9.4). What general conclusion can you draw?

9.18. Continue with the preceding problem but now assume that

$$D_i = 2 \text{ if college graduate}$$
$$= 1 \text{ if noncollege graduate}$$

With this dummy scheme reestimate regression (9.1) using the data of Table 9-1 and compare your results. What general conclusions can you draw from the various dummy schemes?

PART

III

REGRESSION ANALYSIS IN PRACTICE

In this final part of the book consisting of Chapters 10 through 14, we consider several practical aspects of the linear regression model. The classical linear regression model (CLRM) developed in Part II, although a versatile model, is based on several simplifying assumptions which may not hold in practice. In this part we find out what happens if one or more of these assumptions are relaxed or not fulfilled in any given situation.

Chapter 10 on multicollinearity tries to determine what happens if two or more explanatory variables are correlated. Recall that one of the assumptions of the CLRM is that explanatory variables do not have perfect linear relationship(s) among themselves. It is shown in this chapter that as long as explanatory variables are not perfectly linearly related, the ordinary least squares (OLS) estimators are still best linear unbiased estimators (BLUE).

Chapter 11 on heteroscedasticity discusses the consequences of the violation of the CLRM assumption that the error variance is constant. This chapter shows that if this assumption is violated, OLS estimators, although unbiased, are no longer efficient. In short, they are not BLUE. But this chapter shows how with some simple transformations one can get rid of the problem of heteroscedasticity.

Chapter 12 on autocorrelation considers yet another departure from the CLRM by examining the consequences of correlation in error terms. As in the case of heteroscedasticity, in the presence of autocorrelation the OLS estimators, although unbiased, are not efficient; that is, they are not BLUE. But we show in this chapter how with suitable transformation of the data one can minimize the problem of autocorrelation.

Chapter 13 on model selection discusses the unspelled assumption of the CLRM that the model chosen for investigation is the "correct" model. In this chapter we discuss the consequences of various types of misspecification of the regression model and suggest appropriate remedies.

Chapter 14 is a potpourri of some important regression models that have been used in practice extensively. In particular, we discuss three topics: (1) restricted least squares, (2) dynamic regression models, and (3) qualitiative dependent variable regression models. These three topics indicate that the linear regression model is a very flexible model that can handle a variety of practical problems.

As in previous chapters, the concepts introduced in these five chapters are amply illustrated with numerical and concrete economic applications.

CHAPTER

10

MULTICOLLINEARITY: WHAT HAPPENS IF EXPLANATORY VARIABLES ARE CORRELATED

In Chapter 7 we noted that one of the assumptions of the classical linear regression model (CLRM) is that there is no **perfect multicollinearity**—no exact linear relationships among explanatory variables, Xs, included in a multiple regression. In that chapter we explained intuitively the meaning of perfect multicollinearity and reasons for assuming why it should not exist in the population multiple regression (PRF). In this chapter we take a closer look at the topic of multicollinearity. In practice, one rarely encounters perfect multicollinearity, but cases of **near** or **very high multicollinearity** where explanatory variables are *approximately* linearly related frequently arise in many applications. It is important to know what problems these correlated variables pose for the ordinary least squares (OLS) estimation of multiple regression models. Toward that end, in this chapter we seek answers to the following questions:

1. What is the nature of multicollinearity?
2. Is multicollinearity really a problem?
3. What are the theoretical consequences of multicollinearity?
4. What are the practical consequences of multicollinearity?
5. In practice, how does one detect multicollinearity?
6. If it is desirable to eliminate the problem of multicollinearity, what remedial measures are available?

TABLE 10-1
The demand for widgets reconsidered

Y (quantity)	X₂ (price, $)	X₃ (income per week, $)	X₄ (earnings per week, $)
49	1	298	297.5
45	2	296	294.9
44	3	294	293.5
39	4	292	292.8
38	5	290	290.2
37	6	288	289.7
34	7	286	285.8
33	8	284	284.6
30	9	282	281.1
29	10	280	278.8

10.1   THE NATURE OF MULTICOLLINEARITY: THE CASE OF PERFECT MULTICOLLINEARITY

To answer these various questions, we consider first a simple numerical example which is specially "constructed" to "bring home" some crucial points about multicollinearity. Recall from Chapter 6 our demand function for widgets. The data given in Table 6-1 have been reproduced in the first two columns of Table 10-1 with some additional information.

In Table 10-1 we have presented two sets of income figures, X_3, as estimated, say, by a researcher, and X_4, as estimated by another researcher. To distinguish between the two, we call X_3 income and X_4 earnings.

Since besides the price the income of the consumer is also an important determinant of most goods demanded, we write the expanded demand function as

$$Y_i = A_1 + A_2 X_{2i} + A_3 X_{3i} + u_i \tag{10.1}$$

$$Y_i = B_1 + B_2 X_{2i} + B_3 X_{4i} + u_i \tag{10.2}$$

These demand functions differ in the measure of income used. A priori, or according to theory, A_2 and B_2 are expected to be negative (why?) and A_3 and B_3 are expected to be positive (why?).[1]

---

[1] According to economic theory, the income coefficient is expected to be positive for most normal economic goods. It is expected to be negative for what are called "inferior" goods.

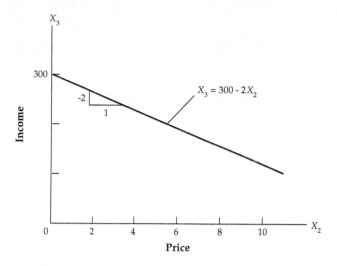

FIGURE 10-1
Scattergram between income (X_3) and price (X_2).

When an attempt was made to fit the regression (10.1) to the data in Table 10-1, the computer "refused" to estimate the regression.[2] What went wrong? Nothing. By plotting variables price (X_2) and income (X_3), we get the diagram shown in Figure 10-1. And by trying to regress X_3 on X_2, we obtain the following results:

$$X_{3i} = 300 - 2X_{2i} \qquad R^2 (= r^2) = 1.00 \qquad (10.3)$$

In other words, the income variable X_3 and the price variable X_2 are **perfectly linearly related;** that is, we have **perfect collinearity** (or **multicollinearity**).[3]

Because of the relationship in Equation (10.3), we cannot estimate the regression (10.1), for if we substitute Eq. (10.3) into Eq. (10.1), we obtain

$$Y_i = A_1 + A_2 X_{2i} + A_3(300 - 2X_{2i}) + u_i$$

$$= (A_1 + 300A_3) + (A_2 - 2A_3) X_{2i} + u_i$$

$$= C_1 + C_2 X_{2i} + u_i \qquad (10.4)$$

---

[2] Usually, you will get a message saying that the X, or data, matrix is not positive definite; that is, it cannot be inverted. In matrix algebra such a matrix is called a singular matrix. Simply put, the computer cannot do the calculations.

[3] Although the term *collinearity* refers to a single perfect linear relationship between variables and the term *multicollinearity* refers to more than one such relationship, we will from now on use the term *multicollinearity* in a generic sense to include both cases. The context will make it clear whether we have just one or more than one exact linear relationship.

where

$$C_1 = A_1 + 300A_3 \qquad (10.5)$$

$$C_2 = A_2 - 2A_3 \qquad (10.6)$$

No wonder we could not estimate (10.1), for as (10.4) shows, we do not have a multiple regression but a simple two-variable regression between Y and X_2. Now, although we can estimate (10.4) and obtain estimates of C_1 and C_2, from these two values we cannot obtain estimates of the original parameters A_1, A_2, and A_3, for in (10.5) and (10.6) we have only two equations but there are three unknowns to be estimated. (From school algebra we know that in order to estimate three unknowns we generally require three equations.)

The results of estimating the regression (10.4) are already given in expression (6.48), which for convenience is reproduced here:

$$\hat{Y}_i = 49.667 - 2.1576X_{2i}$$

$$\text{se} = (0.746)\ (0.1203) \qquad (10.7)$$

$$t = (66.538)\ (-17.935) \qquad r^2 = 0.9757$$

As we can see, $c_1 = 49.667$ and $c_2 = -2.1576$. Try as we might, from these two values there is no way to retrieve the values of the three unknowns, A_1, A_2, and A_3.[4]

The upshot of the preceding discussion is that *in cases of perfect linear relationship or perfect multicollinearity among explanatory variables, we cannot obtain unique estimates of all parameters. And since we cannot obtain their unique estimates, we cannot draw any statistical inferences (i.e., hypothesis testing) about them from a given sample.*

To put it bluntly, in cases of perfect multicollinearity, estimation and hypothesis testing about *individual* regression coefficients in a multiple regression are not possible. It is a dead end issue. Of course, as regressions (10.5) and (10.6) show, we can obtain estimates of a linear combination (i.e., the sum or difference) of the original coefficients, but not each of them individually.

10.2 THE CASE OF NEAR, OR IMPERFECT, MULTICOLLINEARITY

The case of perfect multicollinearity is a pathological extreme. In most applications involving economic data two or more explanatory variables are not exactly linearly related but can be approximately so. That is, collinearity can be "high" but not perfect. This is the case of **near,** or **imperfect,** or **high**

---

[4] Of course, if the value of one of A_1, A_2, and A_3 is fixed arbitrarily, then the values of the other two As can be obtained from the estimated Cs. But these values will not be unique, for they depend on the value arbitrarily chosen for one of the As. To reiterate, there is no way of obtaining unique values of three unknowns (the three As) from two knowns (the two Cs).

multicollinearity. What we mean by "high" collinearity will be explained shortly. *From now on when talking about multicollinearity, we have imperfect multicollinearity in mind.* As we saw in Section 10.1, the case of perfect multicollinearity is a blind alley.

To see what we mean by near, or imperfect, multicollinearity, let us return to our data in Table 10-1, but this time, we run the regression (10.2) with earnings as the income variable. The regression results are as follows:

$$\hat{Y}_i = 145.37 \quad - \quad 2.7975 X_{2i} \quad - 0.3191 X_{4i}$$

$$\text{se} = (120.06) \quad \quad (0.8122) \quad \quad (0.4003) \tag{10.8}$$

$$t = (1.2107) \quad \quad (-3.4444) \quad (-0.7971) \quad \quad R^2 = 0.9778$$

These results are interesting for several reasons:

1. Although the regression (10.1) cannot be estimated, we can estimate the regression (10.2), even though the difference between the two income variables is very small, which can be seen visually from the last two columns of Table 10-1.[5]

2. As expected, price coefficients are negative in both Eqs. (10.7) and (10.8) and the numerical difference between the two is not vast. Each price coefficient is statistically significantly different from zero (why?), but notice, relatively speaking, that the $|t|$ value of this coefficient in Eq. (10.7) is much greater than the corresponding $|t|$ value in Eq. (10.8). Or what amounts to the same thing, comparatively the standard error (se) of the price coefficient in Eq. (10.7) is much smaller than that in Eq. (10.8).

3. The R^2 value in Eq. (10.7) with one explanatory variable is 0.9757, whereas in Eq. (10.8) with two explanatory variables it is 0.9778, an increase of only 0.0021, which does not "appear" to be a great increase. It can be shown that this increase in the R^2 value is not statistically significant.[6]

4. The coefficient of the income (earnings) variable is statistically insignificant, but, more importantly, it has the wrong sign: For most commodities, income has a positive effect on the quantity demanded, unless the commodity in question happens to be an *inferior good.*

5. Despite the insignificance of the income variable, if we were to test the hypothesis that $B_2 = B_3 = 0$ (i.e., the hypothesis that $R^2 = 0$), the hypothesis

---

[5] It is time to let the "cat out of the bag." The earnings figures reported in column 4 of Table 10-1 were "constructed" from the following relation: $X_{4i} = X_{3i} + u_i$, where the us are random terms obtained from a random number table. The 10 values of u are as follows: -0.5, -1.1, -0.5, 0.8, 0.2, 1.7, -0.2, 0.6, -0.9, and -1.2.

[6] This is the topic of "marginal" or "incremental" contribution of an explanatory variable to the regression. This subject is discussed in some detail in Chap. 14, Sec. 14.1. Additional details can be found in Damodar N. Gujarati, *Basic Econometrics*, 2d ed., McGraw-Hill, New York, 1988, pp. 230–231.

can be easily rejected by applying the F test given in expression (7.50). In other words, collectively or together, price and earnings have a significant impact on the quantity demanded.

What explains these "strange" results? As a clue, let us plot X_2 against X_4, price against earnings. (See Figure 10-2.) Unlike Figure 10-1, we see that although price and earnings are not perfectly linearly related, there is a high degree of dependency between the two. This can be seen more clearly from the following regression:

$$X_{4i} = 299.92 \quad - 2.0055X_{2i} + e_i$$

$$\text{se} = (0.6748) \quad (0.1088) \tag{10.9}$$

$$t = (444.44) \quad (-18.44) \qquad r^2 = 0.9770$$

As this regression shows, price and earnings are highly correlated; the coefficient of correlation is -0.9884 (which is the negative square root of r^2). This is the case of **near perfect linear relationship,** or near perfect multicollinearity. If the coefficient of correlation were -1, as in Eq. (10.3), this would be the case of perfect multicollinearity. Notice carefully, in Eq. (10.3) we have not added e_i because the linear relationship between X_{2i} and X_{3i} is perfect, whereas in Equation (10.9) we have added it to show that the linear relationship between X_{4i} and X_{2i} is not perfect.

In passing, note that if there are just two explanatory variables, the coefficient of correlation r can be used as a measure of the degree or strength of collinearity. But if more than two explanatory variables are involved, as we

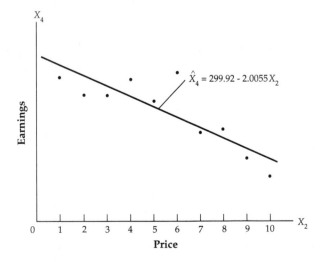

FIGURE 10-2
Earnings (X_4) and price (X_2) relationship.

will show later, the coefficient of correlation may not be an adequate measure of collinearity.

10.3 THEORETICAL CONSEQUENCES OF MULTICOLLINEARITY

Now that we have discussed the nature of perfect and imperfect multicollinearity somewhat heuristically, let us state the consequences of multicollinearity a bit more formally. But keep in mind that from now on we consider only the case of *imperfect* multicollinearity, for perfect mutlicollinearity leads us nowhere.

As we know, given the assumptions of the CLRM, OLS estimators are best linear unbiased estimators (BLUE): In the class of all linear unbiased estimators, OLS estimators have the least possible variance. It is interesting that so long as collinearity is not perfect, OLS estimators still remain BLUE even though one or more of the partial regression coefficients in a multiple regression can be *individually* statistically insignificant. Thus, in Eq. (10.8), the income coefficient is statistically insignificant although the price coefficient is statistically significant. But OLS estimates presented in Eq. (10.8) still retain their BLUE property.[7] Then why all the fuss about multicollinearity? There are several reasons:

1. It is true that even in the presence of near collinearity, the OLS estimators are unbiased. But remember that *unbiasedness is a repeated sampling property*. What this says is that, keeping the values of the X variables fixed, if we obtain several samples and compute the OLS estimates for each of these samples, the average value of the estimates will tend to converge to the true population value of the estimates. But this says nothing about the properties of estimates given in any given sample. In reality, we rarely have the luxury of replicating samples.

2. It is also true that near collinearity does not destroy the minimum variance property of OLS estimators: In the class of all linear unbiased estimators, OLS estimators have minimum variance. This does not mean, however, that the variance of an OLS estimator will be small (in relation to the value of the estimator) in any given sample, as the regression (10.8) shows very clearly. It is true that the estimator of the income coefficient is BLUE, but in the sample at hand its variance is so large compared to the estimate that the computed t value (under the null hypothesis that the true income coefficient is zero) is only -0.7971. This would lead us to "accept" the hypothesis that income has no effect on the quantity of widgets demanded. In short, *minimum variance does not mean the numerical value of the variance will be small*.

3. *Multicollinearity is essentially a sample (regression) phenomenon* in the sense that even if the X variables are not linearly related in the population

---

[7] Since imperfect multicollinearity per se does not violate any of the assumptions listed in Chap. 7, OLS estimators retain the BLUE property.

(i.e., PRF), they can be so related in a particular sample, such as that of Table 10-1. When we postulate the PRF, we believe that all X variables included in the model have a separate or independent effect on the dependent variable Y. But it can happen that in any given sample that is used to estimate the PRF some or all X variables are so highly collinear that we cannot isolate their individual influence on Y. So to speak, our sample lets us down although the theory says that all Xs are important. And this happens because most economic data are not obtained in controlled laboratory experiments: Data on variables such as the gross national product (GNP), prices, unemployment, profits, dividends, etc. are usually observed as they occur and are not obtained experimentally. If data could be obtained experimentally, to begin with, we would not allow collinearity to exist. Since data are usually obtained nonexperimentally, and if there is near collinearity in two or more explanatory variables, often we are in "the statistical position of not being able to make bricks without straw."[8]

For all these reasons, the fact that OLS estimators are BLUE despite (imperfect) multicollinearity is of little consolation in practice. Therefore, we must try to find out what happens or is likely to happen in any given sample. As noted, collinearity is usually a sample-specific phenomenon.

10.4 PRACTICAL CONSEQUENCES OF MULTICOLLINEARITY

In cases of near or high multicollinearity, as in our demand for widget regression (10.8), we are likely to encounter one or more of the following consequences:

1. *Large variances and standard error of OLS estimators.* This is clearly seen from the widget regressions (10.7) and (10.8). As discussed earlier, because of high collinearity between price (X_2) and earnings (X_4), when both variables are included in the regression (10.8), the standard error of the coefficient of the price variable increases dramatically compared with the regression (10.7). As we know, if the standard error of an estimator increases, it becomes more difficult to estimate the true value of the estimator. That is, there is a fall in the *precision* of OLS estimators.

2. *Wider confidence intervals.* Because of large standard errors, confidence intervals for relevant population parameters tend to be large.

3. *"Insignificant" t ratios.* Recall that to test the hypothesis that in our regression (10.8) the true $B_3 = 0$ we use the t ratio $b_3/se(b_3)$ and compare the estimated t value with the critical t value from the t table. But as previously seen, in cases of high collinearity the estimated standard errors increase dramatically, thereby making t values smaller. Therefore, in such cases one will increasingly accept the null hypothesis that the relevant true population coef-

---

[8] J. Johnston, *Econometric Methods*, 2d ed., McGraw-Hill, New York, 1972, p. 164.

ficient is zero. Thus, in the regression (10.8), since the t value is only -0.7971, we might "jump" to the conclusion that in the widget example PRF income has no effect on the quantity demanded.

4. *A high R^2 value but few significant t ratios.* The regression (10.8) shows this clearly. The R^2 in this regression is quite high, about 0.98, but only the t ratio of the price variable is significant. And yet on the basis of the F ratio, we can reject the hypothesis that the price and earnings variable simultaneously have no effect on the quantity of widgets demanded.

5. *OLS estimators and their standard errors become very sensitive to small changes in the data; that is, they tend to be unstable.* To see this, return to Table 10-1. Suppose we change the data on the earnings variable X_4 slightly. The first, fifth, and tenth observations are now 295, 287, and 274, respectively. All other values remain intact. The result of this change gives the following regression:

$$\hat{Y}_i = 100.56 \quad -2.5164X_{2i} -0.16995X_{4i}$$
$$\text{se} - (48.030) \quad (0.35906) \quad (0.1604) \tag{10.10}$$
$$t = (2.0936) \quad (-7.0083) \quad (-1.0597) \qquad R^2 = 0.9791$$

Comparing Eq. (10.8) with regression (10.10), we observe that as a result of a very small change in the data, the regression results change quite substantially. Relatively speaking, standard errors have gone down in Eq. (10.10), as a result of which t ratios have increased in absolute values and the income variable now has become less negative than before.

Why such a change? In the regression (10.8) the coefficient of correlation between X_2 and X_4 was -0.9884, whereas in the regression (10.10) it was -0.9431. In other words, the degree of collinearity between X_2 and X_4 has decreased in going from Eq. (10.8) to Eq. (10.10). Although the decrease in the correlation coefficient does not seem astounding, the change in regression results is noticeable. And this is precisely what happens in cases of near perfect collinearity.

6. *Wrong signs for regression coefficients.* As regressions (10.8) and (10.10) show, the earnings variable has the "wrong" sign, for economic theory would have us believe that for most commodities the income effect is positive. Of course, with an inferior good this is not a wrong sign. Therefore, we have to be careful in attributing the wrong sign to multicollinearity alone, but it should not be ruled out either.

7. *Difficulty in assessing the individual contributions of explanatory variables to the explained sum of squares (ESS) or R^2.* We can illustrate this point again with our widget example. In Eq. (10.7) we regressed quantity (Y) on price (X_2) alone, giving an R^2 value of 0.9757. In regression (10.8) we regressed Y on both price and earnings, obtaining an R^2 of 0.9778. Now if we regress Y on X_4 alone, we obtain the following results:

$$\hat{Y}_i = -263.74 + 1.0438X_{4i}$$

$$\text{se} = (26.929) \qquad (0.0932) \qquad\qquad\qquad (10.11)$$

$$t = (-9.794) \qquad (11.200) \qquad R^2 = 0.9400$$

Lo and behold, earnings X_4 alone explain 94 percent of the variation in the quantity demanded. In addition, the earnings coefficient is not only statistically significant, but it is also positive, in accord with theoretical expectations!

As shown previously, in the multiple regression (10.8) the R^2 value is 0.9778. What part of it is due to X_2 and what part is due to X_4? We cannot tell precisely because the two variables are so highly collinear that when one moves the other moves with it almost automatically, as the regression (10.9) so clearly demonstrates. Therefore, in cases of high collinearity it is futile to assess the contribution of each explanatory variable to the overall R^2.

A question: Can the consequences of multicollinearity that we have illustrated earlier be established rigorously? Yes indeed! But we will skip the proofs here since they can be found elsewhere.[9]

10.5   DETECTION OF MULTICOLLINEARITY

As demonstrated in the previous section, practical consequences of multicollinearity can be far-ranging, the BLUE property notwithstanding. So, what can we do about "resolving" the multicollinearity problem? But before resolving it, we must first find out if we have a collinearity problem to begin with. In short, how do we detect the presence of and severity of multicollinearity? Now we have a problem, for as noted earlier, multicollinearity is **sample-specific;** it is a sample phenomenon. Here it is useful to keep in mind the following warning:[10]

1. Multicollinearity is a question of degree and not of kind. The meaningful distinction is not between the presence and the absence of multicollinearity, but between its various degrees.
2. Since multicollinearity refers to the condition of the explanatory variables that are assumed to be nonstochastic, it is a *feature of the sample* and not of the population.
   Therefore, we do not "test for multicollinearity" but can, if we wish, measure its degree in any particular sample.

Having stated that, we must hasten to add that we do not have a single measure of multicollinearity, for in nonexperimentally collected data we can never be sure about the nature and degree of collinearity. What we have are

---

[9] The proofs are shown in Damodar N. Gujarati, *Basic Econometrics*, 2d ed., McGraw-Hill, New York, 1988, pp. 290–292.

[10] Jan Kmenta, *Elements of Econometrics*, 2d ed., Macmillan, New York, 1986, p. 431.

some rules of thumb, or indicators that will provide us with some clue about the existence of multicollinearity in concrete applications. Some of these indicators follow.

1. *High R^2 but few significant t ratios.* As noted earlier, this is the "classic" symptom of multicollinearity. If R^2 is high, say, in excess of 0.8, the F test in most cases will reject the null hypothesis that the partial slope coefficients are *jointly* or *simultaneously* equal to zero. But individual *t* tests will show that none or very few partial slope coefficients are statistically different from zero. Our widget regression (10.8) bears this out fully.

2. *High pairwise correlations among explanatory variables.* If in a multiple regression involving, say, six explanatory variables, we compute the coefficient of correlation between any pair of these variables using the formula (6.44), and if some of these correlations are high, say, in excess of 0.8, there is the possibility that some serious collinearity exists. Unfortunately, this criterion is not often reliable, for pairwise correlations can be low (suggesting no serious collinearity) yet collinearity is suspected because very few *t* ratios are statistically significant.[11]

3. *Examination of partial correlations.* Suppose we have three explanatory variables, X_2, X_3, and X_4. Let r_{23}, r_{24}, and r_{34} represent the pairwise correlations between X_2 and X_3, between X_2 and X_4, and between X_3 and X_4, respectively. Suppose $r_{23} = 0.90$, indicating "high" collinearity between X_2 and X_3. Now consider this correlation coefficient, called the **partial correlation coefficient,** $r_{23.4}$, which is the coefficient of correlation between X_2 and X_3, *holding the influence of the variable X_4 constant* (the concept is similar to that of the partial regression coefficient discussed in Chapter 7). Suppose $r_{23.4} = 0.43$; that is, holding the influence of the variable X_4 constant, the correlation coefficient between X_2 and X_3 is only 0.43, whereas not taking into account the influence of X_4, it is 0.90. Then, judged by the partial correlation, we cannot say that the collinearity between X_2 and X_3 is necessarily high.

As we can see, in the context of several explanatory variables, reliance on simple pairwise correlations as indicators of multicollinearity can be misleading. Unfortunately, the substitution of simple pairwise correlations by partial correlation coefficients does not provide a definitive guidance toward the presence of multicollinearity or otherwise. The latter provides only another device to check the nature of multicollinearity.[12]

4. *Subsidiary, or auxiliary, regressions.* Since multicollinearity arises because one or more of the explanatory variables are exact or near exact linear combinations of other explanatory variables, one way of finding out which X variable is highly collinear with other X variables in the model is to regress each X variable on the remaining X variables and to compute the correspond-

---

[11] For technical details, see Damodar N. Gujarati, *Basic Econometrics*, 2d ed., McGraw-Hill, New York, 1988, pp. 299–300.

[12] For technical details, see the reference in footnote 11.

ing R^2. Each of these regressions is called a **subsidiary** or an **auxiliary regression,** auxiliary to the main regression of Y on all Xs.

For example, consider the regression of Y on X_2, X_3, X_4, X_5, X_6, and X_7 —six explanatory variables. If this regression shows that we have a problem of multicollinearity because, say, the R^2 is high but very few X coefficients are individually statistically significant, we then look for the "culprit," the variable(s) that may be a perfect or near perfect linear combination of the other Xs. We proceed as follows:

1. Regress X_2 on the remaining Xs and obtain the coefficient of determination, say, R_2^2.
2. Regress X_3 on the remaining Xs and obtain its coefficient of determination, R_3^2.

Continue this procedure for the remaining X variables in the model. In the present example we will have in all six such auxiliary regressions, one for each explanatory variable.

How do we decide which of the X variables are collinear? The estimated R_i^2 will range between 0 and 1. (Why?) If an X variable is not a linear combination of the other Xs, then the R_i^2 of that regression should not be statistically significantly different from zero. And from Chapter 7, Eq. (7.50), we know how to test the assumption that a particular coefficient of determination is statistically equal to zero.

Continuing with our hypothetical example involving six explanatory variables, suppose we want to test the hypothesis that $R_2^2 = 0$; that is, X_2 is not collinear with the remaining five Xs. Now we use Eq. (7.50), which is

$$F = \frac{R^2/(k-1)}{(1-R^2)/(n-k)} \qquad (7.50)$$

where n is the number of observations and k is the number of explanatory variables including the intercept. Let us illustrate.

In our hypothetical example involving six explanatory variables, suppose that we regress each of the X variables on the remaining Xs in a sample involving 50 observations. The R^2 values obtained from the various auxiliary regressions are as follows:

$$R_2^2 = 0.90 \text{ (in the regression of } X_2 \text{ on other } Xs)$$

$$R_3^2 = 0.18 \text{ (in the regression of } X_3 \text{ on other } Xs)$$

$$R_4^2 = 0.36 \text{ (in the regression of } X_4 \text{ on other } Xs)$$

$$R_5^2 = 0.86 \text{ (in the regression of } X_5 \text{ on other } Xs)$$

$$R_6^2 = 0.09 \text{ (in the regression of } X_6 \text{ on other } Xs)$$

$$R_7^2 = 0.24 \text{ (in the regression of } X_7 \text{ on other } Xs)$$

TABLE 10-2
Testing the significance of R^2 [Eq. (7.50)]

Value of R^2	Value of F	Is F significant?
0.90	79.20	Yes*
0.18	1.93	No
0.36	4.95	Yes*
0.86	54.06	Yes*
0.09	0.87	No
0.24	2.78	Yes†

Note: * Significant at the 1% level.
 † Significant at the 5% level.
 In this example $n = 50$ and $k = 6$

The results of applying the F test given in Eq. (7.50) are given in Table 10-2.

As this table shows, the variables X_2, X_4, X_5, and X_7 seem to be collinear with the other Xs, although the degree of collinearity, as measured by R^2, varies considerably. This example points out the important fact that a "seemingly" low R^2, such as 0.36, can still be statistically significantly different from zero. A concrete economic example of auxiliary regressions is given in Section 10.7.

One drawback of the auxiliary regression technique is the computational burden. If a regression contains several explanatory variables, one has to compute several subsidiary regressions, and therefore this method of detecting collinearity can be of limited practical value. But note that many computer packages now can compute the auxiliary regressions without much computational burden.

5. *The variance inflation factor (VIF).* Even if a model does not contain several explanatory variables, the R^2 values obtained from the various auxiliary regressions may not be totally reliable diagnostics of collinearity. This can be seen more clearly if we revert to the three-variable regression discussed more completely in Chapter 7. In Eq. (7.25) and (7.27) we have been given the formulas to compute the variances of the two partial slopes b_2 ad b_3. With simple algebraic manipulations, these variance formulas can be alternatively written as

$$\text{var}(b_2) = \frac{\sigma^2}{\sum x_{2i}^2(1 - R_2^2)}$$

$$= \frac{\sigma^2}{\sum x_{2i}^2} \text{VIF} \tag{10.12}$$

$$\text{var}(b_3) = \frac{\sigma^2}{\sum x_{3i}^2(1 - R_2^2)}$$

$$= \frac{\sigma^2}{\sum x_{3i}^2} \text{VIF} \tag{10.13}$$

(For proofs of these formulas, see problem 10.21.) In these formulas R_2^2 is the coefficient of determination in the (auxiliary) regression of X_2 on X_3 (*Note*: The R^2 between X_2 and X_3 is the same as that between X_3 and X_2).

In the preceding formulas

$$\text{VIF} = \frac{1}{(1 - R_2^2)} \tag{10.14}$$

the expression on the right-hand side of Equation (10.14) is called, very appropriately, the **variance inflation factor (VIF)** because as R^2 increases, the variance, and hence the standard error, of both b_2 and b_3 increase or inflate. (Do you see this?) In the extreme, when this coefficient of determination is 1 (i.e., perfect multicollinearity), these variances and standard errors are undefined (why?). Of course, if R^2 is zero, that is, no collinearity, the VIF will be 1 (why?) and we do not have to worry about the large variances and standard errors that plague the collinearity situations.

Now an important question: Suppose an R_i^2 in an auxiliary regression is very high (but less than 1), suggesting a high degree of collinearity as per the criterion discussed in (4) above. But as Eq. (10.12), (10.13), and (10.14) so clearly show, the variance of, say, b_2, not only depends upon the VIF, but it also depends upon the variance of u_i, σ^2, as well as on the variation in X_2, Σx_{2i}^2. Thus, it is quite possible that an R_i^2 is very high, say, 0.91, but that either σ^2 is low or Σx_{2i}^2 is high, or both, so that the variance of b_2 can still be lower and the t ratio higher. In other words, a high R^2 can be counterbalanced by a low σ^2 or a high Σx_{2i}^2, or both. Of course, the terms *high* and *low* are used in a relative sense.

All this suggests that a high R^2 obtained from an auxiliary regression can only be a *surface* indicator of multicollinearity. It may not necessarily inflate the standard errors of the estimators, as the preceding discussion reveals. To put it more formally, "high R_i^2 is neither necessary nor sufficient to get high standard errors and thus multicollinearity by itself need not cause high standard errors."[13]

What general conclusions can we draw from the various multicollinearity diagnostics just discussed? There are various indicators of multicollinearity and no single diagnostic will give us a complete handle over the collinearity problem. Remember that multicollinearity is a matter of degree and that it is a sample-specific phenomenon. In some situations it might be "easy" to diagnose, but in others one or more of the preceding methods will have to be used to find out the severity of the problem. There is no easy solution to the problem.

Research on multicollinearity diagnostics continues. There are some new

---

[13] G. S. Maddala, *Introduction to Econometrics*, Macmillan, New York, 1988, p. 226. However, Maddala also says that, "if R_i^2 is low, we would be better off."

techniques, such as the *condition index,* that have been developed. But they are beyond the scope of this book and are better left for the references.[14]

10.6   IS MULTICOLLINEARITY NECESSARILY BAD?

Before proceeding to consider remedial measures for the multicollinearity problem, we need to ask an important question: Is multicollinearity necessarily an "evil"? The answer depends on the purpose of the study. If the goal of the study is to use the model to predict or forecast the future mean value of the dependent variable, collinearity per se may not be bad. Returning to our widget demand function Eq. (10.8), although the earnings variable is not individually statistically significant, the overall R^2 of 0.9778 is slightly higher than that of Eq. (10.7), which omits the earnings variable. Therefore, for prediction purposes Eq. (10.8) is marginally better than Eq. (10.7). Often forecasters choose a model on the basis of its explanatory power as measured by the R^2. Is this a good strategy? It may be if we assume that the collinearity observed between the price and earnings data given in Table 10-1 will also continue in the future. In Eq. (10.9) we have already shown how X_4 and X_2, earnings and price, are related. *If the same relationship is expected to continue into the future,* then Eq. (10.8) can be used for the purposes of forecasting. But that is a big *if.* If, in another sample, the degree of collinearity between the two variables is not that strong, obviously, a forecast based on Eq. (10.8) may be of little value.

On the other hand, if the objective of the study is not only prediction but also reliable estimation of the individual parameters of the chosen model, then serious collinearity may be "bad," because we have seen that it leads to large standard errors of the estimators. However, as noted earlier, if the objective of the study is to estimate a group of coefficients (e.g., the sum or difference of two coefficients) fairly accurately, this can be done even in the presence of multicollinearity. In this case multicollinearity may not be a problem. Thus, in Eq. (10.7) the slope coefficient of -2.1576 is an estiamte of $(A_2 - 2A_3)$ [see Eq. (10.6)], which can be measured accurately by the usual OLS procedure, although neither A_2 nor A_3 can be estimated individually.

There may be some "happy" situations where despite high collinearity the estimated R^2 and most individual regression coefficients are statistically significant on the basis of the usual t test at the conventional level of significance, such as 5 percent. As Johnston notes:

> This can arise if individual coefficients happen to be numerically well in excess of the true value, so that the effect still shows up in spite of the inflated standard

---

[14] For a simple discussion of the condition index, see Damodar N. Gujarati, *Basic Econometrics,* 2d ed., McGraw-Hill, New York, 1988, p. 301.

error and/or because the true value itself is so large that even an estimate on the downside still shows up as significant.[15]

Before moving on, let us take time out to consider a concrete economic example illustrating several points made up to this point.

10.7   AN EXTENDED EXAMPLE: THE DEMAND FOR CHICKENS IN THE UNITED STATES, 1960 to 1982

Table 10-3 gives data on per capita consumption of chickens (Y), per capita real (i.e., adjusted for inflation) disposable income (X_2), the real retail price of chicken (X_3), the real retail price of pork (X_4), and the real retail price of beef (X_5) for the United States for the period 1960 to 1982.

Since in theory the demand for a commodity is generally a function of the real income of the consumer, the real price of the product, and real prices of competing or complementary products, the following demand function was estimated: The dependent variable (Y) is the natural log of per capita consumption of chickens in pounds.

Explanatory variable	Coefficient	Standard error (se)	t ratio	
Constant	2.1898	0.1557	14.063	
ln X_2	0.3426	0.0833	4.1140	
ln X_3	−0.5046	0.1109	−4.550	(10.15)
ln X_4	0.1486	0.0997	1.4903*	
ln X_5	0.0911	0.1007	0.9046*	
		$R^2 = 0.9823;$	$\bar{R}^2 = 0.9784$	

* Not significant at the 5% level (two-tailed).

Since we have fitted a log-linear demand function, all slope coefficients are partial elasticities of Y with respect to the appropriate X variable. Thus, the income elasticity of demand is about 0.34 percent, the own-price elasticity of demand is about −0.51, the cross- (pork) price elasticity of demand is about 0.15, and the cross- (beef) price elasticity of demand is about 0.09.

As the previous results show, individually the income and own-price elasticity of demand are statistically significant, but the two cross-price elasticities are not. Incidentally, note that chicken is not a luxury consumption

---

[15] J. Johnston, *Econometric Methods*, 3d ed., McGraw-Hill, New York, 1984, p. 249.

TABLE 10-3
Raw data for the demand for chicken

Y	X_2	X_3	X_4	X_5
27.80000	397.5000	42.20000	50.70000	78.30000
29.90000	413.3000	38.10000	52.00000	79.20000
29.80000	439.2000	40.30000	54.00000	79.20000
30.80000	459.7000	39.50000	55.30000	79.20000
31.20000	492.9000	37.30000	54.70000	77.40000
33.30000	528.6000	38.10000	63.70000	80.20000
35.60000	560.3000	39.30000	69.80000	80.40000
36.40000	624.6000	37.80000	65.90000	83.90000
36.70000	666.4000	38.40000	64.50000	85.50000
38.40000	717.8000	40.10000	70.00000	93.70000
40.40000	768.2000	38.60000	73.20000	106.1000
40.30000	843.3000	39.80000	67.80000	104.8000
41.80000	911.6000	39.70000	79.10000	114.0000
40.40000	931.1000	52.10000	95.40000	124.1000
40.70000	1021.500	48.90000	94.20000	127.6000
40.10000	1165.900	58.30000	123.5000	142.9000
42.70000	1349.600	57.90000	129.9000	143.6000
44.10000	1449.400	56.50000	117.6000	139.2000
46.70000	1575.500	63.70000	130.9000	165.5000
50.60000	1759.100	61.60000	129.8000	203.3000
50.10000	1994.200	58.90000	128.0000	219.6000
51.70000	2258.100	66.40000	141.0000	221.6000
52.90000	2478.700	70.40000	168.2000	232.6000

Source: Data on Y are from *CITIBASE* and on X_2 to X_5 from the U.S. Department of Agriculture. These data were collected by the author's student Robert J. Fisher.

Notes: The real prices were obtained by dividing the nominal prices by the Consumer Price Index for food.

Y = per capita consumption of chickens (pounds)
X_2 = the real disposable income per capita ($)
X_3 = the real retail price (in cents) of chicken per pound
X_4 = the real retail price (in cents) of pork per pound
X_5 = the real retail price (in cents) of beef per pound

item since the income elasticity is less than 1. The demand for chicken with respect to its own price is price inelastic because, in absolute terms, the elasticity coefficient is less than 1.

Although the two cross-price elasticities are positive, suggesting that the other two meats are competing with chicken, they are not statistically significant. Thus, it would "seem" that the demand for chicken is not affected by the variation in the prices of pork and beef. But this might be a hasty conclusion, for we have to guard against the possibility of multicollinearity. Let us therefore consider some of the multicollinearity diagnostics discussed in Section 10.5.

TABLE 10-4
Pairwise correlations between explanatory variables of Eq. (10.15)

	$\ln X_2$	$\ln X_3$	$\ln X_4$	$\ln X_5$
$\ln X_2$	1	0.9072	0.9725	0.9790
$\ln X_3$	0.9072	1	0.9468	0.9331
$\ln X_4$	0.9725	0.9468	1	0.9543
$\ln X_5$	0.9790	0.9331	0.9543	1

Note: The correlation matrix is symmetrical. Thus, the correlation between $\ln X_4$ and $\ln X_3$ is the same as that between $\ln X_3$ and $\ln X_4$.

Collinearity Diagnostics for the Demand Function for Chickens [Equation (10.15)]

The correlation matrix. Table 10-4 gives the pairwise correlations among the (logs of the) four explanatory variables. As this table shows, the pairwise correlations between the explanatory variables are uniformly high; about 0.98 between the log of real income and the log of the price of beef, about 0.95 between the logs of pork and beef prices, about 0.91 between the log of real income and the log price of chicken, etc. Although such high pairwise correlations are no guarantee that our demand function suffers from the collinearity problem, the possibility exists.

The auxiliary regressions. This seems to be confirmed when we regress each explanatory variable on the remaining explanatory variables, which can be seen from the results presented in Table 10-5. As this table shows, all regres-

TABLE 10-5
Auxiliary regressions

$$\widehat{\ln X_2} = \quad 0.9460 - 0.8324 \ln X_3 + 0.9483 \ln X_4 + 1.0176 \ln X_5$$
$$t = \quad (2.5564) \quad (-3.4903) \quad\quad (5.6590) \quad\quad\quad (6.7847)$$
$$R^2 = 0.9846$$

$$\widehat{\ln X_3} = \quad 1.2332 - 0.4692 \ln X_2 + 0.6694 \ln X_4 + 0.5955 \ln X_5$$
$$t = \quad (8.0053) \quad (-3.4903) \quad\quad (4.8652) \quad\quad\quad (3.7848)$$
$$R^2 = 0.9428$$

$$\widehat{\ln X_4} = \; -1.0127 + 0.6618 \ln X_2 + 0.8286 \ln X_3 \; -0.4695 \ln X_5$$
$$t = (-3.7107) \quad (5.6590) \quad\quad\quad (4.8652) \quad\quad\quad (-2.2879)$$
$$R^2 = 0.9759$$

$$\widehat{\ln X_5} = \; -0.7057 + 0.6956 \ln X_2 + 0.7219 \ln X_3 - 0.4598 \ln X_4$$
$$t = (-2.2362) \quad (6.7847) \quad\quad\quad (3.7848) \quad\quad\quad (-2.2870)$$
$$R^2 = 0.9764$$

sions in this table have R^2 values in excess of 0.94; the F test shown in Eq. (7.50) shows that all these R^2s are statistically significant (see Problem 10.24), suggesting that each explanatory variable in the regression (10.15) is highly collinear with other explanatory variables.

Therefore, it is quite possible that in the regression (10.15) we did not find the coefficients of the pork and beef price variables individually statistically significant. But this is all in accord with the theoretical consequences of high multicollinearity discussed earlier. It is interesting that despite high collinearity, the coefficients of the real income and own-price variables turned out to be statistically significant. This may very well be due to the fact mentioned by Johnston (see footnote 15).

As this example shows, one must be careful about judging the individual significance of an explanatory variable in the presence of a high degree of collinearity. We will return to this example in the following section when we consider remedial measures for multicollinearity.

10.8 WHAT TO DO WITH MULTICOLLINEARITY: REMEDIAL MEASURES

Suppose on the basis of one or more of the diagnostic tests discussed in Section 10.5 that we find a particular problem is plagued by multicollinearity. What solution(s), if any, can be used to reduce the severity of the collinearity problem, if not to eliminate it completely? Unfortunately, as in the case of collinearity diagnostics, there is no surefire remedy; there are only a few rules of thumb. This is so because multicollinearity is a feature of a particular sample and not necessarily a feature of the population. Besides, despite near collinearity, OLS estimators still retain their BLUE property. It is true that one or more regression coefficients can be individually statistically insignificant or that some of them can have the wrong signs. If the researcher is bent on reducing the severity of the collinearity problem, then he or she may try one or more of the following methods, keeping in mind that if the particular sample is "ill-conditioned," there is not much that can be done. With this caveat, let us consider the various remedies that have been discussed in the econometric literature.

Dropping a variable(s) from the model. Faced with severe multicollinearity, the "simplest" solution might seem to drop one or more of the collinear variables. Thus, in our demand function for chickens, the regression (10.15), since the three price variables are highly correlated, why not simply drop, say, the pork and beef price variables from the model?

But this remedy can be worse than the disease (multicollinearity). When formulating an economic model, such as the regression (10.15), we base the model on some theoretical considerations. In our example, following economic theory, we expect all three prices to have some effect on the demand for chicken since the three meat products are to some extent competing products. Therefore, economically speaking, the regression (10.15) is an appropriate demand function. Unfortunately, in our regression results based on the particular sample data given in Table 10-3 we were unable to detect the separate influence of the prices of pork and beef on the quantity of chicken demanded. But dropping those variables from the model will lead to what is known as **model specification error,** a topic that we will pursue further in Chapter 13. As we will show then, if we drop a variable from a model simply to eliminate the collinearity problem and to estimate a model without that variable, the estimated parameters of the reduced model may turn out to be biased. To give some idea about this bias, let us present the results of the demand function for chickens without the pork and beef price variables:

$$\widehat{\ln Y} = 2.0328 + 0.4515 \ln X_2 - 0.3722 \ln X_3 \qquad (10.16)$$
$$t = (17.497) \quad (18.284) \qquad (-5.8647)$$

$$R^2 = 0.9801; \quad \bar{R}^2 = 0.9781$$

As these results show, compared to the regression (10.15), the income elasticity has gone up but the price elasticity, in absolute value, has declined. In other words, estimated coefficients of the reduced model seem to be biased. (But more on this in Chapter 13).

As this discussion indicates, there may be a trade-off involved: In reducing the severity of the collinearity problem, we may be obtaining biased estimates of the coefficients retained in the model. *The best practical advice is not to drop a variable from an economically viable model just because the collinearity problem is serious.* Whether a chosen model is economically correct is, of course, an important issue, which we will consider in Chapter 13. In passing, note that in the regression (10.15) the t value of the pork price coefficient was in excess of 1. Therefore, following our discussion in Chapter 7 (see Section 7.11), if we drop this variable from the model, the adjusted R^2 will decrease, which is the case in the present instance.

Acquiring additional data or a new sample. Since multicollinearity is a sample feature, it is possible that in another sample involving the same variables, collinearity may not be as serious as in the first sample. The important practical question is whether one can obtain another sample, for collection of data can be costly.

Sometimes just acquiring additional data—increasing the sample size— can reduce the severity of the collinearity problem. This can be easily seen from formulas (10.12) and (10.13). For example, in the formula

$$\text{var}(b_3) = \frac{\sigma^2}{\sum x_{3i}^2 (1 - R_2^2)} \qquad (10.13)$$

for a given σ^2 and R^2, if the sample size of X_3 increases, $\sum x_{3i}^2$ will generally increase (why?), as a result of which the variance of b_3 will tend to decrease, and with it the standard error of b_3.

As an illustration, consider the following regression of consumption expenditure (Y) on income (X_2) and wealth (X_3) based on 10 observations:[16]

$$\hat{Y}_t = 24.337 + 0.87164 - 0.0349$$

$$\text{se} = \quad (6.2801) \ (0.31438) \quad (0.0301) \tag{10.17}$$

$$t = \quad 3.875 \quad 2.7726 \quad -1.1604 \quad R^2 = 0.9682$$

This regression shows that the wealth coefficient is not statistically significant, say, at the 5% level.

But when the sample size was increased to 40 observations, the following results were obtained:

$$\hat{Y}_i = 2.0907 + 0.7299X_{2i} + 0.0605X_{3i} \tag{10.18}$$

$$t = (0.8713) \quad (6.0014) \quad (2.0641) \quad R^2 = 0.9672$$

Now the wealth coefficient is statistically significant at the 5% level.

Of course, as in the case of obtaining a new sample, getting additional data on variables already in the sample may not be feasible because of cost and other considerations. But, if these constraints are not very prohibitive, by all means this remedy is certainly feasible.

Rethinking the model. Sometimes a model chosen for empirical analysis is not carefully thought out—maybe some important variables are omitted, or maybe the functional form of the model is incorrectly chosen. Thus, in our demand function for chicken, instead of the log-linear specification, the demand function is probably linear in the variables (LIV). It is possible that in the LIV specification the extent of collinearity may not be so high as in log-linear specification.

Returning to the demand function for chicken, we fitted the LIV model to the data given in Table 10-3, with the following results:

$$\hat{Y} = 37.232 + 0.0501X_2 - 0.6112X_3 + 0.1984X_4 + 0.0695X_5 \tag{10.19}$$

$$t = (10.015) \quad (1.0241) \quad (-3.7530) \quad (3.1137) \quad (1.3631)$$

$$R^2 = 0.9426; \quad \bar{R}^2 = 0.9298$$

Compared to the regression (10.15), we now observe that in the LIV specification, the income coefficient is statistically insignificant but the pork price coefficient is. What accounts for this change? Perhaps there is a high degree of collinearity between the income and the price variables. As a matter of fact, we found out from Table 10-5 that this was the case. As noted earlier, in the presence of a high degree of collinearity it is not possible to estimate a single regression coefficient too precisely (i.e., with a smaller standard error.)

In Chapter 13 we will examine the topic of model specification and selec-

---

[16] I am indebted to my colleague Albert Zucker for providing the results given in regressions (10.17) and (10.18).

tion in somewhat more detail, but for now, keep in mind that model misspecification might be the cause of collinearity in the (wrongly) fitted model.

Prior information about some parameters. Sometimes a particular phenomenon, such as a demand function, is investigated time and again. From prior studies it is possible that we can have some knowledge of the values of one or more parameters. This knowledge can be profitably utilized in the current sample. To be specific, let us suppose a demand function for widgets was estimated in the past and it was found that the income coefficient had a value of 0.9, which was statistically significant. But in the data of Table 10-1, as previously seen, we could not assess the individual impact of earnings (a measure of income) on the quantity demanded. If there is reason to believe that the past value of the income coefficient of 0.9 has not changed much, we could reestimate Eq. (10.8) as follows:

$$\text{Quantity} = B_1 + B_2 \, \text{price} + B_3 \, \text{earnings} + u_i$$
$$= B_i + B_2 \, \text{price} + 0.9 \, \text{earnings} + u_i \qquad (10.20)$$
$$\text{quantity} - 0.9 \, \text{earnings} = B_1 + B_2 \, \text{price} + u_i$$

where use is made of the prior information that $B_3 = 0.9$.

Assuming that the prior information is "correct," we have "resolved" the collinearity problem, for on the right-hand side of Equation (10.20) we now have only one explanatory variable and no question of collinearity arises. To run Eq. (10.20), we only have to subtract from the quantity observation 0.9 times the corresponding earnings observation and treat the resulting difference as the dependent variable and regress it on price.[17]

Although an intuitively appealing method, the crux of the method lies in obtaining extraneous, or prior, information, which is not always possible. But, more critically, even if one can obtain such information, to assume that the prior information continues to hold in the sample under study may be a "tall" assumption. Of course, if the income effect is not expected to vary considerably from sample to sample, and if we do have prior information on the income coefficient, this remedial measure can sometimes be employed.

Transformation of variables. Occasionally, transformation of variables included in the model can minimize, if not solve, the problem of collinearity. For example, in a study of the aggregate consumption expenditure in the United States as a function of aggregate income and aggregate wealth we might express aggregate consumption expenditure on a per capita basis, that is, per capita consumption expenditure as a function of per capita income and per capita wealth. It is possible that if there is serious collinearity in the aggre-

---

[17] Note that multicollinearity is often encountered in times series data because economic variables tend to move with the business cycle. Here information from cross-sectional studies might be utilized to estimate one or more parameters in the models based on time series data.

gate consumption function, it may not be so severe in the per capita consumption function. Of course, there is no guarantee that such a transformation will always help, leaving aside for the moment the question whether the aggregate or per capita consumption function to begin with is the appropriate model.

As an example of how a simple transformation of variables can reduce the severity of collinearity, consider the following regression based on the U.S data for 1965–1980:[18]

$$\hat{Y}_t = -108.20 + 0.045X_{2t} + 0.931X_{3t} \tag{10.21}$$

$$t = \quad \text{N.A.*} \quad (1.232) \quad (1.844) \quad R^2 = 0.9894$$

* N.A. = not available.

where

$$Y = \text{imports (\$, in billions)}$$

$$X_2 = \text{the GNP (\$, in billions)}$$

$$X_3 = \text{the Consumer Price Index (CPI)}$$

In theory, imports are positively related to the GNP (a measure of income) and domestic prices.

The regression results show that neither the income nor the price coefficient is *individually* statistically significant at the 5% level (two-tailed).[19] But on the basis of the F test, one can easily reject the null hypothesis that the two (partial) slope coefficients are jointly equal to zero (check this out), strongly suggesting that the regression (10.21) is plagued by the collinearity problem. To resolve collinearity, Salvatore obtained the following regression:

$$\frac{\hat{Y}_t}{X_{3t}} = -1.39 + 0.202\frac{X_{2t}}{X_{3t}} \tag{10.22}$$

$$t = \quad \text{N.A.*} \quad (12.22) \quad R^2 = 0.9142$$

* N.A. = not available.

which shows that real imports are statistically significantly positively related to real income, the estimated t value being highly significant. Thus, the "trick" of converting the nominal variables into "real" variables (i.e., transforming the original variables) has apparently eliminated the collinearity problem.[20]

---

[18] See Dominick Salvatore, *Managerial Economics*, McGraw-Hill, New York, 1989, pp. 156–157. Notation is adapted.

[19] But note that the price coefficient is significant at the 5% level on the basis of the one-tailed t test.

[20] Some authors warn against transforming variables routinely in this fashion. For details, see E. Kuh and J. R. Meyer, "Correlation and Regression Estimates When the Data Are Ratios," *Econometrica*, pp. 400–416, October 1955. Also, see G. S. Maddala, *Introduction to Econometrics*, Macmillan, New York, 1988, pp. 172–174.

Other remedies. The preceding remedies are only suggestive. There are several other "remedies" suggested in the literature, such as combining time series and cross-sectional data, *factor* or **principal component analysis** and **ridge regression.** But a full discussion of these topics would not only take us far afield, it would also require statistical knowledge that is way beyond that assumed in this text.

10.9 SUMMARY

An important assumption of the classical linear regression model is that there is no exact linear relationship(s), or multicollinearity, among explanatory variables. Although cases of exact multicollinearity are rare in practice, situations of near exact or high multicollinearity occur frequently. In practice, therefore, the term *multicollinearity* refers to situations where two or more variables can be highly linearly related.

The consequences of multicollinearity are as follows. In cases of perfect multicollinearity one cannot estimate the individual regression coefficients or their standard errors. In cases of high multicollinearity individual regression coefficients can be estimated and the OLS estimators retain their BLUE property. But the standard errors of one or more coefficients tend to be large in relation to their coefficient values, thereby reducing t values. As a result, based on estimated t values, one can say that the coefficient with the low t value is not statistically different from zero. In other words, one cannot assess the *marginal* or *individual* contribution of the variable whose t value is low: Recall that in a multiple regression the slope coefficient of an X variable is the *partial regression coefficient*, which measures the (marginal or individual) effect of that variable on the dependent variable, holding all other X variables constant. However, if the objective of study is to estimate a group of coefficients fairly accurately, this can be done so long as collinearity is not perfect.

In this chapter we considered several methods of detecting multicollinearity, pointing out their pros and cons. We also discussed the various remedies that have been proposed to "solve" the problem of multicollinearity and noted their strengths and weaknesses.

Since multicollinearity is a feature of a given sample, one cannot foretell which method of detecting multicollinearity or which remedial measure will work in any given concrete situation.

Key Terms and Concepts

The key terms and concepts introduced in this chapter are:

Collinearity and multicollinearity
    a) sample-specific phenomenon
Perfect and imperfect collinearity
    a) near perfect linear relationship

Partial correlation coefficient
Auxiliary regression or subsidiary
    regression
The variance inflation factor (VIF)

Remedial measures for
  multicollinearity
  a) dropping variables; model
    specification error
  b) acquiring a new sample (or
    additional data)

c) rethinking the model
d) extraneous, or prior,
  information
e) transformation of variables
f) other—principal component
  analysis; ridge regression

QUESTIONS

10.1. What is meant by collinearity? And by multicollinearity?

10.2. What is the difference between perfect and imperfect multicollinearity?

10.3. You include the subject's height, measured in inches, and the same subject's height measured in feet in a regression of weight on height. Explain intuitively why ordinary least squares (OLS) cannot estimate the regression coefficients in such a regression.

10.4. Consider the model

$$Y_i = B_1 + B_2 X_i + B_3 X_i^2 + B_4 X_i^3 + u_i$$

where Y — the total cost of production and X = the output. "Since X^2 and X^3 are functions of X, there is perfect collinearity." Do you agree? Why or why not?

10.5. Refer to Eq. (7.21), (7.22), (7.25), and (7.27). Let $x_{3i} = 2x_{2i}$. Show why it is impossible to estimate these equations.

10.6. What are the theoretical consequences of imperfect multicollinearity?

10.7. What are the practical consequences of imperfect multicollinearity?

10.8. What is meant by the variance inflation factor (VIF)? From the formula (10.14), can you tell the least possible and the highest possible value of the VIF?

10.9. Fill in the gaps in the following sentences:
  (a) In cases of near multicollinearity, the standard errors of regression coefficients tend to be _____ and the t ratios tend to be _____.
  (b) In cases of perfect multicollinearity, OLS estimators are _____ and their variances are _____.
  (c) *Ceteris paribus*, the higher the VIF is, the higher the _____ of OLS estimators will be.

10.10. State with reasons whether the following statements are true or false:
  (a) Despite perfect multicollinearity, OLS estimators are best linear unbiased estimators (BLUE).
  (b) In cases of high multicollinearity, it is not possible to assess the individual significance of one or more partial regression coefficients.
  (c) If an auxiliary regression shows that a particular R_i^2 is high, there is definite evidence of high collinearity.
  (d) High pairwise correlations do not necessarily suggest that there is high multicollinearity.
  (e) Multicollinearity is harmless if the objective of the analysis is prediction only.

10.11. In data involving economic time series such as unemployment, money supply, interest rate, consumption expenditure, etc., multicollinearity is usually suspected. Why?

10.12. Consider the following model:

$$Y_t = B_1 + B_2 X_t + B_3 X_{t-1} + B_4 X_{t-2} + B_3 X_{t-3} + u_t$$

where

$$Y = \text{the consumption}$$

$$X = \text{the income}$$

$$t = \text{the time}$$

This model states that consumption expenditure at time t is a linear function of income not only at time t but also of income in two previous time periods. Such models are called *distributed lag models* and represent what are called *dynamic models* (i.e., models involving change over time). (These models are discussed briefly in Chapter 14.)

(a) Would you expect multicollinearity in such models and why?

(b) If multicollinearity is suspected, how would you "get rid" of it?

PROBLEMS

10.13. Consider the following set of hypothetical data:

Y:	-10	-8	-6	-4	-2	0	2	4	6	8	10
X_2:	1	2	3	4	5	6	7	8	9	10	11
X_3:	1	3	5	7	9	11	13	15	17	19	21

Suppose you want to do a multiple regression of Y on X_2 and X_3.

(a) Can you estimate the parameters of this model? Why or why not?

(b) If not, which parameter or combination of parameters can you estimate?

10.14. You are given the annual data in Table 10-6 for the United States for the period 1971 to 1986.

Consider the following aggregate demand function for passenger cars:

$$\ln Y_t = B_1 + B_2 \ln X_{2t} + B_3 \ln X_{3t} + B_4 \ln X_{4t} + B_5 \ln X_{5t} + B_6 \ln X_{6t} + u_t$$

where $\ln = $ the natural log

(a) What is the rationale for the introduction of both price indexes X_2 and X_3?

(b) What might be the rationale for the introduction of the "employed civilian labor force" in the demand function?

(c) What is the role of the interest rate variable X_5 in this model?

(d) How would you interpret the various partial slope coefficients?

(e) Obtain OLS estimates of the preceding model.

10.15. Continue with problem 10.14. Is there multicollinearity in the previous problem? How do you know?

10.16. If there is collinearity in problem 10.14, estimate the various auxiliary regressions and find out which of the X variables is highly collinear.

10.17. Continuing with the preceding problem, if there is severe collinearity, which variable would you drop and why? If you drop one or more X variables, what type of error are you likely to commit?

10.18. After eliminating one or more X variables, what is your final demand function for passenger cars? In what ways is this "final" model better than the initial model that includes all X variables?

10.19. What other variables do you think might better explain the demand for automobiles in the United States?

TABLE 10-6

Year	Y	X_2	X_3	X_4	X_5	X_6
1971	10227	112.0	121.3	776.8	4.89	79367
1972	10872	111.0	125.3	839.6	4.55	82153
1973	11350	111.1	133.1	949.8	7.38	85064
1974	8775	117.5	147.7	1038.4	8.61	86794
1975	8539	127.6	161.2	1142.8	6.16	85846
1976	9994	135.7	170.5	1252.6	5.22	88752
1977	11046	142.9	181.5	1379.3	5.50	92017
1978	11164	153.8	195.3	1551.2	7.78	96048
1979	10559	166.0	217.7	1729.3	10.25	98824
1980	8979	179.3	247.0	1918.0	11.28	99303
1981	8535	190.2	272.3	2127.6	13.73	100397
1982	7980	197.6	286.6	2261.4	11.20	99526
1983	9179	202.6	297.4	2428.1	8.69	100834
1984	10394	208.5	307.6	2670.6	9.65	105005
1985	11039	215.2	318.5	2841.1	7.75	107150
1986	11450	224.4	323.4	3022.1	6.31	109597

Source: Business Statistics, 1986, A Supplement to the *Current Survey of Business,* U.S. Department of Commerce.

Y = new passenger cars sold (thousands), seasonally unadjusted
X_2 = new cars, Consumer Price Index, 1967 = 100, seasonally unadjusted
X_3 = Consumer Price Index, all items, all urban consumers, 1967 = 100, seasonally unadjusted
X_4 = the personal disposable income (PDI), billions of dollars, unadjusted for seasonal variation
X_5 = the interest rate, percent, finance company paper placed directly
X_6 = the employed civilian labor force (thousands), unadjusted for seasonal variation

10.20. In a study of the production function of the United Kingdom bricks, pottery, glass, and cement industry for the period 1961 to 1981, R. Leighton Thomas obtained the following results:[21]

1. $\widehat{\log Q} = -5.04 + 0.887 \log K + 0.893 \log H$
   se = (1.40)   (0.087)   (0.137) $R^2 = 0.878$
2. $\widehat{\log Q} = -8.57 + 0.0272\ t + 0.460 \log K + 1.285 \log H$ $R^2 = 0.889$
   se = (2.99)   (0.0204)   (0.333)   (0.324)

where   Gears T=Time(0)

   Q = the index of production at constant factor cost
   K = the gross capital stock at 1975 replacement cost
   H = hours worked
   t = the time trend, a proxy for technology

---

[21] See R. Leighton Thomas, *Introductory Econometrics: Theory and Applications,* Longman, London, 1985, pp. 244–246.

TABLE 10-7
Hypothetical data on consumption expenditure (Y),
weekly income (X₂), and wealth (X₃)

Dep, Y

Y	X_2	X_3
70	80	810
65	100	1009
90	120	1273
95	140	1425
110	160	1633
115	180	1876
120	200	2252
140	220	2201
155	240	2435
150	260	2686

The figures in parentheses are the estimated standard errors.

(a) Interpret both regressions.

(b) In regression 1 verify that each partial slope coefficient is statistically significant at the 5% level.

(c) In regression 2 verify that the coefficients of t and log K are individually insignificant at the 5% level.

multi — (d) What might account for the insignificance of log K variable in model 2?
coll (e) If you are told that the correlation coefficient between t and log K is 0.980, what conclusion would you draw? *multi is so present*

(f) Even if t and log K are individually insignificant in model 2, would you accept or reject the hypothesis that in model 2 all partial slopes are simultaneously equal to zero? Which test do you use?

(g) In model 1, what are the returns to scale?

10.21. Establish Eqs. (10.12) and (10.13). (*Hint:* Find out the coefficient of correlation between X_2 and X_3, say, R_2).

10.22. You are given the hypothetical data in Table 10-7 on weekly consumption expenditure (Y), weekly income (X₂), and wealth (X₃), all in dollars.

(a) Do an OLS regression of Y on X_2 and X_3.

(b) Is there collinearity in this regression? How do you know?

(c) Do separate regressions of Y on X_2 and Y on X_3. What do these regressions reveal?

(d) Regress X_3 on X_2. What does this regression reveal?

(e) If there is severe collinearity, would you drop one of the X variables? Why or why not?

10.23. Utilizing the data given in Table 10-1, estimate Eq. (10.20) and compare your results.

10.24. Check that all R^2 values in Table 10-5 are statistically significant.

CHAPTER 11

HETEROSCEDASTICITY: WHAT HAPPENS IF THE ERROR VARIANCE IS NONCONSTANT

An important assumption of the classical linear regression model (CLRM) is that the disturbances u_i entering the population regression function (PRF) are *homoscedastic*; that is, they all have the same variance, σ^2. If this is not the case—if the variance of u_i is σ_i^2, indicating that it is varying from observation to observation (notice the subscript on σ^2)—we have the situation of *heteroscedasticity*, or *unequal*, or *nonconstant*, *variance*.

Since the assumption of homoscedasticity is imposed by the CLRM, there is no guarantee in practice that this assumption will always be fulfilled. Therefore, the major goal of this chapter is to find out what happens if this assumption is not fulfilled. Specifically, we seek answers to the following questions:

1. What is the nature of heteroscedasticity?
2. What are its consequences?
3. How does one detect that it is present in a given situation?
4. What are the remedial measures if heteroscedasticity is a problem?

11.1 THE NATURE OF HETEROSCEDASTICITY

To explain best the difference between homoscedasticity and heteroscedasticity, let us consider a two-variable linear regression model in which the dependent variable Y is personal savings and the explanatory variable X is personal disposable, or after-tax, income (PDI). Now consider the diagrams in Figure 11-1 [cf. Figure 6.2(*a*) and 6.2(*b*)].

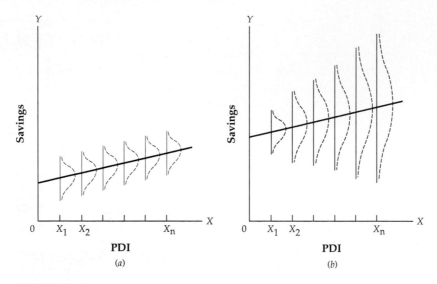

FIGURE 11-1
(a) Homoscedasticity; (b) heteroscedasticity.

Figure 11.1(a) shows that as PDI increases, the mean, or average, level of savings also increases but the variance of savings around its mean value remains the same at all levels of PDI. Recall that the PRF gives the mean, or average, value of the dependent variable for given levels of the explanatory variable(s). This is the case of **homoscedasticity**, or **equal variance**. On the other hand, as Figure 11.1(b) shows, although the average level of savings increases as the PDI increases, the variance of savings does not remain the same at all levels of PDI—here it increases with PDI. This is the case of **heteroscedasticity**, or **unequal variance.** Put differently, Figure 11.1(b) shows that high-income people on the average save more than low-income people, but there is also more variability in their savings. This is not only plausible, it is also borne out by a casual glance at U.S. savings and income statistics. After all, there is very little discretionary income left to save for people on the lower rung of the income distribution ladder. Therefore, in a regression of savings on income, error variances (i.e., variance of u_i) associated with high-income families are expected to be greater than those associated with low-income families.

Symbolically, we express heteroscedasticity as

$$E(u_i^2) = \sigma_i^2 \tag{11.1}$$

Notice again the subscript on σ^2, which is a reminder that the variance of u_i is no longer constant but varies from observation to observation.

Researchers have observed that heteroscedasticity is usually found in **cross-sectional data** and not in time series data.[1] In cross-sectional data one generally deals with members of a population at *a given point in time*, such as individual consumers or their families, firms, industries, or geographical sub-divisions, such as state, county, city, etc. Moreover, these members may be of different sizes, such as small, medium, or large firms, or low, medium, or high income. In other words, there may be some **scale effect.** In time series data, on the other hand, the variables tend to be of similar orders of magnitude because one generally collects data for the same entity over a period of time. Examples are the gross national product (GNP), savings, unemployment rate, etc., say, over the period 1960 to 1990.

As a concrete illustration of heteroscedasticity, we present two examples.

Example 11.1. Brokerage commission on the NYSE after deregulation. Between April and May of 1975 the SEC (Securities and Exchange Commission) abolished the practice of fixed commission rates on stock transactions on the New York Stock Exchange (NYSE) and allowed stockbrokers to charge commission on a competitive basis. Table 11-1 presents data on the average per share commission (in cents) charged by the brokerage industry to institutional investors for selected quarterly periods between April 1975 and December 1978.

Notice two interesting features of this table. There is a downward trend in the commission rate charged since the deregulation. But, more interestingly, there is a substantial difference in the average commission charged and the variance of commission among the four categories of institutional investors shown in the table. The smallest institutional investor, those with share transactions in the range of 0 to 199 shares on the average paid a commission of 46.5 cents per share with a variance of 32.22, whereas the largest institutional investors paid on the average the rate of only 10.1 cents per share but with a variance of only 3.18. All this can be seen more vividly from Figure 11-2.

What explains this difference? Obviously, some scale effect seems to be evident here—the larger the volume of the transaction is, the lower the total cost of transacting is, and therefore the lower the average cost will be. Economists would say that there are *economies of scale* in the brokerage industry data given in Table 11-1. (But this may not necessarily be so. See Example 11.7 in Section 11.5.) Even if there are scale economies in the brokerage industry, why should the variance of the commission rate in the four categories be different? In other words, why is there heteroscedasticity? To attract the business of big institutional investors such as pension funds, mutual funds, etc., brokerage firms compete so

---

[1] This is, strictly speaking, not true. In the so-called *ARCH* (autoregressive conditional heteroscedasticity) models, heteroscedasticity can be observed in time series data also. But this is an involved topic and we will not discuss it in this text. For a discussion of the ARCH model, see G. S. Maddala, *Introduction to Econometrics*, Macmillan, New York, 1988, pp. 218–219.

intensely among themselves that there is not much variability in the commission rates they charge. Small institutional investors may not have the same bargaining clout as large institutions, and hence have more variability in the commission rates that they pay. These and other reasons may explain the heteroscedasticity observed in the data of Table 11-1.

Now if we were to develop a regression model to explain the commission rate as a function of the number of share transactions (and other variables), the error variance associated with high-transaction clients would be lower than that associated with low-transaction clients.

TABLE 11-1
Commission rate trends, April 1975 through December 1978, NYSE

		X_1	X_2	X_3	X_4
April	1975	59.60000	45.70000	27.60000	15.00000
June		54.50000	36.80000	21.30000	12.10000
September		51.70000	34.50000	20.40000	11.50000
December		48.90000	31.90000	18.90000	10.40000
March	1976	50.30000	33.80000	19.00000	10.80000
June		50.00000	33.40000	19.50000	10.90000
September		46.70000	31.10000	18.40000	10.20000
December		47.00000	31.20000	17.60000	10.00000
March	1977	44.30000	28.80000	16.00000	9.800000
June		43.70000	28.10000	15.50000	9.700000
September		40.40000	26.10000	14.50000	9.100000
December		40.40000	25.40000	14.00000	8.900000
March	1978	40.20000	25.00000	13.90000	8.100000
June		43.10000	27.00000	14.40000	8.500000
September		42.50000	26.90000	14.40000	8.700000
December		40.70000	24.50000	13.70000	7.800000

Name	n	Mean	Standard deviation	Variance	Minimum	Maximum
X_1	16	46.500	5.6767	32.225	40.200	59.600
X_2	16	30.637	5.5016	30.268	24.500	45.700
X_3	16	17.444	3.7234	13.864	13.700	27.600
X_4	16	10.094	1.7834	3.1806	7.8000	15.000

Source: S. Tinic and R. West, "The Securities Industry Under Negotiated Brokerage Commissions: Changes in the Structure and Performance of NYSE Member Firms," *The Bell Journal of Economics*, vol 11, no 1, Spring 1980.

Note:

X_1 = commission rate, cents per share (for shares 0 to 199)

X_2 = commission rate, cents per share (for shares 200 to 299)

X_3 = commission rate, cents per share (for shares 1000 to 9999)

X_4 = commission rate, cents per share (for shares 10,000+)

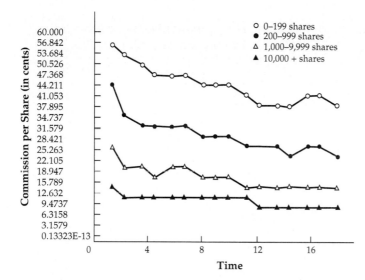

FIGURE 11-2
Commission per share, in cents, NYSE, April 1975 to December 1978 (based on data of Table 11-1).

Example 11.2. R&D expenditure, sales, and profits in U.S. industry. As an example of a purely cross-sectional data with a potential for heteroscedasticity, consider the data given in Table 11-2.[2] These data pertain to the R&D (research and development) expenditure incurred by 18 industry composites (i.e., group-ings) in relation to sales and profits for the year 1988, all data in millions of dollars. Since each industry grouping is a broad category that includes several industries with firms of differing sizes, if one were to regress R&D expenditure, say, on sales, a priori it would be difficult to maintain the assumption of homo-scedasticity because of the diversity of industry groupings. But more on that shortly.

Let us suppose that we want to find out how R&D expenditure is related to sales. For this purpose, suppose we consider the following model:

$$R\&D_i = B_1 + B_2 Sales_i + u_i \tag{11.2}$$

A priori we would expect a positive relationship between the two variables (why?), which seems to be borne out by the scattergram in Figure 11-3, which plots R&D expenditure against sales.

---

[2] In contrast to the data in this table, the data given in Table 11-1 combine both time series and cross-sectional data: The data for any given month for the four transaction categories are cross-sectional, whereas the data for any single transaction category from April 1975 to December 1978 are time series data.

TABLE 11-2

Innovation in America: Research and development (R&D) expenditure in the United States, 1988 (all figures in millions of dollars)

Industry grouping	Sales	R&D expenses	Profits
1. Containers and packaging	6,375.3	62.5	185.1
2. Nonbank financial	11,626.4	92.9	1,569.5
3. Service industries	14,655.1	178.3	276.8
4. Metals and mining	21,869.2	258.4	2,828.1
5. Housing and construction	26,408.3	494.7	225.9
6. General manufacturing	32,405.6	1,083.0	3,751.9
7. Leisure time industries	35,107.7	1,620.6	2,884.1
8. Paper and forest products	40,295.4	421.7	4,645.7
9. Food	70,761.6	509.2	5,036.4
10. Health care	80,552.8	6,620.1	13,869.9
11. Aerospace	95,294.0	3,918.6	4,487.8
12. Consumer products	101,314.1	1,595.3	10,278.9
13. Electrical and electronics	116,141.3	6,107.5	8,787.3
14. Chemicals	122,315.7	4,454.1	16,438.8
15. Conglomerates	141,649.9	3,163.8	9,761.4
16. Office equipment and computers	175,025.8	13,210.7	19,774.5
17. Fuel	230,614.5	1,703.8	22,626.6
18. Automotive	293,543.0	9,528.2	18,415.4

Source: *Business Week*, Special 1989 Bonus Issue, R&D Scorecard, pp. 180–224.

Note: The industries are listed in increasing order of sales volume.

The ordinary least squares (OLS) regression results of Equation (11.2) are as follows:

$$\widehat{R\&D_i} = 192.99 + 0.0319 Sales_i$$

$$se = (990.99) \quad (0.0083) \tag{11.3}$$

$$t = (0.1948) \quad (3.8323) \qquad r^2 = 0.4783$$

This regression line is depicted in Figure 11-3.

What is interesting about Figure 11-3 is not that on the average, the R&D expenditure increases as sales increase, but that the variability of R&D expenditure around the sample regression line seems to increase as sales increase. That is, there *seems* to be some evidence of heteroscedasticity. This can be seen more vividly if we plot the residuals from the regression (11.3) against each individual observation (Figure 11-4): Since the observations are arranged in order of sales volume, this amounts to plotting residuals indirectly against the sales volume.

It is clear from Figure 11-4 that the absolute value of the residuals e_i increase with the sales volume, again *suggesting* that the assumption of homoscedasticity may not be tenable in our illustrative example. Therefore, we will have to rethink about the regression (11.3), which is explicitly based on the assumption of homoscedasticity. We will do this later in the chapter.

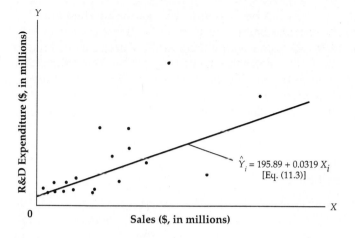

$\hat{Y}_i = 195.89 + 0.0319\ X_i$
[Eq. (11.3)]

FIGURE 11-3
Research and development (R&D) expenditure and sales, U.S. industries, 1988.

A cautionary note: It is true that the residuals e_i are not the same as the disturbances u_i, although they are proxies. Therefore, from the observed variability of the e_i, we cannot categorically conclude that the variance of u_i is also variable. But as we will show later, in practice, we rarely observe u_i, and thus

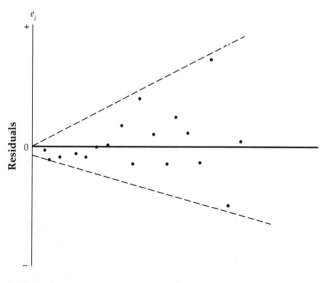

FIGURE 11-4
Residuals from the R&D regression (11.3).

we will have to make do with e_i. In other words, by examining the pattern of e_i, we will have to infer about the pattern of u_i.

Suppose in our R&D regression we believe, say, on the basis of Figures 11-3 and 11-4, that we can have a heteroscedasticity situation. What then? Are the regression results given in the model (11.3), which are based explicitly on the assumption of homoscedasticity, useless?[3] To answer this question, we must find out what happens to the OLS method if there is heteroscedasticity, which is done in the following section.

11.2   CONSEQUENCES OF HETEROSCEDASTICITY

Recall that under the assumptions of the CLRM, OLS estimators are best linear unbiased estimators (BLUE); that is, in the class of linear unbiased estimators least squares estimators have minimum variance—they are efficient. Now assume that all assumptions of CLRM hold except that we drop the assumption of homoscedasticity, allowing for the disturbance variance to be different from observation to observation. The following consequences are stated without proofs:[4]

1. OLS estimators are still linear.
2. They are still unbiased.
3. But they no longer have minimum variance. That is, they are no longer efficient. This is so even in large samples. In short, OLS estimators are no longer BLUE in small as well as in large samples (i.e., asymptotically).
4. The usual formulas to estimate the variances of OLS estimators are generally biased. A priori we cannot tell whether the bias will be positive (upward bias) or negative (downward bias). A positive bias occurs if OLS overestimates the true variances of estimators and a negative bias occurs if OLS underestimates the true variances of estimators.
5. The bias arises from the fact that $\hat{\sigma}^2$, the conventional estimator of true σ^2, namely, $\Sigma \, e_i^2/\text{d.f.}$, is no longer an unbiased estimator of σ^2. [*Note*: The d.f. (degrees of freedom) are $(n - 2)$ in the two-variable case, $(n - 3)$ in the three-variable case, etc.] Recall that $\hat{\sigma}^2$ enters into the calculations of the variances of OLS estimators.
6. As a result, the usual confidence intervals and hypothesis tests based on t and F distributions are unreliable. Therefore, every possibility exists of

---

[3] As a practical matter, when running a regression, we generally assume that all assumptions of the CLRM are fulfilled. It is only when we examine the regression results that we begin to look for some "clues" which might tell us that one or more assumptions of the CLRM may not be tenable. This is not altogether a bad strategy; why "look a gift horse in the mouth"?

[4] Some of the proofs and references to other proofs can be found in Damodar N. Gujarati, *Basic Econometrics*, 2d ed., McGraw-Hill, New York, 1988, Chap. 11.

drawing wrong conclusions if conventional hypothesis-testing procedures are employed.

In short, in the presence of heteroscedasticity, the usual hypothesis-testing routine is not reliable, raising the possibility of drawing misleading conclusions.

Returning to our R&D regression results given in the model (11.3), if there is heteroscedasticity, and we have reason to believe that it might well be the case (the formal tests for the presence of heteroscedasticity are discussed in Section 11.3), we should be very careful about interpreting the results. From regression (11.3) we see that the coefficient of the sales variable is "apparently" significantly different from zero because its t value is 3.83, which for 16 d.f. is "significant" well beyond the 1% level (one-tailed critical t value for 16 d.f. at the 0.01 level is 2.921). Actually, the p value is smaller than 0.0001. But if there is in fact heteroscedasticity, we cannot trust the estimated standard error of 0.0083, and therefore we cannot trust the computed t value. It thus behooves us to find out whether we do, indeed, have the problem of heteroscedasticity.

As the preceding discussion indicates, heteroscedasticity is potentially a serious problem, for it might destroy the whole edifice of the standard, and so routinely used, OLS estimation and hypothesis-testing procedure. Therefore, it is important in any concrete study, especially one involving cross-sectional data, that we determine whether we have a heteroscedasticity problem.

Before turning to the task of detecting heteroscedasticity, however, we should know, at least intuitively, why OLS estimators are not efficient under heteroscedasticity.

Consider our simple two-variable regression model. Recall from Chapter 5 that in OLS we minimize the residual sum of squares (RSS):

$$\sum e_i^2 = \sum (Y_i - b_1 - b_2 X_i)^2 \tag{5.13}$$

Now consider Figure 11-5.

This figure shows a hypothetical Y population against selected values of the X variable. As this diagram shows, the variance of each Y (sub)population corresponding to the given X is not the same throughout, suggesting heteroscedasticity. Suppose we choose at random a Y value against each X value. The Ys thus selected are encircled. As Eq. (5.13) shows, in OLS each e_i^2 receives the same weight whether it comes from a population with a large variance or with a small variance (compare points Y_n and Y_1). This does not seem sensible; ideally, we would like to give more *weight* to observations coming from populations with smaller variances than those coming from populations with larger variances. This will enable us to estimate the PRF more accurately. And this is precisely what the method of *weighted least squares (WLS)* does, a method we discuss later.

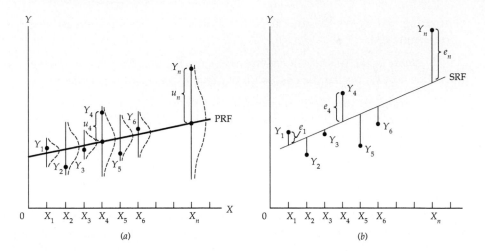

FIGURE 11-5

11.3   DETECTION OF HETEROSCEDASTICITY: HOW DO WE KNOW WHEN THERE IS A HETEROSCEDASTICITY PROBLEM?

Although theoretically it is easy to document the consequences of heteroscedasticity, its detection in a concrete situation is often not so easy. This is understandable because σ_i^2 can be known only if we have the entire Y population corresponding to the chosen Xs, as in the hypothetical population of our widget example given in Table 5-1. Unfortunately, however, we rarely have the entire population available for study. Most generally, we have a sample of some members of this population corresponding to the given values of the X variables. Typically, what we have is a single value of Y for given values of the Xs. And there is no way to determine the variance of the conditional distribution of Y for the given X from a single Y value.[5]

To see this more clearly, return to the R&D data given in Table 11-2. For each industry grouping shown in the table, there is only one R&D figure. From this one R&D figure there is no way to find out the variance of R&D of that group. For example, for the electrical and electronics group the total R&D expenditure was about $6107 (millions of dollars). But there were 171 companies included in this group. Unless we have information about each com-

---

[5] Note that given the Xs, the variance of u and the variance of Y are the same. In other words, the conditional variance of u (conditional on the given Xs) is the same as the conditional variance of Y, as noted in footnote 1 of Chap. 6.

pany, we cannot tell anything about the variability of the R&D expenditure in this group. That is, if we divide $6107 by 171 to obtain about $38 (millions) as the average R&D expenditure of this group, we cannot determine how the R&D expenditure is distributed around this mean value. In other words, we cannot determine what the variance of the R&D expenditure is for this group. The same is true of the other 17 industry groupings shown in Table 11-2.

As a result, from the data given in Table 11-2, if we regress R&D on sales, as was done in Eq. (11.3), we do not know the σ_i^2 associated with each observation (i.e., each R&D figure): The regression (11.3) was run on the assumption that each R&D observation in Table 11-2 had the same (i.e., homoscedastic) variance σ^2, which, as shown in Chapter 6, is estimated by $\hat{\sigma}^2 = \Sigma \, e_i^2/(n - 2)$. And our job here is to find out if that assumption was correct.

Now we are "between the devil and the deep blue sea." If there is heteroscedasticity and we assume it away, we might be drawing misleading conclusions on the basis of the usual OLS procedure because OLS estimators are not BLUE. But since our data are mostly based on a sample, we have no way of finding out the true error variance associated with each observation. If we could find out the true σ_i^2, it is possible to solve the problem of heteroscedasticity, as is shown later in Section 11.4. What is an econometrician to do?

As in the case of multicollinearity, we have no sure method of detecting heteroscedasticity; we only have several diagnostic tools which may aid us in detecting it. Some of the diagnostics follow.

Nature of the Problem

Often the nature of the problem under consideration suggests whether heteroscedasticity is likely to be present. For example, following the pioneering work of Prais and Houthakker[6] on family budget studies, in which they found that the residual variance around the regression of consumption on income increased with income, it is now generally assumed that in similar studies one can expect heteroscedasticity in the error term. As a matter of fact, in cross-sectional data involving heterogeneous units heteroscedasticity may be the rule rather than the exception. Thus, in cross-sectional studies involving investment expenditure in relation to sales, the rate of interest, etc. heteroscedasticity is generally expected if small-, medium-, and large-sized firms are sampled together. Similarly, in a cross-sectional study of the average cost of production in relation to the output, heteroscedasticity is likely to be found if small-, medium-, and large-sized firms are included in the sample. (See Example 11.8 in Section 11.5).

---

[6] S. J. Prais and H. S. Houthakker, *The Analysis of Family Budgets*, Cambridge University Press, New York, 1955.

Graphical Examination of Residuals

In applied regression analysis it is always good practice to examine the residuals obtained from a fitted regression equation. These residuals can be plotted against the observation to which they belong or against one' or more of the explanatory variables or against $\hat{Y}_i$, the estimated mean value of Y_i. Such a plot often gives some clues about whether or not one or more assumptions of the CLRM hold, as we will demonstrate shortly.

We already have a glimpse of this in Figure 11-4, which plots the residuals from the regression (11.3) against sales. As this graph reveals, the (absolute) values of the residuals increase as the sales volume increases. Actually, the graph is in the form of a megaphone. Perhaps some heteroscedasticity is present in the data.

Sometimes instead of plotting the residuals against sales (or any explanatory variable), we can plot e_i^2, the residuals squared, against sales. Although e_i^2 are not the same as u_i^2, they are often good proxies of the latter, especially if the sample size is reasonably large.[7]

Before plotting squared residuals against sales for our data R&D regression (11.3), let us consider some likely patterns of heteroscedasticity that we may encounter when e_i^2 are plotted against an X variable. These patterns are shown in Figure 11-6. Figure 11-6(a) has no discernible systematic pattern between e_i^2 and X, suggesting that perhaps there is no heteroscedasticity in the data. On the other hand, Figure 11-6(b) to (e) exhibits systematic relationships between the squared residuals and the explanatory variable X; e.g., Figure 11-6(c) suggests a linear relationship between the two, whereas Figure 11-6(d) and (e) suggests a quadratic relationship. Therefore, if in an application the squared residuals exhibit one of the patterns shown in Figure 11-6(b) to (e), there is a *possibility* that heteroscedasticity is present in the data.

Keep in mind that the preceding graphical plots are simply a diagnostic tool and that once the suspicion about heteroscedasticity is raised, we should proceed more cautiously to make sure that this suspicion is not just a "red herring." Shortly we will present some formal procedures to do exactly that.

Meanwhile a couple of practical questions can be posed. Suppose we have a multiple regression involving, say, four X variables. How do we proceed then? The most straightforward way to proceed is to plot e_i^2 against each X variable. It is possible that the patterns exhibited in Figure 11-6 can hold true of only one of the X variables. Sometimes we can resort to a shortcut. Instead of plotting e_i^2 against each X variable, plot them against $\hat{Y}_i$, the estimated mean value of Y. Since $\hat{Y}_i$ is a linear combination of the Xs (why?), a plot of squared residuals against $\hat{Y}_i$ might exhibit one of the patterns shown in Figure 11-6(b) to (e), suggesting that perhaps heteroscedasticity is present

---

[7] For the relationship between e_i and u_i, see E. Malinvaud, *Statistical Methods of Econometrics*, North-Holland, Amsterdam, 1970, pp. 88–89.

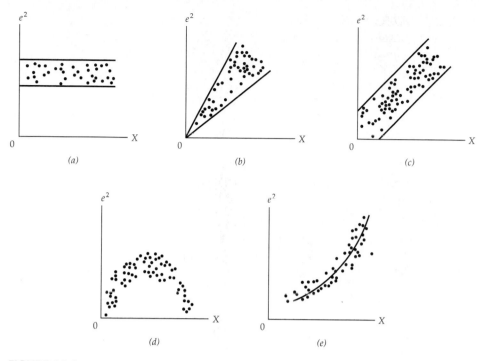

FIGURE 11-6
Hypothetical patterns of e^2.

in the data. This avoids the need for plotting the squared residuals against individual X variables, especially if the number of explanatory variables in the model is very large.

Suppose we plot e_i^2 against one or more X variables or against $\hat{Y}_i$, and further suppose the plot suggests heteroscedasticity. What then? In Section 11.4 we will show how the knowledge that e_i^2 is related to an X variable or to $\hat{Y}_i$ enables us to transform the original data so that in the transformed data there is no heteroscedasticity.

Now let us return to our R&D example. In Figure 11-7 we plot the squared residuals estimated from the regression (11.3) against sales, the explanatory variable in the model.[8]

This figure almost resembles Figure 11-6(b), clearly suggesting that the squared residuals are systematically related to sales. This diagram raises the possibility that the R&D regression (11.3) suffers from the heteroscedasticity problem.

---

[8] Note that we are plotting e_i^2 and not e_i against X_i or $\hat{Y}_i$ because, as pointed out in Chapter 6, footnote 13, e_i has zero correlation with both X_i and $\hat{Y}_i$.

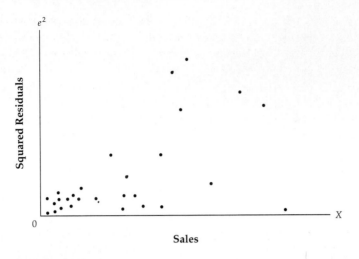

FIGURE 11-7
e_i^2 against sales, R&D regression (11.3).

Park Test[9]

The intuitively and visually appealing graphical test just presented can be formalized. If there is heteroscedasticity, the heteroscedastic variance σ_i^2 may be systematically related to one or more explanatory variables. To see if this is the case, we can regress σ_i^2 on one or more of the X variables. For example, in the two-variable model we can run the following regression:

$$\ln \sigma_i^2 = B_1 + B_2 \ln X_i + v_i \tag{11.4}$$

where v_i is a residual term. This is precisely what Park suggests. The particular functional form (11.4) that he chose was for convenience.

Unfortunately, regression (11.4) is not operational since we do not know the heteroscedastic variance σ_i^2. If we knew it, we could have solved the heteroscedasticity problem easily, as we will show in Section 11.4. Park suggests using e_i as proxies for u_i and running the following regression:

$$\ln e_i^2 = B_i + B_2 \ln X_i + v_i \tag{11.5}$$

Where do we obtain e_i^2? They are obtained from the original regression, such as the model (11.3).

The Park test therefore involves the following steps:

1. Run the original regression despite the heteroscedasticity problem, if any.
2. From this regression, obtain the residuals e_i, square them, and take their logs (most computer programs can do this routinely.)

---

[9] R. E. Park, "Estimation with Heteroscedastic Error Terms," *Econometrica*, vol. 34, no. 4, p. 888, October 1966.

3. Run the regression (11.5) using an explanatory variable in the original model; if there is more than one explanatory variable, run the regression (11.5) against each X variable. Alternatively, run the regression (11.5) against $\hat{Y}_i$, the estimated Y.[10]

4. Test the null hypothesis that $B_2 = 0$; that is, there is no heteroscedasticity. If a statistically significant relationship exists between $\ln e_i^2$ and $\ln X_i$, the null hypothesis of no heteroscedasticity can be rejected, in which case we will have to take some remedial measure(s), which are discussed in Section 11.4.

5. If the null hypothesis is accepted, then B_1 in the regression (11.5) can be interpreted as giving the value of the common, or homoscedastic, variance, σ^2.

Example 11.3 R&D regression and the Park test. Let us illustrate with our R&D regression (11.3). When the residuals obtained from this regression were regressed as in model (11.5), we obtained the following results:

$$\widehat{\ln e_i^2} = 5.6877 + 0.7014 \ln \text{sales}_i$$

$$se = (6.6352) \quad (0.6033)$$

$$t = (0.8572) \quad (1.1626) \qquad\qquad r^2 = 0.0779 \qquad\qquad (11.6)$$

Obviously, the estimated slope coefficient is not statistically significant at the 5% level (one-tailed test) if we choose a 5% level of significance.

Can we therefore accept the hypothesis that in our R&D data we do not have a heteroscedasticity problem? Not so fast. This is because the particular functional form chosen by Park in the regression (11.5) is only suggestive; other functional forms might give us different conclusions. (In Chapter 13 we will have more to say about choosing the "appropriate" model for empirical analysis.) But there is a more serious problem with the Park test, namely, in the regression (11.5), the error term v_i may itself be heteroscedastic! We are back to square one. More testing is needed before we can conclude that our R&D regression (11.3) does not suffer from heteroscedasticity.

Glejser Test[11]

The Glejser test is similar in spirit to the Park test. After obtaining residuals e_i from the original model, Glejser suggests regressing the absolute values of e_i, $|e_i|$, on the X variable that is thought to be closely associated with the

---

[10] The choice of the appropriate functional form to run the regression (11.5) should also be considered. In some cases regressing e_i^2 on X_i might be the appropriate functional form; in some other cases $\ln e_i^2$ may be the appropriate dependent variable.

[11] H. Glejser, "A New Test for Heteroscedasticity," *Journal of the American Statistical Association* (JASA), vol. 64, pp. 316–323, 1969.

heteroscedastic variance σ_i^2. Some functional forms that he has suggested for this regression are

$$|e_i| = B_1 + B_2 X_i + v_i \tag{11.7}$$

$$|e_i| = B_1 + B_2 \sqrt{X_i} + v_i \tag{11.8}$$

$$|e_i| = B_1 + B_2 \left(\frac{1}{X}\right)_i + v_i \tag{11.9}$$

The null hypothesis in each case is that there is no heteroscedasticity, that is, $B_2 = 0$. If this hypothesis is rejected, there is probably evidence of heteroscedasticity.

Example 11.4. R&D regression and the Glejser test.   The results of estimating these models from the residuals obtained from the regression (11.3) are

$$|e_i| = 578.57 + 0.0119 \text{ sales}_i$$
$$t = (0.8525) \quad (2.0931) \qquad\qquad r^2 = 0.2150 \tag{11.10}$$

$$|e_i| = -507.02 + 7.9720 \sqrt{\text{sales}_i}$$
$$t = (-0.5032) \quad (2.3704) \qquad\qquad r^2 = 0.2599 \tag{11.11}$$

$$|e_i| = 2273.7 - 19925000 \frac{1}{\text{sales}_i}$$
$$t = (3.7601) \quad (-1.6175) \qquad\qquad r^2 = 0.1405 \tag{11.12}$$

On the basis of the Glejser test, we see that models (11.10) and (11.11) suggest rejection of the null hypothesis of no heteroscedasticity, for the slope coefficient in each case is statistically significant at about the conventional 5% level (two-tailed test). Model (11.12), on the other hand, suggests that we can accept the hypothesis of homoscedasticity.

A cautionary note regarding the Glejser test: As in the case of the Park test, the error term v_i in the regressions suggested by Glejser can itself be heteroscedastic as well as serially correlated (on serial correlation, see Chapter 12). Glejser, however, has maintained that in large samples the preceding models are fairly good in detecting heteroscedasticity. Therefore, Glejser's test can be used as a diagnostic tool in large samples. Our R&D regression is based on only 18 observations; hence, the results given in regressions (11.10) to (11.12) should be interpreted cautiously.

Other Tests of Heteroscedasticity

The heteroscedasticity tests that we have previously discussed by no means exhaust the list. We mention now several other tests but do not discuss them here because a full discussion would take us far afield.

1. Spearman's rank correlation test (see problem 11.13)
2. Goldfeld-Quandt test
3. Bartlett's homogeneity-of-variance test
4. Peak test
5. Breusch-Pagan test
6. White's general heteroscedasticity test
7. CUSUMSQ test

The interested reader can consult the references for details of these tests.[12]

11.4   WHAT TO DO IF HETEROSCEDASTICITY IS OBSERVED: REMEDIAL MEASURES

As we have seen, heteroscedasticity does not destroy the unbiasedness property of OLS estimators, but the estimators are no longer efficient, not even in large samples. This lack of efficiency makes the conventional OLS hypothesis-testing procedure of dubious value. Therefore, if heteroscedasticity is suspected or diagnosed, it is important to seek remedial measures.

For example, in our R&D example, based on the Glejser test, there was indication that the R&D regression given in Eq. (11.3) probably suffers from the heteroscedasticity problem. How can we solve this problem, if at all? Is there some way in which we can "transform" the model (11.3) so that in the "transformed" model there is homoscedasticity? But what kind of transformation? The answer depends on (1) whether the true error variance, σ_i^2, is known or (2) whether it is unknown.

When σ_i^2 Is Known: The Method of Weighted Least Squares (WLS)

To fix the ideas consider the two-variable PRF

$$Y_i = B_1 + B_2 X_i + u_i \tag{11.13}$$

where Y is, say, R&D expenditure and X is sales. Assume for the moment that the true error variance σ_i^2 is known; that is, the error variance for each observation is known. Now consider the following "transformation" of the model (11.13):

$$\frac{Y_i}{\sigma_i} = B_1\left(\frac{1}{\sigma_i}\right) + B_2\left(\frac{X_i}{\sigma_i}\right) + \frac{u_i}{\sigma_i} \tag{11.14}$$

---

[12] The Spearman's rank correlation, the Goldfeld-Quandt, and the Breusch-Pagan tests are discussed in Damodar N. Gujarati, *Basic Econometrics*, 2d ed., McGraw-Hill, New York, Chap. 11. This text also gives references to the other tests mentioned earlier.

All we have done here is to divide or "deflate" both the left- and right-hand sides of the regression (11.13) by the "known" σ_i, which is simply the square root of the variance σ_i^2.

Now let

$$v_i = \frac{u_i}{\sigma_i} \tag{11.15}$$

We can call v_i the "transformed" error term. Is v_i homoscedastic? If it is, then the transformed regression (11.14) does not suffer from the problem of heteroscedasticity. Assuming all other assumptions of the CLRM are fulfilled, OLS estimators of the parameters in Equation (11.14) will be BLUE and we can then proceed to statistical inference in the usual manner.

Now it is not too difficult to show that the error term v_i is homoscedastic. From Equation (11.15) we obtain

$$v_i^2 = \frac{u_i^2}{\sigma_i^2} \tag{11.16}$$

Therefore,

$$
\begin{aligned}
E(v_i^2) &= E\left(\frac{u_i^2}{\sigma_i^2}\right) \\[2mm]
&= \left(\frac{1}{\sigma_i^2}\right) E\left(u_i^2\right), \quad \text{since } \sigma_i^2 \text{ is known} \\[2mm]
&= \left(\frac{1}{\sigma_i^2}\right) (\sigma_i^2), \quad \text{because of Eq. (11.1)} \\[2mm]
&= 1
\end{aligned}
\tag{11.17}
$$

which is obviously a constant. In short, the transformed error term v_i is homoscedastic. As a result, the transformed model (11.14) does not suffer from the heteroscedasticity problem, and therefore it can be estimated by the usual OLS method.

To estimate the regression (11.14) actually, you will have to instruct the computer to divide each Y and X observation by the "known" σ_i and to run OLS regression on the data thus transformed (most computer packages now can do this routinely.) The OLS estimators of B_1 and B_2 thus obtained are called **weighted least squares (WLS) estimators;** each Y and X observation is weighted (i.e., divided) by its own (heteroscedastic) standard deviation, σ_i. Because of this weighting procedure, the OLS method in this context is known as the *method of weighted least squares (WLS)*.[13] (See problem 11.14.)[14]

---

[13] Note this technical point about the regression (11.14). To estimate it, you will have to instruct the computer to run the *regression through the origin* because there is no "explicit" intercept in Eq. (11.14)—the first term in this regression is $B_1(1/\sigma_i)$. But the "slope" coefficient of $(1/\sigma_i)$ is in fact

When True σ_i^2 Is Unknown

Despite its intuitive simplicity, the WLS method of the model (11.14) begs an important question: How do we know or find out the true error variance, σ_i^2? As noted earlier, knowledge of the true error variance is a rarity. There-fore, if we want to use the method of WLS, we will have to resort to some ad hoc, although reasonably plausible, assumption(s) about σ_i^2 and transform the original regression model so that the transformed model satisfies the homo-scedasticity assumption. OLS can then be applied to the transformed model, for, as shown earlier, *WLS is simply OLS applied to the transformed data.*

In the absence of knowledge about the true σ_i^2 the practical question then is, what assumption(s) can we make about the unknown error variance and how can we use the method of WLS? Here we consider several possibilities, which we discuss with the two-variable model (11.13); the extension to mul-tiple regression models can be made straightforwardly.

Case 1: The error variance is proportional to X_i: The square root transfor-mation. If after estimating the usual OLS regression we plot the residuals from this regression against the explanatory variable X and observe a pattern similar to that shown in Figure 11-8, the indication is that the error variance is linearly related, or proportional, to X.

That is,

$$E(u_i^2) = \sigma^2 X_i \tag{11.18}$$

which states that the heteroscedastic variance is proportional, or linearly related, to X_i; the constant σ^2 (no subscript on σ^2) is the factor of proportion-ality.

Given the assumption (11.18), suppose we transform the model (11.13) as follows:

$$\frac{Y_i}{\sqrt{X_i}} = B_1 \frac{1}{\sqrt{X_i}} + B_2 \frac{X_i}{\sqrt{X_i}} + \frac{u_i}{\sqrt{X_i}}$$

$$= B_1 \frac{1}{\sqrt{X_i}} + B_2 \sqrt{X_i} + v_i \tag{11.19}$$

---

the intercept coefficient B_1. (Do you see this?) On the regression-through-the-origin, see problem 6.15.

[14] Note that in OLS we minimize

$$\sum e_i^2 = \sum (Y_i - b_1 - b_2 X_i)^2$$

but in WLS we minimize

$$\sum \left(\frac{e_i}{\sigma_i}\right)^2 = \sum \left[\frac{Y_i - b_1 - b_2 X_i}{\sigma_i}\right]^2$$

provided σ_i is known. See how in WLS we "deflate" the importance of an observation with larger variance, for the larger the error variances, the larger the divisor will be.

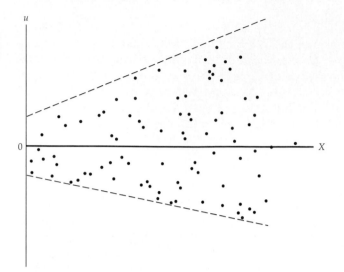

FIGURE 11-8
Error variance proportional to X.

where $v_i = u_i/\sqrt{X_i}$. That is, we divide both sides of the model (11.13) by the square root of X_i. Equation (11.19) is an example of what is known as the **square root transformation**.

Following the development of Eq. (11.17), it can be easily proved that the error variance v_i in the transformed regression is homoscedastic, and therefore we can estimate Eq. (11.19) by the usual OLS method. Actually we are using the WLS method here. (Why?)[15] *It is important to note that in order to estimate Eq. (11.19) we must use the regression-through-the-origin estimating procedure.* Most standard regression software packages do this routinely. (See problem 6.15 for details on the regression-through-the-origin procedure.)

Example 11.5. Transformed R&D regression.   Let us illustrate. For our R&D data, from the diagnostic tests considered earlier we found that heteroscedasticity was probably present in the data. From Figure 11–4 it seems that the error var-

---

[15] Since $v_i = u_i/\sqrt{X_i}$, $v_i^2 = u_i^2/X_i$. Therefore,

$$E(v_i^2) = \frac{E(u_i^2)}{X_i} = \sigma^2 \left(\frac{X_i}{X_i}\right) = \sigma^2$$

that is, homoscedasticity. Note that the X variable is nonstochastic.

iance is proportional to the sales variable. Therefore, if we accept assumption (11.18) and estimate Eq. (11.19), we obtain the following results:

$$\frac{\widehat{Y_i}}{\sqrt{X_i}} = -246.68 \frac{1}{\sqrt{X_i}} + 0.0368 \sqrt{X_i}$$

$$se = (381.13) \qquad (0.0071) \qquad\qquad\qquad (11.20)$$

$$t = (-0.6472) \qquad (5.1723) \qquad r^2 = 0.6258$$

How do these results of WLS compare with those of the OLS regression given in the regression (11.3).

First, the reader may think that the two results are not comparable because the dependent and explanatory variables in the two models are different. But this difference is more apparent than real, for after obtaining Eq. (11.20) we can multiply through by $\sqrt{X_i}$, which will convert Eq. (11.20) into

$$\hat{Y}_i = -246.68 + 0.0368X_i \qquad\qquad (11.21)$$

which can be compared directly with the regression (11.3). There is very little difference between the two slope coefficients. Note, however, that in Eq. (11.20) the coefficient of X is statistically more significant than in the regression (11.3) (why?), suggesting that in the regression (11.3) the OLS actually overestimated the standard error of the X coefficient. As noted before, in the presence of heteroscedasticity OLS estimators of standard errors are biased and one cannot tell which way the bias will go. In the present case the bias is upward; that is, it *overestimates* the standard error. Insofar as the intercept is concerned, it is insignificant in both cases.

It then seems that assumption (11.18) is appropriate for our R&D example and the WLS regression results given in Eq. (11.20) are more trustworthy because we have explicitly accounted for the heteroscedasticity problem.

A question: What happens if there is more than one explanatory variable in the model? In this case we can transform the model as shown in Eq. (11.19) using any one of the X variables that, say, on the basis of graphical plot, seems the appropriate candidate (see problem 11.7). But what if more than one X variable is a candidate? In this case instead of using any of the Xs, we can use the $\hat{Y}_i$, the estimated mean value of Y_i, as the transforming variable, for as we know, $\hat{Y}_i$, is a linear combination of the Xs.

Case 2: Error variance proportional to X_i^2. If the estimated residuals show a pattern similar to Figure 11-9, it suggests that the error variance is not linearly related to X but increases proportional to the square of X. Symbolically,

$$E(u_i^2) = \sigma^2 X_i^2 \qquad\qquad (11.22)$$

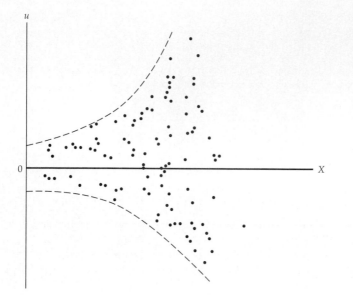

FIGURE 11-9
Error variance proportional to X^2.

In this case the appropriate transformation of the two-variable model considered previously is to divide both sides of the model by X_i, rather than by the square root of X_i, as follows:

$$\frac{Y_i}{X_i} = B_1 \left(\frac{1}{X_i}\right) + B_2 + \left(\frac{u_i}{X_i}\right)$$

$$= B_1 \left(\frac{1}{X_i}\right) + B_2 + v_i$$

(11.23)

where $v_i = u_i/X_i$

Following the earlier development, the reader can easily verify that the error term v in Eq. (11.23) is homoscedastic. Hence, the OLS estimation of Eq. (11.23), which is actually a WLS estimation, will produce BLUE estimators (keep in mind that we are still keeping intact all the other assumptions of the CLRM).

Notice an interesting feature of Eq. (11.23): What was originally the slope coefficient now becomes the "intercept," and what was originally the intercept now becomes the "slope" coefficient. But this change is only for estimation; once we estimate Eq. (11.23), multiplying by X_i on both sides, we get back to the original model.

Respecification of the Model

Instead of "speculating" about σ_i^2, sometimes a respecification of the PRF— choosing a different functional form (see Chapter 8)—can reduce hetero- scedasticity. For example, instead of running the linear-in-variable (LIV) regression, if we estimate the model in the log form, it often reduces hetero- scedasticity. That is, if we estimate

$$\ln Y_i = B_1 + B_2 \ln X_i + u_i \qquad (11.24)$$

the heteroscedasticity problem may be less serious in this transformation because the log transformation compresses the scales in which the variables are measured, thereby reducing a tenfold difference between two values to a twofold difference. Thus, the number 90 is 10 times the number 9, but $\ln 90$ ($= 4.4998$) is only about 2 times as large as $\ln 9 (= 2.1972)$.

   An incidental advantage of the log-linear, or double-log, model, as we have seen in Chapter 8, is that the slope coefficient B_2 measures the elasticity of Y with respect to X, that is, the percentage change in Y for a percentage change in X.

   Whether we should fit LIV or a log-linear model in a given instance has to be determined by theoretical and other considerations, about which more will be said in Chapter 13. But if there is no strong preference for either one, and if the heteroscedasticity problem is severe in the LIV model, we can try the double-log model.

Example 11.6. Log-linear model for the R&D data. For our R&D data, the empirical counterpart of regression (11.24) is as follows:

$$\widehat{\ln Y_i} = -7.3647 + 1.3222 \ln X_i$$

$$se = (1.8480) \qquad (0.16804)$$

$$t = (-3.9852) \quad (7.8687) \qquad r^2 = 0.7947 \qquad (11.25)$$

As this regression shows, in the log form R&D expenditure and sales are posi- tively and statistically significantly related. The estimated elasticity coefficient shows that a 1 percent increase in the amount of sales leads on the average to ≈ 1.32 percent increase in R&D expenditure, *ceteris paribus*.

   In problem 11.9 the reader is asked to examine the preceding regression to find out if heteroscedasticity exists. If the regression (11.25) is not plagued by the heteroscedasticity problem, then this model is preferable to the LIV model, which had this problem present, necessitating the transformation of variables, as in the regression (11.20).

   In passing, note that all the transformations we have discussed earlier to remove heteroscedasticity are known in the literature as **variance stabilizing**

transformations, which is another name for obtaining homoscedastic variances.

To conclude our discussion on remedial measures, we should reiterate that all transformations discussed previously are to some extent ad hoc; in the absence of precise knowledge about true σ_{i}^2, we are essentially speculating about what it might be. Which of the transformations we have considered will work depends upon the nature of the problem and the severity of heteroscedasticity. It may also be noted that sometimes the error variance may not be related to any of the explanatory variables included in the model. Rather, it can be related to a variable that was originally a candidate for inclusion in the model but was not initially included. In this case the model can be transformed using that variable. Of course, if a variable logically belonged in the model, it should have been included in the first place, but more on this subject in Chapter 13.

11.5 SOME CONCRETE EXAMPLES OF HETEROSCEDASTICITY

We end this chapter by presenting two examples to show the importance of heteroscedasticity in applied work.

Example 11.7 Economies of scale or heteroscedasticity. The New York Stock Exchange (NYSE) was initially very much opposed to the deregulation of brokerage commission rates. As a matter of fact, in an econometric study presented to the SEC before deregulation was introduced on May 1, 1975, the NYSE argued that there were economies of scale in the brokerage industry and therefore the (monopolistically determined) fixed rate commissions were justifiable.[16] The econometric study that the NYSE submitted basically revolved around the following regression:[17]

$$\hat{Y}_i = 476{,}000 + 31.348X_i - (1.083 \times 10^{-6})X_i^2$$

$$t = \quad (2.98) \quad\quad (40.39) \quad\quad (-6.54) \quad\quad\quad\quad R^2 = 0.934 \quad\quad\quad\quad (11.26)$$

where Y = the total cost and X = the number of share transactions. From the model (11.26) we see that the total cost is positively related to the volume of transactions. But since the quadratic term in the transaction variable is negative

---

[16] Sometimes economists offer the economics of scale argument to justify monopoly in certain industries, especially in the so-called natural monopolies (e.g., the electric and gas-generating utilities.)

[17] The results given in regressions (11.26) and (11.27) are reproduced from H. Michael Mann, "The New York Stock Exchange: A Cartel at the End of Its Reign" in Almarin Phillips (ed.), *Promoting Competition in Regulated Industries*, Brookings Institution, Washington D.C., 1975, p. 324.

and "statistically significant," it implies that the total cost is increasing at a decreasing rate. Therefore, argued the NYSE, there were economies of scale in the brokerage industry, justifying the monopoly status of the NYSE.

But the antitrust division of the U.S. Department of Justice argued that the so-called economies of scale claimed in the model (11.26) are a mirage, for the regression (11.26) was plagued by the problem of heteroscedasticity. This was because in estimating the cost function (11.26) the NYSE did not take into account that small and large firms were included in the sample. That is, the *scale factor* was not taken into account by the NYSE. Assuming that the error term was proportional to the volume of transaction [see Eq. (11.18)], the antitrust division reestimated Eq. (11.26), obtaining the following result:[18]

$$\hat{Y}_i = 342{,}000 + 25.57X_i + (4.34 \times 10^{-6})X_i^2$$

$$t = \quad (32.3) \qquad (7.07) \qquad (0.503) \qquad\qquad\qquad (11.27)$$

Lo and behold, the quadratic term is not only statistically insignificant, but it has the wrong sign.[19] Thus, there are no economies of scale in the brokerage industry, demolishing the NYSE's argument for retaining its monopoly commission structure.

The preceding example shows dramatically how the assumption of homoscedasticity underlying Eq. (11.26) could have been potentially damaging. Imagine what would have happened if the SEC had accepted Eq. (11.26) on its face value and allowed the NYSE to fix the commission rates monopolistically, as before May 1, 1975!

Example 11.8 Highway capacity and economic growth. In support of his argument that economies with superior surface transportation infrastructure will benefit through higher productivity and per capita income growth, David A. Aschauer[20] obtained the results presented in Table 11-3. Since the study was conducted over a cross section of 48 states in the United States, "there is presumption that the error structure may not be homoskedastic" (p. 18).[21]

---

[18] The actual mechanics consisted in estimating Eq. (11.19) shown in the text. Once this equation was estimated, it was multiplied by $\sqrt{X_i}$ to get back to the original equation, which is presented in Eq. (11.27).

[19] The NYSE in response said that the particular heteroscedasticity assumption used by the antitrust division was not valid. Substitution of other assumptions still supports the antitrust division's finding that there were no economies of scale in the brokerage industry. For details, see the Mann article cited in footnote 17.

[20] This example and the statistical results presented in Table 11-3 are obtained from David A. Aschauer, "Highway Capacity and Economic Growth," *Economic Perspectives*, Federal Reserve Bank of Chicago, pp. 14–23, September/October 1990.

[21] A historical note: Is it heteroscedasticity or heteroskedasticity? It is the latter, but the former is so well established in the literature that one rarely finds the word spelled with a *k* in it.

Happily, in the present instance the presumption of heteroscedasticity was just that since correcting for heteroscedasticity in various ways did not change OLS results much. But this example shows that if there is a presumption of heteroscedasticity, one should look into it rather than assume away the problem. As noted earlier, and as the NYSE economies of scale example so well demonstrates, heteroscedasticity is potentially a very serious problem and must not be taken lightly. It is better to err on the side of safety!

TABLE 11-3
Per capita income growth and highway capacity

Explanatory variable	OLS	WLS[1]	WLS[2]	WLS[3]
Constant	-7.69	-7.94	-8.19	-7.62
	se $= (1.08)$	(1.08)	(1.09)	(1.08)
ln X_2 (in 1960)	-1.59	-1.64	-1.69	-1.58
	se $= (0.18)$	(0.19)	(0.19)	(0.18)
ln X_3	0.30	0.30	0.31	0.30
	se $= (0.06)$	(0.06)	(0.06)	(0.06)
X_4	-0.009	-0.100	-0.011	-0.008
	se $= (0.003)$	(0.003)	(0.003)	(0.003)
D	-31.00	-32.00	-33.00	-31.00
	se $= (0.08)$	(0.08)	(0.08)	(0.08)
	$R^2 = 0.67$	0.49	0.46	0.73

Source: David A. Aschauer, "Highway Capacity and Economic Growth," Economic Perspectives, Federal Reserve Bank of Chicago, Table 1, p. 18, September/October 1990. Notation is adapted.

Notes: Dependent variable Y: Average annual growth of per capita income (1972 dollars) from 1960 to 1980.

X_2 = the level of per capita income (1972 $) in the base year 1960

X_3 = the total existing road mileage, average over 1960 to 1985

X_4 = the percentage of highway mileage of deficient quality in 1982

D = dummy = 1 for midwest region, 0 otherwise.

WLS[1] = weighted least squares using the square root of X_2 [see Eq. (11.19)]

WLS[2] = weighted least squares using the level of X_2 [see Eq. (11.23)]

WLS[3] = weighted least squares using the level of ln X_2.

11.6 SUMMARY

A critical assumption of the classical linear regression model is that the disturbances u_i all have the same (i.e., homoscedastic) variance. If this assumption is not satisfied, we have heteroscedasticity. Heteroscedasticity does not destroy the unbiasedness property of OLS estimators, but these estimators are no longer efficient. In other words, OLS estimators are no longer BLUE. If heteroscedastic variances σ_i^2 are known, then the method of weighted least squares (WLS) provides BLUE estimators.

Despite heteroscedasticity, if we continue to use the usual OLS method not only to estimate the parameters (which remain unbiased) but to establish confidence intervals and test hypotheses, we are likely to draw misleading conclusions, as in the NYSE Example 11.7. This is because estimated standard errors are likely to be biased and therefore the resulting t ratios are likely to be biased, too. Thus, it is important to find out whether we are faced with the heteroscedasticity problem in a specific application. There are several diagnostic tests of heteroscedasticity, such as plotting the estimated residuals against one or more of the explanatory variables or the Park test or the Glejser test or the rank correlation test, among several others.

If one or more diagnostic tests reveal that we have the heteroscedasticity problem, remedial measures are called for. If the true error variance σ_i^2 is known, we can use the method of WLS to obtain BLUE estimators. Unfortunately, knowledge about the true error variance is rarely available in practice. As a result, we are forced to make some plausible assumptions about the nature of heteroscedasticity and to transform our data so that in the transformed model the error term is homoscedastic. We then apply OLS to the transformed data, which amounts to using WLS. Of course, some skill and experience are required to obtain the appropriate transformations. But without such a transformation, the problem of heteroscedasticity is insoluble in practice.

Key Terms and Concepts

The key terms and concepts introduced in this chapter are:

Homoscedasticity (or equal variance)
Heteroscedasticity (or unequal
    variance)
    a) cross-sectional data
    b) scale effect
Detection of heteroscedasticity
    a) Park test
    b) Glejser test
    c) Residual plots
Other tests of heteroscedasticity
    a) Spearman's rank correlation

b) Bartlett's homogeneity-of-
    variance
c) CUSUMSQ
d) Goldfeld-Quandt test
e) Breusch-Pagan test
f) White's general
    heteroscedasticity test
g) Peak test
Weighted least squares (WLS)
The square root transformation
Variance stabilizing transformations

QUESTIONS

11.1. What is meant by heteroscedasticity? What are its effects on
  (a) OLS estimators and their variances?
  (b) Confidence intervals?
  (c) The use of t and F tests of significance?

11.2. State *with brief reasons* whether the following statements are true or false:
  (a) In the presence of heteroscedasticity ordinary least squares (OLS) estimators are biased as well as inefficient.
  (b) If heteroscedasticity is present, the conventional t and F tests are invalid.
  (c) In the presence of heteroscedasticity the usual OLS method always overestimates the standard errors of estimators.
  (d) If residuals estimated from an OLS regression exhibit a systematic pattern, it means heteroscedasticity is present in the data.
  (e) There is no general test of heteroscedasticity that is free of any assumption about which variable the error term is correlated with.

11.3. Would you expect heteroscedasticity to be present in the following regressions?

Y	X	Sample
(a) Corporate profits	Net worth	Fortune 500
(b) Log of corporate profits	Log of net worth	Fortune 500
(c) Dow Jones industrial average	Time	1960–1990 (annual averages)
(d) Infant mortality rate	Per capita income	100 developed and developing countries
(e) Inflation rate	Money growth rate	United States, Canada, and 15 Latin American countries

11.4. Explain intuitively why the method of weighted least squares (WLS) is superior to OLS if heteroscedasticity is present.

11.5. Explain briefly the logic behind the following methods of detecting heteroscedasticity:
  (a) The graphical method
  (b) The Park test
  (c) The Glejser test

PROBLEMS

11.6. In the two-variable PRF, suppose the error variance has the following structure:

$$E(u_i^2) = \sigma^2 X_i^4$$

How would you transform the model so as to achieve homoscedastic error variance? How would you estimate the transformed model? List the various steps.

11.7. Consider the following two regressions based on the U.S. data for 1946 to 1975.[22]
(Standard errors are in parentheses.)

$$\widehat{C_t} = 26.19 + 0.6248 \text{GNP}_t - 0.4398 D_t$$

$$\text{se} = (2.73) \qquad (0.0060) \qquad (0.0736) \qquad R^2 = 0.999$$

$$\left(\frac{C}{\text{GNP}}\right)_t = 25.92 \frac{1}{\text{GNP}_t} + 0.6246 - 0.4315 \frac{D}{\text{GNP}_t}$$

$$\text{se} = (2.22) \qquad\qquad (0.0068) \quad (0.0597) \qquad R^2 = 0.875$$

where

$$C = \text{the aggregate private consumption expenditure}$$

$$\text{GNP} = \text{the gross national product}$$

$$D = \text{the national defense expenditure}$$

$$t = \text{the time}$$

The objective of Hanushek and Jackson's study was to find out the effect of defense expenditure on other expenditures in the economy.

(a) What might be the reason(s) for transforming the first equation into the second equation?

(b) If the objective of the transformation was to remove or reduce heteroscedasticity, what assumption has been made about the error variance?

(c) If there was heteroscedasticity, have the authors succeeded in removing it? How can you tell?

(d) Does the transformed regression have to be run through the origin? Why or why not?

(e) Can you compare the R^2 values of the two regressions? Why or why not?

11.8. In a study of population density as a function of distance from the central business district, Maddala obtained the following regression results based on a sample of 39 census tracts in the Baltimore area in 1970:[23]

$$\widehat{\ln Y_i} = 10.093 - 0.239 X_i$$

$$t = (54.7) \; (-12.28) \qquad R^2 = 0.803$$

$$\widehat{\frac{\ln Y_i}{\sqrt{X_i}}} = 9.932 \frac{1}{\sqrt{X_i}} - 0.2258 \sqrt{X_i}$$

$$t = (47.87) \qquad (-15.10)$$

where $Y = $ the population density in the census tract and $X = $ the distance in miles from the central business district.

(a) What assumption is the author making about heteroscedasticity, if any, in his data?

(b) How can you tell from the transformed (WLS) regression that heteroscedasticity, if present, has been removed or reduced?

---

[22] These results are from Eric A. Hanushek and John E. Jackson, *Statistical Methods for Social Scientists*, Academic, New York, 1977, p. 160.

[23] G. S. Maddala, *Introduction to Econometrics*, Macmillan, New York, 1988, pp. 175–177.

(c) How would you interpret the regression results? Do they make economic sense?

11.9. Refer to the R&D data given in Table 11-2. Regression (11.25) gives the results of the regression of the log of R&D on the log of sales.

(a) Based on the data of Table 11-2, verify this regression.

(b) For this regression, obtain the absolute values of the residuals as well as their squared values and plot each against sales. Is there any evidence of heteroscedasticity?

(c) Do the Park and Glejser tests on the residuals of this regression. What conclusions can you draw?

(d) If heteroscedasticity is found in the double-log model, what kind of WLS transformation would you recommend to eliminate it?

(e) For the linear regression (11.3) there was evidence of heteroscedasticity. If for the log-log model there is no evidence of heteroscedasticity, which model will you choose and why?

(f) Can you compare the R^2s of the two regressions? Why not?

11.10. Continue with the R&D data given in Table 11-2 and now consider the following regressions:

$$R\&D_i = A_1 + A_2\,\text{profits}_i + u_i$$

$$\ln R\&D_i = B_1 + B_2\ln\text{profits}_i + u_i$$

(a) Estimate both regressions.

(b) Obtain the absolute and squared values of the residuals for each regression and plot them against the explanatory variable? Do you detect any evidence of heteroscedasticity?

(c) Verify your qualitative conclusion in part (b) with Glejser and Park tests.

(d) If there is evidence of heteroscedasticity, how would you transform the data to reduce its severity? Show the necessary calculations.

11.11. Consider Figure 11-10, which plots the gross domestic product (GDP) growth, in percent, against the ratio of investment/GDP, in percent, for several countries for 1974 to 1985.[24] The various countries are divided into three groups—those that experienced positive real (i.e., inflation-adjusted) interest rates, those that experienced moderately negative real interest rates, and those that experienced strongly negative interest rates.

(a) Develop a suitable model to explain the percent GDP growth rate in relation to percent investment/GDP rate.

(b) From the preceding figure, do you see any evidence of heteroscedasticity in the data? How would you test its presence formally?

(c) If heteroscedasticity is suspected, how would you transform your regression so as to eliminate it?

(d) Suppose you were to extend your model to take into account the "qualitative" differences in the three groups of countries by representing them with dummy variables. Write the equation for this model. If you had the data and could estimate this expanded model, would you expect heteroscedasticity in the extended model? Why or why not?

---

[24] See *World Development Report, 1989,* the World Bank, Oxford University Press, New York, p. 33.

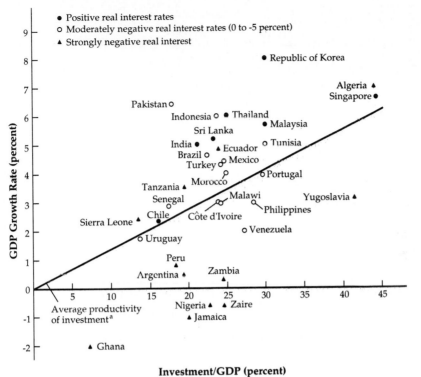

^a Line represents sample average.

FIGURE 11-10
Real interest rates, investment, productivity, and growth in 33 developing countries from 1974 to 1985. (*Source: World Development Report, 1989.* Copyright © by the International Bank for Reconstruction & Development/The World Bank. Reprinted by permission of the Oxford University Press, Inc., p. 33.)

11.12. In a survey of 9966 economists in 1964 the following data were obtained:

Age (years)	Median salary ($)
20–24	7,800
25–29	8,400
30–34	9,700
35–39	11,500
40–44	13,000

Age (years)	Median salary ($)
45–49	14,800
50–54	15,000
55–59	15,000
60–64	15,000
65–69	14,500
70+	12,000

Source: "The Structure of Economists' Employment and Salaries," Committee on the National Science Foundation Report on the Economics Profession, *American Economics Review*, vol. 55, no. 4, p. 36, December 1965.

(a) Develop a suitable regression model to explain median salary in relation to age. For the purpose of regression, assume that median salaries refer to the midpoint of the age interval.
(b) Assuming error variance proportional to age, transform the data and obtain the WLS regression.
(c) Now assume that it is proportional to the square of age. Obtain the WLS regression on this assumption.
(d) Which assumption seems more plausible?

11.13. *Spearman's rank correlation test for heteroscedasticity.* The following steps are involved in this test, which can be explained with the R&D regression (11.3):
(a) From the regression (11.3), obtain the residuals e_i.
(b) Obtain the absolute value of the residuals, $|e_i|$.
(c) Rank both sales (X_i) and e_i in either descending (highest to lowest) or ascending (lowest to highest) order.
(d) Take the difference between the two ranks for each observation, call it d_i.
(e) Compute the Spearman's rank correlation coefficient r_s, defined as

$$r_s = 1 - 6 \left[\frac{\sum d_i^2}{n(n^2 - 1)} \right]$$

where n = the number of observations in the sample.

If there is a systematic relationship between $|e_i|$ and X_i, the rank correlation coefficient between the two should be statistically significant, in which case heteroscedasticity can be suspected.

Given the null hypothesis that the true population rank correlation coefficient is zero and that $n > 8$, it can be shown that

$$\frac{r_s \sqrt{(n - 2)}}{\sqrt{1 - r_s^2}} \sim t_{n-2}$$

follows Student's t distribution with $(n - 2)$ d.f.

TABLE 11-4

Average compensation in relation to productivity by employment size, U.S. manufacturing industries

Employment size (average number of employees) (1)	Average compensation Y ($) (2)	Average productivity X ($) (3)	Standard deviation of compensation σ_i ($) (4)
1–4	3,396	9,355	744
5–9	3,787	8,584	851
10–19	4,013	7,962	728
20–49	4,104	8,275	805
50–99	4,146	8,389	930
100–249	4,241	9,418	1,081
250–499	4,387	9,795	1,243
500–999	4,538	10,281	1,308
1,000–2,499	4,843	11,750	1,112

Source: Data from *The Census of Manufacturing*, U.S. Department of Commerce, 1958. (Figures in table computed by D. N. Gujarati.)

Therefore, if in an application the rank correlation coefficient is significant on the basis of the t test, one can accept the hypothesis that there is heteroscedasticity in the problem. Apply this method to the R&D data given in the text to find out if there is evidence of heteroscedasticity in the data.

11.14. *Weighted least squares.* Consider the data in Table 11-4.

(a) Estimate the OLS regression

$$Y_i = B_1 + B_2 X_i + u_i$$

(b) Estimate the WLS

$$\frac{Y_i}{\sigma_i} = B_1 \frac{1}{\sigma_i} + B_2 \frac{X_i}{\sigma_i} + \frac{u_i}{\sigma_i}$$

(Make sure that you run the WLS through the origin.) Compare the results of the two regressions. Which regression do you prefer? And why?

11.15. Show that the error term v_i in Eq. (11.23) is homoscedastic.

11.16. In a regression of average wages (W) on the number of employees (N) for a random sample of 30 firms, the following regression results were obtained:[25]

$$\hat{W} = 7.5 + 0.009N \tag{1}$$
$$t = \text{N.A.} \ (16.10) \qquad R^2 = 0.90$$

---

[25] See Dominick Salvatore, *Managerial Economics*, McGraw-Hill, New York, 1989, p. 157.

$$\frac{\hat{W}}{N} = 0.008 + 7.8\,\frac{1}{N}$$

$$t = (14.43)\ (76.58) \qquad R^2 = 0.99$$

(2)

(a) How would you interpret the two regressions?

(b) What is the author assuming in going from Eqs. (1) to (2)? Was he worried about heteroscedasticity?

(c) Can you relate the slopes and the intercepts of the two models?

(d) Can you compare the R^2 values of two model? Why or why not?

11.17. From the total cost function given in the NYSE regression (11.26), how would you derive the average cost function? And the marginal cost function? But if Eq. (11.27) is the true (i.e., heteroscedasticity adjusted) total cost function, how would you derive the associated average and marginal cost functions? Explain the difference between the two models.

CHAPTER

12

AUTOCORRELATION: WHAT HAPPENS IF ERROR TERMS ARE CORRELATED

In the previous chapter we examined the consequences of relaxing one of the assumptions of the classical linear regression model (CLRM)—the assumption of homoscedasticity. In this chapter we consider yet another departure from the CLRM assumption, namely, that there is no **serial correlation** or **autocorrelation** among the disturbances u_i entering the population regression function (PRF). Although we discussed this assumption briefly in Chapter 6, we take a long look at it in this chapter in order to seek answers to the following questions:

1. What is the nature of autocorrelation?
2. What are the theoretical and practical consequences of autocorrelation?
3. Since the assumption of nonautocorrelation relates to u_i, which are not directly observable, how does one know that there is no autocorrelation in any concrete study? In short, how does one detect autocorrelation in practice?
4. How does one remedy the problem of autocorrelation if the consequences of not correcting for it are found to be serious?

This chapter is in many ways similar to the preceding one on heteroscedasticity in that *under both heteroscedasticity and autocorrelation ordinary least squares (OLS) estimators, although linear and unbiased, are not efficient; that is, they are not best linear unbiased estimators (BLUE).*

Since our emphasis in this chapter is on autocorrelation, we assume that all other assumptions of the CLRM remain intact.

351

12.1   THE NATURE OF AUTOCORRELATION

The term *autocorrelation* can be defined as "correlation between members of observations ordered in time [as in time-series data] or space [as in cross-sectional data]."[1]

Just as heteroscedasticity is generally associated with cross-sectional data, autocorrelation is usually associated with time series data (i.e., data ordered in temporal sequence), although, as the preceding definition suggests, autocorrelation can occur in cross-sectional data also, in which case it is called **spatial correlation** (i.e., correlation in space rather than in time).

In the regression context the CLRM assumes that such correlation does not exist in disturbances u_i. Symbolically, no autocorrelation means

$$E(u_i u_j) = 0 \qquad i \neq j \tag{12.1}$$

That is, the expected value of the product of two *different* error terms u_i and u_j is zero.[2] In plain English, this assumption means that the disturbance term relating to any observation is not related to or influenced by the disturbance term relating to any other observation. For example, in dealing with quarterly time series data involving the regression of output on labor and capital inputs (i.e., a production function), if, say, there is a labor strike affecting output in one quarter, there is no reason to believe that this disruption will be carried over to the next quarter. In other words, if output is lower this quarter, it will not necessarily be lower next quarter. Likewise, in dealing with cross-sectional data involving the regression of family consumption expenditure on family income, the effect of an increase of one family's income on its consumption expenditure is not expected to affect the consumption expenditure of another family.

But if there is such a dependence, we have autocorrelation. Symbolically,

$$E(u_i u_j) \neq 0 \qquad i \neq j \tag{12.2}$$

In this situation the disruption caused by a strike this quarter can affect output next quarter (it might in fact increase to catch up with the backlog) or the increase in the consumption expenditure of one family can pressure another family to increase its consumption expenditure if it wants to keep up with the Joneses (this is the case of *spatial correlation*).

It is interesting to visualize some likely patterns of autocorrelation and nonautocorrelation, which are given in Figure 12-1. On the vertical axis in the figure we show both u_i (the population disturbances) and their sample counterparts, e_i (the residuals), for as in the case of heteroscedasticity, we do not

---

[1] Maurice G. Kendall and William R. Buckland, *A Dictionary of Statistical Terms*, Hafner, New York, 1971, p. 8.

[2] If $i = j$, Eq. (12.1) becomes $E(u_i^2)$, the variance of u_i, which by the homoscedasticity assumption is equal to σ^2.

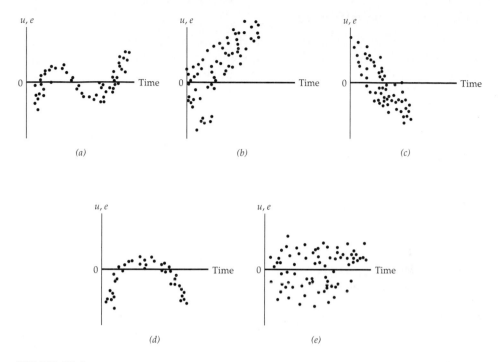

FIGURE 12-1
Patterns of autocorrelation.

observe the former and try to infer their behavior from the latter. Figure 12.1(*a*) to (*d*) shows a distinct pattern among the *u*s while Figure 12.1(*e*) shows no systematic pattern, which is the geometric counterpart of the assumption of no autocorrelation given in Eq. (12.1).

Why does autocorrelation occur? There are several reasons, some of which follow.

Inertia

A distinguishing feature of most economic time series is **inertia** or **sluggishness**. As is well known, time series such as the gross national product (GNP), production, employment, money supply, price indexes, etc., exhibit *business cycles* (recurring and self-sustaining fluctuations in economic activity). Starting at the bottom of the recession, when economic recovery starts, most of these time series start moving upward. In this upswing the value of a series at one point in time is greater than its previous value. Thus, there is a "momentum" built into these time series and the upswing continues until something happens (e.g., an increase in taxes or interest rates, or both) to slow them down. Therefore, in regressions involving time series data successive observations are likely to be interdependent or correlated.

Model Specification Error(s)

Sometimes autocorrelation patterns such as those shown in Figure 12.1(*a*) to (*d*) occur not because successive observations are correlated but because the regression model is not "correctly" specified. By incorrect specification of a model we mean that either some important variables that should be included in the model are not included (this is the case of *underspecification*) or the model has the wrong functional form—a linear-in-variable (LIV) model is fitted whereas a log-linear model should have been fitted. If such **model specification errors** occur, then the residuals from the incorrect model will exhibit a systematic pattern. A simple test of this is to include the excluded variable and to determine if the residuals still show a distinct pattern. If they do not, then the so-called serial correlation observed in the incorrect model was due to specification error. But more on this in the next chapter, where we examine this topic in some depth. (See also problems 12.13 and 12.18.)

The Cobweb Phenomenon

The supply of many agricultural commodities reflects the so-called **cobweb phenomenon,** where supply reacts to price with a *lag* of one time period because supply decisions take time to implement—the gestation period. Thus, at the beginning of this year's planting of crops farmers are influenced by the price prevailing last year so that their supply function is

$$\text{Supply}_t = B_1 + B_2 P_{t-1} + u_t \tag{12.3}$$

Suppose at the end of period t, price P_t turns out to be lower than P_{t-1}. Therefore, in period $(t + 1)$ farmers decide to produce less than they did in period t. Obviously, in this situation the disturbances u_t are not expected to be random, for if the farmers overproduce in year t, they are likely to underproduce in year $(t + 1)$, etc., leading to a cobweb pattern.

Data Manipulation

In empirical analysis the raw data are often "massaged." For example, in time series regressions involving quarterly data, such data are often derived from the monthly data by simply adding three monthly observations and dividing the sum by 3. This averaging introduces "smoothness" into the data by dampening the fluctuations in the monthly data. Therefore, the graph plotting the quarterly data looks much smoother than the monthly data, and this smoothness can itself lend to a systematic pattern in the disturbances, thereby "inducing" autocorrelation.[3]

Before moving on, it should be noted that autocorrelation can be positive

---

[3] It should be pointed out that sometimes the averaging or other data-editing procedures are used because the weekly or monthly data can be subject to substantial measurement errors. The averaging process, therefore, can produce more accurate estimates. But the unfortunate by-product of this process is that it can induce autocorrelation.

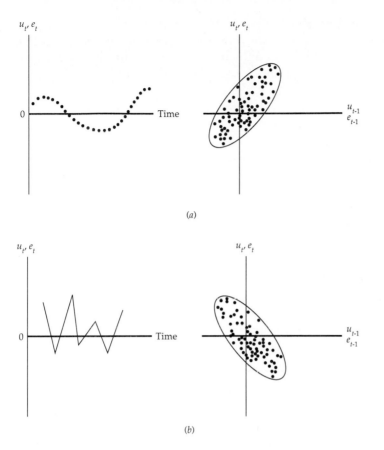

FIGURE 12-2
(a) Positive autocorrelation; (b) negative autocorrelation.

as well as negative, although economic time series generally exhibit positive autocorrelation because most of them either move upward or downward over extended time periods (possibly due to business cycles) and do not exhibit a constant up-and-down movement, such as that shown in Figure 12.2(b).

12.2 CONSEQUENCES OF AUTOCORRELATION

Suppose the error terms exhibit one of the patterns shown in Figure 12.1(a) to (d) or Figure 12.2. What then? In other words, what are the consequences of relaxing assumption (12.1) for the OLS methodology? These consequences are:[4]

---

[4] The proofs can be found in Damodor N. Gujarati, *Basic Econometrics*, 2d ed., McGraw-Hill, 1988, Chap. 12.

1. The least squares estimators are still linear and unbiased.
2. But they are not efficient (i.e., have minimum variance) compared to the procedures that take into account autocorrelation. In short, the usual ordinary least squares (OLS) estimators are not best linear unbiased estimators (BLUE).
3. The estimated variances of OLS estimators are biased. Sometimes the usual formulas to compute the variances and standard errors of OLS estimators seriously *underestimate* true variances and standard errors, thereby *inflating* t values. This gives the appearance that a particular coefficient is statistically significantly different from zero, whereas in fact it might not be the case.
4. Therefore, the usual t and F tests are not generally reliable.
5. The usual formula to compute the error variance, namely, $\hat{\sigma}^2 = RSS/d.f.$ (residual sum of squares/degrees of freedom), is a biased estimator of the true σ^2 and in some cases it is likely to underestimate the latter.
6. As a consequence, the conventionally computed R^2 may be an unreliable measure of true R^2.
7. The conventionally computed variances and standard errors of forecast may also be inefficient.

As the reader can see, these consequences are similar to those of heteroscedasticity, and just as serious in practice. Therefore, as with heteroscedasticity, we must find out if we have the autocorrelation problem in any given application.

12.3 DETECTING AUTOCORRELATION

When it comes to detection of autocorrelation, we face the same dilemma as in the case of heteroscedasticity. There, we did not know the true error variance σ_i^2 because the true u_i are unobservable. Here, too, not only do we not know what the true u_t are, but if they are correlated, we do not know what the true mechanism is that has generated them in a concrete situation: We only have their proxies, the e_ts. Therefore, as with heteroscedasticity, we have to rely on the e_ts obtained from the standard OLS procedure to "learn" something about the presence, or lack thereof, of autocorrelation. With this caveat, we now consider several diagnostic tests of autocorrelation, which we illustrate with an example encountered in Chapter 6.

Example 12.1. The U.S. import expenditure function revisited. In the regression (6.50) we presented the results of the import expenditure function for the United States in relation to the personal disposable income (PDI) for the period 1968 to 1987, all data in 1982 billions of dollars. In Table 12-1 we present the residuals obtained from this regression, the one-period lagged values of these residuals, and the signs of the residuals. The data given in this table are used to illustrate the various diagnostic tests of autocorrelation discussed in this section.

TABLE 12-1
Residuals from the regression (6.50)

	e_t	e_{t-1}	$D = e_t - e_{t-1}$	D^2	e_t^2	Sign e_t
	(1)	(2)	(3)	(4)	(5)	(6)
e_1	16.3642	—	—	—	267.7873	+
e_2	13.3705	16.3642	−2.9937	8.9623	178.7701	+
e_3	2.9212	13.3705	−10.4493	109.1877	8.5334	+
e_4	3.4338	2.9212	0.5126	0.2627	11.7907	+
e_5	11.0128	3.4338	7.5790	57.4419	121.2818	+
e_6	9.3548	11.0128	−1.6580	2.7489	87.5125	+
e_7	7.7123	9.3548	−1.6425	2.6978	59.4795	+
e_8	−24.7218	7.7123	−32.4340	1051.9670	611.1650	−
e_9	0.2837	−24.7218	25.0055	625.2738	0.0805	+
e_{10}	13.6966	0.2837	13.4128	179.9040	187.5956	+
e_{11}	3.6772	13.6966	−10.0193	100.3865	13.5222	+
e_{12}	−3.6072	3.6772	−7.2844	53.0632	13.0119	−
e_{13}	−28.3241	−3.6072	−24.7169	610.9248	802.2545	−
e_{14}	−31.6355	−28.3241	−3.3114	10.9656	1000.8070	
e_{15}	−43.9990	−31.6355	−12.3635	152.8557	1935.913	−
e_{16}	−28.5633	−43.9990	15.4357	238.2615	815.8616	−
e_{17}	6.5193	−28.5633	35.4357	1230.7900	42.3487	+
e_{18}	5.4174	6.5193	−1.1019	1.2141	29.3487	+
e_{19}	25.7603	5.4174	20.3428	413.8302	663.5909	+
e_{20}	41.3268	25.7603	15.5665	242.3160	1707.9010	+
Sum:	0			5093.1400	8558.8	

Note: The figures are rounded to four decimal points.

The Graphical Method

As in the case of heteroscedasticity, a simple visual examination of OLS residuals, *es*, can give valuable insight about the likely presence of autocorrelation among the error terms, the *us*. Now there are various ways of examining the residuals. We can plot them against time, as shown in Figure 12-3, which depicts the residuals of our import expenditure function presented in Table 12-1. Incidentally, such a plot is called a **time-sequence plot**.

An examination of Figure 12-3 shows that the residuals e_ts do not seem to be randomly distributed, as in Figure 12.1(*e*). As a matter of fact, they exhibit a distinct behavior—initially, they are generally positive, then become negative, and after that again turn positive. This can be seen more clearly if we plot the residuals at time *t* against their values lagged in one period; that is, plot e_t given in column 1 of Table 12-1 against e_{t-1} given in column 2, as in Figure 12-4. The general tenor of this figure is that successive residuals are positively correlated, suggesting positive autocorrelation; most residuals are bunched in the first (north-east) and the third (south-west) quadrants.

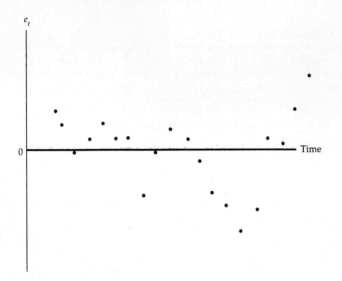

FIGURE 12-3
Residuals from the regression (6.50).

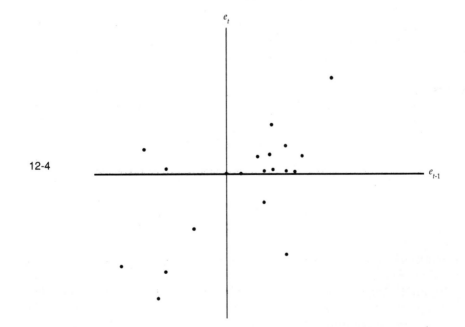

FIGURE 12-4
Residuals e_t against e_{t-1} from the regression (6.50).

The Runs Test

Now that the graphical evidence suggests that there might be (positive) auto-correlation in our import expenditure data, we can supplement this qualitative guess with some formal methods. An examination of the residuals given in Figure 12-3 and Table 12-1, as we have seen earlier, shows that a number of positive residuals are followed by a bunch of negative ones and then again by a bunch of positive ones. If the residuals were strictly random, can we observe such a pattern? Intuitively, it seems very unlikely. This intuition can be checked by the so-called **runs test,** a nonparametric test.[5]

To explain this test, let us simply note down the sign (+ or −) of the residuals from the import expenditure regression given in Table 12-1; column 6 of this table gives the signs of the various residuals. We can write these signs in a slightly different form as follows:

$$(+++++++)(-)(+++)(-----)(++++) \qquad (12.4)$$

Thus, there are 7 positive residuals followed by 1 negative residual, followed by 3 positive residuals, followed by 5 negative residuals, followed by 4 positive residuals, for a total of 20 residuals. We now define a *run* as an uninterrupted sequence of one symbol or attribute, such as + or −. We further define the **length of the run** as the number of elements in the run. In the sequence shown in (12.4), there are 5 runs—a run of 7 pluses (i.e., of length 7), a run of 1 minus (i.e., of length 1), a run of 3 pluses (i.e., of length 3), a run of 5 minuses (i.e., of length 5), and a run of 4 pluses (i.e., of length 4) (for better visual effect we have put the various runs in parentheses).

By examining how runs behave in a strictly random sequence of observations, we can derive a test of randomness of runs. The question we ask is: *Are the 5 runs observed in our example consisting of 20 observations too many or too few as compared with the number of runs expected in a strictly random sequence of 20 observations?* If there are too many runs, it means that the *es* change sign frequently, thus suggesting negative serial correlation [cf. Figure 12.2(*b*)]. Similarly, if there are too few runs, it suggests positive autocorrelation, as in Figure 12.2(*a*).

Now let N = total number of observations ($= N_1 + N_2$)
N_1 = number of + symbols (i.e., + residuals)
N_2 = number of − symbols (i.e., − residuals)
k = number of runs

Then under the hypothesis that the successive outcomes (here, residuals) are independent, Swed and Eisenhart have developed special tables that give critical values of the runs expected in a random sequence of N observations. These tables are given in Appendix B, Table B-6.

---

[5] In nonparametric tests we make no assumptions about the (probability) distribution from which the observations were drawn.

Swed-Eisenhart critical runs test. To illustrate the use of these tables, let us revert to our illustrative example. We have $N = 20$, $N_1 = 14$ (14 pluses), $N_2 = 6$ (6 minuses), and $k = 5$ runs. For $N_1 = 14$ and $N_2 = 6$, the 5% critical value of runs is 5. Now if the actual number of runs is equal to or less than 5, then we can reject the hypothesis that the observed sequence of the es given in (12.4) is random. In our example the actual number of runs is 5. Hence, we reject the null hypothesis of randomness. In other words, we can conclude that our import expenditure data are beset by the autocorrelation problem.

192 9 19   → Time series data so chek for Auto corr

Example 12.2.   The demand function for roses. As another illustration of the runs test, refer to the rose demand function (7.44). As the computer output given for this example in Table 7-3 shows, for this regression we have $N = 16$, $N_1 = 8$, $N_2 = 8$, and $k = 9$. Now from the Swed-Eisenhart tables we observe that the 5% critical values of the runs are 4 and 13. Since the observed runs of 9 lie between these limits, we can conclude that the rose demand function (7.44) does not seem to suffer from the problem of autocorrelation.

n = 16

k = 2   d = pg A3 2.21

Note that the Swed-Eisenhart table is at the most for 40 observations, 20 pluses and 20 minuses. But if the actual sample size is greater, we cannot use these tables. But in that case the distribution of runs can be approximated by the normal distribution. The details of that case can be found in the references.[6]

The Durbin-Watson d Test[7]

The most celebrated test for detecting autocorrelation is that developed by Durbin and Watson, popularly known as the **Durbin-Watson d statistic,** which is defined as

$$d = \frac{\sum_{t=2}^{n} (e_t - e_{t-1})^2}{\sum_{t=1}^{n} e_t^2} \tag{12.5}$$

which is simply the ratio of the sum of squared differences in successive residuals to the RSS. Note that in the numerator of the d statistic the sample size is $(n - 1)$ because one observation is lost in taking successive differences.

A great advantage of the d statistic is its simplicity; it is based on the OLS residuals which are routinely computed by most regression packages. It

---

[6] For details, see Damodar N. Gujarati, *Basic Econometrics*, 2d ed., McGraw-Hill, New York, 1988, pp. 372–373.

[7] J. Durbin and G. S. Watson, "Testing for Serial Correlation in Least-Squares Regression," *Biometrika*, vol. 38, pp. 159–177, 1951.

is now common practice to report the Durbin-Watson d along with summary statistics, such as R^2, adjusted R^2, $(\overline{R}^2)$, t, F ratios, etc.

For our import expenditure regression, we can easily compute the d statistic from the data given in Table 12-1. First, subtract the lagged es given in column 2 of that table from the es given in column 1, square the difference, sum it, and divide the sum by the sum of squared es given in column 5. The necessary raw data to compute d are presented in Table 12-1. Of course, this is now routinely done by the computer. For our example, the computed d value is

$$d = \frac{5093.14}{8558.8} = 0.5951 \tag{12.6}$$

Before proceeding to show how the computed d value can be used to determine the presence, or otherwise, of autocorrelation, it is *very important to note the assumptions underlying the d statistic*:

1. The regression model includes an intercept term. Therefore, it cannot be used to determine autocorrelation in models of regression through the origin.[8]

2. The X variables are nonstochastic; that is, their values are fixed in repeated sampling.

3. The disturbances u_t are generated by the following mechanism:

$$u_t = \rho u_{t-1} + v_t \qquad -1 \le \rho \le 1 \tag{12.7}$$

which states that the value of the disturbance, or error, term at time t depends on its value in time period $(t-1)$ and a purely random term (v_t), the extent of the dependence on the past value, is measured by ρ (rho). This is called the **coefficient of autocorrelation,** which lies between -1 and 1. (*Note*: A correlation coefficient always lies between -1 and 1.) The mechanism, Eq. (12.7), is known as the **Markov first-order autoregressive scheme** or simply the *first-order autoregressive scheme*, usually denoted as the **AR(1) scheme.** The name autoregression is appropriate because Eq. (12.7) can be interpreted as the regression of u_t on itself lagged in one period. And this is first order because u_t and its immediate past value are involved; that is, the maximum lag is one time period.[9]

---

[8] However, R. W. Farebrother has calculated d values when the intercept is absent from the model. See his, "The Durbin-Watson Test for Serial Correlation When There Is No Intercept in the Regression," *Econometrica*, vol. 48, pp. 1553–1563, 1980.

[9] If the model were

$$u_t = \rho_1 u_{t-1} + \rho_2 u_{t-2} + v_t$$

it would be an AR(2) or second-order autoregressive scheme, etc. We note here that unless we are willing to assume some scheme by which the *us* are generated, it is difficult to solve the problem of autocorrelation. This situation is similar to heteroscedasticity in which we also made some assumption about how the unobservable error variance σ_i^2 is generated. For autocorrelation, in practice, the AR(1) assumption has proved to be quite useful.

4. The regression does not contain the lagged value(s) of the dependent variable as one of the explanatory variables. In other words, the test is not applicable to models such as

$$Y_t = B_1 + B_2X_t + B_3Y_{t-1} + u_t \qquad (12.8)$$

where Y_{t-1} is the one-period lagged value of the dependent variable Y. Models like the regression (12.8) are known as *autoregressive models*, a regression of a variable on itself with a lag as one of the explanatory variables. (These models are discussed briefly in Chapter 14).

Assuming all these conditions are fulfilled, what can we say about autocorrelation in our import expenditure regression with a d value of 0.5951? Before answering this question, we can show that for a large sample size Eq. (12.5) can be *approximately* expressed as (see problem 12.20)

$$d \approx 2(1 - \hat{\rho}) \qquad (12.9)$$

where $\approx$ means approximately and where

$$\hat{\rho} = \frac{\displaystyle\sum_{t=2}^{n} e_t e_{t-1}}{\displaystyle\sum_{t=1}^{n} e_t^2} \qquad (12.10)$$

which is an estimator of the coefficient of autocorrelation ρ of the AR(1) scheme given in Eq. (12.7). But since $-1 \le \rho \le 1$, Eq. (12.9) implies the following:

Value of ρ	Value of d (approx.)
1. $\rho = -1$ (perfect negative correlation)	$d = 4$
2. $\rho = 0$ (no autocorrelation)	$d = 2$
3. $\rho = 1$ (perfect positive correlation)	$d = 0$

In short,

$$0 \le d \le 4 \qquad (12.11)$$

that is, *the computed d value must lie between 0 and 4.*

From the preceding discussion we can state that if a computed d value is closer to zero, there is evidence of positive autocorrelation, but if it is closer to 4, there is evidence of negative autocorrelation. And the closer the d value is to 2, the more the evidence is in favor of no autocorrelation. Of course, these are broad limits and some definite guidelines are needed as to when we can

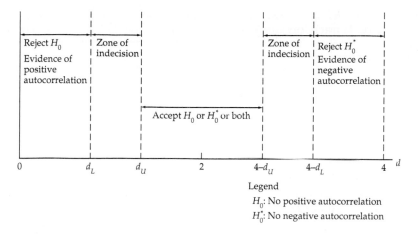

FIGURE 12-5
The Durbin-Watson d statistic.

call a computed d value indicative of positive, negative, or no autocorrelation. In other words, is there a "critical" d value, as in the case of t and F distributions, that will give us some definitive indication of autocorrelation?

Unfortunately, unlike t and F distributions, there are not one but two critical d values.[10] Durbin and Watson have provided a *lower limit* d_L and an *upper limit* d_U, such that if the d value computed from Eq. (12.5) lies outside these bounds, a decision can be made regarding the presence of positive or negative serial correlation. These upper and lower limits, or upper and lower critical values, depend upon the number of observations, n, and the number of explanatory variables, k. These limits for n, from 6 to 200 observations, and for k, up to 20 explanatory variables, have been tabulated by Durbin and Watson for 1% and 5% significance levels and are reproduced in Appendix B, Table B-5. The actual mechanics of the Durbin-Watson test are best explained with Figure 12-5.

The steps involved in this test are as follows:

1. Run the OLS regression and obtain the residuals e_t.
2. Compute d from Eq. (12.5). Most computer programs now do this routinely.
3. Find out the critical d_L and d_U from the Durbin-Watson tables for the given sample size and the given number of explanatory variables.
4. Now follow the decision rules given in Table 12-2, which for ease of reference are also depicted in Figure 12-5.

---

[10] Without going into technicalities, it should be mentioned that the exact critical value of d depends upon the values taken by the explanatory variable(s), which will obviously vary from sample to sample.

TABLE 12-2
Durbin-Watson *d* test: decision rules

Null hypothesis	Decision	If
No positive autocorrelation	Reject	$0 < d < d_L$
No positive autocorrelation	No decision	$d_L \leq d \leq d_U$
No negative autocorrelation	Reject	$4 - d_L < d < 4$
No negative autocorrelation	No decision	$4 - d_U \leq d \leq 4 - d_L$
No positive or negative autocorrelation	Do not reject	$d_U < d < 4 - d_U$

Returning to Example 12.1, we have $d = 0.5951$. From the Durbin-Watson tables we see that for $n = 20$ and one explanatory variable, $d_L = 1.201$ and $d_U = 1.411$ at the 5% level of significance. Since the computed d of 0.5951 is well below the lower bound value of 1.201, following the decision rules given in Table 12-2, we conclude that there is positive autocorrelation in our import expenditure regression residuals. We reached the same conclusion on the basis of the runs test as well as on the basis of the visual inspection of the residuals given in Figures 12-3 and 12-4.

Example 12.3. The demand for roses, again.   As a further illustration of the use of the d statistic, once again return to the rose demand function (7.44). For this example, the computed d value is 2.21. From the Durbin-Watson tables we observe that for $n = 16$ and two explanatory variables, the critical d values are 0.982 and 1.539 (5% level of significance) and 0.737 and 1.252 (1% level of significance). Since the computed d value of 2.21 is above either of the upper limits, we can conclude that there is no evidence of (first-order) autocorrelation in the data, thus reinforcing the conclusion reached on the basis of the runs test.

Example 12.4. The demand for chicken revisited.   Refer to the demand for chicken given in Eq. (10.16). For this example, the computed d value is 1.8756. For $n = 23$ and two explanatory variables, the critical d values are 1.168 and 1.543 (5% level) and 0.938 and 1.291 (1% level). Therefore, we cannot reject the null hypothesis that there is no autocorrelation in the data. Incidentally, for this example, the number of positive residuals is 7, the number of negative residuals is 16, and the number of runs is 9. It is left to the reader to show that on the basis of the runs test we also cannot reject the null hypothesis.

Although popularly used, one drawback of the d test is that if it falls in the *indecisive zone,* or *region of ignorance* (see Figure 12-5), we cannot conclude whether or not autocorrelation does exist. To solve this problem, several authors[11] have proposed modifications of the d test but they are involved and beyond the scope of this book. The computer program SHAZAM performs an exact d test (i.e., true critical value) and those with access to the program may want to use that test if the d statistic lies in the indecisive zone. Since the consequences of autocorrelation can be quite serious, as we have seen, if a d statistic lies in the indecisive zone, it might be prudent to assume that auto-correlation exists and proceed to correct the condition. Of course, the nonpar-ametric runs test and the visual graphics should also be invoked in this case.

To conclude our discussion of the d test, it should be reemphasized that this test should not be applied if the assumptions underlying this test dis-cussed earlier do not hold. In particular, it should not be used to test for serial correlation in autoregressive models like the regression (12.8). If applied mis-takenly in such cases, the computed d value is often found to be around 2, which is the value of d expected in the absence of AR(1). Hence, there is a built-in bias against discovering serial correlation in such models. But if such a model is used in empirical analysis, to test for autocorrelation in such mod-els, Durbin has developed the so-called **h statistic,** which is discussed in prob-lem 12.16.

12.4 REMEDIAL MEASURES

Since the consequences of serial correlation can be very serious and the cost of further testing can be high, and if on the basis of one or more diagnostic tests discussed earlier it is found that we have autocorrelation, we need to seek remedial measures. The remedy, however, depends upon what knowl-edge we have or can assume about the nature of interdependence in the error terms u_t. To keep the discussion as simple as possible, let us revert to our two-variable model:

$$Y_t = B_1 + B_2 X_t + u_t \qquad (12.12)$$

and assume that the error terms follow the AR(1) scheme:

$$u_t = \rho u_{t-1} + v_t \qquad -1 \le \rho < 1 \qquad (12.7)$$

where the vs satisfy the usual OLS assumptions and ρ is known.

Now if somehow we can transform the model (12.12) so that in the trans-formed model the error term is serially independent, then applying OLS to the transformed model will give us the usual BLUE estimators, assuming of course that the other assumptions of CLRM are fulfilled. Recall that we used the same philosophy in the case of heteroscedasticity, where our objective was

---

[11] Some authors maintain that d_U, the upper limit of Durbin-Watson d, is approximately the true significance limit. Therefore, if the calculated d lies below d_U, one can assume that there is (pos-itive) autocorrelation. See, e.g., E. J. Hannan and R. D. Terrell, "Testing for Serial Correlation after Least Squares Regression," *Econometrica*, pp. 646–660, 1966.

to transform the model so that in the transformed model the error term was homoscedastic.

To see how we can transform the regression (12.12) so that in the transformed model the error term does not have autocorrelation, write the regression (12.12) with a one-period lag as

$$Y_{t-1} = B_1 + B_2X_{t-1} + u_{t-1} \qquad (12.13)^{12}$$

Multiply the regression (12.13) by ρ on both sides to obtain

$$\rho Y_{t-1} = \rho B_1 + \rho B_2 X_{t-1} + \rho u_{t-1} \qquad (12.14)$$

Now subtract Eq. (12.14) from Eq. (12.12), to yield

$$(Y_t - \rho Y_{t-1}) = B_1(1 - \rho) + B_2(X_t - \rho X_{t-1}) + v_t \qquad (12.15)$$

where use is made of Eq. (12.7).

Since the error term v_t in Eq. (12.15) satisfies the standard OLS assumption, Eq. (12.15) provides the kind of transformation we are looking for which gives us a model free from serial correlation. If we write Eq. (12.15) as

$$Y_t^* = B_1^* + B_2^*X_t^* + v_t \qquad (12.16)$$

where

$$Y_t^* = (Y_t - \rho Y_{t-1})$$
$$X_t^* = (X_t - \rho X_{t-1})$$
$$B_1^* = B_1(1 - \rho)$$

and apply OLS to the transformed variables Y^* and X^*, the estimators thus obtained will have the desirable BLUE property. Incidentally, note that when we apply OLS to transformed models, the estimators thus obtained are called **generalized least squares (GLS)** estimators: In the previous chapter on heteroscedasticity we also used GLS, except that there we called it WLS (weighted least squares).

We call Eq. (12.15) or (12.16) the **generalized difference equation**; specific cases of the generalized difference equation in which ρ takes a particular value will be discussed shortly. It involves regressing Y on X, not in the original form, but in the *difference form*, which is obtained by subtracting a portion ($= \rho$) of the value of a variable in the previous period from its value in the current time period. Thus, if $\rho = 0.5$, we subtract 0.5 times the value of the variable in the previous time period from its value in the current time period. In this differencing procedure we lose one observation because the first sample observation has no antecedent. To avoid this loss of one observation, the first observation of Y and X are transformed as follows:

$$Y_1^* = \sqrt{1 - \rho^2}(Y_1) \qquad (12.17)$$
$$X_1^* = \sqrt{1 - \rho^2}(X_1)$$

---

[12] If the regression (12.12) holds true at time period t, it must hold true at time period $(t - 1)$ also.

This transformation is known as the **Prais-Winsten transformation**. In practice, though, if the sample size is very large, this transformation is not generally made and we use Eq. (12.15) with $(n - 1)$ observations.

A couple of points about the generalized difference transformation Eq. (12.15) should be made here. First, although we have considered only a two-variable model, the transformation can be generalized to more than one explanatory variable (see problem 12.19). Second, so far we have assumed only an AR(1) scheme, as in Eq. (12.7). But the transformation can be easily generalized to higher-order schemes, such as an AR(2), AR(3), etc.; no new principle is involved in the transformation except some tedious algebra.[13]

It seems that we have a "solution" to the autocorrelation problem in the generalized difference equation (12.15). Alas, we have a problem. For the successful application of the scheme, we must know the true autocorrelation parameter, ρ. Of course, we do not know it, and in order to use Eq. (12.15), we must find ways to estimate the unknown ρ. The situation here is similar to that in the case of heteroscedasticity. There, we did not know the true σ_i^2 and therefore had to make some plausible assumptions as to what it might be. Of course, had it been known, we could have used weighted least squares (WLS) straightforwardly.

12.5 HOW TO ESTIMATE ρ

There is no unique method of estimating ρ, rather, there are several approaches, some of which we present now.

$\rho = 1$: The First Difference Method

Since ρ lies between 0 and ± 1, one can assume any value for ρ in the range -1 to 1 and use the generalized difference equation (12.15). As a matter of fact, Hildreth and Lu[14] proposed such a scheme. But which particular value of ρ?—for even within the confines of the -1 to $+1$ range literally hundreds of values of ρ can be chosen. In applied econometrics one assumption that has been used extensively is that $\rho = 1$; that is, the error terms are perfectly positively autocorrelated, which may be true of some economic times series. If this assumption is acceptable, the generalized difference equation (12.15) reduces to the **first difference equation** as

$$Y_t - Y_{t-1} = B_2(X_t - X_{t-1}) + v_t$$

---

[13] Higher-order autoregressive schemes are discussed in any book on time series analysis. See, e.g., C. Chatfield, *The Analysis of Time Series: An Introduction*, 3d ed., Chapman & Hall, New York, 1984.

[14] G. Hildreth and J. Y. Lu, "Demand Relations with Autocorrelated Disturbances," Michigan State University, *Agricultural Experiment Station*, Technical Bulletin 276, November 1960.

or

$$\Delta Y_t = B_2 \Delta X_t + v_t \tag{12.18}$$

where Δ, called *delta*, is the first difference operator and is a symbol or operator (like the operator E for expected value) for successive differences of two values. In estimating Equation (12.18) all one has to do is to form the first differences of both the dependent and explanatory variable(s) and run the regression on the variable(s) thus transformed.

Note an important feature of the first difference model (12.18): *The model has no intercept*. Hence, to estimate Eq. (12.18), we have to use the regression-through-the-origin routine in the computer package. Naturally, we will not be able to estimate the intercept term in this case directly. (But note that $b_1 = \overline{Y} - b_2\overline{X}$.)

To illustrate the technique of first difference transformation, we apply the method to our import expenditure regression. The results of this regression, along with some other regressions based upon other transformations to be discussed presently, are given in Table 12-4 for comparative purposes toward the end of this section. We will also discuss the outcome of this transformation together with other regressions later. Keep in mind, though, that the first difference transformation is explicitly based upon the assumption that the true $\rho = 1$. If this is not the case, the transformation is not recommended. But how does one find out if ρ is in fact equal to 1? The answer follows.

ρ Estimated from Durbin-Watson d Statistic

Recall earlier that we established the following approximate relationship between the d statistic and ρ:

$$d \approx 2(1 - \hat{\rho}) \tag{12.9}$$

from which we can obtain

$$\hat{\rho} \approx 1 - \frac{d}{2} \tag{12.19}$$

Since the d statistic is now routinely computed by most regression packages, we can easily obtain an approximate estimate of ρ from Equation (12.19).

Once ρ is estimated from d as shown in Eq. (12.19), we can then use it to run the generalized difference equation (12.15); for our import expenditure example, $d = 0.5951$. Therefore,

$$\hat{\rho} \approx 1 - \frac{0.5951}{2} \tag{12.20}$$
$$\approx 0.7025$$

This ρ value is obviously different from $\rho = 1$ assumed for the first difference transformation. The regression results based on ρ obtained from Equation (12.20) are also given in Table 12-4.

Although easy to use, this method of transformation generally gives good estimates of ρ if the sample size is reasonably large. For small samples, another estimate of ρ based on d is suggested by Theil and Nagar, which is discussed in problem 12.21.

ρ Estimated from OLS Residuals, e_t

Recall the first-order autoregressive scheme

$$u_t = \rho u_{t-1} + v_t \tag{12.7}$$

Since the us are not directly observable, we can use their sample counterparts, the es, and run the following regression:

$$e_t = \hat{\rho} e_{t-1} + v_t \tag{12.21}$$

where $\hat{\rho}$ is an estimator of ρ. Statistical theory shows that although in small samples $\hat{\rho}$ is a biased estimator of true ρ, as the sample size increases the bias tends to disappear.[15] Hence, if the sample size is reasonably large, we can use $\hat{\rho}$ obtained from Equation (12.21) and use it to transform the data as shown in Eq. (12.15). An advantage of Eq. (12.21) is its simplicity, for we use the usual OLS method to obtain the residuals. The necessary data to run the regression are given in Table 12-1, and the results of the regression (12.21) are as follows:

$$\hat{e}_t = 0.7339 e_{t-1}$$

$$se = (0.19327)$$

$$t = (3.7947) \qquad r^2 = 0.4435 \tag{12.22}$$

Thus, the estimated ρ is 0.7379, which differs slightly from that obtained from the Durbin-Watson d. Incidentally, the method of estimating ρ as shown in Eq. (12.21) has been refined in the so-called Cochrane-Orcutt method mentioned now.

Other Methods of Estimating ρ

Besides the methods discussed previously, there are other ways of estimating ρ, which are as follows:

1. The Cochrane-Orcutt iterative procedure
2. The Cochrane-Orcutt two-step method
3. The Durbin two-step method

---

[15] Technically, we say that $\hat{\rho}$ is a *consistent* estimator of ρ.

TABLE 12-3
U.S. import expenditure data: original and transformed ($\rho = 0.7339$)

Y_t (1)	$Y_{(t-1)}$ (2)	$\rho Y_{(t-1)}$ (3)	d_1 (4)	X_t (5)	$X_{(t-1)}$ (6)	$\rho X_{(t-1)}$ (7)	d_2 (8)
135.7	—	(92.2485)*	43.45	1551.3	—	(1054.5696)†	496.73
144.6	135.7	99.5224	45.08	1599.8	1551.3	1137.723	462.08
150.9	144.6	106.0496	44.85	1668.1	1599.8	1173.293	494.81
166.2	150.9	110.6700	55.53	1728.4	1668.1	1223.385	505.02
.	.	.	.	.	.	.	.
.	.	.	.	.	.	.	.
.	.	.	.	.	.	.	.
367.9	351.1	257.4967	110.40	2542.8	2469.8	1811.351	731.4487
412.3	367.9	269.8179	142.48	2640.9	2542.8	1864.890	776.01
439.0	412.3	302.3808	136.62	2686.3	2640.9	1936.836	749.46

Notes: Y_t = U.S. expenditure on imports (1982, $ in billions)

X_t = U.S. PDI (1982, $ in billions)

d_1 = the difference between columns 1 and 3 (up to two decimals)

d_2 = the difference between columns 5 and 7 (up to two decimals)

$* = \sqrt{1 - \rho^2}(Y_1)$

$† = \sqrt{1 - \rho^2}(X_1)$

(transformation of the first observation if it is included in the regression à la Prais-Winsten; if it is not included, then the first observation is dropped.)

All remaining entries in the table are to be filled in a similar manner.

4. The Hildreth-Lu search procedure
5. The maximum likelihood method

A discussion of all these methods will take us far afield and thus is left for the references.[16] (But see some of the problems at the end of the chapter.) Whichever method is employed, we use the ρ obtained from that method to transform our data as shown in Eq. (12.15) and run the usual OLS regression.[17] Although most computer software packages do the transformations with minimum instructions, we show in Table 12-3 how the transformed data will look; for illustration we use the value of ρ derived from Eq. (12.22), which is 0.7379.

Before concluding, let us consider the results of applying (1) the first difference transformation, (2) the transformation based on the d statistic, and (3) the transformation based on Eq. (12.22) to our import expenditure data. The results are summarized in Table 12-4. Several observations can be made about these results.

---

[16] For a discussion of these methods, see Damodar N. Gujarati, *Basic Econometrics*, 2d ed., McGraw-Hill, New York, 1988, pp. 381–385.

[17] In large samples the differences in the estimates of ρ produced by the various methods will tend to be small.

TABLE 12-4

Regression results of import expenditure based on transformed data

Method of transformation of regression	ρ estimated from	Intercept	Slope	R^2	Is there autocorrelation in the transformed regression
Original regression	ρ = 0 (assumed)	− 261.09 t = (−8.3345)	0.2452 (16.616)	0.9388	Yes; d = 0.5901
First difference	ρ = 1 (assumed)	t = *	0.3286 (6.4468)	0.9683	Not
Eq. (12.15)‡	ρ = 0.7025 (from Durbin d)	− 405.65 t = (−5.245)	0.3100 (9.1868)	0.9729	Not
Eq. (12.15)§	ρ = 0.7025 (from Durbin d)	− 302.07 t = (−5.606)	0.2674 (10.635)	0.9679	Not
Eq. (12.22)‡	ρ = 0.7334	− 430.03 t = (−5.096)	0.3202 (8.7884)	0.9737	Not
Eq. (12.22)§	ρ = 0.7334	− 307.37 t = (−5.3982)	0.2702 (10.189)	0.9682	Not

Notes: * There is no intercept term in this model. (Why?)
    † Based on the runs test on the estimated residuals.
    ‡ Excludes the first observation.
    § Includes the first observation (i.e., Prais-Winsten transformation).
    The figures in parentheses are the t values.
    All regressions were run on the SHAZAM computer package.

1. The original regression was plagued by autocorrelation, but the various transformed regressions seem to be free from autocorrelation on the basis of the runs tests.[18]

2. Even though the ρ estimated from the first difference transformation and that estimated from the d statistic and Eq. (12.22) are not the same, the estimated slope and intercept coefficients do not differ substantially from one another if we do not include the first observation in the analysis. But the estimates of intercept and slope values are substantially different from the original OLS regression.

3. The situation changes significantly, however, if we include the first observation via the Prais-Winsten transformation. Now the slope coefficients

---

[18] One can obtain the Durbin-Watson d statistic for the transformed regressions too. But econometric theory suggests that the computed d statistic from the transformed regressions may not be appropriate to test for autocorrelation in such regressions because if we were to use it for that purpose, this would suggest that the original error term may not follow the AR(1) scheme. It could, e.g., follow an AR(2) scheme. The runs test does not suffer from this problem since it is a nonparametric test.

in the transformed regressions are very close to the original OLS slope and the intercepts in the transformed models are much closer to the original intercept. As noted, in small samples it is important to include the first observation in the analysis. Otherwise the estimated coefficients in the transformed model will be less *efficient* (i.e., have higher standard errors) than in the model that includes the first observation.

4. The r^2 values reported in the various regressions are not directly comparable because the dependent variables in all models are not the same. Besides, as noted elsewhere (see problem 6.15), for the first difference model, the conventionally computed r^2 is not meaningful.

If we accept the results based upon the Prais-Winsten transformation for our import expenditure example and compare them with the original regression beset by the autocorrelation problem, we see that the original t ratios of the intercept and slope coefficients, in absolute value, have decreased in the transformed regression. This is another way of saying that the original model underestimated the standard errors. But this result is not surprising in view of our knowledge about theoretical consequences of autocorrelation. Fortunately, in this example even after correcting for autocorrelation, the estimated t ratios are statistically significant.[19] But that may not always be the case.

12.6   SUMMARY

The major points of this chapter are as follows:

1. In the presence of autocorrelation OLS estimators, although unbiased, are not efficient. In short, they are not BLUE.
2. Assuming the Markov first-order autoregressive, the AR(1), scheme, we pointed out that the conventionally computed variances and standard errors of OLS estimators can be seriously biased.
3. As a result, standard t and F tests of significance can be seriously misleading.
4. Therefore, it is important to know whether there is autocorrelation in any given case. Among the methods of detecting autocorrelation, we considered three:
   a. graphical plotting of the residuals
   b. the runs test
   c. the Durbin-Watson d test

---

[19] Strictly speaking, this statement is correct if the sample is reasonably large. This is because we do not know the true ρ and estimate it, and when we use the estimated ρ to transform the data, econometric theory shows that the usual statistical testing procedure is valid generally in large samples.

5. If autocorrelation is found, we suggest that it be corrected by appropriately transforming the model so that in the transformed model there is no auto-correlation. We illustrated the actual mechanics with several examples.

Key Terms and Concepts

The key terms and concepts introduced in this chapter are:

Serial correlation or autocorrelation
   a) spatial correlation
Reasons for autocorrelation
   a) inertia or sluggishness
   b) model specification error
   c) the cobweb phenomenon
   d) data manipulation
Detecting autocorrelation
   a) time-sequence plot
   b) the runs test (length of the run; Swed-Eisenhart critical runs values)
   c) The Durbin-Watson d test; coefficient of autocorrelation ρ;

the Markov first-order autoregressive or AR(1) scheme:
   h statistic
Remedial measures for serial or autocorrelation
   a) generalized least squares (GLS) (generalized difference equation)
   b) Prais-Winsten transformation
Estimation of ρ
   a) first difference equation
   b) the Durbin-Watson d statistic
   c) OLS residuals

QUESTIONS

12.1. Explain briefly the meaning of
   (*a*) Autocorrelation
   (*b*) First-order autocorrelation
   (*c*) Spatial correlation

12.2. What is the importance of assuming the Markov first-order, or AR(1), autocorrelation scheme?

12.3. Assuming the AR(1) scheme, what are the consequences of the CLRM assumption that the error terms in the PRF are uncorrelated?

12.4. In the presence of AR(1) autocorrelation, what is the method of estimation that will produce BLUE estimators? Outline the steps involved in implementing this method.

12.5. What are the various methods of estimating the autocorrelation parameter ρ in the AR(1) scheme?

12.6. What are the various methods of detecting autocorrelation? State clearly the assumptions underlying each method.

12.7. Although popularly used, what are some limitations of the Durbin-Watson d statistic?

12.8. State whether the following statements are true or false. Briefly justify your answers.
   (*a*) When autocorrelation is present, OLS estimators are biased as well as in-efficient.

(b) The Durbin-Watson d is useless in autoregressive models like the regression (12.8) where one of the explanatory variables is a lagged value(s) of the dependent variable.

(c) The Durbin-Watson d test assumes that the variance of the error term u_t is homoscedastic.

(d) The first difference transformation to eliminate autocorrelation assumes that the coefficient of autocorrelation ρ must be -1.

(e) The R^2 values of two models, one involving regression in the first difference form and another in the level form, are not directly comparable.

12.9. What is the importance of the Prais-Winsten transformation?

PROBLEMS

12.10. Complete the following table:

Sample size	Number of explanatory variables	Durbin-Watson d	Evidence of autocorrelation
25	2	0.83	Yes
30	5	1.24	. . .
50	8	1.98	. . .
60	6	3.72	. . .
200	20	1.61	

12.11. Use the runs test to test for autocorrelation in the following cases. (Use the Swed-Eisenhart tables.)

Sample size	Number of +	Number of −	Number of runs	Autocorrelation
18	11	7	2	. . .
30	15	15	24	. . .
38	20	18	6	. . .
15	8	7	4	. . .
10	5	5	1	. . .

12.12. For the Phillips curve regression (8.30) given in Chapter 8, the estimated d statistic was 0.6394.

(a) Is there evidence of first-order autocorrelation in the residuals? If so, is it positive or negative?

(b) If there is autocorrelation, estimate the coefficient of autocorrelation from the d statistic.

(c) Using this estimate, transform the data given in Table 8-4 and estimate the generalized difference equation (12.15) (i.e., apply OLS to the transformed data).

(d) Is there autocorrelation in the regression estimated in part (c)? Which test do you use?

12.13. In studying the movement in the production workers' share in value added (i.e., labor's share), the following regression results were obtained based on the U.S. data for the years 1949 to 1964:[20] (t ratios in parentheses).

$$\text{Model A: } \hat{Y}_t = 0.4529 - 0.0041t; \quad r^2 = 0.5284; \quad d = 0.8252$$
$$t = \quad\quad (-3.9608)$$

$$\text{Model B: } \hat{Y}_t = 0.4786 - 0.00127t + 0.0005t^2; \quad R^2 = 0.6629; \quad d = 1.82$$
$$t = \quad\quad (-3.2724) \quad (2.7777)$$

where Y = labor's share and t = the time.

(a) Is there serial correlation in model A? In model B?

(b) If there is serial correlation in model A but not in model B, what accounts for the serial correlation in the former?

(c) What does this example tell us about the usefulness of the d statistic in detecting autocorrelation?

12.14. *Durbin's two-step method of estimating ρ:*[21] Write the generalized difference equation (12.15) in a slightly different but equivalent form as follows:

$$Y_t = B_1(1 - \rho) + B_2X_t - \rho B_2X_{t-1} + \rho Y_{t-1} + v_t$$

In *step 1* Durbin suggests estimating this regression, with Y as the dependent variable and X_t, X_{t-1}, and Y_{t-1} as explanatory variables. The coefficient of Y_{t-1} will provide an estimate of ρ. The ρ thus estimated is a *consistent* estimator; that is, in large samples it provides a good estimate of true ρ.

In *step 2* use the ρ estimated from step 1 to transform the data to estimate the generalized difference equation (12.15).

Apply Durbin's two-step method to the U.S. import expenditure data discussed in the chapter and compare your results with those shown in Table 12-4.

12.15. Consider the following regression model:[22]

$$\hat{Y}_t = -49.4664 + 0.88544X_{2t} + 0.09253X_{3t}; \quad R^2 = 0.9979; \quad d = 0.8755$$
$$t = (-2.2392) \quad (70.2936) \quad (2.6933)$$

where

Y = the personal consumption expenditure (1982 billions of dollars)

X_2 = the personal disposable income (1982 billions of dollars) (PDI)

X_3 = the Dow Jones Industrial Average Stock Index.

The regression is based on U.S. data from 1961 to 1985. $n = 25$

(a) Is there first-order autocorrelation in the residuals of this regression? How do you know?

---

[20] See Damodar N. Gujarati, "Labor's Share in Manufacturing Industries," *Industrial and Labor Relations Review*, vol. 23, no. 1, pp. 65–75, October 1969.

[21] J. Durbin, "Estimation of Parameters in Time-Series Regression Models," *Journal of the Royal Statistical Society*, ser. B, vol. 22, pp. 139–153, 1960.

[22] See Dominick Salvatore, *Managerial Economics*, McGraw-Hill, New York, 1989, pp. 138, 148.

(b) Using the Durbin two-step procedure, the preceding regression was transformed as per Eq. (12.15), yielding the following results:

$$Y_t^* = -17.97 + 0.89X_{2t}^* + 0.09X_{3t}^*; \qquad R^2 = 0.9816; \qquad d = 2.28$$
$$t = \qquad (30.72) \qquad (2.66)$$

Has the problem of autocorrelation been resolved? How do you know?

(c) Comparing the original and transformed regressions, the t value of the PDI has dropped dramatically. What does this suggest?

(d) Is the d value from the transformed regression of any value in determining the presence, or lack thereof, of autocorrelation in the transformed data?

12.16. *Durbin h statistic.* In autoregressive models like Eq (12.8):

$$Y_t = B_1 + B_2X_t + B_3Y_{t-1} + v_t$$

the usual d statistic is not applicable to detect autocorrelation. For such models, Durbin has suggested replacing the d statistic by the h statistic defined as

$$h \approx \hat{\rho}\sqrt{\frac{n}{1 - n \cdot \text{var}(b_3)}}$$

where

n = the sample size
$\hat{\rho}$ = the estimator of the autocorrelation coefficient ρ
var (b_3) = the variance of the estimator of B_3, the coefficient of lagged Y variable

Durbin has shown that for *large samples*, and given the null hypothesis that true $\rho = 0$, the h statistic is distributed as

$$h \sim N(0,1)$$

That is, it follows the standard normal distribution, that is, normal distribution with zero mean and unit variance. Therefore, we would reject the null hypothesis that $\rho = 0$ if the computed h statistic exceeds the critical h value. If, e.g., the level of significance is 5%, the critical h value is -1.96 or 1.96. Therefore, if a computed h exceeds $|1.96|$, we can reject the null hypothesis; if it does not exceed this critical value, we do not reject the null hypothesis of no (first-order) autocorrelation. Incidentally, $\hat{\rho}$ entering the h formula can be obtained from any one of the methods discussed in the text.

Now consider the following demand for money function for India for the period 1948–1949 to 1964–1965:

$$\widehat{\ln M_t} = 1.6027 - 0.1024 \ln R_t + 0.6869 \ln Y_t + 0.5284 \ln M_{t-1}$$
$$\text{se} = (1.2404) \quad (0.3678) \qquad (0.3427) \qquad (0.2007) \qquad R^2 = 0.9227$$

where

M = real cash balances
R = the long-term interest rate
Y = the aggregate real national income

(a) For this regression, find the h statistic and test the hypothesis that the preceding regression does not suffer from first-order autocorrelation.

(b) For the same regression, the Durbin-Watson d statistic is 1.8624. Tell why in this case it is inappropriate to use the d statistic. But note that you can use this d value to estimate ρ ($\hat{\rho} \approx 1 - d/2$).

12.17. Consider the data given in Table 12-5.

TABLE 12-5

Data on stock price index and GNP, United States, 1970 to 1987

Year	Y	X	Year	Y	X
1970	45.72	1015.5	1979	58.32	2508.2
1971	54.22	1102.7	1980	68.10	2732.0
1972	60.29	1212.8	1981	74.02	3052.6
1973	57.42	1359.3	1982	68.93	3166.0
1974	43.84	1472.8	1983	92.63	3405.7
1975	45.73	1598.4	1984	92.46	3772.2
1976	54.46	1782.8	1985	108.09	4019.2
1977	53.69	1990.5	1986	136.00	4240.3
1978	53.70	2249.7	1987	161.70	4526.7

Source: Economic Report of the President, 1989, data on Y from Table B-94, p. 416 and data on X from Table B-1, p. 308.

Note:

         Y = NYSE Composite Common Stock Price Index, (December 31, 1965 = 100)
         X = the GNP ($, in billions)

(a) Estimate the OLS regression

$$Y_t = B_1 + B_2 X_t + u_t$$

(b) Find out if there is first-order autocorrelation in the data on the basis of the d statistic.

(c) If there is, use the d value to estimate the autocorrelation parameter ρ.

(d) Using this estimate of ρ, transform the data as per the generalized difference equation (12.15), and estimate this equation by OLS (1) by dropping the first observation and (2) by including the first observation.

(e) Repeat part (d), but estimate ρ from the residuals as shown in Eq. (12.21). Using this estimate of ρ, estimate the generalized difference equation (12.15).

(f) Use the first difference method to transform the model into Eq. (12.18) and estimate the transformed model.

(g) Compare the results of regressions obtained in parts (d), (e), and (f). What conclusions can you draw? Is there autocorrelation in the transformed regressions? How do you know?

12.18. Using the data given in problem 12.17, the following results were obtained:

$$\hat{Y}_t = 88.543 \quad -0.0454X_t + 0.0000131X_t^2 \qquad R^2 = 0.9577; \qquad d = 1.67$$
$$t = (\ 8.3792)\ (-5.0808) \qquad (8.0045)$$

where X^2 represents the square of the the GNP.

(a) Is there first-order autocorrelation in this regression? If the answer is no, and if you found autocorrelation in the regression of problem 12.17, which did not include the squared GNP term, what can you say about problem 12.17? What is the difference between the two regressions?

(b) Why is the GNP term negative but the squared GNP term positive in the preceding regression? What are the implications?

(c) A priori, would you expect a positive or negative relationship between stock prices and GNP? Justify your answer.

12.19. Consider the following models:

$$Y_t = B_1 + B_2 X_{2t} + B_3 X_{3t} + B_4 X_{4t} + u_t$$

Suppose the error term follows the AR(1) scheme, Eq. (12.7). How would you transform this model so that there is no autocorrelation in the transformed model. (*Hint*: Extend Eq. 12.15).

12.20. Establish Eq. (12.9). [*Hint*: Expand Eq. (12.5) and use Eq. (12.10). Also, note that for a large sample size $\Sigma\ e_{t-1}^2$ and $\Sigma\ e_t^2$ are approximately the same.]

12.21. *The Theil-Nagar ρ based on d statistic.* Theil and Nagar[23] have suggested that in small samples instead of estimating ρ as $(1 - d/2)$, it should be estimated as

$$\hat{\rho} = \frac{n^2(1 - d/2) + k^2}{n^2 - k^2}$$

where

n = the sample size
d = the Durbin-Watson d
k = the number of coefficients (including the intercept)
    to be estimated

Show that for large n, this estimate of ρ is equal to the one obtained by the simpler formula $(1 - d/2)$.

---

[23] See H. Theil and A. L. Nagar, "Testing the Independence of Regression Disturbances," *Journal of the American Statistical Association*, vol. 56, pp. 793–806, 1961.

CHAPTER
13

MODEL SELECTION: CRITERIA AND TESTS

In the preceding chapters we considered several single-equation linear regression models, whether it was the demand function for widgets, the Phillips curve, or the expenditure on foreign imports. In presenting these models we assumed implicitly, if not explicitly, that the chosen model represents "the truth, the whole truth and nothing but the truth"; that is, it "correctly" models the phenomenon under study. More technically, we assumed that there is **no** *specification bias* or *specification error* in the chosen model. A specification error occurs when instead of estimating the "correct" model we estimate another model, although inadvertently. In practice, however, searching for a true model can be like searching for the Holy Grail. One may never know what the true model is; rather, one hopes to find a model that is a "reasonably" accurate representation of reality.

Because of its practical importance, we take a closer look at how to go about formulating an econometric model. Specifically, we consider the following questions:

1. What are the attributes of a "good" or "correct" model?
2. Suppose an omniscient econometrician has developed the "correct" model to analyze a particular problem. However, because of data availability, cost considerations, oversight, or sheer ignorance (which is not always a bliss), the researcher uses another model, and thus, in relation to the "correct" model, commits a specification error. What types of specification errors is one likely to make in practice?
3. What are the consequences of the various specification errors?
4. How does one detect a specification error?

5. What remedies can one adopt to get back to the "correct" model if a specification error has been made?

13.1 THE ATTRIBUTES OF A GOOD MODEL

Whether a model chosen in empirical analysis is "good" or "appropriate" or the "right" model cannot be determined without some reference criteria, or guidelines. A. C. Harvey,[1] a noted econometrician, lists the following criteria by which one can judge a model.

Parsimony. A model can never completely capture the reality; some amount of abstraction or simplification is inevitable in any model building. The Occam's razor or the **principle of parsimony** states that a model be kept as simple as possible.

Identifiability. This means that for a given set of data the estimated parameters must have unique values or, what amounts to the same thing, there is only one estimate per parameter.

Goodness of fit. Since the basic thrust of regression analysis is to explain as much of the variation in the dependent variable as possible by explanatory variables included in the model, a model is judged good if this explanation, as measured, say, by the adjusted R^2 (= $\bar{R}^2$), is as high as possible.[2]

Theoretical consistency. No matter how high the goodness of fit measures, a model may not be judged good if one or more coefficients have the wrong signs. Thus, in the demand function for a commodity if the price coefficient has a positive sign (positively sloping demand curve!), or if the income coefficient has a negative sign (unless the good happens to be an inferior good), we must look at such results with great suspicion even if the R^2 of the model is high, say, 0.92. In short, in constructing a model we should have some theoretical underpinning to it; "measurement without theory" often can lead to very disappointing results.

Predictive power. As Milton Friedman, the Nobel laureate, notes: "the only relevant test of the validity of a hypothesis [model] is comparison of its pre-

---

[1] A. C. Harvey, *The Economic Analysis of Time Series*, Wiley, New York, 1981, pp. 5–7. The following discussion leans heavily on this material. See also D. F. Hendry and J. F. Richard, "On the Formulation of Empirical Models in Dynamic Econometrics," *Journal of Econometrics*, vol. 20, pp. 3–33, October 1982.

[2] Besides R^2, there are other criteria that have been used from time to time to judge the goodness of fit of a model. For an accessible discussion of these other criteria, see G. S. Maddala, *Introduction to Econometrics*, Macmillan, New York, 1988, pp. 425–429.

diction with experience."[3] Thus, in choosing between the monetarist and Keynesian models of the economy, by this criterion, one would choose the model whose theoretical predictions are borne out by actual experience.

Although there is no unique path to a good model, the reader is well advised to keep these criteria in mind in developing an econometric model.

13.2 TYPES OF SPECIFICATION ERRORS

As noted previously, a model should be parsimonious in that it should include key variables suggested by theory and relegate minor influences to the error term u. In this section we consider several ways in which a model can be deficient, which we label **specification errors.** Now we consider several types of specification errors.

Omitting a Relevant Variable: "Underfitting" a Model

As noted in the introduction to this chapter, sometimes a researcher omits one or more explanatory variables that should have been included in the model for a variety of reasons. What are the consequences of such an omission for our ordinary least squares (OLS) estimating procedure?

To be specific, let us revert to the U.S. import expenditure function for the period 1968 to 1987 first given in Eq. (6.50) and subsequently further discussed in Chapter 12. Let us suppose the "true" import expenditure function is as follows:

$$Y_t = B_1 + B_2 X_{2t} + B_3 X_{3t} + u_t \tag{13.1}$$

where

Y = the expenditure on imports

X_2 = the personal disposable income (PDI)

X_3 = the time or trend variable taking values of $1, 2, \ldots$, up to 20

Equation (13.1) states that besides PDI there is another variable, X_3, which also affects the expenditure on imports. It could be a variable such as population, taste, technology, etc., which we represent by a "catch-all" variable, time or trend.[4]

But instead of estimating the regression (13.1), we estimate the following function:

$$Y_t = A_1 + A_2 X_{2t} + v_t \tag{13.2}$$

---

[3] Milton Friedman, "The Methodology of Positive Economics," in *Essays in Positive Economics,* University of Chicago Press, 1953, p. 7.

[4] In time series data it is a common practice to introduce the trend variable to represent the influence of other variables which cannot be precisely pinpointed.

which is the same as Eq. (13.1), except that it excludes the "relevant" variable X_3. Note that v like u is a stochastic error term. Also, notice that we are using the Bs to represent the parameters in the "true" regression and the As to represent the parameters in the "incorrectly specified" regression: Equation (13.2) in relation to Eq. (13.1) is misspecified. As a matter of fact, Eq. (6.50) is simply Eq. (13.2), and therefore if Eq. (13.1) is the correct model, we have committed the specification error of excluding an important variable from the model. What are the consequences of this misspecification, which can be called the **omitted variable bias.** We first state the consequences of dropping the variable X_3 from the model in general terms and then illustrate them with the import expenditure data.

The consequences of omitting X_3 can be as follows:

1. If the omitted, or left-out, variable X_3 is correlated with the included variable X_2, a_1 and a_2 are *biased*; that is, their average, or expected, values do not coincide with the true values.[5] Symbolically,

$$E(a_1) \neq B_1 \quad \text{and} \quad E(a_2) \neq B_2$$

where E is the expectations operator (see Chapter 2). As a matter of fact, it can be shown that[6]

$$E(a_2) = B_2 + B_3 b_{32} \tag{13.3}$$

$$E(a_1) = B_1 + B_3(\overline{X}_3 - b_{32}\overline{X}_2) \tag{13.4}$$

where b_{32} is the slope coefficient in the regression of the omitted variable X_3 on the included variable X_2. Obviously, unless the last term in Equation (13.3) is zero, a_2 will be a biased estimator, the extent of the bias given by the last term. If both B_3 and b_{32} are positive, a_2 will have an *upward bias*—on the average it will overestimate the true B_2. On the other hand, if B_3 is positive and b_{32} is negative, or vice versa, a_2 will be *biased downward*—on the average it will underestimate the true B_2. Similarly, a_1 will be upward biased if the last term in the model (13.4) is positive and downward biased if it is negative.

2. In addition a_1 and a_2 are also *inconsistent*; that is, no matter how large the sample size is, the bias does not disappear generally.

3. If X_2 and X_3 are not correlated, b_{32} will be zero. Then, as the model (13.3) shows, a_2 is unbiased. It is consistent as well. [As noted in Chapter 4, if an estimator is unbiased (which is a small sample property), it is also *consistent* (which is a large sample property). But the converse is not true; estimators can be consistent but may not be necessarily unbiased.] But a_1 still remains

---

[5] A technical point: But shouldn't X_2 and X_3 be uncorrelated by the "no multicollinearity" assumption? Recall from Chap. 7 that the assumption that there is no perfect collinearity among the X variables refers to the population regression (PRF) only; there is no guarantee in a given sample that the Xs may not be correlated.

[6] The proof can be found in Damodar N. Gujarati, *Basic Econometrics*, 2d ed., McGraw-Hill, New York, 1988, p. 209.

biased, unless $\overline{X}_3$ is zero in the model (13.4). Even in this case the consequences mentioned in (4) to (6) below hold true.[7]

4. The error variance estimated from Eq. (13.2) is a biased estimator of the true error variance σ^2. In other words, the error variance estimated from the true model (13.1) and that estimated from the misspecified model (13.2) will not be the same; the former is an unbiased estimator of the true σ^2, but the latter is not.

5. In addition, the conventionally estimated variance of a_2 ($= \hat{\sigma}^2 / \sum x_{2t}^2$) is a biased estimator of the variance of the true estimator b_2. Even in the case where b_{32} is zero, that is, X_2 and X_3 are uncorrelated, this variance remains biased, for it can be shown that[8]

$$E[\text{var}(a_2)] = \text{var}(b_2) + \frac{B_3^2 \sum x_{3i}^2}{(n-2) \sum x_{2i}^2} \tag{13.5}$$

That is, the expected value of the variance of a_2 is not equal to the variance b_2: Since the second term in Equation (13.5) will always be positive (why?), $\text{var}(a_2)$ will on the average overestimate the true variance of b_2. This means it will have a positive bias.

6. As a result, the usual confidence interval and hypothesis-testing procedures are unreliable. In the case of Eq. (13.5), the confidence interval will be wider, and therefore one may tend to accept the hypothesis that the true value of the coefficient is zero (or any other null hypothesis) more frequently than the true situation demands.

Although we have not presented the proofs of the preceding propositions, we will illustrate some of these consequences with our import expenditure function.

Example 13.1. The import demand function revisited. Using the data given in Table 6-2 and adding the data on the trend variable, the empirical counterpart of Eq. (13.1) is as follows:

$$\hat{Y}_t = -859.92 + 0.6470 X_{2t} - 23.195 X_{3t}$$

$$\text{se} = (111.96) \qquad (0.0745) \qquad (4.2704) \tag{13.6}$$

$$t = (-7.6807) \qquad (8.6803) \qquad (-5.4316)$$

$$\hat{\sigma}^2 = 184.05; \qquad R^2 = 0.9776; \qquad \overline{R}^2 = 0.9750; \qquad d = 1.36$$

Whereas the results of the misspecified regression (13.2), which are already given in (6.50) and reproduced here, are as follows:

---

[7] A priori, however, there is no reason to assume $\overline{X}_3$ to be zero.

[8] For proof, see Jan Kmenta, *Elements of Econometrics*, 2d ed., Macmillan, New York, 1986, pp. 444–445. *Note*: This is true only when $b_{32} = 0$, which is not the case in our example, as can be seen from Eq. (13.8), which follows.

$$\hat{Y}_t = -261.09 + 0.2452X_{2t}$$

$$\text{se} = (31.327) \qquad (0.0148) \qquad\qquad\qquad (13.7)$$

$$t = (-8.334) \qquad (16.6160)$$

$$\hat{\sigma}^2 = 475.48; \qquad R^2 = 0.9388; \qquad \bar{R}^2 = 0.9354; \qquad d = 0.5951$$

Note several features of the two regressions.

1. The misspecified equation (13.7) shows that as PDI increases by a dollar, on the average expenditure on imported goods goes up by about 24 cents; that is, the marginal propensity of the import expenditure is 24 cents. On the other hand, the true model (13.6) shows that allowing for the influence of the trend variable, if the PDI increases by a dollar, on the average expenditure on imported goods goes up by about 65 cents. In the present case, then, the misspecified equation *underestimates* the true marginal propensity, that is, it is *downward biased*. The nature of this downward bias can be easily seen if we regress X_3 on X_2 to obtain the slope coefficient b_{32}. The results are

$$\hat{X}_{3t} = -25.817 \quad + 0.0173X_{2t}$$

$$t = (-23.999) \qquad (34.177) \qquad r^2 = 0.9848 \qquad\qquad (13.8)$$

Thus, the slope coefficient b_{32} is 0.0173. Now from Eq. (13.6) we see that the estimated $B_2 = 0.6470$ and $B_3 = -23.195$. Therefore, from model (13.3) we obtain[9]

$$B_2 + B_3b_{32} = 0.6470 + (-23.195)(0.0173)$$

$$= 0.2452[10]$$

which is about the value obtained from incorrectly specified equation (13.7). Note that it is the product of B_3 (the true value of the omitted variable) and b_{32} (the slope coefficient in the regression of the omitted variable on the included variable) that determines the nature of the bias, upward or downward. Thus, by incorrectly dropping the variable X_3 from the model, as in Eq. (13.2), or its empirical counterpart Eq. (13.7), we are not only neglecting the impact of X_3 on Y (B_3) but also the impact of X_3 on X_2 (b_{32}). The "lonely" variable X_2 included in the model thus has to carry the "burden" of this omission, which, so to speak, prevents it from showing its true impact on Y (0.6470 vs. 0.2452).

2. The intercept term is also biased, but here it overestimates the true intercept (note -261 is greater than -859).

3. The error variance estimated from the two models is also substantially different, 184 vs. 475.

4. The standard errors of the intercept and slope coefficient (of X_2) are also substantially different between the two regressions.

---

[9] Note the slightly technical point. Since in the true model b_2 and b_3 are unbiased estimators of true B_2 and B_3, we are using the estimated values of the parameters in the model (13.3); that is, in fact we are using the expression $b_2 + b_3b_{32}$ instead of Eq. (13.3).

[10] Since in the true model $E(b_3) = B_3$, we are using the computed b_3 value in this expression.

All these results are in accord with the theoretical results of misspecification just discussed above. The reader can see at once that if we were to engage in hypothesis testing based upon the misspecified equation (13.7), our conclusions will be of dubious values, to say the least. There is little doubt that dropping relevant variables from a model can have very serious consequences. Therefore, in developing a model, utmost care should be exercised. This is why it is very important that in developing a model for empirical analysis, we should pay close attention to the appropriate theory underlying the phenomenon under study so that all theoretically relevant variables are included in the model. If such relevant variables are excluded from the model, then we are "underfitting" or "underspecifying" the model; in other words, we are omitting some important variables.

Before proceeding further, notice the Durbin-Watson d values in the "correctly" specified model (13.6) and the "incorrectly" specified model (13.7), namely, 1.36 vs. 0.5951. Why such a difference? What does it indicate? We will answer these questions shortly.

Example 13.2. Economies of scale in the brokerage industry, once again In Example 11.7 we saw that the economies of scale found by the New York Stock Exchange (NYSE) were spurious rather than real because of the problem of heteroscedasticity arising from the presence of small and large firms in the sample [see Eq. (11.26)]: When the transaction cost was divided by the (transaction) size variable, we showed in Eq. (11.27) how the so-called economies of scale evaporated.

To show that the economies of scale observed were spurious and not real, we can look at this example from the perspective of specification error. Suppose we continue with the NYSE regression (11.26) but now add to it six dummy variables representing firms of different sizes. The resulting regression results are given in Table 13-1. The striking thing about the results given in Table 13-1 is that the quadratic term is *positive* (and statistically significant at the 10% level), suggesting that the total cost is increasing at an increasing rate, which is in stark contrast to the NYSE finding in the regression (11.26). In other words, there are in fact diseconomies of scale in the brokerage industry. As the results in Table 13-1 clearly show, several dummy coefficients are statistically significant, suggesting that the NYSE had in fact committed a specification error by not explicitly taking into account the size of brokerage transactions.

Inclusion of Irrelevant Variables: "Overfitting" a Model

Sometimes researchers adopt the "kitchen sink" approach by including all sorts of variables in the model, whether or not they are theoretically dictated. The idea behind "overfitting" or "overspecifying" the model (i.e., including unnecessary variables) is the philosophy that so long as you include the the-

TABLE 13-1
NYSE brokerage cost function

Explanatory variable	Coefficient	t
Intercept	384.539	1.906*
X_2	26.760	8.120§
X_2^2	0.877×10^{-6}	1.886*
D_1	670.530	1.775*
D_2	1604.478	2.730‡
D_3	−202.214	0.185
D_4	5760.251	2.490†
D_5	2543.144	0.710
D_6	19488.135	3.690§

$R^2 = 0.94;$ $n = 347$ firms

Sources: Richard R. West and Seha M. Tinic, "Minimum Commission Rates on New York Stock Exchange Transactions," *Bell Journal of Economics*, vol 2, no 2, p. 593, Autumn 1971.

* Significant at 0.10 level.   † Significant at 0.01 level.

‡ Significant at 0.005 level.   § Significant at 0.0005 level.

D_1 = 1 for 40,000 to 100,000 transactions D_5 = 1 for 1,000,000 to 1,800,000 transactions

D_2 = 1 for 100,000 to 200,000 transactions D_6 = 1 for over 1,800,000 transactions.

D_3 = 1 for 200,000 to 500,000 transactions X_2 = the number of transactions.

D_4 = 1 for 500,000 to 1,000,000 transactions

oretically relevant variables, inclusion of one or more unnecessary or "nuisance" variables would not hurt—unnecessary in the sense that there is no solid theory that says they should be included. Such irrelevant variables are often included inadvertently because the researcher is not sure about their role in the model. And this will happen if the theory underlying a particular phenomenon is not well developed. In that case inclusion of such variables will certainly increase R^2 (and adjusted R^2 if the absolute t value of the coefficient of the additional variable is greater than 1), which might increase the predictive power of the model.

What are the consequences of including unnecessary variables in the model, which may be called the (inclusion of) **irrelevant variable bias**. Again, to bring home the point, we consider the case of simple two- and three-variable models. Now suppose that

$$Y_i = B_1 + B_2 X_{2i} + u_i \tag{13.9}$$

is the correctly specified model, but a researcher adds the superfluous variable X_3 and estimates the following model:

$$Y_i = A_1 + A_2 X_{2i} + A_3 X_{3i} + v_i \tag{13.10}$$

Here the specification error consists in overfitting the model, that is, including the unnecessary variable X_3, unnecessary in the sense that a priori it has no effect on Y. The consequences of estimating the regression (13.10) instead of the true model (13.9) are as follows:

1. The OLS estimators of the "incorrect" model (13.10) are *unbiased* (as well as consistent.) That is, $E(a_1) = B_1$, $E(a_2) = B_2$, and $E(a_3) = 0$ (*Note*: Since X_3 does not belong in the true model, the value of B_3 is expected to be zero.)
2. The estimator of σ^2 obtained from regression (13.10) is correctly estimated.
3. The standard confidence interval and hypothesis-testing procedure on the basis of the t and F tests remain valid.
4. However, the as estimated from the regression (13.10) are *inefficient*—their variances will be generally larger than those of the bs estimated from the true model (13.9). As a result, the confidence intervals based on the standard errors of as will be larger than those based on the standard errors of bs of the true model, even though the former are acceptable for the usual hypothesis-testing procedure. What will happen is that the true coefficients will not be estimated as precisely as if we had used the correct model (13.9). In short, the OLS estimators are LUE (linear unbiased estimators), but *not* BLUE.

Notice the difference between the two types of specification errors we have considered thus far. If we exclude a relevant variable (the case of under-fitting), the coefficients of variables retained in the model are generally biased as well as inconsistent, the error variance is incorrectly estimated, the standard errors of estimators are biased, and therefore the usual hypothesis-testing procedure becomes invalid. On the other hand, including an irrelevant variable in the model (the case of overfitting), still gives us unbiased and consistent estimates of the coefficients of the true model, the error variance is correctly estimated, and the standard hypothesis-testing procedure is still valid. The major penalty we pay for the inclusion of the superfluous variable(s) is that the estimated variances of the coefficients are larger, and as a result, our probability inferences about the true parameters are less precise because the confidence intervals tend to be wider. In some cases we will accept the hypothesis that a true coefficient value is zero because of the wider confidence interval; that is, we will fail to recognize significant relationships between the dependent variable and the explanatory variable(s).

An unwarranted conclusion from the preceding discussion is that it is better to include irrelevant variables than to exclude the relevant ones. But this philosophy should not be encouraged because, as just noted, addition of unnecessary variables will lead to loss in efficiency of the estimators (i.e., larger standard errors) and may also lead to the problem of multicollinearity (why?), not to mention the loss of degrees of freedom. That is why.

In general, the best approach is to include only explanatory variables that on theoretical grounds *directly* influence the dependent variable and are not accounted for by other included variables.[11]

Example 13.3. Economies of scale in the brokerage industry, again. Along with Eq. (11.26), the NYSE also estimated the following regression:[12]

$$\hat{Y}_i = 381{,}229 + 33.3445X_i - (2.926 \times 10^{-6})\, X_i^2 + (2.6873 \times 10^{-13})\, X_i^3$$

$$t = (2.0900) \quad (18.2318) \quad (-1.6939) \quad\quad (1.0724)$$

$$R^2 = 0.934 \quad (13.11)$$

where Y = the total cost and X = the number of share transactions.

Since the cubic term in the model (13.11) was staistically insignificant, the NYSE thought that it was a superfluous variable. Hence, it chose to rely on the regression (11.26) to justify its finding that there were economies of scale in the brokerage industry.

Accepting the NYSE regression results on their face value, notice how the inclusion of the "unnecessary" cubic term has increased the standard error of the quadratic term, thereby reducing its t value. This is all in accord with the theoretical consequences just discussed. Of course, we should take the NYSE regression results with a grain of salt because we have already seen that this regression suffers from the heteroscedasticity problem, or omission of a significant variable (size) problem, or both. As a result, the computed standard errors and the t values may not be reliable.

Incorrect Functional Form

We now consider a different type of specification error, which we illustrate with our import expenditure function (13.1). Assume that variables Y, X_2, and X_3 included in the model are theoretically the correct variables. Now consider the following specification of the import expenditure function:

$$\ln Y_t = A_1 + A_2 \ln X_{2t} + A_3 X_{3t} + v_t \tag{13.12}$$

The variables that enter the model in Eq. (13.1) also enter the regression (13.12), except the functional relationship between the variables is different; in the regression (13.12) the (natural) logarithm of Y is a linear function of the (natural) logarithm of X_2 and is a linear function of X_3. Note that in Eq. (13.12) A_2 measures the elasticity of import expenditure with respect to the PDI whereas in Eq. (13.1) B_2 simply measures the rate of change (slope) of import expenditure with respect to the PDI. Obviously, the two are different, as we

---

[11] Michael D. Intriligator, *Econometric Models, Techniques and Applications*, Prentice-Hall, Englewood Cliffs, N.J., 1978, p. 189. Recall also the Occam's razor principle.

[12] These results are reproduced from Richard R. West and Seha M. Tinic, "Minimum Commission Rates on New York Stock Exchange," *Bell Journal of Economics*, vol. 2, no. 2, p. 591, Autumn 1971.

know from Chapter 8: To obtain elasticity of Y with respect to X_2, we have to multiply B_2 by the ratio X_2/Y, which will obviously depend on the values of X_2 and Y that are chosen. For the model (13.12), however, this elasticity coefficient remains the same ($= A_2$) no matter at which X_2 we measure it. Also, in Eq. (13.1), B_3 gives the (absolute) rate of change of import expenditure per time period, whereas the coefficient of the trend variable in the regression (13.12) gives the relative or percentage rate of growth in Y (recall the semilog model from Chapter 8). Again, the two are not the same.

Now the dilemma in choosing between the models (13.1) and (13.12) is that economic theory is usually not strong enough to tell us the functional form in which the dependent and explanatory variables are related. Therefore, if the regression (13.12) is in fact the true model and we fit Eq. (13.1) to the data, we are likely to commit as much a specification error as if the situation were converse, although in both cases the economically relevant variables are included. Without going into theoretical fine points, if we choose the wrong functional form, the estimated coefficients may be biased estimates of the true coefficients.

Example 13.4. The log-linear import demand function. To give a glimpse of this, we present the results of our import expenditure data based on the model (13.12), which are as follows:

$$\widehat{\ln Y_t} = -23.727 + 3.8975 \ln X_{2t} - 0.0526 X_{3t}$$

$$\text{se} = (4.4314) \quad (0.6031) \quad (0.0167) \tag{13.13}$$

$$t = (-5.3542) \quad (6.4623) \quad (-3.1540)$$

$$R^2 = 0.9763; \quad \bar{R}^2 = 0.9735; \quad d = 1.29$$

As this regression shows, the elasticity of import expenditure with respect to PDI is about 3.9 percent; that is, holding other things constant, a 1 percent increase in personal disposable income leads on the average to ≈ 3.9 percent increase in import expenditure. For the linear model (13.1), however, the elasticity computed at the mean values of Y and X_2 is ≈ 5.36, which is obviously much higher than that obtained from the logarithmic model.[13] Also, the model (13.6), which is the estimator of the model (13.1), shows that import expenditure has been decreasing at the rate of $\approx \$23$ billions per year over the time period of the study, whereas Eq. (13.13) shows that it has been decreasing at the rate of ≈ 5.3 percent per year. Dimensionally, these two numbers are not comparable. Also, the R^2 values of Eqs. (13.6) and (13.13) are not comparable because dependent variables in the two models are not the same.

This example shows clearly that in developing a model it is not only important that all theoretically relevant variables that should be included in

---

[13] This elasticity is computed from $b_2 \, (\bar{X}_2/\bar{Y})$, where $\bar{X}_2$ and $\bar{Y}$ are the sample mean values of X_2 and Y.

the model are there but that the functional form in which they interact with each other is also important. In the two-variable regression it is easy to choose the functional form from the visual inspection of the scattergram between dependent and explanatory variables, but once we leave the "comfortable" world of the two-variable model, it is not possible to plot Y against all explanatory variables simultaneously. Unfortunately, the written paper is only a two-dimensional entity. Later on in the section on diagnostics, we will mention a detection device, the so-called Box-Cox transformations, even though we will not pursue it further because of its mathematical demands.

Although there are several other types of specification errors, we will not consider them here for lack of space. But the preceding discussion is warning enough that in developing a suitable model for empirical analysis, one has to be extremely careful. Of course, there is no cause for despair because econometric skills are primarily experience based and will come along with time.

13.3 DETECTING SPECIFICATION ERRORS: TESTS OF SPECIFICATION ERRORS

To know the consequences of specification errors is one thing, but to find out that we have committed such errors is quite another thing, for we (hopefully) do not deliberately set out to commit such errors. Often specification errors arise inadvertently, perhaps from our inability to formulate the model as precisely as possible because the underlying theory is weak, or we do not have the right kind of data to test the theoretically correct model, or the theory is silent about the functional form in which the dependent variable is related to explanatory variables. The practical issue is not that such errors are made, for they sometimes are, but how to detect them. Once it is found that specification errors have been made, the remedies often suggest themselves. If, e.g., it can be shown that a variable is inappropriately omitted from a model, the obvious remedy is to include that variable in the analysis, assuming of course that data on that variable are available. We now consider several tests of specification errors.

Detecting the Presence of Unnecessary Variables

Suppose we have the following four-variable model:

$$Y_i = B_1 + B_2 X_{2i} + B_3 X_{3i} + B_4 X_{4i} + u_i \tag{13.14}$$

Now if theory says that all three X variables determine Y, we should keep them in the model even though after empirical testing we find that the coefficient of one or more of the X variables is not statistically significant. Therefore, the question of irrelevant variables does not arise in this case. However, sometimes we have *control variables* in the model which are only there to prevent omitted variable bias. It may then be the case that if the control variables are not statistically significant and dropping them does not substantially alter our point estimates or hypothesis test results, then dropping them may clarify the model. We can then drop them but mention that they were tried and made no difference.[14] Suppose in the model (13.14) X_4 is the control variable in the sense that we are not absolutely sure whether it really belongs in the model. One simple way to find this out is to estimate the regression (13.14) and test the significance of b_4, the estimator of B_4. Under the null hypothesis that $B_4 = 0$, we know that $t = b_4/\text{se}(b_4)$ follows the t distribution with $(n - 4)$ d.f. (why?). Therefore, if the computed t value does not exceed the critical t value at the chosen level of significance, we do not reject the null hypothesis, in which case the variable X_4 is probably a superfluous variable.[15] Of course, if we reject the null hypothesis, the variable probably belongs to the model.

Example 13.5. The NYSE Regression, Eq. (13.11). This was precisely the logic behind the NYSE's rejection of the regression (13.11) in favor of Eq. (11.26), because in Eq. (13.11) the t value of the cubic term was only 1.0724: Note this regression was based on a sample size of 347 firms. Therefore, the critical t values, using the normal approximation to the t distribution (why?), are 1.96 (5% level) and about 1.65 (10% level). (But keep in mind our warning regarding the heteroscedasticity problem in the NYSE regression.)

But suppose we are not sure that both X_3 and X_4 are relevant variables. In this case we would like to test the null hypothesis that $B_3 = B_4 = 0$. But this can be easily done by the F test discussed in Chapter 7. (For details, see Chapter 14, Section 14.1 on restricted least squares).

Thus, detecting the presence of irrelevant variable(s) is not a difficult task. *But it is very important to remember that in carrying out these tests of specifications, we have a specific model in mind, which we accept as the "true" model.* Given that model, then, we can find out whether one or more X variables are really relevant by the usual t and F tests. But bear in mind that we should not use t and F tests to build a model *iteratively*; that is, we cannot say that initially Y is related to X_2 because b_2 is statistically significant and then expand the model to include X_3 and decide to keep that variable in the model if b_3 turns out to be statistically significant.[16] This strategy, called **data mining,** is not recommended, for if a priori X_3 belonged in the model to begin with, it

---

[14] In this case the researcher should inform the reader that the results including the dropped variables could be made available on request.

[15] We say "probably" because if there is collinearity among X variables, then, as we know, standard errors tend to be inflated relative to the values of the coefficients, thereby reducing estimated t values.

[16] This procedure is known as *stepwise regression*. For a critical review of this subject and the types of stepwise regressions, see Norman Draper and Harry Smith, *Applied Regression Analysis*, 2d ed., Wiley, 1981, Chap. 6.

should have been introduced. Excluding X_3 in the initial regression would then lead to the omission-of-relevant-variable bias with the potentially serious consequences that we have already seen. This point cannot be overemphasized: *Theory must be the guide to model building; measurement without theory can lead up a blind alley.*

Tests for Omitted Variables and Incorrect Functional Forms

The prescription that theory should be the underpinning of any model begs the question: What is theoretically the correct model? Thus, in our Phillips curve example discussed in Chapter 8, although the rate of change of wages (Y) and the unemployment rate (X) are expected to be negatively related, are they?

$$Y_t = B_1 + B_2 X_t + u_t \qquad B_2 < 0$$

or

$$\ln Y_t = B_1 + B_2 \ln X_t + u_t \qquad B_2 < 0$$

or

$$Y_t = B_1 + B_2 \frac{1}{X_t} + u_t \qquad B_2 > 0$$

or some other functional relationship. As noted in the introduction to this chapter, this is one of those questions which cannot be answered definitely. Pragmatically, we proceed as follows. Based upon theory or introspection and prior empirical work, we develop a model that we believe captures the essence of the subject under study. We then subject the model to empirical testing. After we obtain the results, we begin the postmortem, keeping in mind the criteria of a good model discussed earlier. It is at this stage that we come to know if the chosen model is adequate. In determining model adequacy, we look at some broad features of the results, such as:

1. R^2 and adjusted R^2 $(\overline{R}^2)$
2. The estimated t ratios
3. Signs of the estimated coefficients in relation to their prior expectations
4. Durbin-Watson d or the runs statistic
5. Forecasting or prediction error

If these diagnostics are reasonably good, we accept the chosen model as a fair representation of reality.

   By the same token, if the results do not look encouraging because the R^2 is too low, or very few coefficients are statistically significant or have the correct signs, or the Durbin-Watson d value is too low (suggesting possibly positive autocorrelation in the data), or the out-of-sample forecasting error is relatively large, then we begin to worry about model adequacy and to look for remedies: Perhaps we have omitted an important variable, or have used the wrong functional form, or do not have the first differenced time series (see Chapter 12) to remove serial correlation, etc. To aid us in determining whether model adequacy is due to one or more of these problems, we can use some of the methods discussed now.

Examination of residuals. As noted previously, examination of residuals e_i (or e_t, in time series) is a good visual diagnostic to detect autocorrelation or heteroscedasticity. But these residuals can also be examined for model speci-fication errors, such as omission of an important variable or incorrect func-tional form. To see this, return to our models (13.1) and (13.2); the first relates import expenditure to PDI and time trend and the latter drops the trend variable. Now if Eq. (13.1) is in fact the true model in that the trend variable X_3 belongs in the model, but we estimate model (13.2), then we are implicitly saying that the error term in the model (13.2) is

$$v_t = B_3 X_{3t} + u_t \tag{13.15}$$

because it will reflect not only the truly random term u, but also the variable X_3. No wonder in this case residuals estimated from Eq. (13.2) will show some systematic pattern which is due to the excluded variable X_3. This can be seen very vividly from Figure 13-1, which plots the residuals from the inappropri-

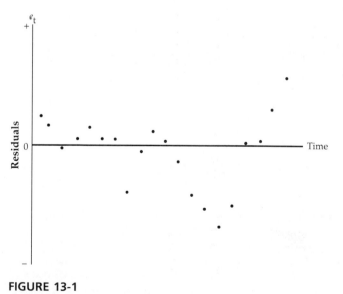

FIGURE 13-1
Residuals from the regression (13.7).

ately estimated regression (13.2) [i.e., (13.7)] of our import expenditure example. As this figure reveals undoubtedly, the residuals do not show a random pattern. But the picture is somewhat different if we plot the residuals estimated from the true model [Eq. (13-1)], which is estimated by Eq. (13.6) (see Figure 13-2).

Now the residuals are much more randomly distributed than before. But even then the scattergram exhibits a discernible pattern. Have we left out any other variable? It is possible that an important variable was not left out, but that the functional form Eq. (13.1), or its empirical counterpart (13.6), is incorrectly specified. Unfortunately, our theory is not robust enough to tell us that.

Example 13.6. Another specification of the import demand function. Suppose that we modify our model (13.1) as follows:

$$Y_t = B_1 + B_2X_{2t} + B_3X_{3t} + B_4X_{3t}^2 + u_t \qquad (13.16)$$

where we have added the squared term in the trend variable, X_{3t}. Recall from Chapter 8 that the regression (13.16) is a second-degree polynominal model in X_3.

The regression results are as follows:

$$\hat{Y}_t = -764.68 + 0.5984\,X_{2t} - 26.549X_{3t} + 0.2912X_{3t}^2$$

$$\text{se} = (89.475) \quad (0.0585) \quad (3.3910) \quad (0.0804) \qquad (13.17)$$

$$t = (-8.5463) \quad (10.231) \quad (-7.8292) \quad (3.6236)$$

$$R^2 = 0.9877; \quad \overline{R}^2 = 0.9854; \quad d = 2.0983$$

The interpretation of this model is, holding other things the same, as the PDI goes up by a dollar, the import expenditure on the average goes up by ≈ 60 cents; that is, the marginal propensity to spend on imports is ≈ 0.60 cents, which is not statistically very much different from the one obtained for the model (13.6), which was ≈ 65 cents (can you demonstrate this formally?). In model (13.6) without the squared trend term we saw that on the average the import expenditure was declining at the *constant* rate of $\approx \$24$ billion per year. In the model (13.17), on the other hand, the import expenditure is not decreasing at a constant rate but at a variable rate.[17] But it is interesting to note that the residuals from the model (13.17) are now practically randomly distributed, as can be seen from Figure 13-3.

The Durbin-Watson d statistic once again. In Chapter 12 we discussed the role of the Durbin-Watson d statistic in detecting autocorrelation. But the same

---

[17] If you have a general quadratic equation like $Y = a + bX + cX^2$, then whether Y increases at an increasing or decreasing rate when X changes will generally depend upon the signs of a, b, c, and the value of X. On this, see Alpha C. Chiang, *Fundamental Methods of Mathematical Economics*, 3d ed., McGraw-Hill, New York, 1984, Chap. 9.

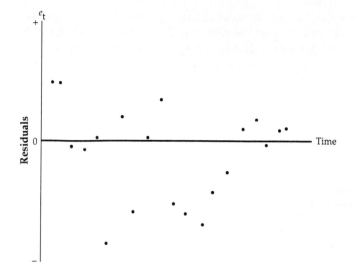

FIGURE 13-2
Residuals from the regression (13.6).

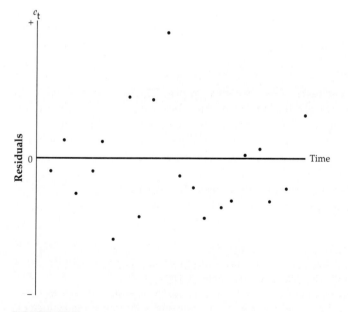

FIGURE 13-3
Residuals from the regression (13.17).

d statistic can also be used to test for specification errors. But how do we know which is which? In other words, how do we find out whether the estimated d value is reflective of pure autocorrelation or of pure specification error? To answer this question, let us consider the d values computed for the various specifications of the import expenditure functions we have considered so far.

Model	d value	Is d significant?
(13.7)	0.5951	Yes*
(13.6)	1.3633	Indecisive†
(13.17)	2.0983	No‡

Note: * For $n = 20$ and $k = 1$, $d_L = 1.201$ and $d_U = 1.411$ (5% level)
   † For $n = 20$ and $k = 2$, $d_L = 1.100$ and $d_U = 1.537$ (5% level)
   ‡ For $n = 20$ and $k = 3$, $d_L = 0.998$ and $d_U = 1.676$ (5% level)

As can be seen from this table, when we go from the model with no trend variable to the model that includes the trend variable and the one that also includes the squared trend variable, the autocorrelation "supposedly" found in the first two models disappears in the third model. We can take the d value in this example more as a measure of specification error than as pure autocorrelation.[18]

The point to note is that sometimes the d statistic, if significant, can suggest the presence of autocorrelation, especially if the data are time series. However, it can also be an indication of specification errors. A simple test of this, as in our illustrative example, is to find out if a significant d statistic becomes insignificant if the original model is respecified, e.g., model (13.7) vs. model (13.17).

Other specification error tests. The residual graph and the Durbin-Watson d test are comparatively simple tests to use. But there are several other tests, with varying degrees of statistical complexity, that we mention but do not discuss because their discussion is beyond the scope of this introductory book. Some of these tests are as follows:[19]

1. **Ramsey's RESET** test (regression error specification test)
2. The likelihood ratio test
3. The **Wald** test

---

[18] There is a somewhat formal method of testing this, which is discussed in Damodar N. Gujarati, *Basic Econometrics*, 2d ed., McGraw-Hill, New York, 1988, p. 410.

[19] Some of these tests are discussed in Damodar N. Gujarati, *Basic Econometrics*, 2d ed., McGraw-Hill, New York, 1988, Chap. 13. A somewhat advanced discussion of these tests can be found in Thomas B. Fomby, R. Carter Hill, and Stanley R. Johnson, *Advanced Econometric Methods*, Springer-Verlag, New York, 1984, Chap. 18.

4. The **Lagrange multiplier** test
5. The **Hausman** test
6. The **Box-Cox transformations** (to determine the functional form of the regression model)

13.4 SUMMARY

The major points discussed in this chapter can be summarized as follows:

1. The classical linear regression model assumes that the model used in empirical analysis is "correctly specified."
2. The term *correct specification* of a model can mean several things, such as:
   a. No theoretically relevant variable has been excluded from the model.
   b. No unnecessary or irrelevant variables are included in the model.
   c. The functional form of the model is correct.
3. If a theoretically relevant variable(s) has been excluded from the model, the coefficients of the variables retained in the model are generally biased as well as inconsistent, and the error variance and the standard errors of the OLS estimators are biased. As a result, the conventional t and F tests remain of questionable value, to say the least.
4. Similar consequences ensue if we use the wrong functional form.
5. The consequences of including irrelevant variables(s) in the model are less serious in that estimated coefficients still remain unbiased and consistent, the error variance and standard errors of the estimators are correctly estimated, and the conventional hypothesis-testing procedure is still valid. The major penalty we pay is that estimated standard errors tend to be relatively large, which means parameters of the model are estimated rather imprecisely. As a result, confidence intervals tend to be somewhat wider.
6. In view of the potential seriousness of specification errors, we considered in this chapter several diagnostic tools to aid us in finding out if we have the specification error problem in any concrete situation. These tools include a graphical examination of the residuals and the Durbin-Watson d statistic. We mentioned several other tests, such as Ramsey's RESET test, the Lagrange multiplier test, the Hausman test, and the Box-Cox transformation.[20]

Since the search for a theoretically correct model can be exasperating, we considered in this chapter several practical criteria that we should keep in mind in this search, such as (1) parsimony, (2) identifiability, (3) goodness of fit, (4) theoretical consistency, and (5) predictive power.

In the ultimate analysis, model building is probably both an art and a

---

[20] For a discussion of these and other tests, see L. G. Godfrey, *Misspecification Tests in Econometrics: The Lagrange Multiplier Principle and Other Approaches*, Cambridge University Press, New York, 1988.

science. A sound knowledge of theoretical econometrics and the availability of an efficient computer program are not enough to ensure success.[21]

Key Terms and Concepts

The key terms and concepts introduced in this chapter are:

Attributes of a good model
  a) parsimony (principle of parsimony)
  b) identifiability
  c) goodness of fit
  d) theoretical consistency
  e) predictive power
(Pure) specification errors and model misspecification errors
  a) underfitting a model (omitted variable bias)
  b) overfitting a model (inclusion of) irrelevant variable bias

  c) incorrect (wrong) functional form bias
Specification error tests
  a) unnecessary variables (data mining)
  b) tests for omitted variables and incorrect functional form
  c) the Durbin-Watson d statistic
  d) other tests (Ramsey's RESET; Lagrange multiplier; Hausman; Box-Cox transformations)

QUESTIONS

13.1. What is meant by specification errors?

13.2. What are the reasons for the occurrence of specification errors?

13.3. What are the attributes of a "good" econometric model?

13.4. What are different types of specification errors? Can one or more of these errors occur simultaneously?

13.5. What are the consequences of omitting a relevant variable(s) from a model?

13.6. When we say that a variable is "relevant" or "irrelevant," what do we mean?

13.7. What are the consequences of including irrelevant variables in the model?

13.8. "Omitting a relevant variable(s) from a model is more dangerous than including an irrelevant variable(s)." Do you agree? Why or why not?

13.9. In looking for the simple Keynesian multiplier, you regress the GNP on investment and find that there is some relationship. Now, thinking that it cannot hurt much, you include the "irrelevant" variable "state and local taxes." To your surprise, the investment variable loses its significance. How can an irrelevant variable do this?

13.10. What would you do if you find yourself in the bind of choosing between a model that satisfies all statistical criteria but does not satisfy economic theory and a model that fits established economic theory but does not fit many statistical criteria?

---

[21] C. W. J. Granger (ed.) *Modelling Economic Series: Readings in Econometric Methodology,* Clarendon, Oxford, U.K. 1990, p. 2. This is a fascinating book that presents the views of leading econometricians on the art and science of model building.

PROBLEMS

13.11. Consider the hypothetical cost and output data given in Table 8-5. Based upon these data, the following cost functions were estimated (see Table 13-2):

TABLE 13-2
Cost functions based on the data given in Table 8.5

Type of cost function	Intercept	X	X^2	X^3	R^2	d
Linear	166.467	19.933	—	—	0.8409	0.716
	se = (19.021)	(3.066)				
Quadratic	222.383	−8.025	2.542	—	0.9284	1.038
	se = (23.488)	(9.809)	(0.869)			
Cubic	141.767	63.478	−12.962	0.939	0.9983	2.70
	se = (6.375)	(4.778)	(0.986)	(0.059)		

The figures in parentheses are the estimated standard errors, X = output, and d = the Durbin-Watson statistic.

(a) For 10 observations and 1, 2, and 3 explanatory variables, what are the critical Durbin-Watson d values at $\alpha = 5\%$?
(b) Is there evidence of "autocorrelation" in the linear cost function? If there is, what is the implication in the present instance?
(c) Is there evidence of "autocorrelation" in the quadratic cost function? If so, what does that mean?
(d) Is there autocorrelation in the cubic cost function? If not, what can you say about the observed autocorrelation in linear and quadratic cost functions?
(e) What is the marginal cost of production in the three cost functions?
(f) Economically speaking, which cost function makes sense and why?

13.12. Table 13-3 gives data on the real gross product, labor input, and real capital input in the Taiwanese manufacturing sector for the years 1958 to 1972. Suppose the theoretically correct production function is of the Cobb-Douglas type, as follows:

$$\ln Y_t = B_1 + B_2 \ln X_{2t} + B_3 \ln X_{3t} + u_t$$

where ln = the natural log.

(a) Given the preceding data, estimate the Cobb-Douglas production function for Taiwan for the sample period and interpret the results.
(b) Suppose capital data were not initially available and therefore someone estimated the following production function:

$$\ln Y_t = A_1 + A_2 \ln X_{2t} + v_t$$

where v = an error term. What kind of specification error is incurred in this case? What are the consequences? Illustrate with the data at hand.

TABLE 13-3

Year	Y	X_2	X_3	X_4
1958	8911.4	281.5	120,753	1
1959	10,873.2	284.4	122,242	2
1960	11,132.5	289.0	125,263	3
1961	12,086.5	375.8	128,539	4
1962	12,767.5	375.2	131,427	5
1963	16,347.1	402.5	134,267	6
1964	19,542.7	478.0	139,038	7
1965	21,075.9	553.4	146,450	8
1966	23,052.0	616.7	153,714	9
1967	26,128.2	695.7	164,783	10
1968	29,563.7	790.3	176,864	11
1969	33,376.6	816.0	188,146	12
1970	38,354.3	848.4	205,841	13
1971	46,868.3	873.1	221,748	14
1972	54,308.0	999.2	239,715	15

Source: Thomas Pei-Fan Chen, "Economic Growth and Structural Change in Taiwan, 1952–1972, A Production Function Approach," unpublished Ph.D. thesis, Department of Economics, Graduate Center, City University of New York, June 1976, Table II.

Note Y = the real gross product, millions of NT $ (new Taiwan dollars)
  X_2 = the labor input, per thousand persons
  X_3 = the real capital input, millions of NT $
  X_4 = the time or trend variable.

(c) Now pretend that the data on labor input were not available initially and suppose you estimated the following model:

$$\ln Y_t = C_1 + C_2 \ln X_{3t} + w_t$$

where w = an error term. What are the consequences of this type of specification error? Illustrate with the data given in Table 13-3.

13.13. Continue with problem 13.12. Since the data are time series there is the possibility of autocorrelation in the data. Check on this possibility with the Durbin-Watson d statistic. If there is in fact (first-order) autocorrelation in the data, use the estimated d value to transform the data as suggested in Chapter 12 and present the results based on the transformed data. Is there a substantial qualitative difference in the two results?

13.14. Consider the following models:

Model I: Consumption$_i = B_1 + B_2$income$_i + u_i$

Model II: Consumption$_i = A_1 + A_2$wealth$_i + v_i$

(a) How would you decide which of the models is the "true" model?
(b) Suppose you regress consumption on both income and wealth. How would this help you to decide between the two models?
(c) Would you expect perfect collinearity between income and wealth? Why or why not?

(d) If there is high but less than perfect collinearity between income and wealth if you include both variables to explain the behavior of consumption, what consequences do you anticipate? In that case, how would you choose between models I and II?

13.15. Refer to problem 6.15 in Chapter 6, which discussed the regression-through-the-origin (i.e., zero intercept) model. If there is in fact an intercept present in the model but you run it through the origin, what kind of specification error is committed? Document the consequences of this type of error with the data given in problem 6.15.

13.16. Table 13-4 gives data on the real rate of return (Y) on common stocks, the output growth (X_2), and inflation (X_3), all in percent for the United States for 1954 to 1981.

(a) Regress Y on X_3.

(b) Regress Y on X_2 and X_3.

(c) Comment on the two regression results in view of Professor Eugene Fama's observation that "the negative simple correlation between real stock returns and inflation is spurious (or false) because it is the result of two structural relationships: a positive relation between current real stock returns and expected output growth and a negative relationship between expected output growth and current inflation."

(d) Do the regression in part (b) for the period 1956 to 1976, omitting the data for 1954 and 1955 due to unusual stock return behavior in those years and compare this regression with the one obtained in part (b), and comment on the difference, if any, between the two.

(e) Suppose you want to run the regression for the period 1956 to 1981 but want to distinguish between the periods 1956 to 1976 and 1977 to 1981. How would you run this regression? (Hint: Think of the dummy variables.)

13.17. Table 13-5 gives data on indexes of aggregate final energy demand (Y), the real gross domestic product, the GDP (X_2), and the real energy price (X_3) for the

TABLE 13-4

Year	Y	X_2	X_3	Year	Y	X_2	X_3
1954	53.0	6.7	−0.4	1968	6.8	2.8	4.3
1955	31.2	2.1	0.4	1969	−13.5	−0.2	5.0
1956	3.7	1.8	2.9	1970	−0.4	3.4	4.4
1957	−13.8	−0.4	3.0	1971	10.5	5.7	3.8
1958	41.7	6.0	1.7	1972	15.4	5.8	3.6
1959	10.5	2.1	1.5	1973	−22.6	−0.6	7.9
1960	−1.3	2.6	1.8	1974	−37.3	−1.2	10.8
1961	26.1	5.8	0.8	1975	31.2	5.4	6.0
1962	−10.5	4.0	1.8	1976	19.1	5.5	4.7
1963	21.2	5.3	1.6	1977	−13.1	5.0	5.9
1964	15.5	6.0	1.0	1978	−1.3	2.8	7.9
1965	10.2	6.0	2.3	1979	8.6	−0.3	9.8
1966	−13.3	2.7	3.2	1980	−22.2	2.6	10.2
1967	21.3	4.6	2.7	1981	−12.2	−1.9	7.3

Source: Jason Benderly and Burton Zwick, "Inflation, Real Balances, Output and Real Stock Returns," *American Economic Review*, vol. 75, no. 5, p. 1117, December 1985.

TABLE 13-5

Year	Y	X_2	X_3	Year	Y	X_2	X_3
1960	54.1	54.1	111.9	1972	97.7	94.3	98.6
1961	55.4	56.4	112.2	1973	100.0	100.0	100.0
1962	58.5	59.4	111.1	1974	97.4	101.4	120.1
1963	61.7	62.1	110.2	1975	93.5	100.5	131.0
1964	63.6	65.9	109.0	1976	99.1	105.3	129.6
1965	66.8	69.5	108.3	1977	100.9	109.9	137.7
1966	70.3	73.2	105.3	1978	103.9	114.4	133.7
1967	73.5	75.7	105.4	1979	106.9	118.3	144.5
1968	78.3	79.9	104.3	1980	101.2	119.6	179.0
1969	83.8	83.8	101.7	1981	98.1	121.1	189.4
1970	88.9	86.2	97.7	1982	95.6	120.6	190.9
1971	91.8	89.9	100.3				

Source: Richard D. Prosser, "Demand Elasticities in OECD: Dynamic Aspects," *Energy Economics*, p. 10, January 1985.

OECD countries—the United States, Canada, Germany, France, the United Kingdom, Italy, and Japan—for the period 1960 to 1982. (All indexes with base 1973 = 100.)

(a) Estimate the following models:

$$\text{Model A: } \ln Y_t = B_1 + B_2 \ln X_{2t} + B_3 \ln X_{3t} + u_{1t}$$
$$\text{Model B: } \ln Y_t = A_1 + A_2 \ln X_{2t} + A_3 \ln X_{2(t-1)} + A_4 \ln X_{3t} + u_{2t}$$
$$\text{Model C: } \ln Y_t = C_1 + C_2 \ln X_{2t} + C_3 \ln X_{3t} + C_4 \ln X_{3(t-1)} + u_{3t}$$
$$\text{Model D: } \ln Y_t = D_1 + D_2 \ln X_{2t} + D_3 \ln X_{3t} + D_4 \ln Y_{(t-1)} + u_{4t}$$

where the *u*s are the error terms. *Note*: models A, B, and C are called *dynamic models*—models that explicitly take into account the changes of a variable over time. Models B and C are called *distributed lag models* because the impact of an explanatory variable on the dependent variable is spread over time, here over two time periods. Model D is called an *autoregressive model* because one of the explanatory variables is a lagged value of the dependent variable as noted in Chapter 12. (The dynamic models are briefly discussed in Chapter 14.)

(b) If you estimate model A only, whereas the true model is either B, C, or D, what kind of specification bias is involved?

(c) Since all the preceding models are log-linear, the slope coefficients represent elasticity coefficients. What are the income (i.e., with respect to GDP) and price elasticities for model A? How would you go about estimating these elasticities for the other three models?

(d) What problems do you foresee with the OLS estimation of model D since the lagged Y variable appears as one of the explanatory variables. (*Hint*: Recall the assumptions of the CLRM.)

13.18. Show that the estimates of the marginal propensity to spend on imports of 0.6470 obtained from Eq. (13.6) and of 0.5984 obtained from Eq. (13.17) are not statistically different from one another.

13.19. Refer to problem 13.12. Suppose you extend the Cobb-Douglas production function model by including the trend variable X_4, a surrogate for technology. Suppose further that X_4 turns out to be statistically significant. In that case, what type of specification error is committed? What if X_4 turns out to be statistically insignificant? Present the necessary calculations.

13.20. *The demand for chicken revisited.* If Eq. (10.15) is the true demand function for chicken and if we substitute Eq. (10.16) for it, what type of specification error is committed? What are the consequences of this specification error? Explain fully.

13.21. In *Bazemore* v. *Friday*, 478 U.S. 385 (1986), a case involving pay discrimination in the North Carolina Extension Service, the plaintiff, a group of black agents, submitted a multiple regression model showing that on the average the black agents' salary was lower than their white counterparts. When the case reached the court of appeals, it rejected the plaintiff's case on the grounds that their regression had not included all the variables thought to have an effect on salary. The Supreme Court, however, reversed the appeals court. It stated:[22]

> The Court of Appeals erred in stating that petitioners' regression analyses were "unacceptable as evidence of discrimination," because they did not include all measurable variables thought to have an effect on salary level. The court's view of the evidentiary value of the regression analysis was plainly incorrect. While the omission of variables from a regression analysis may render the analysis less probative than it otherwise might be, it can hardly be said, absent some other infirmity, that an analysis which accounts for the major factors "must be considered unacceptable as evidence of discrimination." *Ibid.* Normally, a failure to include variables will affect the analysis' probativeness, not its admissibility.

Do you think the Supreme Court was correct in this decision? Articulate your views fully, bearing in mind the theoretical consequences of specification error and practical realities.

---

[22] The following is reproduced from Michael O. Finkelstein and Bruce Levin, *Statistics for Lawyers*, Springer-Verlag, New York, 1989, p. 374.

CHAPTER 14

SELECTED
TOPICS
IN SINGLE
EQUATION
REGRESSION
MODELS

In this final chapter of the textbook we consider three additional topics that are used in applied research quite often. These topics are:

1. Restricted least squares
2. Dynamic economic models
3. The logit model

We discuss the nature of these topics and illustrate them with several examples.

14.1   RESTRICTED LEAST SQUARES (RLS)

In estimating the parameters of a linear regression model, we have used the method of ordinary least square (OLS). The essential idea underlying the OLS is to estimate the unknown parameters so that the residual sum of squares (RSS) Σe_i^2 is minimized. In this minimization process we did not put any "restriction(s)" on the parameters. That is, we did not assume, say, in the three-variable model

$$Y_i = B_1 + B_2 X_{2i} + B_3 X_{3i} + u_i$$

that $B_2 = 2$ (or some such value) or that $(B_2 + B_3) = 1$ (or some other restriction). In other words, so far we estimated these parameters "freely," that is, without any restrictions: Whatever values the minimization of Σe_i^2 produced, we accepted them. In other words we let the given sample give us the best possible values of regression parameters without imposing any prior constraints or restrictions on them. Therefore, the least squares method we have used thus far can be called unrestricted least squares (ULS).

On occasion, however, economic theory suggests that coefficients in a regression model satisfy some restrictions. For example, consider the Cobb-Douglas production function that we have encountered before:

$$\ln Y_i = B_1 + B_2 \ln X_{2i} + B_3 \ln X_{3i} + u_i \tag{14.1}$$

where

$$Y = \text{the output}$$

$$X_2 = \text{the labor input}$$

$$X_3 = \text{the capital input}$$

$$\ln = \text{the natural log}$$

Now if there are *constant returns to scale* (e.g., doubling the inputs simultaneously doubles the output), economic theory suggests that

$$B_2 + B_3 = 1 \tag{14.2}$$

That is, the sum of two output-input elasticities is equal to 1.[1] Equation (14.2) is an example of a *linear equality restriction*.[2]

How does one find out in a concrete study involving Cobb-Douglas-type production functions that there are constant returns to scale, that is, if the restriction Eq. (14.2) is valid? To be specific, let us consider the output-input data for the Taiwanese manufacturing sector given in problem 13.12. In that problem you were asked to fit a Cobb-Douglas production function to those data. The results of fitting the regression (14.1) (i.e., unrestricted least squares) were as follows:

$$\widehat{\ln Y_t} = -8.4010 \quad + 0.6731 \ln X_{2t} + 1.1816 \ln X_{3t}$$

$$\text{se} = \quad (2.7177) \quad (0.15314) \quad (0.30204) \qquad R^2 = 0.9824 \qquad (14.3)$$

$$t = (-3.0912) \quad (4.3952) \quad (3.9121)$$

Now the sum of estimated elasticities is $(b_2 + b_3) = (0.6732 + 1.1814) = 1.8546$. Numerically, this number is greater than 1, but it may not be necessarily greater than 1 statistically because of sampling fluctuations. In other words,

---

[1] Thus, B_2 is the elasticity of output with respect to labor input; it measures the percentage change in output for a percent change in labor input, holding, of course, the capital input constant. Recall that in double-log models slope coefficients are also elasticities.

[2] If $(B_2 + B_3) < 1$, it would be an example of *linear inequality restriction*. To handle such restrictions, we need to use mathematical programming techniques, which are beyond the scope of this book.

the linear restriction Eq. (14.2) can still be statistically valid. How do we find that out? There are several approaches to answer that question, but the one with wider applicability is that of restricted least squares (RLS), which we develop as follows.

Now if the restriction Eq. (14.2) is indeed valid, it follows that

$$B_2 = 1 - B_3 \tag{14.4}$$

(It can also be expressed as $B_3 = 1 - B_2$). Using this, we can express the regression (14.1) as

$$\ln Y_t = B_1 + (1 - B_3) \ln X_{2t} + B_3 \ln X_{3t} + u_t$$

$$= B_1 + \ln X_{2t} + B_3 (\ln X_{3t} - \ln X_{2t}) + u_t$$

That is,

$$(\ln Y_t - \ln X_{2t}) = B_1 + B_3(\ln X_{3t} - \ln X_{2t}) + u_t \tag{14.5}$$

Or

$$\ln \frac{Y_t}{X_{2t}} = B_1 + B_3 \ln \frac{X_{3t}}{X_{2t}} + u_t \tag{14.6}$$

where (Y_t/X_{2t}) = the output/labor ratio (i.e., labor productivity) and (X_{3t}/X_{2t}) = the capital/labor ratio (the amount of capital per unit of labor), quantities of great economic importance.

Equation (14.6) states that the log of labor productivity is a linear function of the log of the capital/labor ratio. Notice several features of Eq. (14.6):

1. It shows how to incorporate directly the restrictions suggested by economic theory, as in Eq. (14.2) or (14.4).
2. It requires the estimation of only two unknowns, whereas Eq. (14.1) requires the estimation of three unknowns.
3. Once B_3 is estimated from Eq. (14.6), B_2 can be easily estimated from Eq. (14.4). Needless to say, this procedure will guarantee that $(B_2 + B_3) = 1$. (Why?)

The procedure outlined in Eq. (14.5) or (14.6) is known as **restricted least squares (RLS)** because we apply the least squares method after we transform the data to take into account the restrictions suggested by the relevant theory. As noted earlier, the usual OLS can be called **unrestricted least squares (ULS)**.

How do regressions (14.1) and (14.6) help us to test for the validity of the restriction Eq. (14.4)? To answer this question, let us first present the results based on the regression (14.6) for the Taiwanese data.

Example 14.1. RLS Cobb-Douglas production function for Taiwan.

$$\ln \frac{\hat{Y}_t}{X_{2t}} = 5.5067 \quad -0.32156 \ln \frac{X_{3t}}{X_{2t}} \quad R^{*2} = 0.9428$$

$$\text{se} = (0.88082) \quad (0.15476) \tag{14.7}$$

$$t = (6.2518) \quad (-2.0777)$$

Equation (14.7) is a **restricted least squares regression,** for it takes into account the restriction imposed by Eq. (14.2). Note these features of the RLS regression (14.7):

1. Since the estimated B_3 is -0.3215, from the model (14.7) the estimate of B_2 can be immediately obtained as $1 - (-0.3215) = 1.3215$; that is, the estimated output-labor elasticity is ≈ 1.32 percent. Obviously, the sum of estimated elasticities is 1. (Why?)
2. Although b_3 in the regression (14.7) is statistically significant (check this out), its value is negative. This does not make economic sense, for economic theory would suggest, *ceteris paribus*, that the higher the capital/labor ratio is, the higher the labor productivity will be.
3. The R^2 of the RLS regression, denoted by R^{*2}, is lower than the R^2 of the original (ULS) regression (14.3). This is generally true. (See the note at the end of the example.)

The fact that the estimated value of the B_3 coefficient is negative, contrary to a prior expectation, would suggest for the Taiwanese manufacturing sector that the restriction $(B_2 + B_3) = 1$—indicating constant returns to scale—does not seem to be valid. But this is only a qualitative inference. We can provide a more direct test of the validity of the restriction(s), as follows:

Let

$$R^2 = R^2 \text{ from the unrestricted regression (14.3)}$$

$$R^{*2} = R^2 \text{ from the restricted regression (14.7)}$$

$$m = \text{the number of linear restrictions imposed (1 in the present case)}^3$$

$$k = \text{the number of parameters estimated in the unrestricted regression (14.3) (three in the present example)}$$

$$n = \text{the number of observations}$$

Assuming the standard assumption that the error term u follows the normal distribution, it can be shown that

$$F = \frac{(R^2 - R^{*2})/m}{(1 - R^2)/(n - k)} \sim F_{m,(n-k)} \tag{14.8}$$

---

[3] The method we have just outlined can be easily extended to more than one linear restriction.

follows the F distribution with m and $(n - k)$ degrees of freedom (d.f.) in the numerator and denominator, respectively. Therefore, if in an application the F value computed from Equation (14.8) is greater than the critical F value at the given level of significance, then the particular restriction imposed by theory is not valid (statistically speaking). On the other hand, if the computed F value is less than the critical F, the validity of the restriction can be accepted, in which case the RLS regression can be preferred to the ULS.

The steps involved in carrying out the F test given in Eq. (14.8) are as follows:

1. Estimate the ULS regression [i.e., the usual ordinary least squares (OLS) regression] and obtain the R^2.
2. Estimate the RLS regression and obtain the corresponding coefficient of determination, denoted by R^{*2}.
3. Find out the number of restrictions (m) and the coefficients estimated in the unrestricted regression (k), and obtain the F value as shown in Eq. (14.8). The null hypothesis is that the restriction(s) is valid.
4. If the F obtained from Eq. (14.8) does not exceed the critical F at the chosen level of significance (i.e., the probability of committing a Type I error), you can accept the null hypothesis (i.e., the given restriction is valid). But if it exceeds the critical F, the imposed restriction(s) is not valid. *Note carefully*: The restrictions can be valid in theory but may not be so in any concrete study.

Returning to our example, the F value corresponding to (14.8) is

$$F = \frac{(0.9824 - 0.9428)/1}{(1 - 0.9824)/(15 - 3)} = 27.13 \tag{14.9}$$

For 1 and 12 d.f., the 5% and 1% critical F values are 4.75 and 9.33, respectively. Obviously, the computed F value far exceeds the critical F value(s), and therefore we reject the hypothesis that for the Taiwanese economy for the period of the study there were constant returns to scale in the manufacturing sector of the economy. The evidence is in favor of increasing returns to scale.

Note: The actual R^2 value of Eq. (14.7) is 0.2493. However, the value of $R^{*2} = 0.9428$ is directly comparable with $R^2 = 0.9824$ given in Eq. (14.3). Recall that to compare two R_2 values the dependent variable must be the same.

The F test given in Eq. (14.8) is quite general and can be applied to study a variety of linear restrictions. All one has to do is to estimate the unrestricted and restricted regressions and use the F test given in Eq. (14.8). If the F statistic is significant, the restricted least squares regression is rejected in favor of the unrestricted one. However, if the F statistic is not significant, the RLS can be chosen over the unrestricted OLS.

Before proceeding further, let us indicate a couple of important points

Example 14.2. The demand for chicken revisited. Refer back to the demand functions for chicken given in Eqs. (10.15) and (10.16). The difference between these demand functions is that the latter exclude the prices of pork and beef, possibly competing products for chicken. Therefore, Eq. (10.15) is the ULS regression and Eq. (10.16) is the RLS regression because we are explicitly assuming that these variables have no effect on the demand for chicken. For Eq. (10.15) $R^2 = 0.9823$ and for the RLS Eq. (10.16) $R^{*2} = 0.9801$. Therefore, from Eq. (14.8) we obtain

$$F = \frac{(0.9823 - 0.9801)/2}{(1 - 0.9823)/(23 - 5)}$$

$$= 1.1186$$

(*Note*: $m = 2$, $n = 23$, and $k = 5$), which has the F distribution with 2 and 18 d.f. in the numerator and denominator, respectively. From the F table we observe that this F value is not significant even at the 10% level of significance. Apparently, the prices of pork and beef do not seem to have significant impact on the demand for chicken. Therefore, the RLS regression (10.16) may be preferred to the ULS regression (10.15).

about the previous example. In Chapter 10 on multicollinearity we stated that if we incorrectly omit a variable from a model, the coefficients of the variables retained in the model tend to be biased (see also Chapter 13). The question now is: Which is the correct model, Eq. (10.15) or (10.16)? Since the F test showed that we can accept the RLS regression (10.16), we can say that probably the correct model is Eq. (10.16). Hence, no question of bias arises in the present instance. Also, as pointed out in Chapter 13, if the regression (10.16) is the true model and we estimate the model (10.15) by including the "superfluous" variables, the prices of pork and beef, OLS estimators still remain unbiased, although they tend to have larger variances.

14.2 DYNAMIC ECONOMIC MODELS: AUTOREGRESSIVE AND DISTRIBUTED LAG MODELS

In all regression models that we have considered up to this point it has been assumed that the relationship between the dependent variable Y and explanatory variables, the Xs, is *contemporaneous*, that is, at the same point in time. This assumption can be tenable in cross-sectional data but not in time series data. Thus, in a regression of consumption expenditure on personal disposable income (PDI) involving time series data it is possible that consumption expenditure depends upon the PDI in the previous time period as well as upon the PDI in the current time period. That is, there may be a noncontemporaneous, or *lagged*, relationship between Y and the Xs.

To illustrate, let Y_t = the consumption expenditure at time t, X_t = the PDI at time t, X_{t-1} = the PDI at time $(t - 1)$, and X_{t-2} = the PDI at time $(t - 2)$. Now consider the model

$$Y_t = A + B_0 X_t + B_1 X_{t-1} + B_2 X_{t-2} + u_t \qquad (14.10)$$

As this model shows, because of the lagged terms X_{t-1} and X_{t-2} the relationship between consumption expenditure is not contemporaneous. Models like Eq. (14.10) are called **dynamic models** (i.e., involving change over time) because the effect of a unit change in the value of the explanatory variable is felt over a number of time periods, three in the model of Eq. (14.10).

More technically, dynamic models like Eq. (14.10) are called **distributed lag models,** for the effect of a unit change in the value of the explanatory variable is spread over, or distributed over, a number of time periods. To illustrate this point further, consider the following hypothetical consumption function:[4]

$$Y_t = \text{constant} + 0.4X_t + 0.3X_{t-1} + 0.2X_{t-2} \qquad (14.11)$$

Suppose a person received a permanent salary increase of $1000, permanent in the sense that the increase in the salary will be maintained. If his or her consumption function is as shown in Eq. (14.11), then in the first year of the salary increase he or she increases his or her consumption expenditure by $400 (0.4 × 1000), by another $300 (0.3 × 1000) the next year, and by another $200 (0.2 × 1000) in the third year. Thus, by the end of the third year the level of his or her consumption expenditure will have increased by (200 + 300 + 400), or by $900; the remaining $100 goes into savings.

Contrast the consumption function Eq. (14.11) with the following consumption function:

$$Y_t = \text{constant} + 0.9X_{t-1} \qquad (14.12)$$

Although the ultimate effect of a $1000 increase in income on consumption is the same in both cases, it takes place with a lag of one year in Eq. (14.12), whereas in (14.11) it is distributed over a period of three years; hence the name *distributed lag model* for models like Eq. (14.11). This can be seen clearly from Figure 14-1.

Before moving on, a natural question arises: Why do lags occur. That is, why does the dependent variable respond to a unit change in the explanatory variable(s) with a time lag? There are several reasons, which we discuss now.

Psychological reasons. Due to the force of habit (inertia), people do not change their consumption habits immediately following a price decrease or an income increase, perhaps because the process of change involves some immediate disutility. Thus, those who become instant millionaires by winning lotteries may not change the lifestyles to which they are accustomed because

---

[4] This example was suggested by Henri Theil, *Introduction to Econometrics*, Prentice-Hall, Englewood Cliffs, N.J., 1978, p. 332.

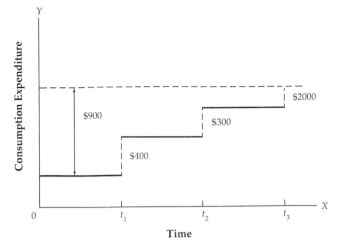

FIGURE 14-1
An example of distributed lag model.

they do not know how to react to such a windfall gain immediately, not to mention the hounding by financial planners, newly discovered relatives, tax lawyers, etc.

Technological reasons. Every time a new-generation personal computer (PC) comes on the market, the prices of existing PCs drop dramatically. Some people who can still use existing PCs would therefore wait for the announcement of a new PC in the hope of purchasing an existing PC at a cheaper price. The same is true of automobiles. The moment, say, the 1991 models are on the market, the prices of 1990 models drop considerably. Consumers thinking of replacing their old cars may wait for the announcement of the new model in anticipation of buying a previous model at a lower price.

Institutional reasons. Since most major collective bargaining agreements are multiyear contracts, union workers have to wait for the expiration of the existing contract to negotiate a new wage rate even though the inflation rate has increased substantially since the signing of the last contract. Likewise, a professional ball player has to wait until the expiration of his contract to negotiate a new one even though his "productivity" has gone up since the contract was signed several years ago. Of course, some players try to renegotiate the existing contract and some do succeed.

For these and other reasons, lags occupy a central role in economics. This is clearly reflected in the short-run/long-run methodology of economics. In the short run the price or income elasticities are generally smaller in absolute value than their long-run counterparts because it takes time to make the necessary adjustment following a change in the values of explanatory variables.

Generalizing Eq. (14.10), we can write a *k-period distributed lag model* as

$$Y_t = A + B_0 X_t + B_1 X_{t-1} + B_2 X_{t-2} + \cdots + B_k X_{t-k} + u_t \qquad (14.13)$$

in which the effect of a unit change in the value of the explanatory variable is felt over k periods.[5] In the regression (14.13) Y responds to a unit change in the value of the X variable not only in the current time period but also in several previous time periods.

In the regression (14.13) the coefficient B_0 is known as the **short-run** or **impact, multiplier** because it gives the change in the mean value of Y following a unit change in X in the same time period. If the change in X is maintained at the same level thereafter, then $(B_0 + B_1)$ gives the change in the mean value of Y in the next period, $(B_0 + B_1 + B_2)$ in the following period, etc. These partial sums are called **interim, or intermediate, multipliers.** Finally, after k periods, we obtain

$$\sum_{i=0}^{k} B_i = B_0 + B_1 + B_2 + \cdots + B_k \qquad (14.14)$$

which is known as the **long-run, or total, multiplier.** Thus, in the consumption function given in the model (14.11), the short-run multiplier is 0.4, the interim multiplier is $(0.4 + 0.3) = 0.7$, and the long-run multiplier is $(0.4 + 0.3 + 0.2) = 0.9$. In the long run, here three periods, a unit change in PDI will lead on the average to a 0.9 unit change in the consumption expenditure. In short, the long-run *marginal propensity to consume (MPC)* is 0.9, whereas the short-run MPC is only 0.4, 0.7 being the intermediate term MPC. Since the impact of the change in the value of the explanatory variable(s) in the distant past is probably less important than the impact in the immediate near period, we would expect that generally B_0 would be greater in value than B_1, which would be greater than B_2, etc. In other words, the values of the various Bs are expected to decline from the first B onward, a fact that will be useful later when we estimate the distributed lag models.

Estimation of Distributed Lag Models

How do we estimate distributed models like the regression (14.13)? Can we still use the usual OLS method? In principle, yes, for if we assume that X_t is nonstochastic, or fixed in repeated sampling, so are X_{t-1} and all other lagged values of the Xs. Therefore, the model (14.13) per se does not violate any of the standard assumptions of the classical linear regression model (CLRM). However, there are some practical problems that need to be addressed.

1. The obvious problem is to determine how many **lagged values** of the explanatory variables to introduce, for economic theory is rarely robust enough to suggest the maximum length of the lag.

2. If we introduce too many lagged values, the degrees of freedom can

---

[5] The term *period* is used generically; it can be a day, a week, a month, a year, or any suitable time period.

become a serious problem. If we have 20 observations and introduce 10 lagged values, we will have only 8 degrees of freedom left—10 d.f. will be lost on account of the lagged values—one on account of the current value and one for the intercept. Obviously, as the number of degrees of freedom dwindles, statistical inference becomes increasingly less reliable. The problem becomes all the more complex if we have more than one explanatory variable in the model, each with its own distributed lag structure. In this case we can consume degrees of freedom very fast—note, for every coefficient estimated, we lose 1 d.f.

3. Even with a large sample where there is not much concern about the degrees of freedom problem, we may run into the problem of *multicollinearity*, for successive values of most economic variables tend to be correlated, sometimes very highly. As noted in Chapter 10, multicollinearity leads to imprecise estimation; that is, standard errors tend to be large in relation to estimated coefficients. As a result, based on the routinely computed t ratios, we tend to declare that a lagged coefficient(s) is statistically insignificant. Another problem that arises is that coefficients of successive lagged terms sometimes alternate in sign, which makes it difficult to interpret some coefficients, as the following example will show.

Example 14.3. An illustrative example: The St. Louis model. To determine whether changes in the nominal gross national product (GNP) can be explained by changes in either the money supply (monetarism) or government expenditure (Keynesianism), the Federal Reserve Bank of St. Louis has developed a model, popularly known as the St. Louis model. One version of this model is

$$\dot{Y}_t = \text{constant} + \sum_{i=0}^{4} A_i \dot{M}_{t-i} + \sum_{i=0}^{4} B_i \dot{F}_{t\ i} + u_t \qquad (14.15)$$

where

$\dot{Y}_t$ = the rate of growth of nominal GNP at time t

$\dot{M}_t$ = the rate of growth in the money supply (M_1 version) at time t

$\dot{E}_t$ = the rate of growth in full or high employment government expenditure at time t

The results based on the quarterly data from 1953-I to 1976-IV using four lagged values of $\dot{M}$ and $\dot{E}$ each were as follows:[6] For ease of reading, the results are presented in tabular form (Table 14-1).

---

[6] These results, with a change in notation, are from Keith M. Carlson, ''Does the St. Louis Equation Now Believe in Fiscal Policy,'' *Review*, Federal Bank of St. Louis, vol. 60, no. 2, p. 17, February 1978. Table Iv. Note

$$\sum_{i=0}^{4} A_i \dot{M}_{t-i} = A_0 \dot{M}_t + A_1 \dot{M}_{t-1} + A_2 \dot{M}_{t-2} + A_3 \dot{M}_{t-3} + A_4 \dot{M}_{t-4}$$

and similarly for $\Sigma_{i=0}^{4} B_i \dot{E}_{t-i}$.

TABLE 14-1
The St. Louis model

Coefficient	Estimate	Coefficient	Estimate
A_0	0.40 (2.96)*	B_0	0.08 (2.26)*
A_1	0.41 (5.26)*	B_1	0.06 (2.52)*
A_2	0.25 (2.14)*	B_2	0.00 (0.02)
A_3	0.06 (0.71)	B_3	-0.06 (-2.20)
A_4	-0.05 (-0.37)	B_4	-0.07 (-1.83)*
$\sum_{i=0}^{4} A_i$	1.06 (5.59)*	$\sum_{i=0}^{4} B_i$	0.01 (0.40)
	$R^2 = 0.40;$	$d = 1.78$	

Note: The figures in parentheses are t ratios.

* Significant at 5% level (one-tailed). The value of the intercept is not presented in the original article.

Notice several features of the results presented in Table 14-1.

1. Not all lagged coefficients are individually significant on the basis of the conventional t test. But we cannot tell whether this lack of significance is genuine or merely due to multicollinearity.

2. The fourth lagged value of $\dot{M}$ has a negative sign, which is difficult to interpret economically because all other lagged money coefficients have a positive impact on $\dot{Y}$. This negative value, however, is statistically insignificant, although we do not know if this is due to multicollinearity. The third and fourth lagged values of $\dot{E}$ are not only negative but are also statistically significant. Again, economically, it is difficult to interpret this negative value, for why should the rate of growth in government expenditure have a negative impact three and four periods in the past while the first two lagged values have a positive impact?

3. The immediate, or short-run, impact of a unit change in $\dot{M}$ is 0.40, whereas the long-term impact is 1.06 (which is the sum of the various A coefficients), and this is statistically significant. The interpretation is that a sustained 1 percent increase in the rate of growth of the money supply will be accompanied by $\approx$ 1 percent increase in the rate of growth of the nominal GNP in about five quarters. Similarly, the short-run impact of 1 percent increase in the rate of growth of government expenditure is $\approx$ 0.08, which is statistically significant, but the long-term impact is only 0.01 (the sum of the B coefficients), which is statistically insignificant.

The implication then is that changes in the growth rates in the money supply have a lasting impact on changes in the growth rate of the GNP (almost one for one) but changes in the growth rates of government expenditure do not. In short, the St. Louis model tends to support monetarism. That is why the St. Louis model is often called the *monetarist model.*

From a statistical viewpoint the obvious question is why did the St. Louis model include only four lags of each explanatory variable? Can some insignificant coefficients be due to multicollinearity? These questions cannot be answered without examining the original data and determining what happens to the model if more lagged terms are introduced. But as the reader can well imagine, this will not be a particularly fruitful line of attack, for there is no way to avoid the problem of multicollinearity if more lagged terms are introduced. Clearly, we need an alternative that will not only rid us of the problem of multicollinearity but will tell us how many lagged terms can legitimately be included in a model.

14.3   THE KOYCK, ADAPTIVE EXPECTATIONS, AND STOCK ADJUSTMENT MODEL APPROACH TO ESTIMATING DISTRIBUTED LAG MODELS[7]

An ingenious approach to reducing both the number of lagged terms in the distributed lag models and the problem of multicollinearity is to adopt the approach used by the so-called **Koyck,** the **adaptive expectations** and **the partial,** or **stock, adjustment model.** Without going into the technical details of these models,[8] a remarkable feature of all these models is that distributed models like Eq. (14.13) can be reduced to the following "simple" model:[9]

$$Y_t = C_1 + C_2 X_t + C_3 Y_{t-1} + v_t \tag{14.16}$$

where v is the error term. This model is called an **autoregressive model** (recall Chapter 12) because the lagged value of the dependent variable appears as an explanatory variable on the right-hand side of the equation. In the regression (14.13) we had to estimate the intercept, current, and k-lagged terms. So,

---

[7] See L. M. Koyck, *Distributed Lags and Investment Analysis,* North-Holland, Amsterdam, 1954; P. Cagan, "The Monetary Dynamics of Hyper Inflations," in M. Friedman (ed.), *Studies in the Quantity Theory of Money,* University of Chicago Press, Chicago, 1956 (for the adaptive expectations model); Marc Nerlove, *Distributed Lags and Demand for Agricultural and Other Commodities,* Handbook No. 141, U.S. Department of Agriculture, June 1958 (for the partial, or stock, adjustment model).

[8] The details can be found in Damodar N. Gujarati, *Basic Econometrics,* 2d ed., McGraw-Hill, New York, 1988, Chap. 16.

[9] Actually, the number of lagged terms in Eq. (14.13) can be many more than k, technically infinite. In passing, note that the Koyck and the other two models implicitly assume that the values of B coefficients decline from the first coefficient onward; that is, numerically B_0 is greater than B_1, which is greater than B_2, etc. This is a plausible assumption because the effect of distant past terms is not likely to be so important as the current ones.

if $k = 15$, we will have to estimate in all 17 parameters, a considerable loss of degrees of freedom, especially if the sample size is not too large. But in the regression (14.16) we have to estimate only three unknowns, the intercept and the two slope coefficients, a tremendous savings in the degrees of freedom. So to speak, all lagged terms in the regression (14.13) are replaced by a single lagged value of Y.

Of course, there is no such thing as a "free lunch." In reducing the number of parameters to be estimated in the model (14.13) to only three, we have created some problems in the model (14.16). First, since Y_t is stochastic, or random, Y_{t-1} is random too. Therefore, to estimate the model (14.16) by OLS, we must make sure that the error term v_t and the lagged variable Y_{t-1} are not correlated; otherwise, as can be shown, *the OLS estimators are not only biased but are inconsistent as well.* If, however, v_t and Y_{t-1} are uncorrelated, it can be proved that the OLS estimators are biased (in small samples), but the bias tends to disappear as the sample size becomes increasingly large. That is, in a large sample (technically, asymptotically) the OLS estimators will be consistent. Second, if, however, v_t is serially correlated (e.g., it follows the first-order Markov scheme, $v_t = \rho v_{t-1} + w_t$, where $-1 \le \rho \le 1$ and the error term w_t satisfies the usual OLS assumptions), OLS estimators are biased as well as inconsistent and the traditional t and F testing procedure becomes invalid. Therefore, in autoregressive models like Eq. (14.16) it is very important that we find out whether the error term v_t follows, say, the first-order Markov, or the AR(1) scheme, discussed in Chapter 12. Third, as we discussed in Chapter 12, in autoregressive models the conventional Durbin-Watson d test is not applicable. In such cases the Durbin h statistic discussed in problem 12.16 can be used to detect first-order autocorrelation, or one can use the runs test.

Before we proceed to illustrate the model (14.16), it is interesting to note that the coefficient C_2 attached to X_t gives the **short-run impact** of a unit change in X_t on mean Y_t and $C_2/(1 - C_3)$ gives the **long-run impact** of a (sustained) unit change in X_t on mean Y_t; this is equivalent to summing the values of all B coefficients in the model (14.13), as shown in Eq. (14.14).[10] In other words, the lagged Y term in the regression (14.16) acts as the workhorse for all lagged X terms in the model (14.13).

Example 14.4.   The impact of adjusted monetary base growth rate on growth rate of nominal GNP, United States, 1960–1988. To see the relationship between the growth rate in the nominal *GNP* ($\dot{Y}$) and the growth rate in the

---

[10] The details can be found in Damodar N. Gujarati, *Basic Econometrics*, 2d ed., McGraw-Hill, New York, 1988, Chapter 16.

adjusted monetary base (AMB),[11] Joseph H. Haslag and Scott E. Hein[12] obtained the following regression results:

$$\hat{Y}_t = 0.004 \quad + 0.238 \text{AMB}_{t-1} + 0.759\dot{Y}_{t-1} \qquad \text{Durbin's } h = 3.35$$

$$\text{se} = (0.004) \quad (0.067) \qquad\qquad (0.054) \qquad\qquad\qquad\qquad (14.17)$$

$$t = (1.000) \quad (3.552) \qquad\qquad (14.056)$$

(*Note*: The authors did not present R^2.)

Note: A dot over a variable represents its growth rate.

Before interpreting these results, notice that Haslag and Hein use a one-period (a year here) lagged value of the AMB as an explanatory variable and not the current period value, but this should cause us no problem because AMB is largely determined by the Federal Reserve system. Besides, AMB_{t-1} is nonstochastic if AMB_t is, which is what we usually assume about any explanatory variable in the standard CLRM. Now to the interpretation of the model (14.17).

From Eq. (14.17) we observe that the *short-run* impact of AMB is 0.238; that is, a one percentage point change in AMB on the average leads to ≈ 0.238 percentage point change in the nominal GNP. This impact seems statistically significant because the computed t value is significant. However, the long-run impact is

$$\frac{0.238}{(1 - 0.759)} = 0.988 \qquad\qquad (14.18)$$

which is almost unity. Therefore, in the long run a (sustained) one percentage point change in the AMB leads to about a one percentage point change in the nominal GNP; so to speak, there is a one-to-one relationship between the growth rates of AMB and the nominal GNP.

The only problem with the model (14.17) is that the estimated h value is statistically significant. As pointed out in problem 12.16, in a large sample the

---

[11] The monetary base (MB), sometimes called **high-powered** money, in the United States consists of currency and total commercial bank reserves. The AMB takes into account the changes in the reserve ratio requirements of the Federal Reserve bank; in the United States all commercial banks are required to keep certain cash or cash equivalents against the deposits that customers keep with the banks. The reserve ratio is the ratio of cash and cash equivalent to the total deposits (which are liabilities of the banks). The Federal Reserve system changes this ratio from time to time to achieve some policy goals, such as containment of inflation or the rate of interest, etc.

[12] See Joseph H. Haslag and Scott E. Hein "Reserve Requirements, the Monetary Base and Economic Activity," *Economic Review*, Federal Reserve Bank of Dallas, p. 13, March 1989. The regression results are presented to suit the format of the model (14.15).

h statistic follows the standard normal distribution. Therefore, the 5% two-tailed critical Z (standard normal) value is 1.96 and the 1% two-tailed critical Z value is ≈ 2.58. Since the observed h of 3.35 exceeds these critical values, it seems that the residuals in the regression (14.17) are autocorrelated, and therefore the results presented in the model (14.17) should be taken with a "grain of salt." But note that the h statistic is a large sample statistic and the sample size in the model (14.17) is 29, which may not be very large. In any case, Eq. (14.17) serves the pedagogical purpose of illustrating the mechanics of estimating distributed lag models via the Koyck, adaptive expectation, or stock adjustment models.

Example 14.5.   Margin requirements and stock market volatility.   To assess the short-run and long-run impact of a margin requirement (which restricts the amount of credit that brokers and dealers can extend their customers), Gikas A. Hardouvelis[13] estimated the following regression (among several others) for the monthly data from December 1931 to December 1987, a total of 673 months, for the stocks included in the Standard & Poor (S&P) index.

$$\widehat{\sigma_t} = 0.112 \quad - 0.112m_t + 0.186\sigma_{t-1}$$

$$\text{se} = (0.015) \quad (0.024) \quad (\quad)^* \qquad R^2 = 0.44 \tag{14.19}$$

where σ_t = the standard deviation of the monthly excess nominal rate of return of stocks (the nominal rate of return minus the one-month T-bill rate at the end of the previous month) calculated from $(t-11)$ to t (in decimals), which is taken as a measure of volatility; m_t = the average official margin requirement from $(t-11)$ to t (in decimals); and the figures in parentheses are the estimated standard errors corrected for heteroscedasticity and autocorrelation. Unfortunately, Hardouvelis does not present the standard error of the lagged volatility coefficient nor the h statistic. Note, though, that the author has corrected his results for autocorrelation.

* The standard error was not presented by the author.

As expected, the coefficient of the margin variable has a negative sign, suggesting that when margin requirements are increased, there is less speculative activity in the stock market, thereby reducing volatility. The value of -0.112 means that if the margin requirement is increased by, say, one percentage point, the volatility of S&P stocks decreases by ≈ 0.11 percentage points. This is, or course, the short-run impact. The long-run impact is

$$-\frac{0.112}{(1-0.186)} \approx -0.138$$

---

[13] See Gikas A. Hardouvelis, "Margin Requirements and Stock Market Volatility," *Quarterly Review*, Federal Reserve Bank of New York, vol. 13, no. 2, Table 4, p. 86, and footnote 21, p. 88.

which obviously is higher (in absolute value) than the short-run impact, but not a whole lot higher.

Although the topic of dynamic modeling is vast and all kinds of newer econometric techniques to handle such models are currently available, the preceding discussion will give the reader just the flavor of what dynamic modeling is all about. For additional details, the reader can consult the references.[14]

14.4   WHAT HAPPENS WHEN THE DEPENDENT VARIABLE IS DUMMY?

In Chapter 9 we examined in detail regression models in which one or more explanatory variables were dummy, or qualitative, in nature but the dependent variable was quantitative. In this section we consider models in which the dependent variable Y is also dummy, or dichotomous, or binary; explanatory variables may be dummy, or quantitative, or a combination of both.

Suppose we want to study labor-force participation of adult males as a function of the unemployment rate, average wage rate, family income, level of education, etc. Now a person is either in or not in the labor force. Hence, the dependent variable, labor-force participation rate, can take only two values: 1 if the person is in the labor force and 0 if the person is not in the labor force. For another example, suppose we want to find out whether a country belongs to the IMF (International Monetary Fund), which can be a function of several factors. Now a country either belongs or does not belong to the IMF. Therefore, the dependent variable, IMF membership, is a dummy variable, taking the value of 1 if the country belongs to the IMF and 0 otherwise. As yet another example, suppose the U.S. parole board is considering paroling an inmate. Now the variable parole is a dummy variable in that the board may or may not grant the parole; the decision to grant it is based upon factors such as the type of offense committed, behavior of the inmate while incarcerated, psychiatric evaluations, etc.

The reader can provide scores of such examples. A unique feature of such examples is that the dependent variable elicits a yes or no response; that is, it is dichotomous in nature. How do we estimate such models? Can we apply OLS straightforwardly to such a model? To answer these and related questions, we first consider a concrete example.

Example 14.6.   The effect of personalized system of instructions (PSI) on course grade in intermediate macroeconomics.   Table 14-2 gives data on the dependent variable, the final grade on the intermediate macroeconomics exam-

---

[14] A good reference is A. C. Harvey, *The Econometric Analysis of Time Series*, 2d ed., MIT, Cambridge, Mass., 1990. But the beginner is warned that some parts of this book can be rough going.

ination (Y), such that $Y = 1$ if the final grade is A and $Y = 0$ if the final grade is a B or C, and explanatory variables GPA = the entering grade-point average, TUCE = the score on an examination given at the beginning of the term to test macroeconomics knowledge of entering students, and PSI = 1 if the new method of the personalized system of instructions is used and is 0 otherwise.

Among other things, the primary objective of the Spector-Mazzeo study was to assess the effectiveness of the new method of teaching (PSI) on the final grade obtained.

Let us suppose we want to apply OLS to the data in Table 14-2 by considering the model

$$Y_i = B_1 + B_2 GPA_i + B_3 TUCE + B_4 PSI + u_i \qquad (14.20)$$

where the dependent variable takes the value of 1 or 0, depending upon whether or not an *A* grade is obtained. If we do that, the resulting model, namely, Equation (14.20) in the present example, is known as the *linear probability model* (LPM) since $E(Y_i)$ can be interpreted as the *conditional probability* (see Chapter 2) that the event Y (i.e., a student will get an A) will occur, conditional on the given values of explanatory variables.[15] Therefore, we can express Eq. (14.20) in two equivalent forms:

$$E(Y = 1 \mid GPA, TUCE, PSI) = B_1 + B_2 GPA_i + B_3 TUCE_i + B_4 PSI_i \qquad (14.21)[16]$$

Or

$$P(Y = 1 \mid GPA, TUCE, PSI) = P_i = B_1 + B_2 GPA_i + B_3 TUCE_i + B_4 PSI_i \qquad (14.22)$$

where P stands for probability. Then,

$$\hat{P}_i = b_1 + b_2 GPA_i + b_3 TUCE_i + b_4 PSI_i \qquad (14.23)$$

will give an estimate of the probability that a student with the given values of explanatory variables will earn an A.

An important question: Up until now we only considered linear regression models in which the dependent variable was quantitative. Since in the model (14.20) this is not the case because Y is a dummy variable, are there any problems with the OLS estimation of the regression (14.20)? Unfortunately, there are. Without going into technicalities, it can be shown that the model (14.20), if estimated by OLS, suffers from the following problems.[17]

---

[15] For proof, see Damodar N. Gujarati, *Basic Econometrics*, 2d ed., McGraw-Hill, New York, 1988, Chap. 15.

[16] *Note*: $(E(Y \mid GPA, TUCE, PSI) = 1.P(Y = 1 \mid GPA, TUCE, PSI) + 0.P(Y = 0 \mid GPA, TUCE, PSI)$
$$= P(Y = 1 \mid GPA, TUCE, PSI)$$

[17] For proofs, see Damodar N. Gujarati, *Basic Econometrics*, 2d ed., McGraw-Hill, New York, 1988, pp. 469–471.

TABLE 14-2
Grade average and related data for 32 students

Observation No.	Y	GPA	TUCE	PSI	Observation No.	Y	GPA	TUCE	PSI
1	0	2.66	20	0	17	0	2.75	25	0
2	0	2.89	22	0	18	0	2.83	19	0
3	0	3.28	24	0	19	0	3.12	23	1
4	0	2.92	12	0	20	1	3.16	25	1
5	1	4.00	21	0	21	0	2.06	22	1
6	0	2.86	17	0	22	1	3.62	28	1
7	0	2.76	17	0	23	0	2.89	14	1
8	0	2.87	21	0	24	0	3.51	26	1
9	0	3.03	25	0	25	1	3.54	24	1
10	1	3.92	29	0	26	1	2.83	27	1
11	0	2.63	20	0	27	1	3.39	17	1
12	0	3.32	23	0	28	0	2.67	24	1
13	0	3.57	23	0	29	1	3.65	21	1
14	1	3.26	25	0	30	1	4.00	23	1
15	0	3.53	26	0	31	0	3.10	21	1
16	0	2.74	19	0	32	1	2.39	19	1

Source: L. Spector and M. Mazzeo, "Probit Analysis and Economic Education," *Journal of Economic Education*, vol. 11, pp. 37–44, 1980.

1. The error term u_i in the model (14.20) does not follow the normal distribution; rather, it follows the *binomial (probability) distribution*. Although we do not need the assumption of normality if the objective is the estimation of parameters only, we need it for the purpose of hypothesis testing. In reality, however, the fact that the error term in the model (14.20) follows the binomial distribution is not a great handicap if the sample size is large. This is because, as the statistical theory shows, as the sample size increases, the binomial distribution converges to the normal distribution.

2. Another problem with the OLS estimation of the model (14.20) is that the error term u_i is heteroscedastic. But this too is not a serious problem in practice because, as seen in Chapter 11 on heteroscedasticity, we can use appropriate transformations to make the error term homoscedastic.

3. The real problem with the model (14.20) is that since it gives the probability that the event Y will occur (e.g., getting an A), the probability of necessity must lie between the limits of 0 and 1. (Why?) Although this is true a priori, when we obtain it by the regression (14.23), there is no guarantee that the estimated P_i will in fact lie between these limits. If, e.g., an estimated P_i is negative, it has no practical meaning, just as if it is greater than 1 it too has no meaning.

4. Another problem with the model (14.20), or its equivalent Eq. (14.21), is that it assumes that the rate of change of probability per unit change in the value of the explanatory variable is constant, given by the value of the slope.

Thus, B_2 tells us that if the GPA increases by a unit, the probability of securing an A increases by the constant amount of B_2 regardless of the value of the GPA from which we measure the unit change, which, in practice, can be an unrealistic assumption. Rather, one would expect that the probability of securing an A would increase at a diminishing rate, if one considers the law of "diminishing returns."

It is because of these reasons, especially reason (3), that models like Eq. (14.20) are generally not estimated by OLS. But before we turn to the alternatives, let us illustrate the model (14.20) with the data given in Table 14-2 to see if reason (3) is present in our example. The straightforward OLS estimation of the model (14.20) is as follows:

$$
\begin{aligned}
\widehat{P_i(Y=1)} = \ &-1.4980 \ + \ 0.4639\text{GPA}_i \ + \ 0.0111\,\text{TUCE}_i \ + \ 0.3786\text{PSI}_i \\
\text{se} = \ &(0.5239) \quad\quad (0.16196) \quad\quad\quad (0.019) \quad\quad\quad\quad (0.13917) \quad (14.24) \\
t = \ &(-2.8594) \quad\ (2.8641) \quad\quad\quad\quad (0.5387) \quad\quad\quad\quad (2.7200)
\end{aligned}
$$

$$R^2 = 0.4159$$

(*Note*: The results are not corrected for heteroscedasticity.)

This model is to be interpreted as follows: Holding all other things constant, if the grade-point average (GPA) goes up by one point, on the average the probability of obtaining an A increases by ≈ 0.48, no matter at what value of the GPA we measure the change. Likewise, for those who have been exposed to PSI, their probability of earning an A increases by ≈ 0.37, *ceteris paribus*. Apparently, in this example TUCE has no discernible impact on the probability of securing an A. Thus, the new method of instruction seems to be effective.

Now if we substitute values of explanatory variables on the right-hand side of Eq. (14.24), we will get the actual estimate of the probability of securing an A. For example, if you take student number 22 and substitute his values on the various explanatory variables in Eq. (14.24), you will obtain

$$-1.5402 + 0.4778(3.62) + 0.0107(28) + 0.3731(1) = 0.85354$$

That is, the probability is ≈ 0.86 that a student with these values of the explanatory variables will secure an A. On the other hand, if you take student number 32 and go through similar calculations, you will find that the probability is only 0.1781. But if you take student number 1 and go through the same exercise, you will find that the probability is -0.0553, a negative probability! As a matter of fact, if you repeat this exercise for each student given in the table, you will find that five students will have a negative probability of obtaining an A! That is, in ≈ 15 percent of the cases, the probability value will turn out to be negative. It is for this reason primarily that the LPM is not a recommended method of estimating models where the dependent variable is dichotomous in nature.

14.5   THE LOGIT MODEL

What are the alternatives? In the literature there are two alternatives that are prominently discussed, the **logit model** and the **probit model.** Since the two models generally give similar results, we will discuss here only the logit model because of its comparative mathematical simplicity.[18] We illustrate the logit model with our illustrative example. As before, let P_i be the probability of obtaining an A grade. Now consider the following model:

$$\ln \left(\frac{P_i}{1 - P_i} \right) = B_1 + B_2 GPA_i + B_3 TUCE_i + B_4 PSI_i + u_i \qquad (14.25)$$

Since P_i is the probability of getting an A and $(1 - P_i)$ is the probability of not getting it, the ratio $P_i/(1 - P_i)$, known as the **odds ratio,** is simply the odds in favor of getting an A. The natural log of this odds ratio is called the logit, and therefore the model (14.25) is called the *logit model.*[19] The logit model tells us that the log of the odds ratio is a linear function of explanatory variables—GPA, TUCE, and PSI in the present case. In this model the slope coefficient, e.g., B_2, gives the change in the log of the odds ratio per unit change in the GPA. Note that, unlike the LPM, the logit model does not give the probabilities directly. Later on we will show how the probabilities can be computed.

What are the special features of the logit model? First, the mathematics of the model guarantees that probabilities estimated from the logit model will always lie within the logical bounds of 0 and 1. Second, unlike the LPM, for this model the probability of securing an A does not increase linearly (i.e., by a constant amount) with a unit change in the value of the explanatory variable. Rather, the probability approaches zero at a slower and slower rate as the value of an explanatory variable gets smaller and smaller and the probability approaches 1 at a slower and slower rate as the value of the explanatory variable gets larger and larger, as shown in Figure 14-2.

Estimation of the Logit Model:
Individual Data

The logit model (14.25) looks like the semilog model discussed in Chapter 8. It would then seem that it can be estimated with the usual OLS method. Unfortunately, this is not the case because to apply OLS to Eq. (14.25), we must know the value of the dependent variable $\ln (P_i/1 - P_i)$, which obvi-

---

[18] For a discussion of the probit and logit models, see Damodar N. Gujarati, *Basic Econometrics,* 2d ed., McGraw-Hill, New York, 1988, Chap. 15.

[19] The logit model derives its name from the *logistic probability distribution function,* which is discussed in Damodar N. Gujarati, *Basic Econometrics,* 2d ed., McGraw-Hill, New York, 1988, pp. 481–482.

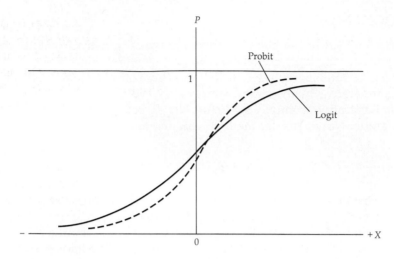

FIGURE 14-2
Logit and probit cumulative distribution functions.

ously is not known. As a matter of fact, our ultimate objective is to find out what P is given the values of the explanatory variable. How then can we estimate models like Eq. (14.25)? The answer depends upon the type of data available for analysis. If we have data on individual observations, we can use the **method of maximum likelihood (ML)** to estimate the model. On the other hand, if we have *grouped* observations (as in Table 14-3), we can then use OLS. Since our data on the GPA is per individual student, we will use the ML method to estimate the parameters of the model (14.25). Although we will not discuss the details of this method, which is beyond the scope of this book, it suffices to note that several computer packages now routinely use the ML method to estimate the logit model. For our illustrative example, we have used the logit ML estimation routine of the SHAZAM computer program. We first present the results of ML estimation for our example. Later we will present another example based upon the grouped data and show how OLS can then be used.

Based upon the SHAZAM program, the empirical counterpart of the model (14.25) is[20]

---

[20] A few technical points: The standard errors and t ratios given in the following regressions are *asymptotic* ones; that is, they are for large samples. Secondly, for the logit model, the usual R^2 is not meaningful. There are several alternatives such as the Maddala, Cragg-Uhler, and McFadden R^2s. In the present example the Maddala and McFadden R^2 values are about the same, although the Cragg-Uhler R^2 is 0.5364.

$$\ln \frac{\hat{P}_i}{1 - P_i} = -13.021 + 2.8261\text{GPA}_i + 0.095\text{TUCE}_i + 2.3787\text{PSI}_i$$

$$\text{se} = \quad (4.9310) \qquad (1.2629) \qquad\qquad (0.142155) \qquad\qquad (1.0645)$$

$$t = (-2.6407) \qquad (2.2378) \qquad\qquad (0.7226) \qquad\qquad (2.2345) \qquad\qquad (14.26)$$

$$\text{Maddala } R^2 = 0.3821$$

The interpretation of this logit regression is as follows. Holding all other things constant, if the GPA goes up by a unit, on the average, the logit, or log of the odds ratio in favor of getting an A, goes up by $\approx$ 2.9 units.[21] Similarly, *ceteris paribus*, the (log of the) odds of getting an A, on the average, goes up by $\approx$ 2.35 units for those who are exposed to PSI. TUCE apparently has no statistically detectable influence on the GPA.

How do we compute the actual probabilities of getting an A? To determine this, let us first show how to calculate the logit values for any student. Putting the values of explanatory variables for each student given in Table 14-2 into Eq (14.26), we get the numerical value of the logit $\ln (P_i/1 - P_i)$. For instance, for student no. 1, the calculated logit is

$$\ln \frac{P_i}{1 - P_i} = -3.6007 \qquad\qquad (14.27)$$

Now if we take the antilog of Eq. (14.27), we obtain

$$\frac{P_i}{1 - P_i} = e\{-3.6174\} \qquad\qquad (14.28)$$

where $e\{\ \}$ means e raised to the power of the expression in $\{\ \}$, which is -3.6174 in the present case. A simple algebraic manipulation of Eq. (14.28) will give

$$P_i = \frac{e\{-3.6174\}}{1 + e\{-3.6174\}} \qquad\qquad (14.29)$$

$$= 0.0266 \qquad\qquad (14.30)$$

Note: $e\{-3.6174\} \approx 0.0268$.

That is, the probability is $\approx$ 3 percent that a student with the given values on explanatory variables will secure an A. On the other hand, if you take student no. 30 and go through similar calculations, his or her logit value is 2.8504, from which the probability can be estimated as 0.94534. This means that the probability that a student with this configuration of explanatory val-

---

[21] Note carefully that the slope coefficient gives the change in the log of the odds ratio for a unit change in the explanatory variable and not the change in the probability itself. The latter change is a little difficult to compute, but the details can be found in Damodar N. Gujarati, *Basic Econometrics*, McGraw-Hill, New York, 1988, p. 488.

ues will get an A is $\approx$ 95 percent. As a general rule, *keep in mind that the higher the value of the logit is, the higher the odds in favor of obtaining an A are, and therefore the higher the probability of getting an A will be.* In problem 14.17 you are asked to compute probabilities of getting an A for the other 30 students whose scores are given in Table 14-2.

Logit Estimation of Grouped Data

Example 14.7. Logit estimation of home ownership. Suppose we want to study home ownership as a function of family income. For this purpose, suppose we have the hypothetical data given in Table 14-3. In this table there are in all 580 families but unlike Table 14-2 we do not have data on each individual family about their income and home ownership status. Instead, these 580 families are *grouped* into 10 broad income classes and we have data on the total number of families belonging to each class and the number of families in each class that actually own a house. Such data are called *grouped data*, whereas the data in Table 14-2 is *micro*, or *individual*, *data*. Now if we take the ratio of n_i to N_i, we obtain

$$p_i = \frac{n_i}{N_i} \tag{14.31}$$

which is simply the *relative frequency* (see Chapter 2), which can be used as an estimator of the true probability P_i, especially if N_i is fairly large.[22] Therefore, in the logit model

$$\ln \frac{P_i}{1 - P_i} = B_1 + B_2 X_i + u_i \tag{14.32}$$

where P_i = the probability of owning a house and X_i = the income, if we substitute p_i obtained from Equation (14.31), the left-hand side of Equation (14.32) can be easily computed, and thus OLS can be directly applied to Eq. (14.32). From the data given in Table 14-3, and using the p_i given in column 4 of that table, we obtain the regression corresponding to Eq. (14.32) as

$$\ln \frac{\hat{p}_i}{1 - p_i} = -3.2438 + 0.0792 X_i$$
$$\text{se} = \quad (0.1708) \quad (0.0041) \tag{14.33}$$
$$t = (-18.992) \quad (19.349) \quad R^2 = 0.9791$$

As these results show, if income increases by a unit (here, $1000), the log of the odds in favor of owning a house goes up by $\approx$ 0.08 units. Of course, we can

---

[22] Recall from our discussion of probability in Chap. 2 that the probability of an event is the limit of the relative frequency as the sample size becomes infinitely large.

actually compute the probability of owning a house at any given income level. For instance, letting $X = 26$, we obtain

$$\ln \frac{p_i}{1 - p_i} = -1.1846$$

Therefore, following Eq. (14.29), we get

$$p_i(\text{given } X = 26) = 0.2342 \qquad\qquad (14.34)$$

whereas the actual probability was 0.20. Other probabilities can be computed similarly (see problem 14.18).

There is one technical point about the regression (14.33): This regression suffers from the problem of heteroscedasticity. This is true of logit models based upon grouped data. But this problem can be easily resolved, although we defer the details to the references.[23]

With the knowledge of the logit model, the reader can now easily handle models in which the dependent variable is dummy or binary. As a matter of fact, one can even run a regression in which the dependent variable as well as all explanatory variables are dummies. Not only that, but one can even consider regression models in which the dependent variable is not only dichot-

TABLE 14-3

Hypothetical data on X_i (income), N_i (number of families at income X_i), and n_i (number of families owning a house)

X ($\$$, in thousands) (1)	N_i (2)	n_i (3)	$p_i = \dfrac{n_i}{N_i}$ (4)
26	40	8	0.20
28	50	12	0.24
30	60	18	0.30
33	80	28	0.35
35	100	45	0.45
40	70	36	0.51
45	65	39	0.60
50	50	33	0.66
55	40	30	0.75
60	25	20	0.80
	580	269	

---

[23] For details, see Damodar N. Gujarati, *Basic Econometrics*, 2d ed., McGraw-Hill, New York, 1988, pp. 485–486.

omous but is also trichotomous (e.g., membership in the Republican party or the Democratic party or a third party), or even has more than three categories. Such models are called *multinominal regression models*, but they are beyond the scope of the present book.[24]

We conclude this chapter by presenting an interesting application of the logit model.

Example 14.8. Predicting bank failure.   Based on call report (i.e., bank examinations) data of 6869 calls between December 1982 and December 1984, Robert Avery and Terrence Belton,[25] estimated a *risk index* (i.e., a logit function) to predict bank failure: A bank was deemed to have failed if it failed within a year following the call—the bank examination. Their results are presented in Table 14-4.

As these results show, *ceteris paribus*, if KTA, the ratio of primary capital (i.e., shareholder equity) to total assets goes up by one percentage point, the log of the odds of bankruptcy goes down by 0.501, which is a sensible result. Similarly, if LNNACCA, the percent ratio of nonaccruing loans to total assets, goes up by a percentage point, the log of odds in favor of bankruptcy goes up by 4.310. The other coefficients are to be interpreted similarly. Statistically, RENEGA and NCOFSA are insignificant and NCOFSA has the wrong sign. (Why?)

Avery and Belton conclude that:

> Although the overall fit of the model suggests that predicting bank failure is difficult, the failed banks in the sample had an average predicted probability of failure of 0.24, a number 69 times larger than the average predicted failure probability of nonfailed banks in the sample. Hence, the model clearly does have some ability to discriminate between high- and low-risk banks.

14.6   SUMMARY

In this chapter we discussed three topics of considerable practical importance. The first topic was that of restricted least squares (RLS). If economic theory suggests that one or more parameters of a regression model should satisfy one or more linear restrictions, then RLS is a way of incorporating such restrictions directly into the estimating procedure. We compare the results of the RLS regression with those obtained from the unrestricted (ULS), or what amounts to the same thing, freely estimated OLS regression. This comparison involves comparing the R^2 values of the restricted and unrestricted regres-

---

[24] For a general description of the logistic models, see David W. Hosmer and Stanley Lemesshow, *Applied Logistic Regression*, Wiley, New York, 1988.

[25] The results given in the table are reproduced from Robert B. Avery and Terrence M. Belton, "A Comparison of Risk-Based Capital and Risk-Based Deposit Insurance," *Economic Review*, Federal Reserve Bank of Cleveland, pp. 20–30, 1987, fourth quarter.

TABLE 14-4
Logit model: Predicting bank failure

Explanatory variable	Coefficient	t value
Constant	−2.420	3.07
KTA	−0.501	−4.89
PD090MA	0.428	5.16
LNNACCA	4.310	4.31
RENEGA	0.269	1.07
NCOFSA	0.223	1.60
NETINCA	0.331	2.68

Source: Robert B. Avery and Terrence M. Belton, "Comparison of Risk-Based Capital and Risk-Based Deposit Insurance," *Economic Review*, Federal Reserve Bank of Cleveland, 1987, fourth quarter.

Note: KTA = the percent ratio of primary capital to total assets
PD90MA = the percent ratio of loans more than 90 days past due to total assets
LNNACCA = the percent ratio of nonaccruing loans to total assets
RENEGA = the percent ratio of renegotiated loans to total assets
NCOFSA = the percent ratio of net loan charge-offs (annualized) to total assets
NETINCA = the percent ratio of net income (annualized) to total assets.

sions. Under the null hypothesis that restrictions are valid, we showed in Eq. (14.8) how the F test enables us to decide whether or not to reject the null hypothesis. If the null hypothesis is not rejected, we can say that the restrictions suggested by the theory are valid. But if the null hypothesis is rejected, the restrictions suggested by the theory are not valid, in which case we will use the unrestricted, or standard, OLS.

The next topic we discussed was dynamic modeling in which time or lag explicitly enters into the analysis. In such models the current value of the dependent variable depends upon one or more lagged values of the explanatory variable(s). This dependence can be due to psychological, technological, or institutional reasons. These models are generally known as distributed lag models. Although the inclusion of one or more lagged terms of an explanatory variable does not violate any of the standard CLRM assumptions, the estimation of such models by the usual OLS method is generally not recommended because of the problem of multicollinearity and the fact that every additional coefficient estimated means a loss of degrees of freedom. Therefore, such models are usually estimated by imposing some restrictions on the parameters of the models (e.g., the values of the various lagged coefficients decline from the first coefficient onward). This is the approach adopted by the Koyck, the adaptive expectations, and the partial, or stock adjustment, models. A unique feature of all these models is that they replace all lagged values of the explanatory variable by a single lagged value of the dependent variable. Because of the presence of the lagged value of the dependent variable among explanatory variables, the resulting model is called an autoregressive model. Although autoregressive models achieve economy in the estimation of distributed lag coefficients, they are not free from statistical problems. In particular, one has to guard against the possibility of autocorrelation in the error term because in the presence of autocorrelation and lagged dependent variable as an explanatory variable, the OLS estimators are biased as well as inconsistent.

In discussing the dynamic models, we pointed out how they help us to assess the short- and long-run impact of an explanatory variable on the dependent variable.

The final topic we discussed in this chapter was the dummy dependent variable, where the dependent variable can take values of either 1 or 0. Although such models can be estimated by OLS, in which case they are called linear probability models (LPM), this is not the recommended procedure since probabilities estimated from such models can sometimes be negative or greater than 1. Therefore, such models are usually estimated by the logit or probit procedures. In this chapter we illustrated the logit model with concrete examples. Thanks to excellent computer packages, estimation of logit and probit models is no longer a mysterious or forbidding task.

Key Terms and Concepts

The key terms and concepts introduced in this chapter are:

Restricted least squares (RLS)
  a) restricted least squares
     regression
Unrestricted least squares (ULS)
Dynamic economic models
  a) distributed lag models
  b) autoregressive models
  c) lagged variables/values (short-
     run, or impact, multiplier;
     interim, or intermediate,
     multiplier; long-run, or total,
     multiplier)

Estimating distributed lag models
  a) the Koyck model
  b) the adaptive expectations model
  c) the partial, or stock adjustment,
     model
Logit model and probit model
  a) odds ratio
  b) method of maximum likelihood
     (ML)

QUESTIONS

14.1. Explain the meaning of the following terms:

(a) Restricted least squares (RLS)
(b) Dynamic models
(c) Distributed lag models
(d) Autoregressive models

14.2. It is generally the case that $R^{*2} \leq R^2$; that is, the R^2 obtained from the RLS is smaller than or at most equal to the R^2 obtained from the unrestricted regression. Can you provide an intuitive justification for this?

14.3. If the restrictions imposed by theory are in fact valid, RLS estimators will be more efficient than unrestricted OLS estimators. Can you justify this intuitively?

14.4. Consider the models:

$$\text{Model A: } Y_i = B_1 + B_2 X_i + u_i$$

$$\text{Model B: } Y_i = A_1 X_i + v_i$$

(a) What is the difference between the two models?

(b) How would you use the RLS to determine which is the appropriate model in a given situation?

(c) Suppose model A is the correct model but you estimate model B. What kind of specification bias is involved? How would you use the RLS to detect this bias?

14.5. Consider the following model:

$$Y_i = B_1 + B_2 X_{2i} + B_3 X_{3i} + B_4 X_{4i} + B_5 X_{5i} + u_i$$

Suppose you want to impose the restrictions that $B_2 = 0$ and $B_4 + B_5 = 1$, how would you set up the RLS model? And how would you test for the validity of the restrictions?

14.6. What are the reasons for the lag in the response of the dependent variable to one or more explanatory variables? Give some examples of distributed lag models.

14.7. What is wrong with the strategy of determining the number of lagged terms in a distributed lag model *sequentially*, that is, adding each successive lagged term if the t value of an added lagged term is statistically significant. In other words, go on adding a lagged term as long as the t value of the added lagged term is statistically significant on the basis of the t test.

14.8. "Since the successive lagged terms in a distributed lag model are likely to be collinear, in such models one should not worry about the statistical significance of any individual lagged coefficient but should consider the statistical significance of the sum of the lagged coefficients as a whole." Comment.

14.9. "Although the logit and probit models may be superior to the LPM model, in practice, one should choose the LPM because of its simplicity as per Occam's razor principle." Do you agree? Why or why not?

14.10. True or false: The greater the value of the logit is, the greater the probability that the particular event will occur.

PROBLEMS

14.11. Corresponding to the regression (14.3), the following is the regression for the agricultural sector of the Taiwanese economy for the years 1958 to 1972.

$$\widehat{\ln Y_t} = -3.3384 + 1.4988 \ln X_{2t} + 0.4899 \ln X_{3i}$$

$$t = (-1.3629) \quad (0.5398) \quad (0.1020) \quad R^2 = 0.8890$$

Imposing the restriction $(B_2 + B_3) = 1$, that is, constant returns to scale, gives the following regression:

$$\ln \frac{\hat{Y}_t}{X_{2t}} = 1.7086 + 0.6130 \ln \frac{X_{3t}}{X_{2t}}$$

$$t = (4.1082) \qquad (6.5702) \qquad\qquad R^{*2} = 0.8489$$

(a) Interpret the two regressions.
(b) Given the preceding regression results, can you tell if there were constant returns to scale in the agricultural sector of Taiwan? Show your calculations.
(c) How do the results given for the agricultural sector differ from those for the manufacturing sector given in the text?

14.12. Table 14-5 gives data on personal consumption expenditure (PCE) and personal disposable income (PDI) for the United States for 1970 to 1987, all figures in billions of 1982 dollars.

TABLE 14-5

Year	PCE	PDI	Year	PCE	PDI	Year	PCE	PDI
1970	1492.0	1668.1	1976	1803.9	2001.0	1982	2050.7	2261.5
1971	1538.8	1728.4	1977	1883.8	2066.6	1983	2146.0	2331.9
1972	1621.9	1797.4	1978	1961.0	2167.4	1984	2249.3	2469.8
1973	1689.6	1916.3	1979	2004.4	2212.6	1985	2354.8	2542.8
1974	1674.0	1896.6	1980	2000.4	2214.3	1986	2455.2	2640.9
1975	1711.9	1931.7	1981	2024.2	2248.6	1987	2521.0	2686.3

Source: Economic Report of the President, 1989, PCE from Table B-15, p. 325 and PDI from Table B-27, p. 339.

Estimate the following models:

$$PCE_t = A_1 + A_2 PDI_t + u_t$$

$$PCE_t = B_1 + B_2 PDI_t + B_3 PCE_{t-1} + v_t$$

(a) Interpret the results of the two regressions
(b) What is the short- and long-run marginal propensity to consume (MPC)?

14.13. Use the data of problem 14.12, but now consider the following models:

$$\ln PCE_t = A_1 + A_2 \ln PDI_t + u_t$$

$$\ln PCE_t = B_1 + B_2 \ln PDI_t + B_3 \ln PCE_{t-1} + v_t$$

where $\ln$ = the natural log.
(a) Interpret these regressions.
(b) What is the short- and long-run elasticity of PCE with respect to PDI?

14.14. To assess the impact of capacity utilization on inflation, Thomas A. Gittings[26] obtained the following regression for the United States for the period 1971 to 1988:

$$\hat{Y}_t = -30.12 + 0.1408X_t + 0.2360X_{t-1}$$
$$t = (-6.27) \quad (2.60) \quad\quad (4.26) \quad\quad\quad R^2 = 0.727$$

where

Y = the GNP implicit deflator, % (a measure of the inflation rate)
X_t = the capacity utilization rate in manufacturing, %
X_{t-1} = the capacity utilization rate lagged one year.

(a) Interpret the preceding regression. A priori, why is there a positive relationship between inflation and capacity utilization?
(b) What is the short-run impact of capacity utilization on inflation? And the long-run impact?
(c) Is each slope coefficient individually statistically significant?
(d) Will you reject the hypothesis that both slope coefficients are simultaneously equal to zero? Which test should you use?
(e) If you had the data and were asked to run the following model

$$Y_t = B_1 + B_2X_t + B_3Y_{t-1} + u_t$$

how would you find out the short- and long-run effects of capacity utilization on inflation? Can you compare the results of this model with the one given by Gittings?

14.15. Table 14-6 gives data on the results of spraying rotenone of different concentrations on the chrysanthemum aphis in ≈ 50 batches.

TABLE 14-6

X	Concentration (mg per liter) log(X)	Total N_i	Deaths n_i	$p_i = \dfrac{n_i}{N_i}$
2.6	0.4150	50	6	0.120
3.8	0.5797	48	16	0.333
5.1	0.7076	46	24	0.522
7.7	0.8865	49	42	0.857
10.2	1.0086	50	44	0.880

Source: D. J. Finney, *Probit Analysis*, Cambridge University Press, London, 1964.
Note: The log is a common log, that is, log to base 10.

Develop a suitable model to express the probability of death as a function of the log of X, the log of dosage, and comment on the results.

14.16. Consider the following model, known as the *logistic (probability) distribution*, where P_i is the probability of owning, say, a house and X_i is income:

---

[26] Thomas A. Gittings, "Capacity Utilization and Inflation," *Economic Perspectives*, Federal Reserve Bank of Chicago, pp. 2–9, May/June 1989.

$$P_i = \frac{1}{1 + \exp\{-B_1 - B_2 X_i\}}$$

where exp { } means e (the base of natural log) raised to the power of the expression in { }. With simple algebraic manipulations, show that

$$\ln \left(\frac{P_i}{1 - P_i} \right) = B_1 + B_2 X_i$$

which is the logit model discussed in the text. The name logit comes from the previous logistic distribution.

14.17. Given the data of Table 14-2 and the regression (14.26), compute the probability of getting an A grade for each individual student.

14.18. From the regression (14.33), compute the probability of owning a house for each income level shown in Table 14-3.

14.19. Based on a sample of 20 couples, Barbara Bund Jackson[27] obtained the following regression:

$$\ln \frac{\widehat{P_i}}{1 - P_i} = -9.456 + 0.3638 \, \text{income}_i - 1.107 \, \text{baby-sitter}_i$$

(*Note*: The author did not present standard errors.)

where

P = the probability of restaurant usage, = 1 if went to a restaurant
    0 otherwise

Income = the income in thousands of dollars

Baby-sitter = 1 if needed a baby-sitter
    0 otherwise

Of the 20 couples, 11 regularly went to a restaurant, 6 regularly used a baby-sitter, and the income ranged from a low of $17,000 to a high of $44,000.

(*a*) Interpret the preceding logit regression.
(*b*) Find out the logit value of a couple with an income of $44,000 who needed a baby-sitter.
(*c*) For the same couple, find out the probability of going to a restaurant.

---

[27] See Barbara Bund Jackson, *Multivariate Data Analysis: An Introduction*, Irwin, 1983, p. 92.

APPENDIX
A

A LIST
OF SELECTED
ECONOMETRIC
SOFTWARE
PACKAGES

We list below some well-known statistical and econometric software packages that can handle most of the econometric techniques discussed in this text. Student versions of some of these packages are available at substantially reduced rates. Some of these packages are also available on mainframe computers. Since these packages are updated regularly, the user is advised to consult the vendor regarding the latest version.

IBM-PC AND COMPATIBLES

BMDP/PC	BMDP Statistical Software Inc., 1440 Sepulveda Blvd., Suite 316, Los Angeles, CA 90025. (213) 479-7799.
DATA-FIT	Oxford Electronic Publishing Company, Oxford University Press, Walton Street, Oxford OX2 6DP, U.K.
ESP	Economic Software Package, 76 Bedford St., Suite 33, Lexington, MA 02173. (617) 861-8852.
ET	William H. Green, Stern Graduate School of Business, New York University, 100 Trinity Place, New York, NY (212) 285-6164.
GAUSS	Aptech Systems Inc., 26250 196th Place SE, Kent, WA 98042. (206) 631-6679.
LIMDEP	William H. Greene, Stern Graduate School of Business, New York University, 100 Trinity Place, New York, NY (212) 285-6164.

MATLAB	Math Work Inc., 20 N Main St., Sherborn, MA 01770. (617) 653-1415.
MICRO TSP	Quantitative Micro Software, 4521 Campus Drive, Suite 336, Irvine, CA 92715. (714) 856-3368
MINITAB	Minitab, 3081 Enterprise Dr., State College, PA 16801. (814) 238-3280.
PC-GIVE	University of Oxford, Institute of Economics and Statistics, St. Cross Building, Manor Rd., Oxford OX1 3UL U.K.
PC-TSP	TSP International, P.O. Box 61015, Palo Alto, CA 94306 (415) 326-1927.
RATS	VAR Econometrics, P.O. Box 1818, Evanston, IL 606204-1818. (312) 864-8772.
SAS/STAT	SAS Institute Inc., P.O. Box 8000, SAS Circle, Cary, NC 27511-8000. (919) 467-8000.
SHAZAM	Kenneth J. White, Department of Economics, University of British Columbia, Vancouver, BC V6T 1Y2 Canada. (604) 228-5062.
SORITEC	The Soritec Group Inc., P.O. Box 2939, 8136 Old Keene Mill Road, Springfield, VA 22152. (703) 569-1400.
SPSS/PC+	SPSS Inc., 444 N. Michigan Ave., Chicago, IL 60611. (312) 329-3600.
STATA	Computing Resource Center, 10801 National Blvd., 3rd Floor, Los Angeles, CA 90064. (800) STATAPC.
STATGRAPHICS	STSC Inc., 2115 E. Jefferson St., Rockville, MD 20852. (800) 592-0050.
STATPRO	Penton Software Inc., 420 Lexington Ave., Suite 2846, New York, NY 10017. (800) 211-3414.
SYSTAT	Systat Inc., 1800 Sherman Ave., Evanston, IL 60201. (312) 864-5670

APPLE MACINTOSH

MATLAB	Math Works Inc., 20 N. Main St., Sherborn, MA 01770. (617)653-1415.
PC-TSP	TSP International, P.O. Box 61015, Palo Alto, CA 93406. (415) 326-1927.
RATS	VAR Econometrics, P.O. Box 1818, Evanston, IL 60204-1818. (312) 864-8772.
SHAZAM	Kenneth J. White, Department of Economics, University of British Columbia, Vancouver, BC V6T 1Y2 Canada. (602) 228-5062.

APPENDIX

B

STATISTICAL
TABLES

TABLE B-1

Areas under the standardized normal distribution

Example

$\Pr(0 \le z \le 1.96) = 0.4750$

$\Pr(z \ge 1.96) = 0.5 - 0.4750 = 0.025$

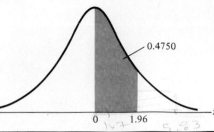

z	.00	.01	.02	.03	.04	.05	.06	.07	.08	.09
0.0	.0000	.0040	.0080	.0120	.0160	.0199	.0239	.0279	.0319	.0359
0.1	.0398	.0438	.0478	.0517	.0557	.0596	.0636	.0675	.0714	.0753
0.2	.0793	.0832	.0871	.0910	.0948	.0987	.1026	.1064	.1103	.1141
0.3	.1179	.1217	.1255	.1293	.1331	.1368	.1406	.1443	.1480	.1517
0.4	.1554	.1591	.1628	.1664	.1700	.1736	.1772	.1808	.1844	.1879
0.5	.1915	.1950	.1985	.2019	.2054	.2088	.2123	.2157	.2190	.2224
0.6	.2257	.2291	.2324	.2357	.2389	.2422	.2454	.2486	.2517	.2549
0.7	.2580	.2611	.2642	.2673	.2704	.2734	.2764	.2794	.2823	.2852
0.8	.2881	.2910	.2939	.2967	.2995	.3023	.3051	.3078	.3106	.3133
0.9	.3159	.3186	.3212	.3238	.3264	.3289	.3315	.3340	.3365	.3389
1.0	.3413	.3438	.3461	.3485	.3508	.3531	.3554	.3577	.3599	.3621
1.1	.3643	.3665	.3686	.3708	.3729	.3749	.3770	.3790	.3810	.3830
1.2	.3849	.3869	.3888	.3907	.3925	.3944	.3962	.3980	.3997	.4015
1.3	.4032	.4049	.4066	.4082	.4099	.4115	.4131	.4147	.4162	.4177
1.4	.4192	.4207	.4222	.4236	.4251	.4265	.4279	.4292	.4306	.4319
1.5	.4332	.4345	.4357	.4370	.4382	.4394	.4406	.4418	.4429	.4441
1.6	.4452	.4463	.4474	.4484	.4495	.4505	.4515	.4525	.4535	.4545
1.7	.4554	.4564	.4573	.4582	.4591	.4599	.4608	.4616	.4625	.4633
1.8	.4641	.4649	.4656	.4664	.4671	.4678	.4686	.4693	.4699	.4706
1.9	.4713	.4719	.4726	.4732	.4738	.4744	.4750	.4756	.4761	.4767
2.0	.4772	.4778	.4783	.4788	.4793	.4798	.4803	.4808	.4812	.4817
2.1	.4821	.4826	.4830	.4834	.4838	.4842	.4846	.4850	.4854	.4857
2.2	.4861	.4864	.4868	.4871	.4875	.4878	.4881	.4884	.4887	.4890
2.3	.4893	.4896	.4898	.4901	.4904	.4906	.4909	.4911	.4913	.4916
2.4	.4918	.4920	.4922	.4925	.4927	.4929	.4931	.4932	.4934	.4936
2.5	.4938	.4940	.4941	.4943	.4945	.4946	.4948	.4949	.4951	.4952
2.6	.4953	.4955	.4956	.4957	.4959	.4960	.4961	.4962	.4963	.4964
2.7	.4965	.4966	.4967	.4968	.4969	.4970	.4971	.4972	.4973	.4974
2.8	.4974	.4975	.4976	.4977	.4977	.4978	.4979	.4979	.4980	.4981
2.9	.4981	.4982	.4982	.4983	.4984	.4984	.4985	.4985	.4986	.4986
3.0	.4987	.4987	.4987	.4988	.4988	.4989	.4989	.4989	.4990	.4990

Note: This table gives the area in the right-hand tail of the distribution (i.e., $z \ge 0$). But since the normal distribution is symmetrical about $z = 0$, the area in the left-hand tail is the same as the area in the corresponding right-hand tail. For example, $P(-1.96 \le z \le 0) = 0.4750$. Therefore, $P(-1.96 \le z \le 1.96) = 2(0.4750) = 0.95$.

TABLE B-2
Percentage points of the t distribution

Example

$\Pr(t > 2.086) = 0.025$

$\Pr(t > 1.725) = 0.05$ for df = 20

$\Pr(|t| > 1.725) = 0.10$

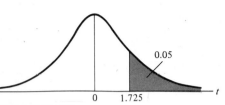

→ 1 Tailed = %. - 1
→ 2 Tailed = %. - 1

Pr df	0.25 0.50	0.10 0.20	0.05 0.10	0.025 0.05	0.01 0.02	0.005 0.010	0.001 0.002
1	1.000	3.078	6.314	12.706	31.821	63.657	318.31
2	0.816	1.886	2.920	4.303	6.965	9.925	22.327
3	0.765	1.638	2.353	3.182	4.541	5.841	10.214
4	0.741	1.533	2.132	2.776	3.747	4.604	7.173
5	0.727	1.476	2.015	2.571	3.365	4.032	5.893
6	0.718	1.440	1.943	2.447	3.143	3.707	5.208
7	0.711	1.415	1.895	2.365	2.998	3.499	4.785
8	0.706	1.397	1.860	2.306	2.896	3.355	4.501
9	0.703	1.383	1.833	2.262	2.821	3.250	4.297
10	0.700	1.372	1.812	2.228	2.764	3.169	4.144
11	0.697	1.363	1.796	2.201	2.718	3.106	4.025
12	0.695	1.356	1.782	2.179	2.681	3.055	3.930
13	0.694	1.350	1.771	2.160	2.650	3.012	3.852
14	0.692	1.345	1.761	2.145	2.624	2.977	3.787
15	0.691	1.341	1.753	2.131	2.602	2.947	3.733
16	0.690	1.337	1.746	2.120	2.583	2.921	3.686
17	0.689	1.333	1.740	2.110	2.567	2.898	3.646
18	0.688	1.330	1.734	2.101	2.552	2.878	3.610
19	0.688	1.328	1.729	2.093	2.539	2.861	3.579
20	0.687	1.325	1.725	2.086	2.528	2.845	3.552
21	0.686	1.323	1.721	2.080	2.518	2.831	3.527
22	0.686	1.321	1.717	2.074	2.508	2.819	3.505
23	0.685	1.319	1.714	2.069	2.500	2.807	3.485
24	0.685	1.318	1.711	2.064	2.492	2.797	3.467
25	0.684	1.316	1.708	2.060	2.485	2.787	3.450
26	0.684	1.315	1.706	2.056	2.479	2.779	3.435
27	0.684	1.314	1.703	2.052	2.473	2.771	3.421
28	0.683	1.313	1.701	2.048	2.467	2.763	3.408
29	0.683	1.311	1.699	2.045	2.462	2.756	3.396
30	0.683	1.310	1.697	2.042	2.457	2.750	3.385
40	0.681	1.303	1.684	2.021	2.423	2.704	3.307
60	0.679	1.296	1.671	2.000	2.390	2.660	3.232
120	0.677	1.289	1.658	1.980	2.358	2.167	3.160
∞	0.674	1.282	1.645	1.960	2.326	2.576	3.090

T &z are =

Note: The smaller probability shown at the head of each column is the area in one tail; the larger probability is the area in both tails.

TABLE B-3

Upper percentage points of the F distribution

Example

$$\Pr(F > 1.59) = 0.25$$
$$\Pr(F > 2.42) = 0.10 \qquad \text{for df } N_1 = 10$$
$$\Pr(F > 3.14) = 0.05 \qquad \text{and } N_2 = 9$$
$$\Pr(F > 5.26) = 0.01$$

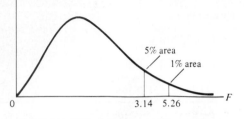

df for denominator N_2	Pr	\multicolumn{12}{c}{df for numerator N_1}

N_2	Pr	1	2	3	4	5	6	7	8	9	10	11	12
1	.25	5.83	7.50	8.20	8.58	8.82	8.98	9.10	9.19	9.26	9.32	9.36	9.41
	.10	39.9	49.5	53.6	55.8	57.2	58.2	58.9	59.4	59.9	60.2	60.5	60.7
	.05	161	200	216	225	230	234	237	239	241	242	243	244
2	.25	2.57	3.00	3.15	3.23	3.28	3.31	3.34	3.35	3.37	3.38	3.39	3.39
	.10	8.53	9.00	9.16	9.24	9.29	9.33	9.35	9.37	9.38	9.39	9.40	9.41
	.05	18.5	19.0	19.2	19.2	19.3	19.3	19.4	19.4	19.4	19.4	19.4	19.4
	.01	98.5	99.0	99.2	99.2	99.3	99.3	99.4	99.4	99.4	99.4	99.4	99.4
3	.25	2.02	2.28	2.36	2.39	2.41	2.42	2.43	2.44	2.44	2.44	2.45	2.45
	.10	5.54	5.46	5.39	5.34	5.31	5.28	5.27	5.25	5.24	5.23	5.22	5.22
	.05	10.1	9.55	9.28	9.12	9.01	8.94	8.89	8.85	8.81	8.79	8.76	8.74
	.01	34.1	30.8	29.5	28.7	28.2	27.9	27.7	27.5	27.3	27.2	27.1	27.1
4	.25	1.81	2.00	2.05	2.06	2.07	2.08	2.08	2.08	2.08	2.08	2.08	2.08
	.10	4.54	4.32	4.19	4.11	4.05	4.01	3.98	3.95	3.94	3.92	3.91	3.90
	.05	7.71	6.94	6.59	6.39	6.26	6.16	6.09	6.04	6.00	5.96	5.94	5.91
	.01	21.2	18.0	16.7	16.0	15.5	15.2	15.0	14.8	14.7	14.5	14.4	14.4
5	.25	1.69	1.85	1.88	1.89	1.89	1.89	1.89	1.89	1.89	1.89	1.89	1.89
	.10	4.06	3.78	3.62	3.52	3.45	3.40	3.37	3.34	3.32	3.30	3.28	3.27
	.05	6.61	5.79	5.41	5.19	5.05	4.95	4.88	4.82	4.77	4.74	4.71	4.68
	.01	16.3	13.3	12.1	11.4	11.0	10.7	10.5	10.3	10.2	10.1	9.96	9.89
6	.25	1.62	1.76	1.78	1.79	1.79	1.78	1.78	1.78	1.77	1.77	1.77	1.77
	.10	3.78	3.46	3.29	3.18	3.11	3.05	3.01	2.98	2.96	2.94	2.92	2.90
	.05	5.99	5.14	4.76	4.53	4.39	4.28	4.21	4.15	4.10	4.06	4.03	4.00
	.01	13.7	10.9	9.78	9.15	8.75	8.47	8.26	8.10	7.98	7.87	7.79	7.72
7	.25	1.57	1.70	1.72	1.72	1.71	1.71	1.70	1.70	1.69	1.69	1.69	1.68
	.10	3.59	3.26	3.07	2.96	2.88	2.83	2.78	2.75	2.72	2.70	2.68	2.67
	.05	5.59	4.74	4.35	4.12	3.97	3.87	3.79	3.73	3.68	3.64	3.60	3.57
	.01	12.2	9.55	8.45	7.85	7.46	7.19	6.99	6.84	6.72	6.62	6.54	6.47
8	.25	1.54	1.66	1.67	1.66	1.66	1.65	1.64	1.64	1.63	1.63	1.63	1.62
	.10	3.46	3.11	2.92	2.81	2.73	2.67	2.62	2.59	2.56	2.54	2.52	2.50
	.05	5.32	4.46	4.07	3.84	3.69	3.58	3.50	3.44	3.39	3.35	3.31	3.28
	.01	11.3	8.65	7.59	7.01	6.63	6.37	6.18	6.03	5.91	5.81	5.73	5.67
9	.25	1.51	1.62	1.63	1.63	1.62	1.61	1.60	1.60	1.59	1.59	1.58	1.58
	.10	3.36	3.01	2.81	2.69	2.61	2.55	2.51	2.47	2.44	2.42	2.40	2.38
	.05	5.12	4.26	3.86	3.63	3.48	3.37	3.29	3.23	3.18	3.14	3.10	3.07
	.01	10.6	8.02	6.99	6.42	6.06	5.80	5.61	5.47	5.35	5.26	5.18	5.11

Source: From E. S. Pearson and H. O. Hartley, eds., *Biometrika Tables for Statisticians*, vol. 1, 3d ed., table 18, Cambridge University Press, New York, 1966. Reproduced by permission of the editors and trustees of *Biometrika*.

				df for numerator N_1										df for denominator N_2
15	20	24	30	40	50	60	100	120	200	500	∞	Pr	
9.49	9.58	9.63	9.67	9.71	9.74	9.76	9.78	9.80	9.82	9.84	9.85	.25	
61.2	61.7	62.0	62.3	62.5	62.7	62.8	63.0	63.1	63.2	63.3	63.3	.10	1
246	248	249	250	251	252	252	253	253	254	254	254	.05	
3.41	3.43	3.43	3.44	3.45	3.45	3.46	3.47	3.47	3.48	3.48	3.48	.25	
9.42	9.44	9.45	9.46	9.47	9.47	9.47	9.48	9.48	9.49	9.49	9.49	.10	2
19.4	19.4	19.5	19.5	19.5	19.5	19.5	19.5	19.5	19.5	19.5	19.5	.05	
99.4	99.4	99.5	99.5	99.5	99.5	99.5	99.5	99.5	99.5	99.5	99.5	.01	
2.46	2.46	2.46	2.47	2.47	2.47	2.47	2.47	2.47	2.47	2.47	2.47	.25	
5.20	5.18	5.18	5.17	5.16	5.15	5.15	5.14	5.14	5.14	5.14	5.13	.10	3
8.70	8.66	8.64	8.62	8.59	8.58	8.57	8.55	8.55	8.54	8.53	8.53	.05	
26.9	26.7	26.6	26.5	26.4	26.4	26.3	26.2	26.2	26.2	26.1	26.1	.01	
2.08	2.08	2.08	2.08	2.08	2.08	2.08	2.08	2.08	2.08	2.08	2.08	.25	
3.87	3.84	3.83	3.82	3.80	3.80	3.79	3.78	3.78	3.77	3.76	3.76	.10	4
5.86	5.80	5.77	5.75	5.72	5.70	5.69	5.66	5.66	5.65	5.64	5.63	.05	
14.2	14.0	13.9	13.8	13.7	13.7	13.7	13.6	13.6	13.5	13.5	13.5	.01	
1.89	1.88	1.88	1.88	1.88	1.88	1.87	1.87	1.87	1.87	1.87	1.87	.25	
3.24	3.21	3.19	3.17	3.16	3.15	3.14	3.13	3.12	3.12	3.11	3.10	.10	5
4.62	4.56	4.53	4.50	4.46	4.44	4.43	4.41	4.40	4.39	4.37	4.36	.05	
9.72	9.55	9.47	9.38	9.29	9.24	9.20	9.13	9.11	9.08	9.04	9.02	.01	
1.76	1.76	1.75	1.75	1.75	1.75	1.74	1.74	1.74	1.74	1.74	1.74	.25	
2.87	2.84	2.82	2.80	2.78	2.77	2.76	2.75	2.74	2.73	2.73	2.72	.10	6
3.94	3.87	3.84	3.81	3.77	3.75	3.74	3.71	3.70	3.69	3.68	3.67	.05	
7.56	7.40	7.31	7.23	7.14	7.09	7.06	6.99	6.97	6.93	6.90	6.88	.01	
1.68	1.67	1.67	1.66	1.66	1.66	1.65	1.65	1.65	1.65	1.65	1.65	.25	
2.63	2.59	2.58	2.56	2.54	2.52	2.51	2.50	2.49	2.48	2.48	2.47	.10	7
3.51	3.44	3.41	3.38	3.34	3.32	3.30	3.27	3.27	3.25	3.24	3.23	.05	
6.31	6.16	6.07	5.99	5.91	5.86	5.82	5.75	5.74	5.70	5.67	5.65	.10	
1.62	1.61	1.60	1.60	1.59	1.59	1.59	1.58	1.58	1.58	1.58	1.58	.25	
2.46	2.42	2.40	2.38	2.36	2.35	2.34	2.32	2.32	2.31	2.30	2.29	.10	8
3.22	3.15	3.12	3.08	3.04	2.02	3.01	2.97	2.97	2.95	2.94	2.93	.05	
5.52	5.36	5.28	5.20	5.12	5.07	5.03	4.96	4.95	4.91	4.88	4.86	.01	
1.57	1.56	1.56	1.55	1.55	1.54	1.54	1.53	1.53	1.53	1.53	1.53	.25	
2.34	2.30	2.28	2.25	2.23	2.22	2.21	2.19	2.18	2.17	2.17	2.16	.10	9
3.01	2.94	2.90	2.86	2.83	2.80	2.79	2.76	2.75	2.73	2.72	2.71	.05	
4.96	4.81	4.73	4.65	4.57	4.52	4.48	4.42	4.40	4.36	4.33	4.31	.01	

TABLE B-3
Upper percentage points of the F distribution (*continued*)

df for denominator N_2	Pr	1	2	3	4	5	6	7	8	9	10	11	12
10	.25	1.49	1.60	1.60	1.59	1.59	1.58	1.57	1.56	1.56	1.55	1.55	1.54
	.10	3.29	2.92	2.73	2.61	2.52	2.46	2.41	2.38	2.35	2.32	2.30	2.28
	.05	4.96	4.10	3.71	3.48	3.33	3.22	3.14	3.07	3.02	2.98	2.94	2.91
	.01	10.0	7.56	6.55	5.99	5.64	5.39	5.20	5.06	4.94	4.85	4.77	4.71
11	.25	1.47	1.58	1.58	1.57	1.56	1.55	1.54	1.53	1.53	1.52	1.52	1.51
	.10	3.23	2.86	2.66	2.54	2.45	2.39	2.34	2.30	2.27	2.25	2.23	2.21
	.05	4.84	3.98	3.59	3.36	3.20	3.09	3.01	2.95	2.90	2.85	2.82	2.79
	.01	9.65	7.21	6.22	5.67	5.32	5.07	4.89	4.74	4.63	4.54	4.46	4.40
12	.25	1.46	1.56	1.56	1.55	1.54	1.53	1.52	1.51	1.51	1.50	1.50	1.49
	.10	3.18	2.81	2.61	2.48	2.39	2.33	2.28	2.24	2.21	2.19	2.17	2.15
	.05	4.75	3.89	3.49	3.26	3.11	3.00	2.91	2.85	2.80	2.75	2.72	2.69
	.01	9.33	6.93	5.95	5.41	5.06	4.82	4.64	4.50	4.39	4.30	4.22	4.16
13	.25	1.45	1.55	1.55	1.53	1.52	1.51	1.50	1.49	1.49	1.48	1.47	1.47
	.10	3.14	2.76	2.56	2.43	2.35	2.28	2.23	2.20	2.16	2.14	2.12	2.10
	.05	4.67	3.81	3.41	3.18	3.03	2.92	2.83	2.77	2.71	2.67	2.63	2.60
	.01	9.07	6.70	5.74	5.21	4.86	4.62	4.44	4.30	4.19	4.10	4.02	3.96
14	.25	1.44	1.53	1.53	1.52	1.51	1.50	1.49	1.48	1.47	1.46	1.46	1.45
	.10	3.10	2.73	2.52	2.39	2.31	2.24	2.19	2.15	2.12	2.10	2.08	2.05
	.05	4.60	3.74	3.34	3.11	2.96	2.85	2.76	2.70	2.65	2.60	2.57	2.53
	.01	8.86	6.51	5.56	5.04	4.69	4.46	4.28	4.14	4.03	3.94	3.86	3.80
15	.25	1.43	1.52	1.52	1.51	1.49	1.48	1.47	1.46	1.46	1.45	1.44	1.44
	.10	3.07	2.70	2.49	2.36	2.27	2.21	2.16	2.12	2.09	2.06	2.04	2.02
	.05	4.54	3.68	3.29	3.06	2.90	2.79	2.71	2.64	2.59	2.54	2.51	2.48
	.01	8.68	6.36	5.42	4.89	4.56	4.32	4.14	4.00	3.89	3.80	3.73	3.67
16	.25	1.42	1.51	1.51	1.50	1.48	1.47	1.46	1.45	1.44	1.44	1.44	1.43
	.10	3.05	2.67	2.46	2.33	2.24	2.18	2.13	2.09	2.06	2.03	2.01	1.99
	.05	4.49	3.63	3.24	3.01	2.85	2.74	2.66	2.59	2.54	2.49	2.46	2.42
	.01	8.53	6.23	5.29	4.77	4.44	4.20	4.03	3.89	3.78	3.69	3.62	3.55
17	.25	1.42	1.51	1.50	1.49	1.47	1.46	1.45	1.44	1.43	1.43	1.42	1.41
	.10	3.03	2.64	2.44	2.31	2.22	2.15	2.10	2.06	2.03	2.00	1.98	1.96
	.05	4.45	3.59	3.20	2.96	2.81	2.70	2.61	2.55	2.49	2.45	2.41	2.38
	.01	8.40	6.11	5.18	4.67	4.34	4.10	3.93	3.79	3.68	3.59	3.52	3.46
18	.25	1.41	1.50	1.49	1.48	1.46	1.45	1.44	1.43	1.42	1.42	1.41	1.40
	.10	3.01	2.62	2.42	2.29	2.20	2.13	2.08	2.04	2.00	1.98	1.96	1.93
	.05	4.41	3.55	3.16	2.93	2.77	2.66	2.58	2.51	2.46	2.41	2.37	2.34
	.01	8.29	6.01	5.09	4.58	4.25	4.01	3.84	3.71	3.60	3.51	3.43	3.37
19	.25	1.41	1.49	1.49	1.47	1.46	1.44	1.43	1.42	1.41	1.41	1.40	1.40
	.10	2.99	2.61	2.40	2.27	2.18	2.11	2.06	2.02	1.98	1.96	1.94	1.91
	.05	4.38	3.52	3.13	2.90	2.74	2.63	2.54	2.48	2.42	2.38	2.34	2.31
	.01	8.18	5.93	5.01	4.50	4.17	3.94	3.77	3.63	3.52	3.43	3.36	3.30
20	.25	1.40	1.49	1.48	1.46	1.45	1.44	1.43	1.42	1.41	1.40	1.39	1.39
	.10	2.97	2.59	2.38	2.25	2.16	2.09	2.04	2.00	1.96	1.94	1.92	1.89
	.05	4.35	3.49	3.10	2.87	2.71	2.60	2.51	2.45	2.39	2.35	2.31	2.28
	.01	8.10	5.85	4.94	4.43	4.10	3.87	3.70	3.56	3.46	3.37	3.29	3.23

Heading over numerator columns: df for numerator N_1

					df for numerator N_1								df for denominator
15	20	24	30	40	50	60	100	120	200	500	∞	Pr	N_2
1.53	1.52	1.52	1.51	1.51	1.50	1.50	1.49	1.49	1.49	1.48	1.48	.25	
2.24	2.20	2.18	2.16	2.13	2.12	2.11	2.09	2.08	2.07	2.06	2.06	.10	10
2.85	2.77	2.74	2.70	2.66	2.64	2.62	2.59	2.58	2.56	2.55	2.54	.05	
4.56	4.41	4.33	4.25	4.17	4.12	4.08	4.01	4.00	3.96	3.93	3.91	.01	
1.50	1.49	1.49	1.48	1.47	1.47	1.47	1.46	1.46	1.46	1.45	1.45	.25	
2.17	2.12	2.10	2.08	2.05	2.04	2.03	2.00	2.00	1 99	1.98	1.97	.10	11
2.72	2.65	2.61	2.57	2.53	2.51	2.49	2.46	2.45	2.43	2.42	2.40	.05	
4.25	4.10	4.02	3.94	3.86	3.81	3.78	3.71	3.69	3.66	3.62	3.60	.01	
1.48	1.47	1.46	1.45	1.45	1.44	1.44	1.43	1.43	1.43	1.42	1.42	.25	
2.10	2.06	2.04	2.01	1.99	1.97	1.96	1.94	1.93	1.92	1.91	1.90	.10	12
2.62	2.54	2.51	2.47	2.43	2.40	2.38	2.35	2.34	2.32	2.31	2.30	.05	
4.01	3.86	3.78	3.70	3.62	3.57	3.54	3.47	3.45	3.41	3.38	3.36	.01	
1.46	1.45	1.44	1.43	1.42	1.42	1.42	1.41	1.41	1.40	1 40	1 40	.25	
2.05	2.01	1.98	1.96	1.93	1.92	1.90	1.88	1.88	1.86	1.85	1.85	.10	13
2.53	2.46	2.42	2.38	2.34	2.31	2.30	2.26	2.25	2.23	2.22	2.21	.05	
3.82	3.66	3.59	3.51	3.43	3.38	3.34	3.27	3.25	3.22	3.19	3.17	.01	
1.44	1.43	1.42	1.41	1.41	1.40	1.40	1.39	1.39	1.39	1.38	1.38	.25	
2.01	1.96	1.94	1.91	1.89	1.87	1.86	1.83	1.83	1.82	1.80	1.80	.10	14
2.46	2.39	2.35	2.31	2.27	2.24	2.22	2.19	2.18	2.16	2.14	2.13	.05	
3.66	3.51	3.43	3.35	3.27	3.22	3.18	3.11	3.09	3.06	3.03	3.00	.01	
1.43	1.41	1.41	1.40	1.39	1.39	1.38	1.38	1.37	1.37	1.36	1.36	.25	
1.97	1.92	1.90	1.87	1.85	1.83	1.82	1.79	1.79	1.77	1.76	1.76	.10	15
2.40	2.33	2.29	2.25	2.20	2.18	2.16	2.12	2.11	2.10	2.08	2.07	.05	
3.52	3.37	3.29	3.21	3.13	3.08	3.05	2.98	2.96	2.92	2.89	2.87	.01	
1.41	1.40	1.39	1.38	1.37	1.37	1.36	1.36	1.35	1.35	1.34	1.34	.25	
1.94	1.89	1.87	1.84	1.81	1.79	1.78	1.76	1.75	1 74	1.73	1.72	.10	16
2.35	2.28	2.24	2.19	2.15	2.12	2.11	2.07	2.06	2.04	2.02	2.01	.05	
3.41	3.26	3.18	3.10	3.02	2.97	2.93	2.86	2.84	2.81	2.78	2.75	.01	
1.40	1.39	1.38	1.37	1.36	1.35	1.35	1.34	1.34	1.34	1.33	1.33	.25	
1.91	1.86	1.84	1.81	1.78	1.76	1.75	1.73	1.72	1.71	1.69	1.69	.10	17
2.31	2.23	2.19	2.15	2.10	2.08	2.06	2.02	2.01	1.99	1.97	1.96	.05	
3.31	3.16	3.08	3.00	2.92	2.87	2.83	2.76	2.75	2.71	2.68	2.65	.01	
1.39	1.38	1.37	1.36	1.35	1.34	1.34	1.33	1.33	1.32	1.32	1.32	.25	
1.89	1.84	1.81	1.78	1.75	1.74	1.72	1.70	1.69	1.68	1.67	1.66	.10	18
2.27	2.19	2.15	2.11	2.06	2.04	2.02	1.98	1.97	1.95	1.93	1.92	.05	
3.23	3.08	3.00	2.92	2.84	2.78	2.75	2.68	2.66	2.62	2.59	2.57	.01	
1.38	1.37	1.36	1.35	1.34	1.33	1.33	1.32	1.32	1.31	1.31	1.30	.25	
1.86	1.81	1.79	1.76	1.73	1.71	1.70	1.67	1.67	1.65	1.64	1.63	.10	19
2.23	2.16	2.11	2.07	2.03	2.00	1.98	1.94	1.93	1.91	1.89	1.88	.05	
3.15	3.00	2.92	2.84	2.76	2.71	2.67	2.60	2.58	2.55	2.51	2.49	.01	
1.37	1.36	1.35	1.34	1.33	1.33	1.32	1.31	1.31	1.30	1.30	1.29	.25	
1.84	1.79	1.77	1.74	1.71	1.69	1.68	1.65	1.64	1.63	1.62	1.61	.10	20
2.20	2.12	2.08	2.04	1.99	1.97	1.95	1.91	1.90	1.88	1.86	1.84	.05	
3.09	2.94	2.86	2.78	2.69	2.64	2.61	2.54	2.52	2.48	2.44	2.42	.01	

TABLE B-3
Upper percentage points of the F distribution (*continued*)

df for denominator N_2	Pr	1	2	3	4	5	6	7	8	9	10	11	12
						df for numerator N_1							
22	.25	1.40	1.48	1.47	1.45	1.44	1.42	1.41	1.40	1.39	1.39	1.38	1.37
	.10	2.95	2.56	2.35	2.22	2.13	2.06	2.01	1.97	1.93	1.90	1.88	1.86
	.05	4.30	3.44	3.05	2.82	2.66	2.55	2.46	2.40	2.34	2.30	2.26	2.23
	.01	7.95	5.72	4.82	4.31	3.99	3.76	3.59	3.45	3.35	3.26	3.18	3.12
24	.25	1.39	1.47	1.46	1.44	1.43	1.41	1.40	1.39	1.38	1.38	1.37	1.36
	.10	2.93	2.54	2.33	2.19	2.10	2.04	1.98	1.94	1.91	1.88	1.85	1.83
	.05	4.26	3.40	3.01	2.78	2.62	2.51	2.42	2.36	2.30	2.25	2.21	2.18
	.01	7.82	5.61	4.72	4.22	3.90	3.67	3.50	3.36	3.26	3.17	3.09	3.03
26	.25	1.38	1.46	1.45	1.44	1.42	1.41	1.39	1.38	1.37	1.37	1.36	1.35
	.10	2.91	2.52	2.31	2.17	2.08	2.01	1.96	1.92	1.88	1.86	1.84	1.81
	.05	4.23	3.37	2.98	2.74	2.59	2.47	2.39	2.32	2.27	2.22	2.18	2.15
	.01	7.72	5.53	4.64	4.14	3.82	3.59	3.42	3.29	3.18	3.09	3.02	2.96
28	.25	1.38	1.46	1.45	1.43	1.41	1.40	1.39	1.38	1.37	1.36	1.35	1.34
	.10	2.89	2.50	2.29	2.16	2.06	2.00	1.94	1.90	1.87	1.84	1.81	1.79
	.05	4.20	3.34	2.95	2.71	2.56	2.45	2.36	2.29	2.24	2.19	2.15	2.12
	.01	7.64	5.45	4.57	4.07	3.75	3.53	3.36	3.23	3.12	3.03	2.96	2.90
30	.25	1.38	1.45	1.44	1.42	1.41	1.39	1.38	1.37	1.36	1.35	1.35	1.34
	.10	2.88	2.49	2.28	2.14	2.05	1.98	1.93	1.88	1.85	1.82	1.79	1.77
	.05	4.17	3.32	2.92	2.69	2.53	2.42	2.33	2.27	2.21	2.16	2.13	2.09
	.01	7.56	5.39	4.51	4.02	3.70	3.47	3.30	3.17	3.07	2.98	2.91	2.84
40	.25	1.36	1.44	1.42	1.40	1.39	1.37	1.36	1.35	1.34	1.33	1.32	1.31
	.10	2.84	2.44	2.23	2.09	2.00	1.93	1.87	1.83	1.79	1.76	1.73	1.71
	.05	4.08	3.23	2.84	2.61	2.45	2.34	2.25	2.18	2.12	2.08	2.04	2.00
	.01	7.31	5.18	4.31	3.83	3.51	3.29	3.12	2.99	2.89	2.80	2.73	2.66
60	.25	1.35	1.42	1.41	1.38	1.37	1.35	1.33	1.32	1.31	1.30	1.29	1.29
	.10	2.79	2.39	2.18	2.04	1.95	1.87	1.82	1.77	1.74	1.71	1.68	1.66
	.05	4.00	3.15	2.76	2.53	2.37	2.25	2.17	2.10	2.04	1.99	1.95	1.92
	.01	7.08	4.98	4.13	3.65	3.34	3.12	2.95	2.82	2.72	2.63	2.56	2.50
120	.25	1.34	1.40	1.39	1.37	1.35	1.33	1.31	1.30	1.29	1.28	1.27	1.26
	.10	2.75	2.35	2.13	1.99	1.90	1.82	1.77	1.72	1.68	1.65	1.62	1.60
	.05	3.92	3.07	2.68	2.45	2.29	2.17	2.09	2.02	1.96	1.91	1.87	1.83
	.01	6.85	4.79	3.95	3.48	3.17	2.96	2.79	2.66	2.56	2.47	2.40	2.34
200	.25	1.33	1.39	1.38	1.36	1.34	1.32	1.31	1.29	1.28	1.27	1.26	1.25
	.10	2.73	2.33	2.11	1.97	1.88	1.80	1.75	1.70	1.66	1.63	1.60	1.57
	.05	3.89	3.04	2.65	2.42	2.26	2.14	2.06	1.98	1.93	1.88	1.84	1.80
	.01	6.76	4.71	3.88	3.41	3.11	2.89	2.73	2.60	2.50	2.41	2.34	2.27
∞	.25	1.32	1.39	1.37	1.35	1.33	1.31	1.29	1.28	1.27	1.25	1.24	1.24
	.10	2.71	2.30	2.08	1.94	1.85	1.77	1.72	1.67	1.63	1.60	1.57	1.55
	.05	3.84	3.00	2.60	2.37	2.21	2.10	2.01	1.94	1.88	1.83	1.79	1.75
	.01	6.63	4.61	3.78	3.32	3.02	2.80	2.64	2.51	2.41	2.32	2.25	2.18

			df for numerator N_1											df for denominator N_2
15	20	24	30	40	50	60	100	120	200	500	∞	Pr		
1.36	1.34	1.33	1.32	1.31	1.31	1.30	1.30	1.30	1.29	1.29	1.28	.25		
1.81	1.76	1.73	1.70	1.67	1.65	1.64	1.61	1.60	1.59	1.58	1.57	.10		22
2.15	2.07	2.03	1.98	1.94	1.91	1.89	1.85	1.84	1.82	1.80	1.78	.05		
2.98	2.83	2.75	2.67	2.58	2.53	2.50	2.42	2.40	2.36	2.33	2.31	.01		
1.35	1.33	1.32	1.31	1.30	1.29	1.29	1.28	1.28	1.27	1.27	1.26	.25		
1.78	1.73	1.70	1.67	1.64	1.62	1.61	1.58	1.57	1.56	1.54	1.53	.10		24
2.11	2.03	1.98	1.94	1.89	1.86	1.84	1.80	1.79	1.77	1.75	1.73	.05		
2.89	2.74	2.66	2.58	2.49	2.44	2.40	2.33	2.31	2.27	2.24	2.21	.01		
1.34	1.32	1.31	1.30	1.29	1.28	1.28	1.26	1.26	1.26	1.25	1.25	.25		
1.76	1.71	1.68	1.65	1.61	1.59	1.58	1.55	1.54	1.53	1.51	1.50	.10		26
2.07	1.99	1.95	1.90	1.85	1.82	1.80	1.76	1.75	1.73	1.71	1.69	.05		
2.81	2.66	2.58	2.50	2.42	2.36	2.33	2.25	2.23	2.19	2.16	2.13	.01		
1.33	1.31	1.30	1.29	1.28	1.27	1.27	1.26	1.25	1.25	1.24	1.24	.25		
1.74	1.69	1.66	1.63	1.59	1 57	1.56	1.53	1.52	1.50	1.49	1.48	.10		28
2.04	1.96	1.91	1.87	1.82	1.79	1.77	1.73	1.71	1.69	1.67	1.65	.05		
2.75	2.60	2.52	2.44	2.35	2.30	2.26	2.19	2.17	2.13	2.09	2.06	.01		
1.32	1.30	1.29	1.28	1.27	1.26	1.26	1.25	1.24	1.24	1.23	1.23	.25		
1.72	1.67	1.64	1.61	1.57	1.55	1.54	1.51	1.50	1.48	1.47	1.46	.10		30
2.01	1.93	1.89	1.84	1.79	1.76	1.74	1.70	1.68	1.66	1.64	1.62	.05		
2.70	2.55	2.47	2.39	2.30	2.25	2.21	2.13	2.11	2.07	2.03	2.01	.01		
1.30	1.28	1.26	1.25	1.24	1.23	1.22	1.21	1.21	1.20	1.19	1.19	.25		
1.66	1.61	1.57	1.54	1.51	1.48	1.47	1.43	1.42	1.41	1.39	1.38	.10		40
1.92	1.84	1.79	1.74	1.69	1.66	1.64	1.59	1.58	1.55	1.53	1.51	.05		
2.52	2.37	2.29	2.20	2.11	2.06	2.02	1.94	1.92	1.87	1.83	1.80	.01		
1.27	1.25	1.24	1.22	1.21	1.20	1.19	1.17	1.17	1.16	1.15	1.15	.25		
1.60	1.54	1.51	1.48	1.44	1.41	1.40	1.36	1.35	1.33	1.31	1.29	.10		60
1.84	1.75	1.70	1.65	1.59	1.56	1.53	1.48	1.47	1.44	1.41	1.39	.05		
2.35	2.20	2.12	2.03	1.94	1.88	1.84	1.75	1.73	1.68	1.63	1.60	.01		
1.24	1.22	1.21	1.19	1.18	1.17	1.16	1.14	1.13	1.12	1.11	1.10	.25		
1.55	1.48	1.45	1.41	1.37	1.34	1.32	1.27	1.26	1.24	1.21	1.19	.10		120
1.75	1.66	1.61	1.55	1.50	1.46	1.43	1.37	1.35	1.32	1.28	1.25	.05		
2.19	2.03	1.95	1.86	1.76	1.70	1.66	1.56	1.53	1.48	1.42	1.38	.01		
1.23	1.21	1.20	1.18	1.16	1.14	1.12	1.11	1.10	1.09	1.08	1.06	.25		
1.52	1.46	1.42	1.38	1.34	1.31	1.28	1.24	1.22	1.20	1.17	1.14	.10		200
1.72	1.62	1.57	1.52	1.46	1.41	1.39	1.32	1.29	1.26	1.22	1.19	.05		
2.13	1.97	1.89	1.79	1.69	1.63	1.58	1.48	1.44	1.39	1.33	1.28	.01		
1.22	1.19	1.18	1.16	1.14	1.13	1.12	1.09	1.08	1.07	1.04	1.00	.25		
1.49	1.42	1.38	1.34	1.30	1.26	1.24	1.18	1.17	1.13	1.08	1.00	.10		∞
1.67	1.57	1.52	1.46	1.39	1.35	1.32	1.24	1.22	1.17	1.11	1.00	.05		
2.04	1.88	1.79	1.70	1.59	1.52	1.47	1.36	1.32	1.25	1.15	1.00	.01		

TABLE B-4
Upper percentage points of the χ^2 distribution

Example

$\Pr(\chi^2 > 10.85) = 0.95$

$\Pr(\chi^2 > 23.83) = 0.25 \qquad$ for df $= 20$

$\Pr(\chi^2 > 31.41) = 0.05$

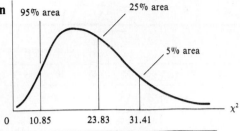

Degrees of Freedom \ Pr	.995	.990	.975	.950	.900
1	$392704 \cdot 10^{-10}$	$157088 \cdot 10^{-9}$	$982069 \cdot 10^{-9}$	$393214 \cdot 10^{-8}$	.0157908
2	.0100251	.0201007	.0506356	.102587	.210720
3	.0717212	.114832	.215795	.351846	.584375
4	.206990	.297110	.484419	.710721	1.063623
5	.411740	.554300	.831211	1.145476	1.61031
6	.675727	.872085	1.237347	1.63539	2.20413
7	.989265	1.239043	1.68987	2.16735	2.83311
8	1.344419	1.646482	2.17973	2.73264	3.48954
9	1.734926	2.087912	2.70039	3.32511	4.16816
10	2.15585	2.55821	3.24697	3.94030	4.86518
11	2.60321	3.05347	3.81575	4.57481	5.57779
12	3.07382	3.57056	4.40379	5.22603	6.30380
13	3.56503	4.10691	5.00874	5.89186	7.04150
14	4.07468	4.66043	5.62872	6.57063	7.78953
15	4.60094	5.22935	6.26214	7.26094	8.54675
16	5.14224	5.81221	6.90766	7.96164	9.31223
17	5.69724	6.40776	7.56418	8.67176	10.0852
18	6.26481	7.01491	8.23075	9.39046	10.8649
19	6.84398	7.63273	8.90655	10.1170	11.6509
20	7.43386	8.26040	9.59083	10.8508	12.4426
21	8.03366	8.89720	10.28293	11.5913	13.2396
22	8.64272	9.54249	10.9823	12.3380	14.0415
23	9.26042	10.19567	11.6885	13.0905	14.8479
24	9.88623	10.8564	12.4011	13.8484	15.6587
25	10.5197	11.5240	13.1197	14.6114	16.4734
26	11.1603	12.1981	13.8439	15.3791	17.2919
27	11.8076	12.8786	14.5733	16.1513	18.1138
28	12.4613	13.5648	15.3079	16.9279	18.9392
29	13.1211	14.2565	16.0471	17.7083	19.7677
30	13.7867	14.9535	16.7908	18.4926	20.5992
40	20.7065	22.1643	24.4331	26.5093	29.0505
50	27.9907	29.7067	32.3574	34.7642	37.6886
60	35.5346	37.4848	40.4817	43.1879	46.4589
70	43.2752	45.4418	48.7576	51.7393	55.3290
80	51.1720	53.5400	57.1532	60.3915	64.2778
90	59.1963	61.7541	65.6466	69.1260	73.2912
100†	67.3276	70.0648	74.2219	77.9295	82.3581

† For df greater than 100 the expression: $\sqrt{2\chi^2} - \sqrt{(2k-1)} = Z$ follows the standardized normal distribution, where k represents the degrees of freedom.

.750	.500	.250	.100	.050	.025	.010	.005
.1015308	.454937	1.32330	2.70554	3.84146	5.02389	6.63490	7.87944
.575364	1.38629	2.77259	4.60517	5.99147	7.37776	9.21034	10.5966
1.212534	2.36597	4.10835	6.25139	7.81473	9.34840	11.3449	12.8381
1.92255	3.35670	5.38527	7.77944	9.48773	11.1433	13.2767	14.8602
2.67460	4.35146	6.62568	9.23635	11.0705	12.8325	15.0863	16.7496
3.45460	5.34812	7.84080	10.6446	12.5916	14.4494	16.8119	18.5476
4.25485	6.34581	9.03715	12.0170	14.0671	16.0128	18.4753	20.2777
5.07064	7.34412	10.2188	13.3616	15.5073	17.5346	20.0902	21.9550
5.89883	8.34283	11.3887	14.6837	16.9190	19.0228	21.6660	23.5893
6.73720	9.34182	12.5489	15.9871	18.3070	20.4831	23.2093	25.1882
7.58412	10.3410	13.7007	17.2750	19.6751	21.9200	24.7250	26.7569
8.43842	11.3403	14.8454	18.5494	21.0261	23.3367	26.2170	28.2995
9.29906	12.3398	15.9839	19.8119	22.3621	24.7356	27.6883	29.8194
10.1653	13.3393	17.1170	21.0642	23.6848	26.1190	29.1413	31.3193
11.0365	14.3389	18.2451	22.3072	24.9958	27.4884	30.5779	32.8013
11.9122	15.3385	19.3688	23.5418	26.2962	28.8454	31.9999	34.2672
12.7919	16.3381	20.4887	24.7690	27.5871	30.1910	33.4087	35.7185
13.6753	17.3379	21.6049	25.9894	28.8693	31.5264	34.8053	37.1564
14.5620	18.3376	22.7178	27.2036	30.1435	32.8523	36.1908	38.5822
15.4518	19.3374	23.8277	28.4120	31.4104	34.1696	37.5662	39.9968
16.3444	20.3372	24.9348	29.6151	32.6705	35.4789	38.9321	41.4010
17.2396	21.3370	26.0393	30.8133	33.9244	36.7807	40.2894	42.7956
18.1373	22.3369	27.1413	32.0069	35.1725	38.0757	41.6384	44.1813
19.0372	23.3367	28.2412	33.1963	36.4151	39.3641	42.9798	45.5585
19.9393	24.3366	29.3389	34.3816	37.6525	40.6465	44.3141	46.9278
20.8434	25.3364	30.4345	35.5631	38.8852	41.9232	45.6417	48.2899
21.7494	26.3363	31.5284	36.7412	40.1133	43.1944	46.9630	49.6449
22.6572	27.3363	32.6205	37.9159	41.3372	44.4607	48.2782	50.9933
23.5666	28.3362	33.7109	39.0875	42.5569	45.7222	49.5879	52.3356
24.4776	29.3360	34.7998	40.2560	43.7729	46.9792	50.8922	53.6720
33.6603	39.3354	45.6160	51.8050	55.7585	59.3417	63.6907	66.7659
42.9421	49.3349	56.3336	63.1671	67.5048	71.4202	76.1539	79.4900
52.2938	59.3347	66.9814	74.3970	79.0819	83.2976	88.3794	91.9517
61.6983	69.3344	77.5766	85.5271	90.5312	95.0231	100.425	104.215
71.1445	79.3343	88.1303	96.5782	101.879	106.629	112.329	116.321
80.6247	89.3342	98.6499	107.565	113.145	118.136	124.116	128.299
90.1332	99.3341	109.141	118.498	124.342	129.561	135.807	140.169

k = # of indep var (x's)

n = # of observations

TABLE B-5a
Durbin-Watson d statistic: Significance points of d_L and d_U at 0.05 level of significance

n	k' = 1 d_L	k' = 1 d_U	k' = 2 d_L	k' = 2 d_U	k' = 3 d_L	k' = 3 d_U	k' = 4 d_L	k' = 4 d_U	k' = 5 d_L	k' = 5 d_U	k' = 6 d_L	k' = 6 d_U	k' = 7 d_L	k' = 7 d_U	k' = 8 d_L	k' = 8 d_U	k' = 9 d_L	k' = 9 d_U	k' = 10 d_L	k' = 10 d_U
6	0.610	1.400	—	—	—	—	—	—	—	—	—	—	—	—	—	—	—	—	—	—
7	0.700	1.356	0.467	1.896	—	—	—	—	—	—	—	—	—	—	—	—	—	—	—	—
8	0.763	1.332	0.559	1.777	0.368	2.287	—	—	—	—	—	—	—	—	—	—	—	—	—	—
9	0.824	1.320	0.629	1.699	0.455	2.128	0.296	2.588	—	—	—	—	—	—	—	—	—	—	—	—
10	0.879	1.320	0.697	1.641	0.525	2.016	0.376	2.414	0.243	2.822	—	—	—	—	—	—	—	—	—	—
11	0.927	1.324	0.658	1.604	0.595	1.928	0.444	2.283	0.316	2.645	0.203	3.005	—	—	—	—	—	—	—	—
12	0.971	1.331	0.812	1.579	0.658	1.864	0.512	2.177	0.379	2.506	0.268	2.832	0.171	3.149	—	—	—	—	—	—
13	1.010	1.340	0.861	1.562	0.715	1.816	0.574	2.094	0.445	2.390	0.328	2.692	0.230	2.985	0.147	3.266	—	—	—	—
14	1.045	1.350	0.905	1.551	0.767	1.779	0.632	2.030	0.505	2.296	0.389	2.572	0.286	2.848	0.200	3.111	0.127	3.360	—	—
15	1.077	1.361	0.946	1.543	0.814	1.750	0.685	1.977	0.562	2.220	0.447	2.472	0.343	2.727	0.251	2.979	0.175	3.216	0.111	3.438
16	1.106	1.371	0.982	1.539	0.857	1.728	0.734	1.935	0.615	2.157	0.502	2.388	0.398	2.624	0.304	2.860	0.222	3.090	0.155	3.304
17	1.133	1.381	1.015	1.536	0.897	1.710	0.779	1.900	0.664	2.104	0.554	2.318	0.451	2.537	0.356	2.757	0.272	2.975	0.198	3.184
18	1.158	1.391	1.046	1.535	0.933	1.696	0.820	1.872	0.710	2.060	0.603	2.257	0.502	2.461	0.407	2.667	0.321	2.873	0.244	3.073
19	1.180	1.401	1.074	1.536	0.967	1.685	0.859	1.848	0.752	2.023	0.649	2.206	0.549	2.396	0.456	2.589	0.369	2.783	0.290	2.974
20	1.201	1.411	1.100	1.537	0.998	1.676	0.894	1.828	0.792	1.991	0.692	2.162	0.595	2.339	0.502	2.521	0.416	2.704	0.336	2.885
21	1.221	1.420	1.125	1.538	1.026	1.669	0.927	1.812	0.829	1.964	0.732	2.124	0.637	2.290	0.547	2.460	0.461	2.633	0.380	2.806
22	1.239	1.429	1.147	1.541	1.053	1.664	0.958	1.797	0.863	1.940	0.769	2.090	0.677	2.246	0.588	2.407	0.504	2.571	0.424	2.734
23	1.257	1.437	1.168	1.543	1.078	1.660	0.986	1.785	0.895	1.920	0.804	2.061	0.715	2.208	0.628	2.360	0.545	2.514	0.465	2.670
24	1.273	1.446	1.188	1.546	1.101	1.656	1.013	1.775	0.925	1.902	0.837	2.035	0.751	2.174	0.666	2.318	0.584	2.464	0.506	2.613
25	1.288	1.454	1.206	1.550	1.123	1.654	1.038	1.767	0.953	1.886	0.868	2.012	0.784	2.144	0.702	2.280	0.621	2.419	0.544	2.560
26	1.302	1.461	1.224	1.553	1.143	1.652	1.062	1.759	0.979	1.873	0.897	1.992	0.816	2.117	0.735	2.246	0.657	2.379	0.581	2.513
27	1.316	1.469	1.240	1.556	1.162	1.651	1.084	1.753	1.004	1.861	0.925	1.974	0.845	2.093	0.767	2.216	0.691	2.342	0.616	2.470
28	1.328	1.476	1.255	1.560	1.181	1.650	1.104	1.747	1.028	1.850	0.951	1.958	0.874	2.071	0.798	2.188	0.723	2.309	0.650	2.431
29	1.341	1.483	1.270	1.563	1.198	1.650	1.124	1.743	1.050	1.841	0.975	1.944	0.900	2.052	0.826	2.164	0.753	2.278	0.682	2.396
30	1.352	1.489	1.284	1.567	1.214	1.650	1.143	1.739	1.071	1.833	0.998	1.931	0.926	2.034	0.854	2.141	0.782	2.251	0.712	2.363
31	1.363	1.496	1.297	1.570	1.229	1.650	1.160	1.735	1.090	1.825	1.020	1.920	0.950	2.018	0.879	2.120	0.810	2.226	0.741	2.333
32	1.373	1.502	1.309	1.574	1.244	1.650	1.177	1.732	1.109	1.819	1.041	1.909	0.972	2.004	0.904	2.102	0.836	2.203	0.769	2.306
33	1.383	1.508	1.321	1.577	1.258	1.651	1.193	1.730	1.127	1.813	1.061	1.900	0.994	1.991	0.927	2.085	0.861	2.181	0.795	2.281
34	1.393	1.514	1.333	1.580	1.271	1.652	1.208	1.728	1.144	1.808	1.080	1.891	1.015	1.979	0.950	2.069	0.885	2.162	0.821	2.257
35	1.402	1.519	1.343	1.584	1.283	1.653	1.222	1.726	1.160	1.803	1.097	1.884	1.034	1.967	0.971	2.054	0.908	2.144	0.845	2.236
36	1.411	1.525	1.354	1.587	1.295	1.654	1.236	1.724	1.175	1.799	1.114	1.877	1.053	1.957	0.991	2.041	0.930	2.127	0.868	2.216
37	1.419	1.530	1.364	1.590	1.307	1.655	1.249	1.723	1.190	1.795	1.131	1.870	1.071	1.948	1.011	2.029	0.951	2.112	0.891	2.198
38	1.427	1.535	1.373	1.594	1.318	1.656	1.261	1.722	1.204	1.792	1.146	1.864	1.088	1.939	1.029	2.017	0.970	2.098	0.912	2.180
39	1.435	1.540	1.382	1.597	1.328	1.658	1.273	1.722	1.218	1.789	1.161	1.859	1.104	1.932	1.047	2.007	0.990	2.085	0.932	2.164
40	1.442	1.544	1.391	1.600	1.338	1.659	1.285	1.721	1.230	1.786	1.175	1.854	1.120	1.924	1.064	1.997	1.008	2.072	0.952	2.149
45	1.475	1.566	1.430	1.615	1.383	1.666	1.336	1.720	1.287	1.776	1.238	1.835	1.189	1.895	1.139	1.958	1.089	2.022	1.038	2.088
50	1.503	1.585	1.462	1.628	1.421	1.674	1.378	1.721	1.335	1.771	1.291	1.822	1.246	1.875	1.201	1.930	1.156	1.986	1.110	2.044
55	1.528	1.601	1.490	1.641	1.452	1.681	1.414	1.724	1.374	1.768	1.334	1.814	1.294	1.861	1.253	1.909	1.212	1.959	1.170	2.010
60	1.549	1.616	1.514	1.652	1.480	1.689	1.444	1.727	1.408	1.767	1.372	1.808	1.335	1.850	1.298	1.894	1.260	1.939	1.222	1.984
65	1.567	1.629	1.536	1.662	1.503	1.696	1.471	1.731	1.438	1.767	1.404	1.805	1.370	1.843	1.336	1.882	1.301	1.923	1.266	1.964
70	1.583	1.641	1.554	1.672	1.525	1.703	1.494	1.735	1.464	1.768	1.433	1.802	1.401	1.837	1.369	1.873	1.337	1.910	1.305	1.948
75	1.598	1.652	1.571	1.680	1.543	1.709	1.515	1.739	1.487	1.770	1.458	1.801	1.428	1.834	1.399	1.867	1.369	1.901	1.339	1.935
80	1.611	1.662	1.586	1.688	1.560	1.715	1.534	1.743	1.507	1.772	1.480	1.801	1.453	1.831	1.425	1.861	1.397	1.893	1.369	1.925
85	1.624	1.671	1.600	1.696	1.575	1.721	1.550	1.747	1.525	1.774	1.500	1.801	1.474	1.829	1.448	1.857	1.422	1.886	1.396	1.916
90	1.635	1.679	1.612	1.703	1.589	1.726	1.566	1.751	1.542	1.776	1.518	1.801	1.494	1.827	1.469	1.854	1.445	1.881	1.420	1.909
95	1.645	1.687	1.623	1.709	1.602	1.732	1.579	1.755	1.557	1.778	1.535	1.802	1.512	1.827	1.489	1.852	1.465	1.877	1.442	1.903
100	1.654	1.694	1.634	1.715	1.613	1.736	1.592	1.758	1.571	1.780	1.550	1.803	1.528	1.826	1.506	1.850	1.484	1.874	1.462	1.898
150	1.720	1.746	1.706	1.760	1.693	1.774	1.679	1.788	1.665	1.802	1.651	1.817	1.637	1.832	1.622	1.847	1.608	1.862	1.594	1.877
200	1.758	1.778	1.748	1.789	1.738	1.799	1.728	1.810	1.718	1.820	1.707	1.831	1.697	1.841	1.686	1.852	1.675	1.863	1.665	1.874

n	$k' = 11$		$k' = 12$		$k' = 13$		$k' = 14$		$k' = 15$		$k' = 16$		$k' = 17$		$k' = 18$		$k' = 19$		$k' = 20$	
	d_L	d_U	d_L	d_U	d_L	d_U	d_L	d_U	d_L	d_U	d_L	d_U	d_L	d_U	d_L	d_U	d_L	d_U	d_L	d_U
16	0.098	3.503	—	—																
17	0.138	3.378	0.087	3.557	—	—														
18	0.177	3.265	0.123	3.441	0.078	3.603	—	—												
19	0.220	3.159	0.160	3.335	0.111	3.496	0.070	3.642	—	—										
20	0.263	3.063	0.200	3.234	0.145	3.395	0.100	3.542	0.063	3.676	—	—								
21	0.307	2.976	0.240	3.141	0.182	3.300	0.132	3.448	0.091	3.583	0.058	3.705	—	—						
22	0.349	2.897	0.281	3.057	0.220	3.211	0.166	3.358	0.120	3.495	0.083	3.619	0.052	3.731	—	—				
23	0.391	2.826	0.322	2.979	0.259	3.128	0.202	3.272	0.153	3.409	0.110	3.535	0.076	3.650	0.048	3.753	—	—		
24	0.431	2.761	0.362	2.908	0.297	3.053	0.239	3.193	0.186	3.327	0.141	3.454	0.101	3.572	0.070	3.678	0.044	3.773	—	—
25	0.470	2.702	0.400	2.844	0.335	2.983	0.275	3.119	0.221	3.251	0.172	3.376	0.130	3.494	0.094	3.604	0.065	3.702	0.041	3.790
26	0.508	2.649	0.438	2.784	0.373	2.919	0.312	3.051	0.256	3.179	0.205	3.303	0.160	3.420	0.120	3.531	0.087	3.632	0.060	3.724
27	0.544	2.600	0.475	2.730	0.409	2.859	0.348	2.987	0.291	3.112	0.238	3.233	0.191	3.349	0.149	3.460	0.112	3.563	0.081	3.658
28	0.578	2.555	0.510	2.680	0.445	2.805	0.383	2.928	0.325	3.050	0.271	3.168	0.222	3.283	0.178	3.392	0.138	3.495	0.104	3.592
29	0.612	2.515	0.544	2.634	0.479	2.755	0.418	2.874	0.359	2.992	0.305	3.107	0.254	3.219	0.208	3.327	0.166	3.431	0.129	3.528
30	0.643	2.477	0.577	2.592	0.512	2.708	0.451	2.823	0.392	2.937	0.337	3.050	0.286	3.160	0.238	3.266	0.195	3.368	0.156	3.465
31	0.674	2.443	0.608	2.553	0.545	2.665	0.484	2.776	0.425	2.887	0.370	2.996	0.317	3.103	0.269	3.208	0.224	3.309	0.183	3.406
32	0.703	2.411	0.638	2.517	0.576	2.625	0.515	2.733	0.457	2.840	0.401	2.946	0.349	3.050	0.299	3.153	0.253	3.252	0.211	3.348
33	0.731	2.382	0.668	2.484	0.606	2.588	0.546	2.692	0.488	2.796	0.432	2.899	0.379	3.000	0.329	3.100	0.283	3.198	0.239	3.293
34	0.758	2.355	0.695	2.454	0.634	2.554	0.575	2.654	0.518	2.754	0.462	2.854	0.409	2.954	0.359	3.051	0.312	3.147	0.267	3.240
35	0.783	2.330	0.722	2.425	0.662	2.521	0.604	2.619	0.547	2.716	0.492	2.813	0.439	2.910	0.388	3.005	0.340	3.099	0.295	3.190
36	0.808	2.306	0.748	2.398	0.689	2.492	0.631	2.586	0.575	2.680	0.520	2.774	0.467	2.868	0.417	2.961	0.369	3.053	0.323	3.142
37	0.831	2.285	0.772	2.374	0.714	2.464	0.657	2.555	0.602	2.646	0.548	2.738	0.495	2.829	0.445	2.920	0.397	3.009	0.351	3.097
38	0.854	2.265	0.796	2.351	0.739	2.438	0.683	2.526	0.628	2.614	0.575	2.703	0.522	2.792	0.472	2.880	0.424	2.968	0.378	3.054
39	0.875	2.246	0.819	2.329	0.763	2.413	0.707	2.499	0.653	2.585	0.600	2.671	0.549	2.757	0.499	2.843	0.451	2.929	0.404	3.013
40	0.896	2.228	0.840	2.309	0.785	2.391	0.731	2.473	0.678	2.557	0.626	2.641	0.575	2.724	0.525	2.808	0.477	2.892	0.430	2.974
45	0.988	2.156	0.938	2.225	0.887	2.296	0.838	2.367	0.788	2.439	0.740	2.512	0.692	2.586	0.644	2.659	0.598	2.733	0.553	2.807
50	1.064	2.103	1.019	2.163	0.973	2.225	0.927	2.287	0.882	2.350	0.836	2.414	0.792	2.479	0.747	2.544	0.703	2.610	0.660	2.675
55	1.129	2.062	1.087	2.116	1.045	2.170	1.003	2.225	0.961	2.281	0.919	2.338	0.877	2.396	0.836	2.454	0.795	2.512	0.754	2.571
60	1.184	2.031	1.145	2.079	1.106	2.127	1.068	2.177	1.029	2.227	0.990	2.278	0.951	2.330	0.913	2.382	0.874	2.434	0.836	2.487
65	1.231	2.006	1.195	2.049	1.160	2.093	1.124	2.138	1.088	2.183	1.052	2.229	1.016	2.276	0.980	2.323	0.944	2.371	0.908	2.419
70	1.272	1.986	1.239	2.026	1.206	2.066	1.172	2.106	1.139	2.148	1.105	2.189	1.072	2.232	1.038	2.275	1.005	2.318	0.971	2.362
75	1.308	1.970	1.277	2.006	1.247	2.043	1.215	2.080	1.184	2.118	1.153	2.156	1.121	2.195	1.090	2.235	1.058	2.275	1.027	2.315
80	1.340	1.957	1.311	1.991	1.283	2.024	1.253	2.059	1.224	2.093	1.195	2.129	1.165	2.165	1.136	2.201	1.106	2.238	1.076	2.275
85	1.369	1.946	1.342	1.977	1.315	2.009	1.287	2.040	1.260	2.073	1.232	2.105	1.205	2.139	1.177	2.172	1.149	2.206	1.121	2.241
90	1.395	1.937	1.369	1.966	1.344	1.995	1.318	2.025	1.292	2.055	1.266	2.085	1.240	2.116	1.213	2.148	1.187	2.179	1.160	2.211
95	1.418	1.929	1.394	1.956	1.370	1.984	1.345	2.012	1.321	2.040	1.296	2.068	1.271	2.097	1.247	2.126	1.222	2.156	1.197	2.186
100	1.439	1.923	1.416	1.948	1.393	1.974	1.371	2.000	1.347	2.026	1.324	2.053	1.301	2.080	1.277	2.108	1.253	2.135	1.229	2.164
150	1.579	1.892	1.564	1.908	1.550	1.924	1.535	1.940	1.519	1.956	1.504	1.972	1.489	1.989	1.474	2.006	1.458	2.023	1.443	2.040
200	1.654	1.885	1.643	1.896	1.632	1.908	1.621	1.919	1.610	1.931	1.599	1.943	1.588	1.955	1.576	1.967	1.565	1.979	1.554	1.991

Source: This table is an extension of the original Durbin-Watson table and is reproduced from N. E. Savin and K. J. White, "The Durbin-Watson Test for Serial Correlation with Extreme Small Samples or Many Regressors," *Econometrica*, vol. 45, November 1977, pp. 1989–96 and as corrected by R. W. Farebrother, *Econometrica*, vol. 48, September 1980, p. 1554. Reprinted by permission of the Econometric Society.

Note: n = number of observations
k' = number of explanatory variables excluding the constant term.

Example. If $n = 40$ and $k' = 4$, $d_L = 1.285$ and $d_U = 1.721$. If a computed d value is less than 1.285, there is evidence of positive first-order serial correlation, if it is greater than 1.721 there is no evidence of positive first-order serial correlation, but if d lies between the lower and the upper limit, there is inclusive evidence regarding the presence or absence of positive first-order serial correlation.

$k' = $ # of indep var $(x's)$

$n = $ # of observations

TABLE B-5b
Durbin-Watson d statistic: Significance points of d_L and d_U at 0.01 level of significance

n	$k'=1$ d_L	d_U	$k'=2$ d_L	d_U	$k'=3$ d_L	d_U	$k'=4$ d_L	d_U	$k'=5$ d_L	d_U	$k'=6$ d_L	d_U	$k'=7$ d_L	d_U	$k'=8$ d_L	d_U	$k'=9$ d_L	d_U	$k'=10$ d_L	d_U
6	0.390	1.142	—	—	—	—	—	—	—	—	—	—	—	—	—	—	—	—	—	—
7	0.435	1.036	0.294	1.676	—	—	—	—	—	—	—	—	—	—	—	—	—	—	—	—
8	0.497	1.003	0.345	1.489	0.229	2.102	—	—	—	—	—	—	—	—	—	—	—	—	—	—
9	0.554	0.998	0.408	1.389	0.279	1.875	0.183	2.433	—	—	—	—	—	—	—	—	—	—	—	—
10	0.604	1.001	0.466	1.333	0.340	1.733	0.230	2.193	0.150	2.690	—	—	—	—	—	—	—	—	—	—
11	0.653	1.010	0.519	1.297	0.396	1.640	0.286	2.030	0.193	2.453	0.124	2.892	—	—	—	—	—	—	—	—
12	0.697	1.023	0.569	1.274	0.449	1.575	0.339	1.913	0.244	2.280	0.164	2.665	0.105	3.053	—	—	—	—	—	—
13	0.738	1.038	0.616	1.261	0.499	1.526	0.391	1.826	0.294	2.150	0.211	2.490	0.140	2.838	0.090	3.182	—	—	—	—
14	0.776	1.054	0.660	1.254	0.547	1.490	0.441	1.757	0.343	2.049	0.257	2.354	0.183	2.667	0.122	2.981	0.078	3.287	—	—
15	0.811	1.070	0.700	1.252	0.591	1.464	0.488	1.704	0.391	1.967	0.303	2.244	0.226	2.530	0.161	2.817	0.107	3.101	0.068	3.374
16	0.844	1.086	0.737	1.252	0.633	1.446	0.532	1.663	0.437	1.900	0.349	2.153	0.269	2.416	0.200	2.681	0.142	2.944	0.094	3.201
17	0.874	1.102	0.772	1.255	0.672	1.432	0.574	1.630	0.480	1.847	0.393	2.078	0.313	2.319	0.241	2.566	0.179	2.811	0.127	3.053
18	0.902	1.118	0.805	1.259	0.708	1.422	0.613	1.604	0.522	1.803	0.435	2.015	0.355	2.238	0.282	2.467	0.216	2.697	0.160	2.925
19	0.928	1.132	0.835	1.265	0.742	1.415	0.650	1.584	0.561	1.767	0.476	1.963	0.396	2.169	0.322	2.381	0.255	2.597	0.196	2.813
20	0.952	1.147	0.863	1.271	0.773	1.411	0.685	1.567	0.598	1.737	0.515	1.918	0.436	2.110	0.362	2.308	0.294	2.510	0.232	2.714
21	0.975	1.161	0.890	1.277	0.803	1.408	0.718	1.554	0.633	1.712	0.552	1.881	0.474	2.059	0.400	2.244	0.331	2.434	0.268	2.625
22	0.997	1.174	0.914	1.284	0.831	1.407	0.748	1.543	0.667	1.691	0.587	1.849	0.510	2.015	0.437	2.188	0.368	2.367	0.304	2.548
23	1.018	1.187	0.938	1.291	0.858	1.407	0.777	1.534	0.698	1.673	0.620	1.821	0.545	1.977	0.473	2.140	0.404	2.308	0.340	2.479
24	1.037	1.199	0.960	1.298	0.882	1.407	0.805	1.528	0.728	1.658	0.652	1.797	0.578	1.944	0.507	2.097	0.439	2.255	0.375	2.417
25	1.055	1.211	0.981	1.305	0.906	1.409	0.831	1.523	0.756	1.645	0.682	1.776	0.610	1.915	0.540	2.059	0.473	2.209	0.409	2.362
26	1.072	1.222	1.001	1.312	0.928	1.411	0.855	1.518	0.783	1.635	0.711	1.759	0.640	1.889	0.572	2.026	0.505	2.168	0.441	2.313
27	1.089	1.233	1.019	1.319	0.949	1.413	0.878	1.515	0.808	1.626	0.738	1.743	0.669	1.867	0.602	1.997	0.536	2.131	0.473	2.269
28	1.104	1.244	1.037	1.325	0.969	1.415	0.900	1.513	0.832	1.618	0.764	1.729	0.696	1.847	0.630	1.970	0.566	2.098	0.504	2.229
29	1.119	1.254	1.054	1.332	0.988	1.418	0.921	1.512	0.855	1.611	0.788	1.718	0.723	1.830	0.658	1.947	0.595	2.068	0.533	2.193
30	1.133	1.263	1.070	1.339	1.006	1.421	0.941	1.511	0.877	1.606	0.812	1.707	0.748	1.814	0.684	1.925	0.622	2.041	0.562	2.160
31	1.147	1.273	1.085	1.345	1.023	1.425	0.960	1.510	0.897	1.601	0.834	1.698	0.772	1.800	0.710	1.906	0.649	2.017	0.589	2.131
32	1.160	1.282	1.100	1.352	1.040	1.428	0.979	1.510	0.917	1.597	0.856	1.690	0.794	1.788	0.734	1.889	0.674	1.995	0.615	2.104
33	1.172	1.291	1.114	1.358	1.055	1.432	0.996	1.510	0.936	1.594	0.876	1.683	0.816	1.776	0.757	1.874	0.698	1.975	0.641	2.080
34	1.184	1.299	1.128	1.364	1.070	1.435	1.012	1.511	0.954	1.591	0.896	1.677	0.837	1.766	0.779	1.860	0.722	1.957	9.665	2.057
35	1.195	1.307	1.140	1.370	1.085	1.439	1.028	1.512	0.971	1.589	0.914	1.671	0.857	1.757	0.800	1.847	0.744	1.940	0.689	2.037
36	1.206	1.315	1.153	1.376	1.098	1.442	1.043	1.513	0.988	1.588	0.932	1.666	0.877	1.749	0.821	1.836	0.766	1.925	0.711	2.018
37	1.217	1.323	1.165	1.382	1.112	1.446	1.058	1.514	1.004	1.586	0.950	1.662	0.895	1.742	0.841	1.825	0.787	1.911	0.733	2.00
38	1.227	1.330	1.176	1.388	1.124	1.449	1.072	1.515	1.019	1.585	0.966	1.658	0.913	1.735	0.860	1.816	0.807	1.899	0.754	1.98
39	1.237	1.337	1.187	1.393	1.137	1.453	1.085	1.517	1.034	1.584	0.982	1.655	0.930	1.729	0.878	1.807	0.826	1.887	0.774	1.97
40	1.246	1.344	1.198	1.398	1.148	1.457	1.098	1.518	1.048	1.584	0.997	1.652	0.946	1.724	0.895	1.799	0.844	1.876	0.749	1.95
45	1.288	1.376	1.245	1.423	1.201	1.474	1.156	1.528	1.111	1.584	1.065	1.643	1.019	1.704	0.974	1.768	0.927	1.834	0.881	1.90
50	1.324	1.403	1.285	1.446	1.245	1.491	1.205	1.538	1.164	1.587	1.123	1.639	1.081	1.692	1.039	1.748	0.997	1.805	0.955	1.86
55	1.356	1.427	1.320	1.466	1.284	1.506	1.247	1.548	1.209	1.592	1.172	1.638	1.134	1.685	1.095	1.734	1.057	1.785	1.018	1.83
60	1.383	1.449	1.350	1.484	1.317	1.520	1.283	1.558	1.249	1.598	1.214	1.639	1.179	1.682	1.144	1.726	1.108	1.771	1.072	1.81
65	1.407	1.468	1.377	1.500	1.346	1.534	1.315	1.568	1.283	1.604	1.251	1.642	1.218	1.680	1.186	1.720	1.153	1.761	1.120	1.80
70	1.429	1.485	1.400	1.515	1.372	1.546	1.343	1.578	1.313	1.611	1.283	1.645	1.253	1.680	1.223	1.716	1.192	1.754	1.162	1.79
75	1.448	1.501	1.422	1.529	1.395	1.557	1.368	1.587	1.340	1.617	1.313	1.649	1.284	1.682	1.256	1.714	1.227	1.748	1.199	1.78
80	1.466	1.515	1.441	1.541	1.416	1.568	1.390	1.595	1.364	1.624	1.338	1.653	1.312	1.683	1.285	1.714	1.259	1.745	1.232	1.77
85	1.482	1.528	1.458	1.553	1.435	1.578	1.411	1.603	1.386	1.630	1.362	1.657	1.337	1.685	1.312	1.714	1.287	1.743	1.262	1.77
90	1.496	1.540	1.474	1.563	1.452	1.587	1.429	1.611	1.406	1.636	1.383	1.661	1.360	1.687	1.336	1.714	1.312	1.741	1.288	1.76
95	1.510	1.552	1.489	1.573	1.468	1.596	1.446	1.618	1.425	1.642	1.403	1.666	1.381	1.690	1.358	1.715	1.336	1.741	1.313	1.76
100	1.522	1.562	1.503	1.583	1.482	1.604	1.462	1.625	1.441	1.647	1.421	1.670	1.400	1.693	1.378	1.717	1.357	1.741	1.335	1.76
150	1.611	1.637	1.598	1.651	1.584	1.665	1.571	1.679	1.557	1.693	1.543	1.708	1.530	1.722	1.515	1.737	1.501	1.752	1.486	1.76
200	1.664	1.684	1.653	1.693	1.643	1.704	1.633	1.715	1.623	1.725	1.613	1.735	1.603	1.746	1.592	1.757	1.582	1.768	1.571	1.77

	$k'=11$		$k'=12$		$k'=13$		$k'=14$		$k'=15$		$k'=16$		$k'=17$		$k'=18$		$k'=19$		$k'=20$	
n	d_L	d_U	d_L	d_U	d_L	d_U	d_L	d_U	d_L	d_U	d_L	d_U	d_L	d_U	d_L	d_U	d_L	d_U	d_L	d_U
16	0.060	3.446	—	—	—	—	—	—	—	—	—	—	—	—	—	—	—	—	—	—
17	0.084	3.286	0.053	3.506	—	—	—	—	—	—	—	—	—	—	—	—	—	—	—	—
18	0.113	3.146	0.075	3.358	0.047	3.357	—	—	—	—	—	—	—	—	—	—	—	—	—	—
19	0.145	3.023	0.102	3.227	0.067	3.420	0.043	3.601	—	—	—	—	—	—	—	—	—	—	—	—
20	0.178	2.914	0.131	3.109	0.092	3.297	0.061	3.474	0.038	3.639	—	—	—	—	—	—	—	—	—	—
21	0.212	2.817	0.162	3.004	0.119	3.185	0.084	3.358	0.055	3.521	0.035	3.671	—	—	—	—	—	—	—	—
22	0.246	2.729	0.194	2.909	0.148	3.084	0.109	3.252	0.077	3.412	0.050	3.562	0.032	3.700	—	—	—	—	—	—
23	0.281	2.651	0.227	2.822	0.178	2.991	0.136	3.155	0.100	3.311	0.070	3.459	0.046	3.597	0.029	3.725	—	—	—	—
24	0.315	2.580	0.260	2.744	0.209	2.906	0.165	3.065	0.125	3.218	0.092	3.363	0.065	3.501	0.043	3.629	0.027	3.747	—	—
25	0.348	2.517	0.292	2.674	0.240	2.829	0.194	2.982	0.152	3.131	0.116	3.274	0.085	3.410	0.060	3.538	0.039	3.657	0.025	3.766
26	0.381	2.460	0.324	2.610	0.272	2.758	0.224	2.906	0.180	3.050	0.141	3.191	0.107	3.325	0.079	3.452	0.055	3.572	0.036	3.682
27	0.413	2.409	0.356	2.552	0.303	2.694	0.253	2.836	0.208	2.976	0.167	3.113	0.131	3.245	0.100	3.371	0.073	3.490	0.051	3.602
28	0.444	2.363	0.387	2.499	0.333	2.635	0.283	2.772	0.237	2.907	0.194	3.040	0.156	3.169	0.122	3.294	0.093	3.412	0.068	3.524
29	0.474	2.321	0.417	2.451	0.363	2.582	0.313	2.713	0.266	2.843	0.222	2.972	0.182	3.098	0.146	3.220	0.114	3.338	0.087	3.450
30	0.503	2.283	0.447	2.407	0.393	2.533	0.342	2.659	0.294	2.785	0.249	2.909	0.208	3.032	0.171	3.152	0.137	3.267	0.107	3.379
31	0.531	2.248	0.475	2.367	0.422	2.487	0.371	2.609	0.322	2.730	0.277	2.851	0.234	2.970	0.196	3.087	0.160	3.201	0.128	3.311
32	0.558	2.216	0.503	2.330	0.450	2.446	0.399	2.563	0.350	2.680	0.304	2.797	0.261	2.912	0.221	3.026	0.184	3.137	0.151	3.246
33	0.585	2.187	0.530	2.296	0.477	2.408	0.426	2.520	0.377	2.633	0.331	2.746	0.287	2.858	0.246	2.969	0.209	3.078	0.174	3.184
34	0.610	2.160	0.556	2.266	0.503	2.373	0.452	2.481	0.404	2.590	0.357	2.699	0.313	2.808	0.272	2.915	0.233	3.022	0.197	3.126
35	0.634	2.136	0.581	2.237	0.529	2.340	0.478	2.444	0.430	2.550	0.383	2.655	0.339	2.761	0.297	2.865	0.257	2.969	0.221	3.071
36	0.658	2.113	0.605	2.210	0.554	2.310	0.504	2.410	0.455	2.512	0.409	2.614	0.364	2.717	0.322	2.818	0.282	2.919	0.244	3.019
37	0.680	2.092	0.628	2.186	0.578	2.282	0.528	2.379	0.480	2.477	0.434	2.576	0.389	2.675	0.347	2.774	0.306	2.872	0.268	2.969
38	0.702	2.073	0.651	2.164	0.601	2.256	0.552	2.350	0.504	2.445	0.458	2.540	0.414	2.637	0.371	2.733	0.330	2.828	0.291	2.923
39	0.723	2.055	0.673	2.143	0.623	2.232	0.575	2.323	0.528	2.414	0.482	2.507	0.438	2.600	0.395	2.694	0.354	2.787	0.315	2.879
40	0.744	2.039	0.694	2.123	0.645	2.210	0.597	2.297	0.551	2.386	0.505	2.476	0.461	2.566	0.418	2.657	0.377	2.748	0.338	2.838
45	0.835	1.972	0.790	2.044	0.744	2.118	0.700	2.193	0.655	2.269	0.612	2.346	0.570	2.424	0.528	2.503	0.488	2.582	0.448	2.661
50	0.913	1.925	0.871	1.987	0.829	2.051	0.787	2.116	0.746	2.182	0.705	2.250	0.665	2.318	0.625	2.387	0.586	2.456	0.548	2.526
55	0.979	1.891	0.940	1.945	0.902	2.002	0.863	2.059	0.825	2.117	0.786	2.176	0.748	2.237	0.711	2.298	0.674	2.359	0.637	2.421
60	1.037	1.865	1.001	1.914	0.965	1.964	0.929	2.015	0.893	2.067	0.857	2.120	0.822	2.173	0.786	2.227	0.751	2.283	0.716	2.338
65	1.087	1.845	1.053	1.889	1.020	1.934	0.986	1.980	0.953	2.027	0.919	2.075	0.886	2.123	0.852	2.172	0.819	2.221	0.786	2.272
70	1.131	1.831	1.099	1.870	1.068	1.911	1.037	1.953	1.005	1.995	0.974	2.038	0.943	2.082	0.911	2.127	0.880	2.172	0.849	2.217
75	1.170	1.819	1.141	1.856	1.111	1.893	1.082	1.931	1.052	1.970	1.023	2.009	0.993	2.049	0.964	2.090	0.934	2.131	0.905	2.172
80	1.205	1.810	1.177	1.844	1.150	1.878	1.122	1.913	1.094	1.949	1.066	1.984	1.039	2.022	1.011	2.059	0.983	2.097	0.955	2.135
85	1.236	1.803	1.210	1.834	1.184	1.866	1.158	1.898	1.132	1.931	1.106	1.965	1.080	1.999	1.053	2.033	1.027	2.068	1.000	2.104
90	1.264	1.798	1.240	1.827	1.215	1.856	1.191	1.886	1.166	1.917	1.141	1.948	1.116	1.979	1.091	2.012	1.066	2.044	1.041	2.077
95	1.290	1.793	1.267	1.821	1.244	1.848	1.221	1.876	1.197	1.905	1.174	1.934	1.150	1.963	1.126	1.993	1.102	2.023	1.079	2.054
100	1.314	1.790	1.292	1.816	1.270	1.841	1.248	1.868	1.225	1.895	1.203	1.922	1.181	1.949	1.158	1.977	1.136	2.006	1.113	2.034
150	1.473	1.783	1.458	1.799	1.444	1.814	1.429	1.830	1.414	1.847	1.400	1.863	1.385	1.880	1.370	1.897	1.355	1.913	1.340	1.931
200	1.561	1.791	1.550	1.801	1.539	1.813	1.528	1.824	1.518	1.836	1.507	1.847	1.495	1.860	1.484	1.871	1.474	1.883	1.462	1.896

Note: n = number of observations

k' = number of explanatory variables excluding the constant term.

Source: Savin and White, op. cit., by permission of the Econometric Society.

TABLE B-6a
Critical values of runs in the runs test

N_1	\	\	\	\	\	\	\	\	N_2	\	\	\	\	\	\	\	\	\
	2	**3**	**4**	**5**	**6**	**7**	**8**	**9**	**10**	**11**	**12**	**13**	**14**	**15**	**16**	**17**	**18**	**19**	**20**
2											2	2	2	2	2	2	2	2	2
3					2	2	2	2	2	2	2	2	2	3	3	3	3	3	3
4				2	2	2	3	3	3	3	3	3	3	3	4	4	4	4	4
5			2	2	3	3	3	3	3	4	4	4	4	4	4	4	5	5	5
6		2	2	3	3	3	3	4	4	4	4	5	5	5	5	5	5	6	6
7		2	2	3	3	3	4	4	5	5	5	5	5	6	6	6	6	6	6
8		2	3	3	3	4	4	5	5	5	6	6	6	6	6	7	7	7	7
9		2	3	3	4	4	5	5	5	6	6	6	7	7	7	7	8	8	8
10		2	3	3	4	5	5	5	6	6	7	7	7	7	8	8	8	8	9
11		2	3	4	4	5	5	6	6	7	7	7	8	8	8	9	9	9	9
12	2	2	3	4	4	5	6	6	7	7	7	8	8	8	9	9	9	10	10
13	2	2	3	4	5	5	6	6	7	7	8	8	9	9	9	10	10	10	10
14	2	2	3	4	5	5	6	7	7	8	8	9	9	9	10	10	10	11	11
15	2	3	3	4	5	6	6	7	7	8	8	9	9	10	10	11	11	11	12
16	2	3	4	4	5	6	6	7	8	8	9	9	10	10	11	11	11	12	12
17	2	3	4	4	5	6	7	7	8	9	9	10	10	11	11	11	12	12	13
18	2	3	4	5	5	6	7	8	8	9	9	10	10	11	11	12	12	13	13
19	2	3	4	5	6	6	7	8	8	9	10	10	11	11	12	12	13	13	13
20	2	3	4	5	6	6	7	8	9	9	10	10	11	12	12	13	13	13	14

Note: Tables D.6a and D.6b give the critical values of runs n for various values of N_1(+symbol) and N_2(−symbol). For the one-sample runs test, any value of n which is equal to or smaller than that shown in Table D.6a or equal to or larger than that shown in Table D.6b is significant at the 0.05 level.

Source: Sidney Siegel, *Nonparametric Statistics for the Behavioral Sciences*, McGraw-Hill Book Company, New York, 1956, table F, pp. 252–253. The tables have been adapted by Siegel from the original source: Frieda S. Swed and C. Eisenhart, "Tables for Testing Randomness of Grouping in a Sequence of Alternatives," *Annals of Mathematical Statistics*, vol. 14, 1943. Used by permission of McGraw-Hill Book Company and *Annals of Mathematical Statistics*.

TABLE B-6b

Critical values of runs in the runs test

									N_2										
N_1	2	3	4	5	6	7	8	9	10	11	12	13	14	15	16	17	18	19	20
2																			
3																			
4			9	9															
5		9	10	10	11	11													
6		9	10	11	12	12	13	13	13	13									
7			11	12	13	13	14	14	14	14	15	15	15						
8			11	12	13	14	14	15	15	16	16	16	16	17	17	17	17	17	
9				13	14	14	15	16	16	16	17	17	18	18	18	18	18	18	
10				13	14	15	16	16	17	17	18	18	18	19	19	19	20	20	
11				13	14	15	16	17	17	18	19	19	19	20	20	20	21	21	
12				13	14	16	16	17	18	19	19	20	20	21	21	21	22	22	
13					15	16	17	18	19	19	20	20	21	21	22	22	23	23	
14					15	16	17	18	19	20	20	21	22	22	23	23	23	24	
15					15	16	18	18	19	20	21	22	22	23	23	24	24	25	
16						17	18	19	20	21	21	22	23	23	24	25	25	25	
17						17	18	19	20	21	22	23	23	24	25	25	26	26	
18						17	18	19	20	21	22	23	24	25	25	26	26	27	
19						17	18	20	21	22	23	23	24	25	26	26	27	27	
20						17	18	20	21	22	23	24	25	25	26	27	27	28	

Example. In a sequence of 30 observations consisting of $20 +$ signs $(=N_1)$ and $10 -$ signs $(=N_2)$, the critical values of runs at the 0.05 level of significance are 9 and 20, as shown by Tables D.6a and D.6b, respectively. Therefore, if in an application it is found that the number of runs is equal to or less than 9 or equal to or greater than 20, one can reject (at the 0.05 level of significance) the hypothesis that the observed sequence is random.

SELECTED
BIBLIOGRAPHY

Introductory

Frank, C. R., Jr.: *Statistics and Econometrics*, Holt, Rinehart and Winston, Inc., New York, 1971.

Hu, Teh-Wei: *Econometrics: An Introductory Analysis*, University Park Press, Baltimore, 1973.

Katz, David A.: *Econometric Theory and Applications*, Prentice-Hall, Inc., Englewood Cliffs, N.J., 1982.

Klein, Lawrence R.: *An Introduction to Econometrics*, Prentice-Hall, Inc., Englewood Cliffs, N.J., 1962.

Walters, A. A.: *An Introduction to Econometrics*, Macmillan & Co., Ltd., London, 1968.

Intermediate

Aigner, D. J.: *Basic Econometrics*, Prentice-Hall, Inc., Englewood Cliffs, N.J., 1971.

Dhrymes, Phoebus J.: *Introductory Econometrics*, Springer-Verlag, New York, 1978.

Dielman, Terry E.: *Applied Regression Analysis for Business and Economics*, PWS-Kent Publishing Company, Boston, 1991.

Draper, N. R. and H. Smith: *Applied Regression Analysis*, 2d ed., John Wiley & Sons, Inc., New York, 1981.

Dutta, M.: *Econometric Methods*, South-Western Publishing Company, Incorporated, Cincinnati, 1975.

Goldberger, A. S.: *Topics in Regression Analysis*, The Macmillan Company, New York, 1968.

Gujarati, Damodar N.: *Basic Econometrics*, 2d ed., McGraw-Hill, New York, 1988.

Huang, D. S.: *Regression and Econometric Methods*, John Wiley & Sons, Inc., New York, 1970.

Judge, George G., Carter R. Hill, William E. Griffiths, Helmut Lütkepohl, and Tsoung-Chao Lee: *Introduction to the Theory and Practice of Econometrics*, John Wiley & Sons, Inc., 1982.

Kelejian, H. A. and W. E. Oates: *Introduction to Econometrics: Principles and Applications*, 2d ed., Harper & Row, Publishers, Incorporated, New York, 1981.

Koutsoyiannis, A.: *Theory of Econometrics*, Harper & Row, Publishers, Incorporated, New York, 1973.

Mark, Stewart B. and Kenneth F. Wallis: *Introductory Econometrics*, 2d ed., John Wiley & Sons, Inc., New York, 1981. A Halsted Press Book.

Murphy, James L.: *Introductory Econometrics*, Richard D. Irwin, Inc., Homewood, Ill., 1973.

Netter, J. and W. Wasserman: *Applied Linear Statistical Models*, Richard D. Irwin, Inc., Homewood, Ill., 1974.

Pindyck, R. S. and D. L. Rubinfeld: *Econometric Models and Econometric Forecasts*, 3d ed., McGraw-Hill Book Company, New York, 1990.

Sprent, Peter: *Models in Regression and Related Topics*, Methuen & Co., Ltd., London, 1969.

Tintner, Gerhard: *Econometrics*, John Wiley & Sons, Inc. (science ed.), New York, 1965.

Valavanis, Stefan: *Econometrics: An Introduction to Maximum-Likelihood Methods*, McGraw-Hill Book Company, New York, 1959.

Wonnacott, R. J. and T. H. Wonnacott: *Econometrics*, 2d ed., John Wiley & Sons, Inc., New York, 1979.

Advanced

Chow, Gregory C.: *Econometric Methods*, McGraw-Hill Book Company, New York, 1983.

Christ, C. F.: *Econometric Models and Methods*, John Wiley & Sons, Inc., New York, 1966.

Dhrymes, P. J.: *Econometrics: Statistical Foundations and Applications*, Harper & Row, Publishers, Incorporated, New York, 1970.

Fomby, Thomas B., Carter R. Hill, and Stanley R. Johnson: *Advanced Econometric Methods*, Springer-Verlag, New York, 1984.

Goldberger, A. S.: *Econometric Theory*, John Wiley & Sons, Inc., New York, 1964.

Goldberger, A. S.: A Course in Econometrics, Harvard University Press, Cambridge, Mass., 1991.

Greene, William H.: *Econometric Analysis*, Macmillan Publishing Company, New York, 1990.

Harvey, A. C.: *The Econometric Analysis of Time Series*, 2d ed., MIT, Cambridge, Mass., 1990.

Johnston, J.: *Econometric Methods*, 3d ed., McGraw-Hill Book Company, New York, 1984.

Judge, George G., Carter R. Hill, William E. Griffiths, Helmut Lütkepohl, and Tsoung-Chao Lee, *Theory and Practice of Econometrics*, John Wiley & Sons, Inc., New York, 1980.

Klein, Lawrence R.: *A Textbook of Econometrics*, 2d ed., Prentice-Hall, Inc., Englewood Cliffs, N.J., 1974.

Kmenta, Jan: *Elements of Econometrics*, 2d ed., The Macmillan Company, New York, 1986.

Madansky, A.: *Foundations of Econometrics*, North-Holland Publishing Company, Amsterdam, 1976.

Maddala, G. S.: *Econometrics*, McGraw-Hill Book Company, New York, 1977.

Malinvaud, E.: *Statistical Methods of Econometrics*, 2d ed., North-Holland Publishing Company, Amsterdam, 1976.

Theil, Henry: *Principles of Econometrics*, John Wiley & Sons, Inc., New York, 1971.

Specialized

Belsley, David A., Edwin Kuh, and Roy E. Welsh: *Regression Diagnostics: Identifying Influential Data and Sources of Collinearity*, John Wiley & Sons, Inc., New York, 1980.

Dhrymes, P. J.: *Distributed Lags: Problems of Estimation and Formulation*, Holden-Day, Inc., Publisher, San Francisco, 1971.

Goldfeld, S. M. and R. E. Quandt: *Nonlinear Methods of Econometrics*, North-Holland Publishing Company, Amsterdam, 1972.

Graybill, F. A.: *An Introduction to Linear Statistical Models*, vol. 1, McGraw-Hill Book Company, New York, 1961.

Rao, C. R.: *Linear Statistical Inference and Its Applications*, 2d ed., John Wiley & Sons, New York, 1975.

Zellner, A.: *An Introduction to Bayesian Inference in Econometrics*, John Wiley & Sons, Inc., New York, 1971.

Applied

Berndt, Ernst R.: *The Practice of Econometrics: Classic and Contemporary*, Addison-Wesley, 1991.

Bridge, J. I.: *Applied Econometrics*, North-Holland Publishing Company, Amsterdam, 1971.

Cramer, J. S.: *Empirical Econometrics*, North-Holland Publishing Company, Amsterdam, 1969.

Desai, Meghnad: *Applied Econometrics*, McGraw-Hill Book Company, New York, 1976.

Kennedy, Peter: *A Guide to Econometrics*, 2d ed., MIT Press, Cambridge, Mass., 1985.

Leser, C. E. V.: *Econometric Techniques and Problems*, 2d ed., Hafner Publishing Company, Inc., 1974.

Rao, Potluri and Roger LeRoy Miller: *Applied Econometrics*, Wadsworth Publishing Company, Inc., Belmont, Calif., 1971.

Note: For a list of the seminal articles on the various topics discussed in this book, please refer to the extensive bibliography given at the end of the chapters in Fomby et al., cited above.

NAME INDEX

SUBJECT INDEX